The Evolution of Human Sexuality
An Anthropological Perspective

Second Edition

David A. Puts
The Pennsylvania State University

 KENDALL/HUNT PUBLISHING COMPANY
4050 Westmark Drive   Dubuque, Iowa 52002

For Khytam

Contents

Preface

Sexuality is one of the most salient and consuming aspects of our lives. Chromosomal sexes and the genders associated with them play major roles in organizing social life in every culture. Romantic relationships are culturally ubiquitous, and marriage occurs in virtually all societies. People everywhere are motivated by desires for sex and romance. Sexual conflict, including sexual violence and rape, is also unfortunately a pervasive feature of human societies. The ways that gender, romance, marriage, and sexual conflict manifest themselves across cultures are conspicuously variable. This variability, both within and across cultures, can help us understand how and why human sexuality takes the forms it does. That is the subject of this book.

But this is not just a book about sex. It is also a book about anthropology—how anthropology is normally done and how anthropology could be done better. Anthropology is a holistic discipline. It aims to further our understanding of humanity on many levels, using many perspectives. Traditionally, the field of anthropology is divided into four main approaches, or subfields. These include *linguistic anthropology, archeology, cultural anthropology,* and *biological* (or *physical*) *anthropology.* Linguistic anthropologists study present and past languages as parts of human cultural behavior. Archeologists are interested in reconstructing past cultures and understanding the processes of culture change through an analysis of material remains. Cultural anthropologists describe and analyze extant cultures and often use these analyses to make cross-cultural comparisons of human lifeways. Biological anthropologists are concerned with describing genetic, morphological, and behavioral variation in humans and their living and extinct primate relatives, and understanding how and why humans evolved the morphologies and behaviors they currently exhibit.

Together, the subfields of anthropology cover a vast terrain, overlapping in scope with many social and natural sciences. Given anthropology's breadth, it is perhaps not surprising that most anthropologists specialize in a single subfield and carry out most of their research in only a small part of that subfield. Such intellectual isolation within anthropology is compounded by theoretical disagreements. Most fundamentally, these disagreements center on differences between sociocultural theories espoused most forcefully within cultural anthropology and the evolutionary biological theories adopted by most biological anthropologists.

This fractionation represents a handicap, for the strength of anthropology lies in its breadth. Knowledge acquired in one area contributes to understanding in other areas. Biological anthropologists, for example, stand to benefit from familiarity with the range and diversity of human behaviors and ideologies and from knowledge of the particulars of human experience that might be overlooked by current evolutionary analyses. Yet such topics are normally the domain of cultural anthropologists. Likewise, cultural anthropologists are liable to profit from an understanding of the evolutionary underpinnings of the human mind. In anthropology, breadth of knowledge leads to depth of knowledge; cultural and biological explanations represent conceptual layers of a more complete understanding. In sum, a multilevel, holistic approach is certain to render a fuller, more coherent, and more robust picture of what it means to be human.

But such an integrated approach to human sexuality will be no easy task. For you, the reader, the major battle will be with your own biases—with getting yourself to see things in slightly different ways, allowing yourself to overcome some conceptual impediments and false dichotomies. To this end, your skepticism is arguably your most valuable asset. Use it as you read this book. Be skeptical about what you read, but be equally skeptical about what you now believe. Ask yourself, what is the *best* explanation for this? Is there another explanation that explains more, that fits better with the other things I know, that is better at predicting things I haven't even seen yet? I hope that in the end you will have a broad, profound, and theoretically rich understanding of human sexuality. I also hope that, in the process, you will have come to agree that a multilevel, holistic approach is not only possible but also desirable.

Book Structure

This book is designed to serve as the primary text/reader for an anthropology course on human sexuality. It consists of seven units. Unit I emphasizes the basic compatibility of cultural and biological perspectives and addresses theoretical and ideological issues that have traditionally presented barriers to a multilevel, holistic approach. Unit II develops evolutionary theory, particularly as it relates to sex and sexuality. Units III through VII have similar formats. Each unit addresses a specific issue or related set of issues in human sexuality, and each is composed of one or two "biological" readings (except for Unit IV, which includes three) and one or two "cultural" readings. Biological readings detail the evolutionary or developmental bases of the phenomena under consideration, and cultural readings illustrate the phenomena as they occur in particular cultures, embedded within sets of social expectations, ideologies, and symbols. Unit III considers the evolution and development of sex differences and their relation to ideas and expressions of gender across cultures. Unit IV develops the idea of reproductive strategies as a means of clarifying human mating competition and mate choice. Unit V builds on the understanding of human reproductive strategies developed in the previous unit to shed light on sexual conflict and its repugnant consequences: sexual harassment, coercion, abuse, and rape. Unit VI considers the development and evolution of homosexual attraction and the role of social expectations on homosexual behavior and identity. Finally, Unit VII discusses the institution of marriage across cultures and the care and abuse of children by their caretakers. Each unit is followed by one or more problem sets with short essay questions that target critical concepts introduced in the text.

Acknowledgments

I would like to give special thanks to Jennifer Baldwin, Christina Jerzyk, and Stephanie Brakeman-Wartell for their helpful comments regarding Chapter 15 and to Carolyn Myers for her input on many topics in this book and her excellent suggestions of readings. I would also like to express my deep gratitude to my friend and mentor, Steven Gaulin, who made many invaluable conceptual and editorial contributions to this book. Finally, I would like to thank Courtney Kennedy, Sarah Knockel, and everyone else at Kendall/Hunt Publishing who worked so patiently with me to make this book possible.

David Puts

Unit I

An Integrated Approach

This unit is brief but critical. It begins with a chapter on an integrated approach to anthropology. In this chapter, I outline aspects of cultural and evolutionary approaches to anthropology as they are normally practiced. I then discuss five barriers to an integrated approach—misunderstandings or logical flaws that consistently impede the integration of cultural and evolutionary approaches. One of the five barriers is the nature/nurture debate. I argue, as others have before, that the nature/nurture debate arises from a failure to distinguish between what causes a person to acquire or develop a trait and what causes variation among individuals in a particular trait.

The nature/nurture debate is also the topic of the second chapter in this unit, "The End of Nature versus Nurture," by Frans de Waal. This article is a thoughtful and articulate critique of this age-old dispute about the causes of human attributes.

The two chapters in this unit are intended to encourage the reader to view evolutionary and cultural anthropology as complementary perspectives and to pave the way for the multi-level thinking that is espoused throughout this volume.

1
An Integrated Approach to Anthropology

David A. Puts

It might be said that the first step toward understanding humanity is realizing how different people are, and the second step is realizing that they are the same. People's beliefs, values, behaviors, and traditions are amazingly variable. To understand humanity we must look beyond our own lives and appreciate the diversity of lifeways that exists around the world. Once we begin to recognize this diversity, it is easy to become bewildered by how different the lives of people in other parts of the world are from ours.

Upon deeper reflection, however, we can see through the obvious differences and realize profound similarities in people's desires, goals, and experiences. People everywhere are happy when they find a mutual attraction, for example, and jealous when they suspect their mates of looking elsewhere. We share a common human experience. Franz Boas, one of the founders of American anthropology, argued in his book *The Mind of Primitive Man* (1938) that human beings everywhere share similar thought processes and mental abilities.

Anthropology is uniquely equipped to show us a picture of humanity that portrays our diversity and simultaneously emphasizes our underlying sameness. To take advantage of what anthropology has to offer, let's begin by examining anthropological approaches as they

are traditionally practiced. We will first consider cultural anthropology, and then we will discuss one perspective adopted by biological anthropologists, an evolutionary perspective. Cultural and biological anthropologists vary widely in how they conceptualize and study humanity, so our discussions of these approaches will necessarily be incomplete. The objective here is not to review and explicate every perspective assumed by cultural and biological anthropologists. Rather, the purpose is to describe some sensible and fruitful approaches taken by researchers in these subfields that can complement one another in a more unified approach. Finally in this chapter, we will consider an integrated approach, some barriers to it, and ways to overcome these barriers.

The Cultural Approach

Cultural anthropology is the study of similarities and differences in the beliefs, values, and behavior of people living in different societies, especially non-Western societies. Cultural anthropologists are interested in looking at how *culture,* or the traditions and customs that characterize a society, influences people's beliefs and behavior. The process by which people's cultural environments influence their beliefs, values, and behavior as they grow and mature is called *enculturation.* An important tenet of cultural anthropology is that differences in beliefs and behavior are caused by differences in the cultural environments in which people are raised. For instance, the enculturation of children into the Sambia culture of New Guinea (a culture that you will encounter in Chapter 19) causes the Sambia to see the world in some very different ways from the way you do. Each culture is viewed as the product of its unique history, including its history of contact with other cultures.

Sometimes cultural anthropologists want to test a specific hypothesis about the beliefs, values, or behavior of people in a particular society or group of societies. For example, the famous anthropologist Margaret Mead wanted to test the hypothesis that the "adolescent angst" characteristic of teenage American girls was due to enculturation in America and would not be found in other cultures such as Samoa. When testing a specific hypothesis, cultural anthropologists have to make some decisions before going into "the field" to do research. They must decide which variables they are interested in collecting information about, how they will measure these variables, and what precisely will be required for them to say that the variables are related in the way they hypothesize.

At other times, cultural anthropologists are simply interested in examining a particular aspect of people's lives, such as family planning issues among the Solomon Islanders of Melanesia, but want to learn more about the topic before trying to explain it. In this case, the cultural anthropologist focuses primarily on description and documentation of the relevant aspects of people's lives in the culture or cultures under investigation. Later, she can go back through her data to see what hypotheses they suggest.

In either case, much cultural anthropology research at some point entails *participant observa-*tion, living among the people being studied, interacting with them, and taking part in their lives for an extended period—usually for at least a year. The reasoning behind this practice is that an outsider cannot easily make sense of the way another group of people constructs an understanding of the world without experiencing what these people experience and living the way they live. While living among the people being studied, cultural anthropologists collect information through observing and recording behaviors, befriending people who seem to be valuable sources of information about the culture, conducting interviews, and, depending on the level of literacy, administering questionnaires. Living with and studying a group of people is called *ethnography,* so this type of research, often involving participant observation, is called *ethnographic research.*

One of the long-term aims of many cultural anthropologists is understanding people's beliefs and behavior across cultures. How are people different across cultures? How are they the same? Why do people in some cultures behave one way, while people in other cultures behave in other ways? Why, for example, do the Mukogodo of Kenya (see Chapter 24) favor their daughters over their sons, while people in some other cultures favor their sons or favor neither sex of offspring? The approach commonly used by cultural anthropologists to answer such questions is called *ethnology.* Ethnology is the comparison of data collected from multiple cultures, generally through ethnographic research.

The Evolutionary Approach

Some biological anthropologists are also interested in understanding similarities and differences in the beliefs and behavior of people across cultures. Like most cultural anthropologists, most evolutionists consider people everywhere to have basically the same underlying psychology. And like cultural anthropologists, evolutionists assume that experience plays a large role in molding the behavior of individuals. Unlike most cultural anthropologists, though, evolutionists tend to be more concerned with understanding why our propensities to learn and respond to our environments as we do—propensities assumed to be shared by all people—evolved in the first place.

Evolutionists Study the Functions of the Mind

Evolutionists want to know why, from the variation in the psychologies of prehistoric people, some psychological traits got passed on to offspring while others did not. The supposition is that some traits helped our ancestors survive and reproduce better than others did. Those traits that most helped their bearers to reproduce got passed on to many offspring, who passed the traits to their offspring and so on, culminating in the set of psychological mechanisms that we all now possess. Evolutionists want to know the *function* that psychological mechanisms served in contributing to survival and reproduction in ancestral environments.

Why emphasize the evolutionary functions of traits rather than their current uses? After all, we are capable of performing all sorts of behaviors, such as driving cars, typing, and playing chess, that were not directly favored by natural selection over our evolutionary history. The human leg provides a useful analogy. Our legs evolved to function in standing, walking, and running, but we also use them for kicking soccer balls and riding bicycles. Examining how our legs kick soccer balls and pedal bicycles can help us understand these limbs. But this focus probably will be less informative than examining how our legs perform the tasks for which they evolved. For instance, the bicycle-pedaling capability of legs neither predicts nor helps us understand the presence of toes. Evolutionists similarly expect that knowing the evolved functions

of the mind will lend greater insight into how the mind is designed. This insight, in turn, is expected to clarify how people learn and how their beliefs and behavior are shaped by culture. As the evolutionary biologist George Williams (1966) inquired, "Is it not reasonable to anticipate that our understanding of the human mind would be greatly aided by knowing the purpose for which it was designed?"

Testing Evolutionary Hypotheses

When evolutionists want to test a hypothesis about the evolutionary function of a trait, they focus on evidence of design for the hypothesized function. To see why, consider this: For decades, it was unclear exactly why male beetles of some species have hornlike structures. Just about every possible function was suggested—defense against predators, tools for digging or for perforating plants to feed on sap, ornaments to attract females, weapons to fight other males for mates, even no function at all. It was not until beetles were carefully observed in the wild that evidence began to accumulate that males use their horns to fight one another and rarely use them for anything else (Fig. 1.1). In fact, beetle horns seem quite well suited for this function. They are used in different species either to

Figure 1.1 Male stag beetles fighting.

Image © Jorge Pedro Barradas de Casais, 2008. Used under license from Shutterstock, Inc.

pry up and push a rival off his site or to grasp, lift, and drop him to the ground (Eberhard 1979).

In other words, researchers were able to determine the evolutionary function of beetle horns by studying them carefully enough to see that they are better designed for male-male combat than for other possible functions. Natural selection is the only evolutionary process known to systematically produce traits that appear engineered for specific functions (Williams 1966). If under close scrutiny a trait looks well suited to a purpose that would have benefited its bearers in the ancestral past, then we can tentatively conclude that it evolved to serve this function. The more efficiently it performs this hypothesized function compared to alternative functions, the stronger the case. But how can we demonstrate this? We need to show that variation in the trait's expression corresponds with variation in its usefulness for the hypothesized function. Such variation can either occur naturally or be induced experimentally.

Naturally Occurring Variation

Traits vary both between and within species, and both of these sources of variation offer potential tests of functional hypotheses. In cross-species comparison, different species are studied to see if the expression of the trait across species is related to the presence of some problem for which the trait putatively provides a solution. If a functional hypothesis about a trait in one species is correct, then species possessing similar traits should have experienced similar problems over their evolution.

For example, recall the hypothesis that horns in male beetles function in contests over females. If this hypothesis is correct, then we should expect horns to occur mostly in beetle species in which males fight for mates, and we would expect them to be rare in beetle species without male contests. However, species can share traits not only because of similar evolutionary pressures, but also because they inherited traits from a common ancestor. Conse-

Figure 1.2 Male elk (stags) fighting.
Image © nialat, 2008. Used under license from Shutterstock, Inc.

quently, the presence of horns (or similar structures) will provide the strongest evidence for our hypothesis if they occur in distantly related species with similar evolutionary pressures. Antlers in many deer species closely resemble beetle horns, for example (Fig 1.2). The fact that male deer use their antlers to fight one another for mates is evidence that horns serve a similar function in beetles.

Traits also vary within species. Our beetle horn hypothesis, for example, predicts relationships between horns and fighting ability among individuals of a given species. We might predict that males with larger horns are more successful in contests with other males, and that horn length is more strongly related to success in male contests than to other possible functions, such as mate attraction or feeding. Sex differences offer another important source of within-species variation. Because males engage in more fighting over mates, we can predict that males will tend to have larger horns.

Finally, traits can vary even within individuals. Behaviors change frequently, of course, but even anatomical traits can change within the lifetime of the individual. For example, many species breed seasonally, and the color of their fur or feathers, and even the presence of entire structures such as antlers, change according to the season. Organisms also change over their development. If male beetles grow horns only (or more rapidly) at sexual maturity, this would support the hypothesis that they function in competition over mates.

Experimental Manipulation

When we find that two variables are related in nature, we cannot be sure which variable affects the other, or whether the two are associated only because they are both affected by an unknown third variable. For example, if we find that beetles with larger horns are better fighters, how do we know that the size of their horns, rather than their overall body size or some other variable, causes them to be more successful? Experimental manipulations allow researchers to show that one variable affects another, while holding all other variables constant. Evolutionary hypotheses can be tested by manipulating a relevant variable to see if the manipulation affects the hypothesized dependent variable. To test the male contest hypothesis for beetle horns, we might take several males back to the laboratory. There, we could match pairs of males against each other and record the outcomes. Then we could artificially enlarge some males' horns (for example, by gluing extra pieces on) to see if this increased their fighting success.

Demonstrating that a trait is well suited to performing a particular function provides evidence that the trait evolved for this function. The more precisely and efficiently the trait serves its hypothesized function, especially compared to other hypothetical functions, the more convincing the case.

Five Barriers to an Integrated Approach

So far, nothing we have discussed regarding the cultural approach or the evolutionary approach contradicts any of the reasoning or assumptions discussed regarding the other. Cultural anthro-pologists concentrate on the historical and more immediate cultural causes of people's behavior and beliefs. Evolutionists concentrate more on the evolutionary, or *pre*historic, causes. Cultural anthropologists do not deny that the abilities of people to learn and respond to cultural and other environmental variables have evolutionary origins. And evolutionists do not deny that cultural experience has a profound influence on human behavior and beliefs.

Yet, as you may have read in the preface to this book, cultural and evolutionary approaches are rarely integrated with one another. Why not? Why do many cultural anthropologists and human behavioral evolutionists see themselves in opposition to one another? This disagreement seems especially paradoxical when one considers the time, energy, and ink spent by so many intelligent and educated researchers trying to resolve it. Some disagreement undoubtedly issues from misunderstandings of philosophically complex issues. But most disagreement probably arises from researchers' misunderstandings of each other's positions. The important task now at hand is being clear ourselves—stating as precisely and as simply as possible what we mean when we try to explain human behavior. To this end, let's now examine what may be called *five barriers to an integrated approach* and, through careful and precise analysis, attempt to overcome them.

Barrier 1: Science and Subjectivity

One persistent criticism of an evolutionary (or any) biological approach to human behavior is that biological approaches are products of the traditions of Western science. A Western scientific approach reflects the biases and history of the Western world and so is merely one of many possible ways of understanding. Moreover, the aspirations of Western science to explain the world objectively can never fully be achieved. Critics of science point out that objectivity is impossible because one can never perceive the world stripped of the influences of personal experience. Indeed, some cultural anthropologists explicitly avoid scientific methods in their research. *Interpretive anthropologists*, for example, study each culture humanistically, as if it were a literary text that must be deciphered within a particular cultural and historical context.

These criticisms are valid. In fact, to one way of looking at things, people explain their world merely by inventing stories that coherently fit together their experiences. From this perspective, all understanding, from the myths of small-scale societies to the scientific theories of the Western world, are subsumed under the same explanatory category. They are culturally biased constructions of reality. Subjectivity is usually discussed in this way—in terms of biases that are common to people socialized in a particular society. But even within a society, the experiences of people differ. And these experiential differences also contribute to differences in how people make sense of their world. Finally, we share a uniquely human bias. We see the world as human beings—not as chimpanzees, dogs, or dust mites, nor as omniscient deities. Our human bias does not contribute to differences among people in how they construct understandings of their worlds. But it is worth bearing in mind that the order, the connectedness, and the *meaning* that seem to characterize the "world out there" may exist not so much out there as in our minds—in the ways that our uniquely human brains acquire, process, and organize information about the world.

Most scientists, especially social scientists, and essentially all philosophers of science are aware of these limitations. These scientists realize that they must operate under the assumption of their own subjectivity and attempt, whenever possible, to be cognizant of their biases. In spite of these limitations, however, there is much to recommend a scientific perspective.

Scientific Explanations Inspire Confidence

Imagine that you and your friend are sitting on a bench watching pairs of male house sparrows competing over some bits of food on the sidewalk. Each time one of the males frightens off the other or otherwise wins the food, your friend informs you that he knew what the outcome would be. He then gives you some dubious-sounding explanation for the outcome. You often suspect your friend of pretending he knows what he's talking about when really he doesn't. How do you know whether to believe your know-it-all friend this time? How can you tell whether he really knows which sparrow will win the food? Wouldn't you want him to tell you the outcome *before* the contest was decided?

Now imagine that your friend tells you how he's predicting the outcome. He tells you that male house sparrows with larger, blacker patches of feathers on their throats tend to be older and dominant to males with smaller, lighter patches (Fig. 1.3). This time, you pay attention to the males' black throats. You notice that the male with the larger, darker patch indeed wins the prize. Still, your friend may have been lucky. But of the next pair, the male with the bigger, blacker throat patch wins again. And again for the next pair! You start feeling guilty for suspecting that your friend was full of hot air. How many times would it take to convince you? Maybe seven out of ten correct predictions? Eight? Nine? We could quibble about just how good at predicting the outcome your friend's explanation would have to be before we decided to believe he was not just lucky. But we can agree that our confidence in his explanation

Figure 1.3 Male house sparrow.

Image © Andrew Williams, 2008. Used under license from Shutterstock, Inc.

would depend on its ability to predict the outcome before the fact.

This is exactly how science works. A hypothesis, like your friend's throat patch-dominance hypothesis, makes predictions. Scientists test these predictions just as you did—they observe nature or they set up the relevant conditions experimentally. If the predictions are right considerably more often than would probably occur by chance alone, then scientists accept the hypothesis for the time being. As observations that contradict the predictions of a hypothesis accumulate, new hypotheses (or modified old ones) are invented to accommodate the new observations. Science thus has a built-in means of adjusting the story to fit the observations—it is *self-correcting*. Careful scientists are especially aggressive in their pursuit of observations that invalidate their hypotheses. When attempts to disprove a hypothesis repeatedly result in failure, scientists begin to express guarded optimism that the hypothesis is a good one.

Because science systematically rejects hypotheses that are bad at making predictions and keeps those that make accurate predictions, scientific theories are generally quite good at predicting. And didn't we agree that this is really the essence of good explanations? It's easy to make up explanations for events after the fact. Indeed, many explanations could easily be invented for a single set of observations. Your friend, if he were creative, could have made up countless stories to explain why one bird or the other won the food. It is only when explanations repeatedly predict things we have not yet seen that we start to have confidence in them. In this realm, science has no rival. As you will see in Chapter 12, for example, scientists have become very adept (although nowhere near perfect) at predicting people's attraction to sex partners.

We could probably agree on some other features as well. For instance, explanations should be based on replicable observations: Someone else observing the world under similar conditions should perceive it in similar ways. This helps remove some individual bias. For example, if your friend reported observing males with larger throat patches winning 99 out of 100 contests, but everyone else who watched male house sparrows competing for food observed a ratio around 50/50, we would not have much confidence in your friend's explanation. Science thus adopts the principle that observations should be replicable.

We could also probably agree that, when choosing among explanations that account for the same observations, as a matter of practicality, the simplest is the most satisfactory. After all, why choose an explanation that is more complicated than necessary? For instance, we could posit that the spirit of a witch always scared off the male with the smaller throat patch. We certainly couldn't *prove* that something that can't be seen, heard, smelled, touched, or otherwise sensed wasn't there. But this would not explain any more observations than your friend's explanation did. Nor would it make any new predictions. In this case, it seems reasonable to stick with the simpler explanation. In science, this is known as the principle of *parsimony*.

Science May Not Be So "Western"; Humans Think in Similar Ways

Are these criteria of science just reflective of the whims of the Western world—as arbitrary as the name of the rose? Perhaps not. Perhaps we should take heart from the fact that we *have* a human bias. Despite the many differences among people in how they perceive and understand the world, there are deeply rooted similarities. People perceive colors similarly, for example, whether their native language includes two basic color terms or eleven (Berlin and Kay 1991). This perceptual similarity results from an underlying commonality in the neurophysiology of color perception. We will discuss later in this chapter how people share many other psychological mechanisms, leading people everywhere to learn particular things in particular ways. These shared mechanisms underpin a uniquely human psychology. These commonalities also suggest that one culture's or one person's explanations can make sense to others—

that people not only perceive but also organize and explain the world in similar ways. The Kapauku of the island of Irian Jaya, Indonesia, for instance,

> hold a rationalistic and logical view of the world that resembles scientific thought. Their outlook on the world is internally consistent, depending upon that which can be perceived through the senses, and follows logically from those perceptions. Once these premises are granted, that which contradicts these expectations is rejected out of hand. Following from this, because the only things that exist are things that can be perceived by the senses, the supernatural does not exist. People believe in it, but it is not real. (Peters-Golden 1997)

Previously, we entertained the possibility that witches cause male house sparrows with small throat patches to lose contests, but we dismissed the conjecture as unnecessarily complicated. But people in some cultures do believe in witches. The Azande of central Africa, for example, are well known for their pervasive belief in witchcraft. According to traditional Azande beliefs, witch spirits cause *every* misfortune, from a broken pot to a stubbed toe to a death from disease (Peters-Golden 1997). Do the Azande see the world completely differently from Westerners? Would Western science make no sense at all to the Azande? The anthropologist Evans-Pritchard (1937) was struck by the Azande's use of witchcraft to explain what appeared to him to be the consequences of completely natural phenomena. When Evans-Pritchard asked them about this, he found that they did in fact recognize the contribution of natural phenomena. A boy who had stubbed his foot on a stump, for example, understood that natural events had placed the tree in his path and that the stump had injured his foot. Witchcraft merely explained why the boy had stubbed his foot *this* time and not other times.

Can you think of an analogous belief in Western culture? You may have thought of the notion of "bad luck." We would say that bad luck had caused the boy to stub his foot. If the misfortune were great, say a loved one getting killed in a car accident, many Westerners might attribute the event to "God's will." Of course, in addition to believing in the supernatural, most Westerners would believe that perfectly natural physical phenomena caused the death of their loved one. "God's will" would simply explain why this misfortune befell *their* loved one. In exactly the same way, the Azande would attribute the accident to witchcraft.

These examples and countless others illustrate the profound similarities between Western thought and the thought of people everywhere. But no matter how much of science is common to people in all cultures and how much is peculiar to a Western way of looking at things, in the final analysis, science works. The use of science has translated into some major achievements. Engineers design planes that fly faster than sound and buildings that can withstand incredible stresses. And modern medicine has all but eradicated many infectious diseases that killed children by the thousands only a century ago.

In sum, science is only one way of making sense of the world. Scientific hypotheses cannot be divorced from individual, cultural, and species-wide bias and so can make no claims about absolute truth. While we can't deny seeing the world through human, cultural, and personal lenses, it would also be foolish to deny the unparalleled success of science at generating and testing useful explanations. Certainly, both humanistic and scientific perspectives can contribute to a fuller understanding of ourselves.

Barrier 2: Explanation on Multiple Levels—Proximate and Ultimate Explanations

Think about what happens when you smell food you like to eat, say, a pizza. Your mouth probably starts to water. And even if you may not have been hungry before, you begin to crave a slice of pizza. Why is that? Perhaps it is because pizza is a popular food in your culture, and you have learned to enjoy its taste. Certainly, people in other cultures enjoy foods that you would not begin to crave after smelling. On the other hand, maybe your craving has to do with the release of certain neurotransmitters in your brain stimulating the brain areas associated with hunger. Or maybe you crave pizza because cravings for fatty, high-calorie foods increased the survival of your ancestors and so were favored by natural selection throughout the course of human evolution.

If you see these explanations as alternatives to one another, you're not alone. In fact, they are *not* competing explanations—they are all possible simultaneously. But people often mistake complementary explanations for competing ones, and this forms yet another barrier to integrating multiple approaches. Notice that the first explanation is a cultural one. People in one culture learn to prefer some types of food, while people in other cultures learn to crave other foods. What are the neurochemical and neuroanatomical mechanisms behind a craving for pizza? The second explanation answers this question. The first and second answers are examples of *proximate* explanations. Proximate explanations address what factors in the lifetime of an organism cause a particular anatomical, physiological, behavioral, or mental attribute to develop or to be expressed.

The final explanation is an evolutionary explanation. It deals with why we evolved the attribute in question. Evolutionary explanations that address the *function* of an attribute of an organism—that is, why natural selection favored the attribute—are called *ultimate* explanations. Pizza is evolutionarily novel, so humans cannot have evolved a preference for pizza per se. However, people have probably evolved the tendency to crave foods that they have seen others eat, have themselves eaten before, have satisfied their preferences for fatty foods, and have not made them sick in the past. An ultimate explanation for your craving for pizza would involve a description of how a tendency like one of these could have contributed to the survival and reproduction of our ancestors.

Although cultural anthropologists tend to focus on proximate explanations and evolution-

ists focus on ultimate explanations, we will examine both types of explanations in this book. Thus, it will be important to keep in mind that proximate and ultimate explanations do not necessarily conflict with one another. They are answers to different questions. Proximate explanations answer the questions, *What mechanisms cause a trait to be expressed?* and *How do these mechanisms develop?* An ultimate explanation addresses the question, *Why did this developmental tendency evolve?* Both types of explanation are necessary for a complete understanding of any human attribute (Mayr 1961, Tinbergen 1963).

Barrier 3: Morality and the Naturalistic Fallacy

In this book, we will consider aspects of human sexuality that we consider undesirable, to put it mildly. In Unit V, for example, we will discuss male sexual violence against women. We will be concerned with understanding the expression of male sexual violence across cultures and the social variables that constrain it. We will also be concerned with understanding sexual violence from an evolutionary perspective. Why did men evolve a tendency to perpetrate sexual violence on women? And given these putative evolutionary functions, what environmental occurrences are likely to precipitate sexual violence?

We want to understand sexual violence for the same reasons we want to understand cancer—not to condone it but to solve a common human problem. There is always the danger, however, that people will interpret an evolutionary explanation as a justification. People mistakenly tend to believe that what is the result of evolution is natural and therefore moral. This assumption is incorrect for at least two reasons. First, there is nothing in evolutionary theory that says evolution will produce only traits that we consider moral or that otherwise increase human happiness. Second, things that are natural are not necessarily good. As Gaulin and McBurney (2001) point out, for example, "Earthquakes, volcanic eruptions, floods, pestilence,

AIDS, cancer, and heart attacks are all natural phenomena" (p. 16). Few people would argue, however, that these phenomena are desirable.

This error in reasoning—that giving an evolutionary explanation for an act means justifying the act—is called the *naturalistic fallacy*. As social scientists, we are concerned with understanding the causes of people's behavior. Some of the behaviors we would most like to understand are those that we consider problematic and immoral, such as sexual violence and rape. It is important to keep the naturalistic fallacy in mind as we attempt to understand both proximate and ultimate causes of human sexual behavior.

Barrier 4: Tabula Rasa (Blank Slate)

In the past, psychologists and other social scientists viewed the human mind as a general-purpose learning machine, capable of acquiring whatever information to which it was exposed. A person was viewed as being born *tabula rasa*, a "blank slate" upon which the idiosyncrasies of culture and experience were etched. While some researchers maintain this viewpoint, many others are beginning to support the idea that minds are instead composed of many somewhat separate mechanisms, each specialized for performing specific functions in how we think, learn, feel, and behave (reviewed in Gaulin and McBurney 2001, Tooby and Cosmides 1992).

Although there is currently no consensus, much depends on how the mind is designed. If the mind is composed of many special-purpose mechanisms, then we can expect evolutionary theory to help us understand how we learn and respond to our environments. We would predict that natural selection has equipped us with specialized mental adaptations for responding to the kinds of survival and reproductive challenges our ancestors faced. If, on the other hand, our minds are not specialized, then evolutionary theory cannot tell us much about how we think, feel, learn, and behave. We would have to conclude that natural selection produced a general-

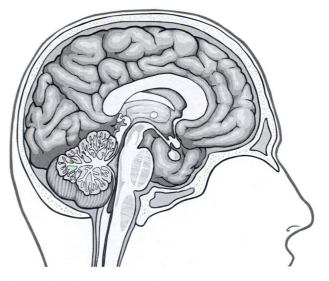

Figure 1.4 The human brain is composed of many specialized parts.

Image © Oguz Aral, 2008. Used under license from Shutterstock, Inc.

purpose learning machine in humans, capable of acquiring whatever information to which the machine was exposed, and leave it at that. Fortunately for those interested in understanding the human mind, the weight of current evidence suggests that our minds are indeed quite specialized.

For instance, we seem to be natural-born experts at learning some complex skills like walking and talking, but have to work quite hard at acquiring others like solving calculus problems and playing the oboe. We often require explicit instruction. How specialized are our capacities to learn? As it turns out, people who are bright in one cognitive area also tend to be bright in other areas. Favorable combinations of genetic and environmental influences apparently cause some people to perform better than others at multiple mental functions. But people such as savants can be exceptional at one or a few cognitive abilities and poor at others. And localized brain damage can impair some mental functions while leaving others intact. This evidence leads us to conclude that many mental functions are distinct from one another—that we do not have one general-purpose thinking machine in our heads.

Perhaps the most "general purpose" of our mental abilities is the ability to learn connections between an occurrence and some stimulus that reliably precedes it, an ability shared with most, if not all, other animal species. The classic example of this type of learning comes from the research of the physiologist Ivan Pavlov, who conditioned dogs to salivate in response to a bell that preceded the presentation of food. This type of learning makes a lot of evolutionary sense. Organisms that can use information from their environment to anticipate and avoid harmful events or take advantage of favorable events will be more successful survivors and reproducers.

However, humans and other animals learn some associations more easily than they learn others. Garcia and Ervin (1968), for example, showed that rats can learn an association between a new taste and the feeling of nausea and between sound and physical pain, but cannot learn to connect taste and physical pain or sound and nausea. These specialized learning abilities also make evolutionary sense; Garcia and Ervin hypothesized that rats evolved only the learning abilities that helped negotiate specific survival and reproductive challenges that recurred over rats' evolution. The ability to pair new tastes with nausea, for example, would have enabled rats to avoid eating foods that were toxic to them. Humans are similarly expected to have evolved learning abilities that helped solve the problems our ancestors faced throughout human evolution. Specialized learning abilities don't fit the tabula rasa concept.

Culturally universal behavior and ideas are also difficult for the tabula rasa concept. For example, cultural taboos against incest (Chapter 11), a tendency to have sex in private (Friedl 1994), and some sex differences in mating psychology, such as greater male preferences for female youth and beauty and greater female preferences for mates with resources (Chapters 12 and 13), are apparent cultural universals or near universals. Such commonality is difficult to explain if human thought and behavior are shaped only by the idiosyncrasies of individual cultures. From the tabula rasa perspective, one might well expect to find cultures in which most women prefer younger men or cultures in which women raid neighboring villages for husbands, for example.

Other aspects of human psychology are patterned in ways that are difficult to attribute to a mind that starts out as a blank slate. For instance, as you will see in Chapter 12, women are more attracted to the scents of men whose bodies are symmetrical and whose immune system genes are compatible with theirs. Some of these preferences exist only when women are near the ovulation phase of their menstrual cycles. It is hard to imagine which aspects of a woman's social environment would inscribe these preferences in a supposedly formless, general-purpose mind. On the other hand, you will see in Chapter 12 that these patterns fit the idea that our minds are composed of many special-purpose mechanisms that have evolved to produce specific patterns of response to the environment. In fact, this "menstrual effect" on women's scent preferences was predicted beforehand using just that idea. (Keep in mind that we generally have the most confidence in the explanations that are good at predicting things before the fact.)

In the past, social scientists considered some behavioral traits learned and some innate or instinctual. But we have just seen that learning is patterned in ways that do not fit the idea that our minds start out as blank slates. As we develop a better understanding of how people learn, feel, think, and behave, we will be able to refine our assessment of how specialized our psychology is. In Chapter 3, we will discuss why natural selection is more likely to build flexible behavior from many specialized mental mechanisms than from one general-purpose one. For now, we may leave the issue by concluding that there is considerable specificity in our responsiveness to our environment. Understanding our specific aptitudes, limitations, and inclinations can help us understand how our environment shapes our thoughts and behaviors.

Barrier 5: The Nature-Nurture "Debate"

In Section 1.1, we discussed the powerful influence of culture in shaping people's behavior and attitudes. So pervasive are culture's effects that the early anthropologist Edward Tylor was inspired to write,

> we can drop individual differences out of sight, and thus generalize on the arts and opinions of whole nations, just as, when looking down upon an army from a hill, we forget the individual soldier, whom, in fact, we can scarce distinguish in the mass. (Tylor in *Applebaum 1987*)

While we may not be as hasty as Tylor to dismiss individual differences, his point is well taken that people tend to conform to the values, ideals, and lifeways of the societies into which they were enculturated. The Sambia of New Guinea act and think like Sambia, and Norwegians act and think like Norwegians. These differences can be extreme. It is the effect of growing up in different cultures, not different genes, that leads to these differences in behavior and thought. If a Sambian infant were adopted at birth by a Norwegian family and raised in Norway, the child would grow up thinking and behaving as a Norwegian, and vice versa.

This is not to say that genetic differences do not cause *any* behavioral or psychological differences among people. We know that genetic differences do indeed cause psychological differences, and in some cases they may be quite profound. But the differences in the prevailing attitudes and behaviors of entire societies result mainly from the exposure of inhabitants to different cultural regimes. These facts are often taken as evidence that genes have a minimal effect on the beliefs, values, attitudes, and behavior of individual people. Thus, it has frequently been argued that behavior is due to culture rather than biology, environment rather than genes, and nurture rather than nature.

These statements lack precision. Whereas the *variation* among people in their psychology and behavior may primarily result from environmental (especially cultural) differences as opposed to genetic ones, the causes of the *acquisition* of behavioral and psychological traits are as much genetic as they are environmental.

This distinction between the causes of trait acquisition and the causes of trait variation is neither simple nor intuitive. It requires us to be much more precise in our discussion of the causes of human behavior than people have tended to be in the past. Indeed, much confusion has been engendered and perpetuated by a lack of clarity in writing (and perhaps in thinking) about these issues. This section is intended to clarify some basic misunderstandings surrounding the causes of human psychological and behavioral attributes so that we may finally undertake a unified approach to their study.

To make our discussion tractable, we must be clear about what is meant by "biology," "genes," and "nature" on the one hand and "culture," "environment," and "nurture" on the other. First of all, the use of the term *biological* to describe behaviors or other psychological traits should be avoided because *every* behavior is biological, even those that might be called *cultural* or *learned*. The environment influences behavior only by influencing the chemistry and physiology of our brains and nervous systems (our biology). Thus, all behavior is biological, and all of it has biological proximate causes (e.g., electrochemical changes in our brains). Why do people have different biologies underlying their different behaviors? They either have different genes, different environments, or both. That is the *only* way it makes sense to talk about biological and cultural causes as being distinct. That is, it only makes sense if by "biological," we mean strictly a difference in DNA. Differences in hormones, brain circuitry, and brain chemistry that cause differences in behavior are not necessarily "biological" causes in this sense because the hormonal or brain differences could be due to different environments rather than different genes. If these causes don't necessarily count as biological causes, then you can see how vague and useless the term *biological* is in this context. Besides, if biology is the study of living things, isn't every aspect of humanity biological, including culture? Similarly, isn't all of humanity part of nature?

On the other hand, as stated previously, it makes sense to talk about the genetic causes of a trait. The word *genotype* refers to all of the genes carried by an individual. In addition to simplifying the discussion by serving as a representative term, this word avoids the confusion that results from using the terms *biology* or *nature*. *Culture, nurture,* and *environment* refer to causes associated with one's surroundings, especially those involving human interaction. The term *environment* will be used to represent this group, as it refers to all aspects of one's surroundings, including social ones. Both the genotype and the environment affect an individual's *phenotype,* the traits that he or she possesses. Now that we have chosen reasonably unambiguous and representative terms, we are prepared to ask the question, *To what extent are human phenotypes determined by the genotype versus the environment?*

Causes of Trait Acquisition: Organization and Activation

What causes people to acquire their phenotypes? Why do we look, think, act, and feel the way we do? Such traits emerge from two processes, which may be called *organization* and *activation*. In reality, there is no line separating these processes; they grade into one another. But this somewhat arbitrary distinction between organization and activation will prove conceptually useful, as you will see.

Organization is the building of our physical traits—from our muscles, skin, and bones to our respiratory, circulatory, digestive, endocrine, reproductive, and nervous systems. The organizational processes that build such sophisticated plumbing and wiring are unimaginably complex. Taken together, these processes are literally too much to wrap one's mind around. But taken individually, they are quite simple. They are no more than chemical reactions. Countless chemical reactions occurring simultaneously all over the body—starting, stopping, speeding up, and slowing down other reactions—underlie our

development from zygote through embryo, infant, and adolescent to adult. It is absolutely awe inspiring to consider how many millions of chemical reactions must go just right and occur at the right times to culminate in a healthy adult person. So how do we do it? What mysterious forces guide these processes?

The easy answer to this question is genes. Genes code for molecules called *enzymes* that control when, where, and how quickly chemical reactions take place. But this answer is incomplete. Genes do not operate in a vacuum. By themselves, genes are just chemically inert strands of DNA. Genes must have materials to work with and chemical reactions to guide. Moreover, genes are not always active. Sometimes they are turned on, and their instructions for making enzymes are expressed, and sometimes genes are silenced. The signals to turn on or turn off genes ultimately come from outside of the cells in which genes reside and often depend on environmental stimuli from outside of the body. Thus, organization is guided by genes interacting with the environment in which they find themselves. Your body, with all of its sophisticated plumbing and wiring, is the house that genes and environment built.

Activation is the operation of your plumbing and wiring. When something happens to you—say you touch a hot stove, smell a fragrant flower, or see a bully picking on a smaller child—your internal machinery is activated. Your systems respond by increasing your heart rate, channeling blood from some tissues toward others, releasing hormones and neurotransmitters, sending electrical signals through your brain and all over your body, causing you to sense, perceive, feel, think, and perhaps act. The nature of your activation—what stimuli you respond to and the intensity, direction, and duration of your response—depends on what machinery you happen to have. How is your circulatory system built? How is your nervous system organized? Because your responses depend on the machinery you have, they result every bit as much from the interaction of genes and environment as the machinery itself.

To say otherwise would be very shortsighted. We would certainly not want to say that only the most recent (environmental) cause was the exclusive or most important cause of our response. Did you ever, as a child (or perhaps as an adult), line up dominoes close to one another so that if you knocked one over, a chain reaction would ensue, knocking over domino after domino until the last one fell? Saying that the stove, the flower, or the bully was more important to your reactions than the gene-environment influences that organized you would be like saying that your brief flick of the first domino was more important to the fall of the last than the way you laboriously and meticulously placed the dominoes. If you *have* set up dominoes in this way, you know this reasoning is patently flawed. If anywhere along the line a domino is aligned improperly or is too far from those that follow it, the chain reaction will come to an anticlimactic halt and the last domino will surely not fall, no matter how you topple the first one.

Regardless of how near or far from the fall of the last domino they are, both genes and environment are equally important, not only for how we are organized, but also for how we are activated—how we think, feel, and behave. Recall that the division between organization and activation is somewhat arbitrary. Here's why: Activation can also be organizing. With varying degrees of permanency, the environmental stimuli that activate you can also alter the machinery of your body. The way activation affects your machinery depends partly on the present organization of your machinery and partly on the resulting gene activity. Activation can change the way you are organized, so that the next time you are activated, you will react differently. You can see this when you exercise. You can also see it when you learn. Learning is an ongoing process, which at every step is guided by the machinery that your genes and environment built, your genes themselves and the environmental influences impinging on them both.

Heritability and the Causes of Variation among Individuals

Every aspect of the phenotype, whether anatomical, physiological, psychological, or behavioral, results equally from the complex interaction of the genotype with its environment. Consequently, although people rarely realize it, it would not make sense to ask how much of a trait of a single individual is caused by genes and how much by environment. To modify an analogy used by Richard Dawkins (1989), it would be like asking how much of the consistency of a cake is caused by the ingredients and how much is caused by the oven. There is simply no way to answer these questions (which means they aren't good questions). One could answer questions like "What proportion of a particular person's weight is due to the water molecules in her body?" or "How much of her standing height is caused by the length of her femur versus the length of her tibia?" We can answer these questions because we are seeking to explain weight and height in terms of the sums of measurable components. But when we ask about components whose interaction produces the trait, we have no basis for parceling out their relative contributions. Thus, one could not profitably ask what proportion of a person's standing height is due to her diet and what proportion is due to her genotype. These factors interact in a way that is not summative. In fact, it is safe to say that the genotype and environment always interact to produce the phenotype of an organism in ways that are not summative.

We can, however, ask another question that differs in a subtle but important way: How much of the *variation* in height among people is due to genetic differences versus environmental differences? This measure, the proportion of a trait's variation in a population caused by genetic differences, is called *heritability*. In a particular environment in a particular population, we can say that, for example, 60% of the variation in IQ results from genetic differences, and the remaining 40% from environmental ones. In other words, IQ would have a heritability of 0.6. But even if IQ had a heritability of zero, both genes and environment would cause the trait. It would simply be the case that there weren't any genetic differences among people that contributed to their IQ differences. These two concepts may seem at odds. How can genes contribute to every trait and yet sometimes contribute to none of the variation in a trait? The answer to this question is so important, and so often misunderstood, that it warrants two examples.

For our first example, let's go back to the cake analogy. The cake's consistency is the "trait" in which we are interested—it can be moist and gooey or dry and crumbly, or somewhere in between. The list of ingredients is the cake's "genotype," and the oven is the cake's environment. Remember that both the ingredients and the oven temperature are essential to the consistency of a cake. We cannot say that one is more important than the other. However, imagine a "population" of a dozen cakes that were all baked in identical ovens at 350 degrees Fahrenheit for 30 minutes but differed in the proportions of their ingredients. Of course, there would be some differences among cakes in their consistency—some might be light and fluffy, others might be dense and moist, and still others might be dry and crumbly. Because all cakes were exposed to the same environmental conditions, all of the variation in consistency would be due to differences in ingredients. The "heritability" of consistency would be nearly equal to one. Yet no one would argue that the environment (30 minutes at 350 degrees) did not contribute to the consistencies of the cakes—it just did not contribute to the variation. Now imagine a different population of twelve cakes, all made with the same proportions of ingredients but this time baked at different temperatures. Again, there would be some variation in consistency, but now virtually all of the variation would be environmental. "Heritability" would now be about equal to zero (Fig. 1.5).

There are several important lessons to take from this example. First, it *never* makes sense to say that either genes or environment contributes

i) All of the variation in cake consistency is due to differences in ingredients (genes). Heritability of cake consistency is 100%.

ii) All of the variation in cake consistency is due to differences in oven temperature (environment). Heritability of cake consistency is zero.

Figure 1.5 Variation in the "trait" cake consistency is represented by different shading. Heritability (the extent to which genes cause variation in a trait) depends on how greatly the relevant genes and environmental factors vary among individuals in a population.

ism. Both ingredients and oven temperature always contribute to the consistency of a cake. Second, it *can* make sense to say that more of the variation among individuals in some trait is due to variation in genes (ingredients) or environment (oven temperature). This is what heritability measures. Third, the heritability of a trait is not some fixed characteristic of the trait. Heritability is peculiar to a given characteristic in a given population under a specified set of environmental conditions. By increasing or decreasing genetic variation in the population or by increasing or decreasing environmental differences among individuals, one can change the heritability of a trait (i.e., the degree to which variation in the trait is genetic).

Let's try a bit more complex example: Imagine a plant (like the garden pea plants studied by Gregor Mendel) that can have one of two different heights, tall or short. Like people, the plant possesses two copies of every gene, although the two copies may be different versions, or *alleles*, of the gene. The tall variety is caused by the tall allele (let's call it *T*), which codes for an enzyme that transforms some chemical precursor into a growth hormone. The short variety is caused by another allele, the *t* allele, which codes for a nonfunctional enzyme. As in Mendel's plants, *T* is dominant to *t*, because having only one *T* allele allows the production of enough of the enzyme to transform all of the precursor into the growth hormone. As a result, the only way for a plant to be short is not to have any copies of the *T* allele and so not to be able to make any of the growth hormone. Plants that have genotypes *TT* or *Tt* are tall, and plants that are *tt* are short. Therefore, height is determined by only one gene, right? The answer is no. But here, admittedly, you were led down a garden path. (Pardon the pun.)

In fact, there was another chemical precursor that had to be transformed into the growth hormone's precursor. This "pre-precursor" was transformed into the final precursor by an enzyme encoded by a second gene. Almost certainly, there was a pre-pre-precursor, and so on. Each step in this long chemical pathway was catalyzed by an enzyme coded for by a different gene (see Fig. 1.6). Thus, there were always many genes that contributed to height—it's just

that variation among individual plants at only one genetic locus contributed to variation in their height. What if we eliminated all of the *t* alleles from the population so that all plants would be tall? There would still be some variation in just how tall different plants were. But these differences would be due entirely to environmental differences, such as exposure to sunlight, water, and local soil quality. Genetic differences would not cause any of the differences in height. The heritability of height would be zero, yet genes would still be playing a crucial role in the height of every plant.

Writers Often Do Not Distinguish between Causes of Trait Acquisition and Causes of Trait Variation

Starting to make sense? Genes and the environment jointly influence every trait of every organism, but the phenotypic variation among organisms can be more genetic or more environmental. Why is understanding this so important? Simply making the distinction between the causes of trait acquisition and the causes of variation in populations goes a long way toward reconciling what biologists know about the genetic causes of psychological traits with the obviously cultural sources of behavioral variation observed by cultural anthropologists and other social scientists. It means that, to be clear,

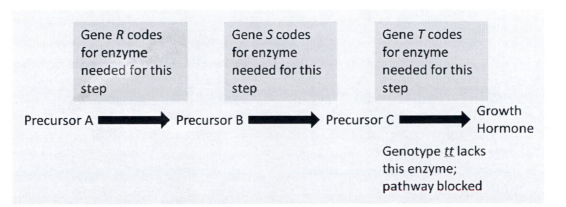

Figure 1.6 This hypothetical metabolic pathway illustrates the difference between the causes of trait acquisition and the causes of trait variation. Multiple genes (*R*, *S*, and *T*, at the minimum) are needed to produce the plant's growth hormone, but variation in growth hormone production is caused by variation in only one of these genes.

we have to be conscientious about making this distinction. The following quote, taken from a popular scientific book, illustrates a common ambiguity:

> The patterns of inheritance that Mendel observed in his pea plants were remarkably simple. The main reason was that, just by chance, all the traits he focused on were controlled by single genes. . . . Mendel's work was further simplified because all of the plants were raised in the same patch, thereby minimizing the effects of environmental variables, such as temperature, rain, and soil quality. (Hamer and Copeland 1994, 77, emphasis added)

As we know, in each pea plant, the traits that Mendel studied were "controlled" by many (if not all) of the plant's genes. What the authors meant was that the variation among pea plants in traits such as height was due mostly to differences in single genes. Likewise, the "effects of environmental variables" can never be minimized in an individual plant's development. Clearly, water, sunshine, carbon dioxide, and nitrogen from the soil, at the very least, are critical for the development of any trait. What could be minimized were the differences among plants resulting from differences in environment.

Here is another similarly ambiguous statement taken from one of the leading cultural anthropology textbooks in the United States:

> The most critical element of cultural traditions is their transmission through learning rather than through biological inheritance. (Kottak 2000, 4)

By "biological inheritance," the author almost certainly means "genes." Thus, this quote *could* be interpreted to mean "People acquire traditional behaviors and ideas because of exposure to the right environments, not because of the genes they inherited." Of course, if we interpret the statement in this way, then it is false. An individual's behaviors and ideas result as much from the influence of genes as from the influence of environmental factors.

On the other hand, as you now know, the *variation* in traits such as cultural behaviors can be due more to genetic or environmental differences. For some psychosocial traits, much of the variation is caused by genetic differences. In Europe and Japan, for example, approximately 80–85% of the variation in schizophrenia is due to genetic differences (Cardno and Gottesman 2000). In other words, the heritability of schizophrenia in these populations is around 80–85%. But in general, we expect traits such as cultural traditions in which learning plays a major role to have low heritability. Thus, if we interpret the previous quote to mean, "People differ in the cultural traditions that they follow mostly because of differences in the cultural traditions to which they were exposed," then not only does the statement make sense, but it is also probably generally correct.

'Genetic' Does Not Mean 'Inflexible'

One final point of clarification on the use of the term *genetic*. This term is often used to describe traits that are relatively unresponsive to changes in the environment. There is a sensible reason for this tendency: Traits with high heritability (i.e., those whose variation is genetic in origin) really do tend to be fairly inflexible. After all, if a trait responded dramatically to environmental changes, then we would probably see substantial population variation caused by environmental differences. This can't be the case if heritability is high. The tendency for highly heritable traits to be relatively inflexible is almost certainly why people say inflexible traits are genetic.

Let's summarize the thinking:

Premise 1: *If a trait is "genetic," then it is heritable*—okay, so long as *genetic* refers to the causes of the trait's variation. (genetic → heritable)

Premise 2: *If a trait is heritable, then it is often inflexible*—a generally reasonable premise. (heritable → inflexible)

Conclusion: *Genetic traits are inflexible.* (genetic → inflexible)

If Premises 1 and 2 are correct, then the conclusion logically follows. That is, if A → B, and

B → C, then A → C. There are, in fact, possible exceptions to Premise 2. Heritable traits are not necessarily inflexible. A trait may be capable of responding to the environment, but the environment may not have changed enough recently for us to observe the trait's response. Thus, the trait may currently be heritable but become less heritable and more obviously flexible were the environment to change appropriately.

Supposing Premise 2 is generally valid, the real problem with the conclusion that genetic traits are inflexible is the same problem that keeps rearing its ugly head. People fail to distinguish between the role of genes in trait acquisition and their role in population variation. Thus, people interpret this otherwise logical conclusion to mean that any trait whose *development* depends largely on genes must be inflexible. Actually, this cannot be. It can't make sense to say that traits whose development depends on genes are inflexible because *all* traits depend on genes for their development—even those that are clearly responsive to the environment, such as behavioral traits.

The point is that we need to be careful to make the distinction between causes of trait acquisition and causes of trait variation. How we interpret statements like those quoted previously can profoundly impact how we study human behavior. If we interpret such statements the wrong way, or fail to make this distinction altogether, we could easily conclude that genes exert at most a trivial influence on behavior. This conclusion could lead to further errors in reasoning, such as the frequently made, but ultimately mistaken, assumption that the study of evolution has little to tell us about human behavior. To the contrary, because genes are essential to the ontogeny of all traits, including psychological ones, and because the genes in human populations today got there as a result of evolutionary forces operating in our past, we can expect evolutionary theory to be very relevant to understanding how we learn, feel, think, and behave.

Summary

These five barriers to an integrated approach are truly a rogues' gallery of some of the biggest problems in the social sciences. If you have understood everything so far, you are well on your way to integrating cultural and biological approaches to the study of human behavior.

You have learned that cultural and evolutionary anthropology need not be viewed as antithetical to one another. An approach that holds that cultural, rather than genetic, differences among people are mostly responsible for differences in cultural behavior is completely consistent with an evolutionary approach. In fact, the two approaches are more than compatible—they are complementary. They offer different levels of explanation for the same phenomena. While one approach can tell us how behavior varies across cultures and to which social and other environmental variables it responds, the other approach can help us understand why we evolved these patterns of response to our environment and why the elements of culture, such as reciprocity, kinship rules, and sexual mores, are such potent determinants of human action. By integrating cultural and evolutionary anthropological approaches, we are better equipped to appreciate both the diversity of ideas and traditions across cultures and the common, underlying psychology that motivates us all.

References

Berlin, B., and P. Kay. 1991. *Basic color terms*. Berkeley: Univ. of California Press.

Boas, F. 1938. *The mind of primitive man*. New York: MacMillan.

Buss, D. 1999. *Evolutionary psychology*. Needham Heights, MA: Allyn and Bacon.

Cardno, A. G., and I. I. Gottesman. 2000. Twin studies of schizophrenia: From bow-and-arrow concordances to star wars Mx and functional genomics. *American Journal of Medical Genetics* 97(1):12–17.

Dawkins, R. 1989. *The extended phenotype*. New York: Oxford University Press.

Eberhard, W. G. 1979. The function of horns in Podischnus agenor (Dynastinae) and other beetles. In *Sexual selection and reproductive competition in insects,* ed. M. S. Blum and N. A. Blum, 231–258. New York: Academic Press.

Evans-Pritchard, E. E. 1937. Witchcraft. In *Oracles and magic among the Azande.* Oxford, England: The Clarendon Press.

Friedl, E.. 1994. Sex the invisible. *American Anthropologist* 96(4):833–44.

Garcia, J., and F. Ervin. 1968. Gustatory-visceral and telereceptor-cutaneous conditioning: Adaptation in internal and external milieus. *Communications in Behavioral Biology, Part A* 1:389–415.

Gaulin, S. J. C., and D. H. McBurney. 2001. *Psychology: An evolutionary approach.* Upper Saddle River, NJ: Prentice Hall.

Hamer, D., and P. Copeland. 1994. *The science of desire.* New York: Simon & Schuster.

Keesing, R. M. 1982. *Kwaio religion: The living and the dead in a Solomon Island society.* New York: Columbia University Press.

Kottak, C. 2000. *Cultural anthropology,* 8th ed. Boston: McGraw-Hill.

Mayr, E. 1961. Cause and effect in biology. *Science, N.Y.* 134:1501–1506.

Peters-Golden, H. 1997. *Culture sketches: Case studies in anthropology,* 2nd ed. Boston: McGraw-Hill.

Tinbergen, N. 1963. On aims and methods of ethology. *Z. Tierpsychol.* 20:410–33.

Tooby, J., and L. Cosmides. 1992. The psychological foundations of culture. In *The adapted mind: Evolutionary psychology and the generation of culture,* ed. J. H. Barkow, L. Cosmides, and J. Tooby. New York: Oxford.

Tylor, E. B. 1987. The science of culture. In *Perspectives in cultural anthropology,* H. Applebaum, ed. Albany: State University of New York Press.

Williams, G. C. 1966. *Adaptation and natural selection.* Princeton, NJ: The Princeton University Press.

The End of Nature versus Nurture

Frans B. M. de Waal

Is human behavior determined by genetics or by environment? It may be time to abandon the dichotomy.

The defenders of nature and nurture have been at each other's throats for as long as I can remember. Whereas biologists have always believed that genes have something to do with human behavior, social scientists have flocked en masse to the opposite position: that we are fully and entirely our own creation, free from the chains of biology.

I felt the heat of this debate in the 1970s whenever, in lectures for general audiences, I mentioned sex differences in chimpanzees, such as that males are more aggressive and more ambitious than females. These would be howls of protest. Wasn't I projecting my own values onto these poor animals? How rigorous were my methods? Why did I even bother to compare the sexes? Did I perhaps have a hidden agenda?

Nowadays the same sort of information makes people yawn! Even direct comparisons between human and ape behavior, something that used to be taboo, fail to get anyone excited. Everyone has heard that men are from Mars and women from Venus. Everyone has seen, in *Time* and *Newsweek,* PET scans of the human brain engaged in various tasks, with different areas lighting up in male and female brains.

This time, however, it is my turn to be troubled. Instead of celebrating the victory of the biological approach, I regard some of the contemporary dichotomies between men and women as gross simplifications rendered politically correct by a fashionable amount of male-bashing (for example, when normal hormonal effects are referred to a "testosterone poisoning"). We remain as far removed as ever from a sophisticated understanding of the interplay between genes and environment. Society has let the pendulum swing wildly back from nurture to nature, leaving behind a numb of bewildered social scientists. Yet we still love to phrase everything in terms of one influence or the other, rather than both.

It is impossible to explore where we may be heading 50 years from now without looking back an equal number of years at the charged history of the nature/nurture controversy. The debate is so emotional because any stance one takes comes with serious political implications.

Positions have ranged from an unfounded faith in human flexibility by reformists to an obsession with blood and race by conservatives. Each in their own way, these positions have caused incalculable human suffering in the past century.

Learning and Instinct

Fifty years ago the two dominant schools of thought about animal and human behavior had opposite outlooks. Teaching animals arbitrary actions such as lever-pressing, American behaviorists came to view all behavior as the product of trial-and-error learning. This process was considered so universal that differences among species were irrelevant: learning applied to all animals, including humans. As B. F. Skinner, the founder of behaviorism, bluntly put it: "Pigeon, rat, monkey, which is which? It doesn't matter."

In contrast, the ethological school in Europe focused on naturalistic behavior. Each animal species is born with a number of so-called fixed-action patterns that undergo little modification by the environment. These and other species-specific behaviors represent evolutionary adaptations. Thus, no one needs to teach humans how to laugh or cry: these are innate signals, universally used and understood. Similarly, the spider does not need to learn how to construct a web. She is born with a battery of spinnerets (spinning tubes connected to silk glands) as well as a behavioral program that "instructs" her how to weave threads together.

Because of their simplicity, both views of behavior had enormous appeal. And although both paid homage to evolution, they sometimes did so in a superficial, arm-waving sort of way. Behaviorists stressed the continuities between humans and other animals, attributing these to evolution. But because for them behavior was learned rather than inborn, they ignored the genetic side, which is really what evolution is all about. While it is true that evolution implies continuity, it also implies diversity: each animal is adapted to a specific way of life in a specific environment. As is evident from Skinner's statement, this point was blithely ignored.

Similarly, some ethologists had rather vague evolutionary notions, emphasizing phylogenetic descent rather than the processes of natural selection. They saw behavioral traits, such as the inhibition of aggression, as good for the species. The argument was that if animals were to kill one another in fights, the species would not survive. This may be true, but animals have perfectly selfish reasons to avoid the escalation of fights that may harm themselves and their relationships. Hence, these ideas have now been replaced by theories about how traits benefit the actor and its kin; effects on the species as a whole are considered a mere by-product.

Behaviorism started losing its grip with the discovery that learning is not the same for all situations and all species. For example, a rat normally links actions with effects only if the two immediately follow each other. So it would be very slow to learn to press a bar if a reward followed minutes later. When it comes to food that makes it sick, however, a delay of hours between consumption and the negative sensation still induces future food aversion. Apparently, animals are specialized learners, being best at those contingencies that are most important for survival.

At the same time that behaviorists were forced to adopt the premises of evolutionary biology and to consider the world outside the laboratory, ethologists and ecologists were laying the groundwork for the neo-Darwinian revolution of the 1970s. The pioneer here was Dutch ethologist Nikolaas Tinbergen, who conducted ingenious field experiments on the survival value of animal behavior. He understood, for instance, why many birds remove eggshells from the nest after the chicks have hatched. Because the outside of a shell is colored for camouflage but the inside is not, predators such as crows easily locate eggs if broken shells are placed next to them. Throwing out the pieces is an automatic response favored by natural selection because the birds that practice this behavior have more surviving offspring.

Others developed theories to explain behavior that at first sight does not seem to help the actor but someone else. Such "altruism" can be seen in ant soldiers giving their lives in defense of their colony or in dolphins lifting a drowning companion to the surface. Biologists assumed that natural selection will allow for assistance among relatives as a means of promoting the same genes. Or, if two animals are unrelated, the favor granted by one must be returned at some future time.

The scientists felt so confident about their explanations of cooperative animal societies that they could not resist extending these ideas to our own species. They saw the hugely cooperative enterprise of human society as based on the same premise of family values and economic tit-for-tat.

It fell to an American expert on ants, Edward O. Wilson, to deliver the news in 1975 that a great deal of human behavior was ripe for the Darwinian perspective and that the social sciences should prepare themselves to work together with biologists on this endeavor. Thus far the two disciplines had led separate lives, but from the perspective of a biologist social science is not much more than the study of animal behavior focused on a single species: ours. Because this is not how social scientists see their work, proposals for a united framework were not kindly received. One of Wilson's outraged opponents even poured cold water over Wilson's head after he gave a lecture. For reasons explained below, his new synthesis, dubbed "sociobiology," was equated with race policies of the past and ultimately with the Holocaust.

Although the criticism was patently unfair—Wilson was offering evolutionary explanations, not policy suggestions—we shouldn't be surprised that the topic of human biology arouses strong emotions.

Burdens of the Past

It is generally believed that some human behavior can easily be changed because it is learned, whereas other behavior resists modification because it is part of our biological heritage.

Ideologues of all colors have grasped this division to argue for the innate nature of certain human characteristics (for example, purported race differences in intelligence) and the plasticity of others (such as the ability to overcome gender stereotypes). Thus, Communism was founded on great confidence in human malleability. Because people, unlike social insects, resist submerging individuality for the greater good, some regimes accompanied their revolutions with massive indoctrination efforts. All of this proved in vain, however. Communism went under because of an economic incentive structure that was out of touch with human nature. Unfortunately, it did so only after having caused great misery and death.

Even more disastrous was the embrace of biology by Nazi Germany. Here, too, the collective (das Volk) was placed above the individual, but instead of relying on social engineering the method of choice was genetic manipulation. People were classified into "superior" and "inferior" types, the first of which needed to be protected against contamination by the second. In the horrible medical language of the Nazis, a healthy Volk required the cutting out of all "cancerous" elements. This idea was followed to its extreme in a manner that Western civilization has vowed never to forget.

Don't think that the underlying selectionist ideology was restricted to this particular time and place, however. In the early part of the 20th century, the eugenics movement—which sought to improve humanity by "breeding from the fitter stocks"—enjoyed widespread appeal among intellectuals in both the U.S. and Great Britain.

Based on ideas going back to Plato's Republic, sterilization of the mentally handicapped and of criminals was considered perfectly acceptable. And social Darwinism—the idea that in a laissez-faire capitalist economy the strong will outcompete the weak, resulting in general improvement of the population—still inspires political agendas today. In this view, the poor should not be aided in their struggle for existence so as not to upset the natural order.

Given these ideologies, it is understandable why suppressed categories of people, such as minorities and women, fail to see biology as a friend. I would argue, however, that the danger comes from both directions, from biological determinism as well as its opposite, the denial of basic human needs and the belief that we can be everything we want to be. The hippie communes of the 1960s, the Israeli kibbutzim and the feminist revolution all sought to redefine humans. But denial of sexual jealousy, the parent-child bond or gender differences can be carried only so far before a countermovement will seek to balance cultural trends with evolved human inclinations.

What makes the present era different is that the genocide of World War II is fading into memory while at the same time the evidence for a connection between genes and behavior is mounting. Studies of twins reared apart have reached the status of common knowledge, and almost every week newspapers report a new human gene. There is evidence for genes involved in schizophrenia, epilepsy and Alzheimer's and even in common behavioral traits such as thrill-seeking. We are also learning more about genetic and neurological differences between men and women, as well as between gay and straight men. For example, a small region of the brain in transsexual men (who dress and behave like women) resembles the same region in women's brains.

The list of such scientific advances is getting longer by the day, resulting in a critical mass of evidence that is impossible to ignore. Understandably, academics who have spent their life condemning the idea that biology influences human behavior are reluctant to change course. But they are being overtaken by the general public, which seems to have accepted that genes are involved in just about everything we do and are. Concurrently resistance to comparisons with other animals has dissipated because of a stream of television nature programs that has brought exotic wildlife into our homes while showing animals to be quite a bit smarter and more interesting than people used to believe.

Studies of chimpanzees and bonobos, such as those by Jane Goodall and myself, show that countless human practices and potentials, from politics and child-rearing to violence and even morality, have parallels in the lives of our closest animal relatives. How can we maintain the dualisms of the past—between humans and animals and between body and mind—in the face of all this evidence to the contrary? Current knowledge about our biological background simply doesn't permit a return to the tabula rasa views of the past.

This doesn't solve the problem of ideological abuse, however. If anything, it makes things worse. So long as people have political agendas, they will depict human nature one way or another for their own purposes. Conservatives like to point out that people are naturally selfish, whereas liberals argue that we have evolved to be social and cooperative. The obvious correctness of both inferences goes to show what is wrong with simple-minded genetic determinism.

The Best of Both Worlds

Because genetic language ("a gene for x") plays into our sound-bite culture, there is all the more reason to educate the public that genes, by themselves, are like seeds dropped onto the pavement: powerless to produce anything. When scientists say that a trait is inherited, all they mean is that part of its variability is explained by genetic factors. That the environment usually explains at least as much tends to be forgotten.

As Hans Kummer, a Swiss primatologist, remarked years ago, to try to determine how much of a trait is produced by genes and how much by the environment is as useless as asking whether the drumming that we hear in the distance is made by the percussionist or by his instrument. On the other hand, if we pick up distinct sounds on different occasions, we can legitimately ask whether the variation is caused by different drummers or by different drums. This is the only sort of question science addresses when it looks into genetic versus environmental effects.

I foresee a continued mapping of the links between genes and behavior, a much more precise knowledge of how the brain works and a gradual adoption of the evolutionary paradigm in the social sciences. Charles Darwin's portrait will finally decorate the walls of departments of psychology and sociology! But one would hope that all of this will be accompanied by continued assessment of the ethical and political implications of behavioral science.

Traditionally, scientists have acted as if it is none of their business how the information they produce is being used. During some periods they have even actively assisted in political abuse. One notable exception was, of course, Albert Einstein, who may serve as a model of the kind of moral awareness needed in the behavioral and social sciences. If history teaches us anything, it is that it is critical that we remain on the alert against misinterpretations and simplifications. No one is in a better position than the scientists themselves to warn against distortions and to explain the complexities.

In which direction the thinking may develop can perhaps be illustrated with an example from the crossroads between cultural and evolutionary anthropology. Sigmund Freud and many traditional anthropologists, such as Claude Lévi-Strauss, have assumed that the human incest taboo serves to suppress sexual urges between family members. Freud believed that "the earliest sexual excitations of youthful

human beings are invariably of an incestuous character." Hence, the incest taboo was seen as the ultimate victory of culture over nature.

In contrast, Edward Westermarck, a Finnish sociologist who lived at about the same time as Freud, hypothesized that early familiarity (such as between mother and child and between siblings) kills sexual desire. Little or no sexual attraction is found, he argued, between individuals who have grown up together. A fervent Darwinian, Westermarck proposed this as an evolved mechanism designed to prevent the deleterious consequences of inbreeding.

In the largest-scale study on this issue to date, Arthur P. Wolf, an anthropologist at Stanford University, examined the marital histories of 14,400 women in a "natural experiment" carried out in Taiwan. Families in this region used to adopt and raise future daughters-in-law, which meant that intended marriage partners grew up together from early childhood. Wolf compared these marriages with those arranged between men and women who did not meet until the wedding day. Using divorce and fertility rates as gauges of marital happiness and sexual activity, respectively, the data strongly supported the Westermarck effect: association in the first years of life appeared to compromise adult marital compatibility. Nonhuman primates are subject to the same mechanism. Many primates prevent inbreeding through migration of one sex or the other at puberty. The migratory sex meets new, unrelated mates, whereas the resident sex gains genetic diversity from the outside. But close kin who stay together also generally avoid sexual intercourse.

Kisaburo Tokuda first observed this in a group of Japanese macaques at the Kyoto Zoo in the 1950s. A young adult male that had risen to the top rank made full use of his sexual privileges, mating frequently with all the females except for one: his mother. This was not an isolated case: mother-son matings are strongly suppressed in all primates. Even in bonobos— probably the most sexually active primates on the earth—this is the one partner combination in which sex is extremely rare or absent. Incest avoidance has now been convincingly demonstrated in a host of primates, and the mediating mechanism is thought to be early familiarity.

The Westermarck effect serves as a showcase for Darwinian approaches to human behavior because it so clearly rests on a combination of nature and nurture. The framework includes a developmental component (learned sexual aversion), an innate component (the effect of early familiarity), a cultural component (some cultures raise unrelated children together, others raise siblings of the opposite sex apart, but most have family arrangements that automatically lead to sexual inhibitions among relatives), a sound evolutionary reason (suppression of inbreeding) and direct parallels with animal behavior. On top of this comes the cultural taboo, which is unique to our species. An intriguing question is whether the incest taboo merely serves to formalize and strengthen the Westermarck effect or whether it adds a substantially new dimension.

The unexpected richness of a research program that integrates developmental, genetic, evolutionary and cultural approaches to a well-circumscribed phenomenon demonstrates the power of breaking down old barriers between disciplines. Most likely what will happen in the next millennium is that evolutionary approaches to human behavior will become more and more sophisticated by explicitly taking cultural flexibility into account. Hence, the traditional either/or approach to learning and instinct will be replaced by a more integrated perspective. In the meantime, students of animal behavior will become more interested in environmental effects on behavior and especially—in animals such as primates and marine mammals—the possibility of cultural transmission of information and habits. For example, some chimpanzee communities use stones to crack nuts in the forest, whereas other communities have the same nuts and stones available but don't do anything with them. Such differences are unexplained by genetic variation.

These two developments together will weaken the dichotomies popular today to the point of eliminating them. Rather than looking at culture as the antithesis of nature, we will be gaining a much more profound understanding of human behavior by silently carrying the old nature/nurture debate to its grave.

References

de Waal, Frans. 1997. *Good Natured: The Origins of Right and Wrong in Humans and Other Animals.* Harvard University Press.

Gould, Stephen Jay. 1996. *The Mismeasure of Man.* Revised edition. W. W. Norton.

Wilson, Edward O. 1975. *Sociobiology: The New Synthesis.* Belknap Press (Harvard University Press), 25th anniversary edition (in press).

Wolf, Arthur P. 1995. *Sexual Attraction and Childhood Association: A Chinese Brief for Edward Westermarck.* Stanford University Press.

Problem Set #1

Nature and Nurture

To do this problem set, you will need to read Chapters 1 and 2.

1. There are many ways of appreciating and understanding the world around us. What are the key features of a scientific understanding?

2. A fear of snakes is one of the most common fears in people.
   a. Give an example of a proximate explanation for this fear.
   b. Give an example of an ultimate explanation for this fear.
   c. What are two ways you might test your ultimate explanation?

3. According to many social scientists, the human mind begins life as a blank slate.

   a. What do they mean by this?

   b. Give three arguments that call the blank-slate view into question.

4. The nature/nurture "debate" really involves the confusion of two quite different questions.

   a. What are these questions?

   b. To which of these two questions is the nature/nurture dichotomy useful?

   c. In the case where it is not useful, explain why not.

5. Schizophrenia is an illness that runs in biological families. For example, adopted children resemble their biological parents on this trait more than they resemble their adoptive parents.

   a. What does this tell you about the ontogeny of schizophrenia?

   b. What does this tell you about the heritability of schizophrenia?

   c. What exactly does heritability tell you about a trait?

Unit II
Sex and Evolution

In this unit, we will consider natural selection, the process that shapes the minds and bodies of organisms and adapts them to the conditions experienced over the evolutionary history of their species.

In Chapter 3, Steven Gaulin and I describe how natural selection works and what is required for it to occur: heritable variation and reproductive differences associated with the variation. The consequences of these conditions are that natural selection ultimately designs organisms for reproduction. Natural selection favors traits that enable organisms to survive and reproduce, and often these traits must change rapidly in response to the environment, as the pupil constricts in response to a bright light. The mind is made of many such environmentally responsive, or *facultative,* adaptations.

Natural selection does not merely design organisms for their own reproduction; it designs organisms for their *genes'* reproduction. And there is another way a gene can get reproduced: It can cause organisms in which it resides to increase the reproduction of *other* organisms in which it resides. Who are these other individuals? Close genetic relatives, of course. This idea—that organisms are designed to increase not only their own reproduction but also the reproduction of their close relatives—is called *kin selection.* It is the overarching modern theory of evolution, and it has been demonstrated thousands of times in countless species.

In Chapter 4, Steven Emlen and his colleagues show in fascinating detail how kin selection has shaped the psychology and behavior of birds called *bee-eaters.* Bee-eaters often perform a shockingly altruistic behavior; they forgo their own reproduction some seasons to help at the nest of other reproducing bee-eaters. Emlen and his colleagues demonstrate carefully and convincingly that kin selection has crafted the psychology of bee-eaters so that they tend to help at the nest in direct proportion to the probability that they share genes with those they help. In other words, bee-eaters tend to help other bee-eaters *facultatively* in response to their genetic relatedness.

With a firm grasp of modern evolutionary theory, the reader is now prepared to apply the theory to some of the most fundamental questions of reproduction. I address these questions in Chapter 5. Why do some organisms reproduce sexually while others do not? Why, in nearly all sexual species, are there two sexes rather than one? Why are some organisms both sexes at the same time, or first one sex and then the other?

Having addressed these questions, we are ready to turn our attention to *gonochorists,* sexual species like human beings in which individuals are either male or female for life. In Chapter 6, John Cartwright describes the major evolutionary process that shapes differences between males and females: *sexual selection.* Sexual selection is the type of natural selection that favors traits that win mating opportunities. Cartwright explores the causes of sexual selection—a biased operational sex ratio (see text)—as well as its consequences—weapons or ornaments in the sex that is more often ready to mate and choosiness in the more slowly reproducing sex. Cartwright ends Chapter 6 (and this unit) by turning the focus briefly on sexual selection in humans, a focus that continues in the next unit and recurs throughout this book.

3

Adaptation and Natural Selection

Steven J. C. Gaulin and David A. Puts

Darwin's Revolutionary Idea

Almost anywhere you look, living things seem well suited to the conditions of their lives. Among the vertebrates, for example, fish have featherlike gills specialized for extracting vital oxygen molecules dissolved in water, whereas land vertebrates have lungs whose multitudes of tiny pockets provide a vast, wet surface across which oxygen can diffuse from the air. It is not a coincidence that aquatic vertebrates have specializations for harvesting oxygen from water and terrestrial vertebrates have specializations for collecting oxygen from air. In 1859, Charles Darwin proposed a mechanism that could explain how such adaptation to the environment occurs.

Darwin called the mechanism *natural selection* to emphasize his idea that nature chooses the designs that work best in any given environment, thus shaping organisms to meet the challenges they face. How could the inanimate force of nature accomplish this creative act? This was Darwin's great discovery. First, he recognized that within any given type of organism there is considerable variation. The members of a species are not identical; for example, they vary slightly in size, shape, coloration, and the size of their various body parts. As these different individuals attempt to live out their lives, some will inevitably be more successful than others, because they are better at escaping predators, better at fending of disease, better at finding food, better at attracting mates, or better at providing for their progeny. In these (and other) ways, some of the naturally occurring variation among individuals turns out to be useful in what Darwin called "the struggle for existence." Individuals who happen to have traits better suited to survival and reproduction under the prevailing conditions end up leaving more offspring. Darwin combined this idea with a fundamental concept of heredity, the fact that offspring tend to resemble their parents.

Now, if some types of individuals survive and reproduce more than others, and if individuals replicate their traits when they reproduce, then traits that contribute to survival and reproduction accumulate in the population over time. And by the same logic, traits that disadvantage individuals in the struggle for existence get passed to relatively few offspring and, over the generations, are eventually eliminated. The favorable traits that accumulate over time because of their contribution to reproduction Darwin called *adaptations*. The spread of many such adaptations over many generations continually refines the fit between organisms and their environment.

Darwin named this process *natural selection* on analogy with the kind of selection that had been practiced by animal and plant breeders for several thousand years. Simply by choosing to breed those individuals with the most desirable characteristics, people had produced cattle with high milk yields, docile sheep that gave large quantities of soft wool, and obedient dogs to herd them both. We call this selective breeding process *artificial selection*. Darwin suggested that, just as a breeder selects which cows to breed by their milk yields, so too could nature "choose" individuals to breed according to their traits. For instance, an arctic environment could metaphorically choose mammals with dense fur coats or thick layers of subcutaneous fat because those without these traits would freeze to death before reproducing. Over time, *natural* selection could lead to significant change in a species, just as *artificial* selection has changed a wolf ancestor into many breeds of domesticated dogs.

Humans have bred pigeons that tumble as they fly, dogs with pathetically short legs, trees that give seedless fruit, and tulips so outrageously fancy that the 17th century Dutch were willing to pay the equivalent of $50,000 for single bulb! Such traits would be quite disadvantageous except under the doting care of humans. For example, direct flight is better for escaping falcons; wild tulips are just big and bright enough to attract their pollinators. The process of natural selection does not change species capriciously. It shapes them for a single ultimate purpose, reproduction. This is true simply because only those that reproduce pass on their traits to the next generation and those that don't reproduce don't pass on anything. Adaptations can thus be thought of as designs for reproduction. Designs for reproduction are transmitted to offspring, and other kinds of designs are not transmitted and therefore disappear. Adaptations are thus preserved by natural selection because they aid reproduction in some way. This idea is central to modern evolutionary theory and deserves further examination.

Natural Selection Builds Adaptations

The reproductive organs are clearly designed for reproduction, but the list of adaptations does not end there. All living things consist of a large set of complicated, integrated functional traits that would impress any engineer. Migratory birds can apparently sense small deviations in the earth's magnetic field and hear the roar of the surf on beaches many miles away. Some frogs can hibernate at the bottom of dried up ponds for a decade, only to reemerge and breed when rains finally come. Bats can "see" by processing the echoes of their voices well enough to intercept an evasive insect in mid-air. Each of these traits was designed by natural selection because it solved some immediate environmental problem such as obtaining food or avoiding danger. This is entirely consistent with our theory. Natural selection can design traits like echolocation, hibernation, and a magnetic sense if—and only if—they contribute to reproduction. For example, if better nourished individuals produce more offspring, then natural selection can shape a wide array of traits that help organisms locate, capture, and digest food, because individuals who lack these traits would leave fewer offspring.

Naturally occurring variations among individuals are always being tested against the environment. Any variation that aids reproduction, whether it happens to be in the heart, the kidneys, or the brain, will be passed to the next generation. For example, an improvement in the brain that aids reproduction is just as much a design for reproduction as an improvement in the gonads. Both are adaptations. Adaptations exist because they improve the fit between the organism and the environment and thereby enhance the chances of reproduction.

Of course, some of the features of organisms are not adaptations. Such nonadaptive features could arise simply by chance, or they could be incidental side effects of other traits that are adaptations. For example, your nose should not be regarded as an adaptation for holding up your sunglasses because it was not designed by natural selection for that purpose. How, then, do we recognize adaptations? Adaptations are often structurally complex, made up of several integrated parts. And they show evidence of design for a particular function, in that the parts work together to efficiently accomplish that function. Let's return to the example of the human nose. Most of its features are much more consistent with the idea that it was designed to filter, humidify, warm, and conduct air to and from the lungs, than with the idea that it was designed to support glasses. If it were merely a sunglasses holder it would lack many of the internal structural features it does have, and it might be expected to have certain external features—a more pronounced ridge perhaps—that it lacks. A few traits may be controversial, but with adequate information it is usually not too difficult to decide whether or not a particular trait is an adaptation.

For example, all the features of the vertebrate eye work together in a way that convinces us it is an adaptation for seeing. Any other idea, such as the suggestion that its parts might have fallen into their present arrangement by chance or that it is really designed for something other than seeing, is inconsistent with what we know about its structure and workings.

Adaptations Are Specialized

Jack-of-all-trades is a master of none. This old saying crystallizes the insight that being competent at many tasks usually compromises the ability to do any one task especially well. This is true for individual humans, tools, or machines and will likewise be true for individual adaptations. Notice that the heart pumps blood, the lungs aerate it, and the liver detoxifies it. We don't have a general "blood-handling" adaptation. Instead, even in the relatively narrow domain of blood handling, each of several organs is specialized for a specific function. To understand why, think about a carpenter's toolbox. It contains drills, saws, planes, hammers, files, clamps—a wide array of specialized implements, each finely tuned for particular tasks. You could cut a board in half by drilling a series of closely spaced holes across the middle. But given the choice, you'd probably use the saw instead; that would be much more efficient and produce a much nicer cut. Present-day toolboxes have drills and saws because round holes and straight cuts are two different kinds of useful outcomes, and each is best produced by a different kind of tool.

Remember that selection is constantly refining adaptations to achieve better and more efficient results. So this general principle that tools are specialized for specific functions applies to adaptations as well as to human-designed tools. Each adaptation tends to be specialized for solving a narrow class of problems simply because less specialized designs didn't work so well and selection tended to weed them out. For example, the vertebrate eye discussed previously shows a marvelous degree of specialization for resolving images from reflected light. It's stunningly good at that task. And it's downright miserable at most others; imagine trying to hear (i.e., detect sound waves) with your eyes! Detecting sound waves is possible—ears are specialized for that task—but it's impossible for eyes because they're designed for, specialized for, a different task.

Darwin's Theory Must Rest on a Theory of Heredity

Part of the elegance of Darwin's theory of adaptation by natural selection is its generality. The most successful variants will spread in any group of reproducers where offspring resemble their parents. The logic of Darwin's idea is inescapable. But Darwin had a difficult time convincing his contemporaries about natural selection because he—and virtually everyone else alive at that time—didn't understand *why* offspring resemble their parents. Thus, the theory of genetics and the theory of evolution by natural selection have inevitably been joined over the last eighty years. Only if we have a coherent theory of heredity can we explain how the advantaged members of one generation manage to pass on their advantages to the next generation.

Genetics

Mendelian Genetics

Although Darwin did not know it, his contemporary, an Austrian monk named Gregor Mendel, had been conducting breeding experiments on garden pea plants that would lead to a better understanding of heredity and a vindication of Darwin's theory. Mendel deduced from his experiments that the units of heredity, which we now call *genes*, pass undiluted from parent to offspring via sex cells called *gametes*. (In humans and other animals, gametes consist of sperm and eggs.) Mendel was able to deduce several other features of the hereditary system. For example, he recognized that normal adults carry two copies of each gene, a condition we call *diploidy*. To maintain this diploid condition over the generations, adults pass only one or the other of these gene copies, not both, to each of their offspring via *haploid* (=half) sex cells. When each of the two parents passes one gene copy, the offspring ends up with the normal double (that is, diploid) dose for each gene.

It is now known that living things carry a huge amount of genetic information. Normal humans, for example, have about 60,000 (30,000 diploid pairs) of genes. These 30,000 pairs constitute the human *genome*. With few exceptions, all the cells in your body contain the entire 30,000-pair genome. These genes are not scattered randomly in the cells. First of all, they are clustered in the cell nucleus. Second, within

the nucleus the genes are grouped together into long sequences, called *chromosomes;* the human genome is grouped into 23 of these sequences. Remembering that humans and most other organisms are diploid, you won't be surprised to learn that we each carry 23 chromosomes received from our mother and a matching set of 23 from our father.

The notion of "matching set" requires a bit of clarification. In some ways the match is very precise, and in other ways the deviation from a perfect match is very important. The precise matches are spatial: The arrangement of genes on the paternal and maternal chromosomes is generally identical. To follow this example we suggest you visit the Web site *http://www.ornl.gov/hgmis/poster/chromosome/chromo01.html* where you can view a map of human chromosome 1. About three-fourths of the way along the chromosome is a gene called "glaucoma." Nearby you'll see a gene that affects susceptibility to atherosclerosis and, a bit farther away, a gene that affects susceptibility to measles. The point is that all normal copies of human chromosome 1, regardless of whether they came from a man or a woman, will have this same identical sequence of these genes. Likewise, all copies of chromosome 2 have a fixed arrangement of the particular genes they contain, as do chromosomes 3, 4, and on down the line. Because these arrangements are fixed, we can build maps—as the Human Genome Project researchers did—and we can talk about the place, or *locus,* where a gene associated with a certain trait occurs. For example, we could talk about the glaucoma locus. Because the paternal and maternal chromosomes have the same arrangement of *loci* (the plural of locus), we say they are *homologous.*

You probably know that glaucoma is a disease that, if untreated, will eventually cause blindness. Why do you have a gene that causes blindness? Fortunately, you probably don't. Here's an explanation for why so many of the genes on the chromosome maps are named for diseases. To figure out what genes do, scientists have to find a defective version of the gene. In other words, they can only tell what job a gene does when it doesn't do its job. You know, "What happens if I unplug this cord?" "Oops!" Thus, scientists have tended to name genes for the problems they cause when they are defective. The notion of a defective gene gives us a window into ways in which the paternal and maternal chromosomes may not match.

The "glaucoma gene" on chromosome 1 is presumably a gene that affects intra-ocular pressure (glaucoma results when this pressure is too high). If we are lucky, we carry the normal version of the gene, which produces a normal level of pressure, and we never develop glaucoma. At least one alternative at this locus is a slightly modified version of this normal gene, an *allele*. Alleles are just alternative versions of a gene that can occur at the same locus. Understanding all this, it might more sense to talk about the "intra-ocular pressure locus" and to recognize that there are (at least) two alleles that could occur at this locus. One of these alleles causes normal pressure and one causes above-normal pressure, making its carrier susceptible to glaucoma.

Thus, one way in which maternal and paternal chromosomes might not match perfectly is that they can carry different alleles. It turns out that well over half of the 30,000 loci in the human genome are *monomorphic,* having only a single gene with no alternative alleles. (This is presumably because selection has eliminated all but the best allele at these loci.) But the remaining 30 to 40 percent of the loci have multiple alleles. For example, you probably know that the blood-type locus on chromosome 9 has three alleles: A, B, and O. Of course this doesn't mean that you have three alleles at your blood-type locus. Remember, you are diploid, so you will have two genes for each locus, one that came from your mother and one from your father. These might simply be two identical copies of the same allele (for example, BB) or they might be two different alleles (such as AO). When a person's two alleles match at a particular locus, we say they are *homozygous* at that locus. When they carry different versions of the gene, different alleles, we say they are *heterozygous*. These terms are easy to remember because *homo* means "the same" and *hetero* means "different."

The ABO system also provides a clear example of another important genetic concept, *dominance*. Dominance refers to a relationship between the effects of alleles. The effects of dominant alleles can be seen if one copy is present. The effects of recessive alleles are noticeable only when two copies are present, that is, in the homozygous state. In heterozygous individuals with either AO or BO genotypes, the O is not expressed. That means that O is recessive to both A and B. It would be equally correct to say that A and B are both dominant to O. Since dominance and recessiveness are relational properties, A's and B's dominance over O tells us nothing about their relation to each other. In fact, in AB heterozygotes, the effects of both alleles are apparent in the phenotype.

Some alternative versions of genes are clearly defective. On the other hand, as the ABO system suggests, there can be multiple alleles at a locus without any of them being "bad." Here's a simple example to show one way this might work. There is a locus on human chromosome 11 that encodes the formula for hemoglobin. Hemoglobin is the protein in red blood cells that allows them to transport oxygen and carbon dioxide. This locus is not monomorphic: There are multiple alleles. One version, the so-called *s* allele, causes sickle-cell anemia in homozygous individuals, that is, in people who received an *s* allele from both parents. Sickle-cell anemia certainly is bad, but what happens when a person has only one copy of the *s* allele and one copy of the normal hemoglobin allele? It turns out that these heterozygous individuals are more resistant to malaria than individuals who are homozygous for the normal allele. Do you see how evolution proceeds in this case? In areas where malarial parasites are common, individuals who have two copies of the normal hemoglobin allele often die of malaria, and those who have two copies of the *s* allele die of anemia. This means that those most likely to survive and reproduce are the heterozygous individuals. Because these individuals carry one copy of each allele, their reproductive success tends to maintain both alleles in the population—thereby keeping the locus polymorphic. If you wanted to test this explanation, you would look to see where the *s* allele is most common. As predicted, it reaches its highest frequency in west-central Africa, where malarial parasites are most abundant.

In this case, two alleles at a locus work together or interact to produce a favorable result. Genes often interact not only with other alleles at the same locus but also with genes at other loci, and with the environment, in building the organism. Here's a practice test. In the ABO system there are six possible diploid genotypes: AA, AO, BB, BO, OO, and AB. Remembering the dominance relationships detailed previously, how many phenotypes are there? The answer is four.

We need to emphasize one more important way in which paternal and maternal genetic contributions might differ. Earlier we mentioned that a normal human genotype consists of 23 pairs of chromosomes. Chromosomes 1 through 22 are always paired, with the qualification that, as you now know, some loci may be heterozygous. "Chromosome 23" is paired in females but unmatched in males. We put "Chromosome 23" in quotes because this is not its normal name: In actuality this final pair is referred to as the sex chromosomes, X and Y. Females have two X chromosomes, whereas males have one X and one Y chromosome. Most of the loci on the X and the Y do not match. Thus females can be heterozygous or homozygous for genes on the X. Males, on the other hand, generally can't be either because there is no possibility of a match between genes on their X and genes on their Y. The technical term for this is *autozygous:* Males are autozygous for most genes on their X and Y chromosomes.

All of this emphasis on matching of the paternal and maternal chromosomes might seem unnecessary, but it turns out to be essential to one of the basic processes of sex. That process is called *meiosis,* but to make its intricacies clear, we'll begin by describing a simpler nonsexual

process called *mitosis.* Remember that all your cells, from bone cells to liver cells to skin cells, have the same genotype—in fact, the very genotype that was first created by the union of your father's haploid sperm and your mother's haploid egg. How has this genotype been conserved and replicated throughout your body? The answer is by mitosis. Mitosis is cell reproduction via cell division. In mitosis the cell grows by accumulating nutrients, but just before it divides, it copies all of its genetic material. The 23 maternal chromosomes copy themselves, and the 23 paternal chromosomes copy themselves. Then, the copies sort themselves out so that, as a new cell membrane divides the cell in half, one complete diploid set of maternal and paternal genes gets distributed to each of the two "daughter" cells. Thus, mitosis is the process that maintains genetic identity throughout the body.

Meiosis, in contrast, is all about diversity. Mitosis occurs almost everywhere in the body, but meiosis occurs only in the gonads, the testes and ovaries, in humans. Beyond their general versus restricted distribution, there are also important differences between the mechanics of mitosis and meiosis. Mitosis conserves the diploid state. Meiosis produces haploid cells from diploid cells by a complicated process of gene shuffling (Fig. 3.1). In meiosis, the set of chromosomes inherited from the father aligns along the equator of the dividing cell with the set of chromosomes inherited from the mother. The maternal chromosome 1 pairs with its homologue, paternal chromosome 1. Maternal chromosome 2 pairs with its homologue from the father, and so forth, so that all homologous chromosomes are paired on the cell's equator. For most paired chromosomes (all but the X and Y in males), a process called *crossing-over* or *recombination* then occurs, in which the two homologous chromosomes swap some of their genes in a precise locus-by-locus fashion. Crossing-over thus has the effect of shuffling the maternally derived and paternally derived chromosomal material. Further variation is generated when the cell divides, as each new haploid cell receives whichever set of chromosomes (a mix-

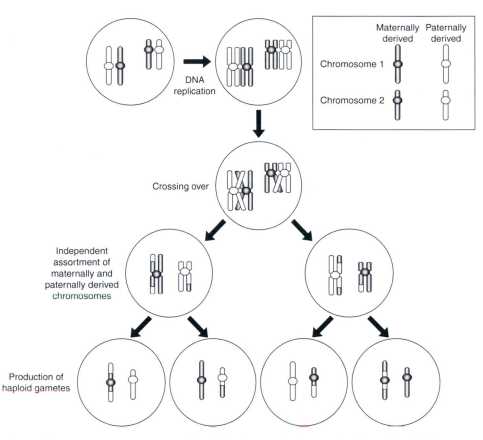

Figure 3.1 Meiosis shuffles maternally and paternally derived genes in the production of haploid gametes.

ture of maternally and paternally derived genes) happened to line up on that side of the dividing cell. Thus, the precise ratio of maternally derived to paternally derived chromosomes that go into a gamete is usually close to 50/50. Because the shuffling is random, a little more of one type of chromosome than the other is likely. Recombination is like shuffling a giant 30,000-card deck, and it all but insures that no two gametes, and hence no two offspring, will ever have the same genotype—except in the case of identical (i.e., monozygotic) twins.

Molecular Genetics

The preceding section explained the mechanics of heredity and gene transmission, but exactly what are genes, and how do they do what they do? Genes are long strands of a molecule called deoxyribonucleic acid (DNA). Since genes are strung one after another to form chromosomes, chromosomes are just very long strands of DNA.

DNA consists of a long sequence of four smaller molecules called bases, which include adenine, cytosine, guanine, and thymine (A, C, G, and T in the language of genetics). A gene is a message written in this four-letter code. The alleles of a gene differ from each other slightly in terms of the sequence of these bases.

In the *cytoplasm* of each cell, outside of its nucleus, the genetic message encoded in the DNA is read and translated. The role of this message is disarmingly simple. DNA directs the synthesis of protein molecules, for example, the hemoglobin molecule discussed previously. The tens of thousands of different genes possessed by oak trees and salamanders and yeast and monkeys code for an equal diversity of proteins. From this perspective, alleles are slightly different versions of a gene's DNA sequence that code for slightly different proteins. Proteins serve many separate functions in organizing, building, and maintaining the phenotypes of organisms. Among animals, proteins function in supporting the body, movement, transporting materials within the body, defense against parasites and pathogens, and as chemical messengers and receptors of chemical messages. But perhaps the most important proteins are *enzymes,* which regulate the chemical reactions of the body.

The properties of organisms, like the properties of all matter, are determined by chemical composition and structure. When enzymes regulate chemical reactions, they are contributing to the properties of the organism in which they reside. Enzymes act as catalysts. They lower the amount of energy required for a chemical reaction to take place within a cell, thus regulating the rate at which various metabolic processes occur. The building up or breaking down of chemical compounds in the body involves *metabolic pathways* (see Fig. 1.6).

A metabolic pathway represents the steps through which one chemical compound must go in order to be transformed into another. At any step, a chemical compound may be transformed into several other compounds. The reaction required for each transformation is catalyzed by a particular enzyme. For example, the purple flower color in Mendel's pea plants is caused by a purple pigment called *anthocyanin,* which is produced from a colorless intermediate compound. The conversion of the colorless compound into anthocyanin is catalyzed by an enzyme encoded by the *P* allele. Having even one copy of the *P* allele allows the plant to transform enough of the colorless intermediate to attain a typical purple coloration. However, having no copies of the *P* allele means that no anthocyanin will be produced, and the plant's flowers will appear white rather than purple.

Thus, to answer the question at the beginning of this section, genes affect the phenotype by coding for proteins, which have important roles in the construction and maintenance of the body. And as you saw, proteins interact with other proteins. For instance, the effects of one enzyme on the phenotype depend on other enzymes acting before it and after it in metabolic pathways. And because proteins are encoded by genes, this means that one gene can

influence the expression of other genes. In fact, the expression of genes is affected not only by the interaction of their associated proteins but also by environmental signals that switch genes on or off. Such signals typically originate from outside of the cells in which genes reside and even depend on circumstances outside of the body. For example, the food you eat and the stimulation of your endocrine system through your senses both affect chemical signals in your body that regulate the expression of genes.

This is fundamentally important, both to the organism and to our understanding of genetics. If an organism had the right combination of genes, it could adjust various biological processes to the environment in an appropriate way. For example, it could adjust its production of a digestive enzyme to the supply of foods that could be processed by that enzyme. This "smart" response would allow the organism to save resources, producing an enzyme only when it is useful. Such patterns of response might seem miraculous, but they are in fact the norm: We are walking collections of thousands of these smart response patterns. The detailed genetic mechanism underlying this sort of digestive response earned its discoverers, François Jacob, André Lwoff, and Jacques Monod, the 1965 Nobel Prize in medicine and physiology.

This realization blows the lid off an old and treasured myth: Genes are destiny; if you have the gene, you have the trait. True, a gene sometimes has a fairly constant effect on a particular aspect of the phenotype. For example, if you have the sickle-cell allele, you will have some red blood cells that are sickle-shaped (see Section 3.3.3). But the phenotypic effects of many genes depend much more heavily on their interactions with other genes and the environment.

The "genes-are-destiny" myth is wrong for another reason. Genes help build traits that track environmental variation and adjust the phenotype in response. For example, your eyes track variation in ambient light and adjust the diameter of your pupils accordingly. These traits are said to be *facultative.* We will discuss facultative traits in greater detail in Section 3.4.2. For now, it is important to note that the existence of both facultative traits and environment-dependent gene expression dispels the myth that genes are destiny. With a little thought, you will also realize that these facts utterly destroy the usefulness of the nature/nurture dichotomy (see Chapter 1).

The Synthesis of Natural Selection Theory and Modern Genetics

Equipped with a basic understanding of modern genetics we are now able to resolve the difficulties of Darwin's theory that resulted from his misunderstanding of the hereditary system.

Mutation: The Ultimate Source of Genetic Variation and Fuel for Natural Selection

Although Darwin could not explain how new hereditary variation was introduced into populations, we now understand its source. While there are many mechanisms within cells that "proofread" newly copied strands of DNA, undetected errors occasionally occur during DNA replication. If such a gene-copying error, or *mutation,* occurs prior to meiosis, a gamete may contain the mutation. And if this gamete is involved in fertilization, the new mutation will be passed on to every cell of the developing offspring. Offspring carrying the mutation that mature and reproduce will pass it on to half of their offspring (on average), and so on.

When a gene mutates by copying itself incorrectly, a new allele, a slightly modified DNA sequence, is created. This new allele will typically specify a slightly different protein, and selection will evaluate the fitness of the phenotypes built by that new protein. Genetic mutations are thus the ultimate source of hereditary variation in populations and the fodder for nat-

ural selection. Ordinarily, copying errors interfere with gene function. The phenotype produced by a new mutant allele typically is less fit than the phenotype produced by the ancestral allele from which it derived. Selection quickly eliminates these harmful new alleles. But every once in a while, by chance, a new mutant allele produces a phenotype that is actually fitter than the one produced by the ancestral allele. This is the stuff of new adaptations. Such beneficial new alleles spread because of the higher reproductive success of the phenotypes they produce. Of course, it can take many generations for the new allele to replace the ancestral one. Thus, sometimes when we see a locus with two alleles, we are just witnessing evolution in progress. A favorable new mutant is in the process of spreading, but it has not yet completely replaced its alternative allele.

Selection cannot create new variants but only chooses among existing alternatives. The alternatives among which selection chooses are the phenotypes produced by alternative alleles. We know that alternative alleles arise by mutation. In other words, the raw material for natural selection originally comes from random errors in the genetic process. This is why selection cannot create variation. Variation comes into existence through genetic, not selective, processes. Selection evaluates these alternatives once they exist, eliminating the harmful ones and spreading the beneficial ones.

Darwinian Selection in a Mendelian World

Darwin wrote in *The Origin of Species* that selection would cause favorable traits to become more common. He said this because he knew that individuals with favorable traits would leave more offspring. And he knew what was obvious to anyone: Parents pass on their characteristics to their offspring. The argument is logical, but a critical detail is missing: Darwin could not say exactly how traits were transmitted to offspring. We now know that, when selection favors a reproductively advantageous trait, selection is *indirectly* favoring the genes associated with the trait. The genes for the advantageous trait get passed on at a higher rate than their alternative alleles, so the trait and the genes associated with it spread in the population. This is an important idea, so let's dissect it a bit more.

Selection cannot evaluate genes directly; it "sees" only the phenotypes they produce. On the other hand, successful phenotypes are not directly passed on to the next generation; only the genes that built the phenotypes are. One analogy would be to say that, in each generation, genes audition for the future by building phenotypes. The phenotypes that perform well get to pass on some (remember, sex cells are haploid) of the genes that directed their performance. In this way, the genes that build the best performers become more common. Thus, the differential reproductive success of phenotypes changes the frequency of the underlying genes.

Let's take a specific example. Remember that in Mendel's peas the *P* allele produces an enzyme that converts a colorless compound into the pigment anthocyanin that shows up in the phenotype by making the flowers purple. When Mendel chose to breed only plants with purple flowers, he was indirectly choosing the *P* allele and selecting out the alternative allele. The offspring's phenotypes resembled their parents' phenotypes because they inherited their parents' genes. This association between genotype and phenotype is absolutely crucial to evolution by natural selection. Selection is only able to spread a favorable trait through the population when phenotypes—flower color in this example—are reliably associated with genotypes.

Selection and Heritability

The association between genotype and flower color in Mendel's pea plants was very strong, so his selective breeding brought about substantial change in the composition of his garden. Nonetheless, there was some variation in flower color that was not caused by variation in geno-

type. Environmental differences between plants in exposure to sunlight, nutrients in the soil, and water almost certainly contributed to some variation in the shade of purple in the flowers.

Recall from Chapter 1 that the strength of the association between phenotype and genotype is measured by *heritability*. To understand heritability precisely, we need three concepts. First, we need the notion of phenotypic variation. This is just a measure of how much variation there is in the population for the trait of interest. For example, we could estimate the phenotypic variation for height just by measuring the height of some reasonable sample of people. We would find considerable variation; people vary widely in height. This phenotypic variation is the result of two other kinds of variation: genetic and environmental. The people in our sample presumably differ from one another in height because of the alleles they carry. Likewise, the people in our sample probably have had different experiences affecting their height; for example, they may have differed in their nutritional regimes while they were growing up. Heritability, then, is ratio of two of these measures. It asks "How much of the total phenotypic variation in the trait of interest is due to the fact that people have different genes affecting the trait?"

Hypothetically, heritability can range from 1 to 0. A value of 1 means that all of the phenotypic variation is due to the fact that people carry different alleles; environment makes no contribution to the differences between individuals. A value of 0 means the reverse: Environment explains all of the phenotypic variation; none of the differences between individuals are caused by genetic differences. You can imagine traits at both ends of this continuum. For example, whether you have sickle-cell anemia or not depends entirely on your genotype. Those with the *ss* genotype have the disease, and those with any other genotype do not. Thus, sickle-cell anemia has a very high heritability, approaching 1. Conversely, speaking English has a very low heritability, near 0. This is because the language you speak depends on the language you happened to hear while you were an infant, on your early experience. Chinese, Russian, or Vietnamese infants adopted by American parents grow up speaking perfect idiomatic English. Genetic differences are more or less irrelevant in shaping what language we speak.

These two examples have no special status other than to make the point that we can easily imagine traits with very high or very low heritability. Most traits, however, have moderate heritabilities, in the range of 0.4 to 0.6. For example, many personality traits such as extroversion, agreeableness, and conscientiousness fall in this range.

All this may get you wondering how heritability is actually measured. The answer is complex and largely beyond the scope of this book (for a full presentation, see Mealey 2000), but you probably already have an informal familiarity with one of the key methods: twin studies. Monozygotic (identical) twins share all their genes and, typically, their environments. Dizygotic (fraternal) twins share only half their genes, and again, their environments. Comparison of the level of similarity between these two classes of twins allows an estimate of genetic contributions to the trait of interest. Likewise, comparing twins reared together versus those reared apart gives useful estimates of environmental contributions.

All of this emphasis on heritability is quite appropriate since heritability is critical to selection. The higher a trait's heritability, the more effectively selection can work on it. Here's why: In Section 3.2.2 you learned that selection spreads genes by allowing some phenotypes to reproduce at higher rates than others. When phenotypes differ because of the genes they carry (high-heritability traits), selection spreads the genes that assemble the better phenotypes. On the other hand, when phenotypes differ principally because of their environments, not because of the genes they carry (low-heritability traits), reproductive advantages have little impact on what genes get passed to the next generation.

With this new understanding of the hereditary system, we can refine our understanding of natural selection. We can now say that the requirements are (1) heritable variation and (2) reproductive differences associated with the variation.

Beyond One-Gene/One-Trait Genetics

Brilliant as he was, Mendel was also quite lucky to have studied the traits he did. All of the traits Mendel examined showed the same inheritance pattern as flower color: Variation among plants in only one gene with two alleles explained almost all of the phenotypic variation among the plants. One allele was always dominant to the other, and environmental differences between plants contributed to only a small amount of the phenotypic variation. We now know that this simple inheritance pattern does not characterize most traits of organisms.

In many cases, the phenotype of a heterozygote does not match the phenotype of either homozygote. Instead, heterozygotes are often intermediate between the two homozygotes. In other words, most traits do not show complete dominance. For example, in snapdragon plants, flower color is determined by alleles at the *I* locus. Snapdragons that have genotype *II* have red flowers, and those that have genotype *ii* have ivory-colored flowers. Unlike garden pea heterozygotes, however, snapdragon heterozygotes *(Ii)* do not resemble either homozygote; instead they have pink flowers, intermediate between the phenotypes of the two homozygotes. Thus, for snapdragon flower color, there are not just two trait values but three. Whereas crosses between heterozygotes for flower color in garden pea plants lead to a phenotypic ratio of 3:1 (due to compete dominance), similar crosses in snapdragons lead to a phenotypic ratio of 1:2:1 (see Fig. 3.2).

This situation accords well with what we see in many traits: a bell-shaped, or *normal*, distribution around the average. But even the snapdragon example is an oversimplification of the typical phenotypic character; for most characters, variation at more than one genetic locus is

a)

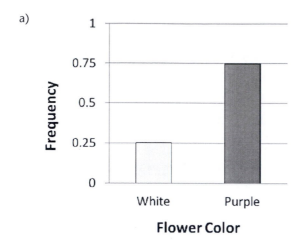

b)

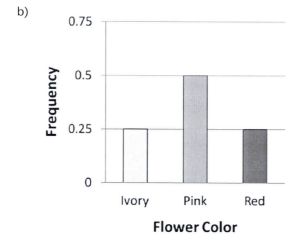

Figure 3.2 Frequency distribution of flower color in (a) garden peas and (b) snapdragons.

a)

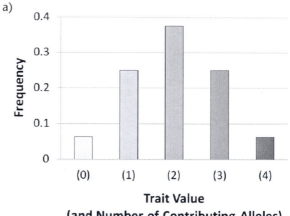

b)

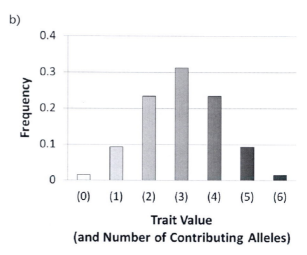

Figure 3.3 Phenotypic variation caused by differences among individuals in (a) two genes having two alleles each, and (b) three genes having two alleles each.

responsible for phenotypic variation. When variation at multiple genetic loci causes variation in a trait, we say the trait is *polygenic*. Figure 3.3 shows how the frequency distribution of flower color would look if it were a polygenic trait with differences at either two or three genetic loci (with two alleles per locus) contributing to variation among phenotypes. Finally, we must include the contribution of environmental differences among individuals to phenotypic variation. Thus, both genetic differences and environmental differences can cause phenotypic differences among individuals. The result is a phenotypic character with a continuous, normal frequency distribution (see Fig. 3.4).

Remember, our primary interest concerns the workings of selection. Thus, as our picture of genetics becomes more sophisticated, we

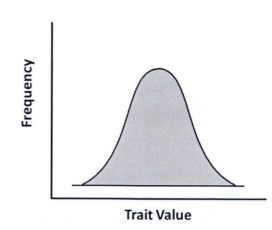

Figure 3.4 Frequency distribution of a continuous (polygenic) trait.

need to continually reconnect it to our picture of evolution. Let's now consider how selection might operate on a polygenic trait with moderately high heritability. Height in humans would be a reasonable example. What would happen if selection favored an increase in human height?

Each individual carries genes at several loci that, in interaction with environmental factors, affect height. On average, tall individuals have more genes for tallness than short individuals do. More precisely, this means that, at the loci affecting height, they have more alleles promoting tallness than do shorter individuals. It follows that if taller individuals are experiencing higher reproductive success, then alleles for tallness are passed on at a higher rate than alleles for shortness are at all of the height-influencing loci.

Alleles for tallness thus increase in frequency, and alleles for shortness decrease in frequency, with three results. First, the average height of the population increases, because the average individual will have more alleles for tallness than was the case before selection. Second, the whole distribution shifts to the right: The shortest types will completely disappear from the population and the tallest individual will be taller than any seen before. This too is a result of the changing mix of genes for tallness and shortness in the population. As genes for shortness decrease in frequency, the combinations of many "short" alleles that produce the shortest individuals become very unlikely. In parallel, as genes for tallness increase in frequency, the combinations that would produce very tall individuals become more likely. In this way, selection on polygenic traits tends to move the entire bell-shaped curve until it becomes centered on the current optimum value. Finally, the *variance*, or spread, of the distribution decreases. This is because some short alleles—and thus some sources of phenotypic variation—have been removed from the population. With fewer different alleles affecting height in the population, there is less variation in height among individuals, and this is reflected in the frequency distribution.

The Precision of Adaptation

Constraints on Perfection

The Constraint of Cost

A common misconception surrounding natural selection is that some traits are universally valuable and thus will always be favored by natural selection. For example, some people might view intelligence as an advantageous trait under any conditions. If so, evolution could be perceived as a progression toward greater intelligence, since greater intelligence would be favored in all species, in all habitats, and at all moments in time. Here's where this line of thinking fails. Building and maintaining a large brain is extremely costly. Your brain represents about 2.5 percent of your total body mass, but it consumes roughly 25 percent of total energy. This is why the brain dies first in cases of oxygen deprivation; it is an energy hog. For such a costly brain to be favored by selection, it must confer substantial fitness benefits. In fact, this is a general idea: Any trait must pay for itself in increased reproductive success; otherwise selection will get rid of it. Bacteria and mosquitoes, for example, produce many offspring very rapidly and have not required a large brain to do so. Eyes would seem to be another advantageous trait, yet hundreds of cave-dwelling and deep sea insect and fish species have lost their eyes over evolutionary time because, in the absence of light, eyes were not worth their production costs. Thus, there is never some universally optimum trait or trait value. The contribution of a trait to reproductive success can be evaluated only in terms of its fitness costs and benefits to particular organisms living under a specified set of environmental conditions.

The Constraint of Variation

Even for a particular species, living under a specified set of circumstances, many adaptations are imperfect. One reason for this is constraints on raw materials. Remember that selection is not like a human engineer. Selection cannot automatically churn out a new design every time it encounters a new environmental challenge. If you've been impressed with the logic of Darwin's argument, you may well ask "Why not?" The answer is that selection only chooses variants; it does not create them. Mutations—blind, random gene-copying errors—are the raw material out of which selection builds adaptations. But selection has no way of *causing* a particular mutation, no matter how useful a trait it might build.

The Constraint of Time

In addition to constraints of costs and materials, there are also temporal constraints. Traits are passed to the present generations because they conferred a reproductive advantage on their possessors in *previous* generations. Traits that harmed the fitness of potential ancestors failed to get themselves into offspring and thus hit evolutionary dead ends. So we expect today's organisms to be adapted to their *ancestors'* environment. If the environment has remained relatively constant, organisms are likely to be adapted to their own environment as well. However, if the environment has changed dramatically, organisms are less likely to have genotypes that are adaptive under the current conditions. This concept is especially important for understanding human adaptation. The environments in which humans find themselves have been changing rapidly for the past ten thousand years or so. For most of our evolution, people probably lived in small, nomadic groups and obtained their subsistence through foraging for animals and plants. This set of environmental conditions is often called the *environment of evolutionary adaptedness*, or *EEA* (Tooby and DeVore 1987). The rapid rate of cultural change since the advent of agriculture has resulted in a set of environmental conditions to which modern humans are in many ways less adapted than they are to the conditions of the EEA. For example, the widespread fears of snakes and spiders are probably better suited to ancestral conditions than to modern society in which such dangers are relatively minimal. On the other hand, few people fear automobiles. Yet in modern Western society automobiles result in hundreds of times more deaths annually than do snakes and spiders combined.

Adaptations That Track Environmental Change

The preceding section argued that environmental change reduces the precision of adaptation. This conclusion is correct for changes at medium time scales, but not so true for slow changes or for rapidly fluctuating conditions. Very slow change doesn't disrupt adaptation because selection can keep pace, making the necessary allele substitutions as environmental conditions shift. Rapid fluctuations within the lifespan of individuals represent an even more interesting case. If we assume, as we have, that different conditions favor different adaptations, how can selection cope with rapidly fluctuating conditions? You have met the answer already: Facultative adaptations track the environment and adjust the phenotype appropriately.

Consider your pupils. At a proximate level, the diameter of the pupil is determined by the constriction or relaxation of the muscles of the iris. Pupil size, in turn, determines how much light reaches the photoreceptive cells of the retina on the back of the eye, thus regulating how much light is available for constructing an image of the world. Too little light results in an image that is dark and poorly defined. On the other hand, too much light results in an image that is too light, appears washed out, and is also poorly defined. A constant amount of light facilitates an optimal pupil diameter that allows as much light as possible to strike the retina but not much that the image is "overexposed" and washed out. The point is, however, that the amount of light in the environment is *not* constant: It changes markedly over the course of the day, ranging from very low light on a moonless

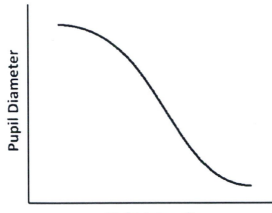

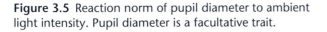

Figure 3.5 Reaction norm of pupil diameter to ambient light intensity. Pupil diameter is a facultative trait.

night to extremely bright light in an open field at midday. Because this environmental variable fluctuates so radically (there are about 10 trillion times as many photons in the sunny field as on the moonless night), natural selection has favored not a single value for pupil diameter in humans but rather a particular pattern of response, called a *reaction norm,* that tracks environmental variation in an adaptive way. Your pupils have a reaction norm to light intensity. They become very wide at night when light intensity is low, letting in as much light as possible, and very small during the day when light intensity is high, keeping too much light from hitting the retina (see Fig. 3.5)

Evolutionarily speaking, why is pupil size variable? Individuals who were not able to adjust their pupil size to the range of normal light conditions were at a disadvantage. They saw well only at one light level and less well under brighter or darker conditions. As a consequence they probably would have produced relatively few offspring. Adjusting pupil size to prevailing light conditions is a good idea. Any mutant genes that contributed to the assembly of mechanisms for making such adjustments had a reproductive advantage. In general, whenever an important environmental feature varies during the ordinary lifetimes of individuals, selection will tend to construct facultative

adaptations that track it. *Obligate* adaptations, adaptations that resist environmental interference, will be favored in cases where the relevant environmental feature changes little, or where the costs of adjusting the phenotype would be too great.

One final caution is appropriate. Some phenotypic changes are not the result of facultative adaptations. Sweating is a facultative response to high environmental temperatures. Bursting into flames is not. Both are phenotypic changes, but only the former is adaptive. For a less dramatic example, sun tanning is a facultative response to high levels of solar radiation, but sun burning is not. Both sun burning and bursting into flames are the result of failures to respond—they are *susceptibilities.* Susceptibilities occur when the facultative responses of the organism are overwhelmed. Remember that, like all adaptations, facultative traits are the result of sculpting by natural selection in real environments. We can respond adequately to cold and heat over a particular temperature range because our ancestors' genes were tested for their ability to cope with that range. Thus, facultative responses occur within the range of historically normal environments and have the effect of keeping fitness prospects high. Failures to respond tend to occur outside the range of normal environments and damage fitness prospects. Now, armed with these insights, try to explain why sun burning occurs in modern humans.

In sum, traits are likely to be obligate when relevant environmental variables are fairly stable or when the trait would be too costly to change. On the other hand, traits are expected to be facultative when relevant environmental variables fluctuate and when the trait is not too costly to modify. In other words, facultative traits are favored by selection when the benefits of flexibility are high and the associated costs are low. Because these conditions generally apply to behavioral traits (energetically inexpensive change can occur rapidly), behaviors are among the quintessential facultative adaptations. Behavioral adaptations are discussed next.

Are Facultative Traits Heritable?

Remember that natural selection is ineffective at shaping low-heritability traits. This may seem to present a problem for facultative traits. After all, by definition facultative traits respond to aspects of the environment. For facultative traits, individuals are likely to differ from one another largely due to environmental differences rather than genetic differences. In other words, the heritability of facultative traits is generally low. For example, the diameter of your pupils is more likely to resemble someone who is genetically unrelated but in the same room than it is to resemble your parents' pupil diameters if they are currently lying on a beach in Jamaica. This apparent paradox is easily resolved: Natural selection shapes facultative adaptations not by favoring single trait values (which have low heritability) but by favoring reaction norms (which can be highly heritable).

Scott Carroll (Carroll 1993, Carroll and Corneli 1995) elegantly demonstrated how natural selection could favor a heritable reaction norm for a facultative behavioral trait. Carroll studied soapberry bugs (also called red-shouldered bugs), insects found in the southeastern United States. Female soapberry bugs may copulate with several males and thus lay eggs fertilized by multiple males. Consequently, males often remain clasped to the female well after copulation to increase the number of eggs they fertilize by preventing other males from copulating with her before she lays. However, such *mate guarding,* as it is called, decreases the number of females with whom a male can mate because it takes time away from locating and courting other females. Thus there are two opposing selection pressures on mate guarding: Too little mate guarding will seriously decrease the number of a female's eggs that are fertilized by the male, whereas too much mate guarding will seriously decrease his number of mates.

You might think that there is an optimal balance between these two opposing forces, one that favors some intermediate level of mate guarding. This idea is generally correct, but the right level depends on both the numbers of competing males (who could fertilize the current mate if the male left her) and the numbers of available females (whose eggs are the reward for leaving the current mate). Thus, Carroll noted that the relative fitness returns from mate guarding depend on the local sex ratio, that is, on the ratio of males to females. If there are many males and few females, the benefits of mate guarding should be high (eliminate lots of competing sperm) and the costs should be low (few additional females are available anyway). On the other hand, if there are few males and many females, mate guarding should be a less useful reproductive tactic.

From our present perspective, an added benefit of Carroll's work is the prediction that in environments where the sex ratio fluctuates markedly, a male's frequency of mate guarding would be facultatively dependent on the sex ratio. When Carroll took soapberry bugs back to the laboratory, this is precisely what he found. Under conditions of a high sex ratio (many males, few females), males were very likely to mate guard. As the sex ratio declined, so did the males' tendency to mate guard.

Carroll carefully plotted each individual male's probability of mate guarding at each experimental sex ratio to determine a reaction norm for each male. He found that there was variation among males in their reaction norms. Some males' probability of mate guarding increased steeply with an increase in the sex ratio, while other males' probability of mate guarding showed a more gradual increase. Carroll also found that these reaction norms were heritable: Sons' reaction norms resembled their fathers' reaction norms. Because he had demonstrated heritable variation in reaction norms, and because there were almost certainly reproductive differences associated with this variation, Carroll concluded that natural selection was working to shape male soapberry bugs' patterns of response to the availability of females.

The Mind Is a Collection of Facultative Adaptations

Let's dissect the behavior of soapberry bugs a bit more. We have said that their mate guarding behavior is facultatively dependent on the sex ratio, and it is. But male soapberry bugs don't just clamp down on thin air whenever the local sex ratio is female-biased. A male must have just copulated with a female to produce this behavior. Thus, mate guarding depends on two environmental variables: the presence of a female with whom a male has just copulated and a female-biased local sex ratio. In addition, male soapberry bugs do not always mate guard even when they have just copulated and the sex ratio is heavily male-biased, so additional variables must affect mate guarding. Perhaps the presence of predators causes a male to seek shelter rather than mate guard, for example. This is certainly a complex behavioral system for such a "dumb" little bug. How do such systems work?

Every facultative relationship is a link between an environmental variable and some flexible response in the phenotype. And each link requires some sort of mechanism that performs the "translation"—that is, that converts the change in the environment to a change in the phenotype. When a response is linked to several features of the environment, as is mate guarding in the present example, several such translation mechanisms are required, with perhaps additional modulators to make sure that the different translators don't interfere with each other and work together in the right way. In the case of behavioral traits, these translators and modulators fall into the broad category of psychological mechanisms. The label *psychological* is appropriate whether we are talking about insects or people.

The point is that complex behavior is made from multiple psychological mechanisms, multiple facultative adaptations, each of which adjusts the behavior in response to a particular feature of the environment. The more complex a behavioral pattern is, the more facultative adaptations must underlie that behavior. Mate guarding in soapberry bugs must depend on at least three facultative adaptations, but more complex behavior such as the parental behaviors of white-fronted bee-eaters, birds that you will encounter in the next chapter, almost certainly depends on many more psychological mechanisms.

Evolutionary psychologists call these mechanisms *mental modules*. The mind is thus said to be *modular,* meaning it is composed of a large set of psychological mechanisms, each helping to adjust some specific sort of behavior in relation to a particular feature of the environment. This modularity does not necessarily imply that mental mechanisms are discretely represented in the neurochemistry or neuro-circuitry of soapberry bugs, bee-eaters, or humans. Mental modules may be distributed widely across the many connections of the nervous systems of organisms. Rather, the term *modular* implies that natural selection has favored specific patterns of response to fitness-related environmental variation; however, these patterns may be wired into the nervous system. Organisms are thus expected to have mental modules that represent adaptive solutions to the survival and reproductive challenges recurring over the evolutionary history of their species. Throughout this book, we will discuss various mental modules (sometimes implicitly, sometimes explicitly) that evolved in humans to solve such problems as locating suitable mates, competing for mates, caring for offspring, and forming alliances with group members. Because human behavior is so varied and so complex, we can be certain that it is guided by a large number of mental modules.

Levels of Selection

The Unit of Selection

Recall that the theory of natural selection is extremely general. Anything that satisfies its preconditions will evolve via natural selection. In fact, these preconditions are satisfied by at least three major levels in the hierarchy of biological organization—populations (and other groups), individuals, and genes. Consequently, natural selection must operate at all of these levels. For example, populations with successful characteristics can increase in size and fission off into new populations with similar characteristics at a higher rate than can other populations. This selective advantage of some populations over others could lead to an increase in the frequency of certain types of populations or even entire groups of species. Similarly, individuals with advantageous characteristics are more likely to produce many offspring, who also bear these characteristics. As a result, traits that are advantageous to individual survival and reproduction spread in populations. Finally, a gene tends to increase in frequency if its phenotypic effects on organisms get the gene copied at a higher rate than its alleles.

Much of the time, there may be no conflict between the selective processes operating at these different levels of organization. By producing traits that increase their own reproduction, alleles increase the reproduction of their bearers and may confer an advantage to the entire group. However, what if things are not so harmonious? What if, for example, a trait that increases its bearers' reproductive success decreases the success of its neighbors in the local group?

The evolutionary biologist John Maynard Smith (1976) analyzed such a scenario to derive the conditions under which group-level or individual-level selection would win out in the case of a conflict between these levels of selection. Maynard Smith considered three kinds of groups: groups composed only of *altruists,* groups composed of only *selfish* individuals, and mixed groups composed of some altruists and some selfish individuals. Altruists are defined as individuals whose traits benefit other members of the group at a cost to the altruists' own fitness. Selfish individuals possess traits that benefit only their own reproduction at the expense of the group. Maynard Smith hypothesized that pure groups of altruists would reproduce more groups by division and migration than would selfish groups because altruist groups would be less likely to go extinct. Mixed groups, on the other

hand, would soon become pure selfish groups. This follows from the fact that, by their definition, altruists decrease their own fitness to increase the fitness of other members of the group. Meanwhile, selfish individuals reap the benefits bestowed on them by altruists and act only to increase their own fitness. Consequently, selfish individuals enjoy higher reproductive success than do altruists. Selfishness thus spreads, turning mixed groups into selfish ones.

Maynard Smith saw that, in order for selection at the level of groups to foster altruism, altruist groups would have to produce new altruist groups faster than they could be "infected" by selfish individuals. *Infection* refers to the migration of selfish individuals from selfish or mixed groups into pure altruist groups. This kind of infection could easily occur in species in which new groups are produced by migration of individuals from existing groups. Every infection puts a formerly altruistic group on a trajectory to being first a mixed group and eventually a pure selfish group. This infection can thus only be cancelled by the eventual extinction of the resulting selfish group. If infections are more common than extinctions—a very likely case in nature—selection at the level of groups will never keep pace with selection at the level of individuals, and group-selected altruism will be eliminated.

Another way to predict the outcome of conflicting selection at different levels is an examination of the degree to which phenomena at each level satisfy the prerequisites for natural selection. Selection should be stronger where its preconditions are more fully satisfied. In this regard, note that the prerequisite of heritable variation is satisfied most completely at the level of the gene. For this criterion to be fully satisfied at the level of the population, populations would have to copy themselves exactly. This is essentially impossible: A new population is very unlikely to be composed of individuals possessing exactly the same characteristics, in exactly the same proportions, as the parent population. Similarly, complete heritability is unrealistic at the level of the individual. Your offspring carry

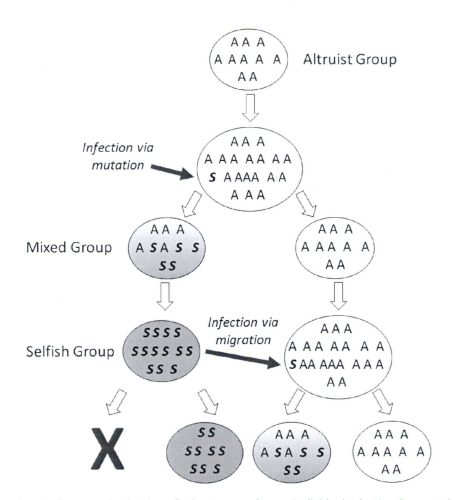

Figure 3.6 Group selection favors traits that benefit the group, whereas individual selection favors traits that increase individual fitness. Group selection sometimes opposes individual selection, as in favoring indiscriminate altruism (designated "A") toward group members. The outcome of conflict between selection at multiple levels is determined by the rate at which pure altruist groups "reproduce" (grow and fission into more groups), relative to the rate at which altruist groups are "infected" by selfish individuals (designated "S") through mutation or migration. Selfishness spreads in altruist groups, turning them into selfish groups, which are more likely to go extinct. Group selection can win out only if the reproductive advantage of altruist groups is large relative to the rate of infection by selfish individuals, an unlikely event in nature.

only half your genes. Even in asexual organisms, environmental differences will always contribute to some measurable phenotypic variation between parent and offspring.

Genes, however, do make exact copies of themselves, except in the very rare event of genetic mutation. Dawkins (1989) proposed that the gene is the largest reproducing "unit" that exactly satisfies all of the preconditions for natural selection. There is variation among genes (alleles) that is transmissible from one generation to the next, and genes affect their own replication by coding for proteins that build phenotypes and thus determine the

gene's chances of being transmitted to the next generation. The gene is therefore the basic unit of selection.

Kin Selection and Inclusive Fitness Theory

Because the gene fits the preconditions for natural selection so well, we can expect selection to have had a major effect at this level of biological organization and to have been somewhat less influential at other levels. As social scientists, however, we are interested not so much in which genes have been successful at propagating themselves as we are in what sorts of traits organisms can be expected to possess. On the other hand, the core of Darwin's legacy is that the answers to these two questions are tightly intertwined. The characteristics of higher levels of biological organization are expected to have benefited the genes that shape these characteristics. As a result, individual organisms are predicted to possess traits that have reliably increased the reproduction of the genes that underlie them.

We can predict what sorts of traits will exist at the individual level by answering a related question: *What phenotypic effects might cause selection to favor a gene over its alleles?* This is a slightly tricky question because a typical gene may be found in many different environments, interacting with many different genes at the same and other loci. For this reason, there are probably very few alleles that always increase reproductive success—that is, that increase reproductive success in every body that carries them. On the other hand, a gene doesn't have to do *that* well to be favored by selection. A gene could be favored by selection by jumping a much lower hurdle: increasing reproduction in some bodies, decreasing reproduction in others, but averaging an increase in reproduction relative to the effects of alternative alleles. For example, a gene that is slightly detrimental to reproductive success in males may be favored over its alleles if it significantly increases the reproductive success of females. Here, we are not assuming that male possessors of a gene actively affect the reproductive success of female possessors of the gene or vice versa—only that a gene's positive effects in some bodies more than compensate for its negative effects in others. This is sufficient to spread and maintain a gene in natural populations.

In teaching about evolution, we call this strategy "the front door to the next generation." A gene that increases the fitness of its average carrier will inevitably spread. This is an important idea, and we should pause to give it proper attention. On the other hand, one of the most exciting evolutionary discoveries of the 20th century was that there is also a "back door to the next generation." At first blush, the idea sounds like science fiction—like a hidden passage to another dimension or time travel. But literally thousands of studies have tested its detailed predictions since the late W. D. Hamilton unveiled his theory of *kin selection* (Hamilton 1964a, b), and it now stands as close to fact as we ever get in science. In a nutshell, Hamilton suggested that a gene could spread if it caused its bearers to *decrease* their own fitness in order to increase the reproduction of *other bearers of the same gene*. In fact, this provides an explanation for altruism, an explanation that the failed theory of group selection could not provide.

Let's dissect the argument supporting kin selection theory. If a gene is to be favored by selection, it must, in total, confer more fitness benefit than cost on its bearers. Of course, it could confer costs on some bearers and benefits on others, as long as the benefits outweighed the costs. When a gene causes one individual to behave altruistically toward another individual, the cost to the gene is simply the reproductive cost to the altruist (let's call this cost *c*). However, the benefit to the gene is slightly more complicated. The *expected* benefit to the "altruist gene" is not merely the reproductive benefit (let's call it *b*) conferred on the recipient of the altruism, because the recipient may not possess the altruist gene. Rather, the expected benefit to the altruist gene is equal to the reproductive benefit *(b)* bestowed on the recipient of the altruism, multiplied by the probability *(r)* that the recipient also possesses the altruist gene. Because such an altruist gene is favored by selection only if the expected benefits to the gene exceed the expected costs, the following relationship obtains:

$$rb > c$$

That is, the benefit to the recipient, multiplied by the probability that the recipient and the altruist share the altruist gene, must be greater than the cost to the altruist. This relationship is known as *Hamilton's rule*. Such altruistic behavior is thus more likely to occur when (1) the cost to the altruist is small, (2) the benefit to the recipient is large, and (3) there is a high probability that the recipient and the altruist share a particular gene.

When is the probability high that the altruist and the recipient share a gene? When the altruist and the recipient are close genetic relatives. In fact, the variable *r* is called the *coefficient of relatedness*. Individuals can share genes by chance, of course, but the only factor that systematically elevates the likelihood of gene sharing above the chance level is kinship. For example, the coefficient of relatedness between full siblings is 0.5; likewise, parents and their offspring are linked by an *r* of 0.5 (because of meiosis). Grandparents and grandchildren have an *r* of 0.25, which is the same as the coefficient of relatedness between aunts and uncles and their nieces and nephews. For first cousins, *r* = 0.125. We can now make a prediction about the sorts of traits we can expect organisms to possess given the strength of gene-level selection: Organisms are expected to possess traits (both morphological and behavioral) that tend to increase their own reproductive success or the reproductive success of their close genetic relatives. The sum of (1) an organism's reproductive success and (2) the organism's effects on the reproduction of its relatives (multiplied by their coefficients of relatedness) is the organism's *inclusive fitness*. We thus expect that organisms will tend to possess traits that, in the evolutionary past, increased inclusive fitness. When organisms use altruism to increase their inclusive fitness, we expect their behavior to be facultatively dependent on the relationship among *r*, *b*, and *c*. A vast literature, spanning creatures from ants through monkeys and apes to people, suggests that these predictions match the behavior of real organisms.

Summary

Natural selection is the engine of adaptive evolution. It is fueled by the trickle of new alleles produced randomly by genetic mutation. Selection differentially preserves any alleles that augment reproduction in the prevailing environment. Phenotypic traits of high heritability—ones where much of the phenotypic variation is due directly to genetic variation—are most subject to natural selection. The outcomes of natural selection are adaptations, designs for reproduction that address recurring environmental challenges. These adaptations may be either obligate or facultative, depending on the temporal patterning of environmental variation and on the costs of mounting a flexible response.

Genes are units of heredity; they are composed of DNA and reside in the nucleus of all our cells. Most cells are diploid, produced by mitosis, and have the full double dose of genes (i.e., homologous paternal and maternal chromosomes). Haploid gametes (e.g., eggs and sperm) are produced by meiosis and contain a single dose of hereditary material that, due to recombination, is a mix of paternal and maternal genes. Genes shape the phenotype by directing the assembly of proteins that interact with each other and with the environment. Variation in a given phenotypic trait may be affected primarily by genes at one locus or, more commonly, by genes at several loci acting in concert.

While natural selection is a powerful force, having designed all the adaptations of all living things, it is constrained by three factors: Some potentially useful adaptations may be too costly, sometimes the necessary variation may be lacking, and in some cases selection will not have had sufficient time to build the needed trait.

Behavioral traits are subject to evolution and, like all other aspects of the phenotype, are shaped by gene-gene and gene-environment interactions. Most behavioral adaptations have significant facultative components; the array of facultative behavioral mechanisms (mental modules) is thought to be quite large.

Selection works most effectively at the lowest levels in the hierarchy of life (i.e., the gene) because its prerequisites are best satisfied there. Selection at the level of the gene can nevertheless explain phenomena at higher levels such as altruism.

References

Carroll, S. P. 1993. Divergence in male mating tactics between two populations of the soapberry bug. 1. Guarding vs. nonguarding. *Behavioral Ecology* 4(2):156–64.

Carroll, S. P. and P. S. Corneli. 1995. Divergence in male mating tactics between two populations of the soapberry bug. 2. Genetic change and the evolution of a plastic reaction norm in a variable social-environment. *Behavioral Ecology* 6(1):46–56.

Dawkins, R. 1989. *The selfish gene* (new ed.). Oxford, England: Oxford University Press.

Hamilton, W. D. 1964a. The genetical evolution of social behaviour I. *Journal of Theoretical Biology* 7:1–16.

Hamilton, W. D. 1964b. The genetical evolution of social behaviour I. *Journal of Theoretical Biology* 7:17–52.

Maynard Smith, J. 1976. Group selection. *Quarterly Review of Biology* 51:277–83.

Mealey, L. 2000. *Sex differences: Development and evolutionary strategies*. San Diego: Academic Press.

Tooby, J., and L. DeVore 1987. The reconstruction of hominid behavioral evolution through strategic modeling. In *Primate models for the origin of human behavior*, ed. W. Kinzey. New York: SUNY Press.

4

Making Decisions in the Family

An Evolutionary Perspective

The complex social interactions in a family of white-fronted bee-eaters are governed by some simple rules of reproductive success.

Stephen T. Emlen, Peter H. Wrege, and Natalie J. Demong

The family has been the fundamental social unit throughout much of human evolutionary history. For countless generations, most people were born, matured and died as members of extended families. However, human beings are not the only animals that form such social structures. Some of the most outstanding examples can be found among birds, of whom nearly 300 species form social bonds that are unquestionably recognizable as family units. In most cases, the family appears to play a crucial role in the socialization and survival of the individual.

The significance of the family to the development of the individual is not lost on biologists, who are inclined to ask whether certain social interactions between family members might be better understood in an evolutionary framework. Given the intensity of the interactions within a family, it is natural to expect that natural selection has shaped many of the behaviors that emerge. Could the same forces that act on birds act also on the human species? Such questions are controversial but compelling.

The evolutionary framework that is used to understand most social interaction is the theory

Stephen Emlen is a professor of animal behavior at Cornell University. His research focuses on cooperation and conflict in animal societies and on animal mating systems. He has also worked on the orientation, navigation and acoustic communication of birds. Peter Wrege is a research associate at Cornell where he received his Ph.D. in 1980 for his studies on the social foraging strategies of the white ibis. Natalie J. Demong is a freelance writer and photographer who specializes in avian field studies. Emlen's address: Department of Neurobiology and Behavior; Mudd Hall, Cornell University, Ithaca, NY 14853-2702. Internet: ste1@cornell.edu

of kin selection, formalized by William D. Hamilton in 1964. Hamilton emphasized that individuals can contribute genetically to future generations in two ways: directly, through the production of their own offspring, and indirectly, through their positive effects on the reproductive success of their relatives. This is because a relative's offspring also carry genes that are identical to one's own by virtue of common descent. The closer the genetic relationship, the greater the proportion of shared genes. The sum of an individual's direct and indirect contributions to the future gene pool is his or her inclusive fitness.

Because of this genetic relatedness, the social dynamics of family life is expected to differ in significant ways from the dynamics of other types of group living. The degree of kinship is predicted to influence the types of behavior exhibited among individuals. All else being equal, closely related individuals are expected to engage in fewer actions that have detrimental reproductive consequences for one another, and more actions with beneficial reproductive consequences. Although we expect significant amounts of cooperation within families, we must also recognize that not all familial interactions will be harmonious. Kinship may temper selfish behavior, but it does not eliminate it. Individuals will often differ in their degrees of relatedness to one another, in their opportunities to benefit from others, and in their abilities to wield leverage over others. These variables should predict the contexts of within-family conflicts, the identity of the participants and even the probable outcomes.

Human beings are notoriously difficult subjects for such studies because so much of our behavior is sculpted by cultural forces. In contrast, family dwelling birds provide excellent opportunities for testing evolutionary predictions about social interactions among relatives. They have a large repertoire of complex social behavior, yet they have few culturally transmitted behaviors that might confound the analysis. They are a natural system in which to search for fundamental biological rules of social interaction.

It is in this light that we spent eight years studying the white-fronted bee-eaters at Lake Nakuru National Park in Kenya. Our original motivation was to study the altruistic behavior of these birds, in particular their tendency to help others at the nest. We came to realize, however, that the birds simultaneously engaged in a number of selfish behaviors as well. Indeed, the birds displayed a wide range of subtle tactics, some mutually beneficial but others clearly exploitative.

An Extended Family

In biological terms, a family exists when offspring continue to interact with their parents into adulthood. This distinguishes families from temporary child-rearing associations in which young members disperse from their parents when they reach sexual maturity. We can further narrow the definition by stipulating that the parents must maintain a preferential social and sexual bond with each other. The white-fronted bee-eaters of Kenya fulfill these qualifications. Indeed, the heart of the bee-eater society is the extended family, a multigenerational group consisting of 3 to 17 individuals. A typical family contains two or three mated pairs plus a small assortment of single birds (the unpaired and the widowed). A young bee-eater matures in a group of close relatives, and most continue to interact with parents, siblings, grandparents, uncles, aunts, nephews and nieces into adulthood. Families can even include step relatives (stepparents and half-siblings) when individuals remate after the death or divorce of a partner. As a result, bee-eater families often have very complex genealogies.

About 15 to 25 families (100 to 200 birds) roost and nest together in a colony. The nests are excavated in sandy cliff faces where the birds dig meter-long tunnels that end in enlarged nesting chambers. Late in the afternoon all bee-eaters congregate at their colony to socialize and roost.

During pair formation, one member leaves its own family and moves to that of the other. This dispersal rule reduces the likelihood of within-family pairings; indeed, we have never witnessed an incestuous pairing among bee-eaters. As a consequence, the resident member of the pair continues to live in a network of

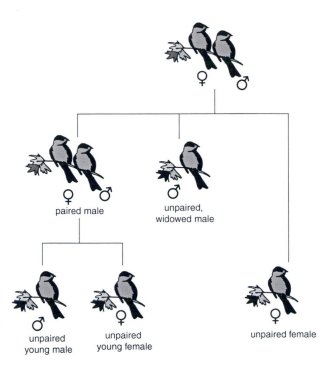

Figure 4.1 Extended family of white-fronted bee-eaters may contain three or more generations of birds. Males remain in their natal families after taking a mate and are surrounded by close genetic relatives throughout most of their lives. When females pair they leave their natal group to live with their mate's family and consequently are not closely related to the birds in their new home. The difference of living with or without genetic relatives is associated with striking differences in the social interactions of paired males and females.

close genetic kin. As in most species of birds, it is the bee-eater females that usually disperse. A paired female becomes socially integrated into her mate's family, but the genetic kinship links are lacking. Unrelated females are the functional equivalents of "in-laws."

Once paired, bee-eaters are socially monogamous, exhibiting high mate fidelity over years. Divorce rates are low with the effect that most individuals remain paired to the same partner for life. Both sexes share equally and heavily in all aspects of parental care.

In many respects, the social structure of bee-eaters has similarities to the supposed organization of ancestral human beings, who are thought to have formed long-term pair bonds, who lived in villages consisting of several extended-family groups, and whose families included both related and unrelated (in-law) members.

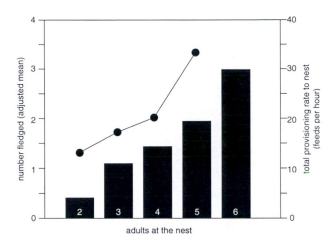

Figure 4.2 Feeding of juveniles by adult members of a family is crucial to the survival of the younger birds. The number of adults at the nest affects the rate at which juveniles are fed, which is closely associated with the number of birds that survive to fledgling status.

Helping Whom?

The most dramatic aspect of bee-eater reproductive behavior is the phenomenon of helping at the nest. Helpers play a major role in almost every aspect of nesting except copulation. Even before breeding begins, helpers aid in digging the nest chamber, a task that may take 10 to 14 days. Helpers also bring food to breeding females during the week in which they are energetically burdened by egg production. After the eggs have been laid, helpers of both sexes undergo physiological changes, enabling them to incubate the clutch. Helpers will defend the young birds for weeks after they are hatched and for several weeks after they are fledged. Helping usually ceases only when the young are completely self-sufficient.

By far the most significant component of helping is providing food for the young. Because the abundance of the bee-eaters' staple food (flying insects) varies unpredictably, the extraparental helpers can have a major effect on a pair's breeding success. In our study, one-half of all nestlings died of starvation before leaving the nest. However, the presence of even a single helper reduced the starvation losses to the point of doubling the fledgling success of an unaided pair!

Because bee-eaters tend to provide aid only to family members (genetic relatives), helpers play a major role in the reproductive success of their nondescendent kin. This means that helpers are indirectly increasing their own inclusive fitness. Interestingly, bee-eater helpers gain no measurable direct benefits from helping. To many other cooperative breeders (species with helpers at the nest or den) the experience of helping often translates into increased personal reproductive success later in life. This is true if the act of helping increases the likelihood that a helper will become a breeder in the future or if helping provides a better breeding slot. It is also true if the experience of helping makes one a better parent in the future. None of these personal benefits accrued to the bee-eater helpers at Nakuru; their helping behavior appears to be maintained entirely through kin selection.

If the major benefit the helpers accrue is through kin selection, bee-eaters should be sensitive to their degree of kinship to different family members. This is indeed the case. When a bee-eater faced the choice of helping one of several relatives, the helper chose to aid the most closely related breeding pair in over 90 percent of the cases (108 of 115).

Kin-selection theory also helps to explain why nearly half (44 percent) of all bee-eaters neither breed nor provide help in any given year. There is little profit in helping distant kin. Indeed, most nonhelpers are individuals with no close relatives in their social group. The largest subset of nonhelpers are the females who separated from their own families at the time of pairing. Helping does not increase the inclusive fitness of such females until they have raised fully grown (and breeding) offspring of their own. At this point, they again become helpers, selectively aiding their breeding sons to produce grand-offspring.

On the other hand, the benefits of helping close kin also explain instances in which birds, whose own nesting attempts fail, change roles and addresses and become helpers at nests of

other breeders in the family. Through such redirected helping, they can recoup much of their lost inclusive fitness. This "insurance" option is typically available only to the males, since they are more likely to be surrounded by close genetic relatives. As predicted, the vast majority (90 percent) of redirected helping involves males. Although females typically relocate to the new nesting chamber with their mate, they rarely participate in rearing unrelated young. The contrasting behaviors of the male and the female are especially striking in the light of all the stimuli—eggs, incubating adults, begging nestlings, and attending adults feeding the nestlings—that would seemingly induce the female to help at the nest.

Coercion by Parents

Since helpers have a large positive effect on nesting success, their services are a valuable resource in a bee-eater family. As a result, we would expect some competition among breeders for a helper's services, and even occasional conflicts between breeders and potential helpers over whether the latter should help. In some instances, helping at the nest might be forcefully "encouraged."

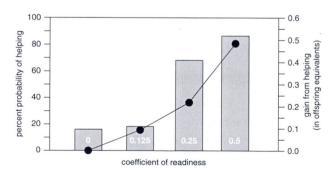

Figure 4.3 Helper's gain in indirect reproductive benefits is proportional to the degree of genetic relatedness between the helper and the juvenile being helped. Not surprisingly, the degree of genetic relatedness is a strong predictor of the probability that one bee-eater will help another.

Bee-eaters do, in fact, engage in seemingly coercive behaviors that result in the disruption of nesting attempts of subordinate birds and their subsequent recruitment as helpers at the nest of the disrupter. Older birds will repeatedly interfere with the courtship feeding of a newly formed pair and block the pair from gaining access to its nesting chamber. Both actions increase the probability that the harassed pair will fail to initiate breeding and that the kin-related subordinate bird will help at the nest of the older bird.

The surprise is that the harassing birds are close genetic relatives of the pair they disrupt. Indeed, parents (mostly fathers) are the most frequent harassers; they disrupt the breeding attempts of their own sons. Over half (54 percent) of one-year-old sons whose parents are breeding fail to breed themselves apparently because they are successfully recruited. This proportion drops as the sons become older and gain in dominance status. By the time sons are three years old, they are practically immune to coercion attempts.

The existence and the resolution of this conflict become understandable when we consider the relatively large net fitness benefit to the breeder and the small net cost to the potential helper when the latter is a son. For one thing, a son is equally related to his own offspring and his parents' offspring (which are his full siblings, provided that no cuckoldry or parasitic egg dumping has occurred). Since an unaided breeder (such as a subordinate son) produces only slightly more young on his own than he does if he contributes as a helper at another's nest, the genetic cost of the tradeoff is minimal to him. Sons apparently do not resist, because the fitness benefits of the two options are nearly equal for them. In contrast, the parents gain considerably more genetic fitness for themselves by using their son to help them increase the production of their own offspring (each of whom shares one-half of a parent's genes by descent) than they would if their son bred and produced grand-offspring (each of whom shares only one-quarter of a grandparent's genes by

descent). In this light, the harassment of the son by the parents makes evolutionary sense.

Other members of the family find themselves in a very different situation. Although a breeder will always gain by recruiting a helper, the cost to the helper increases dramatically when he or she is more distantly related to the harasser. Potential helpers who are distantly related to the harasser should, and do, show much greater resistance to recruitment attempts. An older dominant bird can exert leverage over a younger subordinate, but only to a point. It is not surprising then that harassers preferentially select the youngest, most closely related male family members as their targets.

The Female's Options

Since female bee-eaters break the social bonds with their natal families when they pair, their choice of reproductive options differs from those of male bee-eaters. For one thing, they largely forfeit the ability to obtain indirect benefits by helping. Unlike her mate, a female's inclusive fitness (after pairing) depends almost entirely on her success in breeding.

Since a female bee-eater lives with her mate's family, her breeding success is strongly affected by the composition and social dynamics of his family. The likelihood that the new pair will have helpers of its own, or will be able to breed unharassed by others, depends on the male's social and genealogical position within his family. We would expect females to incorporate social components of male quality in their mating choices. Females should pay attention to the prospective mate's social dominance and to the nature of his kin, who may be potential helpers or harassers.

These predictions have been confirmed. Widowed or divorced, older males with offspring of their own were nearly twice as likely to become paired, as were young males with older close relatives. The older males were more likely to provide the pairing female with helpers at her initial nesting, whereas younger males were more likely to have their initial nesting disrupted.

Unpaired females who postpone the decision to take a mate retain the option of gaining indirect benefits from helping members of their natal family. Females with close breeding kin should be more likely to remain single. Again, this prediction was borne out: Females with both parents breeding were nearly twice as likely to remain single, as were females with only distantly related breeders in their family.

Females appear to be making a very sophisticated assessment of their options. They act as if they compare the expected benefits of helping versus breeding. We compared the females' actual decisions to those predicted on the basis of the expected benefits given their circumstances (the identity of their breeding natal relatives and the status of their chosen mate within his family). We found that more than 90 percent of the females (67 of 74 cases) behaved as our model predicted.

Factors in a female's decision whether to mate or stay in her natal group

Concerns with natal family	• Kinship relationships to breeders
	• Natal group size
Concerns with mate's family	• Mate's kinship relationships
	• Mate's family group size
	• Mate's age
	• Mate's relative dominance position

Figure 4.4 Female bee-eaters appear to make a very sophisticated assessment of their potential fitness benefits when they decide whether to take a mate or stay at home during a breeding season. A female must weigh the indirect fitness benefits she might gain by helping at the nest of close relatives in her family group compared to the potential for direct fitness benefits she could acquire by taking a mate and producing offspring of her own. She must assess whether the potential mate can recruit help from his family on the basis of his genetic relationships and his dominance status, or whether he is likely to be recruited to help at the nest of other members of his family. On the basis of these factors the authors were able to correctly predict the female's decision in 67 of 74 cases.

They paired when a potential mate was in a social position that provided a net increase in their expected inclusive fitness benefits, but they remained in their natal families when their benefits were greater as unpaired helpers. For many females it is better to delay breeding for a season than to accept a mate of poor social standing.

After pairing, a female bee-eater is faced with another series of reproductive choices. If she succeeds in mating with a male in good standing, her problems are solved. But what options remain if her nesting attempts end in failure? Returning to her natal family to help at the nest seems to be an obvious choice, but we have seen this behavior only a handful of times in eight years of studying these birds. We can only speculate that returning home entails some hidden costs. One possibility is that a prolonged separation from one's mate increases the risk of dissolving the pair bond.

It turns out that a female who fails at nesting has another option. If nest failure takes place while she is still at the egg-laying stage, she can deposit her remaining egg(s) in the nest of another bee-eater. The large number of active nests in a colony provides ample opportunity for such parasitic behavior. Indeed, parasitism was common in our study populations: About 16 percent of bee-eater nests were parasitized, and 7 percent of all eggs were laid by foreign females. Despite its frequency, parasitism is a low-yield tactic: Parasitic females usually lay only one egg, and many of these do not survive.

The reproductive costs and benefits of parasitism have resulted in behavioral adaptations by parasites and counter-adaptations by hosts. Breeders and helpers take turns guarding their nests against all trespassers, and breeding females actively remove foreign eggs found in their nest chambers until they have laid their own first egg. Parasites must locate a potential host at the appropriate stage in the nesting cycle and gain access to the chamber when there is a lapse in the host's defenses. Eggs laid too early will be removed, whereas eggs laid too late will fail to hatch before incubation ends.

There is an interesting twist to the story of parasitism among bee-eaters: Not all parasitic females are unrelated to their hosts. About one-third of the parasites are unpaired daughters who were assisting at the nest of their parents. The parasitic daughter actively defends the nest against nonfamily members, but she slips an egg of her own into her mother's (or stepmother's) clutch. In one instance, a daughter removed one of her mother's eggs before laying her own in its place. These intra-familial parasites remain active as helpers at the nest, sharing in incubation and providing food.

How are these females fertilized? We have watched a few such daughters closely: They actively trespassed onto the territory of a neighboring family, where they solicited a copulation with a paired male! Thus their eggs are not the result of an incestuous mating. Rather, parasitism by a daughter appears to be a tactic involving a specific series of complex behaviors.

Intra-familial parasitism offers a single female the option of achieving *direct* fitness benefits in addition to the *indirect* benefits gained by helping. However, the daughter's gain comes at the expense of the parent. It is not clear whether the parents tolerate their daughter's egg dumping to retain her as a helper or whether the daughter is surreptitiously taking advantage of her parents. In either case, the existence of this form of parasitism underscores the flexibility of the bee-eaters' reproductive options and the subtle conflicts that take place in this species.

Conclusion

The tactics that individuals use in their interactions with one another have only recently become the subject of evolutionary analysis. This is because the expression of social tactics is very plastic: Most organisms can adopt a variety of roles according to the situation and the identity of the other participants. Early workers found it difficult to reconcile this plasticity with the view that specific genes literally determine specific behav-

iors. It is now recognized that natural selection can operate on the decision-making process itself.

As long as there is heritable variation in the decision rules that the birds use, natural selection will favor variants that result in the expression of situation-dependent behaviors that maximize the inclusive fitness of the actor. One of the pioneers of this approach, Robin Dunbar of the University College of London speaks heuristically of organisms as "fitness maximizers." They make decisions based on their ability to assess the costs and benefits of the options available to them.

We have observed that bee-eaters behave as if they assess the relative costs and benefits of pursuing different options in very complex social situations. Gender, dominance and kinship all influence the fitness tradeoffs of the various tactical alternatives available to bee-eaters. Knowing these variables allows us to predict with considerable accuracy whether an individual will attempt to breed, whether it will help at a nest and whom it will help. We can also ascertain whether a bird will be harassed and whether harassment will be successful. Differences in the behavior of genetic and nongenetic members in an extended family group would remain mysterious if it were not for the explanatory power of inclusive-fitness theory.

Gender, dominance and kinship should be important predictors of family dynamics in any species that exhibits long-term pair bonding, sex-biased dispersal and interactions where one family member can influence the reproductive success of another. Cases of breeding harassment and even reproductive suppression are common features of many species that live in family-based societies. Analyzing the fitness consequences of such behavior from the perspectives of the various participants provides an evolutionary framework for understanding such social dynamics.

Can we learn anything about the dynamics in a human family from the behavior of the bee-eaters? More than any other species, the behavior of human beings is shaped by culture. The rewards and punishments that accompany human social actions are largely determined by society. The currency human beings use in assessing the costs and benefits of a particular tactic is no longer solely based on reproductive fitness. But this does not mean that we do not possess a set of behavioral predispositions based on flexible decision rules that were adaptive in our evolutionary past. Such tendencies would have been molded during our long history of living in extended family groups. It is these underpinnings that surface more clearly in animal studies of family-dwelling species.

A small but growing number of psychologists and anthropologists are incorporating an evolutionary perspective into their studies of human families. Investigation of the roles of non-parental family members in child-rearing has focused on the role of siblings (especially the mother's brother) and grandparents as human analogues of helpers at the nest. Martin Daly and Margo Wilson of McMaster University have studied the effects of relatedness (parent versus stepparent) on child abuse. Robert Trivers, now of Rutgers University, has looked at the theoretical basis for parent-offspring conflict. Trivers and his colleague Dan Willard have proposed an evolutionary hypothesis to explain why some parents invest unequally in their sons and daughters.

We believe that an evolutionary framework has great potential for increasing our understanding of the social dynamics of family-based societies. By focusing on the fitness consequences of different actions to different individuals, it provides a functional explanation for why particular behavioral predispositions may have evolved. It also provides a theoretical basis for predicting the social roles that different individuals will adopt under differing circumstances. We fully expect that the same general variables found to be important predictors of bee-eater behavior—gender, dominance and kinship—will be important predictors of cooperation, conflict and the resolution of conflict, in most other social species, including human beings. We expect that the incorporation of this Darwinian approach into the social sciences will provide a valuable additional perspective to our understanding of human family interactions.

References

Betzig, L. L., M. Borgerhoff Mulder, and P. Turke. 1988. *Human Reproductive Behaviour: A Darwinian Perspective.* Cambridge: Cambridge University Press.

Daly, M., and M. Wilson. 1985. Child abuse and other risks of not living with both parents. *Ethology and Sociobiology* 6:197–210.

Daly, M., and M. Wilson. 1987. Evolutionary psychology and family violence. In *Sociobiology and Psychology*, C. Crawford, M. Smith, and D. Krebs eds. Hillsdale, New Jersey: Lawrence Erlbaum Associates.

Dunbar, R. 1989. *Reproductive Decisions: An Economic Analysis of Gelada Baboon Social Strategies.* Princeton: Princeton University Press.

Emlen, S. T. 1991. The evolution of cooperative breeding in birds and mammals. In *Behavioural Ecology: An Evolutionary Approach*, J. Krebs and N. Davies eds., pp. 301–337. Blackwell Scientific Publishers.

Emlen, S. T. 1994. Benefits, constraints and the evolution of the family. *Trends in Ecology and Evolution* 9:282–285.

Emlen, S. T., and P. H. Wrege. 1986. Forced copulations and intra-specific parasitism: Two costs of social living in the white-fronted bee-eater. *Ethology* 71:2–29.

Emlen, S. T., and P. H. Wrege. 1988. The role of kinship in helping decisions among white-fronted bee-eaters. *Behavioral Ecology and Sociobiology* 23:305–315.

Emlen, S. T., and P. H. Wrege. 1989. A test of alternate hypotheses for helping behavior in white-fronted bee-eaters. *Behavioral Ecology and Sociobiology* 25:303–319.

Emlen, S. T, and P. H. Wrege. 1991. Breeding biology of white-fronted bee-eaters at Nakuru: The influence of helpers on breeding success. *Journal of Animal Ecology* 60:309–326.

Emlen, S. T., and P. H. Wrege. 1992. Parent-offspring conflict and the recruitment of helpers among bee-eaters. *Nature* 356:331–333.

Emlen, S. T., and P. H. Wrege. 1994. Gender, status and family fortunes in the white-fronted bee-eater. *Nature* 367:129–132.

Hamilton, W. D. 1964. The genetical evolution of social behaviour. *Journal of Theoretical Biology* 7:1–52.

Hegner, R. E., S. T. Emlen, and N. J. Demong. 1982. Spatial organization of the white-fronted bee eater. *Nature* 296:702–703.

Smith, E. A., and B. Winterhalder. 1991. *Ecology, Evolution and Human Behavior.* New York: Aldine de Gruyter.

Trivers, R. L. 1974. Parent-offspring conflict. *American Zoologist* 14:249–264.

Trivers, R. L., and D. E. Willard. 1973. Natural selection of parental ability to vary the sex ratio of children. *Science* 179:90–92.

Wrege, P. H., and S. T. Emlen (1994). Family structure influences mate choice in white-fronted bee-eaters. *Behavioral Ecology and Sociobiology* 35:185–191.

5

Sex, Sexes, and Hermaphroditism

David A. Puts

In this chapter, you will have the chance to apply the concepts you learned in the previous chapters to solve problems as an evolutionist would. You will encounter a fascinating array of modes and patterns of reproduction and be asked to explain them. Why do some organisms not engage in sex at all, while others are completely sexual? Why do most sexual reproducers have males and females instead of just one sex? And why, in these species, are there usually as many males as females? Why are many plants and some animals, such as snails and earthworms, both male and female at the same time? Why do some fish start out life as males and end up as females, or the other way around?

Discovering answers to these questions will not only hone your skills as an evolutionary thinker, it will familiarize you with the diversity of solutions, crafted by natural selection, to the reproductive challenges facing the living world. Perhaps most importantly, this chapter will help you understand where our human piece fits into the evolutionary puzzle of reproduction.

Why Sex?

Sex Is an Evolutionary Puzzle

Sex is an evolutionary puzzle. Some species do it. Others do not. Some species even used to do it but now no longer do. Sexual reproduction is such an essential part of our humanity that we seldom, if ever, consider that reproduction could be otherwise. But from an evolutionary standpoint, this diversity among species' reproductive modes requires an explanation. Why has natural selection favored sex in some species but not in others? As you will see, there are some clear disadvantages to reproducing sexually, so understanding why so many species use sex requires that we search for some compensatory advantages. Knowing why humans and other species reproduce sexually promises us more than a solution to an intriguing mystery, however. The evolutionary function of sex as a reproductive mode lays the groundwork for other aspects of our sexuality, such as what we look for in mates.

What Is Sex?

If you were asked to name as many living things as you could in the next five minutes, it's a fair bet that most would be sexual species. Not only are most of the species with which we are familiar sexual, but the large majority of named species are sexual as well. If we are to understand why natural selection has favored sex in so many species (and favored its absence in others), we must first be clear about what it means to have sex.

To a biologist, sex is not the act of copulation. Sex does not necessarily involve males and females; nor does it even, by definition, involve reproduction. Sex is simply the recombination of DNA from two individuals to produce an organism with a novel genotype. Recombination is the essence of sex. In fact, although protozoa, such as amoebae and paramecia, and bacteria reproduce asexually, they can undergo a process called *conjugation* that fits our definition of sex without exhibiting anything that fits the common definition of reproduction. All protozoa and a few bacteria lack cell walls, so that when two collide, they fuse and combine their genetic material and other cellular contents. Most bacteria have a cell wall that prevents this kind of recombination. Instead, genetic material must be transferred from one bacterium to another through a long, tubelike structure called a *sex pilus*. When, on occasion, two bacteria undergo conjugation, one bacterium duplicates part or all of its single chromosome (depending on the duration of conjugation), spooling it through the sex pilus and into the other bacterium. In the receiving bacterium, the new genetic material lines up alongside the same loci of its original chromosome the way homologous chromosomes pair up during meiosis. Crossing-over incorporates some of the new genes into the receiving bacterium's genome, and any remaining genetic material is broken down. This is sex bacteria-style.

Among organisms that *reproduce* sexually, sex also entails the random shuffling of each donor's genes in the production of gametes. As you may recall from Chapter 3, genetic shuffling occurs during meiosis from crossing-over and the random assortment of maternally derived and paternally derived chromosomes into haploid gametes. For most sexual species, including humans, recombination requires the fusion of two haploid gametes into a zygote during fertilization, or *syngamy*. Syngamy produces an offspring with a new combination of alleles that is unlikely ever to have occurred before. As you will see, this feature of sexual reproduction—the generation of genetically unique offspring—imposes significant fitness costs to sexual reproducers. While sex is very common, many species distributed over a variety of *taxa* (groups of species) reproduce without sex. Before we examine costs and benefits of sex, let's consider the alternative: asexual reproduction.

Asexual reproduction involves producing offspring that share a single parent's genes. In the most common forms, parents either grow large enough to fission into two genetically identical clones of roughly equal size or produce offspring by budding off. A bacterial cell, for example, copies its single, circular chromosome, sends the two copies of the chromosome to opposite ends of the cell, and then divides into two "offspring," each having the same genotype. Under optimal conditions, the entire process takes just over twenty minutes. Some animals and many plants can reproduce by budding off. Plants such as strawberries and spider plants simply send out underground runners that are completely capable of growing and surviving on their own.

In still other asexuals, unfertilized eggs develop into offspring. This form of asexual reproduction is known as *parthenogenesis*. Some such species you may never have seen before, but others you probably have. In several species of the whiptail lizard of the southwestern United States, for example, offspring develop from unfertilized eggs. The interesting thing about parthenogenetic whiptails is that they clearly used to have sex. In

Figure 5.1 Some whiptail lizards can reproduce asexually through a process called parthenogenesis.

Image © David Hamman, 2008. Used under license from Shutterstock, Inc.

fact, in several parthenogenetic species, females (all asexual whiptails are considered females) still require copulation for their eggs to develop. In some of these species, females copulate with other females of their species. In others, females copulate with males of a closely related species. But no matter whom the female copulates with, she retains full genetic parentage of her offspring, for her eggs are already diploid (Fig. 5.1).

Among plants, dandelions also carry the vestiges of sexual reproduction. The most fascinating thing about dandelions is that they have flowers. Ordinarily, flowers are a dead giveaway of sex. Flowers house the sex organs of plants and have been designed by selection specifically to attract pollinators. But in virtually all of the roughly two thousand species of dandelions, sex is no longer possible, and seeds develop without fertilization.

Clearly, natural selection does not always favor sexual reproduction. In fact, as you will soon see, there are so many and such obvious *dis*advantages to sex that evolutionary biologists have had a hard time agreeing on just why sex exists at all. Before we consider some of the proposed reasons for sex, let's examine some of its drawbacks.

Costs of Sex

The Cost of Recombination

The genetic shuffling that characterizes sexual reproduction imposes the first major cost of sex.

After all, in order to reproduce, the parent's particular combination of alleles must have been successful at producing a phenotype that could overcome whatever survival and other reproductive challenges the environment posed. In other words, a parent must have had a genotype that, in a sense, passed the tests of the environment. Sexual reproduction would thus break up a demonstrably fit genotype in the generation of offspring with completely untested combinations of alleles. In contrast to the asexual production of genetically identical offspring, sexual reproduction is therefore quite costly. The cost of breaking up fit genotypes during sexual reproduction is called the *cost of recombination*.

The Cost of Meiosis

A second cost of sexual reproduction is often called the *cost of meiosis* (Williams 1966). Sexual reproducers contribute only half of their genes to each offspring, whereas asexual reproducers can pass on all of theirs. If sexual and asexual reproducers average the same number of offspring, then the number of copies of an asexual reproducer's genes that are represented in the next generation should be double that of a sexual reproducer. Daly and Wilson (1983) call this the "twofold advantage of parthenogenesis." From the individual's perspective, then, sex appears to impose a serious cost in that it produces only half as many copies of the individual's genotype as asexual reproduction does.

However, in a population of sexual reproducers, both parents are expected to possess the genes associated with sexual reproduction. All of the offspring of sexual reproducers receive the genes for sex, and at least for these genes, there is no cost of meiosis. On the other hand, the other costs of sex remain undiminished for sexual genes. Moreover, in such cases of *intragenomic conflict* in which some genes can replicate themselves at the expense of other genes within the same genome, organisms tend to be genetically "democratic." In other words, organisms typically exhibit phenotypes that benefit the majority of their genes. While genes for sex may incur no cost of meiosis, *every* other gene in a sexual organism's genome does. In the words of Richard Dawkins (1989), the genes for sex would be "outlaw genes." A mutation at any other locus that disrupted sexual reproduction and led to asexual reproduction would get copied at twice the rate of its alleles and would quickly increase in frequency in the population.

The Cost of Producing Sons

Some researchers have argued that the disadvantage of sexual reproduction lies not in meiosis, but in producing males. John Maynard Smith (1978) called this the *cost of producing sons*. If we assume that, as was suggested previously, all sexual reproducers really do share the genes for sexual reproduction and all of their offspring inherit these genes, then from the sex gene's perspective, it would seem that sex imposes little cost. But consider the following hypothetical scenario.

Let's start with a population of one male and one female sexual reproducer and one asexual "female." Each sexual pair can be expected to produce, on average, one son and one daughter, which we will assume will both possess any genes for sexual reproduction. Ignoring any deleterious consequences of inbreeding, we can assume these offspring can mate and produce one son and one daughter, so that by the third generation there are still exactly two sexual reproducers. Now turning our attention to the asexual reproducer, let's assume that she too was able to produce two offspring in the first generation. Each of these offspring would then be expected to produce two offspring, so that by the second generation there would be four asexuals compared to the two sexuals. In the next generation, we expect eight asexuals but still only two sexuals, and so forth.

Thus, even if all sexuals possess the genes for sexual reproduction, sexuals produce too few offspring to enable sex genes to keep pace with genes for asexual reproduction. In fact, by assuming two sexuals and only one asexual initially, we gave sexuals a head start—but it was not enough. The real problem for sexual reproducers in this scenario is that males do not produce offspring. From the point of view of the

genes for sexual reproduction, the production of sons is a total waste—hence Maynard Smith's designation, "the cost of producing sons." In a mixed population of sexual and asexual reproducers, asexuals should quickly outstrip sexuals and asexual genes should quickly predominate.

Maynard Smith pointed out that the cost of males would be eliminated if two sexual parents produced twice as many offspring as one asexual parent could alone. Perhaps if both parents contributed more than mere gametes to the production of offspring, this could be realized. After all, two parents working together ought to be able to sequester twice the reproductive resources, provide twice the protection from predators, and so forth. While producing double the number of progeny would offset the cost of producing sons, recombination would seem to make the progeny less viable than asexual offspring. To keep up with asexuals, sexuals would apparently need to produce more than twice as many offspring as asexuals, which seems insurmountable. Even more damaging to the biparental care hypothesis is the fact that most sexual organisms do not exhibit biparental care.

The Cost of Mating

Still another cost of sex is the *cost of mating*. Sexual reproducers must locate mates and produce costly ornaments to attract them, compete for mates and produce weapons to win contests for them, build and maintain the primary and secondary sex traits necessary for copulation, and so on. The act of copulation itself increases vulnerability to predators and *conspecifics* (members of the same species), consumes time and energy, and greatly increases the risk of disease transmission.

Potential Benefits of Sex

With all of the associated costs, it is difficult to imagine how natural selection could ever have caused sexual reproduction to spread in a population of asexual reproducers. (We think the first organisms were asexual.) It is similarly difficult to understand why most sexual populations have not been "infected" and taken over by asexuals as most species of dandelions and several species of whiptail lizards clearly have. In this section, we will examine some proposed compensatory advantages of sex.

The Adaptability Hypothesis

The advantage of sex seems to lie in the variability it generates. Perhaps the increased genetic variation resulting from sexual reproduction, while imposing the cost of recombination, could also somehow afford an advantage. Fisher (1958) suggested that by increasing the amount of variation in the population, sex increases the rate at which populations are able to evolve. A rapid rate of evolution, in turn, enables populations to adapt rapidly to changing environmental conditions and thereby to avoid extinction. For quite a long time, this was believed to be the reason for sex. But in the 1970s, when biologists started thinking more critically about group selection, they realized there must be some more immediate advantage to sex-permitting genes for these genes ever to spread in an asexual population. How could this be accomplished? How could the genes for sex overcome its costs to increase the reproduction of individuals in which they reside? What advantage do genes get from sex?

Because bacterial sex is simple (bacteria are haploid and have only one chromosome), let's consider sex in bacteria. To bacterial genes, sex means having a chance either to mix with new alleles or to get edited out by crossing over. Remember, bacterial genes can get edited out because they were in the part of the recipient's genome that was replaced by donor DNA. Getting edited out is about the worst thing that could happen to a bacterial gene. And mixing with new alleles imposes the cost of recombination. From a bacterial gene's perspective, why put up with sex?

Here's a possibility: Imagine a colony of billions of bacterial cells, descended from a single ancestral cell. Assume that these bacteria reproduce asexually, as do all bacteria, but are capable of mixing genes sexually through conjugation. Since their divergence from a common ancestor, the various lines of descent in this colony of

bacteria will have acquired some mutations. Lineage 1 may have undergone a mutation from the A allele to the a allele. Lineage 2 may not have mutated at the A locus but may instead have undergone a mutation at the B locus, from the B allele to the b allele. And Lineage 3 may have undergone mutation at two loci: a mutation at yet another locus, from C to c, and a later mutation at one of the same loci but to a different allele, from B to b_2. Because of sex, some of these mutations will have recombined into single individuals. While some individuals may have the normal "wildtype" genotype, ABC, others may have any of a number of other possible combinations: ABc, AbC, aBC, Abc, aBc, abC, abc, Ab_2C, Ab_2c, ab_2C, and ab_2c.

Now imagine some dramatic and devastating environmental change for this population of bacteria. If they were living in your body and making you sick, for example, such a change would hopefully occur if your doctor prescribed antibiotics for you. Most bacteria would be wiped out, but a few would survive. Because the wildtype bacteria were adapted to the old (pre-antibiotic) environment, survivors would probably have a different genotype. Sex, in essence, would have given natural selection more from which to choose. Of the various genotypes generated by sexual recombination, one or two just might have what it takes to make it in the new environment.

Let's move on to imagine a parallel asexually reproducing colony undergoing the same environmental change. But unlike the first colony, this one does *not* engage in sex. What is the fate of bacterial genes that find themselves in a lineage that cannot have sex? Not all bacteria in this colony will be genetically identical; some mutations will have occurred and been passed on to descendants. We can even assume for the purposes of argument that the same genetic mutations occurred: A to a, B to b and b_2, and C to c. But genetic variability in this colony will be restricted to mutations that occurred within each bacterial lineage. Different alleles that arose in separate lines cannot be combined in a single individual. As a result, the genotypes in this colony would be limited to *ABC, ABc, AbC, aBC, ABc,* and *Ab₂c*. Half as many genotypes would be generated by mutation alone as were generated by mutation plus recombination. In fact, the difference in number of genotypes between sexuals and asexuals would be considerably greater in real populations with more alleles.

Now when the environment changes dramatically—and eventually it will—it is much less likely that any bacterium in the lineage without sex will have the genetic makeup to survive. All of the bacteria (and their genes with them) will face extinction. Was it worth it for the genes in the sexual colony to "allow" sex? Would a democracy of bacterial genes elect a sex gene to be their president? Or would they accuse it of sexual scandal and declare it an outlaw? In this case, sex was worth it for the bacterial genes, and a gene for sex would probably be quite popular among its peers.

Another way to answer these questions is to consider the fate of a mutation that suppressed sex. How would the mutation fare, compared to an allele that permitted sex? The answer is that at first, the sex-suppressing mutation would do better. The sex-suppressing allele would be present in every descendant of the first bacterium with the allele, whereas the sex-permitting allele would occasionally get edited from a bacterial genome. Furthermore, the sex-permitting allele would incur the cost of recombination and the cost of mating: Conjugation requires the production of a sex pilus and takes time that cannot be spent copying DNA and asexually dividing into more cells. However, as soon as the environment changed appreciably, the initial head start of asexuality would be completely meaningless if the entire asexual population faced sudden extinction. The allele that enjoyed the initial advantage of suppressing sex would pay the ultimate price. In a population of bacteria, some of which carry an allele for sex and some of which carry an allele that prohibits sex, sooner or later the sex allele is likely to win because fewer carriers of the sex allele will die when catastrophe strikes.

The question is, will this benefit come soon enough? This is the single biggest problem fac-

ing the adaptability hypothesis. Indeed, it seems unlikely that sexual genes could overcome the tremendous costs of sex for long enough to avoid being outcompeted for resources by the burgeoning numbers of asexuals. How can sex benefit the individual sexual reproducers long enough for them to stay in the game against asexuals? How can a myopic sex gene, capable of seeing no farther than the present generation, earn its way into the next?

Muller's Ratchet

Muller (1964) suggested a way in which sexuals can gain an immediate advantage over asexuals. Muller's idea follows from the facts that genetic mutations are usually harmful to fitness and that harmful mutations tend to accumulate in asexual lines. Once a mutation occurs in an asexual, it is passed on to all offspring. (In parthenogens, only those mutations contained in the egg will be passed on, but this does not change the argument.) Any mutations that occur in the offspring (or their eggs, in such asexuals) are added to the mutations they inherited from their parents and then passed on to *their* offspring, and so on. Under stable conditions, mutations rarely help fitness, so asexual populations are expected to become progressively less fit. Muller compared the relentless buildup of deleterious mutations in asexual lines to a ratchet, a device composed of a toothed wheel that clicks easily forward but cannot be turned back.

Organisms that engage in sex also undergo some mutation within their lifetimes, and these mutations may be passed on to offspring along with any mutations that were inherited from their parents. However, recombination produces a variety of genotypes, most having a moderate number of mutations, a few having many mutations, and a few having a small number of mutations. Because some sexual individuals in every generation possess no or almost no harmful mutations, even if there are many mutations in the population, they will probably have very high fitness. Individuals with greater numbers of mutations in their genotypes are more likely to fail to reproduce and thus "edit out" harmful mutations from the population. In contrast with parthenogenesis, then, sexual reproduction appears to control the accumulation of harmful genetic mutations in the population, thus slowing the extinction of sexual lines.

Stated this way, Muller's ratchet provides only a long-term, group-level advantage to sex. What is its short-term advantage? What would cause sexual genes to spread in a population? According to Muller's ratchet, the immediate advantage of sex lies in its ability to produce some genotypes with very few mutations. But this advantage of sex depends on a high rate of mutation in the population. Here's why:

Assume that a sex gene appears in a population of asexuals in which mutations are fairly common. On average, individuals possessing the sex gene produce offspring with the same number of mutations as asexuals. And individuals engaging in sex incur the costs of sex. As a result, sexuals are expected to produce offspring with lower fitness than asexuals. The benefit of sexuality in this model is that *some* sexual offspring have fewer mutations than any asexual. If most individuals fail to reproduce because they have too many mutations, then those that *don't* have too many mutations are likely to be the offspring of parents that engaged in sex. The problem is that harmful mutations would have to occur very frequently for the costs of the ratchet to exceed the costs of sex. Kondrashov (1988) estimates the required rate to exceed one harmful mutation per generation.

Perhaps a more serious problem is that the success of a sex gene in a ratcheted-up population should be fairly short-lived. A generation or two of sex should reduce the frequency of harmful mutations in the population, reducing the advantage of sex. A sex-suppressing gene, incurring fewer costs of sex, should get into more offspring and spread rapidly in the population. It is hard to imagine how sex genes could be maintained by selection at anything but low frequencies. Yet most sexual populations are composed entirely of individuals that engage in sex in every generation. While Muller's ratchet gives sex an immediate advantage over asexual reproduction, the advantage appears to be fleeting.

Daly and Wilson (1983) point out that, like the adaptability hypothesis presented previously, Muller's ratchet can help explain why sexual populations are less likely to go extinct. Asexual lines experience a gradual accumulation of harmful mutations that ultimately leads to their extinction. Sexual populations edit out harmful mutations and are likelier to persist. But the advantages of sex according to these hypotheses seem too minor or too ephemeral to explain how the genes for sex overcome the associated costs for each generation to leave increasing numbers of copies of themselves in the next generation. The immediate costs of sex seem overwhelming.

The Lottery Principle

The eminent evolutionary biologist G. C. Williams (1975) suggested a way in which sexual reproducers could reap an individual fitness advantage over asexuals by virtue of the genetic diversity of their offspring. If offspring faced an environment that was likely to be different from their parent's environment, then it might pay a parent to produce offspring with different genotypes. But what genotype would work in the new environment? Williams's idea was that, in the face of a changing or uncertain environment, *any* genotype might work. Thus, the best strategy for a parent would be to produce many offspring of diverse genotypes in the hopes that one or a few would, by chance, be well suited to the prevailing conditions.

This concept has been called the *lottery principle* because Williams suggested that producing offspring is like buying lottery tickets. Sexually producing many different offspring is like purchasing many lottery tickets with different numbers on them. Asexually producing many identical offspring is like purchasing many lottery tickets with the same number on them. If multiple tickets with the same winning number can be redeemed, then when asexuals win, they win big—all or nearly all of their offspring are successful. Likewise, when asexuals lose, they lose big—most or all offspring fail. In this model, asexual reproduction is likely to be successful when the odds of winning are very good. If the odds of winning are low, the chance of winning at least something can be greatly improved by reproducing sexually and diversifying. In a population in which parents have low odds of winning the reproductive sweepstakes, having a decent chance of winning anything provides a considerable edge.

Some evidence indicates that Williams's hypothesis helps explain sex in some species that reproduce sexually. For example, plants and animals such as elms and oysters that send offspring through the air or water into new habitats where parental genotypes are less likely to be successful tend to reproduce sexually. As predicted by the lottery principle, other organisms such as corals, strawberry plants, and many grasses that colonize their local areas (in which their genotype has been successful) send out runners or otherwise tend to reproduce asexually.

For other organisms such as aphids and numerous parasites, the reproductive mode is facultative. These organisms tend to reproduce asexually when the environment is relatively predictable and sexually when the environment fluctuates. Aphids, for example, multiply asexually during the stable summer months but sexually produce offspring that exist as cysts on rosebushes throughout the winter, awaiting the return of warmer weather and whatever conditions it brings. Similarly, many parasites reproduce asexually within the predictable internal environment of their hosts, but reproduce sexually prior to the dispersal of their offspring into new habitats.

However, Williams's explanation applies best to *r strategists,* organisms that produce many offspring, investing little in each. Under these conditions, when offspring mortality is very high, the production of many diverse offspring can be a successful strategy. However, many species do not fit lottery principle conditions. Numerous species, especially those in which we are most interested such as all birds and mammals, are *K strategists,* producers of relatively few offspring that experience comparatively low mortality. How can sex be explained in such species?

Hamilton's Red Queen Hypothesis

Rather than using a lottery as his metaphor for reproduction, Williams could have used target shooting. When a target is large, fixed, and easy to hit, the most efficient tactic is firing a single bullet. When instead the target is, like a clay pigeon, small, moving, and difficult to sight accurately, the best tactic is firing a shotgun shell full of many smaller pieces of shot that spread out as they leave the barrel. To reproduce sexually is to produce offspring in a similar "scattershot" fashion. When the target, the set of environmental conditions relevant to fitness, is in constant motion, such scattershot reproduction is likely to be a parent's best chance for hitting it.

Williams was probably not far off the mark with his lottery principle, even for *K* strategists. Although *K* strategists do not reproduce scattershot by producing many varied offspring in the hopes that one will hit the mark as some *r* strategists do, the environment of *K* strategists is equally a moving target. For *K* strategists, the relevant shifting aspect of the environment is not precipitation, temperature, or another feature of the physical environment. It is the biotic environment. Living things systematically impose strong selection pressures on each other. The speed, weapons, camouflage, and sensory abilities of predators, for example, are powerful selection pressures on their prey. And the speed, weapons, camouflage, and sensory abilities of prey exert strong selection reciprocally on their predators. Every adaptation that evolves in peregrine falcons to make them better suited to capturing pigeons, their prey, sets up a new set of selection pressures on pigeons to circumvent it. Likewise, new anti-predator adaptations in pigeons change the rules of the game for peregrines.

Such *co-evolutionary contests,* or *co-evolutionary arms races* as they are called, were compared by evolutionary biologist Leigh Van Valen (1973) to Alice's meeting with the Red Queen in Lewis Carroll's *Through the Looking Glass* (1871). In Wonderland, the Red Queen takes Alice on a frantic run that seems to get them nowhere.

"Well in our country," said Alice, still panting a little, "you'd generally get somewhere else—if you ran very fast for a long time as we've been doing."

"A slow sort of country!" said the Queen. "Now, here, you see, it takes all the running you can do to keep in the same place. If you want to get to somewhere else, you must run at least twice as fast as that!" (Carroll 1871)

Van Valen's point was that a population seldom *gets* anywhere in terms of becoming better adapted to its environment, because many biological aspects of the environment evolve precisely in ways that make the population less adapted. Pigeons present a landscape for peregrines that moves with them as they run, so peregrines are likely never to become much better predators of pigeons than they are now.

In their mutual arms race, pigeons and peregrine falcons are evenly matched. When the generation time of the two species is roughly the same, they are able to evolve at about the same rate. However, there is a type of co-evolutionary arms race in which pigeons, peregrines, and other *K* strategists are not so evenly matched with their competitors—the arms races with parasites. Because parasites have short generation times and can evolve rapidly, they have an unfair advantage in the co-evolutionary contests with their *K* strategist hosts. By definition, parasites hurt their host's fitness. And because of their rapid rate of evolution, they should be quite good at it. Parasites undergo many generations of natural selection within the lifetime of a host, producing strains of parasites that are superbly adapted to exploiting their host's internal environment.

A host reproducing asexually and producing offspring that were genetically identical to it would be giving them a poor start in life. Offspring inherit not just their parents' genes but their parents' parasites as well. After their host has reproduced asexually, parasites can continue the progress they have made adapting to the parent in the genetically identical body of their new host.

Sexual reproduction changes the rules of the game by producing a genotype that, in all prob-

ability, has never occurred before in the history of life—a genotype to which parasites could not possibly be perfectly adapted to exploiting. At each successive generation in a lineage of hosts, parasites must begin adaptation to their host anew. Sex thus equalizes the co-evolutionary arms races between hosts and their parasites. This was the idea of W. D. Hamilton (1980). For *K* strategists, the redeeming quality of sex may lie in the production of progeny that are resistant to disease.

Several lines of evidence support Hamilton's parasite-host version of the Red Queen hypothesis. First, in species with both sexual and asexual members—that is, with sexual males and females and with parthenogenetic females—the number of males (a telltale sign of sex) tends to diminish as one moves toward environments in which the risk of disease is low. Environments with low disease risk for host species include those in which parasites do not thrive, such as cold, dry environments like those found at high altitudes and polar latitudes, and those in which host population densities, and thus the risk of disease transmission, are low. In insect species with both sexuals and parthenogenetic females, as one approaches environments low in disease risk, males disappear (Glesener and Tilman 1978). Lively (1987) also found that among populations of New Zealand snails, the number of males was highest in areas where parasite loads were greatest (Lively 1987, Ridley 1993).

Further evidence for Hamilton's Red Queen hypothesis comes from rates of genetic recombination. Genetic recombination rates depend on three factors: number of chromosomes, number of crossovers between homologous chromosomes, and degree of outbreeding (Daly and Wilson 1983). Because chromosomes assort independently during meiosis, greater numbers of chromosomes allow more combinations of maternally and paternally derived chromosomes in the production of gametes. Greater numbers of crossovers further increase the reshuffling of alleles into gametes. And more outbreeding increases the number of alleles that are available for recombination. If producing organisms with novel constellations of alleles is the essence of sex, then more recombination equals more sex. Several researchers have used this equation in testing Hamilton's Red Queen hypothesis. For example, recombination rates across various species reflect the parasite loads of the environment, being the highest in regions where parasites are expected to be most prevalent (Levin 1975, Tooby 1982). Additionally, crossover rates in mammals are higher in species with the longest generation times (Gould and Gould 1997). This is a prediction of Hamilton's Red Queen hypothesis because mammals with the longest generation times should be at the greatest disadvantage in arms races with their parasites and so should most benefit most from high rates of genetic recombination.

Some of the most convincing evidence for the Red Queen hypothesis comes from a study indicating that sex actually confers resistance to parasitic infection. Lively, Craddock, and Vrijenhoek (1990) demonstrated that sexually reproducing fish called topminnows were less parasitized than an asexually reproducing hybrid of a topminnow and a closely related fish. Moreover, the most common asexual clones were the most parasitized of all, lending further evidence to the notion that genotypic rarity affords protection from parasites.

Finally, if the production of parasite-resistant progeny is, for some animals, the evolutionary function of sex as a mode of reproduction, then this potential benefit should be reflected in how they choose their mates. In fact, mate choice across a variety of species seems to be predicated, at least in part, on indicators of parasite resistance (see Chapter 12).

Why Sexes?

In considering the costs and benefits of sex, we defined sex as recombination, a phenomenon that does not require males and females. Yet virtually every sexual species has sexes. Why did separate males and females evolve? And for that matter, what do we mean by female and male?

Male and Female

How are males and females different? In later chapters, we will consider many sex differences and examine the evolutionary, genetic, physiological, and environmental (including cultural) causes of these differences. But whatever may come to mind when you consider the differences between the sexes—size, anatomy, behavior, and so on—there is only one difference that holds true across all species: Females produce large gametes, and males produce small gametes. This much is definitional. But why are there nearly always two sexes? Although, as Gould and Gould (1997) suggest, it may take an "effort of will" to imagine, sexual reproduction does not require two different sexes. Sexual reproduction is the contribution of genes from two organisms to produce an individual with a new genotype. Nowhere in this definition of sex is the notion of distinct sexes. As you may remember from our discussion of bacterial conjugation, some protozoa and bacteria engage in sex. Yet they do not have separate sexes—they do not even produce gametes. Algae are plants that produce gametes, but in a few species of algae of the genus *Chlamydomonas,* all gametes are roughly the same size, so individuals cannot be classified as males or females. Why do most sexuals have sexes, and why do some organisms that engage in sex, such as bacteria and *Chlamydomonas,* lack them?

The Evolution of Anisogamy

The question of why sexes exist can be rephrased as "Why did gamete size differences, or *anisogamy* (*an* = not, *iso* = same, *gamy* = gamete), evolve?" For that matter, if sex can occur *without* gametes through conjugation, why produce gametes at all? Because having males and females requires having gametes, let's first consider why some organisms produce gametes and others have sex through conjugation.

Organisms that conjugate are single-celled, while those that produce gametes are multicellular. The evolution of gamete production is almost certainly related to the evolution of multicellular life. The first multicellular organisms probably evolved from colonies of clonally reproducing unicellular organisms around 3.5 billion years ago. Because these single-celled organisms were genetically identical, kin selection would favor high levels of cooperation and altruism between them, causing the colony to behave like a single organism. Most biologists accept this scenario.

When multicellular life evolved, conjugation became impractical. Different conjugation events occurring between the various cells of two multicellular organisms would create "organisms" with cells of diverse genotypes. The sort of kin-selected cooperation and altruism favored between the genetically uniform cells of a clonal colony would disappear, and the resulting conflict between cells in the same "organism" would compromise its fitness. While most early multicellular organisms probably continued to reproduce asexually, gamete production and fertilization became the only efficient means of sexual reproduction. Gamete production allowed sex, while producing multicellular offspring with genetically homogeneous cells.

The Model of Parker, Baker, and Smith

The gametes produced by the first gamete producers would have varied in size, however slightly. Some members of the species would produce slightly larger than average gametes, while other members would produce slightly smaller than average gametes. Limited by finite reproductive resources, producers of larger gametes would not be able to produce as many gametes as producers of smaller gametes could.

Thus, two simultaneous selection pressures would influence gamete production. Selection would favor the production of many gametes, because more gametes would tend to produce more offspring. And selection would favor large gametes, because larger sex cells contain more extra-genetic cellular contents *(cytoplasm)*

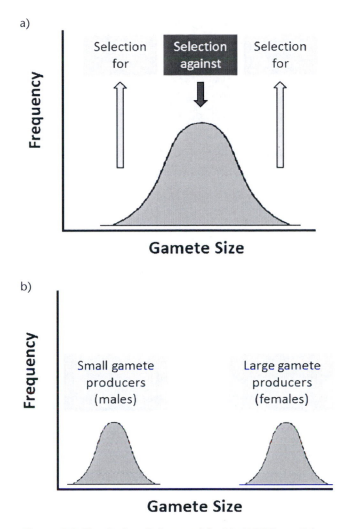

Figure 5.2 The Parker, Baker, and Smith (1972) model of the evolution of anisogamy: (a) Disruptive selection on gamete size, (b) Frequency distribution of gamete size after disruptive selection.

needed by developing embryos. Because organisms cannot simultaneously produce many gametes and large gametes, these selection pressures would conflict and lead to a type of natural selection called *disruptive selection*. Disruptive selection disfavors the mean and favors the extremes in the distribution of a trait. In this case, the extremes in gamete production would be producers of many small gametes at one end and producers of relatively few large gametes at the other (Fig. 5.2).

Parker, Baker, and Smith (1972) demonstrated using mathematical models that producers of medium-sized gametes would make too few gametes to compete successfully with small gamete producers and make too small gametes to compete successfully with large gamete producers. Disruptive selection could lead to an increase in the size difference between small and large gametes until the population consisted of two truly distinct types of gamete producers, males and females.

Further, there would be selection against the small gametes, or proto-sperm, fertilizing other proto-sperm because such fusion would result in a lack of sufficient cytoplasm, and the zygote would be nonviable. There would also be selection on both proto-sperm and proto-ova to avoid fertilizing other gametes produced by the same individual. Self-fertilization prevents the benefits of sex (genetically diverse offspring) while incurring many of the costs. This problem was probably solved in a way similar to that used by single-celled organisms to avoid mating with their clones—through proteins embedded in the cell surface. Proto-sperm would fuse only with cells bearing the type of surface proteins borne by ova, and ova would fuse only with cells bearing the type of surface proteins borne by sperm. While there might be some selection on ova to reject a cytoplasm-deficient sperm in favor of other females' cytoplasm-rich ova, the selection on sperm to bypass any such defenses would be much stronger. After all, if an ovum fails to fuse with another ovum and instead fuses with a sperm, the ovum simply produces a less viable zygote. If a sperm fails to fuse with an ovum, the sperm produces no zygote at all.

From this perspective, the evolution of males appears to be the evolution of a sort of reproductive parasitism. Males evolved because an opportunity existed within the arena of gametic sex to exploit the cytoplasmic investment of large gamete producers. This cannot be a complete explanation for anisogamy, however. As mentioned previously, algae of the genus *Chlamydomonas* are *isogamous*—that is, their gametes are all about the same size. Why did disruptive selection not lead to anisogamy in these species?

The Hypothesis of Cosmides and Tooby

Leda Cosmides and John Tooby (1981) have an answer, and it has to do with symbionts. *Symbionts* are organisms that live in such close association with members of another species that the two can essentially be considered parts of the same organism. Inside animal cells live tiny symbionts called *mitochondria,* descendants of a bacterium that invaded a cell and traded its products for the use of the cell's internal environment. In plant cells, *chloroplasts* are the symbionts. So integral are mitochondria and chloroplasts to the functioning of the cells they occupy that they also go by the name of cell *organelles* ("little organs"). An interesting feature of these organelles is that they still possess their own genes. Mitochondrial and chloroplast genes are replicated and inherited completely independently of nuclear DNA.

Cosmides and Tooby proposed that sexes evolved to prevent the organelles of one parent from competing with the organelles of the other parent after the gametes fused. According to this hypothesis, the organelles from one parent would benefit from destroying organelles from the other to monopolize cytoplasmic resources and ensure exclusive genetic posterity. Because such intracellular competition would weaken the zygote, selection would favor nuclear (parental) genes that caused the cytoplasm, with its organelles, to be discarded during gamete formation. However, *both* zygotes could not shed their cytoplasm because the fusion of two such gametes would result in a nonviable zygote. Selection would favor genes for cell surface proteins or other cell-signaling mechanisms that promoted the fusion of a small gamete (sperm) and a large gamete (ovum) and prevented the fusion of two like gametes.

Hurst and Hamilton (1992) showed using mathematical models that this evolutionary scenario could work. Empirically, it has an advantage over the Parker, Baker, and Smith model in that it explains the odd exceptions noted previously—

the isogamous gametes of *Chlamydomonas*. Gametes from both *Chlamydomonas* parents contain chloroplasts, but soon after syngamy all of the chloroplasts from one parent are destroyed. Some evidence suggests that the destruction results from the opposing chloroplasts' attempts to destroy one another with gene-digesting enzymes (Chiang 1976). Other evidence indicates nuclear genes from one parent "disarm" their respective chloroplast genes (Sager 1977). Hurst and Hamilton concluded that this post-fusion destruction of organelles is one of the two means for preventing cytoplasmic conflict in species whose gametes fuse during fertilization. The other is anisogamy.

Hurst (1991) suggested a variation on the idea that small, streamlined gametes are an adaptation for avoiding cytoplasmic conflict. In addition to minimizing conflict between organelles, sperm may minimize cellular damage from bacteria and viruses that normally inhabit cytoplasm. By stripping sperm of all but their nuclei, males propagate their genes while decreasing disease risks to their progeny. This idea has intrinsic appeal, given that sex itself may exist because it provides offspring with protection from parasitic infection. Moreover, mixing cytoplasmic parasites from two parents may be especially destructive because, like organelles, unrelated parasites inhabiting the same cell are likely to compete for its resources. This competition can lead to the rapid proliferation of formerly dormant bacteria and viruses with devastating effects to the host cell (Ridley 1993).

How Many Males Is Too Many? Sex Ratios in Populations

Whatever the adaptive reasons for sexes turn out to be, the essence of anisogamy seems to involve stripping everything but DNA away from male gametes. Male gametes, so miniaturized, can be produced in huge quantities and, in animals,

equipped with specialized whiplike *flagella* (singular, *flagellum*) for motility. Ova, in contrast, are too large to be manufactured so copiously and tend to be much less mobile. The advantages of producing many gametes or, alternatively, producing large gametes, almost certainly result in the kind of disruptive selection described by Parker, Baker, and Smith (1972). Because males can produce so many gametes, they tend to be the biggest winners in the fertility race. In fact, it is worth considering why such an inexpensive method of generating offspring would not be much more common in populations than the female strategy.

The answer lies in a kind of natural selection called *frequency-dependent selection*. In the simplest cases of frequency-dependent selection, there are two types (phenotypes or alleles) in the population. The fitness associated with one type depends on the frequency of the other. In the case of males and females, the fitness returns from being a male depend on the frequency of females and vice versa. Because every offspring has a father, the average reproductive success of a male will simply be the number of offspring in a particular generation *(G)*, divided by the number of males in the population *(M)*.

(1) Average male fitness = G / M

Likewise, the average reproductive success of a female will be the total number of offspring, divided by the number of females *(F)*.

(2) Average female fitness = G / F

If there are more males than females in the population, then the average reproductive success of a female will be greater than that of a male. You can see this by considering that average male fitness is G divided by M, whereas female fitness is G divided by a smaller number, F. Females have a reproductive advantage and consequently increase in frequency. However, as females increase in frequency, their fitness decreases relative to males. The scales begin to swing and, should females increase too greatly

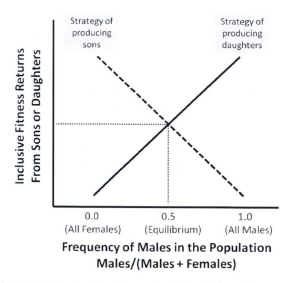

Figure 5.3 Frequency-dependent selection on the sex ratio.

in frequency, males may gain the fitness advantage and begin to increase in frequency relative to females. The scales balance at an equilibrium point where the fitness returns from being a male equal the fitness returns from being a female (see Fig. 5.3).

All things being equal, equilibrium will be achieved when the number of males in the population is the same as the number of females. That is, when $M = F$, then

(3) $G / M = G / F$

However, all things are not always equal, so the story is somewhat more complex. Frequency-dependent selection will favor whichever sex is rare *except* if this sex is too costly to produce. Thus, the relative fitness advantages of males versus females are expected to depend on the current sex ratio in the population *and* the costs of producing males versus females. This argument is generally framed in terms of the inclusive fitness costs to parents of producing sons versus daughters. Parents' production of offspring is expected to reflect these factors. Biasing the sex ratio of offspring toward sons is favored when the number of expected grandchildren per son is greater than the number of grandchildren expected from the daughters that could be produced *with the same reproductive investment*. Equi-

librium is thus reached when the *net* fitness returns from producing sons equals the *net* fitness returns from producing daughters (Fisher 1958). If daughters are costlier to produce, we expect more sons. If sons are costlier, we expect more daughters. Because in most species sons and daughters are about equally costly to produce, sex ratios in nature tend to remain about one-to-one.

Being Both Sexes— The Evolution of Hermaphroditism

We've discussed the sexes so far as if they must occur in different bodies, and they usually do. But in *hermaphroditic* species individuals can be both male and female. It is interesting in its own right to study the evolution of hermaphroditic species whose reproductive modes seem so exotic to us. But a consideration of the evolution of hermaphroditism also helps us understand the broader topic of competition for mates, a topic that will prove central to human sexuality.

What Is a Hermaphrodite?

The word *hermaphrodite* comes from Greek mythology. Hermaphroditus, the son of Hermes and Aphrodite, united into a single body with the nymph Salmacis to produce a person who was both genders. When people talk about hermaphrodites, they often mean a person whose gender is ambiguous. But that is not what a biologist means. To a biologist, a hermaphrodite is an organism that is truly both sexes, capable of reproducing both as a male (producing sperm or pollen) and as a female (producing ova). As far as anyone knows, no person has ever been a hermaphrodite in this sense of the word. Among living things, however, true hermaphrodites are by no means rare. Most flowering plants, or *angiosperms*, for example, have both ovaries (female gonads) and stamens (male gonads) and so reproduce as both sexes.

Hermaphrodites are divided into two general categories: *simultaneous hermaphrodites* and *sequential hermaphrodites*. Simultaneous hermaphrodites are both male and female at the same time. Sequential hermaphrodites begin their reproductive lives as one sex and later become the other. Sequential hermaphrodites can either be *protogynous* (*proto* = first, *gynous* = female), starting their reproductive careers as females and later changing into males, or *protandrous* (*androus* = male), first male and then female. At the end of this section and in following chapters, we will discuss *gonochorists*, organisms like us that are either obligate males or obligate females. The various modes and patterns of reproduction can be organized as in Box 5.1.

Sequential Hermaphrodites and the Size Advantage Model

Now that we have some terminology to work with, let's discuss why these various reproductive patterns may have evolved. Remember from Chapter 3 that natural selection tends to favor facultative adaptations when, over the evolution of a species, selection pressures have changed significantly across individuals' lifetimes. Because sequential hermaphrodites change their sex, it may be useful to ask what shift in selection pressures leads them to do so.

Among animals, most sequential hermaphrodites are fish or other marine animals. One striking aspect of these hermaphroditic species is that, depending on the species, either males or females tend to be larger. This fact led Michael Ghislin (1969) to suggest that sequential hermaphroditism tends to evolve in species in which reproductive success depends more on size in one sex than in the other. Ghislin termed this hypothesis the *size advantage model*. According to the size advantage model, organisms in protogynous species are expected to begin life as relatively small females and to change their sex

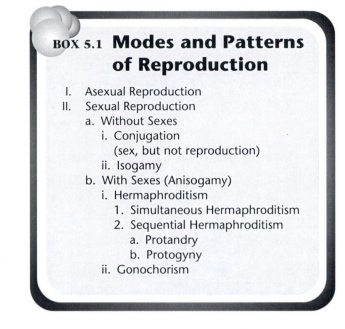

BOX 5.1 Modes and Patterns of Reproduction

I.   Asexual Reproduction
II. Sexual Reproduction
  a. Without Sexes
    i. Conjugation
        (sex, but not reproduction)
    ii. Isogamy
  b. With Sexes (Anisogamy)
    i. Hermaphroditism
        1. Simultaneous Hermaphroditism
        2. Sequential Hermaphroditism
           a. Protandry
           b. Protogyny
    ii. Gonochorism

to reproduce as males when larger. The reverse is expected of protandrous species.

Protogyny

Let's begin our consideration of sequential hermaphrodites by discussing protogynous species. Why might males reap a greater reproductive advantage from being large than would females? An examination of marine fish is informative. Protogynous species of fish tend to inhabit tropical coral reefs where the aquatic environment is divided and subdivided by outcroppings of coral into relatively protected regions. This sort of landscape lends itself easily to territoriality. Indeed, males in many coral reef fish are territorial and cohabit with small "harems" of females, whom the males can readily guard in the sheltered confines of the reef. When a male's territory is invaded by another male, the territorial male must chase off the interloper or risk losing paternity of any eggs that have been laid, or worse, risk losing the harem altogether. Hence the male advantage of large size.

But females do not automatically metamorphose into males when they have attained some predetermined size. The transformation is much more interesting than that. Instead, the female-to-male change requires the removal of the breeding male. When the male dies (or is removed by an experimenter), something truly amazing happens: The *largest* female immediately assumes the role of the territorial male. She begins to perform the aggressive territorial displays and courtship behavior typical of the territorial male, and in at least one species, she rapidly changes to the color of a territorial male (Godwin, Crews, and Warner 1996). Over the next several weeks, her gonads gradually transform from ovarian tissue to testicular tissue until she is fully transformed into a male (Shapiro 1994).

Thus, protogyny tends to occur in species where males use their size to compete with other males for territory and females. Facultative sex change from female to male in these species seems to depend primarily on two variables: the size of the female and the disappearance of a territorial male. While large females are more likely to be successful territorial males, this seems to apply only if the female inherits a harem that has recently become available by the disappearance of a territorial male.

Protandry

In essentially all anisogamous species, larger females are more fecund because they are simply able to produce more and larger eggs. The reproductive advantages obtaining to males of some territorial species outweigh the female benefits of large size. In more monogamous species, however, there is less advantage to be gained from being a large male. Members of the tiny coral reef fish *Amphiprion,* for example, live in monogamously mated pairs in the shelter of the tentacles of a sea anemone (Fig. 5.4). The breeding pair often tolerates several immature members of their species who are not their offspring. Males are not territorial but instead invest fairly heavily in their offspring, guarding their eggs from predation. Male fitness does not increase appreciably with size. Because female egg production *does* increase with size, in these species selection has favored sex change from male to female with growth.

As in protogynous species, sex change in protandrous species is not exclusively a function of body size but is also related to social variables. Males in each breeding pair do not continue to grow and eventually metamorphose into a female. Instead, breeding males change into females only after removal of the breeding female. Similarly, immature (nonbreeding) males living with the breeding pair do not grow appreciably and spontaneously achieve breeding status. Only after the disappearance of the breeding male—by his removal or sex change into a female—does one of the larger immature males change into a breeding male.

Simultaneous Hermaphroditism and the Low Density Model

In sequential hermaphrodites, then, the benefits of changing sex when a better reproductive opportunity presents itself more than compensate for the costs of what must be an energetically expensive transformation. Sequential hermaphrodites must also undergo a period of sex change during which they are often incapable of reproducing at all. As costly as sex change must be, being both sexes simultaneously must be more so. While most of us are kept quite busy performing the roles of one sex, simultaneous hermaphrodites must maintain two separate reproductive systems. On the surface, the reproductive opportunities resulting from such sexual bipotentiality might seem to offset any related costs. But given the great number of species that do not exhibit simultaneous hermaphroditism, we must wonder precisely what circumstances favor its evolution.

Simultaneous hermaphroditism tends to evolve in species where individuals rarely contact one another. Such isolation can result from *sessility* (immobility) or from the sparse distribution of species members in the environment. The evolution of simultaneous hermaphroditism has long been understood as an adaptation to these conditions. Ghislin (1969) termed this explanation the *low density model.* As noted previously, many angiosperm plants are simultaneous hermaphrodites, as are many sessile animals

Figure 5.4 The protandrous fish *Amphiprion* (or clown-fish) in the shelter of a sea anemone.

Image © aliciahh, 2008. Used under license from Shutterstock, Inc.

such as sponges, arrow worms (tube-dwelling, wormlike marine animals), and tunicates (tiny marine chordates). Many mobile animals, such as ctenophores (comb jellies), flatworms, earthworms, snails, and deep-sea fishes are also simultaneous hermaphrodites.

For sessile organisms, the availability of mates is restricted to the region in their immediate vicinity. The dispersal of cheap gametes (sperm or pollen) will soon produce diminishing returns as any ova in the area are fertilized. The production of more expensive ova, however, can increase the number of offspring a sessile organism produces by enabling these gametes to be fertilized as well.

Among mobile animals, simultaneous hermaphroditism occurs in species in which individuals rarely contact one another. Low-contact frequency results from wide dispersion relative to the animals' speed of movement. Thus, slow-moving snails or earthworms can live within a few meters or less of one another yet rarely come into contact. The low density model hypothesizes that when species members seldom meet, there is a great fitness advantage to being able to reproduce as either sex. Developing the reproductive system of one sex and spending your life locating a mate, only to find that the "mate" was your same sex would, from an evolutionary standpoint, be a cruel irony indeed.

Whence Gonochorists?

The size advantage model and the low density model are quite good at explaining the occurrence of hermaphroditism. That is, given a hermaphroditic species, it very probably fits the conditions of one of these models. However, the reverse is not true. A species that fits the conditions of, for example, the size advantage model is not especially likely to be a sequential hermaphrodite. Male elephant seals, for instance, are so much larger than females that the two could easily be confused as separate species. Male elephant seals, like protogynous fish, use their body size to defend breeding territories and the females that inhabit them. Yet elephant seals are obligate gonochorists. Certainly, it seems that the costs of simultaneously maintaining two separate reproductive systems are compensated only in sessile or low-density species. But, like elephant seals, many species are characterized either by larger females or larger males. The absence of sequential hermaphroditism in so many of these species is not completely understood. In the words of David Policansky (1982), "Why don't more organisms change sex?"

Remember from Chapter 3 that one of the main reasons why some traits are obligate is that they would be too costly to change, even if there might be some advantage to doing so. Indeed, most of the reasons that have been proposed for why more organisms don't change sex have to do with the costs of changing sex (Policansky 1982). For one, all land animals descended evolutionarily from aquatic animals, and thus so did their reproductive systems. The transition from water to land entailed many anatomical changes, including considerable modification of the reproductive system for internal fertilization. So the development of highly specialized reproductive systems probably imposes prohibitive costs to sex change in many species of land animals (Warner 1978). In species in which competition for mates is intense, one sex often has elaborate, costly structures (other than simply having large bodies) for winning mates. For the competing sex, these structures likely require channeling resources toward their production rather than to reproduction for a substantial period, thus prohibiting starting one's reproductive career as the opposite sex.

Although none of the reasons so far proposed explains all of the exceptions across species, it is not necessary to assume that one would. It is quite possible that the evolutionary heritage and environmental circumstances of each species determine the relative costs and benefits of gonochorism versus hermaphroditism in different ways.

Summary

We started this chapter by considering the significant costs of sex: the cost of recombination, the cost of producing sons, and the cost of mating. This prompted the question, "Why sex?" We discovered that the variability generated by sex can have some long-term advantages to sexual populations, but that sex probably persists in *K* strategist species like humans because of the short-term advantages it confers. The preeminent explanation today for the persistence of sex in humans and other *K* strategists is Hamilton's Red Queen hypothesis: Sex enables hosts to keep up in the evolutionary arms races with their parasites by producing offspring with novel genotypes to which parasites cannot yet be adapted.

Given sex, we were compelled to ask, "Why sexes?" This amounts to the question of why anisogamy (different-sized gametes) evolved. Males produce relatively small gametes, females produce relatively huge ones. Several advantages may obtain to males and females, including increased numbers or viability of gametes and decreased intracellular competition in zygotes.

The number of males relative to the number of females in the population is called the sex ratio. The sex ratio is maintained by frequency-dependent selection and depends on the costs of

producing sons versus the costs of producing daughters. Frequency-dependent selection favors whichever sex is rare, unless offspring of one sex are more costly to produce than offspring of the other. In this case, frequency-dependent selection favors offspring of whichever sex produces more grand-offspring per unit of cost.

Hermaphrodites are both male and female. That is, they can produce both large and small gametes. Sequential hermaphrodites start out life as one sex and can change later into the other. Protogynous hermaphrodites are first female and then male; protandrous hermaphrodites are the reverse. Simultaneous hermaphrodites can produce both large and small gametes simultaneously and are thus male and female at the same time. Sequential hermaphrodites tend to be species in which one sex gains a greater fitness advantage from large size than does the other sex. In protogynous species, males frequently gain a greater fitness advantage from large size, owing to the benefits of size in defending territories and females from other males. In protandrous species, males gain less fitness from large size, but large females, as in many other species, can produce more and larger eggs. Simultaneous hermaphrodites tend to be immobile or slowly moving relative to their dispersal in the environment. Under these conditions, the ability to reproduce as either sex appears to reduce the difficulty of locating a mate.

Many gonochorists (species in which the sexes are separate) fit the conditions that supposedly favor hermaphroditism, especially those that favor protogyny. That is, in many gonochorist species, larger males gain an advantage in competition with other males for territories or females. While similar fitness advantages might obtain to some gonochorists if they were able to change sex, the costs of doing so are likely prohibitively great, and intense mating competition may favor specialization as one sex. Humans and all of our closest relatives are committed gonochorists. And it is to these species that we will now direct our attention.

References

Carroll, L. 1871. *Through the looking-glass and what Alice found there*. London: Macmillan.

Chiang, K. S. 1976. On the search for a molecular mechanism of cytoplasmic inheritance: past controversy, present progress and future outlook. In *Genetics and biogenesis of chloroplasts and mitochondria* (pp. 305–312), L. Bucher, W. Neupert, W. Sebald, and S. Werner, eds. Amsterdam: North Holland.

Cosmides, L. M., and J. Tooby. 1981. Cytoplasmic inheritance in intragenomic conflict. *Journal of Theoretical Biology*, 89:83–129.

Daly, M., and M. Wilson. 1983. *Sex, evolution, and behavior*, 2nd ed. Belmont, CA: Wadsworth.

Dawkins, R. 1989. *The selfish gene*. Oxford, England: Oxford University Press.

Fisher, R. A. 1958. *The genetical theory of natural selection*, 2nd ed. Oxford, England: Clarendon.

Ghislin, M. T. 1969. The evolution of hermaphroditism among animals. *Quarterly Review of Biology*, 44:189–208.

Glesener, R. R., and D. Tilman. 1978. Sexuality and the components of environmental uncertainty: Clues from geographical parthenogenesis in terrestrial animals. *American Naturalist*, 112:659–73.

Godwin, J., D. Crews, and R. R. Warner. 1996. Behavioural sex change in the absence of gonads in a coral reef fish. *Proceedings of the Royal Society of London* B, 263:1683–88.

Gould, J. L., and C. G. Gould. 1997. *Sexual selection: Mate choice and courtship in nature*. New York: Scientific American Library.

Hamilton, W. D. 1980. Sex versus non-sex versus parasite. *Oikos*, 35:282–90.

Hurst, L. D. 1991. The incidences and evolution of cytoplasmic male killers. *Proceedings of the Royal Society* B, 244: 91–99.

Hurst, L. D. and W. D. Hamilton. 1992. Cytoplasmic fusion and the nature of the sexes. *Proceedings of the Royal Society* B, 247:189–207.

Kondrashov, A. S. 1988. Deleterious mutations and the evolution of sexual reproduction. *Nature*, 336:435–40.

Levin, D. A. 1975. Pest pressure and recombination systems in plants. *American Naturalist*, 109:437–51.

Lively, C. M. 1987. Evidence from a New Zealand snail for the maintenance of sex by parasitism. *Nature*, 328:519–21.

Lively, C. M., C. Craddock, and R. C. Vrijenhoek. 1990. Red Queen hypothesis supported by parasitism in sexual and clonal fish. *Nature*, 344:864–66.

Maynard Smith, J. 1978. *The evolution of sex*. Cambridge, England: Cambridge University Press.

Muller, H. J. 1964. The relation of recombination to mutational advance. *Mutation Research*, 1:2–9.

Parker, G. A., R. R. Baker, and V. G. F. Smith. 1972. The origin and evolution of gamete dimorphism and the male-female phenomenon. *Journal of Theoretical Biology*, 36:529–53.

Policansky, D. 1982. Sex change in plants and animals. *Annual Review of Ecology and Systematics*, 13:471–95.

Ridley, M. 1993. The red queen: Sex and the evolution of human nature. Viking. New York

Sager, R. 1977. Genetic analysis of chloroplast DNA in *Chlamydomonas*. *Advances in Genetics*, 19:287–340.

Shapiro, D. Y. 1994. Sex change in fishes—how and why? In *The Differences Between the Sexes*, ed. R. V. Short and E. Balaban, 105–30. Cambridge, England: Cambridge University Press.

Tooby, J. 1982. Pathogens, polymorphism, and the evolution of sex. *Journal of Theoretical Biology*, 97:557–76.

Van Valen, L. 1973. A new evolutionary law. *Evolutionary Theory*, 1:1–30.

Warner, R. R. 1978. Patterns of sex and coloration in the Galapagos wrasses *Bodianus eclancheri* and *Pimelometopon darwini*. *Not. Galap.* 27:16–18.

Williams, G. C. 1966. *Adaptation and natural selection*. Princeton, NJ: Princeton University Press.

Williams, G. C. 1975. Sex and evolution. In *Monographs in Population Biology*. Princeton, NJ: Princeton University Press.

Sexual Selection

John Cartwright

The senses of man and of the lower animals seem to be so constituted that brilliant colours and certain forms, as well as harmonious and rhythmical sounds, give pleasure and are called beautiful; but why this should be so we know not (Darwin, 1871).

This chapter examines the selective force that operates on males and females as a result of the phenomenon of sexual reproduction and its outcome in shaping the behaviour and morphology of animals. The selective force is a consequence of the fact that a sexually reproducing animal has to surmount a number of hurdles before it can be confident that its gamete has fused with another. It must find a mate, make a judgement on its suitability as a prospective partner and be judged in turn. Once copulation has taken place, competition between males is not necessarily over: the reproductive tract of the female may carry sperm from other males who have also reached this far. Competition now shifts to the level of sperm itself. Sperm competes against sperm in the struggle to fertilize the egg. Even here, the female is no passive recipient and may herself exert some choice over the sperm she wants to retain.

In this chapter, we will show how all these hurdles have left their mark on the physical and behavioural characteristics of animals. Features such as size, behavioural tactics, colouration, the possession of appendages for fighting and the number and type of sperm produced by males, have all been moulded by the force of sexual selection.

Finding a Mate

Natural and Sexual Selection

Natural and sexual selection form the twin pillars of Darwin's adaptationist paradigm. We should be wary, however, of overstating the distinction between these two forms of selection: whether you survive to reproduce because you can run fast to avoid predators, or because you are successful in attracting mates, the same principle of the differential survival of genes is in operation. Indeed, some features that help in avoiding predators, such as body size, may also be of assistance in securing a mate. One way to view the distinction is shown in Box 6.1.

Inter- and Intrasexual Selection

As a rough guide, the degree of choosiness that an individual displays in selecting a partner is related to the degree of commitment and investment that is made by either party. Male black grouse that provide no paternal care will mate with anything that resembles a female black grouse, but females, mindful of their onerous parental duties, are more discriminating. Likewise, male chimpanzees provide little care for their young and are consequently not particularly discriminating in their choice of mate—as long as the female has that irresistible pink swelling announcing oestrus. A male albatross, in contrast, will mate for life and is consequently very choosy about his choice of partner. Among humans, both males and females have a highly developed sense of male and female beauty, and this aesthetic sensibility is similarly consistent with a high degree of maternal and

paternal investment. The more investment that an individual makes, the more important it becomes to choose its mate carefully. All this decision-making results in a selective force, complementary to natural selection, that is known as sexual selection.

We should really distinguish between two types of sexual selection. For reasons already given (see Chapter 5), the sex ratio usually remains close to 1:1, so where conditions favour polygyny, males must compete with other males. This leads to **intrasexual selection** (intra = within). Intrasexual competition can take place prior to mating or after copulation has taken place. On the other hand, a female investing heavily in her offspring or capable of raising only a few offspring in a season or a lifetime needs to make sure that she has made the right choice. There will probably be no shortage of males, but the implications of a wrong choice for the female are graver than for the male, who will be seeking other partners anyway. Females in these conditions can afford to be choosy. This leads to **intersexual selection** (inter = between) (Figure 6.1). The next section examines the intrasexual selection that results from competition before copulation.

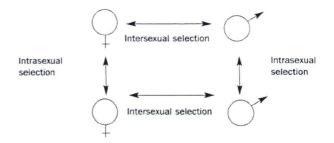

Figure 6.1 Inter- and intrasexual selection.

BOX 6.1 Natural and Sexual Selection as Components of Total Selection

Selection: The differential survival of genes

Natural selection: Traits favoured by non-sexual aspects of survival, for example the avoidance of predators and metabolic efficiency

Natural and sexual selection: Traits favoured by natural and sexual selection, for example size, pathogen resistance, symmetry and motor coordination

Sexual selection: Traits favoured by sexual selection (competing for mates) but disfavoured by natural selection, for example bright colours and courting displays.

Consequences of Intrasexual Selection

Sexual Dimorphism: Size and Weaponry

Fighting between males over access to females is a sight so common that Darwin called it the "law of battle." Such contests are often spectacular affairs and provide good footage for the makers of natural history films. Darwin argued that intrasexual selection was bound to favour the evolution of a variety of special adaptations, such as weapons, defensive organs, sexual differences in size and shape and a whole range of subtle devices to threaten or deter rivals. Some of these structures will be expensive for their possessors and may reduce their ecological (as opposed to sexual) viability.

Such intrasexual contests will lead to arms races since mating success is a product of relative rather than absolute size. It could be imagined that as the escalation of body size or weaponry proceeded through each generation, so natural selection would increase the mortality of males and as a result adult males could begin to become rare. It has even been suggested that the trend towards larger size among some ancient mammals may have led to their extinction (Maynard Smith and Brown, 1986). The whole process of size escalation dampened by natural selection has been modelled on a number of occasions (see, for example, Parker, 1983), the most common result being that, at stable equilibrium, male traits are distributed polymorphically about a mean that is shifted from the ecological optimum. In short, sex has led males to grow too large, and burdened them with appendages that are too demanding for their own ecological good.

The importance of size is illustrated by a number of seal species. During the breeding season, bull elephant seals *(Mirounga angustirostris)*

rush towards each other and engage in a contest of head-butting. Such fighting has led to a strong selection pressure in favour of size, and male seals are consequently several times larger than females. Elephant seals are in fact among the most sexually dimorphic of all animals. In the northern elephant seal *(M. angustirostris)*, a typical male is about three times heavier than a typical female. The mating system is described as female defence polygyny and, to defend a sizeable group of females, a male needs to be large. Competition between males is intense and many males die before reaching adulthood without ever having mated. The variance in the reproductive success of males is correspondingly large (Figure 6.2).

In male-male contests, it may also benefit males to possess fighting weapons. The walrus, elephant and hippopotamus all carry conspicuous tusks. Of the 40 species of deer left today, 36 develop antlers, and in 35 of these species antlers are an exclusively male characteristic. In the case of the European red deer *(Cervus elaphus)*, the body weight of males is about one and a half times that of the females, and the males carry large antlers.

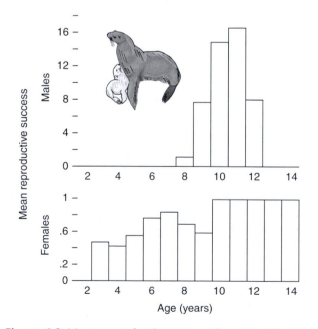

Figure 6.2 Mean reproductive success (measured by number of pups weaned) of male and female elephant seals *(Mirounga angustirostris)*.

(After Le Boeuf and Reiter, 1988, in Andersson, 1994.)

Males battle with their antlers during the rutting season, but during the rest of the year they are tolerant of each other and often move about in groups. It seems probable that antlers also serve as symbols of dominance (Lincoln, 1972).

Some of the most spectacular examples of such weapons are found in beetles such as the stag beetle. The males have large horn-like jaws, absent in the females, which are used only to fight other males. Such differences between males and females are referred to as **sexual dimorphism.** As one would expect, the greater the prize in intramale contests, the greater the degree of sexual dimorphism. Figure 6.3 shows how the degree of dimorphism in body size relates to the size of a harem for seals and ungulates.

Variance in Reproductive Success—Bateman's Principle

Bateman (1948) first quantitatively documented the differential variance in reproductive success between male and female animals (as illustrated in Figure 6.2 for elephant seals) in his classic work on *Drosophila*. The greater variation in the reproductive success of males compared with females has become known as Bateman's principle.

Bateman's work was neglected until it was revived in 1971 by Trivers, then a graduate student, in a paper presented at a symposium commemorating the centenary of Darwin's 1871 work on sexual selection. Trivers illustrated Bateman's principle by his own work on the Jamaican

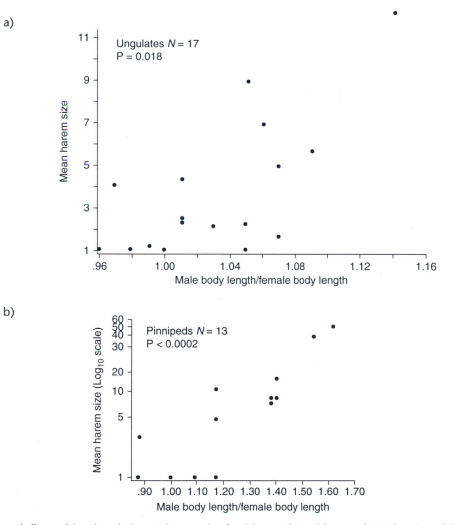

Figure 6.3 Sexual dimorphism in relation to harem size for (a) ungulates (deer and antelope) and (b) pinnipeds (seals). *(Alexander et al., 1979.)*

Intrasexual selection in action: male southern elephant seals (*Mirounga leonina*) fighting.

Image © bierchen, 2008. Used under license from Shutterstock, Inc.

lizard *(Anolis garmani)*. Trivers found that the variance in reproductive success was larger for males than females and that large males tended to have more reproductive success (Trivers, 1972). The key concept to note here is that a difference in the variance in reproductive success between males and females indicates the operation of **intrasexual competition.** If male variance is greater, this tends to suggest that the mating system is averaging out at polygyny. These signs and principles are important when we come to examine human mating behaviour in later chapters.

It would be wrong to conclude that males are always larger than females. A useful test of the principle that large body size is favoured in the sex that competes for the other is to look at cases in which the usual **sex roles** are reversed. If we find species where males invest more than females in the production of offspring, we would predict that female reproductive success should vary more than that of males, that females should be larger than males and that males should be careful in their choice of mating partner. A number of species are known that bear out these predictions fairly well. In the common British moorhen *(Gallinula chloropus)*, for example, males perform about 72 percent of the incubation and lose about 10 percent of their body weight as a consequence. Petrie (1983) has observed that competition for mates is more intense among females than males and that heavier females win fights more often. Females are larger than males and occasionally mate polyandrously.

Intrasexual competition is not the only cause of sexual dimorphism. Darwin suggested in 1871 that the larger size of some female animals could be a consequence of the fact that large size favours increased egg production. In most mammalian species, males are larger than females, and intrasexual competition seems able to account for this, but there are some species, for example, rabbits, hares and two tribes of small antelope (*Cephalophini* and *Neotragini*), in which females are the larger sex. In these cases, natural selection seems to override sexual selection. Ralls' explanation is the "big mother hypothesis" that large mothers can produce larger babies with a better chance of survival. A larger mother can also provide better maternal care, such as defending and carrying the young (Ralls, 1976). A summary of the selective factors that influence body size in males and females is shown in Box 6.2.

Another physiological characteristic that can assist males is "sexual enthusiasm" or the capacity to be easily aroused. In many polygynous species, males have a low threshold for sexual arousal. Some species of frog will, in the mating season, cling to anything that resembles a female frog, and males will often attempt to mate with the wrong species and even the wrong sex. Another feature of the sex drive of the male is the "Coolidge effect," so named after the United States' President Coolidge. The story goes that, while visiting a farm, President and Mrs. Coolidge were shown a yard containing many hens and only one cockerel. When Mrs. Coolidge asked why only one cockerel was necessary, she was told that he could copulate many times each day. "Please tell that to the President," she said. When the President was informed, he asked whether the cockerel copulated with the same hen and was told no; his reply was "Tell that to Mrs. Coolidge" (Goodenough *et al.*, 1993). The Coolidge effect has been observed in many species. In a study on Norway rats *(Rattus norvegicus)*, Fisher (1962) found that whereas a male rat with a single female reached sexual satiation after about 1.5 hours, some males could be kept sexually active for up to 8 hours by the introduction of novel females at appropriate intervals.

BOX 6.2 Selective Pressures on Body Size for Males and Females

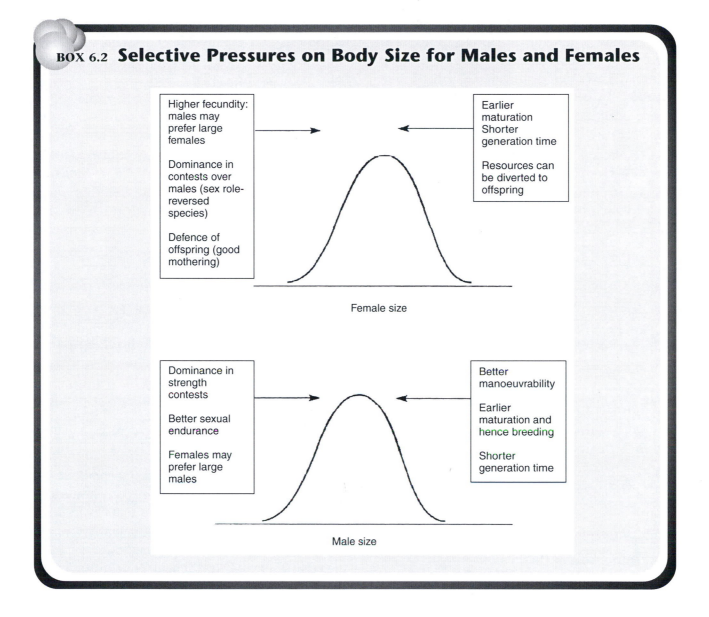

Higher fecundity: males may prefer large females

Dominance in contests over males (sex role-reversed species)

Defence of offspring (good mothering)

Earlier maturation
Shorter generation time

Resources can be diverted to offspring

Female size

Dominance in strength contests

Better sexual endurance

Females may prefer large males

Better manoeuvrability

Earlier maturation and hence breeding

Shorter generation time

Male size

Parental Investment, Reproductive Rates and Operational Sex Ratios

Problems with the Concept of Parental Investment

When Trivers advanced his concept of **parental investment** in 1972, it seemed to promise, and indeed to a degree did deliver, a coherent and plausible way of examining the relationship between parental investment, sexual selection and mating behaviour. The sex that invests least will compete over the sex that invests most, while the sex that invests most will have more to lose by a poor match and will thus be more exacting in its choice of partner.

Trivers defined parental investment as:

any investment by the parent in an individual offspring that increases the offspring's chance of surviving (and hence reproductive success) at the cost of the parent's ability to invest in other offspring. (Trivers, 1972, p.139)

Using this definition, Trivers concluded that the optimum number of offspring for each parent would be different. In the case of many mammals, a low-investing male will have the potential to sire more offspring than a single female could produce, and a male will therefore increase his reproductive success by increasing the number of his copulations. It has proved very difficult, however, to measure such terms as increase in "offspring's chance of surviving" and "cost to parents," so deciding which sex invests the most is not always easy.

In considering the expenditure of time and energy that an organism makes in mating, it is helpful to divide reproductive effort into mating effort and parenting effort such that:

Total reproductive effort = Mating effort
+ Parenting effort

We have already noted that, as a broad generalisation for mammals, we could say that mating and parenting efforts are unequally distributed across each sex. Although this distinction is useful, difficulties still arise in deciding how to allocate particular activities to the two categories. A **nuptial gift** from a male to a female or the effort a male makes in guarding a valuable resource could be thought of as mating effort since it enables him to attract females, or as parental effort in that his offspring may benefit from the resources provided. One concept that may help to circumvent these difficulties is that of potential reproductive rates.

Potential Reproductive Rates: Humans and Other Animals

It can be misleading to focus on anisogamy as a clear sign of an unequal investment by males and females. It is true that males produce sperm in vaster numbers than females produce ova, and that sperm are minute compared with eggs, but we must remember that males deliver millions of sperm, together with seminal fluid, in the hope of reaching one egg. In terms of energy investment, that of the ejaculate of the male probably exceeds that needed to produce one

egg by the female. In mammals, it is not the size of the egg but the involvement in gestation and nurturing that places limitations on the reproductive opportunities of females.

On this theme, Clutton-Brock and Vincent (1991) have suggested that a fruitful way of understanding mating behaviour is to focus on the potential offspring production rate of males and females rather than trying to measure investment *per se*. As a guide to understand sexual selection, these authors suggest that it is important to identify the sex that is acting as a "reproductive bottleneck" for the other. This approach works particularly well for some species of frog, bird and fish in which males are responsible for parental care. In some of these species, brightly coloured large females compete for smaller, duller males while in others, large, brighter males compete for choosy females—even though the paternal care of offspring (and thus high male parental investment) is common to both sets. Table 6.1 shows two cases in which, even though males provide parental care, it is the reproductive rate rather than the amount of parental investment that predicts selection.

In the same study, data on the potential reproductive rates of males and females from 29 species in which high levels of paternal care are found were extracted. The results are summarized in Table 6.2. The general conclusion is that the sex with the highest potential reproductive rate competes for that with the least and that this is therefore a better predictor of competition than is investment as such.

Humans are a special case in point in that the range of parental investment possible from a male ranges from near zero, if the male deserts, to equal or more than that of the female. Given this wide range, it is difficult to measure the investment that human males make. One could turn to hunter-gatherer tribes, but again there is cross-cultural diversity as well as variation within a culture. Another approach might be to look at the potential reproductive rate. The record often claimed for the largest number of children from one parent is 888 for a man and 69 for a woman. The father was Ismail the Bloodthirsty

(1672–1727), an Emperor of Morocco, the mother a Russian lady who experienced 27 pregnancies with a high number of twins and triplets. It is a safe bet that you are more astonished by the female record than the male.

The figure of 888 looks extreme compared with most cases of fatherhood, but *prima facie* would seem to be a practical possibility. Ismail died at the age of 55 and could have enjoyed a period of fertility of 40 years. Over this time, he could have had sex with his concubines once or twice daily. The record claimed for Ismail has, however, recently been questioned by Dorothy Einon of University College London (Einon, 1998). She analyses the mathematical probability of conception by members of his harem. The problem for a breeding male with access to a large number of females is, first, that he is uncertain when they are ovulating. The fact that ovulation takes place 14–18 days before the next menstruation was not known until 1920. Copulating with a woman once every day over her ovarian cycle would only give a probability of hitting the right day of about 10 percent, which could be raised to 15 percent if days of menstruation were avoided. Second, only half of all menstrual cycles are fertile. Further reductions then have to be made for probabilities of conception, implantation and miscarriage. The end result becomes that if Ismail had coitus three times per week, without interruption caused by illness or exhaustion, he would have produced a lifetime total of 79 children, and with coitus 14 times per week a total of 368 children.

It is of course possible that men subconsciously know when ovulation is taking place and are thus able to target their reproductive efforts better. Even so, Einon's calculations give us pause to reflect that the male reproductive rate is not as high at it may seem at first sight. It is reduced of course by the concealment of ovulation. If Ismail knew exactly when women were ovulating, he could direct his efforts accordingly. The concealment of ovulation may have

Table 6.1 Two Examples of Sexual Selection in Relation to the Potential Reproductive Rate of the Two Sexes (*Data from Clutton-Brock and Vincent, 1991.*)

Species	Behaviour	Ratio of Female to Male Reproductive Rate	Dimorphism/ Sex-Specific Behaviour
Three-spined stickleback (*Gasterosteus aculeatus*)	Males can guard up to ten clutches of eggs at any one time on their own territory Females can lay only one clutch every 3–5 days	<1	Males brightly coloured
Pipefish (*Nerophis ophidion*)	Males carry fertilized eggs Females can lay more eggs in a season than males can carry	>1	Females compete for males

Table 6.2 Intersexual Competition for Mates in Cases of High Paternal Investment in Relation to Reproductive Rates Out of Total of 29 Species Examined (*After Clutton-Brock and Vincent, 1991.*)

Ratio of Female to Male Reproductive Rate	Competition for Mates More Intense in Males	Competition for Mates More Intense in Females
<1	Fish 10 species Frogs 3 species	0 species
>1	Fish 1 species Birds 1 species	Fish 3 species Birds 11 species

evolved as a tactic by females to elicit more care and attention from males.

It is probably true to say that, in modern *Homo sapiens,* the limiting factor in reproduction resides marginally with the female. This would by itself predict some male versus male competition and sexual selection, and certainly an increased intensity of these factors in the evolutionary lineage of the hominoids before ovulation was concealed. We should also note that most men in history have not been emperors, and the harem that Ismail enjoyed would not have been a regular feature of our evolutionary past.

The Operational Sex Ratio

The potential reproductive rate and the **operational sex ratio** are closely related concepts. In Chapter 4, it was suggested that the spatial distribution of females determines the environmental potential for polygyny. Spatially clumped females could in principle be monopolised by a male who could thereby achieve polygyny, but such spatial concentration is only useful to the male if the females are fertile. In this respect, we can think of females as also being temporally distributed in the sense of their sexual receptivity at any one time. This idea is contained in the concept of the operational sex ratio:

$$\text{Operational sex ratio} = \frac{\text{Fertilisable females}}{\text{Sexually active males}}$$

When this ratio is high, females could be more willing to mate than males and might engage in competition. If the male pipe-fish, as shown in Table 6.1, can hold fewer eggs in a season than a female can lay, the operational sex ratio exceeds 1 and is said to be female biased. In these circumstances, females will compete for males. When the operational sex ratio is low, this situation is reversed and males will vie with other males for the sexual favours of fewer females.

Of the many factors that can affect the operational sex ratio, food availability is one of the most important. Studies on the orthopteran katydids or bush crickets *(Tettigonidae)* have shown this effect dramatically. Male katydids transfer sperm in a large nutritious spermatophore during copulation. This nuptial gift provides an important source of food for the female and affects her fecundity (Gwynne, 1988). A number of studies have been carried out on these creatures. The overall effect of food availability on male and female behaviour across several species of bush cricket is shown in Table 6.3.

The bush crickets illustrate how food supply, operational sex ratios and sexual competition are intertwined (Table 6.3). A general model of the way in which these and other factors may influence the operational sex ratio, and the way this in turn affects mating competition, is summarized in Figure 6.4. The manner in which intrasexual competition varies with the opera-

Table 6.3 Food Supply, Operational Sex Ratios, and Intraspecific Competition among Various Species of Bush Cricket (*Data from Various Sources, Reviewed by Andersson, 1994.*)

	Food Plentiful	**Food Scarce**
Males	Rapid production of spermatophores	Production of spermatophores slow and difficult
Operational sex ratio	Reduces, that is, male biased	Increases, that is, female biased
Competition	Reduction in female competition for males	Females compete for males
Male investment	Low*	High*
Reproductive bottleneck	Females	Males

*The fact that we can say that male investment is high when food is scarce and the production of spermatophores is slow stresses the need to define investment carefully. When food is limited, a small spermatophore produced by a male may represent a high investment of time and energy.

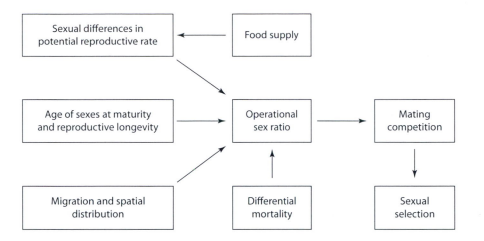

Figure 6.4 Influences on the operational sex ratio and the relationship between this and sexual selection.
(Image © bierchen, 2008. Used under license from Shutterstock, Inc.)

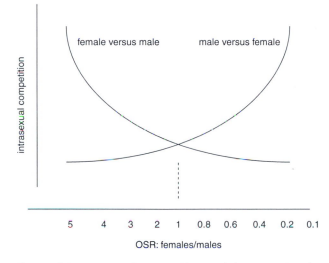

Figure 6.5 Intrasexual competition and the operational sex ratio (OSR).

(Adapted from Kvarnemo and Ahnesjo, 1996.)

tional sex ratio can also be conjectured along the lines shown in Figure 6.5.

The Operational Sex Ratio and Humans

Using the concept of the reproductive bottleneck, it is tempting to say that females are the limiting resource for male fecundity. After all, a man could impregnate a different woman every day for a year whereas over this same period a woman can become pregnant only once. But we need to proceed carefully. Imagine a male that mates with 56 different women over 56 days and a female that mates with 56 different men over the same period. The woman is likely to become pregnant and bear one offspring in the same year. Using the reasoning advanced by Einon earlier, if the male avoids the time of menstruation, he has about a 15 percent chance of impregnating a woman during her fertile period. Only half of the female ovarian cycles will be fertile, some women will be infertile themselves anyway, and implantation will only take place about 40 percent of the time. The number of women a man could expect to make pregnant is one. Over a year, this could be raised to about 6 (365/56 = 6.5). Women are in one sense a limiting resource but not to the extreme sometimes claimed. It is, however, significant that men engage in competitive display tactics and are more likely to take risks than are women. It is also men who tend to pay for sex—one way of increasing the supply of the limiting resource.

The operational sex ratio (females to males) for a group of humans with a 1:1 sex ratio will be less than one if we measure it in terms of males or females that are fertile. There will be more sexually fertile males than females; this arises from the fact that men experience a longer period of fertility compared with women. It is counterbalanced to some degree, but not entirely, by the higher mortality rate for men than women. The picture is, however, complicated if the population is growing. In these circumstances, the fact that women tend to prefer to marry slightly older men will mean more younger women than there are slightly older men available, since the cohort of marriageable men will be smaller than the number of marriageable women in the expanding cohort below. Guttentag and Secord (1983) have argued that this can in itself be a contributory factor to the development of social mores. In the United States from 1965 to the 1970s, because of the post-war baby boom, there was an oversupply of women, with the effect of decreasing male-male competition and increasing female-female competition. This allowed men to pursue their own reproductive preferences, especially in terms of an increased number of partners, to a greater extent than women could pursue theirs. These authors suggest that this could be a factor contributing to the liberal sexual mores of those decades, characterized by a high divorce rate, a lower level of paternal investment and a relaxed attitude to sex. They stress that sex ratios by themselves are not a sufficient cause for such social changes but that they may be part of the equation (Guttentag and Secord, 1983).

A more realistic application of sex ratio thinking may be found in the analysis of traditional cultures in which social values shift less rapidly. In South America, there are two indigenous Indian groups with a different sex ratio. The Hiwi tribe shows a surplus of men while the Ache people have a sex ratio of females to males of about 1.5 (Hill and Hurtado, 1996). The ecology of the two groups is otherwise similar, but whereas among the Ache people extramarital affairs are common and marriages are unstable, marital life is more stable among the Hiwi. This pattern is what one would expect from the anticipated effect of sex ratio on mating strategies.

A man who attempts to impregnate several women in the course of a year faces another problem apart from the concealment of ovulation: other men will probably want to do the same thing. The reproductive tract of a female could therefore contain the sperm of more than one male at any one time. This is where sperm competition begins.

Post-Copulatory Intrasexual Competition

Sperm Competition

It may seem that once copulation has taken place, intrasexual competition is over; one male must surely have won. The natural world, however, has more surprises in store. Some females mate with many males and retain sperm in their reproductive tracts; such sperm compete inside them to fertilize the egg. The concept of **sperm competition** illuminates many features of male and female anatomy in nonhuman animals. Male insects are particularly adept at neutralising or displacing sperm already present in the female. The male damselfly (*Calopteryx maculata*) has evolved a penis designed both to transfer sperm and, by means of backward-pointing hairs on the horn of the penis, to remove any sperm already in the female from a rival male.

We should not, however, think of females as passive in this process of sperm competition. A female may choose to mate with many males (as is the case with female chimps) to ensure that the sperm reaching her egg is competitive. The female may also exercise choice over the sperm once it is inside her (Wirtz, 1997). Female sand lizards (*Lacerta agilis*) have been reported to accept sperm from nearly every male that courts them, including close relatives. Given that mating between close relatives is likely to reduce genetic fitness, it is a plausible hypothesis that females exert some control over the sperm that they eventually allow to fertilize their eggs. Olsson *et al.* (1996) have found support for this. When males are genetically similar to females, the probability of producing an offspring from this union is reduced.

Many female insects store sperm that they use to fertilize their eggs at oviposition (egg-laying) as the eggs pass down the female's reproductive tract. It has been suggested that the function of the female orgasm in humans is to assist the uptake of sperm towards the cervix (Baker and Bellis, 1995). Thornhill *et al.* (1994) carried out a study to show that the bodily **symmetry** of the male is a strong predictor of whether or not a female will experience a copulatory orgasm. Symmetry is thought to be an indicator of genetic fitness and the possession of a good immune system (Thornhill *et al.*, 1994). The orgasm therefore ensures that sperm from exciting and desirable males, who are presumably genetically fit and unlikely to be transmitting a disease, stand a good chance of meeting with the female's egg. In a sense, the human female is extending her choice beyond courtship (Baker and Bellis, 1995).

In some ways, all intrasexual competition is a form of sperm competition in that the winning male is the one which produced the sperm that fertilizes the egg. The term "sperm competition" is, however, usually reserved for interejaculate competition, that is, competition between sperm from different males after ejaculation. Sperm competition also takes place in species in which the eggs are fertilized outside the female's body, as in many invertebrates, fish and amphibians, since several males can release their sperm in the vicinity of eggs from the female.

The theory of sperm competition was first developed by Geoffrey Parker, a biologist at the University of Liverpool, in a classic series of papers (Parker, 1970). Its importance was first recognized in insects, but the advent of sophisticated paternity assignment techniques such as DNA fingerprinting has revolutionized the detection of sperm competition. There is now abundant evidence for the existence of sperm competition in virtually every animal taxon (Birkhead and Parker, 1997).

Anisogamy and Sperm Warfare

The theoretical rationale for the production of a large number of small mobile sperm by males has already been discussed in the context of anisogamy (see Chapter 5). In this respect, one could argue that the very existence of two sexes is a result of sperm competition. Anisogamy probably began in conditions of external fertilization, and the advantages of small mobile sperm are clear to see. However, in situations where a single male fertilizes an egg internally, we may question the point of retaining anisogamy. If there are no competitors, the millions of sperm produced by monogamous mammals are simply wasted. So why not return to isogamy and have males producing larger gametes, say 50 percent of the optimum size for a zygote? The answer is, as pointed out by Parker (1983), that only a mild degree of sperm competition is required to maintain anisogamy.

Consider cattle. A cow's ovum is typically about 20,000 times larger than a bull's sperm. If a mutant bull were to appear that reduced the number of sperm by half but increased their size by a factor of two, the biomass of the fertilized egg would be increased by 1 in 20,000, or 0.005 percent—a trivial amount. If this bull and another now mate with the same cow, and sperm competition takes place, the chances of the mutant bull (assuming that the larger sperm behave the same as the smaller ones) are reduced from 50 percent to 33.3 percent—a significant reduction. It follows from this argument that even a mild degree of sperm competition can maintain anisogamy. It also follows that animals that are anisogamous and classified as monogamous have developed monogamy fairly recently in their evolutionary lineage or else are not 100 percent monogamous.

The more sperm produced, the greater the chance of one finding an egg: 50 million sperm are twice as effective as 25 million and so on. In situations in which sperm competition is rife, we would expect males to produce more sperm than are typically produced when sperm competition is less intense. This could be expected to apply both within and across species. This prediction has been supported indirectly between species by measurements on the level of sperm expenditure as measured by testis size. Species facing intense sperm competition have larger testes than those in which sperm competition is less pronounced. Measurements of the size of sperm do not, however, fit so neatly and it may be that the ability of larger sperm to swim faster is a confounding variable.

Within a given species, it is at least a theoretical possibility that males could adjust the number of sperm they ejaculate according to the risk of sperm competition. Given that it requires energy to produce sperm, it would be in the interests of any male to reduce the number of sperm introduced into a female when he suspects the level of competition to be low—as with a socially monogamous partner that he has guarded—and conversely increase the number in the case of **extrapair copulation** with an already mated female.

Baker and Bellis at Manchester University provide evidence to support the idea that the number of sperm in the ejaculate of men is adjusted according to the probability of sperm competition taking place. In one study, when couples spent all their time together over a given period, the male was found to ejaculate about 389×10^6 sperm during a subsequent sexual act. When the couple only spent 5 percent of their time together, men typically ejaculated 712×10^6 sperm. Baker and Bellis interpret this as being consistent with the idea that the male increases the number of sperm in the latter case to compete better against rival sperm in the case of any infidelity on behalf of the female. Baker and Bellis have been successful in generating new ideas in an area of research that faces innumerable experimental and ethical difficulties (Baker and Bellis, 1995). They have also been successful in disseminating their ideas, helped partly by a prurient media and partly by the popularisation of their work in such books as *Sperm Wars* (Baker, 1996). Some aspects of their work, especially the

sensational and lurid presentation in the latter work, have caused some concern in academic circles (Birkhead *et al.*, 1997).

In the "sperm wars," males can adopt various tactics: they can produce sperm in large numbers, attempt to displace rival sperm, insert copulatory plugs or produce sperm that actively seek out to destroy rivals. In moths and butterflies (the Lepidoptera) males produce two types of sperm. One type, "eupyrene" sperm, carries genetic material and can fertilize eggs. The other type, "apyrene" sperm, typically furnishes half the number in any ejaculate but is lacking in genetic material and thus cannot fertilize the female egg. The function of apyrene sperm is something of a mystery. One intriguing hypothesis proposed by Silberglied *et al.* (1984) is that apyrene sperm play a role in sperm competition. Either they "seek and destroy" active sperm from other males, or they serve as a cheap "filler" that reduces the receptivity of females to further matings. Baker and Bellis (1995) have developed this into a "kamikaze sperm hypothesis," claiming that a wide variety of animals, including humans, produce sperm whose function is to block or destroy rival sperm.

Copulatory plugs are plugs of a thick, viscous material left by the male in the reproductive tract of the female. They could be a functionless artifact of insemination, but it seems much more probable that they either help to seal in the sperm from the last male to deposit sperm, or serve as "chastity enforcers" to reduce the likelihood of successful insemination by a rival male (Voss, 1979). In the common honeybee *(Apis mellifera)*, males produce mating plugs that attempt to seal off the reproductive tract of the queen to prevent further injections of sperm from competitors. Interestingly, the female is not as concerned to secure the sperm from only one male, and in this case the queen still manages to carry multiple-origin sperm in her body. In the case of deer mice *(Peromyscus maniculatus)*, experiments by Dewsbury (1988) suggest that the plug serves to retain the sperm from a male. Perhaps the most determined example of copulatory plugging occurs when males of the fly *Johannseniella nitidia* leave behind their genitalia while the rest of their body is eaten by the female. Baker and Bellis (1995) claim that there is evidence for somewhat less extreme copulatory plugging in human mating.

Long before sperm competition takes place, however, a male has to be accepted by a female or vice versa. Passing this test of approval has also left its mark on anatomy and behaviour. It has given rise, of course, to the force of intersexual selection, and it is to this process that we now turn.

Intersexual Selection

Mechanisms of Intersexual Selection

In sexually reproducing species, the outcrossing of genes is the gateway through which all genes must pass. The fusion of gametes to yield a fertilized zygote represents a type of genetic rite of passage. Darwin realized that, during all the preliminaries to this process, when mate choice takes place the preferences of one sex can exert a selective pressure on the behaviour and physical features of the other. This is the essence of intersexual selection.

Darwin's suggestion that female choice could over time bring about an extreme change in the appearance of males was poorly received in the patriarchal climate of Victorian Britain (Cronin, 1991). Darwin's insight has, however, emerged triumphantly since the 1970s and is now the basis of a flourishing school of research. As noted in Chapter 2, Darwin had difficulty in explaining in adaptionist language why females find certain features attractive. Numerous ancillary theories have emerged recently to address this problem, tending to fall into two schools: the "good sense" school and the "good taste" school.

The good taste school of thought stems largely from the ideas of Fisher, who tackled the problem in the 1930s. Consider a male character such as tail length that females may find attractive. Fisher argued that a runaway effect would result, leading to long tails, if some time in the past an arbitrary drift of fashion led a large number of females in a population to prefer long tails. Once this fashion took hold, it would become despotic and self-reinforcing. Any female that bucked the trend, and mated with a male with a shorter tail, would leave sons with short tails that were unattractive. Females that succumbed to the fashion would leave "sexy sons" with long tails and daughters with the same preference for long tails. The overall effect is to saddle males with increasingly longer tails, until the sheer expense of producing them outweighs any benefit in attracting females. But since attracting females is fundamental, very long tails indeed could be produced by this process. In this Fisherian view, tail length need serve no other purpose than a simple fashion accessory to delight the senses of the opposite sex.

The good sense view suggests that an animal is responding to, and estimating the quality of, the genotype of, a prospective mate through the signals that he or she sends out prior to mating, or alternatively, that a judgement is made on the level of resources that a mate is likely to be able to provide. The idea that females are choosing good genes when selecting a mate was also suggested by Fisher, who in 1915 spoke of the "profitable instincts of the female bird" in choosing features such as "a clearly-marked pattern of bright feathers," which afforded "a fairly good index of natural superiority" (quoted in Andersson, 1994, p. 27). The idea was raised again and developed by Williams (1966) and others, now being one of the most promising lines of inquiry in sexual selection theory.

Table 6.4 shows a breakdown of the different possibilities of intersexual selection. This division of sexual selection into the neat categories shown should not, however, deceive us into thinking that the natural world is so simple. Darwin himself despaired of the possibility of being able to distinguish between natural and sexual selection in all cases. Pheasants, for

Table 6.4 Mechanisms of Intersexual Competition

Category	Mechanism
Good taste (Fisherian runaway process)	Initial female preference becomes self-reinforcing. A runaway effect results in elaborate and often dysfunctional (in terms of natural selection) appendages, for example the peacock's train.
Good sense (genes)	The female may use signals from the male to indicate the resistance of the male to parasites. Symmetry could be inspected as a clue to general metabolic efficiency.
Good sense (resources)	The female may inspect resources held by the male and his willingness to invest resources (potential for good behaviour). This could also serve as indication of genetic quality.

example, have long tails, which would seem to be a classic case of intersexual selection. The tarsal spurs on their legs used in fighting would appear to be products of intrasexual selection. Yet, in the case of the golden pheasant (*Chysolophus pictus*), the tail is used for support while fighting, and among ring-tailed pheasants (*C. colchinus*), the females judge males according to the quality of their spurs (Krebs and Davies, 1991). The picture is also clouded by the fact that, in some species, the females seem to encourage the males to fight and then choose the winners. This is found with the spider *Linyphra litigosa*. Females attract into their nests a succession of males that fight one another to stay there until she is ready to mate (Watson, 1990).

At the gene level, the distinction is of course even more blurred. Both intra- and intersexual selection are forms of competition between male genotypes, whether they are instrumental in displaying to a female or fighting another male. With these qualifications in mind, we will examine the good taste and good sense views in turn.

Good Taste: Fisher and Runaway Sexual Selection

For many of Darwin's followers, the problem with his theory of sexual selection was that it did not adequately explain the origin and adaptive purpose of female choice. This perceived weakness was attacked in ironic tones by the Nobel Prize winning geneticist Thomas Hunt Morgan:

Shall we assume that still another process of selection is going on . . . that those females whose taste has soared a little higher than that of the average (a variation of this sort having appeared) select males to correspond, and thus the two continue heaping up the ornaments on one side and the appreciation of these ornaments on the other? No doubt an interesting fiction could be built up along these lines, but would anyone believe it, and if he did could he prove it? (Morgan, quoted in Andersson, 1994, p. 24)

The irony backfires since the answer to Morgan's questions is probably yes. The idea of female taste that could not be entertained seriously by Morgan was taken up and developed by Fisher into one of the classic theories for the existence of conspicuous male traits.

Fisher's original account of his model was rather brief, but later refinements have established that a number of conditions need to hold if it is to function properly. In the simplest accounts, these conditions are:

- Variation in a male trait that is heritable
- Variation in female preference that is heritable
- Individuals having genes for both trait and preference (linkage disequilibrium) but only expressing the character appropriate to their sex.

Thus males carry preference genes for a particular trait as well as genes prescribing that trait, but only the genes for the trait are expressed. It is also assumed that genes for high trait values are linked with genes for preferring high trait values.

Suppose that females have a preference (p) for a particular tail length, and that this and the value of tail length in males (t) are both normally distributed. If values of p and t have the same mean values, neither will change, and stability will result. Females with particular values of p will tend to mate with males having corresponding t values, and any individual will carry matched values of t and p.

The precise conditions under which this Fisherian process becomes unstable have been subject to numerous attempts at modelling (see Harvey and Bradbury, 1991). The simplest condition is when (perhaps through drift) the mean value of the tail length that females prefer (expressed by preference value p) is higher than the mean population value of the male trait itself (t). Females will thus choose males with higher than average t values. Such males will also carry higher than average values of p; conversely, low-t males with correspondingly low p values will not fare as well. The net result will be that, in the next generation, the mean values of p and t will both increase, but since p is now larger than t (because the next generation contains descendants of females with high p values), this will continue in a runaway process. The process stops when natural selection forces a halt to the size of the male trait as it becomes increasingly burdensome (Box 6.3).

We could still ask why a set of p genes should exist at all; in other words, why females should be at all fussy about the value of any trait such as tail length. The answer that Fisher gave, and one that still seems probable, is that the value of a particular trait was initially correlated with fitness.

There is a problem at the heart of Fisher's theory of runaway sexual selection, and that is the "lek paradox" (see also Chapter 4). Leking species such as grouse and peacocks are strongly sexually dimorphic: males have elaborate ornaments that look like the products of a Fisherian runaway process. Since males in leking species practice polygyny, the generation following a mating season will be descended from just a few males with higher than average t values. The problem is that, after a few generations, all the variation in t will be exhausted. All males will be descended from a small number of male ancestors, and they will all have the highest t values allowed by the gene pool. Put another way, males will tend to converge on a particular trait value. If all males eventually have the same value, there is no point to choosing, and t cannot increase any further. This is the lek paradox: how can a trait value t increase in a runaway fashion if, after a few generations, the variation in t reduces to zero? The most satisfactory answer so far relies upon mutation. Lande (1981) and others have pointed out that a feature such as tail length will not be the expression of a single gene but will be influenced by a large number of polygenes. The combined effect of outcrossing and mutation will, according to Lande, always ensure that there is enough variation for female preference to exert its effect.

Empirical Tests of Fisher

It has in fact proved difficult to test Fisher's ideas. One approach has been to examine the geographical variation of both trait and preference. They should be found in close proximity if Fisher's ideas about the co-evolution of male traits and female preferences are correct. A number of studies have shown this to be the case for the guppy (*Poecilia reticulata*). The distribution of bright orange colouration in males was found to be strongly correlated with the strength of female preference for orange (Endler and Houde, 1995).

Further evidence that is at least consistent with Fisher's ideas comes from breeding experiments on sticklebacks. It has been known for many years that some females find the bright red breeding patch on a stickleback highly attractive. The redness of the patch on males is geographically variable. Bakker (1993) bred from male sticklebacks with either dull or bright red nuptial colouration. It was found that the sons of bright red males also tended to have bright

BOX 6.3 Diagrammatic Representation of the Effect of Natural and Sexual Selection on the Mean Value of Trait *t*

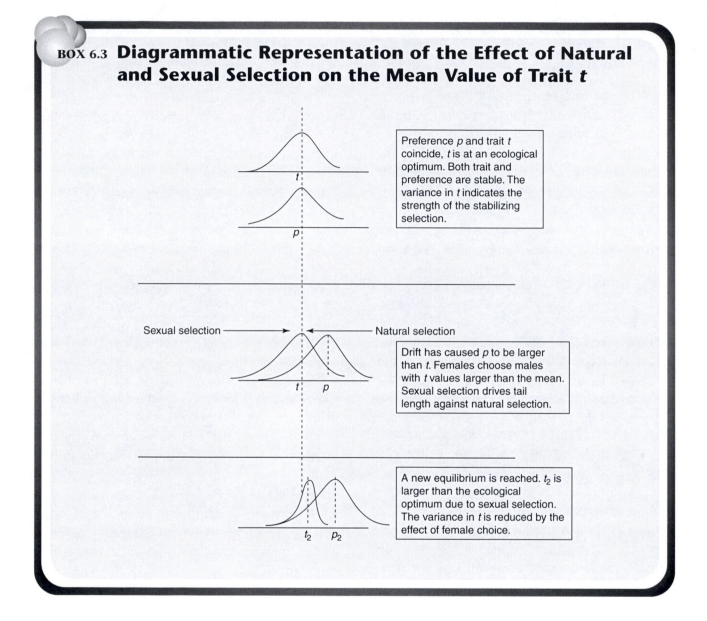

Preference *p* and trait *t* coincide, *t* is at an ecological optimum. Both trait and preference are stable. The variance in *t* indicates the strength of the stabilizing selection.

Sexual selection —→   ←— Natural selection

Drift has caused *p* to be larger than *t*. Females choose males with *t* values larger than the mean. Sexual selection drives tail length against natural selection.

A new equilibrium is reached. t_2 is larger than the ecological optimum due to sexual selection. The variance in *t* is reduced by the effect of female choice.

red patches and the daughters of red males preferred red to dull males. The daughters of dull males showed no particular preference for male colour. Such experiments offer support for the linkage that Fisher posited between male traits and female preferences. The general problem with much of the empirical evidence so far is that it does not give unique support for Fisher, other processes still being possible. Andersson refers to the problem of deciding between Fisherian and other mechanisms as "one of the greatest present challenges in the field of sexual selection" (Andersson 1994, p. 51).

Good Genes and Indicator Mechanisms

The **good genes** dimension of good sense would explain why, in polygynous mating systems, females share a mate with many other females, even though there may be plenty of males without partners and despite the fact that males contribute nothing in the way of resources or parental care. Females are in effect looking for good genes. The fact that the male is donating them to all and sundry is of no concern to her. It is suggested that the female is able to judge the quality of the male's genotype from the **"honest signals"** he is forced to send. Thus, for example, size, bodily condition, colour of plumage, symmetry and size of territory held are all signals providing the female with information about the potential of her mate. Human females find some men sexually attractive even though they know they may be unreliable, philandering and something of a cad.

There are several ways in which selected features may be a signal from a male of genetic prowess. Two models we will consider are handicap and parasite exclusion.

Handicap Models

Imagine that two competitors enter a running race. One is dressed in appropriate sportswear, the other is similarly attired but with the addition of a rucksack full of pebbles. The result of the race is a dead heat. Which competitor is most impressive? Most would agree the contestant with the extra load is probably the most physically fit and able. The analogy is not perfect, but this is roughly how the **handicap principle** proposed by Zahavi (1975) is supposed to work. Females choose males that sport a costly handicap since the very fact that they have survived with such a handicap is itself an indication that they are genetically fit. A. Zahavi (1975, p. 213) says:

> The handicap principle as understood here suggests that the marker of quality should evolve to handicap the selected sex in a character which is important to the selecting sex, since the selecting sex tests, through the handicap, the quality of its potential mate in characters which are of importance.

Since its publication, this idea has met with a very mixed response, and the literature has become technically complicated. Intuitively, it might seem as if any handicap carried by a male simply cancels out any superior fitness that a male may possess in developing one. Although population geneticists originally rejected the idea, support has been rallying over the last few years. Zahavi's original idea has been refined into a number of versions. In one, the "qualifying handicap," only males with a high viability can survive to display the handicap. The handicap serves as a sort of fitness filter. In another, the "revealing handicap," males perform some onerous task such as growing a long tail or developing bright colours as an "honest signal" of their otherwise hidden qualities.

Whatever the outcome of Zahavi's theory, it has been valuable in introducing the concept of "honest signalling" into the study of animal behaviour. It is now generally accepted that many animals, including humans, carry "badges" advertising their worth. It is probable that such badges generally evolve towards honest advertising, not because honesty is a virtue but because **dishonest signals** are eventually ignored. One such honest signal could be the possession of a good immune system to ward off parasites.

Coping with Parasites—The Model of Hamilton and Zuk

William Hamilton and Marlene Zuk (1982) tackled the question of how male ornamentation could be a reliable indication of the male's health and nutritional status. They suggested that secondary sexual characteristics such as elaborate ornamentation are indicators of the parasite burden of the host since a male infected by parasites produces a poorer display than males not so infected. The conditions in which this process could operate are as follows:

- Host fitness decreases with increasing parasite burden
- Ornament condition decreases with increasing parasite burden
- Resistance to parasites has a heritable component
- Female choice favours the most ornamented males since these are the least parasitised
- Host and parasite are locked into a genetic arms race, each striving to stay ahead of the other's resistance.

The last point also helps to explain the lek paradox—the problem that after a few generations of choice, males will tend to look alike and females will have no variation to choose from. In a world of parasite-infected males, the females will always be choosing a slightly different set of genes since males must constantly change genes to keep parasites at bay. If the genes "stood still," males would quickly show signs of increased parasite load and appear less attractive to females.

Since Hamilton and Zuk (1982) published their ideas, a mass of experimental and observational data have accumulated in relation to their hypothesis. On the whole, the data have been positive in its support. It has proved most difficult to establish whether or not parasite resistance is heritable, but the evidence is generally favourable. For three species (guppy, pheasant and swallow) all five conditions cited above are found to hold (see Andersson, 1994, for a review).

Parasite resistance may also apply to human mate choice. The American evolutionary psychologist David Buss has done much work on delineating the features that humans find attractive in the opposite sex. Buss and his co-workers found that males in all cultures rated female beauty very highly, but especially so where there was a risk of serious parasitic infection such as malaria or schistosomiasis. If you live in a culture where parasites are common, it is even more important to choose your mate carefully and use every cue available to estimate his or her physical health status (Gangestad and Buss, 1993).

Males and females can send signals about their health and reproductive status in a variety of ways. One time-honoured principle of fashion is that "If you have it flaunt it; if you haven't, hide it." This applies to cosmetics as much as clothes. One study has suggested a function of bodily markings such as those produced by the scarification and tattooing practiced in some cultures. Devendra Singh and Matthew Bronstad of the University of Texas found a correlation between the degree of bodily marking on females and the strength of pathogen prevalence in that culture. They hypothesize that females draw attention to sexually dimorphic features such as waist and breast measurements by the use of body markings. In the cultures examined, they did not find any correlation for male markings (Singh and Bronstad, 1997).

Hamilton and Zuk's work has been of enormous heuristic value, but there remains the problem that much of the experimental work is still open to other interpretation. It could be, for example, that females are simply avoiding the transmission of parasites to themselves and not judging the condition of the males with a view to choosing good genes. In many relationships, however, females are looking for something more substantial than just parasite-resistant genes.

Good Resources and Good Behaviour

In the leking species discussed earlier, the males provide nothing except a few drops of sperm. The females have come to expect nothing except genes, so if they are choosy, it will be for good genes. In many species, however, males are expected to bring something to mating in addition to their DNA. In effect, the female may only consent to mating once she has exacted some resources from the male. She may thus judge the ability of the male to provide resources before and after copulation. Resource provision could be in the form of a nesting site, food, territory, parental care or some combination of these.

The donation of resources and genes may be linked. A courtship period in which nuptial gifts are exchanged is a common sight in the animal world. A female may use this period to assess whether the male is able to gather resources and, just as importantly, be willing to devote them to the relationship. In many bird species (for example, European crossbills), males pass food to the females during courtship. A female could use this as a signal of foraging ability and a willingness to feed offspring. Such resources may be crucial in raising young and may, as a bonus, also indicate the genetic fitness of a male to gather such resources. In human hunter-gatherer societies, there is evidence that food is often exchanged for sex and that wealthy men are able to secure more partners. In modern societies, the phenomenon of the "sugar daddy" is well known. Rich and powerful men seem to be able to attract younger and highly attractive females as their partners. This dimension to human mating will be examined in more thoroughly in Chapter 12.

Intra- and intersexual selection often overlap. We have already noted that where one sex provides a significant commitment in terms of parental investment, such as a large egg, nurturing a fetus or caring for the young, this sex is often the limiting factor for the reproductive success of the other sex. The least investing sex will compete for the sex that constrains its reproductive potential. The limiting sex can afford to be choosy and may look for good genes, good behaviour (indications of future investment) or more tangible resources. The insect world is full of examples of males transferring nutritious offerings before or during sex. In the scorpionfly *Harpobatticus nigriceps,* females lay more eggs with males who provide larger gifts of prey that they have captured. Females also lay more eggs fertilized by larger males, so females may in this species be choosing for good genes as indicated by large size of male, and for good resources (which may indirectly indicate good genes anyway) by preferring larger prey offerings (Trivers, 1972).

In previous discussions on resource defence polygyny, we saw how this system allows the males to achieve polygyny. From a female perspective, it may be that females are choosing males who are able to provide resources. Studies have shown that the number of females per male is strongly influenced by the resources in the territory of the male (see, for example, Kitchen, 1974). In polygyny, there will of course be male competition, and only vigorous males will be able to command the territory to attract females. In these cases once again, it is not always easy to establish whether females are choosing good genes, good resources or both.

Courtship has other functions as well as providing a forum for the inspection of genes and the passing of gifts. Monogamous species often engage in lengthy courtship rituals prior to actual mating. Courtship has many functions, such as the identification of species and the advertisement of readiness to mate, but it seems more than likely that courtship also enables each sex to "weigh up" its prospective partners in terms of their commitment to a relationship. In the case of the behaviour of the common tern *(Sterna hirundo),* it looks highly probable that females choose males on the basis of their willingness to invest. When on the feeding grounds, females rarely provide their own food and instead rely upon males to bring food to them. The amount of food brought by the male strongly influences the size of the clutch laid. In the first phase of courtship, the male provides food as part of pair formation, and a female will only pair with a male who is carrying a fish (Trivers, 1972). The female is in effect acting to increase the investment made by the male. The more investment a male makes, the less likely he is to desert.

Case Studies: The Peacock and the Widow-Bird

The Peacock's Train

The peacock's train has become a paradigm case for the theory of sexual selection. The train looks precisely like the product of some crazy runaway Fisherian process. It is clearly a handicap and, in the Indian native home of the *peafowl (Pavo cristatus),* tigers often bring down male birds by their train as they struggle to take flight. It could also be an honest signal that males with highly elaborate and "beautiful" trains are relatively free from parasites. Deciding between these hypotheses has proven very difficult, but the work of Petrie *et al.* (1991; Petrie, 1994) on the peafowl population of Whipsnade Park in the United Kingdom has thrown considerable light on the factors involved.

The behaviour of peafowl is typical of leking species in that males attempt to secure a display

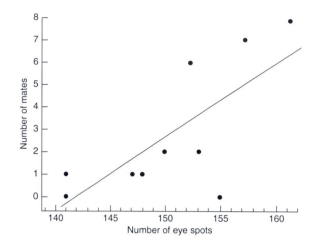

Figure 6.6 Relationship between the number of eye spots and mating success in a group of ten peacocks.

(Data from Petrie et al., 1991.)

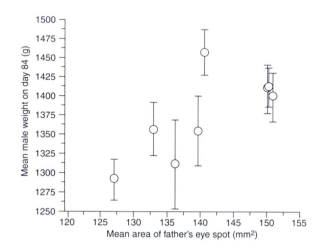

Figure 6.7 Relationship between the eye spot area of males and the fitness of offspring.

(From Petrie, 1994.)

site within the lek and only those which secure a site will display. Females never mate with the first male to court them and will reject several before deciding. As in many polygynous mating systems, there is a large variance in reproductive success. The key predictor of reproductive success in the first studies turned out to be the number of eye spots in the train (Figure 6.6).

It could be argued of course that the number of spots correlates with some other variable such as age of the male or his overall symmetry, or that the number of spots is related to something that males use in intrasexual competition. The question also arises of what peahens gain by choosing males with plenty of spots. In an effort to address this last question, Petrie took eight free-ranging displaying males (whose mating success varied) from Whipsnade Park and transferred them to pens, where they were each mated individually with four randomly chosen young peahens. The eggs and the young that resulted from these matings were carefully measured. It was found that the weight of the young after 84 days and their chances of surviving when introduced back into Whipsnade Park (both of which can be used as a indication of condition and fitness) varied strongly with the average area of each eye spot on the male's train and the overall length of the train (Figure 6.7).

The result of intersexual selection: a male of the common peafowl (*Pavo cristatus*) displaying.

(Image © Jill Lang, 2008. Used under license from Shutterstock, Inc.)

These results suggest that peahens may be choosing peacocks for good "viability" genes for their offspring and that Fisherian runaway selection may be coupled with something that also indicates the genetic quality of the males.

The Widow-Bird

Another way in which to approach the problem of what females look at in assessing males is to manipulate experimentally the male character that attracts females. Andersson (1982) did this for an African bird called the long-tailed widowbird (*Euplectes progne*). Early in the breeding season, Andersson caught 36 widow-birds, having

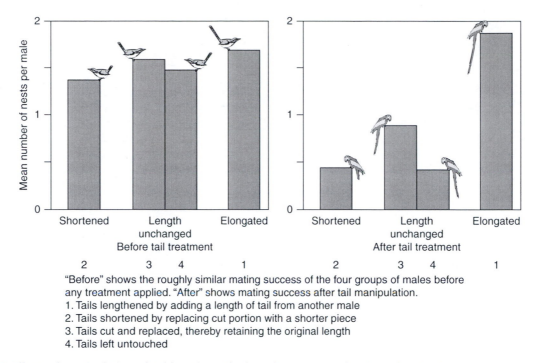

"Before" shows the roughly similar mating success of the four groups of males before any treatment applied. "After" shows mating success after tail manipulation.
1. Tails lengthened by adding a length of tail from another male
2. Tails shortened by replacing cut portion with a shorter piece
3. Tails cut and replaced, thereby retaining the original length
4. Tails left untouched

Figure 6.8 Effects of manipulation of tail length on the breeding success of male widow-birds.
(Data from Andersson, 1982; modified from Hall and Halliday, 1992.)

first recorded the number of nests in their territories, which in this species is an indication of the number of females that a male has attracted. Andersson then divided them into four groups and, by cutting off portions of their tails, manipulated their tails as follows:

- Group 1: males whose tails were lengthened by replacing the cut-off portion with a piece longer than the one removed

- Group 2: males whose tails were shortened by replacing the cut-off portion with a shorter piece

- Group 3: males whose tails were kept the same length by gluing back the cut-off portion

- Group 4: males whose tails were left untouched.

After this cosmetic surgery, the birds were released and the number of additional nests that each male secured was counted. As Figure 6.8 shows, the elongated-tail birds fared better than any of the others, even those who were returned to the wild in the same condition. Females pre-

fer long tails, and the longer the better it seems. The results seem to indicate that the perceptual apparatus of the female long-tailed widow-bird is geared up to prefer a length even above the male population average. As Francis Bacon commented in the 17th century, "there is no beauty without some strangeness of proportion."

Sexual Selection in Humans— Some Questions

Humans show sexual dimorphism in a range of traits (Figure 6.9), and it is probable that many of these are the results of sexual selection. The fact that human infants need prolonged care would ensure that females were alert to the abilities of males to provide resources. In addition, the fact that a female invests considerably in each offspring would make mistakes (in the form of weak or sickly offspring that are unlikely to reproduce) very expensive. It has been estimated that human females of the Old Stone Age would have raised successfully to adulthood only two or three children. Females would therefore be on the lookout for males who showed signs of being

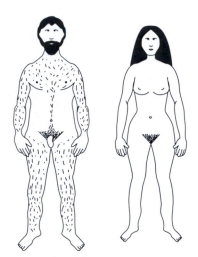

Males Compared with Females

On average, males have:

    Greater upper body strength

    More facial and bodily hair

    Greater height and mass

    Deeper voices

    Riskier life histories and higher juvenile mortality

    Later sexual maturity

    Earlier death

    Broader and more prominent chins

    Lower levels of fat deposited on buttocks and hips

Figure 6.9 Human sexual dimorphism.

genetically fit and healthy, and who were able to provide resources. Both of these attributes, genetic and material, would ensure that her offspring receive a good start in life.

One problem to address is whether features that attract the opposite sex are the products of sexual selection for good genes (health, fertility, parasite resistance and so on) or the products of an arbitrary Fisherian runaway process. If features were the result of the latter, we would expect some or all of the following:

- The expression of the trait is not correlated with any other reliable indicator(s) of fitness

- Differences in traits between people are based on genetic differences

- Any cross-cultural differences are not related to ecological factors; hence trait is arbitrary with respect to natural selection

- Extreme expressions of the trait will be more attractive than average ones: size does matter.

On the other hand, the good genes argument would predict that:

- The trait is correlated with a variety of fitness indicators, for example immunocompetence, fertility and metabolic efficiency

- Symmetrical traits will be preferred to unsymmetrical ones. The logic here is that sexually selected traits are challenging to physiological mechanisms that develop and maintain symmetry, and hence revealing of overall genetic efficiency and fitness. Parasites or environmental stress reduce symmetry.

The theory is clear enough, but it turns out that when tackling human morphology, it is difficult to find crucial evidence that will falsify one approach and support another. Two particular enigmatic features of human anatomy that may have been shaped by sexual selection are the female breast and the human brain.

The Female Breast

In Western cultures, and probably many more, there is a fascination with the enlarged mammary glands of the human female. There are strong cultural mores about when they can be revealed, or should be concealed or only half revealed. The femininity of a woman is strongly associated with her breasts. Women sometimes pay large sums of money and experience much discomfort to have them reduced or enlarged. Bra manufacturers expend much time and effort researching how best to make a product to support them in the right shape. There is agreement between the sexes that they are essential objects of desire, but what are they for? Most people would take this to be a pointless question since it is obvious that they are there to provide infants with milk. A consideration of the facts below forces a rethink on this issue:

- Breasts are strongly sexually dimorphic and appear at puberty
- Permanently enlarged breasts are not found among any other primates: most primates have enlarged breasts only during pregnancy and lactation
- Large breasts, although attractive to males, interfere with locomotion, and women athletes engaged in running sports tend to have small breasts
- There is some cross-cultural variation in breast morphology but with no obvious ecological correlates
- The size of a woman's breasts bears very little relationship to her ability to lactate. Women with much smaller breasts could supply the necessary nutrition to a baby.

It looks then as if breasts have not been shaped by natural selection, women would move better without them and their permanently enlarged state is not essential in order to supply milk. Acting as a storage device for fat is a possibility, but storage around the waist would be mechanically more efficient. Breasts are thus

Young men and women at a disco. Sexual selection in action or just having a good time?

(Image © Yuri Arcurs, 2008. Used under license from Shutterstock, Inc.)

prime candidates for good genes or runaway sexual selection. Some studies have shown that breast symmetry correlates with fertility, which suggests a role in the honest advertisement of good genes. The fact that breast size is not negatively correlated with asymmetry runs counter to this, however, since a sexual trait that increases in size should become more asymmetrical as the demands of size growth take their toll on symmetry (Thornhill and Gangestad, 1994).

Until more conclusive evidence is forthcoming, the consensus seems to be that they have been sexually selected, but the precise mechanism is not certain.

The Brain

One human feature that some have claimed shows signs of runaway sexual selection is the brain. Between about 6 million and 3 million years ago, our ancestors roamed the African savannah with brains about the size of those of a modern chimpanzee (450 cm^3). Then, 2 million years ago, there began an exponential rise in brain volume that gave rise to modern humans with brains of about 1300 cm^3. A tripling of brain size in 2 million years is rapid by evolutionary standards. One force that can bring about such rapid change is sexual selection (Miller, 1998).

Miller suggests that humans would have examined potential partners to estimate health, age, fertility, social status and cognitive skills. It is this latter criterion that might have set up a runaway growth in brain size. Miller sees this as beginning with females choosing males who were amusing and inventive, and had creative brains. Language accelerated the process since the exchange of information could then be used to judge the suitability of a potential partner. Although brain growth was driven by female choice, both sexes gradually acquired larger brains since brains were needed to decode and appreciate inventive male displays. Miller makes a remarkable, and what will prove to be a controversial, assertion:

Males produce about an order of magnitude more art, music, literature . . . than women, and they produce it mostly in young adulthood. This suggests that . . . the production of art, music, and literature functions primarily as a courtship display. (Miller, 1999, p.119)

It is an intriguing thought that much of what passes for culture may be a form of sexual display. The view that art and literature represent the outpourings of testosterone-fuelled males strutting their stuff is a wonderful image destined to infuriate at least half of the academic community and most female artists and writers, but it has a poetic plausibility that may carry more than a few grains of truth when we consider the strength of the libido and the sexual activities of successful artists and musicians.

There are of course other theories to account for the rapid brain growth (encephalisation) of hominids. The "Machiavellian intelligence" hypothesis suggests an arms race between mind-reading and deception. In this view, success depended on anticipating and manipulating the actions of others. Large brains helped early humans to understand each other's minds; this allowed deception, which in turn stimulated brain growth to detect and avoid deception, and so the process ran on, causing an escalation of brain size. This is examined in more detail in the next chapter.

Summary

- Sexual selection results when individuals compete for mates. Competition within one sex is termed intrasexual selection, and typically gives rise to selection pressures that favour large size, specialised fighting equipment and endurance in struggles.

- Individuals of one sex also compete with each other to satisfy the requirements laid down by the other sex. An individual may require, for example, some demonstration or signal of genetic fitness or the ability to gather and provide resources. Selective

pressure resulting from the choosiness of one sex for the other is studied under the heading of intersexual selection. Such pressure often gives rise to elaborate courtship displays or conspicuous features that may indicate resistance to parasites, or may possibly be the result of a positive feedback runaway process.

- The precise form that mating competition takes (such as which sex competes for the other) is related to the relative investments made by each sex and the ratio of fertile males to females. If females, for example, by virtue of their heavy investments in offspring or scarcity, act as reproductive bottlenecks for males, males will compete with males for access to females, and females can be expected to be discriminatory in their choice of mate.

- In cases where a female engages in multiple matings and thus carries the sperm of more than one male in her reproductive tract, competition between sperm from different males may occur. The theory of sperm competition is successful in explaining various aspects of animal sexuality, such as the high number of sperm produced by a male, the frequency of copulation and the existence of copulatory plugs and infertile sperm.

- It is probable that many features of human physiognomy and physique have been sexually selected. In examining females, males can be expected to look for features that indicate youth and fertility (nubility), health and resistance to parasites. Females can be expected to look for strength, wealth, health and status as well as parasite resistance in prospective male partners. Symmetry is an attribute valued by both sexes and may correlate with physiological fitness. The rapid increase in brain size among hominids that started about 2 million years ago is a candidate for sexual selection.

Key Words

Dishonest signals • Extrapair copulation • Good genes • Handicap principle • Honest signals • Intersexual selection • Intrasexual selection • Nuptial gift • Operational sex ratio • Parental investment • Sex role reversal • Sexual dimorphism • Sperm competition • Symmetry

Further Reading

Andersson, M. (1994) *Sexual Selection*. Princeton, NJ, Princeton University Press.
Extremely thorough book that reviews a wide range of research findings. Tends to concentrate on non-human animals.

Geary, D. C. (1998) *Male, Female: The Evolution of Human Sex Differences*. Washington DC, American Psychological Association.
Geary explains the principles of sexual selection and how these can be used to understand differences between males and females. Good discussion of the evidence for real cognitive differences between males and females.

Gould, J. L, and Gould, C. G. (1989) *Sexual Selection*. New York, Scientific American.
Readable, well structured and well illustrated. Its main drawback is a lack of references in the text to support the evidence. Mostly covers non-human animals.

Ridley, M. (1993) *The Red Queen*. London, Viking.
An enjoyable and well-written account of sexual selection theory and its application to humans.

References

Alexander, R. D., Hoogland, J. H., Howard, R. D., *et al.* 1979. Sexual dimorphisms and breeding systems in pinnipeds, ungulates, primates and humans. In *Evolutionary Biology and Human Social Behavior: An Anthropological Perspective*, N. I. A. Chagnon and W. Irons, eds. North Scituate, MA: Duxbury.

Andersson, M. 1982. Female choice selects for extreme tail length in a widowbird. *Nature* 299:818–820.

Andersson, M. 1994. *Sexual Selection*. Princeton University Press. Princeton, New Jersey.

Baker, R. R. 1996. *Sperm Wars*. London: Fourth Estate.

Baker, R. R., and Bellis, M. A. 1995. *Human Sperm Competition*. London: Chapman and Hall.

Bakker, T. C. M. 1993. Positive genetic correlation between female preference and preferred male ornament in sticklebacks. *Nature* 363:255–257.

Bateman, A. J. 1948. Intra-sexual selection in *Drosophila*. *Heredity* 2:349–368.

Birkhead, T. R., and Parker, G. A. 1997. Sperm competition and mating systems. In *Behavioural Ecology*, J. R. Krebs and N. B. Davies, eds. Oxford: Blackwell Science.

Birkhead, T. R., Moore, H. D. M., and Bedford, J. M. 1997. Sex, science and sensationalism. *Trends in Ecology and Evolution* 12(3):121–122.

Clutton-Brock, T. H., and Vincent A. C. J. 1991. Sexual selection and the potential reproductive rates of males and females. *Nature* 351:58–60.

Cronin, H. 1991. *The Ant and the Peacock*. Cambridge: Cambridge University Press.

Darwin, C. 1871. *The Descent of Man, and Selection in Relation to Sex*. Murray, London.

Dewsbury, D. A. 1988. A test of the role of copulatory plugs in sperm competition in deer mice (*Peromyscus maniculatus*). *Journal of Mammals* 69:854–857.

Einon, D. 1998. How many children can one man have? *Evolution and Human Behavior* 19:413–426.

Endler, J. H., and Houde, A. E. 1995. Geographic variation in female preferences for male traits in *Poecilia reticulata*. *Evolution* 49:456–458.

Fisher, A. E. 1962. Effects of stimulus variation on sexual satisfaction in the male rat. *Journal of Comparative Physiological Psychology* 55:614–620.

Gangestad, S. W., and Buss, D. M. 1993. Pathogen prevalence and human mate preference. *Ethology and Sociobiology* 14:89–96.

Goodenough, J., McGuire, B., and Wallace, R. 1993. *Perspectives on Animal Behavior*. New York: Wiley.

Guttentag, M., and Secord, P. 1983. *Too Many Women?* Beverly Hills, CA: Sage.

Gwynne, D. T. 1988. Courtship feeding and the fitness of female katydid (Orthoptera: Tettigoniidae). *Evolution* 42:545–555.

Hall, M., and Halliday, T. 1992. *Behaviour and Evolution*, Book 1, *Biology: Brain and Behaviour*. Milton Keynes, Open University Press.

Hamilton, W. D., and Zuk, M. 1982. Heritable true fitness and bright birds: A role for parasites? *Science* 218:384–387.

Harvey, P. H., and Bradbury, J. W., 1991. Sexual selection. In *Behavioural Ecology*, J. R. Krebs and N. B. Davies, eds. Oxford: Blackwell Science.

Hill, K., and Hurtado, M. 1996. *Demographic/Life History of Ache Foragers*. Hawthorne, NY: Aldine de Gruyter.

Kitchen, D. W. 1974. Social behavior and ecology of the pronghorn. *Wildl. Monogr.* 38:1–96.

Krebs, J. R., and Davies, N. B., eds. 1991. *Behavioural Ecology*. Oxford: Blackwell Science.

Kvarnemo, C., and Ahnesjo, I. 1996. The dynamics of operational sex ratios and competition for mates. *Trends in Evolution and Ecology* 11:4–7.

Lande, R. 1981. Models of speciation by sexual selection on polygenic traits. *Proc. Natl. Acad. Sci. USA* 78:3721–3725.

Lincoln, G. A. 1972. The role of antlers in the behaviour of red deer. *Journal of Experimental Zoology* 182:233–50.

Maynard Smith, J., and Brown, R. L. W. 1986. Competition and body size. *Theoretical Population Biology* 30:166–179.

Miller, G. F. 1999. Sexual selection for cultural displays. In *The Evolution of Culture*, R. Dunbar, C. Knight, and C. Power, eds. Edinburgh: Edinburgh University Press.

Olsson, M., Shine, R., and Madsen, T., *et al.* 1996. Sperm selection by females. *Nature* 383:585.

Parker, G. 1983. Arms race in evolution: an ESS to the opponent-independent costs game. *Journal of Theoretical Biology* 101:619–648.

Parker, G. A. 1970. Sperm competition and its evolutionary consequences in the insects. *Biology Review* 45:525–567.

Petrie, M. 1983. Female moorhens compete for small fat males. *Science* 220:413–415.

Petrie, M. 1994. Improved growth and survival of offspring of peacocks with more elaborate trains. *Nature* 371:598–599.

Petrie, M., Halliday, T., and Saunders, C. 1991. Peahens prefer peacocks with elaborate trains. *Animal Behaviour* 41:323–331.

Ralls, K. 1976. Mammals in which females are larger than males. *Quarterly Review of Biology* 51:245–276.

Silberglied, R. E., Shepherd, J. G., and Dickenson, J. L. 1984. Eunuchs: the role of apyrene sperm in Lepidoptera. *American Naturalist* 123:255–265.

Singh, D., and Bronstad, P. M. 1997. Sex differences in the anatomical locations of human body scarification and tattooing as a function of pathogen prevalence. *Evolution and Human Behaviour* 18:403–416.

Thornhill, R., and Gangestad, S. 1994. Human fluctuating asymmetry and sexual behavior. *Psychological Science* 5, 297–302.

Trivers, R. R. 1972. Parental investment and sexual selection. In B. Campbell, ed., *Sexual Selection and the Descent of Man, 1871–1971*, 136–179. Heinemann, London.

Voss, R. 1979. Male accessory glands and the evolution of copulatory plugs in rodents. *Museum of Zoology, University of Michigan. Occasional Papers* 968:1–27.

Watson, P. J. 1990. Female-enhanced male competition determines the first mate and principal sire in the spider *Linyphia litigiosa*. *Behavioural Ecology and Sociobiology* 26:77–90.

Williams, G. C. 1966. *Adaptation and Natural Selection: A Critique of Some Current Evolutionary Thought.* Princeton University Press, Princeton, NJ.

Wirtz, P. 1997. Sperm selection by females. *Trends in Ecology and Evolution* 12(5):172–173.

Zahavi, A. 1975. Mate selection—a selection for handicap. *J. Theor. Biol.* 53:205–214.

Problem Set #2

Adaptation and Natural Selection

To do this problem set, you will need to read Chapter 3.

1. Organisms are products of evolution. This claim justifies the assumption that organisms can be viewed as "designs for reproduction."

   a. How does the theory of evolution by natural selection justify this assumption?

   b. In this context, define *adaptation*.

2. What are the essential prerequisites for the operation of natural selection? Why is each necessary?

3. Natural selection is powerful, but the adaptations it constructs are not always perfect. Give three reasons for evolved imperfection.

4. Some adaptations are obligate and some are facultative.

   a. What is the difference?

   b. What is the difference between a facultative adaptation and a susceptibility?

   c. When will selection favor facultative adaptations over obligate ones?

5. The following questions concern the mating behavior of soapberry bugs (*Jadera haematoloma*).

   a. Imagine that male soapberry bugs grasp every single female of the species they encounter. Would such grasping behavior be obligate?

b. Imagine that male soapberry bugs grasp every female with which they copulate. In this case, would males' grasping behavior be obligate?

c. In fact, whether males grasp females after copulation depends on a feature of their environment. What is this feature?

d. What is the adaptive logic of this dependence? In other words, why does it make sense for male grasping behavior to depend on this feature of the environment?

Problem Set #3

Levels of Selection

To do this problem set, you will need to read Chapters 3 and 4.

1. In "harem" species, breeding groups consist of a breeding male and several adult females. There is a lot of competition to be a harem-holding male; many males don't have harems and attack harem-holding males in efforts to take over. In several mammal species, a successful invader kills the dependent young. This causes nursing females to stop lactating and return to a state where they can conceive new offspring. Some biologists have argued that such infanticide serves the function of population regulation, keeping the number of individuals down, so they will not exhaust their food supply.

   a. In the population-regulation explanation, at what level is selection supposedly acting?

   b. If the population-regulation explanation is correct, when would you expect this behavior to occur? In other words, on what should it be facultatively dependent?

c. On what does it seem to be facultatively dependent?

d. How do these facts affect your confidence in the population-regulation explanation?

e. Can you offer any other ultimate explanation for this facultative infanticide? Hint: Who might benefit by it, and how might they benefit?

2. Just like infanticide, altruism is a bit of an evolutionary puzzle.

   a. Define altruism.

   b. Traits spread because the genes that shape those traits are good at getting passed on to the next generation. What kinds of things could a gene do to help itself get passed on? (Remember, there is a "front door" and a "back door" to the next generation—be sure to address both.)

3. Hamilton's theory about the "back door" is called "kin selection." Explain the logic behind that term.

4. Hamilton's rule for adaptive altruism is $rb > c$. Explain Hamilton's rule.

5. How would you test Hamilton's theory about the evolutionary causes of altruism? Hint: What does Hamilton's rule predict?

Problem Set #4

Evolution of Sex

To do this problem set, you will need to read Chapter 5.

1. Sexual reproduction involves two processes: meiosis and recombination.

   a. Define each.

   b. Each amounts to a cost of sexual reproduction. Explain.

   c. What is another cost of sexual reproduction?

2. Sexual reproduction must produce some benefits that are sufficient to outweigh these costs; otherwise it would not have become so widespread. One idea is that, through meiosis, it increases the diversity of genotypes in the population and thus makes it more likely that the population will be able to adapt to environmental change. How likely is this as an explanation for the spread of sexual reproduction?

3. These questions concern the lottery principle.

   a. What is the supposed benefit of sex, according to the lottery principle?

   b. Who supposedly gets this benefit?

   c. Is this benefit likely to explain all cases of sexual reproduction? Why or why not?

4. These questions concern the Red Queen hypothesis.

   a. What is the supposed benefit of the Red Queen hypothesis?

   b. Who supposedly gets this benefit?

   c. Is this benefit equally important in all environments? Why or why not?

5. Sexual reproduction is logically possible without sexes: An individual could combine its gametes with the gametes of any other member of its species.

   a. Define male and female.

   b. Why did sexes evolve?

6. These questions concern hermaphroditism.

   a. What is a hermaphrodite?

   b. What are the three types of hermaphrodites?

   c. For each type of hermaphroditism, state what selective conditions might favor its existence.

Problem Set #5

Sexual Selection

To do this problem set, you will need to read Chapter 6.

1. What is sexual selection? How, if at all, does it differ from natural selection?

2. Distinguish between inter- and intrasexual selection, being sure to state:

   a. The dynamics of each process (what kinds of things are happening).

   b. The kinds of traits that are favored by each process.

3. Sometimes, sexual selection seems to be acting more strongly on one sex than on the other; these questions deal with attempts to explain this observation.

   a. What is Bateman's principle?

   b. Contrast *Anolis* lizards and British moorhens in regard to Bateman's principle.

   c. What is the operational sex ratio?

   d. What variables influence the operational sex ratio?

   e. Why might the operational sex ratio affect the intensity of sexual selection on each sex?

4. These questions are about the Coolidge Effect.

   a. What is it?

   b. Why might it be adaptive?

   c. Would it be likely to yield similar evolutionary payoff for males and females?

5. When sex A competes for mates, sex B gets to choose among the competitors.

   a. What kinds of preferences have evolved?

   b. Do any of these seem to be related to the adaptive reason for sexual reproduction? Explain.

Unit III
Sexes and Genders

In any society, most people can easily be classified as either male or female on the basis of their primary sex organs and secondary sex characteristics. Some behavioral differences between men and women are also cross-culturally universal. For example, in every society most men are primarily attracted to women and vice versa. Many culturally ubiquitous sex differences probably reflect an evolutionary history of differential selection on males and females. Divergent selection pressures have favored different developmental plans—different organizational processes—in men and women, especially during fetal development and puberty.

However, such culturally universal trends break down at the individual level. For example, in apparently every society, some people are attracted primarily to members of their own sex. Nor does sexual binarism map perfectly onto other cultural expectations about one's identity, behavior, rights, and obligations associated with sex and sexuality—in short, onto one's gender. Some cultures, both past and present, recognize three genders, or four. And Kulick (Chapter 10) argues in this unit that in at least one Latin American culture with two genders, gender may be defined not by sex but by the role one plays in sexual intercourse. This unit will explore the relationships between these important features of sexuality: an evolutionary history of differential selection on males and females, sex differences in development, and gender roles across cultures.

The Evolution and Ontogeny of Sex Differences

We will begin with a chapter from Martin Daly and Margo Wilson's "Homicide" (1988), which considers how sexual selection has operated differently on men and women. Daly and Wilson argue that differential selection on men and women has led to sex differences in behavior. The authors provide evidence that at least one behavioral sex difference, higher rates of same-sex homicide in men than in women, is cross-culturally universal. The ultimate explanation that Daly and Wilson propose for this sex difference is compelling: Men have experienced an evolutionary history of high-risk, high-stakes competition for mates. Those males who were unsuccessful competitors died without reproducing, and their traits died with them. We are instead the descendents of males whose propensity for physical aggression against other men contributed to mating success.

What is the proximate cause of such sex differences in behavior? Certainly, the treatment and expectations of women and men differ in every society, and these differences contribute to psychological and behavioral differences between women and men. But is the differential treatment of women and men stable enough across societies to cause such universal sex differences as the difference in rates of same-sex homicide? Daly and Wilson turn the question of the proximate causes of behavioral sex differences around and pose the question, "Would treating girls and boys alike make them similar in adulthood, or would we have to treat them differently?" The evidence, as presented by Daly and Wilson, indicates that the latter is true, that there are developmental factors differing between the sexes that would lead to sex differences in behavior over a wide range of environments, even environments in which girls and boys were socialized identically. That sexual selection could produce behavioral sex differences that would persist even if males and females were not treated differently should come as no surprise. The world is replete with insect, fish, and reptile species that exhibit dramatic sex differences in behavior that cannot have resulted from differential upbringing for the simple reason that they *have* no upbringing.

The next reading, by Doreen Kimura, considers some of the developmental events that lead to later sex differences in behavior. Kimura discusses how a minor genetic difference between males and females, the possession by males of the *Sry* gene residing on the Y chromosome, sets off a developmental pathway leading men to diverge anatomically and behaviorally from women. The *Sry* gene causes the undifferentiated fetal gonads to develop into testes rather than ovaries. Kimura explores how different amounts of sex hormones secreted into the bloodstream by testes and ovaries lead to sexual differentiation of not only internal and external genitals and breasts but also the sexual differentiation of the brain and behavior. Sex differences in behavior thus often reflect sexually divergent selection pressures on fetal development, hormonal regimes, and the like.

Genders and Gender Variants

Common sex differences can lead to similar expectations across cultures about male and female behavior. In light of Daly and Wilson's research on same-sex homicide, for example, it's a fair bet that males are generally expected to be more physically violent than females. But expectations about the roles of males and females also vary considerably across cultures in relation to local traditions, beliefs, and values, as you will see. The roles and expectations associated with males and females within a society comprise *gender*. From birth, a person's identity and behavior are influenced by gender roles—by cultural beliefs about what is normal and acceptable behavior for members of one's sex.

In every culture, males who conform to societal expectations about maleness are included in one gender category *(men)* and females who conform to societal expectations about femaleness are included in another gender category *(women)*. But some males and females do not closely fit societal expectations about their sex. Often these people are included in the usual gender categories for their sex. For example, in the United States, males who are perceived as not acting "manly" and females who are viewed as not acting "womanly" are nevertheless placed in the gender categories of men and women, respectively. But sometimes sex role nonconformists are placed into gender categories that are not the norm for their anatomical sex. Across cultures, this takes only two or three forms: male gender variant categories, female gender variant categories and, possibly, categories occupied by both females and gender variant males.

By far the most common alternative gender system is the classification of males with sex-atypical behavioral patterns into a third gender. A third gender can be identified through the presence of specific labels, symbols, and other linguistic practices that distinguish a class of individuals from both men and women and through the attribution of a "constellation of traits comparable to those used to define other genders" (Roscoe 1995). Third genders can also be recognized through the presence of rites of passage and origin myths associated with such roles (Roscoe 1995). Examples include the xanith of Oman, the mahu of Tahiti, the hijra of India (Nanda 1990), and the berdache of many North American Indian cultures (Nanda 2000).

In this unit, Serena Nanda examines North American Indian societies that often included three gender categories: men, women, and male gender variants called *berdaches*. Nanda also discusses some North American Indian societies in which females with sex-atypical behavioral patterns were placed into a fourth gender. Apparently, such females never occupied their own gender category within a society unless males with sex-atypical behavioral patterns occupied their own gender. Nanda considers the variation among Native American societies in the degree to which gender variants were integrated and accepted and in the ways in which gender variants were understood and expected to behave.

Kulick, in this unit, argues that gender variant males may also be placed into the same gender category as females. Kulick explores the integration (or its absence) of effeminate male homosexuals into Brazilian culture, in which gender roles are strictly dichotomous. Kulick contends that in Brazilian culture, males who enjoy being anally penetrated by other males belong with females in "the same classificatory category . . . [that they] share, in other words, a gender" (p. 580). Kulick's evidence comes mainly from two sources. First, in Brazil (as in numerous other cultures), a male who engages in same-sex sexual relations is not necessarily considered effeminate or homosexual if he plays only the insertor role in sex. Second, the *travestis* (effeminate homosexual male prostitutes), with whom Kulick interacted, viewed their role as the insertee in homosexual sex as crucial to their femininity and the insertor role of their boyfriends as critical to their boyfriends' masculinity.

Kulick admits his idea that travestis and women share a gender is contentious. ". . . Brazilians generally contest and mock individual travestis' claims to femininity" (p. 582). Tellingly, travestis face discrimination "throughout Brazil at the hands of gay men, many of whom feel that travestis compromise the public image of homosexuals and give gay men a bad name" (p. 580). Such conflict underscores the tension between sexual identity and gender roles. Those who conform to neither the cultural expectations of a man nor those of a woman face the dilemma of fitting into a gender category, even where a satisfactory category may not exist. Travestis, in their own eyes, may fit best into the gender category of *women*. This does not seem to be the prevalent view in Brazil, but Kulick's argument is, in part, rhetorical. Gender classification depends on how one defines gender categories. Kulick is making the point that ideas about masculinity and femininity are culturally variable. While some societies, such as the United States and Western Europe, emphasize one's sexual partners, other societies, such as Brazil, place more emphasis on the role one plays in sexual intercourse.

Dissecting Gender

We have already discussed how cross-cultural sex differences in development contribute to a universal *man/woman* gender dichotomy, however this dichotomy manifests itself culturally. Is there a similar way to understand the existence of gender variants? Is there something to connect all of them as a singular phenomenon? There seems to be. Everywhere, regardless of the gender system, gender variants behave in some ways that are typical of the opposite sex in their culture, including expressing homosexual orientation (see Unit VI). In his forward to Serena Nanda's (1990) well-known ethnography of the hijras, John Money describes gender variant males across cultures:

> It is feasible to compare all of these groups with one another insofar as they all share one defining characteristic. That characteristic is that, whereas they are not born as females and declared to be girls, they grow up so that, at some stage in life and to some degree, they act like women.

Money goes on to say,

> This worldwide similarity points to the conclusion that [gender variant male behavior] is of similar origin, no matter where it appears, and that the differences in its outcome are a secondary overlay, shaped by local traditions. (Money 1990, p. xiii)

Why is there a tendency for gender variant males the world over to "act like women," including preferring males as sex partners? Why did female gender variants among North American Indians show "an affinity for the occupations of the other gender" (Nanda 2000, p. 23), commonly dress like men, and have sexual relationships with women? Perhaps an inclination to behave like the opposite sex causes some people to identify with a gender variant role. Or maybe identification with a gender variant role causes people to act like the opposite sex. These are both real possibilities, but neither is probably a complete answer. The first begs the question, What causes a tendency to act like the opposite sex? And the second forces us to ask, What causes identification with a gender variant role?

More probably, both gender variant identification and homosexual preferences are influenced by another factor. Effeminate, homosexual men and masculine, homosexual women appear to exist in every society, so we cannot look to the peculiarities of any particular society to explain their presence. And no social variable (e.g., childhood abuse) has been identified to explain, for example, why some men within a society are effeminate homosexuals and others are not (Bell, Weinberg, and Hammersmith 1981; Stoller and Herdt 1985). Citing experimental hormonal manipulation in rodents and non-human primates and research on congenital hormonal variation in humans, Kimura (1999) suggests that sex-atypical hormonal levels during fetal development may contribute to homosexual orientation and other sex-atypical behavior.

A growing corpus of genetic, endocrinological, and neuroanatomical evidence supports this possibility, as you will see in Unit VI. Of course, deviations from sex-typical developmental pathways cannot perfectly predict cross-gender behavior. Most, if not all, societies probably sufficiently stigmatize gender variant behavior so that many people *behave* according to the expectations of their sex despite having some inclinations to the contrary. And the specific manifestation of a predisposition for cross-gender behavior depends on socialization. Vern and Bonnie Bullough (1993, p. 326) describe the formation of cross-gender identities as a three-step process:

1. "A genetic predisposition for a cross-gender identity is present . . . ."

2. "Prenatal hormonal stimulation supports that genetic predisposition . . . During the prenatal period, the hormonal stimulation indelibly marks the neural pathways so the pattern that produced the cross-gender identity is continued after birth."

3. "A socialization pattern shapes the specific manifestation of the predisposition."

Common developmental causes help explain the presence of cross-gender behavior across cultures and help explain gender classificatory systems. Societies differ in how accepting they are of sex-atypical behavior. Some societies have institutionalized gender variant roles for cross-gender individuals. Others do not recognize gender variance. An interesting and unresolved question is why societies differ in their recognition and acceptance of gender variance. But where institutionalized gender variant roles exist, they always function to classify people who in some ways fit the expectations of the opposite sex.

Summary

The interplay between relatively obligate developmental events and culturally variable gender roles highlights the necessity of a holistic approach. As you examine the readings in this unit, consider the interactions between these factors. A history of sexual selection has favored different developmental plans in males and females. These different genetic and hormonal influences *in utero,* and variations on them, contribute to divergent brain architecture and behavioral predispositions. However, it is only within particular sociocultural milieus that these variations in tendencies are manifested as differences in gender identity and behavior. Ultimately, an understanding of gender and associated behaviors will come only from considering how developmental processes, hormonal levels, and the like interact with cultural values, ideologies, and meanings.

References

Bell, A. P., M. S. Weinberg, and S. K. Hammersmith. 1981. *Sexual preference: Its development in men and women.* Bloomington: Indiana University Press.

Bullough, V. L., and B. Bullough. 1993. *Crossdressing, sex, and gender.* Philadelphia: University of Pennsylvania Press.

Daly, M., and M. Wilson. 1988. *Homicide.* New York: Aldine de Gruyter.

Hamer, D. H., S. Hu, V. L. Magnuson, N., Hu, and A. M. L. Pattatucci. 1995. A linkage between DNA markers on the X chromosome and male sexual orientation. *Science,* 261:321–27.

Kallman, F. J. 1952. Comparative twin study on the genetic aspects of male homosexuality. *Journal of Nervous and Mental Disorders,* 115:283–98.

Kimura, D. 1999. *Sex and cognition.* Cambridge, MA: MIT Press.

Money, J. 1990. Forward to the book *in* Nanda, S. *Neither man nor woman:The Hijras of India,* xi–xiv, Belmont, CA: Wadsworth.

Nanda, S. 1990. *Neither man nor woman:The Hijras of India.* Belmont, CA: Wadsworth.

Nanda, S. 2000. Multiple genders among North American Indians. In *Gender diversity cross cultural variations,* Chapter 1, 11–26. Long Grove, IL: Waveland Press.

Robinson, S. J., and J. T. Manning. 2000. The ratio of 2nd to 4th digit length and male homosexuality. *Evolution and Human Behavior,* 21:333–45.

Roscoe, W. 1995. How I became a queen in the empire of gender. Presented at conference, Lesbian and Gay History: Defining a Field. Center for Lesbian and Gay Studies, City University of New York, October 7, 1995.

Stoller, R. J., and G. H. Herdt. 1985. Theories of origins of male homosexuality: A cross-cultural look. *Archives of General Psychiatry,* 42:399–404.

Why Men and Not Women?

Martin Daly and Margo Wilson

Why was the last chapter entirely about *men?* We have proposed that dangerous altercations derive from status competition, and that the inclination to compete for status has evolved because high status has been contributory to fitness throughout human history. If this proposal is sound, why should it not apply equally to women?

Recall the Yanomamo headman Shinbone and his 11 wives. As we noted earlier, the fact that one man monopolizes several women means that others are consigned to celibacy. Indeed in any polygynous system, the fact that a few males each have more children than any one female could ever bear, necessarily implies that males are also much more likely than females to leave very few descendants, or none. And that is demonstrably the case. In a demographic survey of the Xavante Indians of Brazil (Salzano, Neel, and Maybury-Lewis, 1967), for example, 40 percent of the married men were polygynous. Other adult men were thus unmarried, although no woman of fertile age was without a husband. By 20 years of age, only 1 out of 195 women had not yet borne a child. By contrast, 6 percent of men who reached the age of 40 were still childless. The maximum number of children for a man was 23, for a woman, 8.

So we are primarily concerned with reproductive competition among men rather than women, not out of arbitrary sexism, but because the differentials among males are larger, and the competition is therefore more severe. A man has a higher ceiling upon his potential fitness than does a woman, but he also has a greater likelihood of going to his grave with no descendants at all (Ellison, 1985). There is, in other words, a sex difference in *fitness variance,* and this difference is causally linked to a host of other sex differences, the explication of which will require an excursion into basic evolutionary theory.

Sexual Selection and "Parental Investment"

Charles Darwin published his great work on natural selection in 1859. His second greatest contribution, the concept of *sexual selection,* he elaborated 12 years later (Darwin, 1871), but this idea had rather little impact for almost 100 years.

Whereas most adaptive attributes of animals are clearly of service in the struggle to survive, certain features—particularly those used by males in courtship—seem positively to *detract* from survival. The peacock's gaudy tail, for example, may charm the peahen, but it is conspicuous to potential predators too, and it is an impediment to flight. How could such traits persist if the more spectacular males tend to die sooner than their duller rivals? Darwin's answer was that mere longevity was not the same thing as reproductive success. A trait might be penalized by "natural" selection and yet win out by "sexual" selection, a process that occurs whenever some attribute contributes to success either in wooing the opposite sex or in vanquishing members of one's own sex in competition for mates. But just why sexual selection should appear to apply primarily to males—that is to say why males generally court and fight over females rather than the reverse—was not clearly elucidated for several decades, until the publication of a laboratory study, not of a spectacular wooer like the peacock nor a battler like the elk, but of the innocuous little fruit fly, *Drosophila*.

In 1948, the British geneticist A. J. Bateman published in the journal *Heredity* the results of his experiments on the reproduction of these tiny animals, when maintained in jars on the laboratory shelf, with each jar containing equal numbers (3, 4, or 5) of each sex. Bateman constituted the groups in such a way that he could attribute offspring to particular parents on the basis of distinct "genetic markers," characteristics analogous to human eye color or birth marks. By observing the behavior of the flies directly, and subsequently counting the progeny of each individual, he was able to relate individual differences in mating behavior to eventual reproductive success.

What Bateman found was that the reproductive success of a male is dependent upon his behavior in a very different way from that of a female. A fly of either sex might be observed to mate with anywhere from 0 to 4 individuals. In the case of females, fitness was unaffected by the precise number of mates: Assuming she mated at all, a female could expect to produce about 60 to 80 offspring, and it did not matter whether she had copulated with one male or with several. In the case of males, however, eventual reproductive success was a linear function of the number of sexual partners: Those who copulated with one female produced about 40 young, those who copulated with two produced about 80, and so forth. Related to this sex difference in the effects of differential mating frequency is a further difference: Whereas one female laid more or less the same number of eggs as another, the maximum being limited by her physiological capacity to produce them, a minority of males did much better than average, and a much greater proportion of males than of females produced no young at all. In other words, the variance in male fitness greatly exceeded the variance in female fitness.

With a little thought these phenomena may seem rather obvious, but Bateman was the first scientist to document such sex differences and to discuss their broader implications. Noting that the "greater dependence of males for their fertility on frequency of insemination" is "an almost universal attribute of sexual reproduction," he suggested that selection would produce tactics of male mating competition, as well as "an undiscriminatory eagerness in the males and a discriminatory passivity in the females." Thus Bateman explained Darwin's observation that in the animal kingdom generally, "the males are almost always the wooers": Male fitness is directly limited by access to fertile females, whereas a female's fitness is limited not by access to males but by access to the material resources necessary for reproduction, or, when resources are abundant, by her limited intrinsic capacities to convert them to babies.

Essentially the same argument applies to *Homo sapiens*. Female reproduction in people (and other mammals) is not, of course, limited simply by egg production capacity as in the case of the fruit fly: A woman may produce hundreds of eggs in a lifetime, but that does not mean that she could produce hundreds of children. However, in mammals, as in fruit flies, it is still the case that female productivity has a much lower potential maximum and a much lower variance than male productivity.

As Robert Trivers (1972) has elaborated Bateman's argument, the common denominator in fruit flies and ourselves is that females typically make a greater *parental investment* (PI) in each offspring than do males, with the result that female PI is, in effect, the "resource" that limits male fitness, and hence is a commodity for which males have been selected to compete. In the fly, the sex difference in PI resides in the greater material cost of a batch of eggs as compared to the ejaculate that fertilizes them. In a woman, the investment includes a 9-month gestation, lactation (lasting many months in the environments in which we evolved), and much subsequent nurture. While men *may* supply some of this later PI, women never had many options (at least before the domestication of milk animals). So a man—like a male fruit fly—could always increase his expected fitness by gaining sexual access to one more fertile female, regardless of whether he presently has no mates or fifty, whereas a woman—like a female fruit fly—typically would not enhance her expected fitness by gaining sexual access to every fertile male on the planet.

Her female rivals may limit a woman's fitness, to be sure—it is not our point to disparage the selective consequences of competition among females. And having multiple suitors may often provide material and protective advantages over monogamy (Hrdy, 1981). Nevertheless, male fitness is limited by access to the opposite sex much more directly than is female fitness, with the result that females compete *for mates* much less than do males. Partly for that reason, the competition between females is often less direct and confrontational than that between males. Competition among females for limited food resources, for example, is often a "scramble" in which the competitors do not even encounter one another. But the still more

important sex difference is quantitative. Competition among males is more intense than that among females in a simple objective sense: The variance in male fitness is greater than the variance in female fitness. Among men as compared to women, the big winners win bigger, and the losers are more likely to be total losers. As Richard Alexander (1979) has written, "as a general consequence, the entire life history strategy of males is a higher-risk, higher-stakes adventure than that of females" (p. 241).

Polygyny Is a Matter of Degree

Our point in discussing sexual selection and parental investment is not to make a facile comparison between fruit flies and people. Nor is it to claim that "competitiveness" is an attribute of maleness in the animal world generally. On the contrary, there is a sizable minority of animal species—some birds, for example, some frogs, a few insects, and others—in which the sex differences discussed above are reversed. In such species, the males make the greater parental investment and have the lower reproductive potential, and this being so, sexual selection has operated more intensely on the females, who are larger and more combative, have greater fitness variance, and tend to die younger than the males. Such reversals provide some of the strongest evidence for the Bateman-Trivers theory, because they support the idea that it is parental investment disparities that drive the system.

The interesting point for our purposes is comparative: Animal species vary in a large number of correlated traits, all of which turn out to be related to the species-typical magnitude of the sex difference in parental investment, in fitness variance, and in sexual selection. And *Homo sapiens,* it so happens, can be readily situated within this comparative scheme.

A *monogamous breeding system* can be defined for present purposes as one in which individuals breed only with a single member of the opposite sex. If eight children represent the maximum for a female, for example, then under monogamy, eight will be the maximum for a male as well. The frequency distribution of numbers of offspring is identical for females and males, and the fitness variances are equal (if the sexes are about equally numerous). Now, whereas monogamy implies equal fitness variance, the reverse is not true: Both sexes could change partners frequently and still have identical fitness distributions. However, we refer to any case in which female and male variances are equal as "effectively monogamous" because sexual selection is likely to have had approximately equal impact upon the two sexes in any case where the variances are equal, just as in true monogamy.

Where male fitness variance exceeds female fitness variance, we refer to the system as "effectively polygynous." Note that effective polygyny is a matter of degree (see Daly and Wilson, 1983, pp. 151–156). The degree of effective polygamy can be approximated as the ratio of male variance over female variance. A value of 1 is effective monogamy, greater than 1 is effective polygyny, and less than 1 is effective polyandry (a state of affairs that exists in the "sex-reversed" animals alluded to earlier, but probably does not characterize any human society, although a tiny minority practice polyandrous marriage; Murdock, 1967).

The data on animal breeding systems are seldom good enough to permit precise quantification of the degree of effective polygamy. However, we can often get a reasonable estimate from proxy measures such as the number of females in a sexually active male's "harem." By such measures, we find dramatic differences in polygamy among closely related species. Certain species of African antelopes (see, e.g., Jarman, 1974), for example, are monogamous. In some other related species, a successful male may sire the calves of three or four females in a single season, while other males lose out. In still other species, the most successful males may sire dozens, while the majority of males never get to breed at all. (See Clutton-Brock, 1988, for recent studies of lifetime reproductive success and the degree of effective polygamy in animal breeding systems.)

What is most interesting about this variability in the degree of effective polygamy among animal species is that other traits vary along with it. Among monogamous antelope species, for example, female and male are about the same size, are of similar build and markings, and may indeed be virtually indistinguishable. When we then examine other antelope species with increasingly polygynous breeding systems, we find that males are larger and larger relative to the females, and the sexes exhibit increasingly dramatic differences in armament. As the degree of polygyny increases, so too does the fitness prize to the most successful males, and so does the probability of total reproductive failure.

Sexual Success versus Survival?

One might imagine that a polygynous male's large size and armament would contribute to his survival as well as to his competitive success. But that is demonstrably not the case. Within a comparative series such as the antelopes, the trend toward greater polygyny and increasing size difference between the sexes parallels another trend toward a greater and greater sex difference in mortality, and it is the powerful males who are the more vulnerable sex. In highly polygynous species, males die in combat, of course, but they also suffer greater mortality than females in other contexts as well, sometimes because of starvation, sometimes because of greater conspicuousness to predators, sometimes because of relative immobility in hard conditions such as deep snow. Thus sexual selection for intraspecific competitive ability often acts counter to natural selection for ecological efficiency and survival capability. As the intensity of sexual selection in an effectively polygynous breeding system increases, the male's design for survival is more and more compromised by the requirements for success in reproductive competition.

The fact that the males of a polygynous species may expect to die younger than the females means that selection operates differently on the sexes, with respect to any trait that might enhance present fitness at a cost in long-term maintenance of bodily condition or survival capability. If we intervene to remove the normal extrinsic causes of mortality, maintaining the animal in a sheltered captivity, we would typically expect to find that males and females of a monogamous species exhibit similar life spans before senescing and dying, whereas males senesce more rapidly than females in those species that are effectively polygynous. Elevated function of adrenals and gonads, for example, contributes to the competitive success of males of the Australian small mammal genus *Antechinus* during the single breeding season that a male ordinarily lives to see; the same hormonal events contribute to anemia, hemorrhages, and the suppression of the immune system, which guarantee the male's death soon after the mating season ends, while the females live on to raise their litters and perhaps to breed again another year (Lee *et al.*, 1977).

The same arguments of course apply to psychological attributes and behavioral propensities: A more polygynous system selects for riskier behavior by males competing for mating opportunities, whether the risks in question are incurred in combat with rivals or in less directly competitive pursuits, such as exposing oneself to predation in order to visit scattered females. Animals, as we have said before, are not designed to live forever, but to outreproduce their rivals. The more polygamous the breeding system, the greater is the difference between the sexes in how long each is designed to live.

The Sexual Selective History of *Homo sapiens*

The relevance of all this to the human case should be obvious. What do the sexually differentiated characteristics of this particular animal reveal about its history of sexual selection? The clear answer is that we are the products of a mild but sustained polygynous competition.

Within the primates generally, the ratio of male body length to female body length is strongly correlated with effective polygyny (Alexander *et al.*, 1979). Moreover, there is some evidence that the females of polygynous primate species are closer than the males to a body size that is optimal for the species' feeding ecology (Gaulin and Sailer, 1985); males, in other words, are "oversized," presumably for the sake of combative prowess. The ratio of male body length to female body length in our own species is greater than in such monogamists as gibbons or marmosets, less than in such extreme polygynists as baboons or gorillas. An independent vestige of our polygynous selective history can be seen in the fact that males senesce more rapidly than females. Still another is that females are sexually mature a little before males; a sex difference in the age at maturity is yet another correlate of the species-characteristic degree of effective polygamy in comparative studies, apparently because whichever sex is the more competitive requires longer to attain sufficient competitive abilities to make a first breeding attempt worthwhile. All the available evidence is consistent in suggesting that our sexual selective history has been one of effective polygyny.

Sexual dimorphism and violent male-male competition are ancient and enduring elements of our evolutionary history. Fifty thousand years ago, there was approximately the same degree of sexual size dimorphism among Neanderthals as we find in modern men and women (Trinkaus,

1980). Indeed, our nearest living relatives, the anthropoid apes, are all sexually dimorphic and effectively polygynous, and the same appears to have been true of the earliest fossil anthropoids (Fleagle *et al.,* 1980).

There can be no doubt that men have killed one another at high rates for as long as there have been men. Twenty years ago, this claim engendered great controversy, but we have learned a lot in the interim.

Where ethologists once believed that intraspecific killing was rare in the animal world in general and among our close kin in particular, we have since found that attacks by conspecifics are a major cause of mortality in many (probably most) mammals, including those most closely related to ourselves. At the same time, novel theoretical work has elucidated the conditions under which intraspecific violence would be adaptive for the aggressor, providing an impetus for researchers to record and study such violence, instead of attributing it to pathology. As a result, careful field studies have demonstrated that male-male combat is a leading cause of death in polygynous, dimorphic mammals. In our closest relatives, the chimpanzees, males form alliances, partly along kinship lines, and conduct prolonged campaigns of intergroup hostility (see Goodall, 1986).

Most importantly, we have discovered in the past 20 years a great deal about the violent history of man himself. The old idea that hunter-gatherers are nonviolent was an ideologically motivated myth that never matched the evidence: Old and recent ethnography alike provide ample testimony of murder and prolonged blood feuds among Australian aborigines, Plains Indians, Eskimos, Kalahari San, and other hunter-gatherers. Moreover, the evidence of prehistoric violence has accumulated greatly (and paleontological detective work has become much more sophisticated) since Raymond Dart's controversial claim that australopithecines staved in one another's skulls. In some ancient skeletal samples, for example, one can observe and count cranial fractures (evidently by clubbing) and rib fractures (evidently by stabbing), both healed and fatal. Sometimes the wounds still contain fragments of the weapon. It is regularly found that male skeletons exhibit more such wounds than female skeletons, and moreover that men (more than women) are more often wounded on the left than on the right side, evidently by right-handed antagonists (e.g., Walker, 1985). The earliest known victim of human weapons was a Neanderthal man, frontally stabbed in the chest by a right-handed antagonist more than 50,000 years ago (Trinkaus and Zimmerman, 1982).

We still cannot say to what extent human sex differences in size and bodily structure reflect specific sexually selected adaptation to male-male combat. It is possible, for example, that the selective pressure for male body size and power resides primarily in hunting rather than in fighting. What is certain is that men have fought and killed one another for tens of thousands of years. It is hard to doubt that the winners in such combat generally outreproduced the losers.

What evidence we have on modern human populations indicates that the selective circumstance of an effectively polygynous breeding system persists. Polygynous marriage was available to successful men the world 'round until recently. And even now, in societies with legislated monogamy, men have a longer potential reproductive life span than women, remarry and raise successive families with different mates more often than do women, and are more likely than women never to marry. Moreover, there is, in many cases, reason to suspect some degree of clandestine polygyny or reproductive concubinage. Thus, although data on men's fertility histories are sparse (and of dubious validity, thanks to uncertain paternity), it seems very likely that the variance in men's fitness must still exceed that of women.

Intrasexual Competition and Violence

Competition is a subcategory of conflict, arising when two (or more) individuals aspire to make similar use of a resource that is not sufficiently abundant to satisfy both (or all). Not all conflict is competitive. If a female spurns one suitor for another, for example, then she and the rejected male have a conflict of interest, but they are not competitors (whereas the rival suitors are).

Competition for limited resources is predominantly intrasexual: female against female, male against male. It is not *entirely* intrasexual: A female and a male might both desire the same food item, for example, and might fight or even kill over it. But competition is *predominantly* intrasexual because same-sex individuals are usually more similar in the resources they require than are opposite-sex individuals. In particular, individuals of the opposite sex are often the "resource" that same-sex individuals compete for.

According to the Bateman-Trivers theory, access to the sex that makes the greater parental investment tends to become the crucial resource limiting the fitness of individuals of the less investing sex, so that selection favors competition among the latter for access to mates. Fitness variance is a measure of the intensity of competition, and the more intense that competition— that is to say, the more disparate the outcomes— then the more likely it becomes that selection will favor a psychology prone to risky competitive tactics, including escalated fighting even to the point of death. This point is elaborated with a game-theoretical model in Chapter 8. Note that the Bateman-Trivers theory of sexual selection leads to predictions about sex differences, but not to the simplistic account of sex differences that is so often misattributed to biologists, namely that there is something about "maleness"—androgens, in one popular version—that

leads to inevitable aggressivity and violence. On the contrary, the theory predicts that sex differences will themselves differ from one species to another in their magnitude and even in their direction, and it predicts the nature of that variability in considerable detail (Trivers, 1972).

The comparative evidence is abundant, and it is clearly supportive of the theory. In monogamous wolves or gulls or gibbons, the fitness variance of females is as great as that of males, and females are about as hostile to one another as are males. In a polyandrous species such as the spotted sandpiper of North America (Maxson and Oring, 1980), females have the greater fitness variance, and thus have more to fight over; as we would expect, the females' battles are more spectacular and evidently dangerous than those of the males. In polygynous species, it is predominantly the males who fight, and their fights are more severe the more polygynous the species. Although there are still many puzzling cases and additional complications, these general cross-species correlations are not controversial (see, for example, Daly and Wilson, 1983).

In Chapter 6, we proposed that a large proportion of the homicides in America—and in particular most of those traditionally dismissed as being the results of "trivial altercations"— have to be understood as the rare, fatal consequences of a ubiquitous competitive struggle among men for status and respect. These social "resources" have come to be valued by the male psyche because of their positive fitness consequences. Since our selective history has been one of effective polygyny (and our present circumstances apparently maintain the sex difference in fitness variance), and since differential fitness is demonstrably more strongly correlated with differential status in males than in females, we may expect men to be more inclined to risky, confrontational intrasexual interactions than women, and we may expect this difference to be much more generally manifested than in America alone. So what are the facts?

Table 7.1 presents the numbers of male-male and female-female homicides that have been recorded in various studies in a wide range of

Table 7.1   Same-Sex Homicides in Various Studies

References	Male Killed Male	Female Killed Female	Proportion Male
Canada, 1974–1983	2968	175	.944
Miami, 1925–1926; Wilbanks, 1984	111	5	.957
North Carolina, 1930–1940; Garfinkel, 1949	603	28	.956
Birmingham, 1937–1944; Harlan, 1950	277	20	.933
Cleveland, 1947–1953; Bensing & Schroeder, 1960	417	14	.968
Philadelphia, 1948–1952; Wolfgang, 1958	333	16	.954
Houston, 1958–1961; Pokorny, 1965	246	16	.939
Chicago, 1965; Voss & Hepburn, 1968	219	10	.956
Pittsburgh, 1966–1974; Costantino *et al.*, 1977	382	16	.960
Detroit, 1972; Wilson & Daly, 1985	345	16	.956
St. Louis, 1973; Herjanic & Meyer, 1976	135	2	.985
Miami, 1980; Wilbanks, 1984	369	1	.997
Gros Ventre (USA), 1850–1885; Flannery, 1953	13	0	1.000
Tzeltal Mayans (Mexico), 1938–1965; Nash, 1967	37	0	1.000
Belo Horizonte (Brazil), 1961–1965; Yearwood, 1974	228	6	.974
New South Wales, (Australia, 1968–1981); Wallace, 1986	675	46	.936
Oxford (England), 1296–1398; Hammer, 1978	105	1	.991
England, 13th century; Given, 1977	1409	73	.951
England and Wales, 1982; Edwards, 1985	241	22	.916
Scotland, 1953–1974; Gillies, 1976	172	12	.935
Iceland, 1946–1970; Hansen & Bjarnason, 1974	10	0	1.000
Denmark, 1933–1961; Siciliano, 1965	87	15	.853
Baden-Wurttemburg, (Germany) 1970–1971; Sessar, 1975	94	4	.959
Bison-Horn Maria, (India), 1920–1941; Elwin, 1950	69	2	.972
Munda (India); Saran, 1974	43	0	1.000
Oraon (India); Saran, 1974	40	0	1.000
Bhil (India), 1971–1975; Varma, 1978	85	1	.988
Kung San (Botswana), 1920–1955; Lee, 1979	19	0	1.000
Congo (now Zaire), 1948–1957; Sohier, 1959	156	4	.975
Tiv (Nigeria), 1931–1949; Bohannan, 1960b	96	3	.970
BaSoga (Uganda), 1952–1954; Fallers & Fallers, 1960	46	1	.979
Gisu (Uganda), 1948–1954; LaFontaine, 1960	72	3	.960
BaLuyia (Kenya), 1949–1954; Bohannan, 1960	88	5	.946
JoLuo (Kenya); Wilson, 1960	31	2	.939
Alur (Uganda), 1945–1954; Southall, 1960	37	1	.974

societies. *The difference between the sexes is immense, and it is universal.* There is no known human society in which the level of lethal violence among women even begins to approach that among men.

The sex differences in Table 7.1 are huge, but they indubitably underestimate the actual sex difference in intrasexual competitive violence. This is so because the table includes homicides that are not properly construed as the outcomes of competition, and these constitute a higher proportion of the female cases than of the male cases. The single female-female homicide in Miami in 1980, for example, was an infanticide, and so was the single case in 14th-century Oxford. As we saw in Chapters 3 and 4, killing one's own dependent offspring is a very different matter from an intrasexual, competitive altercation, and such cases weigh heavily in Table 7.1. The Danish data set, for example, exhibits the smallest ratio of male-male to female-female cases ("only" 5.8 to 1), but *all* 15 of the latter were cases in which mothers killed dependent children. Similarly, the second smallest ratio ("only" 11 to 1) is that for England and Wales in 1982, but there were 27 father-son cases among the 241 male-male killings, and 18 mother-daughters among the 22 female-female; so between unrelated men, lethal same-sex violence was more than 50 times as numerous as between unrelated women.

In our 10-year Canadian sample, the tabulated data indicate 16.9 times as many male-male cases as female-female ones. However, more than half of the latter were cases in which mothers killed preschool-age daughters, whereas only 3 percent of male-male cases were father-son cases (still a larger absolute number than mother-daughter cases). If we remove these parental homicides from the comparison, there remain 2861 male-male cases and just 84 female-female cases; the former are now 34.1 times as numerous as the latter. To slice the pie

yet another way, we might propose that competition tends to occur primarily between peers, and hence that the competitive element is probably greater in cases where the ages of victim and killer are not very different. If we therefore select those Canadian cases in which the parties' ages differed by no more than 10 years, we find 1519 male-male cases and a mere 39 female-female cases, the former being 38.9 times as numerous. All in all, it appears that *the sex difference in intrasexual competitive homicides is even more extreme than the data in Table 7.1 would suggest.*

In the United States, a great deal of publicity has recently been granted to allegations of an alarming rise in female criminality. It is widely believed that behavioral differences between American women and men are on the wane as a result of "women's liberation." This belief is exploited by conservative critics of feminism, who cite rising female crime statistics as the "dark side" of progress toward equality. But the bogeyman of violent crime by women is a fiction. The statistics in question are the Federal Bureau of Investigation's national arrest data for "serious crimes," and while the proportion of arrestees that are women has indeed increased more or less continuously over the past 30 years, this is *entirely* because of an increased representation of women among those arrested for "larceny-theft" (and even this difference may not represent a change in the behavior of women, but rather a change in the willingness of police to arrest them). The female proportion among arrestees for *violent* crimes—and in particular for homicide—has in fact declined slightly over the same period. There is no evidence that women in modern America are approaching the level of violent conflict prevailing among men. Indeed there is no evidence that the women in any society have *ever* approached the level of violent conflict prevailing among men in the same society.

Margaret Mead and New Guinea

The sex difference that is illustrated in Table 7.1 is so universally an aspect of human experience that it should surprise no one. Yet it is part of the mythology of the social sciences, particularly as they have developed in North America, that any such differences between women and men are culturally arbitrary and easily reversed. "In our culture," writes Marvin Wolfgang, trying to explain the enormous sex difference in his study of Philadelphia homicides, the female is "less given to or expected to engage in physical violence than the male" (1958, p. 163). In other writings, he has attributed the same phenomenon to "socialization" and "the theme of masculinity in American culture" (1978, p. 87). The clear implication is that things are otherwise in other cultures. But they are not.

The myth that the familiar sex difference in violence is reversed in other societies can be laid at the door of the famous anthropologist and popular writer Margaret Mead. Her study of three New Guinea tribes, published in 1935 under the title *Sex and Temperament in Three Primitive Societies,* has been presented to literally millions of college undergraduates as a demonstration that differences in the traits of men and women are arbitrary and reversible cultural artifacts. As she summed up the matter in her preface to the 1950 edition,

> *Here, admittedly looking for light on the subject of sex differences, I found three tribes all conveniently within a hundred mile area. In one, both men and women act as we expect women to act—in a mild parental responsive way; in the second, both act as we expect men to act—in a fierce initiating fashion; and in the third, the men act according to our stereotype for women—are catty, wear curls and go shopping, while the women are energetic, managerial, unadorned partners.*

These peoples were the "gentle Arapesh," the "violent, cannibalistic Mundugumor," and the sex-reversed Tschambuli, respectively.

Imagine a 2 × 2 matrix: aggressivity vs. passivity in males times the same alternatives in females. The dark forces of ethnocentrism and sexism would have had us believe that aggressive-male/passive-female constituted the only possible combination. Suddenly, Mead had demolished that claim by filling in the other three cells of the matrix at a single stroke! What could be neater?

Mead was a major public figure and propagandist for humane causes. For over a decade, *Redbook* magazine ran a popular monthly column called "Margaret Mead Answers." The reading public could ask her anything from "Do primitive people keep pets?" to "Is the U.S. State Department right to forbid Americans to travel to Cuba?," and could count on a thoughtful answer. By 1975, 3 years after her death, Mead's bibliography of publications—the books, scientific papers, book reviews, interviews, letters, columns—ran to 1397 items (Gordon, 1976). But Mead's ideological and popularizing goals seriously compromised her ethnographic research, as has recently been made painfully clear by Derek Freeman's (1983) surgical exposé of the fantastic misrepresentation of Samoan culture that constituted Mead's doctoral thesis and made her famous. What then, of her later work in New Guinea? What *did* Margaret Mead observe in those three tribes?

As it happens, Mead published extensively only on the "gentle" Arapesh. She never provided details on who her informants were in the other cultures, nor what they actually told her, let alone present any behavioral data. The bases for the wonderful story of sex-role arbitrariness are entirely contained in the two popular books *Sex and Temperament* and *Male and Female.* Mead's goal, following the "culture and personality" program of her friend and mentor Ruth Benedict, was to characterize each society's "temperament" in broad, artistic strokes. And that she certainly did. Let us consider the three societies, one by one.

Mead insisted that the Arapesh of both sexes were "gentle" and "passive," but whatever these terms were intended to convey, nonviolence was not the point. Mead herself described homicides and spear-throwing battles ("mainly over women"), and somehow the participants in such violence were exclusively male. Subsequent ethnographers, especially Donald Tuzin (1977, 1980), have documented the bloody preoccupations of Arapesh men, and in particular the obligation that a young man must commit homicide in order to be initiated into adulthood. Four years after *Sex and Temperament* appeared, Mead's former husband and collaborator, Reo Fortune (1939), published a paper on "Arapesh Warfare" in the *American Anthropologist*. Fortune dramatically illustrated the chronic violence among these "gentle" men, and explicitly contradicted Mead's claim that the Arapesh idealize an identical temperament for men and women. Mead neither changed her story nor refuted Fortune's paper; she simply added it to her reference list.

Enough said about the gentle Arapesh. What about the Mundugumor, of whom Mead (1935) claimed, "Both men and women are expected to be violent, competitive, aggressively sexed, jealous and ready to see and avenge insult, delighting in display, in action, in fighting" (p. 225)? Alas, this is a society much less well documented than the others, and on a return visit in 1973, Mead concluded that the traditional culture had been completely extinguished by missionaries and other modern influences. Neither Mead nor Fortune ever got around to working up their Mundugumor materials for scholarly publication, but there are hints about the nature of male and female violence in Mead's popular books. The men, it seems, were avid polygynists, raiding neighboring tribes for wives, and for heads. Women, of course, did not raid, neither for heads nor for husbands. A young man, but not a woman, was again evidently obliged to kill an enemy before achieving fully adult status.

Though both sexes were "violent in their love-making," Mundugumor women otherwise manifested their violence differently than did men. Mead (1949) writes, for example, that they "express their active aggressive impulses by fishing and eating better than men, or serving dishes tastier than their co-wives [sic] to a common husband" (p. 122). Some further insight into the nature of female violence comes from Mead's (1935) allusion to

> aberrant personalities who are so violent that even Mundugumor standards have no place for them. A man of this sort becomes too continuously embroiled with his fellows, until he may be finally killed. . . . A woman of equal violence, who continually tries to attach new lovers and is insatiable in her demands, may in the end be handed over to another community to be communally raped. (p. 232)

These quotes exhaust the available material on the "violence" of Mundugumor women.

And what, finally, can be said about the "Tschambuli," the remarkable society in which, in Mead's words, "we found a genuine reversal of the sex-attitudes of our culture"? Well, whatever is meant by "sex-attitudes," they do not extend to violent conflict. Like the Arapesh, the Tschambuli (called Chambri in recent literature) have been studied further. Like the other Sepik River societies, they have a long history of warfare, in which they have totally annihilated certain neighboring tribes (Gewertz, 1983). As in all tribal societies, warfare is a male monopoly. As in the Arapesh and the Mundugumor, killing his first enemy is an important milestone in a young man's life. In fact, it entitles him to wear the make-up that Mead found so feminine. So wherein lies the famous sex-reversal? Well, the Tschambuli women are "dominant," insisted Mead (1935), "And yet the men are after all stronger, and a man can beat his wife, and this possibility serves to confuse the whole issue of female dominance" (p. 264).

Indeed.

Biophobia

The "culture and personality" program to which Margaret Mead subscribed is anthropological history. It failed—like so many other failed perspectives in the social sciences—because it overextended a weak analogy between societies and individuals. "A people" does not have "a personality."

Today, Mead's descriptions of the various tribal peoples she studied appear quaintly typological, as must any attempt to characterize the "temperament" of an entire society. Indeed, Mead asserted, without evident awareness of her own ethnocentrism, that the cultural differences between any two neighboring American families were as large as those "between New Guinea tribes." Her research is scarcely cited in anthropological texts nowadays, with the result that many of her professional colleagues considered Freeman's (1983) debunking of her Samoan story to be gratuitous viciousness.

But the myths that Margaret Mead gave us live on, in adjacent disciplines, in journals of opinion, in the American world view. According to a recent survey of 61 current psychology textbooks (Minderhout, 1986), Mead is the most frequently cited anthropologist, and *Sex and Temperament* is her most frequently cited work. She is also the most cited anthropologist in 51 sociology texts (tied with Ruth Benedict).

Mead's "discovery" that differences between the sexes are reversed in other societies created a sensation, and it is impossible to exaggerate its impact upon the attitudes of the educated public. It has been retold in print many hundreds of times, and, like any good tale, it has frequently been embellished in the retelling. Here, for example, is an excerpt from a page-long version, collected from a recent popular book (Nowak, 1980):

Human nature, the Arapesh believe, is basically peaceful, but people can be taught to be aggressive in the defense of others. When to the wonderment of the Arapesh, some men or women do become violent, the Arapesh resign themselves and try not to provoke these unfortunate souls. (p. 34)

And here (in its entirety) is a short, punchy version, collected from a recent introductory psychology textbook (multiauthored, in the current fashion, so that each section has been written by a specialist in the relevant field) (Schlenker and Severy, 1979):

Margaret Mead (1949) in her classic work Males and Females [sic], describes various New Guinea cultures wherein it is the female who is responsible, makes all the decisions, and is aggressive—with the males being docile, submissive, and homebodies. (p. 518)

"Makes all the decisions" and "homebodies" are timely little touches for the contemporary American scene. Does it really matter that Mead herself made no such claims?

Our point is not to blame the late Dr. Mead for the liberties that others have taken with the myth she created. What is of interest is how *the myth fills the need* for social scientists and commentators. It seems to demonstrate that our social natures are pure cultural artifacts, as arbitrary as the name of the rose, and that we can therefore create any world we want, simply by changing our "socialization practices." (This may sound a remarkably totalitarian vision, but it's not, you see, because the new, improved socialization practices will be designed by *nice* people with everyone's best interests at heart, and not by nasty, self-interested despots.) The social science that is used to legitimize this ideology can only be described as *biophobic*.

We wish we were exaggerating, but we are not. American social scientists fear and despise biology, although few of them have troubled to learn any. We can get a hint about the sources of their biophobia from the following words of Marvin Wolfgang (1978), dean of American criminologists, boosting a sociological approach by disparaging other disciplines:

> *Biological needs and psychological drives may be declared uniformly distributed and hence of no utility in explaining one form of behavior relative to another. . . . Neither biology . . . nor psychology . . . helps to explain the overwhelming involvement in crime of men over women, slums over suburbs, youth over age, urban over rural life.* (p. 87)

Psychologists will take vigorous exception to Wolfgang's caricature of their discipline, and rightly so. "Uniformly distributed drives"? Why, the entire subject matter of psychology has to do with the multitudinous causes of behavioral variation! But will the same psychologists recognize that biology is no less caricatured?

Again and again in the writings of social scientists, we find "biological" equated with "invariant" or "genetic" or "instinctive," and contrasted with "social," with "cultural," with "learned." This usage betrays an incomprehension of the domain of biology. Theoretical and empirical work on social behavior abounds in biological research journals, for example. Developmental biologists are engaged in elucidating how environmental variations interact with and influence the organism as it grows. Behavioral ecologists are concerned with the strategies by which creatures acquire information, that is to say, how they learn, and how they utilize what they have learnt.

Here is a dictionary definition of biology (Morris, 1969):

> *The science of life and life processes, including the structure, functioning, growth, origin, evolution, and distribution of living organisms.*

That is pretty well what biologists mean by it, too. By this definition, the social sciences are branches of biology, and we think that they would profit by considering themselves to be just that. Our point has nothing to do with interdisciplinary imperialism, nor is it a mere

quibble about definitions. The important point is not simply that biology *definitionally* encompasses all the life sciences, but that it provides an encompassing *conceptual* framework, which the social sciences ignore to their disadvantage. Progress in every subfield of what is usually called biology is predicated upon evolutionary insights, and most of it upon an understanding of selection. Little wonder, since selection is the creative process that "designed" organisms and all their constituent parts from cell membranes to minds. As George Williams (1966) has written, "Is it not reasonable to anticipate that our understanding of the human mind would be aided greatly by knowing the purpose for which it was designed?" (p. 16).

Suppose that an archaeologist were advised to study the processes of sedimentation, but refused, scorning geology as "reductionism." The archaeologist's research could, of course, proceed, and some valid conclusions might be attained. But the risk of wasted efforts and nonsensical interpretations would be higher than necessary. The phenomena that archaeologists study are partly the products of well-understood geological processes, and the archaeologist who does not want to know about those processes operates under a self-imposed handicap. Of course, no archaeologist would be so foolish. But the biophobic social scientist is in an analogous position.

Consider the following argument, advanced by an eminent anthropologist (Harris, 1974):

> *Knowing only the facts of human anatomy and biology, one could not predict that females would be the socially subordinate sex. . . . If I had knowledge only of the anatomy and cultural capacities of men and women, I would predict that women rather than men would be more likely to gain control over the technology of defense and aggression. . . . I would expect women to concentrate their efforts on rearing solitary and aggressive females rather than males. . . . I would predict that women would monopolize the headship of local groups. . . . Finally, I would expect that the ideal and most prestigious form of marriage would be polyandry—one woman con-*

trolling the sexual and economic services of several men. (pp. 84–85)

In this passage, Marvin Harris, leader of the "cultural materialist" school of American anthropology, clearly imagines that he has demonstrated the futility of biologizing. Instead, he has demonstrated his ignorance of evolutionary theory. Armed with the theory of sexual selection that is outlined in this chapter, and with no more knowledge of *Homo sapiens* than that provided by a few skeletons, a biologist from outer space would guess right about every aspect of male-female relations that Harris would get wrong.

Harris's playful "predictions" are indeed in never-never land, but not because of biology's impotence, as he implies; the "predictions" follow not from "anatomy" but from Harris's incomprehension of what the male-female phenomenon is fundamentally about. Why assume, for example, that women should be much *interested* in controlling "the technology of aggression" or "the sexual services of several men"? (A widespread and ironically sexist presumption is that "liberated" women will think and act like men.) Marvin Harris is by no means the only outstanding social scientist suffering from biophobia. What a waste.

On the Causes of Sex Differences

It is our conviction that the biophobia that is rampant in the social sciences is founded more in ignorance than in a reasoned critique of evolutionary theory. But that is not to say that there are no substantive points of contention. There appears to be a genuine difference of opinion about why sex differences like that in Table 7.1 exist.

A popular explanation for sex differences is "culture." A sociologist studying spousal homi-cide in Canada, for example, echoes Marvin Wolfgang (Chimbos, 1978):

The marked differences of violent crimes . . . between the sexes . . . can be partly explained in terms of cultural conditioning. For example, in North America, aggressiveness and physical prowess are important to male development while softness and gentleness are emphasized in female development. (p. 21)

But why invoke North American culture to explain a sex difference that is universal? The clear implication of this paragraph is that men would not be more violent than women if "conditioned" by some other culture. No such culture has ever been discovered. It is particularly ironic that both Wolfgang and Chimbos should attribute to North American culture a sex difference (rates of violent crime) that is apparently smaller in modern North America than in any other human society, present or past.

When the same universal sex difference is observed in other societies it is again likely to be attributed to cultural peculiarities. *Amok*, for example, is a regularly recurring phenomenon in several southeast Asian societies, in which a young man embarks on a frenzied homicidal rampage until killed or subdued. And why don't women do the same? Well, here is the explanation offered by a psychiatrist (Westermeyer 1973):

The total absence of amok women from all studies over the last century and a half can perhaps also be understood from the psychosocial perspective. By virtue of their socially subordinate status to men, they have not been so vulnerable to social upheaval; prestige and a reliable social role are available to them in the home. Where stress does mount, their cultures offer behavioral alternatives which channel anger into nondestructive syndromes such as latah. In Laos, where men are expected to keep a "cool heart" in public, women can loudly vent their feelings at home. Thus, women in these cultures appear more able to show hostility in their arena (the home); where they cannot do so, the socially prescribed syndromes do not lead to irremediable violence. (p. 875)

Fine, but homicidal rampages analogous to the amok syndrome are not peculiar to southeast Asia, and mass murderers are invariably men, never women. Have women but not men "socially prescribed" means to "vent their hostile feelings" in *all* societies? Westermeyer's proposed explanation is vacuous.

One more example. An historian encounters the familiar sex difference in homicidal violence in records from 13th-century England, and seeks an explanation in terms of contemporary social practices (Given, 1977):

> To an extent, the low level of female participation in homicide, both as killers and victims, may be explained by the different social roles that contemporaries expected the sexes to play. The use of violence was regarded as inappropriate for women. . . . The strong social and cultural inhibitions against the use of force by women as a means of settling disputes is [sic] reflected in the verdicts handed down on women accused of homicides. . . . Women . . . stood a greater chance of being executed. (pp. 134–137)

The trouble with this "explanation" is that women continue to behave far less violently than men when they are the sex that is penalized less severely, as for example in contemporary North America. More generally, the basic strategy of attempting to explain cross-culturally universal phenomena in terms of culturally and historically peculiar causes is surely futile.

In Chapter 1, we briefly outlined Donald Symons's useful analysis of what is at issue beneath the polemics and mutual misunderstandings of the "sociobiology debate." Symons (1987) suggested that "imaginations informed by Darwinism" tend generally to expect that the human brain/mind will comprise a large and complex set of special-purpose behavioral control mechanisms that have been shaped by natural and sexual selection. The alternative view is that the brain/mind is a general-purpose machine guided in its development by the principles of learning and by a few "primary reinforcers." (That, at least, has been the mainstream view within psychology, which is the only social

science to have addressed the question of the explicit nature of "socialization" and other ontogenetic processes. Recently, psychologists themselves have become increasingly inclined to postulate a complex repertoire of evolved mental mechanisms; see, for example, Fodor, 1984; Shepherd, 1984; Cosmides, 1985.)

For the case of sex differences, the issue may be stated as follows. Are behavioral sex differences entirely the products of differential personal histories of socially administered reinforcement and sex-role socialization? Or has selection differentially shaped the psyches of males and females by enlisting a variety of sexually differentiated developmental processes other than those that are usually encompassed by the term "socialization"?

Note that this issue has nothing to do with greater or lesser roles of genes or environments as causal agents in development. *All* developmental processes from the single-cell stage to death are *entirely* dependent upon both gene action and environmental influence. Another thing that is not the issue is whether sex-typical behavior happens to be learned. Those phenotypic attributes that arise as a result of "learning" are every bit as susceptible to modification by natural and sexual selection as are those phenotypic attributes that arise by developmental processes that do not happen to include "learning." And finally, it is not the issue whether the causal sequence leading to any particular behavioral difference between women and men can be traced back to a genetic difference, for it always can. It is, after all, a genetic difference between the sexes that is causally antecedent to fetal gonadal differentiation, which is, in turn, causally antecedent to the structural differentiation that allows parents to identify the sex of their child and to socialize it accordingly. It follows that even those sex differences that are induced by arbitrary culture-specific sex-role socialization are nevertheless "traceable to genetic differences." No doubt some readers will think this argument is a semantic trick, but in fact, this is all that is *ever* meant by the claim that some trait is "genetic": There is some sort of chain of causal links from the alternative traits back to alternative genotypes.

Let us approach sex differences in another way. If, for some reason, it were our ambition to eliminate the behavioral differences between women and men, what sort of ontogenetic engineering would be likely to achieve the desired end? Would treating girls and boys alike make them similar in adulthood, or would we have to treat them differently?

The conventional wisdom in the social sciences is the former: that men and women are not psychologically different except by virtue of having been treated differently. However, several lines of evidence suggest that this is unlikely to be true. We know, for example, that males and females behave differently in ways that are not merely cross-culturally consistent, but are furthermore just as one would predict from sexual selection theory and from the morphological dimorphism of our particular species. These sex differences include not only the violence illustrated in Table 7.1, but various aspects of interactions between the sexes as well (see, e.g., Symons, 1979; Daly and Wilson, 1983). We also know that gonadal hormones are secreted according to different schedules in young males and females, and that such patterns of secretion influence the developing brain in every animal in which the matter has been studied experimentally (e.g., MacLusky and Naftolin, 1981); of course, such experiments have not been done on people. We know that the sexes differ in a number of perceptual and information-processing domains that are difficult to attribute to sex-role socialization. Little boys exhibit significantly longer postrotatory nystagmus than little girls (Crowe, Deitz, and Siegner, 1984), to take a recent, arbitrary example; men process materials presented to their left versus right visual half-fields at different speeds whereas women do not, for another (Heister, 1984). We do not know much about the functional significance of these differences, if any, nor much about their implications for sex-typical cognitive styles, but it would be rash to assume that there are *no* such implications.

Moreover, people have begun to discover anatomical differences between the brains of women and men, too (e.g., Swaab and Fliers, 1985). The most dramatic such difference to date is the much larger posterior corpus callosum in females (Lacoste-Utamsing and Holloway, 1982), a morphological difference that is apparent before birth, and that might well have been predicted from the mounting evidence that women have superior interhemispheric communication while men's cortical functions are more lateralized (see McGlone, 1980).

On the other side of the issue, the direct evidence for an important influence of sex-role socialization upon sexually differentiated behavior is astonishingly thin (see, e.g., Pleck, 1981). In fairness, it must be remarked that the problem is one of exceptional methodological difficulty. If parents punish boys more than girls, for example, or assign more child-care duties to girls, it may be that the parents are reacting to behavioral sex differences at least as much as they are creating them. Indeed, in these particular examples, there is evidence that boys are punished more because they transgress more, and that boys are less likely than girls to comply with parental requests to mind younger siblings, so that parents eventually prefer to assign such tasks to the more willing daughters (see, e.g., Maccoby and Jacklin, 1974).

A recent study of parental behavior and later intellectual skills of the children (Bee *et al.*, 1984) speaks directly to the issue as we stated it above. In this study, individual differences in early parental behavior were found to be predictive of individual differences in the children's later performance, with the child's sex proving to be an important variable in a possibly surprising way. Parents did not treat the sexes differently, but within sexes, the ways in which measures of parental behavior were predictive of the child's subsequent performance were different for girls than for boys. As the authors of this study (Bee *et al.*, 1984) conclude, "The combination of these two groups of findings—lack of difference on measures of environment and parent-child interaction, and the presence of differences in prediction—suggest that the same experiences produce different effects for boys and girls" (p. 783).

The last four paragraphs have outlined a number of empirical reasons why it would be very surprising to discover that men's and women's psyches develop similarly except as a result of differential sex-role socialization. But there is a still more powerful reason to doubt this conventional wisdom. The fitness of males and females is differentially affected by numerous variables. (One obvious example is what Bateman, 1948, called "the greater dependence of males for their fertility on frequency of insemination.") If the conventional wisdom were true—that is, if the psyches of women and men have *not* been differentially shaped by selection—then someone has to explain *why* not. Why should patterns of differential reproduction have been without selective consequences in this one sphere, namely behavioral sex differences, when they have so clearly been effective in shaping morphological sex differences, and in shaping those aspects of behavioral control systems that are not sexually differentiated?

So the problem with the conventional wisdom as a scientific theory is not just that there is little evidence in favor of it and much that speaks against it. The even bigger problem is that no theoretical framework has yet been proposed within which a sexually undifferentiated psychology would be anticipated, or even explicable. Why, then, is this incoherent and unsupported theory still popular? A partial answer is the biological illiteracy of most social scientists, which interacts with an ideological reason: By virtue of their equating biology with "determinism," many social scientists are motivated to denigrate all biologically informed approaches to the study of sex differences. Fortunately, this biophobia is on the wane, but the improbable idea of a sexually undifferentiated psychology is still textbook fare, where it is regularly asserted not as hypothesis but as dogma. We believe that such assertions are motivated not by scientific reasoning, good or bad, but by

good intentions and bad philosophy combining to produce the conviction that human equality (a moral objective) somehow rests upon human equipotentiality.

The developmental causes of sex differences may be legitimately controversial, but the fact of difference is not. Whatever is eventually discovered about the sources of sex differences—and whatever it would take to engineer a rearing environment in which behavioral sex differences were abolished—this much is clear: *Intrasexual competition is far more violent among men than among women in every human society for which information exits.*

References

Alexander, R. D. (1979). *Darwinism and human affairs.* Seattle, WA: University of Washington Press.

Bateman, A. J. (1948). Intra-sexual selection in *Drosphila. Heredity,* 2, 349–368.

Bee, H. L., Mitchell, S. K., Barnard, K. E., Etres, S. J., and Hammond, M. A. (1984). Predicting intellectual outcomes: Sex differences in response to early environmental stimulation. *Sex Roles,* 10, 783–803.

Bensing, R. C. and Schroeder, O. (1960). *Homicide in an urban community.* Springfield, IL: Thomas.

Bohannan, P. (Ed.). (1960a). *African homicide and suicide.* Princeton, NJ: Princeton University Press.

Chimbos, P. D. (1978). *Marital violence: A study of interspouse homicide.* San Fransisco, CA: R & E Research Associates.

Clutton-Brock, T. H. (Ed.) (1988). *Reproductive success.* Chicago, IL: University of Chicago Press, in press.

Cosmides, L. (1985). Deduction or Darwinian algorithms? An explanation of the "elusive" content effect on the Wason selection task. Unpublished Ph.D. dissertation, Harvard University.

Costantino, J. P., Kuller, L. H., Perper, J. A., and Cypess, R. H. (1977). An epidemiological study of homicides in Allegheny County, Pennsylvania. *American Journal of Epidemiology,* 106, 314–324.

Crowe, T. K., Deitz, J. C., and Siegner, C. B. (1984). Postrotatory nystagmus response of normal four-year-old children. *Physical and Occupational Therapy in Pediatrics,* 4, 19–28.

Daly, M. and Wilson, M. (1983). *Sex, evolution and behavior* (2nd ed.). Boston, MA: Willard Grant.

Darwin, C. (1871). *The descent of man, and selection in relation to sex.* NY: D. Appleton.

Flannery, R. (1953). *The Gros Ventres of Montana: Part 1, Social Life.* Washington, DC.: Catholic University of America.

Fleagle, J. G., Kay, R. F., and Simons, E. L. (1980). Sexual dimorphism in early anthropoids. *Nature (London), 287,* 328–330.

Fodor, J. (1984). *The modularity of mind.* Cambridge, MA: MIT Press.

Fortune, R. (1939). Arapesh warfare. *American Anthropologist, 41,* 22–41.

Freeman, D. (1983). Margaret Mead and Samoa. *The making and unmaking of an anthropological myth.* Cambridge, MA: Harvard University Press.

Garfinkel, H. (1949). Research notes on inter- and intra-racial homicides. *Social Forces, 27,* 369–381.

Gaulin, S. J. C. and Sailer, L. D. (1985). Are females the ecological sex? *American Anthropologist, 87,* 111–119.

Gewertz, D. B. (1983). *Sepik River societies.* New Haven, CT: Yale University Press.

Gillies, H. (1976). Homicide in the West of Scotland. *British Journal of Psychiatry, 128,* 105–127.

Given, J. B. (1977). *Society and homicide in thirteenth-century England.* Stanford, CA: Stanford University Press.

Goodall, J. (1986). *The chimpanzees of Gombe.* Cambridge, MA: Harvard University Press.

Gordon, J. (Ed.). (1976). *Margaret Mead: The complete bibliography 1925–1975.* The Hague: Mouton.

Hammer, C. I. (1978). Patterns of homicide in a medieval university town: Fourteenth century Oxford. *Past and Present, 78,* 1–23.

Hansen, J. P. H. and Bjarnason, O. (1974). Homicide in Iceland 1946–1970. *Forensic Science, 4,* 107–117.

Harlan, H. (1950). Five hundred homicides. *Journal of Criminal Law and Criminology, 40,* 736–752.

Harris, M. (1974). *Cows, pigs, wars and witches.* NY: Random House.

Herjanic, M. and Meyer, D. A. (1976). Notes on epidemiology of homicide in an urban area. *Forensic Science, 8,* 235–245.

Hrdy, S. B. (1981). *The woman that never evolved.* Cambridge, MA: Harvard University Press.

Jarman, P. J. (1974). The social organization of antelope in relation to their ecology. *Behaviour, 48,* 215–267.

Locoste-Utamsing, C. de and Holloway, R. L. (1982). Sexual dimorphism in the human corpus callosum. *Science, 216,* 1431–1432.

Lee, A. K., Bradley, A. J., and Braithwaite, R. W. (1977). Corticosteroid levels and male mortality in *Antechinus stuartii.* In B. Stonehouse and D. Gilmore (Eds.), *The biology of marsupials.* Baltimore, MD: University Park Press.

Lee, R. B. (1979). *The !Kung San: Men, women, and work in a foraging society.* Cambridge: Cambridge University Press.

Maccoby, E. E. and Jacklin, C. N. (1974). *The psychology of sex differences.* Palo Alto, CA: Stanford University Press.

McGlone, J. (1980). Sex difference in human brain asymmetry: A critical survey. *The Behavioral and Brain Sciences, 3,* 215–263.

MacLusky, N. J. and Naftolin, F. (1981). Sexual differentiation of the central nervous system. *Science, 211,* 1294–1303.

Maxson, S. J. and Oring, L. W. (1980). Breeding season time and energy budget of the polyandrous spotted sandpiper. *Behaviour, 74,* 200–263.

Mead, M. (1935). Sex and temperament in three primitive societies. NY: William Morrow.

Mead, M. (1949). *Male and female.* NY: Morrow.

Mead, M. (1950). *Sex and temperament,* Preface. NY: Morrow.

Minderhout, D. J. (1986). Introductory texts and social sciences stereotypes. *Anthropology Newsletter, 27* (3), 20, 14–15.

Morris, W. (1969). *The American heritage dictionary of the English language.* Boston: Houghton Mifflin.

Murdock, G. P. (1967). *Ethnographic atlas.* Pittsburgh, PA: University of Pittsburgh Press.

Nash, J. (1967). Death as a way of life: The increasing resort to homicide in a Maya Indian community. *American Anthropologist, 69,* 455–470.

Nowak, M. (1980). *Eve's rib.* NY: St. Martin's Press.

Pleck, J. H. (1981). *The myth of masculinity.* Cambridge, MA: MIT Press.

Pokorny, A. (1965). A comparison of homicides in two cities. *Journal of Criminal Law, Criminology and Police Science, 56,* 479–487.

Salzano, F. M., Neel, J. V., and Maybury-Lewis, D. (1967). Further studies on the Xavante Indians. I. Demographic data on two additional villages: Genetic structure of the tribe. *American Journal of Human Genetics, 19,* 463–489.

Saran, A. B. (1974). *Murder and suicide among the Munda and the Oraon.* Delhi: National Publishing House.

Schlenker, B. R. and Severy, L. J. (1979). Perspectives on social issues. In M. E. Meyer (Ed.), *Foundations of contemporary psychology.* NY: Oxford University Press.

Sessar, K. (1975). The familial character of criminal homicide. In I. Drapkin and E. Viano (Eds.), *Victimology: A new focus.* Vol. IV: *Violence and its victims.* Lexington, MA: Lexington.

Shepherd, R. N. (1984). Ecological constraints on internal representation: Resonant kinematics of perceiving, imagining, thinking and dreaming. *Psychological Review, 91,* 417–447.

Siciliano, S. (1965). *l'Omicidio.* Padova: Case Editrice Dott. Antonio Milani.

Sohier, J. (1959). *Essai sur la criminalite dans la province de Leopoldville.* Brussels: J. Duculot.

Southall, A. W. (1960). Homicide and suicide among the Alur. In P. Bohannan (Ed.), *African homicide and suicide.* Princeton, NJ: Princeton University Press.

Swaab, D. F. and Fliers, E. (1985). A sexually dimorphic nucleus in the human brain. *Science, 228,* 1112–1115.

Symons, D. (1987). If we're all Darwinians, what's the fuss about? In C. Crawford, M. Smith and D. Krebs (Eds.), *Sociobiology and psychology.* Hillsdale, NJ: Erlbaum.

Trinkaus, E. (1980). Sexual differences in Neanderthal limb bones. *Journal of Human Evolution, 9,* 377–397.

Trinkaus, E. and Zimmerman, M. R. (1982). Trauma among the Shanidar Neanderthals. *American Journal of Physical Anthropology, 57,* 61–76.

Trivers, R. L. (1972). Parental investment and sexual selection. In B. Campbell (Ed.), *Sexual selection and the descent of man 1871–1971.* Chicago, IL: Aldine.

Tuzin, D. F. (1977). *The Ilahita Arapesh.* Berkley, CA: University of California Press.

Tuzin, D. F. (1980). *The voice of the Tambaran.* Berkley, CA: University of California Press.

Varma, S. C. (1978). *The Bhil Kills.* Delhi: Kunj Publication House.

Voss, H. L. and Hepburn, J. R. (1968). Patterns in criminal homicide in Chicago. *Journal of Criminal Law, Criminology and Police Science, 59,* 499–508.

Walker, P. L. (1985). Cranial injuries as evidence of violence in prehistoric southern California. Unpublished manuscript.

Wallave, A. (1986). *Homicide: The social reality.* Sydney: New South Wales Bureau of Crime Statistics and Research.

Westermeyer, J. (1973). On the epidemiology of amok violence. *Archives of General Psychiatry, 28,* 873–876.

Wilbanks, W. (1984). *Murder in Miami.* Lanham, MD: University Press of America.

Williams, G. C. (1966). *Adaptation and natural selection.* Princeton, NJ: Princeton University Press.

Wilson, G. M. (1960). Homicide and suicide among the Joluo of Kenya. In P. Bohannan (Ed.), *African Homicide and Suicide.* Princeton, NJ: Princeton University Press.

Wilson, M. and Daly, M. (1985). Competitiveness, risk taking, and violence: The young male syndrome. *Ethology and Sociobiology, 6,* 59–73.

Wolfgang, M. E. (1958). *Patterns in criminal homicide.* Philadelphia, PA: University of Pennsylvania Press.

Wolfgang, M. E. (1978). Family violence and criminal behavior. In R. L. Sadoff (Ed.), *Violence and responsibility.* NY: Spectrum.

Yearwood, J. H. E. (1974). Firearms and interpersonal relationships in homicide: Some cross-national comparisons. In M. Riedel and T. P. Thornberry (Eds.), *Crime and delinquency: Dimensions of deviance.* NY: Praeger.

8

How Males and Females Become Different

Doreen Kimura

In humans, the genetic makeup required for becoming a male is having an X and a Y chromosome on the 23rd pair of chromosomes, and for becoming a female, having two X chromosomes. It might seem that nothing else is required to produce the two sexes, but it turns out it's not that simple. XY persons do typically become males, and XX persons do generally become females, but the process, at least in the case of males, is not direct or inevitable.

Most of the differences between males and females are *secondary* consequences of the presence or absence of the Y chromosome. The Y chromosome, in the normal course of events, determines that testes (male gonads) rather than ovaries (female gonads) will form; the testes, in turn, help determine most of the other differences between the sexes.

Many of the details we know about sexual differentiation come from studies on rats and mice. Most animal species are said to be bipotential in terms of sex, that is, they initially have undifferentiated gonads that can become testes or ovaries. The early embryo's basic structure can become either male or female. So the critical first step in the production of a male is the formation of testes which produce the male sex hormones needed to finish the job, including

among other things, forming the male genitals. The "testis-determining factor" has been assumed to be carried on the Y chromosome, but until recently its precise location and nature were unknown. Currently a strong candidate for testis determination is the Sry gene on the Y chromosome. Koopman (Koopman, Gubbay, Vivian, Goodfellow, and Lovell-Badge, 1991) has shown that transplanting the Sry gene into a female (XX) mouse embryo can result in formation of a male whose testes secrete male hormones. Such a mouse will copulate normally with female mice, but is sterile, that is, it produces no sperm.

If there are no male hormones, a female will form, and it appears that no special hormonal milieu is needed to yield a female. Males, however, are formed only when testosterone is produced by the testes, and when the tissue in the organism reacts to the testosterone or its derivatives. We can summarize the process of sexual differentiation by saying that the "default" or "basic" form in mammals is a female, and that the male might be considered a variation on the female. In the embryo, testes develop earlier than ovaries do, perhaps to overcome the natural tendency for a female to form.

From *Sex and Cognition* by Doreen Kimura, pp. 17–29. Publisher MIT Press. Reprinted by permission of MIT Press.

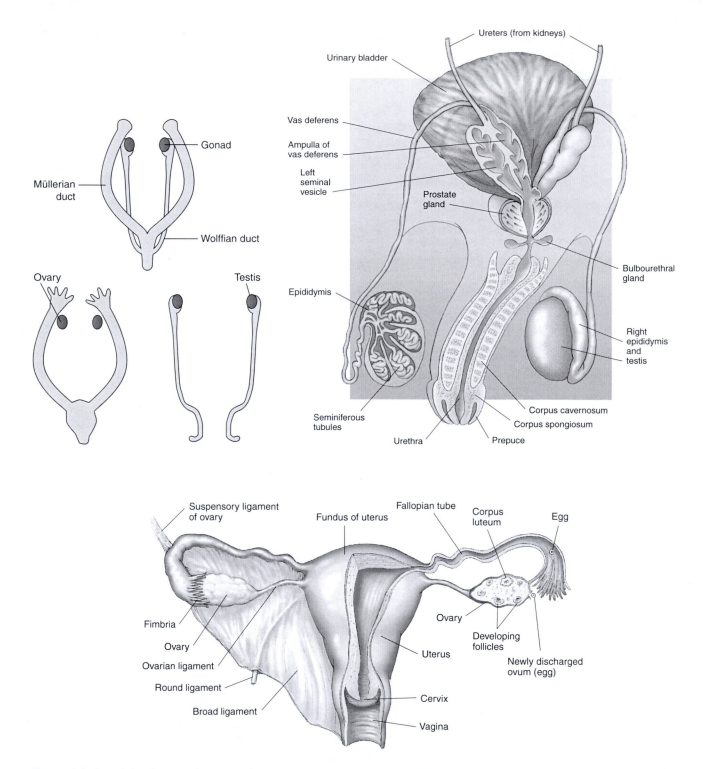

Figure 8.1 (Top left) The undifferentiated gonad and two sets of ducts (Müllerian—female; Wolffian—male) eventually become the ovary, uterus, and fallopian tubes (female); or the testis, seminal vesicles, and vas deferens (male). (Top right) Adult male reproductive anatomy. (Bottom) Adult female reproductive anatomy.

(© Kendall Hunt Publishing Company.)

Two sets of ducts, only one of which typically survives, are initially present in both male and female mammals. Wolffian ducts ultimately form male internal reproductive structures and the Müllerian ducts form female internal structures. If testes are present, two things happen in the ducts as a result of two different substances produced by the testes-testosterone and Müllerian regression factor (MRF). Testosterone develops the Wolffian ducts and MRF causes the Müllerian ducts to dissolve. In females, who have ovaries, there is of course no MRF, so the Müllerian ducts are able to develop, but the Wolffian ducts do atrophy. Why the Wolffian ducts disappear in females is unclear, except that they do require testosterone to develop.

The next major step in making a male is formation of the external genitals, the penis and scrotum, the latter being the pouch which will contain the testes outside the body cavity later in life. Testosterone (T) is critical also for this step, but it works by being converted to a related compound, dihydrotestosterone (DHT). Conversion from T to DHT is achieved by an enzyme called 5-alpha-reductase, which is normally present in the genital tissue of both males and females; it is only effective when sufficient T is available, that is, in males. If for some reason the quantity of 5-alpha-reductase is insufficient or the enzyme is absent, the external genitals look female, even though there are testes inside the abdomen, and even though the Wolffian ducts are developed and the Müllerian ducts have regressed. As you can see, there are several stages of development into a male when variation from the "norm" can occur, whereas so far as we know at present, hormonal support is not critical in producing the genital structures of a female.

It is a reasonable assumption that all mammals have roughly similar mechanisms of sexual differentiation, and what facts we have support the idea that human sex is determined in a fashion parallel to that of the rodent. Some of this evidence comes from human sexual anomalies. For example, some genetic males (XY) are born without sensitivity to androgens, the group of hormones which includes testosterone, DHT, androstenedione, and others that have masculinizing effects. The body cells of such people have no androgen "receptors," small structures within the cell that respond to the hormones to produce their effects. These androgen-insensitive individuals form testes in the usual way (though they remain inside the abdominal cavity), and the testes produce testosterone, but the body tissues do not respond. As a consequence, the male or Wolffian ducts don't develop, and the female or Müllerian ducts usually disappear because the testes produce effective quantities of MRF. Because the genital tissue is insensitive to T and DHT, the scrotum and penis do not develop.

These genetic males therefore look like females and are only discovered to be males at puberty, when they fail to menstruate. In fact they are typically quite curvaceous females, although, because of the androgen insensitivity, they have sparse pubic hair. Breasts form at the usual time, because the testes also produce some estrogen, and breast formation is related to the ratio of estrogen to effective testosterone in the tissue.

Another interesting developmental anomaly, discovered some time ago in the Dominican Republic, confirms the role of DHT in the formation of external genitals in human males. These XY individuals were born looking externally like girls, and were raised as girls. At puberty, however, male genitals began to form and the testes descended into a scrotum. These males had a genetic deficiency in 5-alpha-reductase, the enzyme that converts testosterone to dihydrotestosterone. As a result, although they had functional internal testes, and developed Wolffian ducts, the penis and scrotum did not develop. At puberty, however, when the testes produced larger amounts of testosterone, even partial conversion to DHT was apparently sufficient to masculinize the external genitals (Imperato-McGinley, Guerrero, Gautier, and Peterson, 1974). Nearly all of these males seem to have adapted well to the change in sex, most have married, but to date none has been known to produce offspring.

Finally, to make the story in humans even more convincing, there are the cases of what is called congenital adrenal hyperplasia (CAH). These are individuals (male and female) who have been exposed to an excess of androgens from their adrenal glands. The adrenals produce some androgens, notably androstenedione. Because these people are deficient in an important enzyme that converts other adrenal substances to cortisol, their brains send out signals to the adrenals to pour out more hormones. As a result, the adrenal glands produce more androgens as well. In girls, the increased androgen can have a masculinizing effect, and some of them are born with partially "virilized" or male genitals. This can be corrected by surgery, and the hormone production can be stopped by medications begun shortly after birth.

All these cases illustrate the powerful masculinizing effect of androgens in humans. Although we tend to speak of androgens as male hormones, and estrogens as female hormones, males and females both produce both types of hormones. The ovaries initially produce androgens, most of which are quickly converted in the ovary to estrogens. This conversion is done by a process called aromatization, which requires the presence of an enzyme called aromatase. The testes, in addition to producing testosterone, also convert some testosterone to estrogen. To further complicate the picture, as we just mentioned, the adrenal glands in both sexes produce androgens. Finally, the ovaries also produce a hormone called progesterone which is important during pregnancy.

So far we have been discussing the obvious structural differences between males and females—internal and external genitals, and breast formation. For males and females to adopt differing complementary roles in sexual behavior and reproduction, their brains must also somehow be made to work differently. Again, we can use other mammalian species as models to find out how this happens. In rodents, the typical sexual behavior involves, on the part of the female, certain inviting movements such as ear wiggling and hopping, as well

as downward arching of the back (lordosis) and moving the tail aside, to allow the penis to enter the vagina. The male must have in his repertoire mounting behavior, in which he climbs partially onto the female's back and holds her with the forepaws, as well as intromission (placing the penis into the vaginal canal), thrusting movements, and finally ejaculation, the deposit of semen.

As with structural sexual differentiation, behavioral or brain sexual differentiation appears to depend, for the male, on the presence of sex hormones early in life. These early effects of sex hormones, which have lifelong irreversible effects on behavior, are called *organizational effects* (see Goy and McEwen, 1980). In the absence of sex hormones before and immediately after birth, the female pattern develops. We have come to know about this through a number of studies in which the hormonal state of an animal has been altered either before or just after birth. As it happens, the rodent brain remains sensitive to the effects of sex hormones for a few days immediately after birth, when the genital structures are already formed. This means that we can change the behavior so that it no longer corresponds, as an adult, to the structural or genital sex.

One common way of doing this is by castration (removing the testes but leaving the penis intact), thus stopping or significantly reducing the flow of androgens to the brain. If this is done to a rat in the first few days of life, then when the animal is full grown it will, with some priming from female sex hormones (called an *activational* effect), display *female* sexual behavior, such as lordosis, but little or no male sexual behavior. An adult male rat not castrated at birth will not show female behavior when given the same kind of hormonal priming, so the early exposure to androgens must somehow prevent it.

Removing the ovaries from a female rat right after birth does not affect either her adult sexual behavior or maternal behavior, in parallel with the way female genital structures differentiate. Of course, since without ovaries she cannot produce young, the maternal behavior has to be tested with another mother's litter. The general pattern seems to be that ovarian hormones are not essential for female brain organization, which occurs without the influence of sex hormones. However, some have argued that either the female's own ovarian hormones or her mother's hormones prenatally provide a low level of estrogen which is necessary to complete the "feminization" of the female brain (Dohler *et al.* 1984). In other words, they believe that female behavioral characteristics do not develop fully in the *absence* of sex hormones. This is currently an unresolved issue.

In the rodent, researchers have identified two fairly independent processes in the development of male sexual behavior. One is *masculinization,* the organization of such male behaviors as mounting, intromission, etc. The other, called *defeminization,* refers to the inhibition of female behaviors like lordosis, which will occur if not actively suppressed. Obviously both masculinization and defeminization must happen if normal male behavior is to occur. McEwen (1987) has suggested that defeminization occurs primarily after birth through the process of changing testosterone (paradoxically) to estrogen, through aromatization. So defeminization depends on the action of estrogen on estrogen receptors in the brain. Masculinization is thought to depend on the same route, plus the conversion of testosterone to DHT, via 5-alpha-reductase, and the consequent interaction of DHT with androgen receptors in the brain. The reader will recall that DHT was also essential for the formation of external male genitals. In primates, such as monkeys and perhaps humans, the testosterone-to-estrogen conversion may play a less important role, and the androgens a more salient one.

We know what we do about these processes through the use of several other methods, besides castration, of changing the animal's hormonal environment. These include administering sex hormones (for example, androgens or estrogens) to females right after birth; administering anti-androgens, such as flutamide, substances that block the effect of androgens, usually by occupying the receptors the androgens

would affect; administering anti-estrogens such as tamoxifen; and employing compounds that block the conversion (aromatization) of testosterone to estrogen.

One puzzle that arises is why the female brain, which we would expect to be bombarded by the estrogen produced by the ovaries, is not also defeminized and partially masculinized by it. The tentative answer has been that in females the estrogen is captured in the bloodstream by a substance called alpha-fetoprotein, which keeps estrogen from entering the brain cells. This substance is present in infants of both sexes, but since it does not bind to androgens, has no effect on males.

The fact that sexual behavior in rodents and primates can be radically altered by early exposure to sex hormones has raised the possibility that variation in exposure to hormones might be the basis for variation in sexual orientation in humans. One objection to this idea is that the hormones influence the likelihood that certain behaviors (for example, lordosis or mounting) will occur; whereas it is not necessarily particular behaviors which differentiate heterosexual and homosexual individuals, but a preference for the type of partner—same-sex or opposite-sex. Recent research by Brand and co-workers, however, has suggested that early hormonal manipulation in rats can also alter adult partner preference, making it somewhat more likely that sexual orientation in humans could result from a parallel mechanism (Brand, Kroonen, Mos, and Slob, 1991; Brand and Slob, 1991). The fact that girls with CAH, who have early overexposure to androgens, tend to have a higher incidence of homosexual fantasy and preference than their unaffected sisters (Dittman, Kappes and Kappes, 1992) supports such a position. Of course, these findings do not rule out other contributing factors.

The importance of early organizational factors in influencing the lifelong pattern of humans is also suggested in a recent review by Diamond and Sigmundson (1997) of cases in which the penis has been damaged shortly after birth. Because it is easier to construct a vagina than a penis, the common solution in such cases used to be to remove the testes as well, and attempt to rear the child as a girl. Diamond gives a detailed account of one boy whose penis was accidentally burnt off during surgery, at the age of eight months. At about one year of age his testicles were removed, and a vagina was later constructed. The apparent success with which he adopted a girl's role, reported much earlier by Money and Ehrhardt (1972), was widely accepted as evidence that human males and females are psychologically undifferentiated at birth.

Longer-term followup of this case, however, told quite a different story. Even in childhood this person showed play patterns and toy preferences more typical of boys than of girls. His walk and physique were reminiscent of males and resulted in a great deal of teasing from other children. He even tried to stand up to urinate! By the age of eight or nine years, he felt strongly that he was a boy. He rebelled at taking the estrogen prescribed at age twelve to induce breast formation, and finally at fourteen decided to live as a male. Only then did the parents reveal his early history, which he learned with great relief. He subsequently underwent breast removal surgery and had a penis constructed. Eventually he married a woman with two children, whom he adopted. He never had any sexual interest in males.

Several other cases in the literature have apparently run a similar course. If it is found to be generally true that such individuals prefer a male role despite an inadequate penis and being reared as girls, this would of course suggest that in humans also, as well as rodents, some aspects of behavioral masculinization are complete at birth or within a short period thereafter.

The masculinizing influence of sex hormones is not limited to reproductive behavior. In fact, it appears to operate for all behaviors so far studied that are sexually dimorphic—that is, in which males and females differ. For example, juvenile male rodents as well as monkeys show a high level of "rough-and-tumble" play, or play-fighting. This consists of boisterous activity in

which there is a great deal of body contact, though the juveniles do not harm each other. Juvenile females normally show very little of this behavior, but at the same ages, female monkeys appear to spend a fair amount of time in infant-carrying behavior, within the limits permitted by the mother (Meaney, Lozos, and Stewart, 1990). In most human societies too, boys are reported to show a higher level of rough-and-tumble play than girls do. This is not merely a difference in activity level (in which boys and girls are more equivalent), but in a preponderance of rough-housing, characterized by close physical contact.

Michael Meaney (Meaney and McEwen, 1986) has worked out the probable brain and hormonal mechanisms in rodents for the organization of this play-fighting activity in rodents. It appears to depend on testosterone-to-DHT conversion, with DHT having its effect primarily on androgen receptors in a brain structure called the amygdala. The amygdala is known to be important in the expression of fear and aggression. If male rats are deprived of androgens, or female rats are exposed to them shortly after birth, as juveniles they will show sex-atypical behavior. The deprived males show less, and treated females more, rough-and-tumble play.

There may be a parallel mechanism in humans, since girls with CAH are reportedly more "tomboyish" than unaffected girls. They also are more active in sports involving rough body contact (Hampson, Rovet, and Altmann, 1995). Equally interesting is the finding that CAH girls have toy preferences that are strikingly similar to boys. It is well established that boys and girls differ in some toy preferences, with most boys preferring to play with vehicles and construction toys, and most girls preferring dolls or stuffed animals. Many people (at least until they have children of their own) believe that these preferences are taught by parents and other adults. However, CAH girls show a strong preference for "boys" toys, and there is every reason to believe that the parents of CAH girls are at least as likely to encourage them to be feminine, and thus to play with girls' toys, as other parents are. Despite this probable socializing influence, the CAH girls play with dolls less, and with vehicles more, than normal girls (Berenbaum and Hines, 1992). There is also some evidence that CAH girls tend to have less interest in real infants than unaffected girls do, and that they don't differ from boys in this respect (Leveroni and Berenbaum, 1998). So there is a strong probability that prenatal exposure to hormones is the basis for the difference normally seen between boys and girls in toy and baby-tending preferences.

One of the important features of the early organizing effect of sex hormones on behavior is that not all behaviors are susceptible to these influences at the same time. Recall that one of the important components of masculine sexual behavior in rats is mounting onto the partner's back. Administering testosterone to mothers prenatally would result in exposure of the fetal brain to androgens, and would therefore be expected to increase mounting behavior in the female offspring when they are adult. Goy has shown that, in monkeys, testosterone is most effective in increasing mounting in the daughters if it is administered early in the mother's pregnancy (Goy, Bercovitch, and McBrair, 1988). In these early-treated females, rough-and-tumble play is only slightly increased. However, testosterone administered later in gestation has a minimal effect on the daughters' mounting behavior, but greatly increases the play-fighting.

This must mean that the nervous system mechanisms for mounting and for rough-and-tumble play develop at different times before birth. We have already mentioned that masculinization and defeminization of sexual behavior in the male rat also occur at somewhat different times. These findings are important because they open up the possibility that prenatal hormonal variation that is restricted in time can affect some aspects of behavioral masculinization but leave others unaffected. Such phenomena may be relevant, for example, to human homosexuality, where gender identification and many other behaviors are sex-typical, but partner preference is not.

Summary

Most of the differences between male and female mammals are a secondary consequence of the presence or absence of the Y chromosome. Typically, the Y chromosome results in formation of male gonads, testes, which secrete the androgens that guide the formation of male genitalia, and of male-typical behavior. In the absence of effective androgens, a female develops.

Anomalies of human hormonal development suggest that the human situation is similar to that of other mammals. Thus, XY individuals without functional androgen receptors look and act like females, whereas XX individuals with excess early exposure to androgens may be born with virilized genitals and show some male-typical behaviors later in life.

There is evidence that the early sensitive time periods for masculinization of different behaviors, such as mounting and rough-and-tumble play, may be different. This fact might be relevant to sexual orientation, suggesting how homosexually-oriented persons could be sex-atypical in partner preference, but nevertheless show sex-typical gender identity.

References

Berenbaum S. A. & Hines M. (1992) Early androgens are related to sex-typed toy preferences. *Psychological Science*, 3, 203–206.

Brand T. & Slob A. K. (1991) On the organization of partner preference behavior in female Wistar rats. *Physiology & Behavior*, 49, 549–555.

Brand T., Kroonen J., Mos J., & Slob A.K. (1991) Adult partner preference and sexual behavior of male rats affected by perinatal endocrine manipulations. *Hormones & Behavior*, 25, 323–341.

Diamond M. & Sigmundson K. (1997) Sex reassignment at birth. *Archives of Pediatric & Adolescent Medicine*, 151, 298–304.

Dittman R. W., Kappes M. E., & Kappes M. H. (1992) Sexual behavior in adolescent and adult females with congenital adrenal hyperplasia. *Psychoneuroendo-crinology*, 17, 153–170.

Dohler K. D., Hancke J. L., Srivastava S. S., Hofmann C., Shryne J. E., & Gorski R. A. (1984) Participation of estrogens in female sexual differentiation of the brain; neuroanatomical, neuroendocrine and behavioral evidence. In G. J. DeVries, J. P. C. DeBruin, H. B. M. Uylings, & M. A. Comer (Eds.), *Sex differences in the brain. Progress in Brain Research,* 61, Amsterdam: Elsevier, pp. 99–117.

Goy R. W., Bercovitch F. B., & McBrair M. C. (1988) Behavioral masculinization is independent of genital masculinization in prenatally androgenized female rhesus macaques. *Hormones & Behavior,* 22, 552–571.

Goy R. W. & McEwen B. S. (1980) *Sexual differentiation of the brain.* Cambridge: MIT Press. (Discusses the concepts of "organizational" and "activational" influences of hormones on behavior.)

Hampson E., Rovet J. F., & Altmann D. (1995) Sports participation and physical aggressiveness in children and young adults with congenital adrenal hyperplasia. *Proceedings of the International Behavioral Development Symposium. Biological basis of sexual orientation and sex-typical behavior.* Minot, North Dakota, p. 39.

Imperato-McGinley J., Guerrero L., Gautier T., & Peterson R. E. (1974) Steroid 5-alpha-reductase deficiency in man: an inherited form of male pseudo-hermaphroditism. *Science,* 186, 1213–1215.

Koopman P., Gubbay J., Vivian N., Goodfellow P., & Lovell-Badge R. (1991) Male development of chromosomally female mice transgenic for Sry. *Nature,* 351, 117–121.

Leveroni C. L. & Berenbaum S. A. (1998) Early androgen effects on interest in infants: Evidence from children with congenital adrenal hyperplasia. *Developmental Neuropsychology,* 14, 321–340.

McEwen B. S. (1987) Observations on brain sexual differentiation: A biochemist's view. In J. M. Reinisch, L. A. Rosenblum, & S. A. Sanders (Eds.), *Masculinity/femininity.* New York: Oxford Univ. Press, pp. 68–79.

Meaney M. J., Lozos E., & Stewart J. (1990) Infant carrying by nulliparous female vervet monkeys (*Cercopithecus aethiops*). *Journal of Comparative Psychology,* 104, 377–381.

Meaney M. J. & McEwen B. S. (1986) Testosterone implants into the amygdala during the neonatal period masculinize the social play of juvenile female rats. *Brain Research,* 398, 324–328.

Money J. & Ehrhardt A. A. (1972) *Man & woman. Boy & girl.* Baltimore: Johns Hopkins.

Nelson R. J. (1995) An introduction to behavioral endocrinology. Sunderland, Mass: Signer. (Includes an overview of the process of sexual differentiation.)

Quigley C. A., Debtless A., Marschke K. B., El-Awady M. K., Wilson E. M., & French F. S. (1995) Androgen receptor defects: Historical, clinical and molecular perspectives. *Endocrine Reviews,* 16, 271–321.

9

Multiple Genders among North American Indians

Serena Nanda

The early encounters between Europeans and Indian societies in the New World, in the fifteenth through the seventeenth centuries, brought together cultures with very different sex/gender systems. The Spanish explorers, coming from a society where sodomy was a heinous crime, were filled with contempt and outrage when they recorded the presence of men in American Indian societies who performed the work of women, dressed like women, and had sexual relations with men (Lang 1996; Roscoe in 1995).

Europeans labeled these men "berdache," a term originally derived from an Arabic word meaning male prostitute. As such, this term is inappropriate and insulting, and I use it here only to indicate the history of European (mis)understanding of American Indian sex/gender diversity. The term berdache focused attention on the sexuality associated with mixed gender roles, which the Europeans identified, incorrectly, with the "unnatural" and sinful practice of sodomy in their own societies. In their ethnocentrism, the early European explorers and colonists were unable to see beyond their own sex/gender systems and thus did not understand the multiple sex/gender systems they encountered in the Americas. They also largely overlooked the specialized and spiritual functions of many of these alternative sex/gender roles and the positive value attached to them in many American Indian societies.

By the late-nineteenth and early-twentieth centuries, some anthropologists included accounts of North American Indian sex/gender diversity in the ethnographies. They attempted to explain the berdache from various functional perspectives, that is, in terms of the contributions these sex/gender roles made to social structure or culture. These accounts, though less contemptuous than earlier ones, nevertheless largely retained the emphasis on berdache sexuality. The berdache was defined as a form of "institutionalized homosexuality," which served as a social niche for individuals whose personality and sexual orientation did not match the definition of masculinity in their societies, or as a "way out" of the masculine or warrior role for "cowardly" or "failed" men (see Callender and Kochems 1983).

Anthropological accounts increasingly paid more attention to the association of the berdache with shamanism and spiritual powers and also noted that mixed gender roles were often central and highly valued in American Indian cultures, rather than marginal and deviant. These accounts were, nevertheless, also ethnocentric in misidentifying indigenous gender diversity with European concepts of homosexuality, transvestism, or hermaphroditism, which continued to distort their indigenous meanings.

In American Indian societies, the European homosexual/heterosexual dichotomy was not culturally relevant and the European labeling of the berdache as homosexuals resulted from their own cultural emphasis on sexuality as a central, even defining, aspect of gender and on sodomy as an abnormal practice and/or a sin. While berdache in many American Indian societies did engage in sexual relations and even married persons of the same sex, this was not central to their alternative gender role. Another overemphasis resulting from European ethnocentrism was the identification of berdache as **transvestites.** Although berdache often cross-dressed, transvestism was not consistent within or across societies. European descriptions of berdache as **hermaphrodites** were also inaccurate. Considering the variation in alternative sex/gender roles in native North America, a working definition may be useful: the berdache in the anthropological literature refers to people who partly or completely take on aspects of the culturally defined role of the other sex and who are classified neither as women nor men, but as genders of their own (see Callender and Kochems 1983:443). It is important to note here that berdache thus refers to variant gender roles, rather than a complete crossing over to an opposite gender role.

In the past twenty-five years there have been important shifts in perspectives on sex/gender diversity among American Indians and anthropologists, both Indian and non-Indian (Jacobs, Thomas, and Lang 1997:Introduction). Most current research rejects institutionalized homosexuality as an adequate explanation of American Indian gender diversity, emphasizing the importance of occupation rather than sexuality as its central feature. Contemporary ethnography views multiple sex/ gender roles as a normative part of American Indian sex/gender systems,

rather than as a marginal or deviant part (Albers 1989:134; Jacobs *et al.* 1997; Lang 1998). A new emphasis on the variety of alternative sex/gender roles in North America undercuts the earlier treatment of the berdache as unitary phenomenon across North (and South) America (Callender and Kochems 1983; Jacobs *et al.* 1997; Lang 1998; Roscoe 1998). Current research also emphasizes the integrated and often highly valued position of gender variant persons and the association of sex/gender diversity with spiritual power (Roscoe 1996; Williams 1992).

A change in terminology has also taken place. Berdache generally has been rejected, but there is no unanimous agreement on what should replace it. One widely accepted suggestion is the term **two-spirit** (Jacobs *et al.* 1997; Lang 1998), a term coined in 1990 by urban American Indian gays and lesbians. Two-spirit has the advantage of conveying the spiritual nature of gender variance as viewed by gay, lesbian, and transgendered American Indians and also the spirituality associated with traditional American Indian gender variance, but the cultural continuity suggested by two-spirit is in fact a subject of debate. Another problem is that two-spirit emphasizes the Euro-American gender construction of only two genders. Thus, I use the more culturally neutral term, variant genders (or gender variants), and specific indigenous terms wherever possible.

Distribution and Characteristics of Variant Sex/Gender Roles

Multiple sex/gender systems were found in many, though not all, American Indian societies. Male gender variant roles (variant gender roles assumed by biological males) are documented for 110 to 150 societies. These roles occurred most frequently in the region extending from California to the Mississippi Valley and upper-Great Lakes, the Plains and the Prairies, the Southwest, and to a lesser extent along the Northwest Coast tribes. With few exceptions, gender variance is not historically documented for eastern North America, though it may have existed prior to European invasion and disappeared before it could be recorded historically (Callender and Kochems 1983; Fulton and Anderson 1992).

There were many variations in North American Indian gender diversity. American Indian cultures included three or four genders: men, women, male variants, and female variants (biological females who by engaging in male activities were reclassified as to gender). Gender variant roles differed in the criteria by which they were defined; the degree of their integration into the society; the norms governing their behavior; the way the role was acknowledged publicly or sanctioned; how others were expected to behave toward gender variant persons; the degree to which a gender changer was expected to adopt the role of the opposite sex or was limited in doing so; the power, sacred or secular, that was attributed to them; and the path to recruitment.

In spite of this variety, however, there were also some common or widespread features: transvestism, cross-gender occupation, same sex (but different gender) sexuality, some culturally normative and acknowledged process for recruitment to the role, special language and ritual roles, and associations with spiritual power.

Transvestism

The degree to which male and female gender variants were permitted to wear the clothing of the other sex varied. Transvestism was often associated with gender variance but was not equally important in all societies. Male gender variants frequently adopted women's dress and

hairstyles partially or completely, and female gender variants partially adopted the clothing of men; sometimes, however, transvestism was prohibited. The choice of clothing was sometimes an individual matter and gender variants might mix their clothing and their accoutrements. For example, a female gender variant might wear a woman's dress but carry (male) weapons. Dress was also sometimes situationally determined: a male gender variant would have to wear men's clothing while engaging in warfare but might wear women's clothes at other times. Similarly, female gender variants might wear women's clothing when gathering (women's work), but male clothing when hunting (men's work) (Callender and Kochems 1983:447). Among the Navajo, a male gender variant, **nádleeh,** would adopt almost all aspects of a woman's dress, work, language and behavior; the Mohave male gender variant, called **alyha,** was at the extreme end of the cross-gender continuum in imitating female physiology as well as transvestism (the transvestite ceremony is discussed later in this chapter). Repression of visible forms of gender diversity, and ultimately the almost total decline of transvestism, were a direct result of American prohibitions against it.

Occupation

Contemporary analysis emphasizes occupational aspects of American Indian gender variance as a central feature. Most frequently a boy's interest in the implements and activities of women and a girl's interest in the tools of male occupations signaled an individual's wish to undertake a gender variant role (Callender and Kochems 1983:447; Whitehead 1981). In hunting societies, for example, female gender variance was signaled by a girl rejecting the domestic activities associated with women and participating in playing and hunting with boys. In the arctic and subarctic, particularly, this was sometimes encouraged by a girl's parents if there were not enough boys to provide the family with food (Lang 1998). Male gender variants were frequently considered especially skilled and industrious in women's crafts and domestic work (though not in agriculture, where this was a man's task) (Roscoe 1991; 1996). Female gender crossers sometimes won reputations as superior hunters and warriors.

Male gender variants' households were often more prosperous than others, sometimes because they were hired by whites. In their own societies the excellence of male gender variants' craftwork was sometimes ascribed to a supernatural sanction for their gender transformation (Callender and Kochems 1983:448). Female gender variants opted out of motherhood, so were not encumbered by caring for children, which may explain their success as hunters or warriors. In some societies, gender variants could engage in both men's and women's work, and this, too, accounted for their increased wealth. Another source of income was payment for the special social activities of gender variants due to their intermediate gender status, such as acting as go-betweens in marriage. Through their diverse occupations, then, gender variants were often central rather than marginal in their societies.

Early anthropological explanations of male gender variant roles as a niche for a "failed" or cowardly man who wished to avoid warfare or other aspects of the masculine role are no longer widely accepted. To begin with, masculinity was not associated with warrior status in all American Indian cultures. In some societies, male gender variants were warriors and in many others, men who rejected the warrior role did not become gender variants. Sometimes male gender variants did not go to war because of cultural prohibitions against their using symbols of maleness, for example, the prohibition against their using the bow among the Illinois. Where male gender variants did not fight, they sometimes had other important roles in warfare, like treating the wounded, carrying supplies for the war party, or directing postbattle ceremonials

(Callender and Kochems 1983:449). In a few societies male gender variants became outstanding warriors, such as Finds Them and Kills Them, a Crow Indian who performed daring feats of bravery while fighting with the United States Army against the Crow's traditional enemies, the Lakota Sioux (Roscoe 1998:23).

Gender Variance and Sexuality

Generally, sexuality was not central in defining gender status among American Indians. But in any case, the assumption by European observers that gender variants were homosexuals meant they did not take much trouble to investigate or record information on this topic. In some American Indian societies, same-sex sexual desire/practice did figure significantly in the definition of gender variant roles; in others it did not (Callender and Kochems 1983:449). Some early reports noted specifically that male gender variants lived with and/or had sexual relations with women as well as men; in other societies they were reported as having sexual relations only with men, and in still other societies, of having no sexual relationships at all (Lang 1998:189–95).

The bisexual orientation of some gender variant persons may have been a culturally accepted expression of their gender variance. It may have resulted from an individual's life experiences, such as the age at which he or she entered the gender variant role, and/or it may have been one aspect of the general freedom of sexual expression in many American Indian societies. While male and female gender variants most frequently had sexual relations with, or married, persons of the same biological sex as themselves, these relationships were not considered homosexual in the contemporary Western understanding of that term. In a multiple gender system the partners would be of the same sex but different genders, and homogender, rather than homosexual, practices bore the brunt of negative cultural sanctions. The sexual partners of gender variants were never considered gender variants themselves.

The Navajo are a good example (Thomas 1997). The Navajo have four genders; in addition to man and woman there are two gender variants: masculine female-bodied nádleeh and feminine male-bodied nádleeh. A sexual relationship between a female nádleeh and a woman or a sexual relationship between a male-bodied nádleeh and a man were not stigmatized because these persons were of different genders, although of the same biological sex. However, a sexual relationship between two women, two men, two female-bodied nádleeh or two male-bodied nádleeh, was considered homosexual, and even incestual, and was strongly disapproved of.

The relation of sexuality to variant sex/ gender roles across North America suggests that sexual relations between gender variants and persons of the same biological sex were a result rather than a cause of gender variance. Sexual relationships between a man and a male gender variant were accepted in most American Indian societies, though not in all, and appear to have been negatively sanctioned only when it interfered with child-producing heterosexual marriages. Gender variants' sexual relationships varied from casual and wide-ranging (Europeans used the term promiscuous), to stable, and sometimes even involved life-long marriages. In some societies, however, male gender variants were not permitted to engage in long-term relationships with men, either in or out of wedlock. In many cases, gender variants were reported as living alone.

There are some practical reasons why a man might desire sexual relations with a (male) gender variant: in some societies taboos on sexual relations with menstruating or pregnant women restricted opportunities for sexual intercourse; in other societies, sexual relations with a gender variant person were exempt from punishment for extramarital affairs; in still other societies, for example, among the Navajo, some gender variants were considered especially lucky and a man might hope to vicariously partake of this quality by having sexual relations with them (Lang 1998:349).

Biological Sex and Gender Transformations

European observers often confused gender variants with hermaphrodites. Some American Indian societies explicitly distinguished hermaphrodites from gender variants and treated them differently; others assigned gender variant persons and hermaphrodites to the same alternative gender status. With the exception of the Navajo, in most American Indian societies biological sex (or the intersexedness of the hermaphrodite) was not the criterion for a gender variant role, nor were the individuals who occupied gender variant roles anatomically abnormal. The Navajo distinguished between the intersexed and the alternatively gendered, but treated them similarly, though not exactly the same (Thomas 1997; Hill 1935).

And even as the traditional Navajo sex/ gender system had biological sex as its starting point, it was only a starting point, and Navajo nádleeh were distinguished by sex-linked behaviors, such as body language, clothing, ceremonial roles, speech style, and work. Feminine, male-bodied nádleeh might engage in women's activities such as cooking, weaving, household tasks, and making pottery. Masculine, female-bodied nádleeh, unlike other female-bodied persons, avoided childbirth; today they are associated with male occupational roles such as construction or firefighting (although ordinary women also sometimes engage in these occupations).

Traditionally, female-bodied nádleeh had specific roles in Navajo ceremonials.

Thus, even where hermaphrodites occupied a special gender variant role, American Indian gender variance was defined more by cultural than biological criteria. In one recorded case of an interview with, and physical examination of, a gender variant male, the previously mentioned "Finds Them and Kills Them," his genitals were found to be completely normal (Roscoe 1998).

If American Indian gender variants were not generally hermaphrodites, or conceptualized as such, neither were they conceptualized as transsexuals. Gender transformations among gender variants were recognized as only a partial transformation, and the gender variant was not thought of as having become a person of the opposite sex/gender. Rather, gender variant roles were autonomous gender roles that combined the characteristics of men and women and had some unique features of their own. This was sometimes symbolically recognized: among the Zuni a male gender variant was buried in women's dress but men's trousers on the men's side of the graveyard (Parsons quoted in Callender and Kochems 1983:454; Roscoe 1991:124, 145). Male gender variants were neither men—by virtue of their chosen occupations, dress, demeanor, and possibly sexuality—nor women, because of their anatomy and their inability to bear children. Only among the Mohave do we find the extreme imitation of women's physiological processes related to reproduction and the claims to have female sexual organs—both of which were ridiculed within Mohave society. But even here, where informants reported that female gender variants did not menstruate, this did not make them culturally men. Rather it was the mixed quality of gender variant status that was culturally elaborated in native North America, and this was the source of supernatural powers sometimes attributed to them.

Sacred Power

The association between the spiritual power and gender variance occurred in most, if not all, Native American societies. Even where, as previously noted, recruitment to the role was occasioned by a child's interest in occupational activities of the opposite sex, supernatural sanction, frequently appearing in visions or dreams, was also involved. Where this occurred, as it did mainly in the Prairie and Plains societies, the visions involved female supernatural figures, often the moon. Among the Omaha, for example, the moon appeared in a dream holding a burden strap—a symbol of female work—in one hand, and a bow—a symbol of male work—in the other. When the male dreamer reached for the bow, the moon forced him to take the burden strap (Whitehead 1981). Among the Mohave, a child's choice of male or female implements heralding gender variant status was sometimes prefigured by a dream that was believed to come to an embryo in the womb (Devereux 1937).

Sometimes, by virtue of the power associated with their gender ambiguity, gender variants were ritual adepts and curers, or had special ritual functions (Callender and Kochems 1983:453, Lang 1998). Gender variants did not always have important sacred roles in native North America, however. Where feminine qualities were associated with these roles, male gender variants might become spiritual leaders or healers, but where these roles were associated with male qualities they were not entered into by male gender variants. Among the Plains Indians, with their emphasis on the vision as a source of supernatural power, male gender variants were regarded as holy persons, but in California Indian societies, this was not the case and in some American Indian societies gender variants were specifically excluded from religious roles

(Lang 1998:167). Sometimes it was the individual personality of the gender variant rather than his/her gender variance itself, that resulted in occupying sacred roles (see commentary following Callender and Kochems 1983). Nevertheless, the importance of sacred power was so widely associated with sex/gender diversity in native North America that it is generally agreed to be an important explanation of the frequency of gender diversity in this region of the world.

In spite of cultural differences, some significant similarities among American Indian societies are particularly consistent with multigender systems and the positive value placed on sex/gender diversity (Lang 1996). One of these similarities is a cosmology (system of religious beliefs and way of seeing the world) in which transformation and ambiguity are recurring themes. Thus a person who contains both masculine and feminine qualities, or one who is transformed from the sex/gender assigned at birth into a different gender in later life, manifests some of the many kinds of transformations and ambiguities that are possible, not only for humans, but for animals and objects in the natural environment. Indeed, in many American Indian cultures, sex/gender ambiguity, lack of sexual differentiation, and sex/gender transformations play an important part in the story of creation. American Indian cosmology may not be "the cause" of sex/gender diversity, but it certainly (as in India) provides a hospitable context for it (Lang 1996:187).

The Alyha: A Male Gender Variant Role among the Mohave

One of the most complete classic anthropological descriptions of a gender variant role is from the Mohave, a society that lives in the southwest desert area of the Nevada/California border. The following description, based on interviews by anthropologist George Devereux (1937) with some old informants who remembered the transvestite ceremony and had heard stories about gender variant individuals from their elders, indicates some of the ways in which gender variance functioned in native North America.

The Mohave had two gender variant roles: a male role called alyha and a female role called **hwame.** In this society, pregnant women had dreams forecasting the anatomic sex of their children. Mothers of a future alyha dreamt of male characteristics, such as arrow feathers, indicating the birth of a boy, but their dreams also included hints of their child's future gender variant status. A boy indicated he might become an alyha by "acting strangely" around the age of 10 or 11, before he had participated in the boys' puberty ceremonies. At this age, young people began to engage seriously in the activities that would characterize their adult lives as men and women; boys, for example, learned to hunt, ride horses, make bows and arrows, and they developed sexual feelings for girls. The future alyha avoided these masculine activities. Instead he played with dolls, imitated the domestic work of women, tried to participate in the women's gambling games, and demanded to wear the female bark skirt rather than the male breechclout.

The alyha's parents and relatives were ambivalent about this behavior. At first his parents would try to dissuade him, but if the behavior persisted his relatives would resign themselves and begin preparations for the transvestite ceremony. The ceremony was meant to take the boy by surprise; it was considered both a test of his inclination and an initiation. Word was sent out to various settlements so that people could watch the ceremony and get accustomed to the boy in female clothing. At the ceremony, the boy was led into a circle of onlookers by two women, and and the crowd began singing the transvestite songs. If the boy began to dance as women did, he was confirmed as an alyha. He was then taken to the river to bathe and given a girl's skirt to wear. This initiation ceremony confirmed his changed gender status, which was considered permanent.

After this ceremony the alyha assumed a female name (though he did not take the lineage name that all females assumed) and would resent being called by his former, male name. In the frequent and bawdy sexual joking characteristic of Mohave culture, an alyha resented male nomenclature being applied to his genitals. He insisted that his penis be called a clitoris, his testes, labia majora, and anus a vagina. Alyha were also particularly sensitive to sexual joking, and if they were teased in the same way as women they responded with assaults on those who teased them. Because they were very strong, people usually avoided angering them.

Alyha were considered highly industrious and much better housewives than were young girls. It is partly for this reason that they had no difficulty finding spouses, and alyha generally had husbands. Alyha were not courted like ordinary girls, however (where the prospective husband would sleep chastely beside the girl for several nights and then lead her out of her parents' house), but rather courted like widows, divorcees, or "wanton" women. Intercourse with an alyha was surrounded by special etiquette. Like Mohave heterosexual couples, the alyha and her husband practiced both anal and oral intercourse, with the alyha taking the female role. Alyha were reported to be embarrassed by an erection and would not allow their sexual partners to touch or even comment on their erect penis.

When an alyha found a husband, she would begin to imitate menstruation by scratching herself between the legs with a stick until blood appeared. The alyha then submitted to puberty observations as a girl would, and her husband also observed the requirements of the husband of a girl who menstruated for the first time. Alyha also imitated pregnancy, particularly if their husbands threatened them with divorce on the grounds of barrenness. At this time they would cease faking menstruation and follow the

pregnancy taboos, with even more attention than ordinary women, except that they publicly proclaimed their pregnancy, which ordinary Mohave women never did. In imitating pregnancy, an alyha would stuff rags in her skirts, and near the time of the birth, drank a decoction to cause constipation. After a day or two of stomach pains, she would go into the bushes and sit over a hole, defecating in the position of childbirth. The feces would be treated as a stillbirth and buried, and the alyha would weep and wail as a woman does for a stillborn child. The alyha and her husband would then clip their hair as in mourning.

Alyha were said to be generally peaceful persons, except when teased, and were also considered to be cowards. They did not have to participate in the frequent and harsh military raids of Mohave men. Alyha did participate in the welcoming home feast for the warriors, where, like old women, they might make a bark penis and go through the crowd poking the men who had stayed home, saying, "You are not a man, but an alyha."

In general, alyha were not teased or ridiculed for being alyha (though their husbands were teased for marrying them), because it was believed that they could not help it and that a child's inclinations in this direction could not be resisted. It was believed that a future alyha's desire for a gender change was such that he could not resist dancing the women's dance at the initiation ceremony. Once his desires were demonstrated in this manner, people would not thwart him. It was partly the belief that becoming an alyha was a result of a "temperamental compulsion" or predestined (as forecast in his mother's pregnancy dream) that inhibited ordinary Mohave from ridiculing alyha. In addition, alyha were considered powerful healers, especially effective in curing sexually transmitted diseases (also called alyha) like syphilis.

The alyha demonstrates some of the ways in which gender variant roles were constructed as autonomous genders in North America. In many ways the alyha crossed genders, but the role had a distinct, alternative status to that of both man and woman (as did the hwame). Although the alyha imitated many aspects of a woman's role—dress, sexual behavior, menstruation, pregnancy, childbirth, and domestic occupations—they were also recognized as being different from women. Alyha did not take women's lineage names; they were not courted like ordinary women; they publicly proclaimed their pregnancies; and they were considered more industrious than other women in women's domestic tasks.

In spite of the alyha's sexual relations with men, the alyha was not considered primarily a homosexual (in Western terms). In fact, among ordinary Mohave, if a person dreamed of having homosexual relationships, that person would be expected to die soon, but this was not true of the alyha. Most significantly, the alyha were believed to have special supernatural powers, which they used in curing illness.

Female Gender Variants

Female gender variants probably occurred more frequently among American Indians than in other cultures, although this has been largely overlooked in the historic and ethnographic record (but see Blackwood 1984; Jacobs *et al.* 1997; Lang 1998; Medicine 1983).

Although the generally egalitarian social structures of many American Indian societies provided a hospitable context for female gender variance, it occurred in perhaps only one quarter to one half of the societies with male variant roles (Callender and Kochems, 1983:446; see also Lang 1998:262–65). This may be explained partly by the fact that in many American Indian societies women could—and did—adopt aspects of the male gender role, such as warfare or hunting, and sometimes dressed in male clothing, without being reclassified into a different gender (Blackwood 1984; Lang 1998:261; Medicine 1983).

As with men, the primary criteria of changed gender status for females was an affinity for the occupations of the other gender. While this inclination for male occupations was often displayed in childhood, female gender variants entered these roles later in life than did males (Lang 1998:303). Among some Inuit, "men pretenders" would refuse to learn women's tasks and were taught male occupations when they were children, by their fathers. They played with boys and participated in the hunt. Among the Kaska, a family who had only daughters might select one to "be like a man"; by engaging in the male activity of hunting, she would help provide the family with food. Among the Mohave, too, hwame refused to learn women's work, played with boys, and were considered excellent providers, as well as particularly efficient healers (Blackwood 1984:30; Lang 1998:286). Among the Cheyenne, the *hetaneman* (defined as a hermaphrodite having more of the female element) were great female warriors who accompanied the male warrior societies into battle. In all other groups, however, even outstanding women warriors were not recast into a different gender role (Roscoe 1998:75). Female gender variants also sometimes entered specialized occupations, becoming traders, guides for whites, or healers. The female preference for male occupations might be motivated by a female's desire to be independent, or might be initiated or encouraged by a child's parents, and in some societies was sanctioned through supernatural omens or in dreams.

In addition to occupation, female gender variants might assume other characteristics of men. Cocopa *warrhameh* wore a masculine hairstyle and had their noses pierced, like boys (Lang 1998:283). Among the Maidu, the female *suku* also had her nose pierced on the occasion of her initiation into the men's secret society. Mohave hwame were tattooed like men instead of women. Transvestism was commonly though not universally practiced: it occurred, for example, among the Kaska, Paiute, Ute, and Mohave.

Like male gender variants, female gender variants exhibited a wide range of sexual relationships. Some had relationships with other females, who were generally regarded as ordinary women. Only rarely, as among a southern Apache group, was the female gender variant (like her male counterpart) defined in terms of her sexual desire for women. Mohave hwame engaged in sexual and marriage relationships with women, although they courted them in a special way, different from heterosexual courtships. If a hwame married a pregnant woman, she could claim paternity of the child, although the child belonged to the descent group of its biological father (Devereux 1937:514). Like an alyha's husband, a hwame's wife was often teased, and hwame marriages were generally unstable. Masahai Amatkwisai, the most well known hwame, married women three times and was also known to have sexual relationships with many men. Masahai's wives were all aggressively teased by male Mohave who viewed "real" sexual relations only in terms of penetration by a penis. At dances Masahai sat with the men, described her wife's genitals, and flirted with girls, all typical male behavior. Masahai's masculine behavior was ridiculed, and the men gravely insulted her (though never to her face) by referring to her by an obscene nickname meaning the female genitals. The harassment of Masahai's wives apparently led to the eventual breakup of her marriages.

Sexual relationships between women in American Indian societies were rarely historically documented, but in any case, were generally downplayed in female gender variant roles, even when this involved marriage. One female gender variant, for example, Woman Chief, a famous Crow warrior and hunter, took four wives, but this appeared to be primarily an economic strategy: processing animal hides among the Crow was women's work, so that Woman Chief's polygyny (multiple spouses) complemented her hunting skills.

While most often American Indian women who crossed genders occupationally, such as Woman Chief, were not reclassified into a gen-

der variant role, several isolated cases of female gender transformations have been documented historically. One of these is Ququnak Patke, a "manlike woman" from the Kutenai (Schaeffer 1965). Ququnak Patke had married a white fur trader and when she returned to her tribe claimed that her husband had transformed her into a man. She wore men's clothes, lived as a man, married a woman and claimed supernatural sanction for her role change and her supernatural powers. Although whites often mistook her for a man in her various roles as warrior, explorer's guide, and trader, such transformations were not considered a possibility among the Kutenai, and many thought Ququnak Patke was mad. She died attempting to mediate a quarrel between two hostile Indian groups.

It is difficult to know how far we can generalize about the relation of sexuality to female gender variance in precontact American Indian cultures from the lives of the few documented female gender variants. These descriptions (and those for males, as well) are mainly based on ethnographic accounts that relied on twentieth-century informants whose memories were already shaped by white hostility toward gender diversity and same-sex sexuality. Nevertheless, it seems clear that although American Indian female gender variants clearly had sexual relationships with women, sexual object choice was not their defining characteristic. In some cases, female gender variants were described "as women who never marry," which does not say anything definitive about their sexuality; it may well be that the sexuality of female gender variants was more variable than that of men.

Occasionally, as with Masahai and Ququnak Patke, and also for some male gender variants, contact with whites opened up opportunities for gender divergent individuals (see Roscoe 1988; 1991). On the whole, however, as a result of Euro-American repression and the growing assimilation of Euro-American sex/gender ideologies, both female and male gender variant roles among American Indians largely disappeared by the 1930s, as the reservation system was well under way. And yet, its echoes may remain. The current academic interest in American Indian multigender roles, and particularly the testimony of contemporary two-spirits, remind us that alternatives are possible and that understanding American Indian sex/gender diversity in the past and present makes a significant contribution to understandings of sex/gender diversity in the larger society.

References

Albers, Patricia C. 1989. "From Illusion to Illumination: Anthropological Studies of American Indian Women." In *Gender and Anthropology: Critical Reviews for Research and Teaching,* edited by Sandra Morgen. Washington, DC: American Anthropological Association.

Blackwood, Evelyn. 1984. "Sexuality and Gender in Certain Native American Tribes: The Case of Cross-Gender Females." *Signs: Journal of Women in Culture and Society* 10:1–42.

Callender, Charles, and Lee M. Kochems. 1983. "The North American Berdache." *Current Anthropology* 24 (4): 443–56 (Commentary, pp. 456–70).

Devereux, George. 1937. "Institutionalized Homosexuality of the Mohave Indians." *Human Biology* 9:498–587.

Fulton, Robert, and Steven W. Anderson. 1992. "The Amerindian 'Man-Woman': Gender, Liminality, and Cultural Continuity." *Current Anthropology* 33 (5): 603–10.

Hill, Willard W. 1935. "The Status of the Hermaphrodite and Transvestite in Navaho Culture." *American Anthropologist* 37:273–79.

Jacobs, Sue-Ellen, Wesley Thomas, and Sabine Lang, eds. 1997. *Two-Spirit People: Native American Gender Identity, Sexuality, and Spirituality.* Urbana and Chicago: University of Illinois.

Lang, Sabine. 1996. "There Is More than Just Men and Women: Gender Variance in North America." In *Gender Reversals and Gender Culture,* edited by Sabrina Petra Ramet, pp. 183–96. London and New York: Routledge.

Medicine, Beatrice. 1983. "Warrior Women: Sex Role Alternatives for Plains Indian Women." In *The Hidden Half: Studies of Plains Indian Women,* edited by P. Albers and B. Medicine, pp. 267–80. Lanham Park, MD: University Press of America.

Roscoe, Will. 1991. *The Zuni Man-Woman.* Albuquerque: University of New Mexico Press.

Schaeffer, Claude E. 1965. "The Kutenai Female Berdache: Courier Guide, and Warrior." *Ethnohistory: The Bulletin of the Ohio Valley Historic Indian Conference* 12 (3): 173–236.

Thomas, Wesley. 1997. "Navajo Cultural Constructions of Gender and Sexuality." In *Two-Spirit People: Native American Gender Identity, Sexuality, and Spirituality,* edited by Sue-Ellen Jacobs, Wesley Thomas, and Sabine Lang, pp. 156–73. Urbana and Chicago: University of Illinois.

Whitehead, Harriet. 1981. "The Bow and the Burden Strap: A New Look at Institutionalized Homosexuality in Native North America." In *Sexual Meanings: the Cultural Construction of Gender and Sexuality,* edited by Sherry B. Ortner and Harriet Whitehead, pp. 80–115. Cambridge: Cambridge University Press.

Williams, Walter. 1992. *The Spirit and the Flesh: Sexual Diversity in American Indian Culture.* Boston: Beacon.

10

The Gender of Brazilian Transgendered Prostitutes

Don Kulick

Males who enjoy being anally penetrated by other males are, in many places in the world, an object of special cultural elaboration. Anywhere they occur as a culturally recognized type, it is usually they who are classified and named, not the males who penetrate them (who are often simply called "men"). Furthermore, to the extent that male same-sex sexual relations are stigmatized, the object of social vituperation is, again, usually those males who allow themselves to be penetrated, not the males who penetrate them. Anywhere they constitute a salient cultural category, men who enjoy being penetrated are believed to think, talk, and act in particular, identifiable, and often cross-gendered manners. What is more, a large number of such men do in fact behave in these culturally intelligible ways. So whether they are the *mahus, hijras, kathoeys, xaniths,* or *berdaches* of non-Western societies, or the mollies and fairies of our own history, links between habitual receptivity in anal sex and particular effeminate behavioral patterns structure the ways in which males who are regularly anally penetrated are perceived, and they structure the ways in which many of those males think about and live their lives.[1]

One area of the world in which males who enjoy being anally penetrated receive a very high degree of cultural attention is Latin America. Any student of Latin America will be familiar with the effervescent figure of the effeminate male homosexual. Called *maricón, cochón, jeto, marica, pajara, loca, frango, bicha,* or any number of other names depending on where one finds him (see Murray and Dynes 1987 and Dynes 1987 for a sampling), these males all appear to share certain behavioral characteristics and seem to be thought of, throughout Latin America, in quite similar ways.[2]

One of the basic things one quickly learns from any analysis of Latin American sexual categories is that sex between males in this part of the world does not necessarily result in both partners being perceived as homosexual. The crucial determinant of a homosexual classification is not so much the fact of sex as it is the role performed during the sexual act. A male who anally penetrates another male is generally not considered to be homosexual. He is considered, in all the various local idioms, to be a "man"; indeed, in some communities, penetrating another male and then bragging about it is one way in which men demonstrate their mas-

Reproduced by permission of the American Anthropological Association from *American Anthropologist* Volume 99(3), 1997. doi:10.1525/aa1997.99.3.574. Not for sale or further reproduction.

Don Kulick is an associate professor in the Department of Social Anthropology, Stockholm University, 10691 Stockholm, Sweden.

culinity to others (Lancaster 1992:241; cf. Brandes 1981:234). Quite different associations attach themselves to a male who allows himself to be penetrated. That male has placed himself in what is understood to be an unmasculine, passive position. By doing so, he has forfeited manhood and becomes seen as something other than a man. This cultural classification as feminine is often reflected in the general comportment, speech practices, and dress patterns of such males, all of which tend to be recognizable to others as effeminate.

A conceptual system in which only males who are penetrated are homosexual is clearly very different from the modern heterosexual-homosexual dichotomy currently in place in countries such as the United States, where popular understanding generally maintains that a male who has sex with another male is gay, no matter how carefully he may restrict his behavior to the role of penetrator.[3] This difference between Latin American and northern Euro-American understandings of sexuality is analyzed with great insight in the literature on male same-sex relations in Latin America, and one of the chief merits of that literature is its sensitive documentation of the ways in which erotic practices and sexual identities are culturally organized.

Somewhat surprisingly, the same sensitivity that informs the literature when it comes to sexuality does not extend to the realm of gender. A question not broached in this literature is whether the fundamental differences that exist between northern Euro-American and Latin American regimes of sexuality might also result in, or be reflective of, different regimes of gender. This oversight is odd in light of the obvious and important links between sexuality and gender in a system where a simple act of penetration has the power to profoundly alter a male's cultural definition and social status. Instead of exploring what the differences in the construction of sexuality might mean for differences in the construction of gender, however, analysis in this literature falls back on familiar concepts. So just as gender in northern Europe and North America consists of men and women, so does it consist of men and women in Latin America, we are told. The characteristics ascribed to and the behavior expected of those two different types of people are not exactly the same in these two different parts of the world, to be sure, but the basic gender categories are the same.

This article contests that view. I will argue that the *sexual division* that researchers have noted between those who penetrate and those who are penetrated extends far beyond sexual interactions between males to constitute the basis of the *gender division* in Latin America. Gender, in this particular elaboration, is grounded not so much in sex (like it is, for example, in modern northern European and North American cultures) as it is grounded in sexuality. This difference in grounding generates a gender configuration different from the one that researchers working in Latin America have postulated, and it allows and even encourages the elaboration of cultural spaces such as those inhabited by effeminate male homosexuals. Gender in Latin America should be seen not as consisting of men and women, but rather of men and not-men, the latter being a category into which both biological females and males who enjoy anal penetration are culturally situated. This specific situatedness provides individuals—not just men who enjoy anal penetration, but everyone—with a conceptual framework that they can draw on in order to understand and organize their own and others' desires, bodies, affective and physical relations, and social roles.

The Body in Question

The evidence for the arguments developed here will be drawn from my fieldwork in the Brazilian city of Salvador, among a group of males who enjoy anal penetration. These males are effeminized prostitutes known throughout Brazil as *travestis* (a word derived from *transvestir*, to cross-dress).[4]

Travestis occupy a strikingly visible place in both Brazilian social space and in the Brazilian cultural imaginary.[5] All Brazilian cities of any size contain travestis, and in the large cities of Rio de Janeiro and Sao Paulo, travestis number in the thousands. (In Salvador, travestis numbered between about 80 and 250, depending on the time of year.)[6] Travestis are most exuberantly visible during Brazil's famous annual Carnival, and any depiction or analysis of the festival will inevitably include at least a passing reference to them, because their gender inversions are often invoked as embodiments of the Carnival spirit. But even in more mundane contexts and discourses, travestis figure prominently. A popular Saturday afternoon television show, for example, includes a spot in which female impersonators, some of whom are clearly travestis, get judged on how beautiful they are and on how well they mime the lyrics to songs sung by female vocalists. Another weekly television show regularly features Valéria, a well-known travesti. *Tieta,* one of the most popular television *novelas* in recent years, featured a special guest appearance by Rogéria, another famous travesti. And most telling of the special place reserved for travestis in the Brazilian popular imagination is the fact that the individual widely acclaimed to be the most beautiful woman in Brazil in the mid-1980s was . . . a travesti. That travesti, Roberta Close, became a household name throughout the country. She regularly appeared on national television, starred in a play in Rio, posed nude (with demurely crossed legs) in *Playboy* magazine, was continually interviewed and portrayed in virtually every magazine in the country, and had at least three songs written about her by well-known composers. Although her popularity declined when, at the end of the 1980s, she left Brazil to have a sex-change operation and live in Europe, Roberta Close remains extremely well-known. As recently as 1995, she appeared in a nationwide advertisement for Duloren lingerie, in which a photograph of her passport, bearing her male name, was transposed with a photograph of her looking sexy and chic in a black lace undergarment. The caption read, "Você não imagina do que uma Duloren é capaz" (You can't imagine what a Duloren can do).

Regrettably, the fact that a handful of travestis manage to achieve wealth, admiration, and, in the case of Roberta Close, an almost iconic cultural status says very little about the lives of the vast majority of travestis. Those travestis, the ones that most Brazilians only glimpse occasionally standing along highways or on dimly lit street corners at night or read about in the crime pages of their local newspapers, comprise one of the most marginalized, feared, and despised groups in Brazilian society. In most Brazilian cities, travestis are so discriminated against that many of them avoid venturing out onto the street during the day. They are regularly the victims of violent police brutality and murder.[7] The vast majority of them come from very poor backgrounds and remain poor throughout their lives, living a hand-to-mouth existence and dying before the age of 50 from violence, drug abuse, health problems caused or exacerbated by the silicone they inject into their bodies, or, increasingly, AIDS.

The single most characteristic thing about travestis is their bodies. Unlike the drag performers examined by Esther Newton (1972) and recently elevated to the status of theoretical paragons in the work of postmodernist queer scholars such as Judith Butler (1990), travestis do not merely don female attributes. They incorporate them. Sometimes starting at ages as young as 10 or 12, boys who self-identify as travestis begin ingesting or injecting themselves with massive doses of female hormones in order to give their bodies rounded features, broad hips, prominent buttocks, and breasts. The hormones these boys take either are medications designed to combat estrogen deficiency or are contraceptive preparations designed, like "the pill," to prevent pregnancy. In Brazil such hormones are cheap (a month's supply, which would be consumed by a travesti in a week or less, costs the equivalent of only a few dollars) and are sold over the counter in any pharmacy.

Boys discover hormones from a variety of sources. Most of my travesti friends told me that they learned about hormones by approaching adult travestis and asking them how they had achieved the bodies they had. Others were advised by admirers, boyfriends, or clients, who told them that they would look more attractive and make more money if they looked more like girls.

Hormones are valued by travestis because they are inexpensive, easy to obtain, and fast working. Most hormones produce visible results after only about two months of daily ingestion. A problem with them, however, is that they can, especially after prolonged consumption, result in chronic nausea, headaches, heart palpitations, burning sensations in the legs and chest, extreme weight gain, and allergic reactions. In addition, the doses of female hormones required to produce breasts and wide hips make it difficult for travestis to achieve erections. This can be quite a serious problem, since a great percentage of travestis' clients want to be penetrated by the travesti (a point to which I shall return below). What usually happens after several years of taking hormones is that most individuals stop, at least for a while, and begin injecting silicone into their bodies.

Just as hormones are procured by the individual travestis themselves, without any medical intervention or interference, so is silicone purchased from and administered by acquaintances or friends. The silicone available to the travestis in Salvador is industrial silicone, which is a kind of plastic normally used to manufacture automobile parts such as dashboards. Although it is widely thought to be illegal for industrial outlets to sell this silicone to private individuals, at least one or two travestis in any city containing a silicone manufacturing plant will be well connected enough to be able to buy it. Whenever they sense a demand, these travestis contact their supplier at the plant and travel there in great secrecy to buy several liters. They then resell this silicone (at a hefty profit) to other travestis, who in turn pay travestis who work as

bombadeiras (pumpers) to inject it directly into their bodies.

Most travestis in Salvador over the age of 17 have some silicone in their bodies. The amount of silicone that individual travestis choose to inject ranges from a few glasses to up to 18 liters. (Travestis measure silicone in liters and water glasses *(copos)*, six of which make up a liter.) Most have between two and five liters. The majority have it in their buttocks, hips, knees, and inner thighs. This strategic placement of silicone is in direct deference to Brazilian aesthetic ideals that consider fleshy thighs, expansive hips, and a prominent, teardrop-shaped *bunda* (buttocks) to be the hallmark of feminine beauty. The majority of travestis do *not* have silicone in their breasts, because they believe that silicone in breasts (but not elsewhere in the body) causes cancer, because they are satisfied with the size of the breasts they have achieved through hormone consumption, because they are convinced that silicone injections into the chest are risky and extremely painful, or because they are waiting for the day when they will have enough money to pay for silicone implants *(prótese)* surgically inserted by doctors. A final reason for a general disinclination to inject silicone into one's breasts is that everyone knows that this silicone shifts its position very easily. Every travesti is acquainted with several unfortunate others whose breasts have either merged in the middle, creating a pronounced undifferentiated swelling known as a "pigeon breast" *(peito de pomba)*, or whose silicone has descended into lumpy protrusions just above the stomach.

The Body in Process

Why do they do it? One of the reasons habitually cited by travestis seems self-evident. Elizabeth, a 29-year-old travesti with 1½ liters of silicone in her hips and one water-glass of silicone in each breast, explained it to me this way: "To mold my body, you know, be more feminine, with the body of a woman." But why do travestis want the body of a woman?

When I first began asking travestis that question, I expected them to tell me that they wanted the body of a woman because they felt themselves to be women. That was not the answer I received. No one ever offered the explanation that they might be women trapped in male bodies, even when I suggested it. In fact, there is a strong consensus among travestis in Salvador that any travesti who claims to be a woman is mentally disturbed. A travesti is not a woman and can never be a woman, they tell one another, because God created them male. As individuals, they are free to embellish and augment what God has given them, but their sex cannot be changed. Any attempt to do so would be disastrous. Not only do sex-change operations not produce women (they produce, travestis say, only *bichas castradas*, castrated homosexuals), they also inevitably result in madness. I was told on numerous occasions that, without a penis, semen cannot leave the body. When trapped, it travels to the brain, where it collects and forms a "stone" that will continue to increase in size until it eventually causes insanity.

So Roberta Close notwithstanding, travestis modify their bodies not because they feel themselves to be women but because they feel themselves to be "feminine" *(feminino)* or "like a woman" *(se sentir mulher)*, qualities most often talked about not in terms of inherent predispositions or essences but rather in terms of behaviors, appearances, and relationships to men.[8] When I asked Elizabeth what it meant when she told me she felt feminine, for example, she answered, "I like to dress like a woman. I like when someone—when men—admire me, you know? . . . I like to be admired, when I go with a man who, like, says: 'Sheez, you're really pretty, you're really feminine.' That . . . makes me want to be more feminine and more beautiful every day, you see?" Similar themes emerged when travestis talked about when they first

began to understand that they were travestis. A common response I received from many different people when I asked that question was that they made this discovery in connection with attraction and sexuality. Eighteen-year-old Cintia told me that she understood she was a travesti from the age of seven:

> I already liked girls' things, I played with dolls, played with . . . girls' things; I only played with girls. I didn't play with boys. I just played with these two boys; during the afternoon I always played with them . . . well, you know, rubbing penises together, rubbing them, kissing on the mouth. [Laughs.]

Forty-one-year-old Gabriela says that she knew that she was a travesti early on largely because "since childhood I always liked men, hairy legs, things like that, you know?" Banana, a 31-year-old travesti, told me "the [understanding that I was a] travesti came after, you know, I, um, eight, nine years, ten years old, I felt attracted, really attracted to men."

The attraction that these individuals felt for males is thus perceived by them to be a major motivating force behind their self-production as travestis, both privately and professionally. Travestis are quick to point out that, in addition to making them feel more feminine, female forms also help them earn more money as prostitutes. At night when they work on the street, those travestis who have acquired pronounced feminine features use them to attract the attention of passing motorists, and they dress (or rather, undress) to display those features prominently.

But if the goal of a travesti's bodily modifications is to feel feminine and be attractive to men, what does she think about her male genitals?

The most important point to be clear about is that virtually every travesti values her penis: "There's not a better thing in the whole world," 19-year-old Adriana once told me with a big smile. Any thought of having it amputated repels them. "Deus é mais" (God forbid), many of them interject whenever talk of sex-change operations arises. "What, and never cum (i.e., ejaculate, *gozar*) again?!" they gasp, horrified.

Despite the positive feelings that they express about their genitals, however, a travesti keeps her penis, for the most part, hidden, "imprisoned" *(presa)* between her legs. That is, travestis habitually pull their penises down between their legs and press them against their perineums with their underpanties. This is known as "making a cunt" *(fazer uma buceta).* This cunt is an important bodily practice in a travesti's day-to-day public appearance. It is also crucial in another extremely important context of a travesti's life, namely in her relationship to her *marido* (live-in boyfriend). The maridos of travestis are typically attractive, muscular, tattooed young men with little or no education and no jobs. Although they are not pimps (travestis move them into their rooms because they are impassioned [*apaixonada*] with them, and they eject them when the passion wears thin), maridos are supported economically by their travesti girlfriends. All these boyfriends regard themselves, and are regarded by their travesti girlfriends, as *homens* (men) and, therefore, as nonhomosexual.

One of the defining attributes of being a homem (man) in the gender system that the travestis draw on and invoke is that a man will not be interested in another male's penis. A man, in this interpretative framework, will happily penetrate another male's anus. But he will not touch or express any desire for another male's penis. For him to do so would be tantamount to relinquishing his status as a man. He would stop being a man and be reclassified as a *viado* (homosexual, faggot), which is how the travestis are classified by others and how they see themselves.

Travestis want their boyfriends to be men, not viados. They require, in other words, their boyfriends to be symbolically and socially different from, not similar to, themselves. Therefore, a travesti does not want her boyfriend to notice, comment on, or in any way concern himself with her penis, even during sex. Sex with a boyfriend, consists, for the most part, of the travesti sucking the boyfriend's penis and of her boyfriend penetrating her, most often from behind, with the travesti on all fours or lying on her stomach on the bed. If the boyfriend touches the travesti at all, he will caress her breasts and perhaps kiss her. But no contact with the travesti's penis will occur, which means, according to most travestis I have spoken to, that travestis do not usually have orgasms during sex with their boyfriends.

What surprised me most about this arrangement was that the ones who are the most adamant that it be maintained are the travestis themselves. They respect their boyfriends and maintain their relationships with them only as long as the boyfriends remain "men." If a boyfriend expresses interest in a travesti's penis, becomes concerned that the travesti ejaculate during sex, or worst of all, if the boyfriend expresses a desire to be anally penetrated by the travesti, the relationship, all travestis told me firmly, would be over. They would comply with the boyfriend's request, they all told me, "because if someone offers me their ass, you think I'm not gonna take it?" Afterward, however, they were agreed, they would lose respect for the boyfriend "You'll feel disgust *(nojo)* toward him," one travesti put it pithily. The boyfriend would no longer be a man in their eyes. He would, instead, be reduced to a viado. And as such, he could no longer be a boyfriend. Travestis unfailingly terminate relationships with any boyfriend who deviates from what they consider to be proper manly sexuality.

This absolute unwillingness to engage their own penises in sexual activity with their boyfriends stands in stark contrast to what travestis do with their penises when they are with their clients. On the street, travestis know they are valued for their possession of a penis. Clients will often request to see or feel a travesti's penis before agreeing to pay for sex with her, and travestis are agreed that those travestis who have large penises are more sought after than those with small ones. Similarly, several travestis told me that one of the reasons they stopped taking hormones was because they were losing clients. They realized that clients had begun avoiding them because they knew that the travesti could not achieve an erection. Travestis maintain that one of the most common sexual services they are paid to perform is to anally penetrate their clients.

Most travestis enjoy this. In fact, one of the more surprising findings of my study is that travestis, in significant and highly marked contrast to what is generally reported for other prostitutes, enjoy sex with clients.[9] That is not to say they enjoy sex every time or with every client. But whenever they talk about thrilling, fulfilling, or incredibly fun sex, their partner is always either a client or what they call a *vício*, a word that literally means "vice" or "addiction" and that refers to a male, often encountered on the street while they are working, with whom they have sex for free. Sometimes, if the vício is especially attractive, is known to have an especially large penis, or is known to be especially versatile in bed, the travesti will even pay *him*.

The Body in Context

At this point, having illustrated the way in which the body of a travesti is constructed, thought about, and used in a variety of contexts, I am ready to address the question of cultural intelligibility and personal desirability. Why do travestis want the kind of body they create for themselves? What is it about Brazilian culture that incites and sustains desire for a male body made feminine through hormones and silicone?

By phrasing that question primarily in terms of culture, I do not mean to deny that there are also social and economic considerations behind the production of travesti bodies and subjectivities. As I noted above, a body full of silicone translates into cash in the Brazilian sexual marketplace. It is important to understand, however—particularly because popular and academic discourses about prostitution tend to frame it so narrowly in terms of victimization, poverty, and exploitation—that males do not

become travestis because they were sexually abused as children or just for economic gain. Only one of the approximately 40 travestis in my close circle of acquaintances was clearly the victim of childhood sexual abuse. And while the vast majority of travestis (like, one must realize, the vast majority of people in Brazil) come from working-class or poor backgrounds, it is far from impossible for poor, openly effeminate homosexual males to find employment, especially in the professions of hairdressers, cooks, and housecleaners, where they are quite heavily represented.

Another factor that makes it problematic to view travestis primarily in social or economic terms is the fact that the sexual marketplace does not require males who prostitute themselves to be travestis. Male prostitution (where the prostitutes, who are called *michês*, look and act like men) is widespread in Brazil and has been the topic of one published ethnographic study (Perlongher 1987). Also, even transgendered prostitution does not require the radical body modifications that travestis undertake. Before hormones and silicone became widely available (in the mid-1970s and mid-1980s, respectively) males dressed up as females, using wigs and foam-rubber padding *(pirelli)*, and worked successfully as prostitutes. Some males still do this today.

Finally, it should be appreciated that travestis do not need to actually have sex with their clients to earn money as prostitutes. A large percentage (in some cases, the bulk) of a travesti's income from clients is derived from robbing them. In order to rob a client, all that is required is that a travesti come into close physical proximity with him. Once a travesti is in a client's car or once she has begun caressing a passerby's penis, asking him seductively if he "quer gozar" (wants to cum), the rest, for most travestis, is easy. Either by pickpocketing the client, assaulting him, or if she does have sex with him, by threatening afterward to create a public scandal, the travesti will often walk away with all the client's money (Kulick 1996a). Thus it is entirely possible to derive a respectable income from prostitution and still not consume hormones and inject silicone into one's body.

In addition to all those considerations, I also phrase the question of travestis in terms of culture because, even if it were possible to claim that males who become travestis do so because of poverty, early sexual exploitation, or some enigmatic inner psychic orientation, the mystery of travestis as a sociocultural phenomenon would remain unsolved. What is it about the understandings, representations, and definitions of sexuality, gender, and sex in Brazilian society that makes travesti subjectivity imaginable and intelligible?

Let me begin answering that question by noting an aspect of travesti language that initially puzzled me. In their talk to one another, travestis frequently refer to biological males by using feminine pronouns and feminine adjectival endings. Thus the common utterance "ela ficou doida" (she was furious) can refer to a travesti, a woman, a gay male, or a heterosexual male who has allowed himself to be penetrated by another male. All of these different people are classified by travestis in the same manner. This classificatory system is quite subtle, complex, and context sensitive; travestis narrating their life stories frequently use masculine pronouns and adjectival endings when talking about themselves as children but switch to feminine forms when discussing their present-day lives. In a similar way, clients are often referred to as "she," but the same client will be referred to with different gendered pronouns depending on the actions he performs. When a travesti recounts that she struggled with a client over money or when she describes him paying, for example, his gender will often change from feminine to masculine. The important point here is that the gender of males is subject to fluctuation and change in travesti talk. Males are sometimes referred to as "she" and sometimes as "he." Males, in other words, can shift gender depending on the context and the actions they perform. The same is not true for females. Females, even the several extremely brawny and conspicuously unfeminine lesbians who associate with

the travestis I know, are never referred to as "he" (Kulick 1996b). So whereas the gender of females remains fixed, the gender of males fluctuates and shifts continually.

Why can males be either male or female, but females can only be female? The answer, I believe, lies in the way that the gender system that the travestis draw on is constituted. Debates about transgendered individuals such as eighteenth-century mollies, Byzantine eunuchs, Indian hijras, Native American berdaches, U.S. transsexuals, and others often suggest that those individuals constitute a third, or intermediate, gender, one that is neither male or female or one that combines both male and female.[10] Journalists and social commentators in Brazil sometimes take a similar line when they write about travestis, arguing that travestis transcend maleness and femaleness and constitute a kind of postmodern androgeny.

My contention is the opposite. Despite outward physical appearances and despite local claims to the contrary, there is no third or intermediate sex here; travestis only arise and are only culturally intelligible within a gender system based on a strict dichotomy. That gender system, however, is structured according to a dichotomy different from the one with which many of us are familiar, anchored in and arising from principles different from those that structure and give meaning to gender in northern Europe and North America.

The fundamental difference is that, whereas the northern Euro-American gender system is based on sex, the gender system that structures travestis' perceptions and actions is based on sexuality. The dominant idea in northern Euro-American societies is that one is a man or a woman because of the genitals one possesses. That biological difference is understood to accrete differences in behavior, language, sexuality, perception, emotion, and so on. As scholars such as Harold Garfinkel (1967), Suzanne Kessler and Wendy McKenna (1985[1978]), and Janice Raymond (1979) have pointed out, it is within such a cultural system that a transsexual body can arise, because here biological males, for example, who do not feel or behave as men should, can make sense of that difference by reference to their genitals. They are not men; therefore they must be women, and to be a woman means to have the genitals of a female.

While the biological differences between men and women are certainly not ignored in Brazil, the possession of genitals is fundamentally conflated with what they can be used for, and in the particular configuration of sexuality, gender, and sex that has developed there, the determinative criterion in the identification of males and females is not so much the genitals as it is the role those genitals perform in sexual encounters. Here the locus of gender difference is the act of penetration. If one *only* penetrates, one is a man, but if one gets penetrated, one is not a man, which, in this case, means that one is either a viado (a faggot) or a mulher (a woman). Tina, a 27-year-old travesti, makes the parallels clear in a story about why she eventually left one of her ex-boyfriends:

1. TINA: For three years [my marido] was a man for me. A total man *(foi homíssimo)*. Then I was the man, and he was the faggot (viado).

2. DON: What?

3. TINA: Do you see?

4. DON: Yes. . . . But no, how?

5. TINA: For three years he was a man for me, and after those three years he became a woman *(ele foi mulher)*. I was the man, and he was the woman. The first three years I was together with him, do you see, he penetrated me *(ele me comia)* and I sucked [his penis]. I was his woman.

6. DON: Yeah . . .

7. TINA: And after those three years, I was his man. Do you understand now? Now you get it.

8. DON: But what happened? What, what made him . . .

9. TINA: Change?

10. DON: Change, yeah.

11. TINA: It changed with him touching my penis. . . . He began doing other kinds of sex things. "You don't have to cum [i.e., have orgasms] on the street [with clients]" [he told me], "I can jerk you off *(eu bato uma punhetinha pra você)*. And later on we can do other new things." He gives me his ass, he gave me his ass, started to suck [my penis], and well, there you are.

Note how Tina explains that she was her boyfriend's woman, in that "he penetrated me and I sucked [his penis]" (line 5). Note also how Tina uses the words *viado* (faggot) and *mulher* (woman) interchangeably (lines 1 and 5) to express what her boyfriend became after he started expressing an interest in her penis and after he started "giving his ass" to her. This discursive conflation is similar to that used when travestis talk about their clients, the vast majority of whom are believed by travestis to desire to be anally penetrated by the travesti—a desire that, as I just explained, disqualifies them from being men and makes them into viados, like the travestis themselves. Hence they are commonly referred to in travestis' talk by the feminine pronoun *ela* (she).

Anal penetration figures prominently as an engendering device in another important dimension of travestis' lives, namely, their self-discovery as travestis. When I asked travestis to tell me when they first began to understand that they were travestis, the most common response, as I noted earlier, was that they discovered this in connection with attraction to males. Sooner or later, this attraction always led to sexuality, which in practice means that the travesti began allowing herself to be penetrated anally. This act is always cited by travestis as crucial in their self-understanding as travestis.

A final example of the role that anal penetration plays as a determining factor assignment is the particular way in which travestis talk about gay men. Travestis frequently dismiss and disparage gay men for "pretending to be men" ([*andar/passar*] *como se fosse homem*), a phrase that initially confounded me, especially when it was used by travestis in reference to me. One Sunday afternoon, for example, I was standing with two travesti friends eating candy in one of Salvador's main plazas. As two policemen walked by, one travesti began to giggle. "They see you standing here with us," she said to me, "and they probably think you're a man." Both travestis then collapsed in laughter at the sheer outrageousness of such a profound misunderstanding. It took me, however, a long time to figure out what was so funny.

I finally came to realize that as a gay man, a viado, I am assumed by travestis to *dar* (be penetrated by men). I am, therefore, the same as them. But I and all other gay men who do not dress as women and modify their bodies to be more feminine disguise this sameness. We hide, we deceive, we pretend to be men, when we really are not men at all. It is in this sense that travestis can perceive themselves to be more honest, and much more radical, than "butch" (*machuda*) homosexuals like myself. It is also in this sense that travestis simply do not understand the discrimination that they face throughout Brazil at the hands of gay men, many of whom feel that travestis compromise the public image of homosexuals and give gay men a bad name.

What all these examples point to is that for travestis, as reflected in their actions and in all their talk about themselves, clients, boyfriends, vícios, gay men, women, and sexuality, there are two genders; there is a binary system of opposites very firmly in place and in operation. But the salient difference in this system is not between men and women. It is, instead, between those who penetrate (*comer,* literally "to eat" in Brazilian Portuguese) and those who get penetrated (*dar,* literally "to give"), *in a system where the act of being penetrated has transformative force.*

Thus those who only "eat" (and *never* "give") in this system are culturally designated as "men"; those who give (even if they also eat) are classified as being something else, a something that I will call, partly for want of a culturally elaborated label and partly to foreground my conviction that the gender system that makes it possible for travestis to emerge and make sense is one massively oriented towards, if not determined by, male subjectivity, male desire, and male pleasure, as those are culturally elaborated in Brazil: "not men." What this particular binarity implies is that females and males who enjoy being penetrated belong to the same classificatory category, they are on the same side of the gendered binary. They share, in other words, a gender.

This sharing is the reason why the overwhelming majority of travestis do not self-identify as women and have no desire to have an operation to become a woman even though they spend their lives dramatically modifying their bodies to make them look more feminine. Culturally speaking, travestis, because they enjoy being penetrated, are structurally equivalent to, even if they are not biologically identical to, women. Because they already share a gender with women, a sex-change operation would (again, culturally speaking) give a travesti nothing that she does not already have. All a sex-change operation would do is rob her of a significant source of pleasure and income.

It is important to stress that the claim I am making here is that travestis share a gender with women, not that they *are* women (or that women are travestis). Individual travestis will not always or necessarily share individual women's roles, goals, or social status. Just as the worldviews, self-images, social statuses, and possibilities of, say, a poor black mother, a single mulatto prostitute, and a rich white businesswoman in Brazil differ dramatically, even though all those individuals share a gender, so will the goals, perspectives, and possibilities of individual travestis differ from those of individual women, even though all those individuals share a gender. But inasmuch as travestis share the same gender as women, they are understood to share (and feel themselves to share) a whole spectrum of tastes, perceptions, behaviors, styles, feelings, and desires. And one of the most important of those desires is understood and felt to be the desire to attract and be attractive for persons of the opposite gender.[11] The desire to be attractive for persons of the opposite gender puts pressure on individuals to attempt to approximate cultural ideals of beauty, thereby drawing them into patriarchal and heterosexual imperatives that guide aesthetic values and that frame the direction and the content of the erotic gaze.[12] And although attractive male bodies get quite a lot of attention and exposure in Brazil, the pressure to conform to cultural ideals of beauty, in Brazil as in northern Euro-American societies, is much stronger on females than on males. In all these societies, the ones who are culturally incited to look (with all the subtexts of power and control that that action can imply) are males, and the ones who are exhorted to desire to be looked *at* are females.

In Brazil, the paragon of beauty, the body that is held forth, disseminated, and extolled as desirable—in the media, on television, in popular music, during Carnival, and in the day-to-day public practices of both individual men and women (comments and catcalls from groups of males at women passing by, microscopic string bikinis, known throughout the country as *fio dental* [dental floss], worn by women at the beach)—is a feminine body with smallish breasts, ample buttocks, and high, wide hips. Anyone wishing to be considered desirable to a man should do what she can to approximate that ideal. And this, of course, is precisely what travestis do. They appropriate and incorporate the ideals of beauty that their culture offers them in order to be attractive to men: both real men (i.e., boyfriends, some clients, and *vícios*), and males who publicly "pretend to be men" (clients and *vícios* who enjoy being penetrated).

Conclusion: Penetrating Gender

What exactly is gender and what is the relationship between sex and gender? Despite several decades of research, discussion, and intense debate, there is still no agreed-upon, widely accepted answer to those basic questions. Researchers who discuss gender tend to either not define it or, if they do define it, do so by placing it in a seemingly necessary relationship to sex. But one of the main reasons for the great success of Judith Butler's *Gender Trouble* (and in anthropology, Marilyn Strathern's *The Gender of the Gift*) is surely because those books called sharp critical attention to understandings of gender that see it as the cultural reading of a precultural, or prediscursive, sex. "And what is 'sex' anyway?" asks Butler in a key passage:

> Is it natural, anatomical, chromosomal, or hormonal, and how is a feminist critic to assess the scientific discourses which purport to establish such "facts" for us? Does sex have a history? Does each sex have a different history, or histories? Is there a history of how the duality of sex was established, a genealogy that might expose the binary options as variable construction? Are the ostensibly natural facts of sex discursively produced by various scientific discourses in the service of other political and social interests? If the immutable character of sex is contested, perhaps this construct called "sex" is as culturally constructed as gender; indeed, perhaps it was always already gender, with the consequence that the distinction between sex and gender turns out to be no distinction at all. [1990:6–7]

It is only when one fully appreciates Butler's point and realizes that sex stands in no particularly privileged, or even necessary, relation to gender that one can begin to understand the various ways in which social groups can organize gender in different ways. My work among travestis has led me to define gender, more or less following Eve Sedgwick (1990:27–28), as a social and symbolic arena of ongoing contestation over specific identities, behaviors, rights, obligations, and sexualities. These identities and so forth are bound up with and productive of male and female persons, in a hierarchically ordered cultural system in which the male/female dichotomy functions as a primary and perhaps a model binarism for a wide range of values, processes, relationships, and behaviors. Gender, in this rendering, does not have to be about "men" and "women." It can just as probably be about "men" and "not-men," a slight but extremely significant difference in social classification that opens up different social configurations and facilitates the production of different identities, understandings, relationships, and imaginings.

One of the main puzzles I have found myself having to solve about Brazilian travestis is why they exist at all. Turning to the rich and growing literature on homosexuality in Latin America was less helpful than I had hoped, because the arguments developed there cannot account for (1) the cultural forces at work that make it seem logical and reasonable for some males to permanently alter their bodies to make them look more like women, even though they do not consider themselves to be women and (2) the fact that travestis regularly (not to say daily) perform both the role of penetrator and penetrated in their various sexual interactions with clients, vícios, and boyfriends. In the first case the literature on homosexuality in Latin America indicates that it should not be necessary to go to the extremes that Brazilian travestis go to (they could simply live as effeminate, yet still clearly male, homosexuals), and in the second case, the literature leads one to expect that travestis would restrict their sexual roles, by and large, to that of being penetrated.[13] Wrong on both counts.

What is lacking in this literature, and what I hope this essay will help to provide, is a sharper understanding of the ways in which sexuality and gender configure with one another throughout Latin America. My main point is that for the

travestis with whom I work in Salvador, gender identity is thought to be determined by one's sexual behavior.[14] My contention is that travestis did not just pull this understanding out of thin air; on the contrary, I believe that they have distilled and clarified a relationship between sexuality and gender that seems to be widespread throughout Latin America. Past research on homosexual roles in Latin America (and by extension, since that literature builds on it, past research on male and female roles in Latin America) has perceived the links to sexuality and gender to which I have drawn attention (see, for example, Parker 1986:157; 1991:43–53, 167), but it has been prevented from theorizing those links in the way I have done in this article because it has conflated sex and gender. Researchers have assumed that gender is a cultural reading of biological males and females and that there are, therefore, two genders: man and woman. Effeminate male homosexuals do not fit into this particular binary; they are clearly not women, but culturally speaking they are not men either. So what are they? Calling them "not quite men, not quite women," as Roger Lancaster (1992:274) does in his analysis of Nicaraguan cochones, is hedging: a slippage into "third gender" language to describe a society in which gender, as Lancaster so carefully documents, is structured according to a powerful and coercive binary. It is also not hearing what cochones, travestis, and other effeminate Latin American homosexuals are saying. When travestis, maricas, or cochones call each other "she" or when they call men who have been anally penetrated "she," they are not just being campy and subcultural, as analyses of the language of homosexual males usually conclude; I suggest that they are perceptively and incisively reading off and enunciating core messages generated by their cultures' arrangements of sexuality, gender, and sex.

I realize that this interpretation of travestis and other effeminate male homosexuals as belonging to the same gender as women will seem counterintuitive for many Latin Americans and students of Latin America. Certainly in

Brazil, people generally do not refer to travestis as "she," and many people, travestis will be the first to tell you, seem to enjoy going out of their way to offend travestis by addressing them loudly and mockingly as "o senhor" (sir or mister).[15] The very word *travesti* is grammatically masculine in Brazilian Portuguese *(o travesti),* which makes it not only easy but logical to address the word's referent using masculine forms.[16]

There are certainly many reasons why Brazilians generally contest and mock individual travestis' claims to femininity, not least among them being travestis' strong associations with homosexuality, prostitution, and AIDS—all highly stigmatized issues that tend to elicit harsh condemnation and censure from many people. Refusal to acknowledge travestis' gender is one readily available way of refusing to acknowledge travestis' right to exist at all. It is a way of putting travestis back in their (decently gendered) place, a way of denying and defending against the possibilities that exist within the gender system itself for males to shift from one category to the other.[17]

During the time I have spent in Brazil, I have also noted that the harshest scorn is reserved for unattractive travestis. Travestis such as Roberta Close and some of my own acquaintances in Salvador who closely approximate cultural ideals of feminine beauty are generally not publicly insulted and mocked and addressed as men. On the contrary, such travestis are often admired and regarded with a kind of awe. One conclusion I draw from this is that the commonplace denial of travestis' gender as not-men may not be so much a reaction against them as gender crossers as it is a reaction against unattractiveness in people (women and other not-men), whose job it is to make themselves attractive for men. Seen in this light, some of the hostility against (unattractive) travestis becomes intelligible as a reaction against them as failed women, not failed men, as more orthodox interpretations have usually argued.

Whether or not I am correct in claiming that the patterns I have discussed here have a more widespread existence throughout Latin America remains to be seen. Some of what I argue here may be specific to Brazil, and some of it will inevitably be class specific. In a large, extraordinarily divided, and complex area like Latin America, many different and competing discourses and understandings about sexuality and gender will be available in different ways to different individuals. Those differences need to be investigated and documented in detail. My purpose here is not to suggest a monolithic and immutable model of gender and sexuality for everyone in Latin America. I readily admit to having close firsthand understanding only of the travestis with whom I worked in Salvador, and the arguments presented in this essay have been developed in an ongoing attempt to make sense of their words, choices, actions, and relationships.

At the same time, though, I am struck by the close similarities in gender and sexual roles that I read in other anthropologists' reports about homosexuality and male-female relations in countries and places far away from Salvador, and I think that the points discussed here can be helpful in understanding a number of issues not explicitly analyzed, such as why males throughout Latin America so violently fear being anally penetrated, why men who have sex with or even live with effeminate homosexuals often consider themselves to be heterosexual, why societies like Brazil can grant star status to particularly fetching travestis (they are just like women in that they are not-men, and sometimes they are more beautiful than women), why women in a place like Brazil are generally not offended or outraged by the prominence in the popular imagination of travestis like Roberta Close (like women, travestis like Close are also not-men, and hence they share women's tastes, perceptions, feelings, and desires), why many males in Latin American countries appear to be able to relatively unproblematically enjoy sexual encounters with effeminate homosexuals and travestis (they are definitionally not-men, and hence sexual relations with them do not readily call into question one's self-identity as a man), and why such men even pay to be penetrated by these not-men (for some men being penetrated by a not-man is perhaps not as status- and identity-threatening as being penetrated by a man; for other men it is perhaps more threatening, and maybe, therefore, more exciting). If this essay makes any contribution to our understanding of gender and sexuality in Latin America, it will be in revitalizing exploration of the relationship between sexuality and gender and in providing a clearer framework within which we might be able to see connections that have not been visible before.

Notes

Acknowledgments. Research support for fieldwork in Brazil was generously provided by the Swedish Council for Research in the Humanities and Social Sciences (HSFR) and the Wenner-Gren Foundation for Anthropological Research. The essay has benefited immensely from the critical comments of Inês Alfano, Lars Fant, Mark Graham, Barbara Hobson, Kenneth Hyltenstam, Heather Levi, Jerry Lombardi, Thaïs Machado-Borges, Cecilia McCallum, Stephen Murray, Bambi Schieffelin, Michael Silverstein, Britt-Marie Thurén, David Valentine, Unni Wikan, and Margaret Willson. My biggest debt is to the travestis in Salvador with whom I work and, especially, to my teacher and coworker Keila Simpsom, to whom I owe everything.

1. Chauncey 1994; Crisp 1968; Jackson 1989; Nanda 1990; Trumbach 1989; Whitehead 1981; Wikan 1977.

2. See, for example, Almaguer 1991; Carrier 1995; Fry 1986; Guttman 1996; Lancaster 1992; Leiner 1994; Murray 1987, 1995; Parker 1991; Prieur 1994; and Trevisan 1986.

3. One of the few contexts in which ideas similar to Latin American ones are preserved in North American and northern European understandings of male sexuality is prisons. See, for example, Wooden and Parker 1982.

4. This article is based on 11 months of anthropological fieldwork and archival research and more than 50 hours of recorded speech and interviews with travestis between the ages of 11 and 60 in Salvador, Brazil's third-largest city, with a population of over 2 million people. Details about the fieldwork and the transcriptions are in Kulick n.d.

5. Travestis are also the subject of two short anthropological monographs in Portuguese: de Oliveira 1994 and Silva 1993. There is also an article in English on travestis in Salvador: Cornwall 1994. As far as I can see, however, all the ethnographic data on travestis in that article are drawn from de Oliveira's unpublished master's thesis, which later became her monograph, and from other published sources. Some of the information in the article, such as the author's claim that 90 percent of the travestis in Salvador are devotees of the Afro-Brazilian religion *candomblé,* is also hugely inaccurate.

6. In the summer months leading up to Carnival, travestis from other Brazilian cities flock to Salvador to cash in on the fact that the many popular festivals preceding Carnival put men in festive moods and predispose them to spend their money on prostitutes.

7. de Oliveira 1994; Kulick 1996a; Mott and Assunção 1987; Silva 1993.

8. The literal translation of *se sentir mulher* is "to feel woman," and taken out of context, it could be read as meaning that travestis feel themselves to be women. In all instances in which it is used by travestis, however, the phrase means "to feel like a woman," "to feel as if one were a woman (even though one is not)." Its contrastive opposite is *ser mulher* (to be woman).

9. In her study of female prostitutes in London, for example, Day explains that "a prostitute creates distinctions with her body so that work involves very little physical contact in contrast to private

sexual contacts. Thus . . . at work . . . only certain types of sex are acceptable while sex outside work involves neither physical barriers nor forbidden zones" (1990:98). The distinctions to which Day refers here are inverted in travesti sexual relationships.

10. Bornstein 1994; Elkins and King 1996; Herdt 1994.

11. One gendered, absolutely central, and culturally incited desire that is almost entirely absent from this picture is the desire for motherhood. Although some readers of this article have suggested to me that the absence of maternal desires negates my thesis that travestis share a gender with women, I am more inclined to see the absence of such desire as yet another reflex of the famous Madonna-Whore complex: travestis align themselves, exuberantly and literally, with the Whore avatar of Latin womanhood, not the Mother incarnation. Also, note again that my claim here is not that travestis are women. The claim is that the particular configurations of sex, gender, and sexuality in Brazil and other Latin American societies differ from the dominant configurations in northern Europe and North America, and generate different arrangements of gender, those that I am calling men and not-men. Motherhood is indisputably a crucial component of female roles and desires, in that a female may not be considered to have achieved full womanhood without it (and in this sense, travestis [like female prostitutes?] can only ever remain incomplete, or failed, women). I contend, however, that motherhood is not *determinative* of gender in the way that I am claiming sexuality is.

12. I use the word *heterosexuality* purposely because travesti-boyfriend relationships are generally considered, by travestis and their boyfriends, to be *hetero*sexual. I once asked Edilson, a 35-year-old marido

who has had two long-term relationships in his life, both of them with travestis, whether he considered himself to be heterosexual, bisexual, or homosexual. "I'm heterosexual; I'm a man," was his immediate reply. "I won't feel love for another heterosexual," he continued, significantly, demonstrating how very lightly the northern Euro-American classificatory system has been grafted onto more meaningful Brazilian ways of organizing erotic relationships: "[For two males to be able to feel love], one of the two has to be gay."

13. One important exception to this is the Norwegian sociologist Annick Prieur's (1994) sensitive work on Mexican jotas.

14. Note that this relationship between sexuality and gender is the *opposite* of what George Chauncey reports for early twentieth-century New York. Whereas Chauncey argues that sexuality and gender in that place and time were organized so that "one's sexual behavior was necessarily thought to be determined by one's gender identity" (1994:48), my argument is that for travestis in Salvador, and possibly for many people throughout Latin America, one's gender identity is necessarily thought to be determined by one's sexual behavior.

One more point here. I wish to note that Unni Wikan, upon reading this paper as a reviewer for the *American Anthropologist,* pointed out that she made a similar claim to the one I argue for here in her 1977 article on the Omani xanith. Rereading that article, I discovered this to be true (see Wikan 1977:309), and I acknowledge that here. A major difference between Wikan's argument and my own, however, is that it is never entirely clear whether Omanis (or Wikan) conceptualize(s) xaniths as men, women, or as a third gender. (For a summary of the xanith debate, see Murray 1997.)

15. The exceptions to this are boyfriends, who often—but, interestingly, not always—use feminine grammatical forms when speaking to and about their travesti girlfriends, and clients, who invariably use feminine forms when negotiating sex with travestis.

16. In their day-to-day language practices, travestis subvert these grammatical strictures by most often using the grammatically feminine words *mona* and *bicha* instead of *travesti*.

17. The possibility for males to shift gender—at least temporarily, in (hopefully) hidden, private encounters—seems to be one of the major attractions that travestis have for clients. From what many different travestis told me, it seems clear that the erotic pleasure that clients derive from being anally penetrated is frequently expressed in very specific, heavily gender-saturated, ways. I heard numerous stories of clients who not only wanted to be penetrated but also, as they were being penetrated, wanted the travesti to call them *gostosa* (delicious/sexy, using the feminine grammatical ending) and address them by female names. Stories of this kind are so common that I find it hard to escape the conclusion that a significant measure of the erotic delight that many clients derive from anal penetration is traceable to the fact that the sexual act is an engendering act that shifts their gender and transforms them from men into not-men.

References

Almaguer, Tomás 1991. *Chicano Men: A Cartography of Homosexual Identity and Behavior. Differences* 3:75–100.

Bornstein, Kate 1994. *Gender Outlaw: On Men, Women and the Rest of Us.* London: Routledge.

Brandes, Stanley 1981. Like Wounded Stags: Male Sexual Ideology in an Andulusian Town. In *Sexual Meanings: The Cultural Construction of Gender and Sexuality.* S. B. Ortner and H. Whitehead, eds. pp. 216–239. Cambridge: Cambridge University Press.

Butler, Judith 1990. *Gender Trouble: Feminism and the Subversion of Identity.* London: Routledge.

Carrier, Joseph 1995. *De los Otros: Intimacy and Homosexuality among Mexican Men.* New York: Columbia University Press.

Chauncey, George 1994. *Gay New York: Gender, Urban Culture and the Making of the Gay Male World, 1890–1940.* New York: Basic Books.

Cornwall, Andrea 1994. Gendered Identities and Gender Ambiguity among Travestis in Salvador, Brazil. In *Dislocating Masculinity: Comparative Ethnographies.* A. Cornwall and N. Lindisfarne, eds., pp. 111–132. London: Routledge.

Crisp, Quentin 1968. *The Naked Civil Servant.* New York: New American Library.

Day, Sophie 1990. Prostitute Women and the Ideology of Work in London. In *Culture and AIDS.* D. A. Feldman, ed., pp. 93–109. New York: Praeger.

de Oliveira, Nenza Maria 1994. *Damas de paus: O jago aberto dos travestis no espelho da mulher.* Salvador, Brazil: Centro Editorial e Didático da UFBA.

Dynes, Wayne 1987. Portugayese. In *Male Homosexuality in Central and South America.* S. O. Murray, ed., pp. 183–191. San Francisco: Instituto Obregón.

Elkins, Richard, and Dave King 1996. *Blending Genders: Social Aspects of Cross-dressing and Sex-changing.* London: Routledge.

Fry, Peter 1986. Male Homosexuality and Spirit Possession in Brazil. In *The Many Faces of Homosexuality: Anthropological Approaches to Homosexual Behavior.* E. Blackwood, ed., pp. 137–153. New York: Harrington Park Press.

Garfinkel, Harold 1967. *Studies in Ethnomethodology.* Englewood Cliffs, NJ: Prentice-Hall.

Guttman, Matthew C. 1996. *The Meanings of Macho: Being a Man in Mexico City.* Berkeley: University of California Press.

Herdt, Gilbert, ed. 1994. *Third Sex, Third Gender: Beyond Sexual Dimorphism in Culture and History.* New York: Zone Books.

Jackson, Peter A. 1989. *Male Homosexuality in Thailand: An Interpretation of Contemporary Thai Sources.* New York: Global Academic Publishers.

Kessler, Suzanne J., and Wendy McKenna 1985[1978]. *Gender: An Ethnomethodological Approach.* Chicago: University of Chicago Press.

Kulick, Don 1996a. Causing a Commotion: Public Scandals as Resistance among Brazilian Transgendered Prostitutes. *Anthropology Today* 12(6):3–7.

Kulick, Don 1996b. *Fe/male Trouble: The Unsettling Place of Lesbians in the Self-images of Male Transgendered Prostitutes in Salvador, Brazil.* Paper presented at 95th annual meeting of the American Anthropological Association, San Francisco.

Kulick, Don n.d. *Practically Woman: The Lives, Loves and Work of Brazilian Travesti Prostitutes.* Manuscript under review.

Lancaster, Roger N. 1992. *Life Is Hard: Machismo, Danger, and the Intimacy of Power in Nicaragua.* Berkeley: University of California Press.

Leiner, Marvin 1994. *Sexual Politics in Cuba: Machismo, Homosexuality and AIDS.* Boulder, CO: Westview Press.

Mott, Luis, and Aroldo Assunção 1987. Gilete na carne: Etnografia das automutilações dos travestis da Bahia. *Revista do Instituto de Medicina Social de São Paulo* 4(1):41–56.

Murray, Stephen O. 1997. The Sohari Khanith. In *Islamic Homosexualities: Culture, History, and Literature.* S. O. Murray and W. Roscoe, pp. 244–255. New York: New York University Press.

Murray, Stephen O., ed. 1995. *Latin American Male Homosexualities.* Albuquerque: University of New Mexico Press.

Murray, Stephen O. 1987. *Male Homosexuality in Central and South America.* San Francisco: Instituto Obregón.

Murray, Stephen O., and Wayne Dynes 1987. Hispanic Homosexuals: Spanish Lexicon. In *Male Homosexuality in Central and South America.* S. O. Murray, ed., pp. 170–182. San Francisco: Instituto Obregón.

Nanda, Serena 1990. *Neither Man nor Woman: The Hijas of India.* Belmont, CA: Wadsworth Publishing.

Newton, Esther 1991. *Bodies, Pleasures and Passions: Sexual Culture in Contemporary Brazil.* Boston: Beacon Press.

Newton, Esther 1972. *Mother Camp: Female Impersonators in America.* Englewood Cliffs, NJ: Prentice-Hall.

Parker, R. G. 1991. *Bodies, Pleasures, and Passions: Sexual Culture in Contemporary Brazil.* Boston: Beacon Hill.

Parker, Richard G. 1986. Masculinity, Femininity, and Homosexuality: On the Anthropological Interpretation of Sexual Meanings in Brazil. In *The Many Faces of Homosexuality: Anthropological Approaches to Homosexual Behavior.* E. Blackwood, ed., pp. 155–163. New York: Harrington Park Press.

Perlongher, Nestor 1987. *O negócio do michê: Prostituição viril em São Paulo.* São Paulo: Editora Brasiliense.

Prieur, Annick 1994. *Iscensettelser av kønn: Tranvestitter og machomenn i Mexico by.* Oslo: Pax Forlag.

Raymond, Janice 1979. *The Transsexual Empire.* London: Women's Press.

Sedgwick, Eve Kosofsky 1990. *Epistemology of the Closet.* Berkeley: University of California Press.

Silva, Hélio R. S. 1993. *Travesti: A invenção do feminino.* Rio de Janeiro: Relume-Dumará.

Strathern, Marilyn 1988. *The Gender of the Gift: Problems with Women and Problems with Society in Melanesia.* Berkeley University of California Press.

Trevisan, João Silvério 1986. *Perverts in Paradise.* London: Gay Men's Press.

Trumbach, Randolph 1989. The Birth of the Queen: Sodomy and the Emergence of Gender Equality in Modern Culture, 1660–1750. In *Hidden from History: Reclaiming the Gay and Lesbian Past.* M. B. Duberman, M. Vicinus, and G. Chauncey Jr., eds., pp. 129–140. New York: New American Library.

Whitehead, Harriet 1981. The Bow and the Burden Strap: A New Look at Institutionalized Homosexuality in Native North America. In *Sexual Meanings: The Cultural Construction of Gender and Sexuality.* S. B. Ortner and H. Whitehead, eds., pp. 80–115. Cambridge: Cambridge University Press.

Wikan, Unni 1977. Man Becomes Woman: Transsexualism in Oman as a Key to Gender Roles. *Man,* n.s., 12:304–319.

Wooden, Wayne S., and Jay Parker 1982. *Men behind Bars: Sexual Exploitation in Prison.* New York: Da Capo Press.

Problem Set #6

Sexes and Genders

To do this problem set, you will need to read Unit III.

1. According to Daly and Wilson, why, evolutionarily, is there more violence among men than there is among women?

2. These questions concern sex hormones.

   a. Where are they produced?

   b. What is their function?

   c. How do they work?

   d. What is the difference between organizational and activational effects of sex hormones?

3. These questions concern congenital adrenal hyperplasia (CAH).

   a. What is CAH?

   b. How is it related to spatial ability, childhood toy preferences, childhood play patterns, and sexual orientation?

4. What are genders, and how do they differ from sexes?

5. How are Brazilian *travestis* like North American Indian *alyha*?

Unit IV
Mating Strategies: Competition and Choice

How do people choose mates? What characteristics do women and men prefer? And how do they go about winning the objects of their desire, especially when their choices often conflict with the aims of potential mates and same-sex competitors? In this unit, we will explore the complex *strategies* that people employ to select and acquire mates.

The term *strategy* is used in a specific way here. People often consciously strategize about winning the attentions of desired mates and thwarting the maneuvers of unwanted mates or competitors. But we can also talk about women and men as strategists without implying such conscious intent. In this way, we can also speak of the strategy of a flowering plant for attracting pollinators. The production of an apple blossom, for instance, with its bright colors, fragrant smells, and nutritious nectar, may be viewed as part of an apple tree's strategy for getting its ova fertilized and pollen dispersed by bees. Of course, bright, fragrant petals and sweet nectar are simply traits preserved by natural selection because they got their associated genes passed on to future generations. Apple trees do not actually strategize. But apple trees *appear* as if they are strategizing to attract pollinators, and humans likewise appear to choose and compete for mates as if they are strategizing to increase their inclusive fitness. This is the sense in which we will use the term *strategy* to discuss competition and mate choice.

We will begin with a reading on the "fundamental rule of human mate choice": incest avoidance. In this reading, Adrian Forsyth articulates the genetic and evolutionary rationales behind the "incest taboo"—the universal tendency of people to avoid mating with their relatives. Forsyth points out that inbreeding avoidance is widely shared among animals, predates the evolution of human beings, and thus cannot have originated in human culture. Yet incest does sometimes occur, and marriage systems across cultures are complexly organized in ways that do not solely reflect incest avoidance. How can a simple rule such as inbreeding avoidance account for these patterns? Forsyth explains:

> To understand mating patterns, it is essential not just to factor in the cost of inbreeding depression but to include other elements, like the costs and benefits of dispersal and various material considerations, such as the intensity of sibling rivalry, intrasexual competition and the possibility of inheritance of territories and resources.

169

Incest avoidance is thus one of many influences on human mate choice that must compete with sociopolitical and economic concerns, the availability of mates, and a variety of other mate choice criteria that vary in relative importance among individuals and across cultures.

In the next reading, Gaulin and McBurney examine the mating consequences of sex differences in reproduction. Men can reproduce faster than women and have more offspring, and they are more likely to die without reproducing. Women, through gestation and lactation, can invest in offspring with their bodies and typically invest more than men, who can invest only by providing resources, protection, child care, and the like. These sex differences have had profound effects on the mating psychologies of men and women.

For males, acquiring more mates has meant leaving more offspring over human evolutionary history. Consequently, sexual selection has favored relative eagerness in males to have sex with multiple fertile partners. Women get fewer opportunities to reproduce because of their greater parental investment. Thus, women have evolved the tendency to be relatively more discriminating about their mates' qualities: Does this male have status and wealth, or is he lowly and poor? Will he invest in his mate and children or abandon them?

Because human infants are born helpless, both women and men invest in their offspring. When a man invests, his energy and resources become unavailable to other women and form the basis for competition. These conditions have led to greater competition for mates among women than is typically found among female mammals and greater choosiness among men than is typically found among male mammals. Because women gestate and nurse their children, women can take several years for each reproductive venture. As a result, the acquisition of a mate by one man makes that mate reproductively unavailable to other men for a substantial period of time. This fosters competition among men. And with more fitness to be gained or lost, reproductive competition typically reaches more extreme levels among men than among women, as Gaulin and McBurney discuss in this unit (and as you learned in Chapter 7).

Because women and men invest differently, sexual selection has favored different mate selection patterns in the two sexes. Whereas men tend to prefer physical features that indicate a woman's fertility (e.g., youth and a small waist relative to hip width), women tend to prefer indicators of a man's ability to invest materially in offspring (e.g., status and wealth). Gaulin and McBurney review evidence that these patterns are expressed cross-culturally. Thus, broadly speaking, women can be said to employ a strategy of pursuing high-quality, investing mates, and men can be said to employ a strategy of pursuing multiple fertile mates.

However, women and men are also expected to prefer mates of high genetic quality. Gaulin and McBurney consider evidence that people choose mates on the basis of features such as facial symmetry that indicate underlying genetic quality. Choosing mates based on both genetic quality and investment capacity leads to a potential conflict for women: Good genes and investment are not always packaged together. In fact, there is a tendency for males' genetic quality and investment to be negatively correlated (Gangestad 1993, Gangestad and Thornhill 1997). This means that women who enter sexually exclusive relationships with investing males may not necessarily be recruiting the best genes for their offspring. And women who have sexual encounters with males of high genetic quality are less likely to garner male investment.

A possible solution is the use of a *mixed reproductive strategy*. From a woman's perspective, the most evolutionarily rational strategy may sometimes be to enter a long-term, committed relationship with an investing male and have so-called "extra-pair" sexual liaisons with good-genes males on the side.

While this arrangement may not conflict with the strategies of extra-pair males, it poses serious problems for investing males. Men are expected to have evolved strategies to avoid investing their resources in other men's offspring—a very real possibility when (at least before genetic testing) the paternity of offspring was *never* certain. Gaulin and McBurney discuss women's mixed reproductive strategies and the counter-strategies, including sexual jealousy, employed by men to avoid investing in other males' children.

Gaulin and McBurney also examine the other side of the coin—the mixed reproductive strategy available to men. Men can invest primarily in one mate and their (putatively) mutual offspring, while seeking extra-pair mating opportunities. As discussed previously, multiple mating opportunities are likely to have significantly increased the fitness of males over human evolutionary history. But females often demand some investment from males before they are willing to mate. And a male may switch the focus of his primary investment to a new mate. Extra-pair matings are thus likely to draw some, if not all, of a male's investment and resources away from his primary mate. And women are expected to have responded by evolving their own counter-strategies, such as emotional jealousy, to prevent their mates from channeling resources away from them.

Not all men and women employ mixed reproductive strategies. Many are faithful investors in a single mate. Others seek as many partners as they can get. We have already seen that a male's genetic quality may be associated with his reproductive strategy. Males with good genes may tend to invest less, presumably because women find them attractive and are often willing to engage in sex with them after little investment. But what determines a female's reproductive strategy? Gaulin and McBurney discuss one major factor, a female's expectations about the likelihood of male investment. Women who were reared in father-absent homes and women who report lower expectations for male investment appear to employ a strategy of seeking multiple partners and forming less stable emotional bonds. Males, too, appear to base their reproductive strategies partly on their expectations about the societal prevalence of male investment. Males who believe other men are willing to invest are likelier to display their willingness and ability to invest.

In the next reading, Elizabeth Cashdan examines in greater detail the reproductive strategies of women. Cashdan begins by asking what women would want if they could "have it all"—a mate in good condition with resources and high status. She goes on to examine the consequences of the conflicts of interest that necessarily arise when the choices of multiple women converge on the same males. Women "use a variety of weapons" to win mates, including *direct* competitive tactics, such as derogating their competitors and engaging in physical violence, and *indirect* competitive tactics that involve making themselves more attractive to men by increasing their appearance of youth and chastity and occasionally by providing their own resources through dowries. Finally, Cashdan examines the conflicts of interest that arise between women and men when women attempt to employ mixed reproductive strategies and when they enter into direct competition with men in the economic marketplace.

In the final reading of this unit, Jim Bell considers mate choice and romance among the Taita of Kenya. Bell, through his interviews with informants, dispels the myths propagated by early racist missionaries that Africans were incapable of feeling romantic love and capable only of lust. He finds that modern Taita express mate preferences like those described by Gaulin and McBurney (Chapter 12) and Cashdan (Chapter 13): "Males emphasize physical attributes, whereas females, as in our society, focus on personality and social standing." Among the Taita, first marriages are often arranged between couples who may be indifferent to one another and marry out of economic and political obligations to their families. But later, polygynous marriages and extramarital affairs often follow romantic interests "based on deep admiration and intense affection for one another." Such passionate or romantic love, Bell concludes, was integral to African culture before the arrival of Europeans.

References

Gangestad, S. W. 1993. Sexual selection and physical attractiveness: Implications for mating dynamics. *Human Nature,* 4:205–35.

Gangestad, S. W., and R. Thornhill. 1997. *An evolutionary psychological analysis of human sexual selection: Developmental stability, male sexual behavior, and mediating features.* Unpublished manuscript, University of New Mexico, Albuquerque.

11

Incest and Outcest

Adrian Forsyth

"Almost everyone carries the equivalent of more than one lethal gene in the recessive heterozygous condition."

—L. L. Cavalli-Sforza and W. F. Bodmer
The Genetics of Human Races

Greenland Inuit have a legend about the sun and the moon. To amuse themselves in the dark of winter, the inhabitants of an igloo would set their seal-oil lamps outside the igloo. In the darkened igloo, they could then make love anonymously. No one could be exactly sure who his or her partner was. A girl who joined this game every evening began to suspect that her brother was making love to her. One night, she coated her hands with soot and smeared her lover's face. She then ran outside to get a torch. Her lover followed, and by the light of her torch, she could see that he was indeed her brother. She touched her torch and began to run, and he began to chase her, carrying his own torch. They ran on and on, faster and faster, until they began to rise, spiraling into the sky, "and the girl, warm and shining, / Became the sun / And her brother, dark and cold, / Became the moon."

Biologists should see a genetic moral in the story. The woman who ran from incest is given a favorable light, the sun, giver of light and warmth. The incestuous brother is diminished,

dark and cold. But why should Inuit abhor incest? There are some stringent geographical reasons that might favor some tolerance for incest in the high Arctic.

On the top of our planet, people used to live a harsh isolated life. Inuit villages could survive only at special sites where hunting conditions were suitable. Often, communities were separated by hundreds of miles, distances made even vaster and more formidable by the cold and by winters during which the night darkness lasted for months at a stretch. For a human in search of a mate, such obstacles might seem to favor inbreeding. It would be far easier to find someone within the group, even if he or she were closely related. And yet by their legends and taboos and their mate-choice behavior, Inuit show no tendency to inbreed. Marriages between even sixth cousins were once prohibited before acculturation took place. Inuit, like humans the world over, had rules of mate choice.

The fundamental rule of human mate choice is this: incest is taboo. The difference between classical anthropological explanations of human incest taboos and a biological explanation comes down to two perspectives: those who see selection in terms of individuals and those who see selection in terms of groups. No one disputes that humans abhor incest. With a few minor exceptions to be discussed later, every culture prohibits primary incest—that is, brother-sister or offspring-parent matings. Most forbid marriages between cousins. But the simple biological explanation of this has not been universally accepted.

The biological explanation of incest avoidance is simply that incest is selected against by a phenomenon known as "inbreeding depression," in which the offspring produced by incestuous matings are less fit than those from outbred matings. This explanation is easily followed if one is willing to wade through a little genetic jargon.

Inbreeding depression follows inevitably from the mechanics of our genetic system. Organisms such as ourselves are diploid, meaning we contain two sets of chromosomes, two sets of genes arranged and organized into particular sequences and combinations. Because we have two sets, every gene within an individual can exist in two forms. These alternative forms are called alleles. For example, the gene that controls brown eyes can have several allelic forms. At any given gene, an individual can carry two alleles that can be identical or different. If they are identical, the gene is said to be homozygous; if they are different, it is heterozygous.

Some allelic forms are nonfunctional, or harmless, or they may be dangerous, coding for a protein that causes death or reduces the vigor of the carrier. If these deleterious effects are directly expressed, natural selection will quickly remove them from the population. But some defective alleles are not expressed if they occur in the company of a functional allele. Consider, for example, a gene that controls the production of skin pigment. An individual might contain an albino allele that was defective and would result in no protective pigment being produced, but if the other allele was functional, it would code for pigment production, and the individual would appear normal. Thus functional alleles may "dominate" and mask the effect of an unexpressed, or "recessive," and deleterious allele. They would lower the rate at which such deleterious recessives are exposed to the culling action of natural selection.

These deleterious recessives are part of what geneticists call the "genetic load" of a population. Every population carries significant numbers of deleterious alleles, and every individual usually carries deleterious alleles that can lower his or her fitness. The amount of the genetic load is measured in "lethal equivalents." For example, if an allele lowers an individual's fitness by 20 percent and an individual contains five similarly deleterious alleles, then that individual carries five times 20 percent, which equals one lethal equivalent. Human populations are estimated to carry an average of two to five lethal equivalents per person. Similar estimates have been made for fruit flies, flour beetles and pine trees.

Since most of these deleterious alleles exist in an individual as unexpressed recessives masked by functional, dominant alleles, an individual rarely suffers their effects. Their deleterious effects are usually expressed only when an individual happens to have two deleterious alleles of the same gene, in which case their defective nature is exposed.

For individuals who breed with nonrelatives, there is a very low probability that they will both contribute the same set of deleterious alleles to their offspring. Each individual contains tens of thousands of genes, and there may be many allelic forms of each gene, so the chance of an offspring getting the identical deleterious recessive alleles at several genes is low. But under incest, the probability of inbreeding depression shoots up.

Consider the deleterious recessive allele that causes feeble-minded phenylketonuria when it is expressed in the homozygous state; that is, when an individual has two alleles for this gene which are identical and defective. The defective allele exists in populations with a frequency of 0.01, meaning that if we counted alleles of this gene drawn at random from the population, 1 out of 100 would be the defective form. Therefore, the probability of an individual being homozygous for this gene and suffering the disease is 0.01 multiplied by 0.01, or 1 in 10,000. In other words, we expect 1 in 10,000 children from outbred matings to suffer feeble-minded phenylketonuria. Simple laws of probability show that this risk goes way up for incestuous matings. Children from brother-sister matings are 576 times more likely to produce children suffering the disease. This is because a brother and sister share half of their allelic forms. They each got half of their genes from their mother and half from their father. There is a high chance—0.5, or 1 in 2—that they carry the same deleterious alleles and that their progeny will be homozygous at many genes.

Knowing the average number of lethal equivalents carried by a population enables one to calculate the mortality of children produced by primary incest. For example, if humans carry 2.2 lethal equivalents, it can be shown that a brother-sister mating would produce children of which 42 percent would not survive to reproduce. This is a theoretical prediction that human geneticists have documented with data from several human populations.

In one study conducted in Czechoslovakia, the fate of 160 children born to women through incestuous matings with sons, brothers or fathers was compared with another set of 95 children born to the same women but with a nonrelative as the father. Close to half of the incestuously produced children failed to survive to reproduce, whereas almost 90 percent of the nonincestuous children were able to reproduce. First-cousin marriages bear a lesser but still significant cost. In Sweden, about 4 to 6 percent of children not born of incestuous relations suffer from genetic disease. When the children come from first-cousin marriages, the incidence of genetic disease rises to 16 to 28 percent. In France, a study of children from first-cousin marriages showed that they were twice as likely to die before adulthood as children from unrelated crosses. The same difference has been reported in Japan. As expected, second-cousin marriages produce children of intermediate vigor.

The high cost of incest through inbreeding depression is well established for many other plant and animal species. Thus we expect organisms to evolve mechanisms for avoiding inbreeding. Plants and animals may accomplish this by having massive synchronized reproductive bouts or by having one sex disperse from the area in which it was born. Both of these may also be explained as adaptations to reduce predation or as competitive strategies. But neither predation risk nor intrasexual competition explains the ability of many animals and plants to distinguish between kin and non-kin. Some plants have recognition alleles that enable them to discriminate against pollen which is too closely related. Various marine organisms also possess recognition alleles that allow them to distinguish between genetic relatives. We expect this ability in highly colonial, altruistic animals such as social insects, in which extended families compete with other families. But kin recognition based on odor is well developed in many mammals, including various rodents and monkeys that have a much more flexible social system.

Humans seem to possess a similar kind of recognition system in which we learn an aversion to siblings. We learn to be sexually uninterested in siblings and thereby minimize incest. This argument was implied in the writings of psychologists such as Hans Westermark and Havelock Ellis, who found suggestions of a link between childhood familiarity and lack of erotic interest.

The best evidence that this is so comes from studies of Israeli kibbutzim. Originally designed to be self-sufficient units, kibbutzim were composed of largely unrelated people. Children were reared communally. When the marriage patterns of a group of 2,769 children raised in kibbutzim were analyzed, it was found that not one marriage occurred between children who had been raised together. The children were largely unrelated, so the finding at first makes little sense in terms of natural selection. But communal children rearing on this scale does not approximate the condition under which humans evolved; for most of our history, humans have existed as nuclear families. In kibbutzim, children raised together develop the same erotic aversion to each other that exists among siblings—familiarity apparently breeds contempt.

Many anthropologists have offered different explanations of the human incest taboo, and many are openly hostile to the biological explanation based on inbreeding depression. They see the incest taboo as fulfilling a variety of strong social functions that could account for its existence. In the past, most standard anthropological explanations for incest taboos used good-of-the-group arguments, which proceed from the notion that cultural practices exist for the good of society. Freud argued that the incest taboo developed because it prevented cultural stagnation. Individuals who outbred married into social units different from the family units in which they were reared, and this increased social diversity and kept the society dynamic. This same sort of argument is found in the work of such giants in anthropology as Margaret Mead and Claude Levi-Strauss. In writing about marriage rules, Mead claims that "the primary task of any society is to keep men working together in some sort of cooperation." Levi-Strauss concurs, saying: "The prime role of culture is to ensure the group's existence as a group," and he made famous the idea that incest taboos and marriage rules evolved as rules for wife trading. He hypothesized that a required outbreeding enables male kinship groups to trade and exchange women for material and political gain. This trading is used to form political alliances that strengthen the group.

As evolutionary biologist J. Maynard-Smith has pointed out, anthropologists have made too much of the cultural significance of the incest taboo: "When Levi-Strauss (1969) asserts that the incest taboo is the characteristic feature which originated human culture, it is in one sense tautological and in another manifestly false. If the emphasis is on the cultural connotation of the word 'taboo,' the statement is tautological, since there can be no culture without culture. If the statement implies that animals do not have practices which avoid incest, then the statement is false."

He goes on: "It seems to me more plausible that the differences between the customs of different societies call for a cultural interpretation of which has little to do with inclusive fitness. But to attempt a general explanation of human marriage customs and incest taboos which ignore the fact that in all probability, our ancestors avoided mating with close relatives long before they could talk would be foolishly parochial." A more biological view of culture is that it is nothing more than an abstract construct representing the sum of individual decision-making and behavioral patterns. It is individuals that must create, implement or ignore taboos and rules and enjoy the attendant costs and benefits. Individual costs and benefits are the mechanisms that give rise to cultural patterns. It is also true that humans are social. They live in groups and compete against other groups. This creates a second and higher order of selective pressure. An individual's action is influenced not only by its immediate costs and benefits to the individual and his or her children or kin but also by how it will affect the fortunes of the group in which the individual must exist. Individuals may sacrifice personal gains or be coerced by other members or by historical rules to alter their selfish behavior in the interests of the group. However, it should be borne in mind that the interests of the group or the culture are genetically important only because they influence the success of the individuals and kin groups which make up the group and act out the culture of the group.

Part of the conflict between the individualist and the group-selection view of cultural rules is because of the different levels of focus, the forest-and-the-trees problem. The biologist is interested in the primary-incest taboo; anthropologists have been perplexed by the ornate complexity of systems determining marriage patterns beyond the primary-incest taboos. Many marriage possibilities that do not involve incest are prohibited. Furthermore, there is nothing in the primary-incest taboos that precludes the use of marriage rules to accomplish such ends as cementing political alliances.

Parsimony of explanation is a goal of science. But one cannot choose among factors in a multifarious process. Instead, one must build a model that incorporates them all. This is unsatisfying but necessary. To understand mating patterns, it is essential not just to factor in the cost of inbreeding depression but to include other elements, like the costs and benefits of dispersal and various material considerations, such as the intensity of sibling rivalry, intrasexual competition and the possibility of inheritance of territories and resources. The goal is not to find a single law that explains the incest taboo but to model a process and explore the operation and conflict of various forces.

In this light, the fact that some human groups routinely practiced incest between siblings or close cousins is not a fatal flaw but material for testing a model. The people who routinely sanctioned and even encouraged incest did so for economic reasons and acted to their own personal advantage. They do not represent a random selection from human cultures. Incest was a prerogative of royalty in Iran, Peru, Hawaii and possibly Samoa. As Sir James Frazer argued in *The Golden Bough,* when the throne is passed down through the female bloodline, it profits the king to commit incest with his daughter whenever his wife, the queen, dies. Similarly, incest with siblings is a way to keep family inheritances and holdings intact, and the pattern of nieces marrying uncles is a way to retain dowries within the extended family. Incest is a resource monopolization strategy in the cases in which substantial material benefits are counted as more valuable than the cost of inbreeding depression. A family willing to eliminate malformed children by means of infanticide further reduces the cost of incest. This practice was well known in most incestuous groups, and the longer the incest is practiced, the lower its cost, because deleterious alleles are exposed to selection and removed from the lineage.

The costs and benefits of incest also vary for the two different sexes. In general, males will experience a lower cost for an incestuous mating than will females. A woman who bears a defective offspring has substantially reduced her lifetime reproductive success, but the man who fathers it has not diminished his reproductive success much. In fact, if little parental investment is exacted from him for the offspring, he will have raised his reproductive success. Thus we expect to see males be more inclined to commit incest than females. We also expect individuals nearing the end of their reproductive career to be willing to commit incest. They, too, have little to lose and much to gain.

Anecdotes hardly suffice to prove anything, but I will recount one about the costs and benefits of incest among Inuit as described by French anthropologist Jean Malurie in his magnificent book *The Last Kings of Thule.* "The Eskimo is above all a realist—don't worry about how you live, he says, just see that you survive—and he adapts his rules to fit the circumstances. The 'exofamilial' solution was to marry outside of the family altogether; this widened a man's choice of mate but also extended the obligations to give financial help that he incurred through his marriage. The 'endofamilial' solution for the hunter who was a widower, isolated and unable to find a second wife either among his relatives or elsewhere, was to sleep with his own daughter and so ensure himself a true partner. I know of such a case in northeastern Canada. The widower, who was a good hunter and had had many children, had spent two years in a fruitless search among neighboring groups for a new wife; only then did he decide on this course, provoking the silent disapproval of his neighbors and causing great sorrow to his oldest daughter, on whom his choice had fallen. His search had been useless, and no wives were to be had because the rate of female infanticide in the area had been very high between 1930 and 1940."

Avoidance of inbreeding depression is only part of the cost-benefit equation. It is also necessary to consider the costs of outbreeding.

Dispersal itself is costly. For some insects, it can be shown that there is a trade-off between the energy consumed by dispersal and that required for reproduction. One may be more likely to be eaten when dispersing. And it is possibly harder to acquire a territory in a new and unfamiliar area.

There are also genetic costs to outbreeding. Plants, at least, seem to become locally adapted to a certain area. The mixing of genes from distantly separated individuals will break up that match between the genotype and the environment, and it may break up particularly favorable gene sequences. In some plants, outbreeding depression takes place on an amazingly small scale. Nicolas Waser and Mary Price have done the first studies documenting this effect on a small scale. They worked with *Delphinium nelsonii,* a dark blue larkspur that grows in the alpine meadows of the Colorado Rockies. They cross-pollinated plants by hand, moving pollen from plants at distances varying from three feet to more than 3,000 feet apart. No one was surprised that they found inbreeding depression in the crosses from only three feet apart. *Delphinium* seeds are relatively heavy and probably do not disperse far, so the plants growing within three feet of each other may be close relatives. What was surprising was that maximum seed set, an indicator of the success of the pollination, occurred in plants only 30 feet apart. The matings from a separation of more than 3,000 feet were lower. The interpretation of this is that if mating partners are too dissimilar genetically, then there is a lack of compatibility in the resulting offspring. Waser and Price have shown that the natural pollinators of *Delphinium,* such as various bumblebees and hummingbirds, transfer little pollen beyond the optimal 30-foot distance. This means that over time, the individuals of a given spot will tend to be made up from genetic combinations that are both favorable and drawn from a highly local pool. Bringing in pollen from great distances breaks up this local coadaptation of genetic combinations.

The logical extension of this argument is that plants with different seed- and pollen-dispersal systems should have different scales of optimal outcrossing. There are several other works studying optimal-outcrossing neighborhoods in plants that have high rates of long-distance pollen transfer. Bat-pollinated trees or desert plants—whose seeds are washed great distances down flash-flooding arroyos—have optimal-outcrossing neighborhoods on the order of several miles.

As a human example, we can consider the geographic variation of blood groups, which are genetically determined. If a woman with Rhesus-negative (Rh-negative) blood mates with a Rhesus-positive (Rh-positive) man, then she often has a so-called blue baby during later pregnancies. She develops an immune reaction to the foreign Rhesus blood-group factors found in her baby but not in her own blood. During the first pregnancy, there is usually no problem, because there is little mixing of blood between the mother and the fetus, but at birth, considerable mixing occurs. As a result, the mother develops antibodies in her blood against Rh-positive blood, and during the next pregnancy, these antibodies can enter and destroy the blood of the Rh-positive baby. Rh-positive blood is widespread in Europe, and blue babies are rare. In China, most people are Rh-negative, therefore matings between European males and Chinese women are at a significantly greater risk for blue babies.

Of all the things that humans do, mating and reproducing would seem most likely to influence evolution. They are, and have always been, far more important than, say, one's taste in music. Thus it comes as a surprise that the discussion of the biology of incest avoidance should have provoked negative reactions from many scientists. Any discussion of human biology always seems accompanied by the fear that evolutionary interpretations of our behavior will justify the behavior or discourage and prevent us from changing our behavior. For example, sociobiologist E. O. Wilson aroused the ire of many anthropologists and psychologists when he argued in *On Human Nature* that the sociobiological explanation of the incest taboo "identifies a deeper, more urgent cause, the heavy physiological cost imposed by inbreeding." A caustic reviewer, experimental psychologist N. L. Macintosh, counterclaimed that "biological explanations simply cannot preempt sociological explanations this way. We could accept that the biological function of incest taboos was to prevent inbreeding, but this would not serve to exclude the possibility that they served social functions as well and not just as secondary contributing factors. Nor would the identification of any such biological function allow one to choose between an infinity of possible proximate (social and psychological) causes." Granted, but it is also true that the social func-

tions cannot develop uninfluenced by the genetic cost of inbreeding.

There is no doubt that a family marooned on a desert island could overcome its aversion to incest or that royalty would permit a son to bed a daughter if it meant keeping the family fortune intact or that a tribe might prohibit marriages which led to strife or weakness. Biologists concede the point that humans are able to understand, use and culturally modify biological tendencies—in this case, the avoidance of inbreeding depression. But the corollary concession is also necessary. Evolutionary history affects cultural practices. It does not rigidly bind or predict them, but it is an influence. We cannot, however we might wish it, escape the fact that we are animals and minds within bodies and within history.

The Psychology of Human Mating

Steven J. C. Gaulin and Donald H. McBurney

The military was able to fulfill congressional and popular demands for ethnic and skin-colour integration with notable success. But trying to do the same with women has been a major intellectual failure, because the military has operated on the incorrect assumption that skin colour and sex are equally important classifications. They are not. There is nothing we can know about a person's nature by knowing his skin colour. Sexuality, on the other hand, is an all-important, all-pervasive force in the lives of people, especially the 19- to 30-year-olds who predominate in military life. (Tiger, 1997, p. A15)

There are some significant differences between men and women, a fact that traditional psychology tends to neglect. Consider the following experiment. Attractive men and women were paid to approach strangers of the opposite sex and, after a brief conversation, asked one of three questions: "Would you go out with me tonight?" "Would you come over to my apartment tonight?" "Would you go to bed with me tonight?" The experimenters were interested in how people would respond. Do you think men and women responded similarly? To all of the questions?

Men and women seem to be equally interested in dating. About 50 percent of each sex agreed to a date with the person they had just met. But the sexes differed greatly in their interest in the other two activities. Only 6 percent of women agreed to the apartment visit, whereas 69 percent of men did so. And not a single woman said she would have sex, but 75 percent of the men accepted this invitation (Clark & Hatfield, 1989). How would you explain these differences? In this chapter we consider the results of this and other experiments that illuminate human mating strategies. In the process we explore how sexual selection has shaped the psychologies of women and men.

Sexual Selection in Humans

As you will recall from Chapter 6, sexual selection is caused by sex differences in reproductive rate. Obviously, then, the first question must be, Do men and women differ in reproductive rate? This question deserves more than a simple yes or no answer, because the situation is complicated.

Reproductive Rates of Women and Men

Except in the relatively rare cases of twinning, a woman can produce only one child annually because her commitment to gestation and preparing her body for another pregnancy require about a year. Over most of human evolution, when breast milk was the only suitable food for infants and young children, her minimal commitment might have been more like 3 or 4 years. This estimate is based on what we know of reproduction in chimpanzees (Tutin & McGinnis, 1981), our closest living relatives, and on contemporary hunter-gatherers like the !Kung San of Botswana (Howell, 1979).

Notice that having multiple mating partners would do little to increase a woman's reproductive rate. This is because her fertility is limited by the constraints of gestation and lactation, not by any shortage of mates or sperm.

> **Trail Marker:** A woman's reproduction is limited by her physiological investment capacity.

What are the comparable figures for men? If a man made little commitment to rearing the children, and if he had multiple partners, he could reproduce much more rapidly than a woman ever could. Each of his partners could, in principle, produce one offspring per year, so his reproductive rate would be the sum of the rates of his partners. Unlike a woman's, a man's fertility *is* limited by access to mates. Consider this example. Moulay Ismail, who lived from 1672 to 1727, was the last Sharifian emperor of Morocco. By 1703 (when he was 31 years old), he had produced 525 sons and 342 daughters; his 700th son was born in 1721, and he presumably continued to produce children for the remaining six years of his life. Of course, this high reproductive output was only possible because Moulay Ismail had hundreds of wives.

> **Trail Marker:** A man's reproduction is limited by his access to fertile women.

Moulay Ismail is fact, not fantasy, but his reproductive output is highly unusual, earning him a citation in the *Guinness Book of Records* (McFarlan et al., 1992; but see Einon, 1998). Men will seldom be able to reproduce much more quickly than women. Among contemporary humans everywhere, men do invest in offspring. How much they invest varies from society to society, but men are seldom like the deer, discussed in Chapter 6, who simply copulate and depart. Men's paternal investment slows down their reproduction. Paternal investment takes time and resources that might otherwise be spent on courting additional mates. Also, human mating practices impose limits on men's reproductive rate. In a perfectly monogamous system the sexes would have identical reproductive rates. If all of a man's children were produced with his one monogamous partner, his reproductive rate would necessarily be the same as hers. This idea provides a baseline. We would not want to naively claim that human mating systems are perfectly monogamous. But, to the degree that they approach monogamy, they tend to reduce the sex difference in reproductive rate.

So, what are human mating systems actually like? Is monogamy the norm? Marriage practices offer one sort of evidence, and these practices vary quite a lot from one society to the next. North Americans are often surprised to learn that 85 percent of well-described human societies allow polygyny—the practice of one man marrying several women (Murdock, 1967). The reason this surprises people is that most of the large nation-states that readily come to mind prohibit polygyny. Most of the more than 1,000 societies that permit polygyny are small tribal groups. Anthropological and historical records suggest that prohibitions on polygyny are, evolutionarily speaking, very recent, nowhere dating back more than 500 years (e.g., MacFarlane, 1986).

> **Trail Marker:** Monogamy is evolutionarily novel in humans.

Of course, marriage practices are not a perfect reflection of mating practices. Even societies that prohibit and punish polygyny are not fully monogamous for two reasons: marital infidelity and the combination of divorce and remarriage. Marital infidelity results in defacto polygyny because, as we saw above, having multiple partners raises a man's reproductive rate more than it raises a woman's. In principle, a man's wife and his lover could be pregnant simultaneously. But having a lover will not help a married woman produce more children; how could it? Through in-depth interviews, Susan Essock-Vitale and Michael McGuire (1985) studied the sexual and reproductive histories of a random sample of 35 to 45 year-old, middle-class white women living in Los Angeles. Of the 283 women who had been married at some time in their lives, 23 percent reported having at least one extramarital affair. But having more than one mate had not increased their reproductive success. Those who reported having affairs had an average of 2.2 children; those who did not averaged 2.3 children.

Trail Marker: Even in monogamous societies, infidelity, divorce, and remarriage allow effective polygyny.

Divorce and remarriage also affect the reproductive rates of men and women. The important fact is that regardless of age, men are more likely to remarry than are women. The difference between the sexes in their prospects of remarriage increases with age. For example, among people in the United States who divorce between the ages of 25 and 29, men are 30 percent more likely to remarry than are the women they divorce. For partners divorcing between the ages of 50 and 54, men are four times more likely to remarry! These patterns are not unique to North America. A study of remarriage patterns based on data from 47 countries showed that on a worldwide basis, men are more likely to remarry after divorce than are women, often much more likely (Chamie & Nsuly, 1981). Further, when men divorce and remarry, they tend to marry women younger than their previous

wife (Mackey, 1980). In this way they "capture" the fertile years of more than one woman. The effect of remarriage on fertility is potentially large; by 1980 nearly 40 percent of all marriages in the United States involved one partner who was remarrying (Chamie & Nsuly, 1981). The conclusion is that both infidelity and patterns of divorce and remarriage turn nominally monogamous societies like our own into at least mildly polygynous ones.

Human Parental Investment

Since male parental care—more precisely, male parental investment—is what slows men's reproductive rates, it is worth exploring this concept in more detail. **Parental investment** (Trivers, 1972) is a technical concept in biology. It includes anything that a parent does for a particular offspring that helps the offspring (reproductively, of course) and reduces the parent's ability to invest in other offspring. It is a limited resource, just like your income or allowance—what you spend on one purchase is unavailable for something else. Gestation and lactation are clear examples of parental investment. So are groceries, medical fees, clothing, tuition, and time spent preparing the child to compete effectively in the world. When both parents typically contribute in these ways, we say the species has **biparental investment.**

The Evolution of Biparental Investment

Why, if males could accelerate their reproductive rate by acquiring more mates, do they slow themselves down by investing? The answer is that under some circumstances, offspring who receive investment from two parents do much better than offspring who receive it from only one. Consider two hypothetical kinds of males: one who merely fertilizes females and then departs to seek additional mates, and one who gives up some mating opportunities to stay around and help rear his offspring. If offspring who receive biparental investment have a big enough advantage, then investing males might end up with more grandchildren than males who fail to help.

> **Trail Marker:** Biparental investment is more likely to evolve in species with helpless young.

This is sensible enough, but biparental care is rare among mammals (Kleiman, 1977). Is there anything special about humans that might have made the additional investment of a dad especially valuable? Yes; human infants are very helpless and take a very long time to grow to adulthood. This fact too requires explanation. The current idea is that changes in the pelvis associated with an upright, bipedal gait made it more difficult for our female ancestors to give birth. The solution was to give birth earlier in the gestational cycle, resulting in smaller but more helpless infants. In this way, the extreme dependence of human infants may have favored the evolution of biparental investment in our species. This biparental investment has consequences for the outcome of sexual selection in our species.

Dynamics of Mating Competition and Choice Humans

To summarize, human mating systems are not perfectly monogamous, but neither are they as polygynous as those of many nonhuman mammals. Men are much more committed fathers than are most of their mammalian counterparts. This involvement limits their opportunities for polygyny and thus slows down their reproduc-

tive rate. In Chapter 6 you learned that members of the fast sex compete, while members of the slow sex choose. In perfectly monogamous species, where reproductive rates are equal, sexual selection favors similar traits in females and males. Thus, in monogamous species females and males tend to be equally competitive, and they also tend to be equally choosy. Given what we know about the reproductive rates of men and women, how will sexual selection have acted in humans?

> **Trail Marker:** Because of a tendency toward weak polygyny, women are expected to be somewhat choosier, men somewhat more competitive.

The human situation, neither strongly polygynous nor fully monogamous, leads to an interesting prediction about the effects of sexual selection. Both sexes will evolve to compete for mates, with the competition among men being somewhat more intense. Both sexes will evolve to be choosy about their mating partners as well, with women being more selective. This might seem like a prediction that can accommodate any finding, but it cannot. For example, it predicts a clear sex difference on both choosiness (women choosier) and competitiveness (men more competitive). It also predicts that relative to what we see in polygynous mammals such as chimpanzees and gorillas, human females will be more competitive and human males more choosy.

Sex Differences in Choosiness

Reticence to initiate sexual relations is one clear indicator of choosiness. Sex partners are potential co-parents. Individuals who are relatively indiscriminate about their sex partners are not being very choosy. Thus the Clark and Hatfield (1989) study discussed at the beginning of this chapter is clear evidence for a sex difference in choosiness. Women were just as eager as men to go on a date with the person they had just met, but men were 11 times more likely than women to agree to visit this person's apartment. Not a single woman agreed to sexual relations, while

75 percent of the men did. This study is especially relevant because the participants presumably thought the solicitations were genuine and that their answers would have real consequences: Either they would or would not find themselves in bed with their new acquaintance. Men generally found the idea appealing, whereas women did not.

Note, however, that one-quarter of the men declined the sexual proposition. Such a rejection would be very unlikely in the vast majority of mammalian species. Unless a more dominant male were standing by, ready to punish the transgressor, a male deer, male baboon, or male chimpanzee would seize virtually any opportunity to mate with any fertile female. David Buss and David Schmitt (1993) provide evidence showing that while men are less choosy than women, men are not indiscriminate when it comes to mating. Buss and Schmitt asked women and men to rate how likely they would be to consent to sexual intercourse with someone they viewed as desirable, given that they had known the person for various periods of time from 1 hour to 5 years. Participants rated

their willingness on a scale from –3 (definitely not) to +3 (definitely yes). The data are shown in Figure 12.1.

Men consistently indicate a greater willingness to engage in sexual intercourse than women do; the gap does not close until they have known each other for 5 years. So, men are clearly less choosy than women. But note also that men do not have a flat response at +3. For relationships of less than 1 week duration, they also rate their willingness as on the negative side of neutral; and they reach a plateau closer to +2 than to +3.

Trail Marker: On average, women are choosier about their sex partners, but men are not wholly indiscriminate.

In a seminal book on evolutionary psychology Donald Symons (1979) points out that homosexuals provide an interesting window on the sexual inclinations of men and women. As we have just outlined, men are more interested in having a large number of sex partners than women are. From a heterosexual man's view-

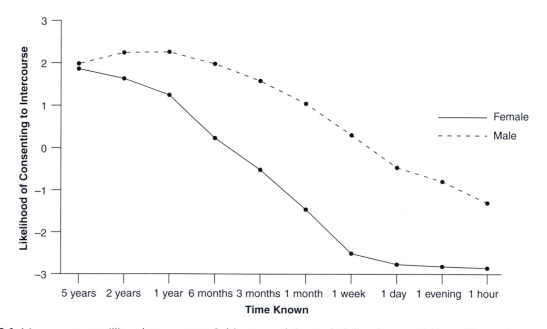

Figure 12.1 Men are more willing than women. Subjects rated the probability they would be willing to have sexual intercourse with an attractive partner they had know for various periods of time.

(From "Sexual Strategies Theory: An Evolutionary Perspective on Human Mating," D. Buss and D. Schmitt, in Psychological Review, *1993, 100, pp. 204–232. Copyright © 1993 by American Psychological Association.)*

point, that creates a problem: The people with whom he must negotiate his sexual desires are women, whose desires differ! Homosexual men, on the other hand, negotiate their sexual activity with other men, whose desires are presumably more coincident. Thus we would expect that homosexual men would be more successful in achieving large numbers of sexual partners than are heterosexual men. Indeed, this seems to be the case; homosexual males often report having hundreds or even thousands of partners. Fear of dangerous sexually transmitted diseases such as AIDS may have narrowed the gap somewhat, but even as late as the early 1990s homosexual men were still reporting significantly more sexual partners than were heterosexual men.

J. Michael Bailey and his collaborators have explored this issue in more detail. For example, this difference in promiscuity is not the result of differences in underlying interest. Homosexual and heterosexual men show no difference in their self-reported desire for uncommitted sex, only in their success in satisfying this desire. This is because gay men are negotiating their sexual activity with other men, whose desires are presumably convergent. To complete the story, lesbian and straight women do not differ on average in their numbers of sexual partners (Bailey et al., 1994).

With respect to their eagerness to copulate, it seems that men are behaving as if they constitute the fast sex, the sex with the potentially higher reproductive rate. This chapter presents tests of many predictions derived from this assumption. But first we need to examine a mystery that has some surprising twists: When we are choosy about mates, what are we choosing for?

Choosiness for What?

An analogy will be helpful in launching the discussion. We are attracted to both sweet and fatty foods. This is because, in the EEA, sweetness and

fattiness consistently signaled nutritional benefits. Those proto-humans who were attracted to and ate sweet and fatty foods were better nourished as a consequence and were thus more likely to be ancestors than those who rejected these foods. The key idea here is that attraction is not an intrinsic feature of the "attractive" object. Our sensory systems are not passive receptors; they have been designed by selection with particular built-in biases. Simply put, we perceive certain stimuli as positive, as attractive, because those stimuli were reliable signals of fitness-enhancing opportunities.

What data are available on human mate-choice criteria? You might think of looking at people's marriage choices. Aren't they a clear behavioral indication of mating preferences? In fact, actual marriages may not accurately reflect evolved mating preferences. Let's return to the dietary analogy. If you crave a particular food, then, within very wide bounds, you can just eat it. The food on the supermarket shelves has no strategies of its own. For this reason the stuff that modern humans eat is probably a reasonable indicator of what we evolved to find appetizing. But in the realm of mating, our cravings can be frustrated by the rather different cravings of our intended. Marriage is the result of a successful negotiation between two partners, and it is reasonable to assume that each has made some compromises in reaching the agreement. Realizing this, some researchers have tried to assess what people want in a mate rather than what they are willing to accept.

Trail Marker: Marriage patterns are not a "pure" indicator of mating preferences because marriages involve compromise.

It will not be surprising that physical attractiveness is important in mate choice (Berscheid & Walster, 1974). Contrary to some popular notions, criteria of physical attractiveness are not all that variable from one culture to another (e.g., Jones, 1996). For example, Nancy Anderson and her colleagues showed facial photographs of Asian women to a sample that included Japanese-, Korean-, Chinese-, and European-Americans. She asked these judges to rate the attractiveness of each face and to say whether it was most likely to be Japanese, Korean, or Chinese. While the various groups of judges focused on quite different facial features in rating the ethnicity of the faces, they agreed closely on which faces were the most and least attractive, and on the particular facial dimensions that contributed to attractiveness (Anderson, Park, Johnston, & Giddon, 1999).

Trail Marker: "Beauty is in the adaptations of the beholder." (Symons 1995)

Despite focusing on the consequences of attractiveness, traditional psychology has ignored the question of what it is. Donald Symons (1995) has stressed the evolutionary perspective: "Beauty is in the adaptations of the beholder." Studying the dimensions of sexual choosiness amounts to asking, What are the mating analogues of sweet and fatty? What are the reliable cues to a fitness-enhancing mate? A first approach to an answer is not very difficult. Mates provide two kinds of resources: genes and parental investment. The best mates are the ones that provide both good genes and good investment. The question of how we select such mates is a central focus of this chapter.

Choosing Good Genes

The arguments and evidence on this point are among the most fascinating in all of biology— and are tied to the fundamental question of why sex exists. Think about it. Asexual forms pass on all their genes each time they reproduce, whereas sexual forms pass on only half. Sexual reproduction also carries with it other significant costs, such as the cost of finding and courting mates and the cost of producing offspring with previously untested genotypes. Despite

these costs, there are reasonable explanations for sexuality in organisms that produce very large numbers of progeny. But in low-fertility organisms like ourselves there is currently only one plausible reason for sexual reproduction: to cope with the parasites and pathogens that make us sick (Hamilton & Zuk, 1982; Tooby, 1982).

The Red-Queen Model

Parasites and pathogens are small, rapidly reproducing organisms that eat us from the inside out. They can kill us or seriously reduce our fitness. Because they reproduce rapidly, they evolve and adapt quickly. Their environment is their host's body, and thus, over time, they get better and better at exploiting that host. Of course, hosts evolve defenses too. But, because hosts have much longer generation times than these "micro-predators" do, parasites and pathogens have the upper hand in an evolutionary arms race. (See Chapter 5 to remind yourself why generation time affects the rate of revolution.)

Trail Marker: According to the Red-Queen model, sex evolved as a defense against rapidly evolving pathogens.

By the time a typical host reaches reproductive age, he or she will have provided a stable environment for *tens of thousands* of generations of parasites and pathogens. If hosts reproduce asexually, they pass an identical copy of their genotype to their offspring. Since their own parasites and pathogens are already adapted to that genotype, this burdens the offspring with many well-adapted enemies. Wouldn't the offspring have a better start in life if it had a new and different genotype? According to Bill Hamilton and Marlene Zuk's (1982) **Red-Queen model**, this is why we mix our genes with our mate's: to change the rules of the game for our parasites and pathogens. Their further insight was that if we have sex to help our offspring escape pathogens, shouldn't we choose mates on the basis of their pathogen resistance? In other words, shouldn't the evolutionary reason for sex have shaped the way we choose mates? If Hamilton and Zuk are correct, we should have evolved to view signs of consistent good health as attractive.

Trail Marker: Mate choice criteria ought to be linked to the ultimate function of sex.

Obviously, a parasite- and pathogen-resistant individual will show clear signs of health and vigor. Thus we should have evolved to rate signs of health and vigor as attractive. Many signs of health are visible in the face. Clear skin, bright eyes, and shiny hair all suggest an individual in good physiological condition, one not too stressed by parasites. You know this is so, because if one of your friends is not well, a mere glance at his face reveals this fact. But faces reveal even more.

Symmetry as an Indicator of Parasite-Pathogen Resistance

Faces provide more than a current health report. They also constitute a life-long "medical record." The reason is that because they drain the body's resources, parasites and pathogens disturb normal processes of growth and development. Such disturbances leave a permanent, though small, trace. Like many other animals, humans are bilaterally symmetrical. Viewed from the outside at least, our right side is nearly a mirror image of the left. However, the disruptions of growth and development caused by parasites and pathogens perturb our symmetry and leave a permanent trace in terms of slight right-left differences. Thus deviations from right-left symmetry constitute a medical record that is also a matter of public record, since any potential mate can read it at a glance.

Trail Marker: Health, vigor, and symmetry are key components of attractiveness.

No face is perfectly symmetrical (see Figure 12.2). However, a number of recent studies indicate that the smaller the deviation from perfect symmetry, the more attractive the face is judged to be. This is true for both men's and

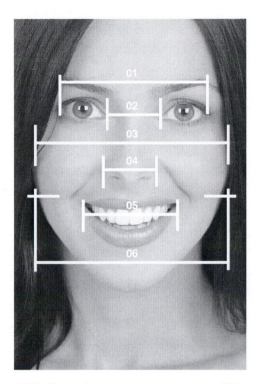

Figure 12.2 How is facial symmetry measured? Here's one technique. First, the distance between right and left facial landmarks is measured. Then the midpoint of each measurement is computed. On the most symmetrical faces these midpoints line up.

(Image © Kurhan, 2008. Used under license from Shutterstock, Inc.)

women's faces (Grammer & Thornhill, 1994). Using a computer "morphing" technique, Hume and Montgomerie (1999) were able to increase the symmetry of digital photographs of normal faces. They found a clear-cut relationship: The more a face was modified to approach perfect symmetry, the more attractive it was judged to be.

In a particularly intriguing study, Steve Gangestad, Randy Thornhill, and Ronald Yeo (1994) computed right-left asymmetry of nonfacial features (for example, elbow, ankle, and wrist diameters) for 72 undergraduates and then took standardized facial photographs of these same volunteers. The facial photographs were then rated for attractiveness by another group of subjects. Those individuals who were more symmetrical on the basis of nonfacial measurements were judged to have more attractive faces. This is presumably because the kind of developmental insults that produce asymmetry affect all parts of the body: Those with nonfacial asymmetries also had less symmetrical faces. Research indicates that, among males at least, more symmetrical individuals have first sexual intercourse at younger ages and have more sex partners over their lifetimes (Thornhill & Gangestad, 1994).

Complementarity of Immune Weapons

The Red-Queen model suggests that we select mates so as to produce the most parasite- and pathogen-resistant offspring. This is not precisely the same as selecting the most parasite- and pathogen-resistant mates. What is important is the health and vigor of the offspring, not the mate. So here is the challenge: We should try to choose a mate whose genes, *when mixed with our own*, will produce the healthiest progeny. This means choosing a mate who will provide different weapons in the fight against parasites and pathogens than we can provide, thus giving the offspring a diverse arsenal of defenses.

Thanks to various kinds of medical research, we know that our arsenal of defenses lies in our immune system (Janeway, 1993), and we know that the so-called MHC genes build our immune systems. Now, humans generally prefer mates similar to themselves on a variety of dimensions—height, intelligence, political views, to name just a few. But the Red-Queen model predicts a mating preference for individuals who have *dis*similar MHC genes. This very preference was documented in rodents even before its theoretical basis was understood (Yamazaki et al., 1976; Yamazaki et al., 1978; Egid & Brown, 1989; Penn & Potts, 1999). This preference for MHC-discordant mates is based on odor.

Trail Marker: The Red-Queen model predicts a preference for mates with complementary immune weapons.

Research indicates that humans also prefer MHC-discordant mates (Ober et al., 1997). Some of the clearest data comes from so-called "t-shirt studies" (Wedekind et al., 1995; Wedekind & Furi, 1997). People are given a clean t-shirt and asked to wear it without showering or using scented products for two days. At the end of that period, they contribute these shirts to be used as stimuli in scent-preference tests and donate a small blood sample for MHC genotyping. A different set of individuals serve as subjects. Their MHC genotypes are also measured; but instead of contributing shirts, they are asked to express preferences among several of the previously scented shirts. The results are fairly clear. Subjects prefer shirts worn by MHC-discordant individuals; women's preferences are stronger than men's; and women's preferences are disrupted—in fact, reversed—by the use of oral contraceptives.

These results are readily interpretable in terms of the theories you have learned. The basic preference for MHC-discordant partners would lead to the production of more pathogen-resistant offspring. Women are expected to be choosier than men because of their slower reproductive rates. Separate research confirms that women rate odor as a more important criterion of mate choice than men do; in fact women rate odor as the *most important* physical characteristic of a potential mate (Herz & Inzlicht, 2002). Finally, oral contraceptives simulate pregnancy, a time when there is no current need to discriminate among potential mates.

If further research confirms the effects of "the pill" on mating preferences, these findings would have great practical as well as theoretical significance. The widespread use of oral contraceptives could be fueling divorce rates! Suppose a women uses the pill while she's dating. Any long-term partner choice she makes on the basis of MHC will be tend to be "wrong." Thus she may begin to feel less attracted to her mate when, as a married couple, they discontinue contraception in order to start a family. Conversely, imagine a woman who begins using oral contraceptives soon after marrying, to delay reproduction for educational or career objectives. This woman too will experience a reversal in her odor-based mate preferences. The divorce rate did increase after the introduction of the birth-control pill; just how much of this increase is due to its effects on mating preferences remains to be seen.

Choosing Good Parental Investment

We have seen that women are more choosy—for example, requiring a longer friendship before copulating and being more selective about their partner's scent. In other words, so far it seems that women and men use the same mate-choice criteria, but women simply set a higher standard or cutoff. It turns out that in choosing for good parental investment the sexes have evolved not just different cutoffs but also different criteria. This is because, to some degree, women and men provide different kinds of parental investment.

Sex Differences in Parental Investment

There are some underlying asymmetries in *how* women and men invest. For example, some very important components of female parental investment—gestation and lactation—are physiological. At least in this early phase of child rearing, women in better physiological condition will be better parents and therefore better choices as mates.

In contrast, men's parental investment is not physiological but economic, in the broadest sense of this word. Men are involved in harvesting resources from the environment, which they may channel to offspring (or to courtship). This is not to say that women never harvest resources. They clearly provide for their (older) children in this way too. The key point is that men *only* harvest resources. They never commit their own bodily resources to children. So, a man's "economic" well-being may provide a better indication of his value as a mate than does his physiological state.

Trail Marker: Both sexes invest economically in offspring; only women invest physiologically.

These differences in how men and women invest in offspring have implications for the kinds of mates they are expected to prefer. Try to predict men's and women's mating preference based on what you have just learned. Much of the rest of this chapter presents evidence that will allow you to test your predictions.

In a series of studies reaching back to the 1930s researchers have asked North American women and men about the characteristics they find important in potential mates. For example, Reuben Hill (1945) asked participants to rate a series of 18 different traits in terms of how indispensable they were in a marriage partner. Women's and men's preferences are, overall, quite similar. For example, both sexes rate a sense of humor and various personality characteristics at the top of their lists. Of course, this is to be expected on commonsense grounds and also because, unless sexual selection is favoring differences between the sexes, natural selection will keep them quite similar. Because we are exploring the effects of sexual selection, we will concentrate on the areas where men's and women's preferences differ.

Women's Preferences

Hill (1945) found that women rate financial status as about twice as important as do men, despite that the sexes differed little in the importance they placed on many other attributes. David Buss (1989a) used the same methodology with a sample of about 1,500 North Americans in the mid-1980s and obtained the same result, as did studies in the intervening decades (McGinnis, 1958; Hudson & Henze, 1969). More recently, a representative sample of unmarried Americans between the ages of 19 and 35 confirmed that this sex difference is not limited to college students and seems to be stable despite a growing emphasis on similar socialization for boys and girls (Sprecher et al., 1994).

Analysis of personal advertisements in newspapers leads to a similar conclusion. In a sample of more than 1,100 heterosexually oriented advertisements (Wiederman, 1993), both sexes indicated that they were seeking financial resources in a prospective mate, but for every man who mentioned this criterion, 11 women did! In another study of 1,000 such advertisements that appeared in a British newspaper, women mentioned financial criteria 3.7 times as often as men did (Greenlees & McGrew 1994).

Trail Marker: Women prefer partners with good economic potential.

At least one more line of evidence is relevant here. Many of us have a clear idea of what we want in a mate. But to the extent that we agree with members of our own sex, we will be thrown into competition for the most desirable members of the opposite sex. Publically criticizing or putting down rivals can be an effective tactic in this sort of competition. Of course, the put-downs will only be effective if they criticize aspects of the competitor that matter to the opposite sex. David Buss and Lisa Dedden (1990) studied the use of such derogation tactics among both undergraduates and newlyweds. They found that men are significantly more likely to denigrate other men's resources or resource acquisition potential than women are to criticize women in this way.

But perhaps this sex difference is just a response to the modern Western socioeconomic scene. After all, don't mate-choice criteria vary widely from one culture to another? This is an empirical question, and fortunately there are plenty of crosscultural data. With a large number of collaborators, David Buss (1989a) undertook a study of mating preferences in 37 cultures from 33 different countries. The study included over 10,000 participants representing "a tremendous diversity of geographic, cultural, political, ethnic, religious, racial and economic groups" (Buss, 1989a). Buss and his collaborators asked participants to rate or rank the importance of various criteria in their choice of a mate. Some of these were *distractor* variables, that is, mate-choice criteria on which the sexes were not expected to differ. Others were *target* variables— criteria expected to be of greater importance to

one sex than to the other. Distractors included such items as "sociable," "intelligent," and "dependable character." Target variables included items like "good financial prospect" and "good looking."

In every one of the 37 cultures, women scored "good financial prospect" as a more important criterion of mate choice than men did, and the difference between women's and men's rankings was statistically significant in 36 of the 37 cultures (Table 12.1). This is a striking regularity considering the diversity of cultures sampled. Could this be an evolved sex difference, universal among contemporary humans?

The Structural Powerlessness Hypothesis

Before drawing that conclusion, you may want to consider other hypotheses. Perhaps women value economic potential not because men have invested that way for millions years, but because women have access to economic resources primarily through their mates. This idea is called the "structural powerlessness hypothesis" (Buss & Barnes, 1986). According to this view,

> . . . women's relative preferences for economic resources in a mate may be byproducts of the culturally determined differential economic status of men versus women. If women are typically excluded from power . . . then women may seek mates possessing characteristics associated with power and resource acquisition skills (e.g., earning capacity). . . . In short, the structural powerlessness hypothesis implies that as economic differences between men and women diminish, men and women become more alike in their mate selection preferences. (Wiederman & Allgeier, 1992:117)

So do women with relatively good access to economic resources relax their standards with respect to the earning potential of prospective mates, as the structural powerlessness hypothesis predicts? In short, the answer is "no."

Trail Marker: Structural powerlessness does not explain women's preference for economically promising partners.

Table 12.1 Emphasis Placed on Financial Prospects of Potential Mates by Men and Women in 37 Cultures

Sample	Men	Women
African		
Nigeria	1.37	2.30
S. Africa (whites)	0.94	1.73
S. Africa (Zulu)	0.70	1.14
Zambia	1.46	2.33
Asian		
China	1.10	1.56
India	1.60	2.00
Indonesia	1.42	2.55
Iran	1.25	2.04
Israel (Jewish)	1.31	1.82
Israel (Palestinian)	1.28	1.67
Japan	0.92	2.29
Taiwan	1.25	2.21
European-Eastern		
Bulgaria	1.16	1.64
Estonian S.S.R.	1.31	1.51
Poland	1.09	1.74
Yugoslavia	1.27	1.66
European-Western		
Belgium	0.95	1.36
France	1.22	1.68
Finland	0.65	1.18
Germany-West	1.14	1.81
Great Britain	0.67	1.16
Greece	1.16	1.92
Ireland	0.82	1.67
Italy	0.87	1.33
Netherlands	0.69	0.94
Norway	1.10	1.42
Spain	1.25	1.39
Sweden	1.18	1.75
North American		
Canada (English)	1.02	1.91
Canada (French)	1.47	1.94
USA (Mainland)	1.08	1.96
USA (Hawaii)	1.50	2.10
Oceanian		
Australia	0.69	1.54
New Zealand	1.35	1.63
South American		
Brazil	1.24	1.91
Colombia	1.72	2.21
Venezuela	1.66	2.26

(Data from Buss, 1989a.)

In a study of 100 newlywed couples, Buss (1989b) collected data on both income and mate-choice priorities. Among the men in his sample, Buss found no association between income and the importance placed on the partner's income. But among women, a positive correlation was observed: Women with higher incomes placed a *greater* emphasis on a mate's earning potential than did women with lower incomes. Similarly, John Townsend (1989) found that in a sample of 20 female medical students, each of whom expected a very good salary of her own, all stressed earning potential as an important criterion of mate choice.

Michael Wiederman and Elizabeth Allgeier (1992) pursued the same question with nearly 1,000 college students and a sample of 282 individuals from the wider community. In neither sample did men's expected earnings affect their own mate preferences. In the college sample, women again showed a significant positive correlation: Those who expected to earn more placed more, not less, emphasis on a potential mate's income. In the broader community sample there was no relationship between earnings and women's mate-choice priorities. Remember, the structural powerlessness hypothesis predicts a negative correlation: If women prefer men with good earning potential because women in general have poor financial prospects, those women with the best financial prospects should care less about the earning potential of suitors. But no study has reported this negative relationship. Most report a significant positive relationship, and one sample suggests no relationship. Thus the structural powerlessness hypothesis has received no support, and its usefulness as an explanation for the sex difference in mating preferences is therefore in doubt.

Men's Preferences

Given that a significant fraction of a woman's parental investment is physiological, men are expected to value signs of good physiological (rather than financial) condition. Men should have evolved to pay attention to signs of physiological well-being. Any such signs will surely be physical. So, unlike women, men will have evolved to attend disproportionately to the physical attributes of potential mates and to see as attractive those features most strongly correlated with physiological investment capacity.

Trail Marker: Men prefer physically attractive partners.

The first prediction is abundantly verified. The same series of studies that examined the importance of financial status in mate choice also evaluated the extent to which men and women value physical attractiveness in their mates (Hill, 1945; McGinnis, 1958; Hudson & Henze, 1969; Buss, 1989a). Men consistently rate physical attractiveness as significantly more important in a mate than women do. This is not to say that the emphasis placed on physical attractiveness is unmodifiable. Over the 50 years spanned by these studies, both men and women have shifted in the direction of placing more emphasis on physical attractiveness. But throughout this period, the magnitude of the difference between the sexes has been essentially unchanged (Buss, 1994; Sprecher et al., 1994). By a steady margin, men rate physical attractiveness as more important in potential partners than women do.

Personal advertisements support these findings. In a large North American sample of such solicitations, men were 3.7 times as likely as women to be seeking a physically attractive partner (Wiederman, 1993). Crosscultural data match the North American pattern. In every one of the 37 cultures studied by Buss (1989a), men rated physical attractiveness as a more indispensable trait of potential mates than women did, and the difference between men's and women's ratings was statistically significant in all but three cultures (Table 12.2). Derogation tactics exhibit the same sex bias. Women are much more likely to put down a rival's physical appearance than are men (Buss & Dedden, 1990).

Table 12.2 Emphasis Placed on Physical Attractiveness of Potential Mates by Men and Women in 37 Cultures

Sample	Men	Women
African		
Nigeria	2.24	1.82
S. Africa (Whites)	1.58	1.22
S. Africa (Zulu)	1.17	0.88
Zambia	2.23	1.65
Asian		
China	2.06	1.59
India	2.03	1.97
Indonesia	1.81	1.36
Iran	2.07	1.69
Israel (Jewish)	1.77	1.56
Israel (Palestinian)	2.38	1.47
Japan	1.50	1.09
Taiwan	1.76	1.28
European-Eastern		
Bulgaria	2.39	1.95
Estonian S.S.R.	2.27	1.63
Poland	1.93	1.77
Yugoslavia	2.20	1.74
European-Western		
Belgium	1.78	1.28
France	2.08	1.76
Finland	1.56	0.99
Germany-West	1.92	1.32
Great Britain	1.96	1.36
Greece	2.22	1.94
Ireland	1.87	1.22
Italy	2.00	1.64
Netherlands	1.76	1.21
Norway	1.87	1.32
Spain	1.91	1.24
Sweden	1.65	1.46
North American		
Canada (English)	1.96	1.64
Canada (French)	1.68	1.41
USA (Mainland)	2.11	1.67
USA (Hawaii)	2.06	1.49
Oceanian		
Australia	1.65	1.24
New Zealand	1.99	1.29
South American		
Brazil	1.89	1.68
Colombia	1.56	1.22
Venezuela	1.76	1.27

(Table from "Sex Differences in Human Mate Preferences: Evolutionary Hypotheses Tested in 37 Cultures" by D. Buss, *Behavioral and Brain Sciences,* 12 (1989), pp. 1–49. Copyright © 1989.)

After puberty, a woman's physiological investment capacity declines with age. Women are less fertile at 30 years of age than at 20, and less fertile at 40 than at 30. On the other hand, economic investment capacity may, for a time at least, increase with age as experience and social influence grow. These patterns may underlie the consistently divergent age preferences expressed by men and women. In Buss's (1989a) crosscultural study, men preferred mates younger than themselves and women preferred mates older than themselves in every culture, and the difference was statistically significant in all 37 cases.

Trail Marker: Men prefer youthful partners.

Of the three variables we have examined so far—financial capacity, physical attractiveness, and age—we have been able to predict and verify the direction of the expected sex difference. It turns out that an evolutionary view also allows a more precise prediction with respect to age criteria. Averaged across the 37 cultures studied by Buss, men preferred a wife who was about 2.7 years younger than themselves. But what does that tell us? Are males expected to prefer a mate because she is x years younger than he is or because she is y years old? Clearly, a woman's fertility is related to her own age, not to how much younger she is than her husband. This suggests that as men age they are expected to prefer a progressively greater age difference between themselves and their partners.

Data from disparate societies support this prediction (Kenrick & Keefe, 1992). Men younger than 20 years of age tend to marry women their same age. In their 20s men marry women 3 to 4 four years younger. Men marrying in their 30s select wives who average 6 to 8 years younger. The trend continues: The wives of men marrying in the 40s, 50s, and 60s are 13, 15, and 16 to 19 years younger respectively. The data for women marrying at progressively later ages show no such pattern. In fact, regardless of their age at marriage, women tend to marry men who are 1 to 6 years older than themselves.

Are men attending to any other traits in their attractiveness judgments? Devendra Singh (1993) has an interesting answer. As a consequence of sex hormone regimes, men and women deposit body fat differently. Estrogen, a reproductively important female hormone, inhibits fat deposition in the abdominal region and fosters its deposition on the hips, thighs, and buttocks, producing the so-called "gynoid" fat distribution. In contrast, male hormones, called androgens, foster fat deposits that are concentrated abdominally and on the upper body, the "android" fat distribution. The difference between gynoid and android patterns is immediately clear from a simple ratio of waist to hip measurements. Healthy premenopausal women have waist-hip ratios in the range of 0.67 to 0.80, whereas healthy men typically have waist-hip ratios between 0.85 and 0.95. The distributions of healthy women and men do not even overlap on this trait! Most important is that, among women, high (that is, android) waist-hip ratios are correlated with low fertility and higher susceptibility to a range of degenerative diseases. In other words, a woman's waist-hip ratio honestly reveals her reproductively relevant hormone profile. See Figure 12.3.

Trail Marker: Men prefer partners with a low waist-hip ratio.

Given this, and given the negative fitness consequences of high waist-hip ratios in women, men should have evolved to prefer mates with low waist-hip ratios. In personal advertisements, men are 9.5 times more likely than women to mention body shape in describing the kind of partner they seek (Weiderman, 1993). But this test is indirect. Using a range of methods, Singh explicitly examined the effects of waist-hip ratio on men's evaluation of female attractiveness. Low waist-hip ratios are consistently preferred not only in North America (Singh, 1993) but across a range of cultures (Singh & Luis, 1995).

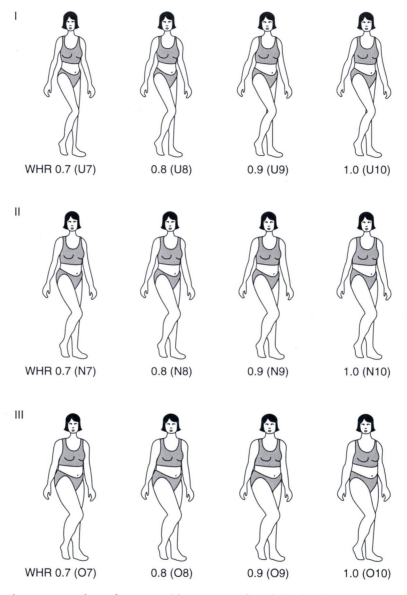

Figure 12.3 Stimuli used to assess male preferences with respect to female body shape. Men consistently prefer the left-most figure in the second row; this figure depicts a women of normal weight with a waist-hip ratio of 0.7.

(From "Adaptive Significance of Female Physical Attractiveness: Role of Waist-to-Hip Ratio," D. Singh, in Journal of Personality and Social Psychology, 1993, 65. Copyright © 1993 by American Psychological Association. Reprinted by permission.)

To sum up, women provide large amounts of physiological investment for their offspring, whereas men's investment emphasizes the provision of resources. An evolutionary view predicts that women's and men's mate-choice criteria would reflect these different patterns of investment. The available data support this view. Compared to men, women focus on the resources a potential mate might provide, and they seem to emphasize this criterion more when they are relatively well-off, so their preference is probably not motivated by a lack of access to resources. Compared to women, men look for signs of fertility in potential mates, such as physical attractiveness, a low waist-hip ratio, and youth. Data from around the world suggest that these patterns are not artifacts of western culture, but rather universal features of male and female mating psychology. Even in the realm of their sexual fantasies—a domain that is presumably little influenced by arbitrary social conventions—women and men exhibit this same pattern of differences (Ellis & Symons, 1990).

Mixed Reproductive Strategies

Our discussion of mate-choice criteria has focused on the fact that we can recruit both genes and parental investment from our partners. Up to a point at least, a woman's genes and her investment necessarily flow to the same offspring. This is because (barring the evolutionarily novel technique of egg transplantation) she will invariably gestate only offspring that carry her genes. But a man's investment is not automatically linked to his genetic progeny.

Another way of stating this asymmetry is that a woman's child definitely bears her genes, but a man's child . . . well, that's just the point: Who is a man's child? His wife's children are not automatically his own. Thus there is a large sex difference in what evolutionists call **parental confidence,** the ability to accurately identify one's own offspring. A great deal follows from this sex difference. Because a man's investment and his genes are not automatically linked, women could recruit the two separately. Some males may offer better genes than investment, and others may offer the reverse. In the final analysis, selection would favor women who get the best possible genes and the best possible investment, even if they come from different sources. Likewise, because a man's investment and his genes are not automatically linked, men can separate their contributions, giving only genes to some of their offspring. The male's potential to achieve higher reproductive rates means that there is at least some selection on men to desert their partners and children and seek additional mates.

These opportunities define what evolutionary biologists call **mixed reproductive strategies.** In playing a mixed reproductive strategy, an individual tries to "get the best of both worlds." Without falling prey to the naturalistic fallacy—in other words, remembering that what is natural is not necessarily virtuous— let's explore the mixed reproductive strategies open to men and women.

A woman's reproductive ends would be best served if she had a reliable partner able and willing to invest lots of resources in her offspring and if she could recruit the very best genes for those offspring as well. (The notion of good genes is discussed under the heading "Evolution of Mating Preferences: Physical Attractiveness.") The amount of resources a man has to invest may be partly related to his genotype; men with good genes may be somewhat better at getting resources. But luck and historical accident affect a man's resources too. So, the men with the best genes are not always the ones with the most resources. Thus women will sometimes find themselves with a difficult choice: recruit a mate with good genes or one with good resources. Either of these "pure" strategies may deprive a woman of some of the benefits men can provide. The mixed strategy is to recruit genes and investment separately, choosing the best source of each.

Trail Marker: Women playing a mixed reproductive strategy would accept genes and investment from different men.

Similarly, males also face conflicting reproductive goals. A man can benefit by having a fertile mate capable of high-quality maternal investment. But men also can raise their reproductive rates by having multiple mates. Should they settle down or play the field? Whichever they choose, they sacrifice something. For a male, the best of both worlds—the mixed reproductive strategy—is to have one fertile partner and invest in her offspring, but to also commit just enough resources to gain reproductive access to a number of other women.

Trail Marker: Men playing a mixed reproductive strategy would invest heavily in one partner but still attempt to attract additional mates.

Obviously, these mixed reproductive strategies violate the ideal of marital fidelity for both sexes. But we know that marital infidelity occurs. Estimates of the actual rate of adultery vary greatly, from 26 percent to 70 percent for women and from 33 percent to 75 percent for men (Buss & Schmitt, 1993, and contained references). Of course, some of this may just be sexual bragging, and some of the estimates have come from self-selected samples (e.g., readers of *Playboy* or *Cosmopolitan*). But even very careful studies based on random samples make it clear that true rates of infidelity are likely to be well above zero. For example, remember that in Essock-Vitale and McGuire's (1985) random sample, 23 percent of ever-married Los Angeles women reported extramarital affairs. That said, does extramarital sex seem to be motivated by the evolutionary incentives of mixed reproductive strategies?

Douglas Kenrick and his associates used an innovative technique to assess whether people change their level of choosiness when seeking different kinds of relationships. Other studies have asked which characteristics of a potential partner are important and which are unimportant. For example, from Buss's studies, we know that men prefer attractive mates, but we do not know what level of attractiveness they would find acceptable: We do not know how selective they are. Kenrick and his colleagues (1993) studied selectivity. Basically, they asked people to specify the minimum ranking of an acceptable partner on a series of characteristics, such as status, agreeableness, and attractiveness. (They explained that, for example, a person at the 60th percentile of status would be above 60 percent of other people but below 39 percent on this trait.) They also asked about these minimum percentile rankings for several levels of involvement, including a single date, steady dating, one-night stands, and marriage. Figure 12.4 shows their data for four characteristics. There are several points you should notice.

The Kenrick team found that for most levels of involvement and for most characteristics,

women set higher standards—they specified higher minimum percentile rankings—than men did. (The only exception here is that, in agreement with previous findings, men tend to set higher standards for the physical attractiveness of their partners.) Men's generally lower standards could be predicted from what we have said about male reproductive strategy. Remember, men's mixed reproductive strategy involves gaining access to multiple partners. In comparison to women, men are expected to emphasize partner number more and partner quality less. Setting high standards eliminates potential mates. Thus relaxed standards function to increase the size of the potential mate pool for men.

Trail Marker: Women are especially selective about the physical attractiveness of their one-night-stand partners.

Overall, and for most individual traits, both men and women set the highest standards for marriage partners. The greater the commitment, the more people insist on a high-quality partner. But there is one notable exception: Women set even higher standards for the attractiveness (and only for attractiveness) of their one-night-stand partners than they do for their marriage partners. (For comparison, men exhibit the more typical pattern of lowered standards for all the characteristics of one-night-stand partners, including attractiveness.) Since attractiveness is the best proxy measure for assessing genetic quality, the Kenrick team's findings have an obvious evolutionary interpretation. When women marry and thus expect to get investment as well as genes, they are willing to compromise somewhat on genetic quality. But in the context where they can expect to get nothing but genes (the one-night stand) they set maximal standards for genetic quality and relax all other criteria. These patterns would be difficult to explain without the guidance of an evolutionary framework.

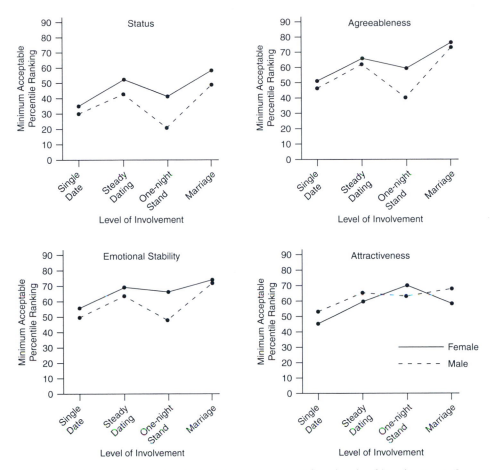

Figure 12.4 Women's and men's selectivity for four characteristics over four levels of involvement. See text for a discussion of the data.

Counterstrategies

Selection has favored these mixed reproductive strategies because, on average, they increased the fitness of the women and men who displayed them. But how do mixed reproductive strategies affect the fitness of partners? The answer is obvious: negatively. When a man forms a union with a woman and invests in her children, he suffers serious fitness costs if those children are not his.

To see why this is so, again imagine two kinds of males: one who invests selectively, by aiding only his own (genetic) offspring, and one who invests indiscriminately in anyone's offspring. By targeting his investment at his own

offspring, the selective investor helps his own genes spread. In comparison, the indiscriminate investor suffers two fitness costs. First, any genetic offspring he might have will suffer because much of his investment goes elsewhere. Second, his investment is not just wasted; it aids the offspring of his competitors. There is a word for being duped into investing in another man's children: *cuckoldry*. Obviously, genes for indiscriminate investment would lose out in competition with genes for investing in one's own children. Precisely because women can sometimes gain by drawing genes and investment from different men, men are expected to have evolved defenses against giving only investment, against being cuckolded. (If this argument starts you wondering about adoption, see Box 12.1).

Likewise, women should have evolved counterstrategies to men's mixed reproductive

BOX 12.1 Adoption

If selection disfavors investing in other people's offspring, why does anyone ever adopt? This is an interesting question. The first thing to note about adoption is that our practices in the modern West are unusual. On a worldwide basis most adoptions involve relatives (Silk, 1990). If the parents die or are otherwise unable to care for children, the children are typically adopted by a closely related individual. This pattern matches the predictions of kin selection theory (Hamilton 1964a, 1964b; see Chapter 3). If my sister is able to raise her offspring (my nieces and nephews), then I should let her. But suppose she is incapacitated in some way—then my choice could be between letting her children die and taking them in. Under some circumstances, the costs of adopting them may be compensated by their increased chance of reproducing genes we share. So, the general pattern of kin adoption fits with our expectations from modern evolutionary theory.

But in countries like the United States a large number of adoptions are by non-kin. How can these be explained? There are two kinds of cases. First, a stepparent may adopt his or her stepchildren (Kirk, 1981). This too is fairly easy to understand. If you marry someone who has children by a previous union (your stepchildren), you can help to cement your new marriage and signal a common purpose by adopting your mate's children. Assuming the marriage can produce genetic progeny for you, the benefits of adoption may again outweigh the costs.

The second kind of case is even more interesting. In this case a married couple adopt a child to whom neither is related. Such adoptions are regular in the United States, accounting for almost half of all adoptions in the 1950s and 1960s (Silk, 1990), and they might seem to defy evolutionary explanation. But remember, neither human beings nor any other animal is designed to consciously compute the likely fitness outcomes of alternative strategies. We are simply designed to respond to a system of internal and external rewards that ordinarily signal high fitness.

To take a pragmatic example, we might ask, why does sex feel good? Presumably because individuals who found sex unpleasant avoided it and thus left few offspring. What does this have to do with non-kin adoption? Sex is just one step in reproduction. Selection designed us to enjoy the other phases as well. Most people find parenting genuinely rewarding and feel some degree of dissatisfaction when they are deprived of those rewards. Adoption provides an outlet for these motivations. This predicts that the majority of non-kin adoptions would be by people who have tried to reproduce and been unsuccessful, a prediction which accords well with the available data (Bonham, 1977).

One way to think about whether this analysis makes sense is to consider the following social experiment. When a woman leaves the hospital after giving birth, she is given an infant to take home—the one most ready to be discharged in the opinion of the medical staff—without regard to whose infant it actually is. Do you think parents would, in general, be happy with this arrangement?

strategies. A woman might sometimes opt to mate with a male who will give her little investment, if he demonstrates sufficient evidence of high genetic quality. But she pays a price if her husband plays the same role to other women. The price can take several forms. First, because women are generally selective in their mating, any mating will require the male to make some investment in courtship. The time and other resources spent on this courtship necessarily reduce what he has available for parental investment. Second, women are favored by selection to get as many resources as they can from their partners. When a man's extramarital partner captures some of his resources, she depletes what is available to his wife's children. Finally, a husband might completely desert his wife and commit all of his resources to a woman who initially was an extramarital partner. In short, women stand to lose at least some, and possibly all, of their husband's investment when he takes a lover. Women are expected to have evolved defenses against losing this valuable resource.

Trail Marker: Both women and men are expected to guard against the mixed reproductive strategies of their partner.

What form do these male and female counterstrategies take? The male's problem is cuckoldry, and he has two lines of defense. He can attempt to secure a sexually faithful mate; if he fails at that, he can divorce his partner and minimize his investment in her offspring. We address these in turn.

In two separate studies Buss and Schmitt (1993) asked men to rate over 60 characteristics of long-term mates (that is, wives) and short-term mates (for example, casual sex partners). From the array of characteristics, men rated sexual fidelity as the single most important characteristic of a long-term mate and sexual infidelity as the most negative possible trait of such a partner. Indeed, the positive and negative ratings of these two traits closely approached the limits of the rating scale. In contrast, in the short-term mating context where men expect to invest few resources, they rated both fidelity and infidelity much more neutrally.

Women seem to use men's sensitivity to the risk of cuckoldry in competing for mates. For example, women attempt to make their competitors less attractive to men by stressing the competitors' promiscuity:

> Calling a rival a tramp, saying that the rival is loose, or telling others that a rival sleeps around a lot emerge in the top 10 percent of effective derogation tactics for women. Newlywed couples also maintain that women are significantly more likely than men to derogate their rival's promiscuity. (Buss, 1994, 114–115)

Men are much more likely than women to engage in physical aggression over potential mates (Daly & Wilson, 1988). But physical aggression is not uncommon among teenage girls of low socioeconomic status. In this group, one of the surest ways to trigger violence is to call a rival promiscuous (Campbell, 1995; Marsh & Patton, 1986). Girls are willing to fight to protect their sexual reputations.

Even if a man finds he has been cuckolded, there are some available strategies. About 1,300 men living in or near Albuquerque, New Mexico, in the early 1990s were interviewed about a wide range of reproductive issues. Of the 2,952 children born to the partners of these men, the men identified 36 (1.2 percent) as low-paternity-confidence children. The point is not that this is a large percentage (it isn't); the point is how the men responded. Men were roughly 10 times more likely to divorce women who bore them low-paternity-confidence children and invested much less in these particular children after divorce (Anderson, Kaplan, & Lancaster, 1999).

Jealousy

When their mates play a mixed reproductive strategy, women need to guard against the loss of resources. In other words, the cuckoldry risk that men face and the resource threats that women face are both triggered by infidelity. Is there any evidence that men and women have different sexual psychologies, tracking the different risks that infidelity poses for the two sexes? The most relevant studies focus on sex differences in jealousy (Buss et al., 1992; Harris, 2002). Methodologies vary somewhat, but here is a widely used approach: Men and women are asked to picture themselves in a serious, committed romantic relationship and then presented two alternative scenarios: (A) their romantic partner forming a deep emotional attachment to someone else, and (B) their partner having sexual intercourse with someone else.

Trail Marker: Patterns of sexual jealousy may reflect the different risks that men and women face.

Buss and his colleagues expected that men would find sexual infidelity more threatening because, over human evolution, sexual infidelity would have signaled a significant risk of cuckoldry. They predicted that women would find emotional infidelity more threatening because this would signal a weakening in the commitment of her partner and therefore the potential loss of some or all of his paternal investment. Sexual jealousy has been measured in a variety of ways. Subjects have been asked to report which of the two scenarios (sexual or emotional infidelity) would upset or distress them more. Also, physiological measurements have been taken in some studies. These included two indicators of autonomic arousal: pulse rate and skin conductance (measured with a standard polygraph or "lie-detector" test). In addition, brow muscle contraction was measured (electromyographically), because this muscle is typically contracted in facial displays of unpleasant emotion (Fridlund, Ekman, & Oster, 1987).

Buss and his associates (1992) found large sex differences in self-reported distress. Only 17 percent of women reported that sexual infidelity of a partner was more distressing than emotional infidelity. But 60 percent of males selected this alternative. Physiological measurements matched these self reports. Men showed consistently stronger physiological responses to the sexual-infidelity scenario than to the emotional-infidelity scenario. Women showed the reverse pattern, responding more strongly to the prospect of emotional infidelity.

Recent studies, however, have produced contradictory findings (e.g., DeSteno & Salovey, 1996; Harris & Christenfeld, 1996). There are several sources of disagreement. First, it seems to matter how the questions are posed. Some researchers have used a "forced-choice" format, asking their subjects to designate one of the two scenarios as worse. In this format there tends to be a clear sex difference, with males more likely to choose sexual infidelity as worse (Buss, 1994; Harris, 2002). If, instead, subjects are asked to rate the unpleasantness of a mate's infidelity along a 5-point or 7-point scale, then men and women rate the unpleasantness of both scenarios quite similarly (e.g., Harris 2002).

A second source of debate is the imprecision of the prediction being tested. It has been argued that men are expected to find sexual infidelity more threatening than emotional infidelity. Does this mean that *most men* will answer that way; or does it merely mean that *more men than women* will answer that way? At present it seems that the empirical evidence supports only

the latter interpretation. Finally, as Buss and his collaborators originally suggested, people may respond differently to these kinds of questions depending on their own levels of experience with relationships and infidelity. Some new evidence suggests that among those who have experienced the infidelity of a mate, men and women react very similarly (Harris, 2002).

Monitoring Physical Resemblance

A recent study suggests that men's cuckoldry risks have also influenced their sensitivity to physical resemblance cues. Of course, resemblance is complicated and difficult to study in real families, in part because researchers can never be sure that the alleged father is the actual father. To solve this problem, Steven Platek and his collaborators took resemblance into their own hands. First, they assembled a collection of facial photographs of young children. Subsequently, when each of their adult subjects arrived in the laboratory, they secretly used a computer morphing technique to blend the facial features of the subject with those of a randomly selected child. Then, in the data-collection phase, each subject saw five photographs: the subject-child composite and four unmodified photographs of children. Each subject was asked a series of positive and negative questions: "Which child would you be more likely to adopt?" "Which child would you punish more severely if it had damaged something valuable of yours?" If there were no effect of resemblance, the morphed faces would have been selected 20 percent of the time (one in five). That describes the performance of the female, but not the male, subjects. Men showed highly significant bias, picking the self-morphed face more often than chance for the positive questions and less often than chance for the negative ones (Platek et al., 2002).

Facultative Influences on Reproductive Strategy

What shapes the reproductive strategies of individuals? Some men are faithful investors, while others seek as many partners as they can. Some women remain faithful to a single mate, while others have children by several different men. Are these differences in any way predictable? One key factor may be expectations about the frequency of these strategies in the population (Draper & Harpending, 1982; Cashdan, 1993, 1996; see Chapter 5 for an explanation of frequency-dependent selection).

For example, imagine that the population includes many men who are both able and willing to invest in offspring. Under these circumstances it would pay a female to secure an investing mate. In such a population many offspring will receive biparental care; and those who do not will therefore be at a competitive disadvantage. Thus a woman who secures an investing mate avoids handicapping her offspring. Because of the risks of cuckoldry, even investing men are expected to withhold resources when there are significant threats to their paternity. Hence when investing males are sufficiently common, women are expected to offer the sexual fidelity that fosters male investment.

In contrast, when investing men are scarce, different female strategies may be favored. Short-term investment can be extracted from men in return for sexual access. In this case a woman might increase the amount of investment she harvests by increasing her number of sexual partners. This strategy would surely decrease her attractiveness to marital partners but could be her best option where few males are willing or able to provide long-term investment.

There are parallel alternatives facing men. If investing males are common, women can reasonably expect to attract one. Women should

evolve to recognize the difference between investing and noninvesting males because mistaking the latter for the former is very costly. Once women evolve this capacity to discriminate, noninvesting males might expend considerable time and effort on courtship with very limited success. Better to be an investing male and produce offspring with one female than to be rejected by all.

Conversely, if there are few investing males in the population, men may have higher reproductive success simply by maximizing the number of sexual partners they have. If most offspring receive only maternal investment, a male handicaps his offspring little when he abandons them to seek additional matings. With few investing males in the population, women could not expect to secure such a mate and hence will not be in a position to categorically reject noninvestors. This will mean that at least some attempts at courtship will bear reproductive fruit.

These scenarios suggest that the local availability of paternal investment is a key environmental variable. Just as the level of uv_b predicts the costs and benefits of melanin production (see Chapter 3), the abundance of investing men predicts the payoffs of alternative reproductive strategies. In a groundbreaking paper, Patricia Draper and Henry Harpending (1982) argued that children show lasting, critical-period responses to the presence or absence of an investing father during their early years. It seems that children read the absence of a father as an indication that investing males are scarce. Males who grow up in father-absent homes engage in more interpersonal manipulation and dominance striving; women reared in father-absent homes engage in sexual activity at earlier ages and more indiscriminately, and form less stable bonds with their mates.

Trail Marker: Both men and women adjust their mating strategies to their expectations about the availability of male investment.

Elizabeth Cashdan (1993) tested a critical assumption of this model. She investigated the relationship between people's own reproductive strategy and their beliefs about the need for and likelihood of securing male parental investment. First, she examined the paternal investment expectations of her subjects. Here is a sample item from the men's questionnaire:

"Bob says 'A woman can raise children success-fully on her own.' Don says 'Children need to have their father present when they are growing up.' " (Cashdan 1993: 10)

Subjects were asked to locate their beliefs along a continuum between Don's and Bob's views. A series of these scales probed several related beliefs about men's willingness to support children, the stability of marriage, and economic factors affecting men's ability to invest. Similar items presented from a female perspective made up the women's questionnaire. Then, each participant was asked to rate, on a 5-point scale, how often they used particular mate-attraction tactics, such as "showed I wasn't interested in dating anyone else," "wore sexy clothes," or "paid for dinner at a nice restaurant."

Cashdan found that the subjects' own expectations about the necessity and likelihood of male parental investment were correlated with their mate-attraction tactics. Women who believed investing males to be scarce were significantly more likely to use overtly sexual mate-attraction tactics such as wearing sexy clothes and copulating. In contrast, women who expected considerable male parental investment downplayed their sexuality and were reluctant to copulate, instead offering higher sexual fidelity and thus greater assurances of paternity. Men too seemed to adjust their mating tactics to their own parental investment expectations. Like women, men who downplayed the importance of male parental investment relied on overtly sexual mate-attraction tactics. Men who thought high levels of male parental investment were the norm were significantly more likely to attract mates by displaying both their ability and willingness to invest. In other words, each sex responded to their beliefs about the kind of mating arena in which they were competing. When they assume male investment to be rare, both men and women show mate-attraction behaviors that reduce the likelihood of long-term bonding. When they perceive long-term bonding between an investing man and woman to be the norm, they behave in ways that maximize their chances of securing such a relationship.

In summary, although men and women are very similar in many respects, they approach dating, mating, and marriage somewhat differently. They emphasize different traits in choosing partners, and they compete for partners using different tactics. These sex differences seem to be universal in that they are present across a very wide range of cultures. These differences also are predictable from a consideration of sex differences in parental investment.

Monogamy is an evolutionary novelty for humans, because polygyny was permitted everywhere until the last few hundred years. For this reason, both men and women often exhibit mixed reproductive strategies. That is, women and men have been designed by selection to form cooperating reproductive pairs, but also to monitor—and sometimes seize—opportunities for extra-pair copulation. Mixed reproductive strategies have in turn selected for counterstrategies in both sexes.

Over the course of development, culture seems to shape our expectations about the durability of pair bonds and the opportunities for extra-pair copulations. This facultative effect seems to shape the reproductive strategies of both sexes, leading them to behave in ways that maximize their chances of success, given their beliefs about prevailing mating patterns.

Summary

1. Sex differences generally evolve in species where females and males can reproduce at different rates.

2. Despite considerable male parental investment, humans exhibit sex differences in reproductive rate: females are the slower sex. Hence humans are likely to have evolved reproductively signifacant sex differences.

3. Among humans, as among other mammals, females are generally more selective about their sexual partners than males are.

4. People choose mates for at least two attributes: genetic quality and investment quality.

5. As predicted by the Red-Queen model, genetic quality is signaled by cues to parasite- and pathogen-resistance.

6. Humans seem to prefer both signs of absolute pathogen-resistance (as revealed by symmetry) and signs of complementarity in anti-pathogen strategy (as revealed by MHC-associated odors).

7. Women invest physiologically (as well as economically) in offspring, whereas men's investment is never physiological.

8. This difference in parental investment leads to sex differences in mate-choice criteria.

9. Compared to women, men place more emphasis on physical attractiveness of potential partners, and in this regard they seem to value indicators of high fertility, such as youth, health, and a low waist-hip ratio.

10. Compared to men, women place more emphasis on the resources and social dominance of potential partners.

11. These findings are crossculturally valid.

12. These patterns are not due to economic inequities between the sexes. For example, when women have high earning potential, they show no tendency to relax their standards; in fact they raise them, insisting on even wealthier partners.

13. Both women and men have the option of using mixed reproductive strategies.

14. For a woman, this would involve recruiting genes for her progeny from one man and parental investment from another.

15. For a man, this would involve having a primary mate in whose offspring he invests considerably and one or more secondary mates in whom he invests just enough to gain or maintain reproductive access.

16. Both men and women should have evolved to guard against the mixed reproductive strategies of the opposite sex.

17. Women are expected to guard against the loss of male parental investment to competitors.

18. Men are expected to guard against cuckoldry.

19. Patterns of jealousy, patterns of derogation of competitors, patterns of mating selectivity, and differential sensitivity to resemblance cues all support the idea that mixed strategies have been important during human evolution.

20. Both men and women set higher standards for marriage partners than for mere sex partners, with one exception: Women set higher physical-attractiveness standards for one-night-stand partners (when they can expect nothing but genes) than they do for husbands.

21. The tactics men and women use in competing for mates seem to be facultatively dependent on local levels of male parental investment.

13

Women's Mating Strategies

Elizabeth Cashdan

Key words: mating strategies, mate choice, sexual selection, women, aggression

What does a woman want? The traditional evolutionist's answer to Freud's famous query is that a woman's extensive investment in each of her children implies that she can maximize her fitness by restricting her sexual activity to one, or at most, a few high-quality males. Because acquiring resources for her offspring is of paramount importance, a woman will try to attract wealthy, high-status men who are willing and able to help her. She must be coy and choosy, limiting her attentions to men who are worthy of her and emphasizing her chastity so as not to threaten the paternity confidence of her mate.

The lady has been getting more complicated of late, however. As Sarah Hrdy predicted, we now have evidence that women, like other female primates, are also competitive, randy creatures. Women have been seen competing with their rivals using both physical aggression and more subtle derogation of competitors. While they are still sometimes coy and chaste, women have also been described recently as sexy and sometimes promiscuous creatures, manipulating fatherhood by the timing of orgasm and using their sexuality to garner resources from men.

The real answer to Freud's query, of course, is that a woman wants it all: a man with the resources and inclination to invest, and with genes that make him attractive to other women so that her sons will inherit his success. Her strategies for attaining these somewhat conflicting aims, and her success in doing so, are shaped by her own resources and options and by conflicts of interest with men and other women.

I begin this review by considering women's mating preferences unconstrained by resource limitation or conflicts of interest. The literature has only recently begun to tackle the interesting problem of how women get what they want in spite of other women who want the same thing and men whose preferences differ from theirs. Most of this paper is concerned with the trade-offs engendered by these conflicts of interest.

Evolutionary Anthropology by Elizabeth Cashdan. Copyright © 1990 Wiley-Liss, Inc., a Wiley Co. Reproduced with permission of John Wiley & Sons, Inc.

Elizabeth Cashdan is an Associate Professor of Anthropology at the University of Utah. This paper was completed at the King's College Research Centre, Cambridge University. She has conducted fieldwork among Kalahari foragers and food producers as well as Utah undergraduates. She is interested in human behavioral adaptation and the evolution of human nature. Cashdan@anthro.utah.edu

A caveat is in order before I explore these issues. The preferences and strategies discussed here are assumed to be evolved psychological tendencies. They are not necessarily conscious strategies, nor are they necessarily desirable, except within the limited framework of fitness maximization. Here, as elsewhere in evolutionary anthropology, the assumption is that natural selection has favored preferences and behaviors that maximize reproductive success. There is nothing in evolutionary theory to suggest that the route to high fitness is necessarily the route to happiness, or that it forms a useful guide for living.

What Type of Man Does a Woman Want?

Good Condition

Women, like men, want healthy mates. We might expect a man in good physical condition to be desirable both because he is likely to be a better provider than others and because the basis for his good health may be heritable, and hence of genetic benefit to offspring. The trouble, here as always, is how to detect an honest signal of good condition. Such a signal must be one that is not easily displayed by cheaters, either because it is sufficiently expensive that it cannot easily be faked or because failure to display it is a natural byproduct of ill health. The most intriguing example of the latter is the recent finding that women prefer males with low fluctuating asymmetry; the deviation from symmetry in bilateral features that are normally symmetrical, is assumed to result from disruptions in development that might be caused by parasites or environmental toxins. An individual with the genetic constitution to withstand such environmental insults will show less fluctuating asymmetry, and, other things being equal, should be favored as a mate.

Gangestad, Thornhill, and Yeo measured the bilateral asymmetry in seven nonfacial features in their subjects and took photographs of the subjects' faces. Subjects with the lowest fluctuating asymmetry were judged to have the most attractive faces, especially in women's judgments of men. Men with low fluctuating asymmetry also had more sexual partners, on the average, and had their first sexual encounter at an earlier age. Although it is not yet known what facial cues women are using to assess fluctuating asymmetry, it is clear that natural selection has shaped female preferences to be acute evaluative mechanisms for good condition in a mate.

Resources

Females in a wide variety of species (insects, birds, and mammals) prefer males with resources, and the same is true for humans. Buss's cross-cultural questionnaire study of 37 societies showed that women in all of them placed a higher value on the financial prospects of a prospective mate than men did, although the actual values were not as high as might be expected. Women cross-culturally also expressed a preference for mates who had attributes likely to correlate with financial success—maturity, ambition, and industriousness. Closer questioning of an American sample showed that women prefer immediate access to resources when seeking short-term matings but place greater value on cues to future resource acquisition when evaluating long-term mates.

If women act on these stated preferences, we would expect wealthy men to have more mates, and there is ample cross-cultural evidence that they do (see Low and citations therein). The importance of resources to women is apparent even in egalitarian societies such as the Ache and the Sharanahua, in which the best hunters are able to attract the most sexual partners.

The relationship between wealth and male mating success is consistent with female choice for wealthy males. However, this could also indicate differences in competitive ability among men, for a wealthy high-status man is more likely to out-compete his rivals for control over women. It is difficult to disentangle these causes of polygyny, and a discussion of this problem is beyond the scope of this paper. It seems likely, nevertheless, that female choice for wealthy, high-status males (or the choice of her kinsmen on her behalf) is an important factor in many polygynous societies. The best evidence that polygyny is a consequence of women's preferences for wealthy men is Borgerhoff Mulder's field work among the agro-pastoral Kipsigis. In a longitudinal study that followed the marriage histories of pioneers over 17 years, Borgerhoff Mulder showed that women new to the area were more likely to choose as husbands men who could offer them more land (i.e., land available to the prospective wife after division among existing wives). Total wealth (i.e., before division) was unrelated to a man's chances of getting a mate, which indicates that female choice rather than direct male competition is the key to polygamy in this society

Status

High-status men are wealthy men in a wide range of societies, from subsistence pastoralists and agriculturists to complex stratified states. However, status may hold other attractions as well. The children of high-status men may be treated better by others and may inherit the traits that led their father to high status. A powerful, high-status man may also be more likely to protect a woman from the unwanted attentions of other men.

It is not surprising, therefore, that women value indicators of status. Some of these indicators, such as large size, strength, and maturity, have ancient phylogenetic roots. Women cross-culturally prefer men who are taller and older than themselves. In our own society, tall men tend to be wealthier; the politically important "big men" in nonstate societies are sometimes described as being physically big as well. Maturity is also associated with higher status, at least in males, and this apparently translates into attractiveness in the eyes of women. Keating

manipulated various facial features, using the identification materials developed for police agencies, and found that women judge men with more mature facial features (a prominent jaw, bushy eyebrows, small eyes, and thin lips) to be both more dominant and more attractive. The female preference for testosterone-associated features such as broad shoulders relative to waist and hip size is probably also related to social dominance.

Chagnon has shown the importance of status, irrespective of its associated material benefits, for the Yanomamo. In this economically egalitarian population, men who have killed enemies have both higher status and more wives. At least some of this appears to be due to their greater attractiveness as mates.

While wealth and status may be attractive to women the world over, societies differ in the ways that wealth and status are attained. The particular traits most desired by women can be expected to vary accordingly. Hill and Hurtado have shown that male hunting success is associated with fertility among forest-living Ache foragers, whereas socio-economic status, but not hunting success, is associated with fertility on the reservation. They infer from this that "Ache women have probably shifted mate choice criteria from favoring good hunters to favoring those who accumulate resources through farming and wage labor" (p. 318).

Conflicts of Interest with Other Women

The ideal man is worth competing for, and women may use a variety of weapons to do so. Some methods are direct, such as hitting their opponent or spreading nasty rumors about them. Others are indirect, such as enticing men with the promise of fidelity, youthful attractiveness, and sometimes dowries. What circumstances favor these different tactics?

Direct Competition

Daly and Wilson have clearly shown that same-sex homicide is overwhelmingly a male affair, as would be expected in a polygynous species in which males compete more strongly for females than vice versa. Nonetheless, women sometimes do resort to violence against other women. In a cross-cultural survey, Burbank found that female-female aggression, when it did occur, usually took place between women who were competing for the attentions of a man. Cowives in polygynous societies are often reported to be hostile toward each other, particularly in agricultural, as opposed to pastoral, societies. Even in monogamous societies, jealousy among women can erupt into violence.

Accusations of promiscuity or infidelity are a frequent cause of female-female aggression. Campbell, who studied working-class British school girls, found that 73 percent of her sample had been involved in at least one fight with another girl, usually involving punching, kicking, or slapping. The most frequent cause of fighting among these girls, and among the youngest of the lower-class teenage girls studied by Marsh and Paton, was defense of a girl's integrity and sexual reputation. A reputation for fidelity clearly is important to a woman who wants to secure a long-term mate, because men are often unwilling to invest in a child who is not their own. Paternity issues, such as accusations that a rival's children have been fathered by many men, are a frequent cause of fighting among women on the Venezuelan island of Margarita. Even among American college women, derogation of female competitors usually takes the form of attacking the other woman's sexual reputation.

In her British samples, Campbell found that fighting, especially among older girls and women, was sometimes provoked by jealousy over a particular romantic partner. The same was true for the adult urban Zambian women studied by Schuster, among whom the chief cause of female-female aggression was fighting over a particular man. Schuster reported fierce competition in this society for high-status men and the resources they provide; one woman's attempts to attract another's man frequently resulted in violent aggression and sometimes serious injury.

My readers may be surprised at the level of female aggression reported by these authors, but most of you probably did not come of age in the types of communities these authors studied. What circumstances, then, are likely to make fighting worth the risk? Campbell argues that competitive aggression should be favored where women are able to choose their own mates, where there is a shortage of men, and where there is high variability in male quality. High effective variance in male quality should be exacerbated in stratified societies with socially imposed monogamy; shortage of males should be most acute in the lower classes of such societies, where male homicide rates are high and more males are in prison. Perhaps, then, the large number of same-sex fights among girls in working-class urban communities is not so surprising.

Yet there are unresolved questions about this picture. Why should teenage girls be more concerned with their reputations, whereas adult women are more likely to fight about getting and keeping a particular man? And why the concern with a reputation for fidelity in societies where male investment is low? Paternal investment has been described as being low in both Zambia and Margarita. It is also typically low in poor communities within complex societies, so the same may be true of the British schoolgirls. If so, why should these young women be concerned with a reputation for fidelity? Societies with low paternal investment are generally associated with sexual freedom for women. American women who expect little paternal investment are more likely to flaunt their sexuality than are women who expect to find investing men. Shouldn't the concern with a reputation for fidelity be more acute among the latter, and lower in societies such as Zambia and Margarita, where paternal investment is low? So why are women in societies with investing males less likely to fight? Two things that merit further consideration in answering these questions are how likely women are to form sexual relationships with other women's mates, and how age changes both what a woman wants and how much paternal investment she expects.

Adult women, both in the United States and Zambia, are in competition for material resources and the men who provide them. The Zambian sub-elite women studied by Schuster were described as being sexually assertive. The matrilineal tradition of most Zambian tribes suggests that paternal confidence would not be high even among more traditional Zambians. The same is likely to be true in the matrifocal communities found toward the bottom of the social ladder in stratified industrial societies. A woman in such a community, therefore, could expect many direct attempts by other women to attract her mate for a short-term relationship. Such attempts would be less of a threat to women in communities where male investment is high and women are less interested in short-term relationships. A larger number of sexually unrestricted competitors, rather than just a shortage of desirable men, may lie behind the greater female-female aggression found in communities with low male parental investment.

Among the young adolescent girls studied by Campbell and by Marsh and Paton, fighting over reputation may stem from age effects on their economic circumstances and their expectations of male investment. They presumably were living at home and perhaps were less in need of resources than they will be later. They may also have been more optimistic about securing the investment of a high-status mate. Schuster described the Zambian women she studied as being optimistic and "starry-eyed" when young, expecting "to find a handsome, wealthy, educated man and marry, then to go on to life in a big house, with the ideal four children . . ." After a series of disappointing encounters, however, they typically became tough, acquired a number of boyfriends, and became manipulative toward men. In the words of one jaded Zambian woman, "Why put all your eggs in one basket, especially since nearly all of them are rotten anyway?" (pp. 66–91). Concern with a good sexual reputation may have mattered when they were young, but the women faced other problems later. Optimism about finding a desirable mate has also been described among young women in Abidjan, Ivory Coast, for whom "youth is a temporary asset that they utilize to the fullest extent. [Among those who] have been befriended by more successful men . . . a particular combination of entrepreneurship and delusion often prevails" (p. 172).

A period of mating optimism among young adult women may be a regular feature of female psychology. A woman's reproductive value, and hence her chance of marrying upward in the social scale, is at its height when she is young. These odds may favor the type of sexual restraint and concern with sexual reputation that would make finding such a mate more likely. As a woman ages, particularly if she experiences disappointments that suggest she is unlikely to get what she wants, a shift in mating tactics may be expected. Schuster's informants, in other words, may have behaved quite rationally. It would be interesting to know if their experience is widely shared. There was a hint of this shift in Marsh and Paton's teenage girls. These authors reported that the younger girls were ambivalent about their aggressiveness because they were aware that it is not regarded as feminine, whereas the older teens were uninhibited about their aggressiveness and were not concerned about appearing unfeminine.

Indirect Competition

The literature paints a consistent picture of what a man wants in a woman: she should be young (at an age when her reproductive value is highest), beautiful (healthy, fertile, and young), chaste (except with him), and rich. She should also, though the evidence here is indirect, be careful not to threaten his reputation for dominance with his peers. One way in which women compete for men is to give them more of what they want.

Looking Youthful

Because youth and health are strong indicators of fertility, it is not surprising that smooth skin, good muscle tone, and other indicators of youth and health are considered attractive by men. Men the world over prefer and mate with women who are younger than they are. Furthermore, women with youthful facial features are judged to be the most attractive. Women who avail themselves of cosmetics and other beauty aids in a quest for "younger-looking skin," therefore, are rationally attempting to manipulate evolved male preferences. A figure with a small waist relative to hip size (low waist-hip ratio) is also judged to be particularly attractive, not only by American males and females, but by those in other ethnic groups as well. Low waist-hip ratio, an estrogen-dependent trait, is a particularly effective marker of good female condition because it is associated with both high fertility and low susceptibility to many degenerative diseases. Fashion, of course, has found many ways to mimic and exaggerate this trait.

Appearing Faithful

Because men are more willing to invest in offspring when they can be assured of their paternity, women have good reason to reassure them on this score. Mothers—but not fathers!—are more likely to report that their newborn infants look just like Dad. In societies where men invest heavily in their offspring, women are more likely to behave in ways that will ensure greater paternity confidence. Dickemann argued that concern about female chastity reaches a peak in highly stratified polygynous societies, in which "large numbers of beggars, outcasts, floater males, and celibates exist at the bottom while intense polygyny in the form of secondary wives, concubines, and harems occurs at the top." Extreme concern about female chastity is adaptive for husbands in these societies, not only because of high male investment but because of increased competition from a sea of unmated men with little to lose. It is noteworthy that claustration and other forms of sexual control are often enforced by women, not just by men. Clitoridectomy and infibulation, usually viewed as a form of male control over female sexuality, are performed on women by women. Mothers willingly put their daughters through these brutal procedures, presumably because without them their daughters will be unable to secure a desirable mate.

Dowry

Men worldwide value female beauty and fidelity, and it is reasonable to expect that women worldwide are concerned to advertise these traits, though to variable degrees. Sweetening the pot with economic incentives through dowry, however, is limited to comparatively few societies. Where do we find dowry, and why?

Dowry has been viewed as a form of female-female competition for high quality mates, and Gaulin and Boster predict that it should be found where such competition is most acute. What circumstances give rise to such intense competition? When resources held by males differ widely in quality, polygyny is normally favored; yet polygyny itself acts to mitigate these differences because wealthy males have to share their resources among more wives. The fiercest competition among women for desirable men, therefore, should be in societies that are both highly stratified and strictly monogamous. As predicted, Gaulin and Boster's cross-cultural analysis shows that the co-occurrence of stratification with socially imposed monogamy is the best predictor of dowry, although dowry is also found in the upper strata of some extremely stratified polygynous societies. We might wish to add to the criteria of stratification and socially imposed monogamy the additional one of degree of female dependence on male investment. Competition for investing mates should be most intense when the pay-offs of such investment are highest. Hence, greater economic independence of women might be expected to discourage the prevalence of dowry payments, even in monogamous, stratified societies. These arguments suggest that the direction of marriage payments may be a useful proxy for the relative strength of male-male versus female-female mate competition.

Conflicts of Interest with Men

Because males and females can best enhance their fitness in different ways, conflicts of interest between women and men are, unfortunately, an intrinsic part of the mating game. A man can enhance his fitness by investing in his children and maximizing his number of mates, but time and resources devoted to one interfere with the other. These trade-offs lead to variation in male strategies, with the polar types, in the words of Draper and Harpending, being "cads" (low-investment males seeking to maximize mating opportunities) and "dads" (high-investment males committed to one sexual partner).

The trade-offs facing men define the choices facing women. Should a woman try to secure an investing mate, who may have lower mate value in other respects, or should she content herself with getting good genes and immediate resources from a non-investing cad? She will have trouble doing both at the same time, because flaunting her sexuality, the behavior that attracts a cad, will put off a dad, who wants evidence of fidelity, and vice versa.

Having It Both Ways: Mixed Strategies

Recent research suggests that the difficulty of having it both ways is not always insurmountable. Women may try to get investment from one man while mating with another who is desirable in different respects. Baker and Bellis have found that when married women have affairs, matings with the "extra-pair" male occur

disproportionately during the woman's fertile period. This finding suggests that one goal of short-term matings for women is to secure "good genes" from another mate, and that women may use deception to play a mixed sexual strategy.

The detailed investigations of Baker and Bellis on human sexual behavior show that this strategy also exists on a more covert level. They have found that "high retention" female orgasms (those that lead to retention of the largest number of sperm) are those occurring between one minute before and forty-five minutes after the male's ejaculation. Questionnaire data from a large sample of women indicate that those who had extra-marital affairs were more likely to have high-retention orgasms with the extra-pair partner than with their regular mate. Baker and Bellis argue, further, that noncopulatory orgasms also affect sperm retention, thereby endowing women with considerable flexibility in attaining their reproductive aims. These data suggest, among other things, that males have good reason to be concerned about the sexual satisfaction of their partners.

The good-genes interpretation of short-term liaisons is supported by the finding that women place a higher value on physical attractiveness in a short-term partner than in a long-term mate. Other reasons that have been suggested for women's short-term matings are the securing of immediate resources, the promotion of sperm competition, the evaluation of men as prospective marriage partners, and enhanced survival of offspring through confusion of paternity.

Making a Choice: Sexual Restrictedness

Proximate Determinants

Male vigilance limits a woman's ability to play the mixed strategy I have described, and this forces her to make a choice. Should she flaunt her sexuality to win a high-quality cad (with good genes, immediate resources, and perhaps the possibility of changing his mind later) or should she advertise her fidelity and other charms to attract a long-term, investing dad? Gangestad and Simpson have measured how much time and commitment a woman requires before entering a sexual relationship (a variable they call sexual restrictedness), and have explored its genetic underpinnings with twin studies. They have argued that some of the personality traits underlying this behavior are heritable, and that the genetic variation is bimodally distributed. This finding is consistent with the notion that the costs and benefits of sexual restrictedness impose trade-offs, and that a woman may be better off trying to maximize one thing or the other.

There is also evidence supporting the role of early learning in sexual restrictedness, although it is difficult to separate this effect from genetic influence. Hetherington did behavior observation studies of "father-absent" adolescents (those whose mothers had divorced when they were very young) and compared them to adolescents whose fathers were present when they were growing up and to adolescents whose mothers were widowed rather than divorced. The girls who were father-absent due to divorce behaved more seductively toward men than did girls in either of the other two groups. These and related results have been interpreted as evidence of early learning of appropriate mating strategies. If true, the difference between daughters whose mothers were divorced and those whose mothers were widowed suggests that they are learning about men from their mothers, not from their fathers' absence per se. The lesson they are learning is, presumably, "Don't count on male investment—get what resources you can through short-term liaisons with high-status men." The proximate mechanisms leading to differences in sexual restrictedness may of course, be both genetic and environmental. Evidence for one does not rule out the other.

Adaptive Explanations

What factors favor these different female strategies? Much probably depends on a woman's other economic options. Much also depends on the likelihood that a woman will be able to secure an investing mate. In a study of undergraduates, I found that women were less likely to flaunt their sexuality and engage in sex with their romantic partners when their expectations of paternal investment were high. High expectations of paternal investment and its associated female mating strategies should be favored in the following circumstances: a) when the ratio of men to women is high, creating from the female perspective a "buyer's market;" b) other women are restricted in their sexuality, so that a man cannot obtain sexual access without investment; c) males are able to provide significant investment; and d) male investment significantly enhances the survival of offspring. There is some evidence in favor of these propositions, which I will discuss in turn.

Can males get what they want without having to invest? Low sex ratios make it more likely, because an excess of marriageable women in the relevant age brackets increases competition for males. The baby boom in the United States between 1946–1957 created such a situation. Women born during this period were seeking mates from the smaller cohort born a few years earlier. Guttentag and Secord have related this phenomenon to the sharp increase in illegitimate births, unmarried couples living together, divorce, and matrifocal families—all reflections of weakened commitment that began in the 1960s. The effects of the marriage squeeze have also been felt by South American (Hiwi and Ache) foragers. Among the Hiwi, a shortage of available women has promoted monogamy and high male investment in spite of relatively low returns from that investment, while the greater availability of women among the Ache has favored males with a low investment strategy. This is true in spite of the fact that fathers have a greater effect on offspring survival among the Ache than the Hiwi. This underscores the fact that a man's investment patterns are shaped as much by his other reproductive options as by the fitness returns on his investment.

Do males have the resources to invest? An inability to provide significant investment resulting from high unemployment has frequently been suggested as a factor promoting matrifocal families in the lower classes of stratified societies in the United States and elsewhere. On the other hand, where there is heterogeneity among the males available to a woman, a man with few material resources may compensate in other ways, such as by providing more direct care of infants and children. This appears to be the case for Aka foragers, among whom hunters who do less holding of infants are more likely than other men to have high status, an influential father, and multiple brothers.

Does paternal investment pay significant returns? This question is complicated by the fact that when men acquire and distribute resources, and perhaps even when they care directly for children, they may be doing so more to attract additional mates than to enhance the survival of their offspring. This raises the question of whether it is even appropriate to classify such behavior as "paternal investment." Irrespective of the father's motivation, however, the fitness benefits to offspring from a given amount of male effort should be lower when women are able to provide their children with abundant resources without the father's help. Such a woman should also be less willing to make compromises in the interest of securing male investment. For these reasons, we can expect economic self-sufficiency for women to be associated with higher divorce rates and greater female sexual freedom.

Economic independence from men can come from a woman's own efforts, from state aid (as in wealthy socialist countries), or from the help of female kin. Irons has argued that "marriage becomes attenuated when female coalitions are more effective at gaining what is scarce in a particular environment than are either individual men or male coalitions." The clearest example of this is found in matrilocal horticultural societies, where a woman's closest relationships typically are with her female kin, and where the women of the kin group are responsible for most of the food production. Matrilineal, matrilocal societies are famous for the independence of their women and for their comparative lack of concern with female chastity. The same dynamic appears to operate in matrifocal households in lower-class stratified societies. The unreliability of male support in these communities favors investment from maternal kin, particularly a woman's mother. In one poor black community with little male investment, women explicitly favored teen-age child-bearing because it enabled the child's grandmother to be young and healthy enough to take on the main child-rearing role.

The causal nature of the relationship between women's economic independence and low male investment could logically go both ways. Where a woman's economic independence comes from supportive female kin or from her own efforts in the labor market, it may sometimes be a response to low male investment (brought on by low sex ratios or unemployment) rather than a cause of it. The role of women's economic independence in causing lower male investment is perhaps most compelling in wealthy socialist countries such as Sweden, where economic independence is a result of state support. In Sweden "the taxpayers effectively provide what husbands formerly provided, freeing women from their economic dependence on men. Thus, practically no Swedish women are virgins at marriage and hence the value men place on chastity has commensurately declined to a worldwide low" (pp. 68–69).

Making a Choice: Competing against Men

Women may find the combination of economic self-sufficiency and an investing, long-term mate to be desirable but difficult to attain. Men should be less likely to invest when returns on their investment are small, as they are likely to be if the mother is economically self-sufficient. In addition, maturity, dominance, and successful competition with men, the very traits that favor economic success, may make her less attractive as a mate if they threaten the man's status with his peers.

There is some evidence that mature features in a woman inhibit both sexual interest and investment from men. Women with youthful facial features are, as we have seen, judged to be more attractive. But attractive for what? Cunningham found that a set of neonatal facial features (large eyes, small nose and chin) as well as two mature facial features (narrow cheeks and wide cheekbones) made women more attractive to his American male subjects. The subjects reported that they would also be more likely to hire women with these features for a job. However, only the neonatal features, not the mature ones, made a woman more attractive for sex and more likely to elicit male monetary investment, physical risk, and self-sacrifice. It is not clear whether youthful features have this effect because they signal high reproductive value or because neonatal features elicit caretaking (or both), but the fact that they do suggests that women face a dilemma.

This dilemma is even more clearly seen in the self-deprecating behavior that women often display around males. Women and girls have been found to perform less well when competing against males than when competing in all-female groups. This has been shown for a variety of tasks, both stereotypically masculine and sex-neutral (see review by Weisfeld). Women also use more subordinate body postures in mixed-sex than in same-sex group discussions, and girls from coed elementary schools are less likely to overrate their toughness than are girls in all-girls' schools.

I have considered the possibility that this type of behavior advertises a woman's need for investment. Some of my data support this expectation; for example, women who expect little paternal investment are more likely than other women to display their own competence and resources as a way of attracting a mate. However, the hypothesis was not well supported by other data from my study. Another plausible explanation is that a woman who is more suc-cessful than her mate threatens his position in the male hierarchy. In other words, economic success may make a woman an attractive mate but, in the process of attaining it, she must be careful not to threaten her man's status, particularly when other men are watching. Either explanation poses a dilemma between the attainment of economic self-sufficiency and the acquisition of a desirable mate. As with the dilemma about sexual restrictiveness (should she flaunt sexuality to attract many short-term mates or advertise fidelity to attract a long-term one?), a woman's best strategy here may depend on her chances of finding an investing mate as well as on her own resources and competitive ability.

Conclusion

We have learned a great deal in the last decade about what women want in a mate. It is clear that women value wealthy, high-status men in good physical condition, both for the resources such men can provide and for the genetic quality they can give offspring. Women particularly value high-quality men who are willing as well as able to invest.

Much less research has focused on how women secure such a mate in the face of competition from other women and conflicts of interest with the men they seek. We have known for a long time that one way women compete with other women is by making themselves more attractive. We are now learning that women also compete more directly, and that physical aggression is part of the repertoire. The challenge in both cases is understanding when women choose one competitive "weapon" over another. Thus far, it appears that physical aggression may be favored in populations where there is a shortage of desirable mates and an abundance of women desirous of short-term liaisons with a variety of men.

Women face conflicts of interest with men also, for men are better able to maximize their reproductive success by mating with a variety of women. In search of this aim, men will be attracted to youthful, sexually unrestricted women, but may be unwilling to invest in a woman's offspring unless she can assure him that the children are his. He will be attracted to an economically independent woman but he may be less likely to invest in her, and he will not want his status with his peers to be threatened by her pursuit of economic success. Women sometimes try to get around these trade-offs by playing a mixed sexual strategy, but male vigilance places limits on this ability and imposes choices. Should a woman compete openly with men, which will enhance her economic independence but may make her less desirable as a mate? Should she flaunt her sexuality, which will attract males but at the risk of losing a male's continued investment? Here, too, the challenge is understanding the factors that favor one strategy over the other. In general, it appears that a woman's optimal strategy will be affected by her other economic options and by her expectations of paternal investment. There is evidence that the likelihood of male investment is affected by the sex ratio, the sexual restrictiveness of other women, the economic position of the men she is able to attract, and the payoffs to male investment. We are only just beginning to understand how women's strategies are shaped by these factors. Clarifying this matter remains the primary challenge for future research.

Acknowledgments

I am grateful to Kristen Hawkes, Sarah Hrdy, Eric Smith, Alan Rogers, Randy Thornhill, and Margo Wilson for their suggestions and comments.

References

Aries E (1982) Verbal and nonverbal behavior in single-sex and mixed-sex groups: Are traditional sex roles changing? *Psychol Reports* 51:127–134.

Baker R R, Bellis M A (1993) Human sperm competition: Ejaculate manipulation by females and a function for the female orgasm. *Anim Behav* 46:887–909.

Baker R R, Bellis M (1995) *Human Sperm Competition: Copulation, Masturbation and Infidelity.* New York: Chapman and Hall.

Bellis M A, Baker R R (1990) Do females promote sperm competition? Data for humans. *Anim Behav* 40:997–999.

Belsky J, Steinberg L, Draper P (1991) Childhood experience, interpersonal development, and reproductive strategy: An evolutionary theory of socialization. *Child Dev* 62:647–70.

Betzig L (1986) *Darwinism and Differential Reproduction: A Darwinian View of History.* Hawthorne, NY: Aldine de Gruyter.

Borgerhoff Mulder M (1987) On cultural and reproductive success: Kipsigis evidence. *Am Anthropol* 89:617–634.

Borgerhoff Mulder M (1990) Kipsigis women prefer wealthy men: Evidence for female choice in mammals? *Behav Ecol Sociobiol* 27:255–264.

Borgerhoff Mulder M (1992) Women's strategies in polygynous marriage: Kipsigis, Datoga, and other East African cases. *Hum Nat* 3:45–70.

Burbank V (1987) Female aggression in cross-cultural perspective. *Behav Sci Res* 21:70–100.

Burton L W (1990) Teenage childbearing as an alternative life-course strategy in multigenerational black families. *Hum Nat* 1:123–143.

Buss D M (1989) Sex differences in human mate preferences: Evolutionary hypotheses tested in 37 cultures. *Behav Brain Sci* 12:1–49.

Buss D M (1994) *The Evolution of Desire: Strategies of Human Mating.* New York: Basic Books.

Buss D M, Dedden L A (1990) Derogation of competitors. *J Social Personal Rel* 7:395–422.

Buss D M, Schmitt D P (1993) Sexual strategies theory: An evolutionary perspective on human mating. *Psychol Rev* 100:204–232.

Campbell A (1995) A Few Good Men: Evolutionary psychology and female adolescent aggression. *Ethol Sociobiol* 16:99–123.

Cashdan E (1993) Attracting mates: Effects of paternal investment on mate attraction strategies. *Ethol Sociobiol* 14:1–24.

Chagnon N (1988) Life histories, blood revenge, and warfare in a tribal population. *Science* 239:985–992.

Cook H B K (1992) Matrifocality and aggression in Magariteño society. In Björqvist K, Niemelä P (eds), *Of Mice and Women: Aspects of Female Aggression*, pp 149–162. San Diego: Academic Press.

Cunningham M R (1986) Measuring the physical in physical attractiveness: Quasi-experiments on the sociobiology of female facial beauty. *J Pers Soc Psychol* 50:925–935.

Daly M, Wilson M (1983) *Sex, Evolution and Behavior* (second ed). Boston MA: Willard Grant.

Daly M, Wilson M (1988) *Homicide*. Hawthorne, NY: Aldine de Gruyter.

Daly M, Wilson M I (1982) Whom are newborn babies said to resemble? *Ethol Sociobiol* 3:69–78.

Dickemann M (1981) Paternal confidence and dowry competition: A biocultural analysis of purdah. In Alexander R D, Tinkle D W (eds), *Natural Selection and Social Behavior*, pp 417–438. New York: Chrion Press.

Draper P, Harpending H H (1982) Father-absence and reproductive strategy: An evolutionary perspective. *J Anthropol Res* 38:255–273.

Ellis B J (1992) The evolution of sexual attraction: Evaluative mechanisms in women. In Barkow, Cosmides L, Tooby J (eds*)*, *The Adapted Mind: Evolutionary, Psychology and the Generation of Culture*, pp 267–288. New York: Oxford University Press.

Gangestad S N V, Simpson J A (1990) Toward an evolutionary history of female sociosexual variation. *J Pers* 58:69–96.

Gangestad S W, Thornhill R, Yeo R A (1994) Facial attractiveness, developmental stability, and fluctuating asymmetry. *Ethol Sociobiol* 15:73–85.

Gaulin S J C, Boster J S (1990). Dowry as female competition. *Am Anthropol* 93:994–1003.

Gaulin S J C, Schlegel A (1980) Paternal confidence and paternal investment: A cross-cultural test of a sociobiological hypothesis. *Ethol Sociobiol* 1:301–309.

Guttentag M, Secord P F (1983) *Too Many Women? The Sex Ratio Question*. Beverly Hills: Sage.

Hartung J (1985) Matrilineal inheritance: New theory and analysis. *Behav Brain Sci* R:661–688.

Hawkes K (1996) Foraging differences between men and women: Behavioral ecology of the sexual division of labor. In Steele J, Shennan S (eds), *The Archaeology of Human Ancestry*, pp 283–305. New York: Routledge.

Hetherington E M (1972) Effects of father absence on personality development in adolescent daughters. *Dev Psychol* 7:313–326.

Hewlett B S (1988) Sexual selection and paternal investment among Aka pygmies. In Betzig L, Borgerhoff Mulder M, Turke P (eds), *Human Reproductive Behaviour: A Darwinian Perspective* pp 263–276. Cambridge: Cambridge University Press.

Hill K, Hurtado A M (1996) *Ache Life History: The Ecology and Demography of a Foraging People*. Hawthorne, New York: Aldine de Gruyter.

Horvath T (1979) Correlates of physical beauty in men and women. *Social Behav Pers* 7:145–151.

Hrdy S B (1981) *The Woman that Never Evolved*. Cambridge, MA: Harvard University Press.

Hurtado A M, Hill K R (1992) Paternal effect on offspring survivorship among Ache and Hiwi hunter-gatherers: Implications for modeling pair-bond stability: In Hewlett B (ed), *Father-Child Relations: Cultural and Biosocial Contexts*, pp 31–55. Hawthorn, NY: Aldine de Gruyter.

Irons W (1979) Cultural and biological success. In Chagnon N, Irons W (eds), *Evolutionary Biology and Human Social Behavior: An Anthropotogical Perspective*, pp 257–272. North Scituate, MA: Duxbury Press.

Irons W (1983) Human female reproductive strategies. In Wasser S K (ed), *Social Behavior of Female Vertebrates*, pp 169–213. New York: Academic Press.

Jones D (1995) Sexual selection, physical attractiveness, and facial neoteny: Cross-cultural evidence and implications. *Curr Anthropol* 36:723–748.

Kaplan H, Hill K (1985) Hunting ability and reproductive success among male Ache foragers. *Curr Anthropol* 26:131–133.

Keating C (1985) Human dominance signals: The primate in us. In Ellyson S L, Dovidio J F (eds), *Power, Dominance and Nonverbal Behavior*. New York: Springer-Verlag.

Lewis B (1977) Economic activity and marriage among Ivoirian urban women. In Schlegel A (ed), *Sexual Stratification: A Cross-Cultural View*, pp 161–91. New York: Columbia University Press.

Low B S (1993) Ecological demography: A synthetic focus in evolutionary anthropology. *Evol Anthropol* 1:177–187.

Marsh P, Paton R (1986) Gender, social class and conceptual schemas of aggression. In Campbell A, Gibbs J J (eds), *Violent Transactions: The Limits of Personality*. New York: Basil Blackwell.

Martin M K, Voorhies B (1975) *Female of the Species*. New York: Columbia University Press.

Parker R, Omark D R (1980) The social ecology of toughness. In Omark D R, Strayer F F, Freedman D G (eds), *Dominance Relations: An Ethological View of Human Conflict and Social Interaction*, pp 415–426, New York: Garland STPM Press.

Schuster I (1983) Women's aggression: An African case study. *Aggressive Behav* 9:319–331.

Schuster I M G (1979) *New Women of Lusaka.* Palo Alto, CA: Mayfield Publishing.

Singh D (1993) Body shape and women's attractiveness: The critical role of waist-to-hip ratio. *Hum Nat* 4:297–321.

Singh D, Luis S (1994) Ethnic and gender consensus for the effect of waist-to-hip ratio on judgement of women's attractiveness. *Hum Nat* 6:51–65.

Siskind J (1973) *To Hunt in The Morning.* New York. Oxford University-Press.

Smuts B B (1992) Male aggression against women: An evolutionary perspective. *Hum Nat* 3: 1–44.

Smuts B B, Gubernick D J (1992) Male-infant relationships in nonhuman primates: Paternal investment or mating effort? In Hewlett B (ed), *Father-Child Relations: Cultural and Biosocial Contexts,* pp 1–30. Hawthorn, New York: Aldine de Gruyter.

Symons D (1979) *The Evolution of Human Sexuality,* pp 158–165. New York: Oxford University Press.

Symons D (1995) Beauty is in the adaptations of the beholder: The evolutionary psychology of human female sexual attractiveness. In Abramson P R, Pinkerton S D (eds), *Sexual Nature Sexual Culture,* pp 80–118. Chicago: University of Chicago Press.

Thornhill R, Gangestad S W (1994) Human fluctuating asymmetry and sexual behavior. *Psychol Sci* 5:297–302.

Weisfeld C C (1986) Female behavior in mixed-sex competition: A review of the literature. *Dev Rev* 6:278–299.

14

Notions of Love and Romance among the Taita of Kenya

Jim Bell

Throughout the nineteenth and twentieth centuries a prevailing European image of Africa held that the native was nonhuman and thus driven entirely by animalistic desires for sexual satisfaction. This image, which Katherine George (1958) calls "antagonistic fantasy," found its strongest voice in the works of some Western missionaries (Hulstaert 1938; Johnston 1911; Lugard 1904; MacDonald 1916; Noble 1899; and others). Their early accounts of daily African life are filled with tales of lust and other forms of "sexual debauchery." They are silent, however, about the presence of passionate love. For most it was a moot point: the African was not capable of experiencing passionate love, so there was nothing to discuss.

The proper business of missionaries was to save souls, which meant that they had to instruct the Africans on how to live according to the Christian ideals of family and virtue. They seldom were successful in this endeavor. Donald Fraser's (1928) account of Africans' inability to achieve the Western ideal of good family is highly representative. He writes:

In spite of all that we have said of the magical sanctions which preserve a comparatively high fidelity between husband and wife in primitive African society, the standards of social purity are shockingly low. The cases that demand most of the attention of the native and magisterial courts are breaches of the seventh commandment [adultery is forbidden] (1928:107).

Another missionary, Ellen Parsons (1906), working among the Taveta (a close neighbor of the Taita), also noted similar behavior. She writes:

One great hindrance stood in the way—sensuality. The awfulness of the bondage to the flesh in which the people are enthralled only incites their teachers the more to point them to Christ the Liberator, for He is able to so renew their minds that even they can learn to say, "In thy presence is fullness of joy; at thy right hand are pleasures for evermore." (1906:173)

The Christian obsession with "proper" family structure and sexual behavior prevented a clear understanding of romance among Africans. In many ways this misunderstanding, first expressed in the early missionary accounts, continues as a predominant Euro-American image of Africa (Jablow and Hammond 1977:16).

In this essay I examine the ideal of lust, love and romance, as they are remembered, lived, and performed among the Taita (sometimes also referred to as the Wataita, or Wadawida) of Kenya, East Africa. I argue that the notion of marriage for love (or passionate love) may not be new to Taita culture and might not depend on European contact. Rather, passionate love or romantic love existed before the arrival of what Ali Mazrui (1986) calls "European Christianity" and, as such, has been an integral part of African culture.

Missionaries and the Development of Passionate Love

For most missionaries the primary evil in African society was the widespread custom of females and males becoming deeply involved with one another (for whatever reason and on whatever terms) *outside* the institution of *monogamous* marriage—with an equal emphasis on both words: *outside* and *monogamous*. This emphasis on standard marriage and monogamy services to blur the notion of romantic love.

The religious preoccupation with monogamous marriage helped to prevent recognition of an important human phenomenon. Because the missionaries favored monogamous marriage over polygynous marriage, they actively sought to persuade all converts of the cultural and religious superiority of monogamy through the introduction of symbols and rituals that glorified monogamous marriage. In this way early missionaries (cf. Clark 1890, Lovett 1899, Parsons 1906, Thomas 1885, and others) who toiled in the African bush strove to introduce a number of Western-inspired cultural features, including certain forms of romantic expression, into contemporary African marriage and daily life.

The words "love, honor, and obey" in the marriage rite is one such introduction. Promotion of monogamous marriage was initiated with the moral imperative to "cleave to one wife or husband." Further evidence of the missionaries' misunderstanding of the variety of expressions that love can take, both inside and outside of marriage, can be found in their depictions of polygynous marriage among the Kikuyu. The missionaries believed this practice was based on the principle that women were chattel. Jomo Kenyatta, a Kikuyu who was also Oxford-educated, insists, however, that the "*Gikuyu* [or Kikuyu] have always been free to choose a mate without any interference on the part of the parents on either side" (Kenyatta 1959:165). He further insists that in traditional Kikuyu society "love" was a strong motive in mate selection. Kenyatta also notes that when a "boy falls in love with a girl he cannot tell her directly that he loves her or display his devotion to her in public, as this would be regarded by Gikuyu as impolite and uncultured" (1959:165). The early missionaries were ignorant of such customs of public decorum and politeness.

I found among the Taita a similar attitude toward choice and public decorum. For example, younger Taita women prefer becoming involved with what they call a "chosen lover," usually a member of their age group. Many of these involvements arise out of a sense of deep affection, physical attraction, romantic love, or a mixture of all three. In the last case, some of these relationships last a lifetime. Given the missionaries' obsession with reporting on the "native's" sexual behavior, this type of love arrangement was, perhaps, predictably, condemned in some accounts and curiously ignored in others.

For the Taita two cultural features are important: 1) European missionaries tried to change the indigenous ideals of marriage and love affairs. Marriage practices have changed; polygyny, however, remains a popular institution. 2) Romantic love appears to have always been part of Taita history. Consequently, love affairs (and not just sexual liaisons) are a regular fact of daily Taita life. As one old and thoughtful grandmother informed me, "Lovers will continue to walk the hills of Dawida (the mountain range in which she lives)."

Lust, Love, and Beauty in the Taita Hills

The Taita are highland farmers who have inhabited a mountainous area in southern Kenya for four or five hundred years. During this period the Taita have engaged in wars with the nomadic Maasai and the slave-trading Arab and Swahili peoples from the coast. In addition, the culture has, for at least 140 years, sought to assimilate and accommodate European missionary efforts to alter their view of the world. These efforts have led to the adoption of certain Western linguistic expressions like *love* and *lust*. Nevertheless, Taita informants assert that prior to European contact *ashiki* (lust) and *pendo* (love) were terms already in existence. It would stand to reason therefore that just as these experiences were found in European cultures before the French coined the word romance in the twelfth century, the emotions underlying them would have existed before the linguistic invention of the term itself. Although the Taita have adopted many aspects of Christian cosmology, which frame and filter their descriptions and accounts of lust, love, and romance, their adoptions only constitute a gloss over indigenous human sentiments. In short, the terminology reflects feelings of private experience that have always been present, if not warmly celebrated, in Taita culture.

An examination of East African folklore finds that there are only a few pre-contact tales of romance. Because folklorists initially showed some interest in narratives of subsistence and warfare tales, they did not collect very many love tales. The small number of love stories collected does not therefore mean that the sentiment was foreign to the Taita. It only suggests that the phenomenon was ignored by earlier students of Africa and, in particular, students of the Taita. When the folklore of the entire region is analyzed, I suspect that future folklorists will find the Taita to be correct in their contention that the lack of East African love stories is due to the failure of previous anthropologists to identify the presence of romantic love, and is, thus, more a product of ethnographic oversight than the lack of indigenous desire or interest.

The Ideal Mate: Beauty as a Factor in Love and Marriage

Observers of polygynous family life often ignore the fact that within the nuclear family each co-wife and her offspring form their own social unit. For centuries the Taita have practiced arranged marriages, which advance the interests of the larger family group. The criteria for these marriages seldom focus on an individual's physical beauty. Rather, the senior generation looks for evidence of health and an accommodating personality. Individual desire is deemed irrelevant. It is understood by everyone that the welfare of the family, and not the individual, is the primary objective of arranged marriages. Nevertheless, Taita males have definite ideas of female beauty, and beauty plays no small part in the selection of a mate. Although there are differences in opinion, there is a general consensus over what constitutes a beautiful woman. Many young men describe their ideal mate as possessing the following attributes:

A full face, with "bright eyes and a pretty nose that flares broad on the face." She should "have a full mouth and thick lips, with a large smile, white teeth, and fresh breath." Her neck should "possess

smoothness and be thick near the shoulders."
Together these features "make for a pleasant
woman to look upon." In addition, a beautiful
woman has soft skin and "delicate eyes and sharp
cheeks (high cheek-bones)." The last feature is a
sign of "a woman who will love you for life."
Finally, her ears should be small and close to the
head. The young males were all certain that these
particular features of beauty are self-evident and,
thus, universal.

Women's hair, never heretofore a specially expressed element of beauty among the Taita, today has a place in the attributes of beauty looked for by young men. Some young men expressed preference for the traditional close-cropped head, where the shape of the head is clearly seen and the hair is clean and shiny. Others preferred long hair, plated in some style resembling the European styles commonly seen in magazines. Either way, the face and neck must be accentuated.

The eyes, as mentioned, should be "delicate" and reflect what many young men claim is "the heart of the girl's mind." The darker the eyes, the better. Since the Taita are a combination of several different East African ethnic groups, some have light brown eye coloring while others exhibit the almost olive-shaped black eyes found among coastal peoples. It is the dark-eyed women that young men find so attractive. A young man in his early twenties told me, "Such eyes of a woman speak of love in late evening, just prior to the setting of the sun."

The ideal body shape of a beautiful female is hefty overall, with large breasts (for feeding children), thick legs, and small ankles. She should walk "as if floating in the air" and "she should smell of fresh flowers always." Her buttocks "should be round and firm, moving to the sway of her hips in such a manner as to appear to be in a dance as she walks." Finally, all agreed that the women must have a pleasing personality. Such a personality is a sign of great beauty.[1]

A Female View of Males as Love Objects

Taita females, also have an image of the "ideal" man. Young women (fifteen to twenty years old) spoke of the men they *would like* to marry, although most admitted it would be unlikely they would have such a husband. The ideal man for a few Taita women is someone who is honest and kind. Others thought the ideal man should be "tall and handsome." Everyone interviewed stressed that a husband should be intelligent and a good farmer/provider. Clearly, a male's physical attractiveness is not as important as how he interacts with his wife and how he treats her. Some of the informants, however, believed that a man could enhance his manliness if he bathed everyday (an activity Taita women do daily). A man should have "a strong look to his face, with no hair on it." Facial hair connotes a dirty person. Or as several informants put it, "white men have hair on their face and they are dirty for that reason."

The ideal man's eyes "should shine with life like the morning sun on the grasses." His mouth "should smile often to reveal his kind nature." One young woman told me, "Some men believe they must speak in a loud voice, but a man should speak in a low tone so others will respect him." His head "should have a close cut with the hair. It should be kept clean and carefully managed." Men should possess "a thick neck so as to carry his head in a proud manner."

Most women were not as forthcoming about the ideal male body (perhaps because I was male and a foreigner). Nevertheless, a few women of various ages did agree that a male must not have small genitals or a penis that is too large. In addition, "his arms and legs should show musculature, and he should be the dark color of the sky before sunrise (a copper brown or a reddish brown), with dark eyes."

In the main, both males and females hold different ideals of beauty and personality that influence the choice of lovers they select, or would select, if completely free to do so. Males emphasize physical attributes, whereas females, as in our society, focus on personality and social standing. Both Taita men and women prefer a lover who exhibits the proper cultural graces.

Love and Romance among the Taita

My Taita informants distinguished between three kinds of love that are commonly found within their gender interactions outside of arranged marriages, from childhood through adult courtship rituals. Each kind has a different style of romantic expression. It must be noted that such emotions are considered by the Taita to have been present before European contact. Since contact occurred more than 140 years ago, it is difficult to corroborate my informants' statements. It is important to note, however, that many older Taita believe the introduction of English only provided convenient terms to express the emotions. I assume that myth and reality may cross somewhere back in time. The first kind of love is infatuation (what we might call puppy love), which is characterized by an irresponsible feeling of longing and deep attraction toward another person. It resembles in every way Western notions of passionate (or romantic) love. However, the Taita do not, as such, make this distinction. Moreover, it is the senior generation who insist that this type of love passion is nothing more than a misguided infatuation, "a kind of sickness." This kind of love tends to occur in the early stages of life (around ten to eleven years old), usually lasts only a few weeks or months, and then disappears forever.

A second notion of love closely resembles lust. This condition arises whenever someone desires another sexually. Although the Taita believe that relationships based entirely on sexual desire are a form of love, they acknowledge that this is not romantic love and seldom lasts for a long time.

For both men and women cultural restrictions in mate selection contribute to the production of erotic fantasies. Many young (eighteen-through twenty-four-year-old) Taita males, for example, experience a sexual desire for a woman (in their thirties through forties) just slightly younger than their mothers. To fulfill their sexual fantasy, some males engage prostitutes in this age group. Conversely, young females (fifteen through seventeen) prefer males who are their age mates (eighteen through twenty-two) but whom they will rarely marry.

The third kind of love is called romantic love, which is used to connote those relationships that combine passion and enduring affection. It differs from infatuation in being a more permanent affectionate bond. The Taita, at the beginning of the relationship, however, cannot determine whether it is driven by infatuation or genuine romantic sentiment. In this way the Taita notion of romantic love incorporates images of companionate love (or attachment love) and passionate love (or romantic love).

The Taita, however, never refer—at least in conversation—to this kind of love sentiment as companionship love but insist instead on calling it romantic love. Romantic love, the "love for life," or "love out of the heart," etc., is love that the younger Taita can often observe between a father and a "favorite wife." It is based upon deep admiration and intense affection for one another.

Many young informants believe it is "the best kind of love" and, as such, constitutes one of the primary life goals. Young males readily pointed out that this love can be a motive for fathers (i.e., any male relative who is in their father's generation) marrying a second, third, or fourth wife.

Young females also spoke in envy over the "luck" of older siblings who married for love. Even when a couple involved cannot marry, they often continued their affair for years. Several parents informed me that they knew of many such affairs in the community. One important point is that love is considered a valid motive for entering into both a short- and a long-term relationship. Therefore, not every Taita marriage is organized around a concern with alliance building or economic necessity. Marriages can and do arise out of momentary infatuation and long-lasting romantic commitment.

Lovers and Other Strangers: Affairs and Marriage

Taita culture is organized around a patrilineal descent and residence system that honors, as an ideal, the larger lineage over the individual interests. The Taita are not atypical in this regard. According to David Maybury-Lewis,

> Many traditional societies recognize and value the kind of passion that our love stories are made of. They encourage it, but they contrive to keep it distinct from their formal marriage arrangements. They try to ensure that it does not destroy the lives of the lovesick or those around them, and above all, they try to prevent personal passion from disturbing the social order (1992:100).

Unmarried Taita are not allowed to carry their love interests too far. To do otherwise might undermine their commitment to the family. Taita men therefore strive primarily, but not always, to meet their familial obligations in the first marriage and thus fulfill their duties to the lineage. Once those duties are achieved, however, romantic passion can, and often does, become a primary consideration in selecting a new wife. This sentiment can arise both inside

and outside of marriage. In fact, several Taita, who had arranged marriages, were romantically indifferent to their wife while passionately committed to their "outside lover." Many Taita admit to wanting, from time to time, to be involved with a particular person, but few admit to having done so. When these "affairs of the heart" did arise, however, they were unexpected and often directed toward someone unattainable. One informant remarked that "it can happen that your heart is lost to one you can never marry, but you love that person for your life." A middle-aged parent concurred, saying that "this notion is not a rare one." Many older men expressed their love for a woman who "belonged to another man." Some informants assured me that they had lovers elsewhere or that some of the children I had interviewed were the offspring of lovers who "played in the forest together." Such affairs of love and romance are not new to Africa or the Taita Hills.

David Maybury-Lewis, speaking of affairs among the Wodaabe of West Africa, notes the commonality and acceptance of them, and summarizes Wodaabe attitudes meant to help maintain social order: "What the eyes do not see did not happen, which means that rumors and suspicions have to be ignored" (1992:102). The Taita are extremely covert in their extramarital affairs and they have a somewhat elaborate set of rules similar to those found among the Wodaabe. Taita lovers, being discreet, seldom even hint at duplicity in public. Whenever they meet they act as if they are strangers. Or, to paraphrase Maybury-Lewis, "What people cannot imagine cannot be rumor or suspicion."

In sum, Taita seek to balance individual desires and family duty by insisting there are different motives for marriage.[2] They also strive to allow individual desires to be expressed without undermining the prevailing social order. The first and, perhaps, the second marriage may honor family obligations; thereafter a man's lust and/or love interest *can* constitute the primary motivation for taking a new bride. In this way, both the so-called lovesick that Maybury-Lewis discusses and the needs of "the social order" are fulfilled.

Old Ladies and Old Men Tell of Better Days

I came to know many older people (sixty to eighty years old) in my travels around the Taita Hills. Whenever I engaged in conversations about love and romance with younger people, older people noted that they had either experienced or knew someone who had been involved in a romantic encounter in their youth. What follows is a brief sample of Taita senior citizens' remembrances of love lost.

A woman, in her middle seventies, reported that she was infatuated with three or four men at different times during her early teenage years. Her father had, however, arranged a marriage for her with one of *his* peers. She had eight children. She recalled:

> *A man from a highland village (nearer to her own age) was my lover. My husband would leave me for months at a time, and I would travel at night to a place we [she and her lover] would meet and "play in the forest" for plenty of time. My husband never caught me, and only one of my sisters (co-wives) knew of this. She would not reveal me because I had once caught her with her lover in the act.*

Several old men remembered their affairs in sharp detail, as though they happened yesterday rather than some forty or fifty years earlier. One gentleman, nearly eighty years of age, described his fourth wife:

> *She was the wife of my heart. We were almost similar in age. I loved her in the early days when she was married to another. Her family had arranged it that way. When she was widowed and I passed my stages and become an elder, I married her out of love. She and I had love. I would sit with her for hours on that hill (pointing to a hill behind his homestead). I could look at her and she at me—no words would pass, just a smile. We did this for several years before she died.*

A woman, also in her seventies, stressed (through an interpreter) that "even when I was a young girl, women were having babies before marriage. And others had lovers in the forest after marriage. That which we speak of at the moment is not a new thing. It has always been here."

In this informal survey older people were quite open about their views on lust and love. Some felt it was acceptable for people to experiment with sex. Others thought it was rude and bad for people, especially girls. Young girls who become pregnant by lovers before marriage often reduced their bride price. Still, such "accidents" do not usually prevent the girl from entering into an arranged marriage. All of the older people I spoke with agreed that this is no longer as serious a situation as it was when they were young. Time, apparently, has changed the attitudes toward unwed mothers.

The Politics of Romance among the Taita

In the literature on African polygynous systems, there is some mention of the favorite wife, but little is detailed as to what makes her "favorite." Is this status related to love, economic arrangement, family association, or clan politics? The Taita believe such a concept evolves around "love out of the heart." Some males indicated that a favorite wife could include some economic attachment to prime landholdings or business dealings; only a few men in the older generation conceded such economic considerations in the designation of favorite wife. Instead, as a rule, most Taita asserted that favorite status goes to the woman who is the man's true love, or, in some cases, to the woman whom the husband finds more sexually pleasing. Either love or sexuality could be the basis for the status, but most Taita men and women believed it indicated true love.

Another consideration must account for the role of the favorite wife with in the context of the co-wife relationship. She must get along with the other women of the family with whom she shares a husband and a life. Co-wives usually try to maintain cooperative unions with one another. They attempt to secure the other wives as allies, attempting to set up clear working relationships while striving for peace and harmony within the larger family unit. This serves them well in times of emotional and physical difficulties (i.e., sickness, birth, or the death of a child). The wife who has married out of love may be the husband's favorite wife, and the husband may love her more than any of the others, but he cannot allow her to supplant the authority and status of the other wives, especially that of the first wife. Other members of the extended family will also not allow it. Such an obvious show of disrespect and breach of decorum toward the first wife, her family, those other wives who came before the favorite, and their families would challenge the social order prized by the Taita. It is important to note that the wives' families share in the favorite's honor or dishonor after marriage. For a wife to lose her honor, or status, within her husband's family is a loss of status and honor for her birth family as well. Since these other marriages were arranged and, in the course of daily life, formed alliances with other family groups, it is extremely vital to foster good relations with a wife's family. Loss of honor can also result in a loss of a business partnership.

It is often reported that a husband will not endeavor to replace one wife's status within his family, or her position in the extended family, with his favorite. Men seek to keep control over their polygynous families by maintaining as much harmony between wives as possible. A "wife out of love" would find it difficult to disrupt a family unit by manipulating her husband's feelings toward her for political gain

inside the family. This is precisely where the Taita ideal of personality as part of female beauty comes into play, forestalling any serious wifely conflict. The favorite wife should be as pleasing as possible around the other wives to show her husband that she is indeed "beautiful."

Sometimes, however, co-wives just do not get along with one another. In such cases wives are kept in separate locations or homesteads rather than in the single compound that is the norm. In this instance the woman married out of love is often given special gifts of land, animals to tend and use for her needs, and other compensations for not being high in the family's female hierarchy.

However, a woman married out of love is not likely to cause disruption. She knows she is at a slight disadvantage. The other wives know that the husband regards her as special and that he places her above them in romantic sentiment. It is to the favorite wife's advantage to hide her feelings and maintain a cooperative attitude toward co-wives. To experience constant attack from two or three other women, with whom one *must* cooperate on a daily basis, can be very damaging to her sensibilities as well as disrupt her status in the extended family. In spite of the harmonious ideal and pragmatic orientation to daily interaction, each co-wife pursues her own interests, with passionate love often being a very important concern.

The Taita have adopted a fail-safe system that serves to control, and thus minimize, the expression of this sentiment. Because the first wife has certain rights, privileges, and obligations that are never transferred to the other co-wives, she is able to maintain an active position within the family. Within the extended family group first wives are likely to be mother to all younger co-wives. Moreover, it is only after the first wife's economic needs are met that the other co-wives' economic needs can be discussed. Given the first wife's enormous fund of power, a favorite wife must move very cautiously.

Conclusion

The earliest missionary writings are unabashedly ethnocentric and focus more on the "lust of the flesh" than on exploring other human sentiments such as empathy, cooperation, and love. In time indigenous populations in Africa, especially the Taita, became the victims of erroneous observations and, thus, incorrect cultural interpretations. Some missionary writings reinforced the idea that the African was incapable of experiencing any other love emotion than lust. Thus, the ethnocentric assumptions that produced a Western racist ideology also contributed to strengthening the belief that love and romance were a European contribution to human history (cf. Jankowiak and Fisher 1992).

When Taita behavior is examined within the context of sexual encounters, it is apparent that they exhibit thoughts and concerns typically, though not necessarily of equal intensity, found among the average American teenager. Accordingly, Taita males expressed fear of rejection while Taita females giggled at the prospect of having an affair with a man *they* deemed "handsome" or "manly." In this way, lust, love, and romance are in the air on any weekend night in the hills of Taita, where people are seldom surprised when someone marries for love of the heart.

Notes

The information that forms this paper was collected in 1981 over a twelve-month period among the Taita of Kenya. The research was partially funded by the National Science Foundation.

1. The Taita see personality as an intricate part of physical beauty. An ugly personality distracts from a pretty face or a charming body. Older men informed me how it was sometimes necessary to "beat a pleasing personality into a woman, especially a young woman who does not like the arrangements her family has made for her." Thus, a pleasing female personality is one that is of little or no trouble to a man. She is kind and thoughtful toward his relatives. She is respectful to him in public and serves him proper meals. She is pleasant for him to be around, and she acknowledges that he is the head of the household. Many Taita men repeatedly qualified their statement that they would never find such an ideal woman. In fact, I observed a few relationships where men were obviously attracted to women who did not, in any way, possess these attributes.

2. Kissing and fondling appear to be European-derived contributions to Taita culture. The older generation believes that both these methods of showing affection came to the Taita Hills with Europeans. I cannot refute this with any hard data, except to say that fondling seems quite common among East African peoples and, therefore, as a practice or a prelude to love-making, it may have its origins among the peoples of this region and was not therefore imported by Europeans.

References

Clark, H. E. 1890. *The Story of Friends Mission in Madagascar.* London: Friends Missionary Society.

Fraser, D. 1928. *The New Africa.* New York: Missionary Education Movement of the United States and Canada.

George, K. 1958. "The Civilized West Looks at Primitive Africa: 1400–1800." Isis 49:62–72.

Hulstaert, G. 1938. *Le Marriage des Nkunde.* Bruxelles: Given Campenhout.

Jablow, A., and D. Hammond. 1977. *The Myth of Africa.* New York: Library of Social Science.

Jankowiak, W., and E. Fischer. 1992. "A Cross-Cultural Perspective on Romantic Love." *Ethnology* 31(2):149–155.

Johnson, H. H. 1911. *The Opening of Africa.* New York: University Books.

Kenyatta, J. 1953. *Facing Mount Kenya.* London: Seeker and Warburg.

Lovett, R. 1899. *History of the London Missionary Society.* London: Oxford University Press.

Lugard, F.D. 1904. Uganda and Its People. Edinburgh: Mansfield.

Lugard, F.D. 1922. *The Duel Mandate in British Tropical Africa*. Edinburgh: Blackwood.

MacDonald, A.J.M. 1916. *Trade, Politics, and Christianity in Africa and the East*. New York: Longman's Green.

Maybury-Lewis, D. 1992. *Millennium: Tribal Wisdom and the Modern World*. New York. Viking.

Mazrui, A. 1986. *The Africans: A Triple Heritage*. Boston: Little, Brown.

Noble, F.R 1899. *The Redemption of Africa*. New York: Fleming H. Revell.

Parsons, E. 1906. *Christus Liberator: An Outline Study of Africa*. London: Macmillan.

Thomas, J. 1885. *Through Masai Land: Eastern Equatorial Africa*. London: Houghton, Mifflin.

Problem Set #7

Sexual Selection in Humans

To do this problem set, you will need to read Chapter 12.

1. What variables drive sexual selection, and what is your assessment of these variables in humans?

2. Do men exhibit any of the traits typically found in the faster sex among mammals? Explain.

3. How, in general, do mate choice criteria evolve? What are the variants that selection is evaluating, and why do some spread?

4. If men and women choose mates on the basis of good genes, how will they choose?

   a. Will the two sexes focus on the same or different traits?

   b. What will those traits be?

   c. Why?

5. If men and women choose mates on the basis of parental investment capacity, how will they choose?

   a. Will the two sexes focus on the same or different traits?

   b. What will those traits be?

   c. Why?

6. These questions are about mixed reproductive strategies.

   a. What does the phrase *mixed reproductive strategy* mean?

   b. Why do mixed reproductive strategies evolve?

   c. What are the essential features of the mixed reproductive strategies of men and women?

7. What kinds of environmental information might be relevant to the ontogeny (development) of women's and men's reproductive strategies?

Problem Set #8

Female Mating Strategies and Love

To do this problem set, you will need to read Chapters 13 and 14.

1. According to Cashdan, women want three attributes in a mate: good condition, resources, and status. Give the evolutionary logic that explains each of these preferences.

2. Female-female competition is more prominent in our species than it is in our close relatives among the apes.

   a. Why, evolutionarily speaking, do women compete?

   b. What forms does female-female competition take?

   c. For two of these forms, predict what environmental variables trigger it.

3. Just as women may confront evolutionary conflicts of interest with each other, their reproductive strategies may conflict with those of men.

   a. Identify at least two of these conflicts.

   b. What is the source of each type of conflict (i.e., what might benefit one sex but harm the other)?

   c. Identify relevant counter-strategies.

4. "Romantic love" could be viewed as an alternative to evolutionary explanations of mating preferences. In other words, we don't cynically seek out partners with good genes or good earning potential; we just "fall in love."

   a. Can you think of any way to integrate the two approaches (i.e., is there a way to think about love as an evolved motivational system)?

   b. If that integrated approach is correct, what predictions would you make about the cross-cultural occurrence and triggers of love?

   c. What can you say about the occurrence of romantic love among the Taita of Kenya that is relevant to this issue?

Unit V
Rape and Sexual Conflict

Rape is a vicious, murderous relation. Rape creates a chasm of mutual incomprehension between women and men. The will to rape is impossible to comprehend for women, and the consequences of rape for the victim-survivor may be equally difficult to understand and to empathize with for men. (Moreno, this volume).

This unit attempts to narrow the "chasm of mutual incomprehension between women and men" by considering women's experiences of rape and other forms of sexual violence and by examining the proximate and ultimate causes of these transgressions.

Chapter 15 adopts an explicitly evolutionary perspective on male aggression against women. In this chapter, it is especially important for the reader to remember the concept of the *naturalistic fallacy* introduced in Chapter 1. Natural selection favors traits that tend to augment the inclusive fitness of their bearers, whether these traits are considered noble (like parental love) or morally repugnant (like rape). Evolutionists examine the evolutionary causes of behaviors in attempts to understand, but not to justify them. Certainly, in order to ameliorate a social affliction, it helps to understand its causes.

In Chapter 15, I consider male aggression against women as an outcome of conflicts between the reproductive strategies of women and men. Men appear to perpetrate sexual violence against women when men's sexual access or paternity certainty is threatened.

In addition to the naturalistic fallacy, it is important for the reader to remember that behavior is *facultative*—it responds to the environment (see Chapter 3). Thus, sexual aggression is not some fixed and immutable feature of maleness; most men do not rape, and the incidence of rape varies across cultures. The relevant evolutionary question is: Under what circumstances has male aggression been especially *mal*adaptive for men over our evolutionary history? When brothers or other relatives come to a woman's aid? When female alliances are strong, and women can cooperate against male aggressors? When women are not economically dependent on men and so are not forced to tolerate their husbands' aggression? I conclude Chapter 15 by summarizing five such sociocultural variables hypothesized by the evolutionary anthropologist Barbara Smuts to modulate male aggression against women.

Chapter 16 is written by a female anthropologist under the pseudonym of Eva Moreno. In this chapter, Moreno recounts her attempted rape at the hands of a male assistant she hired during her

fieldwork in Ethiopia. Moreno describes vividly and in great detail the events leading up to and immediately following her traumatic experience. She then discusses the reactions of various individuals to
the rape, including her own reactions, and places them in the context of gender differences in the
understanding of rape. Moreno offers the following conclusion regarding rape: "It concerns all of us,
women and men, and it warrants a strong place on the mainstream anthropological agenda."

In Chapter 17, Rogaia Mustafa Abusharaf addresses the issue of female "circumcision," a form of
ritual genital mutilation practiced in several parts of Africa and Asia. Abusharaf discusses the health
problems caused by this practice and considers the social conditions that perpetuate it. Although
women directly perform and encourage female circumcision, the practice appears to be motivated by
desires to protect the chastity of female relatives. Chastity is presumed to be valued because it makes a
woman a more attractive wife to men. Thus, this ritual has, at its roots, a conflict between the welfare
of women and the reproductive motivations of men.

15

Sexual Conflict and Male Aggression toward Women

David A. Puts

Eva was 28 years old. She had traveled to Ethiopia from her native Sweden to conduct fieldwork toward her doctoral degree in anthropology. She needed a research assistant, someone educated and proficient in English. After interviewing several candidates she had learned of through university contacts, Eva hired Yonas, an eager and self-assured man of Eva's own age. Eva and Yonas traveled to the town of Ketema, where Eva would conduct her research. There, she rented two hotel rooms while she scouted out more permanent lodgings. A couple of nights into their stay at the hotel, Yonas appeared at the door to Eva's room. He was in his underwear, and he declared that it was time for them to become lovers. Eva explained that she had a permanent partner in Sweden and didn't take Yonas's declaration seriously. When Eva found a suitable house to rent, she even offered Yonas a room, partly to save the cost of renting separate lodgings for him, and partly for the company.

But Yonas's sexual interests were not quelled. Over the following weeks, Yonas nagged and begged Eva for sex. When this didn't work, Yonas began secretly to sabotage Eva's fieldwork, hoping to convince her that she needed his help. This also failed. Yonas's frustration and anger boiled over as he accused Eva of sleeping with everyone but him. He quit work-

ing for her to show her that she needed him. This, too, failed. Yonas returned and began brandishing his pistol and bullets menacingly in front of her. When at last Eva announced that she was leaving town, Yonas realized it was his last chance. That night, he forced himself into her room and, using his gun, he made her acquiesce to sex.

An anthropologist writing under the pseudonym of Eva Moreno vividly recounts this campaign of sexual harassment launched at her twenty years earlier by the man she hired to help her (see Chapter 16). Such stories of men forcing sex on women are disturbing and all too common. Rape is so traumatic for women that it is difficult to imagine a comparable trauma for men. Why do some men rape women? Why do some men perpetrate other kinds of sexual aggression against women, such as assault and harassment? This chapter will explore the ultimate and proximate causes of male sexual aggression against women, consider female counter-adaptations to sexual aggression, and examine some sociocultural variables that may affect its occurrence.

The perspective toward male aggression adopted in this chapter—an evolutionary perspective—has much to offer those who are interested in combating sexual violence. As the most powerful theoretical tool available to modern behavioral biologists, selection theory has repeatedly clarified the behaviors of organisms across the living world. You have just seen in Unit IV, for example, how selection thinking elucidates the mating behavior of human beings.

Yet, many social scientists have received the application of selection theory to sexual violence with skepticism and antipathy. Evolutionary theory has encountered this reception partly because it contradicts more widely accepted social science explanations. These viewpoints will be discussed in detail in this chapter. Evolutionary theory has also encountered this reception in part because some believe that its application to sexual violence is motivated by sexism and perhaps a desire to justify sexually violent behaviors. Certainly, any tool can be wielded with malice no matter how innocent the intentions of its inventor. But you know from Chapter 1 that evolutionary explanations cannot morally justify sexism or any other behavior. To believe the contrary is to fall victim to the naturalistic fallacy.

Rather than justifying sexual violence, this chapter is intended to foster a more complete understanding of sexual violence by placing it in an evolutionary theoretical framework. Why handicap our ability to understand and manage a social problem like rape by denying ourselves the use of such a potent theoretical tool? It is hoped that explanation at the ultimate level will lead to proximate-level solutions to this widespread social affliction.

The Social Science Explanation of Rape

One approach to understanding male sexual aggression is to examine the contexts in which it occurs and identify some common elements that might hint at its causes. For example, Peggy

Sanday (1981) found that rape was more prevalent in tribal societies in which men raid other groups and capture wives and in societies in which women have little socioeconomic or political power. Sanday concluded that rape is caused by a "socio-cultural script" (p. 24) in which men express themselves through interpersonal violence and toughness. This conclusion echoes the view popularized by Susan Brownmiller (1976) that rape is an act of aggression and not an act of lust. Thus, there are two main elements to this prevalent perspective on rape. First, men's capacity to rape is the result of socialization—men *learn* to rape. Second, rape is not fundamentally a sexual act involving violence—it is a violent act involving sex. Rape is a sexual manifestation of a male desire to dominate women.

There are some potential political advantages to viewing rape in this way. For example, this perspective may ensure that rapists are held accountable for their actions. The danger is, perhaps, that if rape is not viewed as learned and fundamentally an act of violence, then it may be seen as a crime of passion or worse, an "innate" part of maleness. And if rape were believed to be "innate," then rapists might be thought unable to have done otherwise and therefore less responsible, if not altogether innocent. Punishment would serve little purpose because it could not prevent rapists from repeating their crimes, nor could it deter other men from committing rape. To avoid this seemingly hopeless situation, many social scientists have adopted the viewpoint that rape is learned and not motivated by lust. Although well intentioned, this view, referred to by Thornhill and Palmer (2000) as the *social science explanation,* suffers from several logical as well as empirical flaws.

Is Rape Learned?

First and foremost, implicit in the social science explanation is the idea that rape has mainly social causes—that men learn from their social environment to be physically aggressive and to disrespect and dominate women. Certainly, sexual violence against women is more likely to occur in social environments where male aggression and toughness are encouraged and where women are subordinated. But while rape varies in frequency across cultures, cross-cultural data indicate that rape occurs in most, if not all, human societies. For example, Sanday (1981) found only five of ninety-five tribal cultures with no evidence of rape, and Palmer (1989) subsequently brought into question the absence of rape in even these five cultures. Furthermore, as Barbara Smuts (1996) notes, male sexual aggression toward females, including rape, is common in nonhuman primates. And rape occurs in many species of marine mammals, birds, reptiles, amphibians, fish, and insects (reviewed in Thornhill and Palmer 2000).

The cross-cultural frequency of rape, coupled with its presence in many species of nonhuman animals with no socialization at all, challenges the notion that men commit rape primarily because they are exposed to socialization patterns that encourage it. To the contrary, although social factors certainly contribute to rape across cultures, most social prescriptions concerning male sexuality "are intended to suppress [rape], not to foster it" (Symons 1979, p. 303). In laboratory studies, male sexual arousal in response to rape depictions depends on the *costs* of rape, indicating that rape occurs not so much because it is encouraged as because it is not appropriately penalized (Thornhill and Palmer 2000).

Thus, social factors are indeed related to the incidence of rape. But, as we have seen, it is unlikely that rape is *only* the result of particular socialization regimes. Rather, people are born with specific behavioral predispositions—with patterns of learning and responding to the environment—that have been shaped by a long and continuous history of natural selection. The propensity to rape probably reflects aspects of evolved male sexual psychology, just as the abhorrence of rape reflects aspects of evolved female sexual psychology. Our understanding of

the roles played by environmental variables in promoting or inhibiting rape is likely to be aided by an understanding of the role of rape in the evolved sexual psychology of men.

Is Rape a Sex Crime?

The second major conclusion of the social science explanation is that rape is a crime of violence and power rather than a crime of sexual passion. There is certainly some truth to this; violence and issues of power are very much components of rape. But claims that rape is "a crime of" or "an act of" power, aggression, violence, domination, and so on are vague. For whom is rape an act of violence rather than sex? What are the *relationships* between rape, violence, and sex?

Rape clearly elicits strong feelings of violation and powerlessness for rape victims. For the victims, rape is reasonably considered an act of violence. Rape involves elements of power and aggression for the perpetrators as well. Convicted rapists often report the desire to dominate their victims (Groth 1979). But with sexual acts so intimately involved in rape, it is worth asking what role sex plays.

The social science explanation holds that the ultimate goal of rape is power and domination, and the tactic used to achieve this goal is sexual aggression. In this view, men desire a feeling of potency and commit acts of forced sex to achieve this end. According to Barbara Rodabaugh and Melanie Austin (1981, p. 40), "the rapist is primarily motivated by hostility and anger, with a strong need to dominate and humiliate his victim." But as Rodabaugh and Austin continue, "[t]he major unanswered question is why the need for power and control is expressed by means of sexual assault."

Indeed, if rape were motivated primarily by a need for control, one might expect those easiest to dominate, such as children and elderly women, to be victimized by rapists most often. But this prediction contradicts available data. Most rape victims are in their twenties, the age group most willing and able to resist their assailants. According to Thornhill and Palmer (2000, p. 73),

> young adult females are vastly overrepresented and female children and post-reproductive-age females are greatly underrepresented in the population of rape victims. This pattern has been shown so many times, across so many settings, by so many methods, that it is established beyond any reasonable doubt.

On the other hand, the hypothesis that rape is motivated mainly by a desire for power could make exactly the opposite prediction. Perhaps young women, precisely because they are at the peak of their abilities to resist male aggression, present the greatest challenge to rapists' feelings of power and control. Perhaps rapists target young women because overcoming the challenge such victims present can best fulfill the need for control. While this would explain why young women are overrepresented as rape victims, it is also probably incorrect.

Rapes *are* often sufficiently premeditated to afford rapists the opportunity to choose their victims carefully. A study of 75 violent rapists, for example, found that "[t]he majority of offenders intended to rape someone that day and planned their attacks. Over half of the sample said that they were 'out looking for a victim to rape' " (Queen's Bench Foundation 1976, quoted in Rodabaugh and Austin 1981, p. 39). But there is considerable evidence that rapists seek out vulnerable victims rather than challenging ones. For example, rapists report looking for victims who appear defenseless, and attempted rapes are more likely to be completed if the rapist perceives the victim to be frightened (Rodabaugh and Austin 1981). Moreover, rape tends to occur across cultures when females are most vulnerable (Groth 1979), such as during war, when rapists are essentially anonymous and females are unprotected.

Thus, rapists preferentially target vulnerable women in vulnerable situations. So why do they target the *least* vulnerable age category? That is, why do rapists target the age group of women

most able to resist while simultaneously preferring vulnerable victims? And why is this true for rape but not for other forms of male aggression? Although older women are far less likely to be raped, they are equally likely to be victims of other violent crimes perpetrated by men, such as aggravated assault (Buss 1994). The obvious answer to these questions is that rape is sexually motivated. Despite rapists' desires for vulnerable victims, they target the least vulnerable age group because these women are the most fertile, and men have evolved sexual preferences for traits associated with female fertility. When the form of male aggression is not sexual, young, fertile women are relatively less frequently victimized.

Because of lower rates of prosecution for cases of acquaintance rape, the available data, obtained primarily from *convicted* rapists, almost certainly overrepresent incidences of stranger rape. Stranger rape and acquaintance rape probably differ in some important respects. For example, stranger rape probably more often involves "preferential rape," a sexual preference for coercive sexual activity. However, acquaintance rape also seems to be motivated at least in part by male sexual desires. This is illustrated by the description of Eva Moreno's rape by "Yonas" at the beginning of this chapter.

In Moreno's account, one can see Yonas undergo a psychological transformation. Initially, he harbors little resentment toward her. He is attracted to her and confidently believes they will have sex. As he discovers otherwise, he begins to plead. Here, it is clear that Yonas is more sexually interested in Moreno than interested in dominating her: He is *begging* for sex. He wants her *charity*. It is only Yonas's repeated failure to wear Moreno down, probably coupled with his initial assumption of sex, that frustrates him. Moreno's sexuality holds a power over Yonas. His frustration becomes resentment and finally anger as Yonas forms an image of Moreno that is concordant with his growing hatred—an image of a promiscuous, spiteful woman who would sleep with anyone but him. For Yonas, physical violence was clearly a last resort. He had tried every imaginable tactic—

from a confident proposal to begging, nagging, pleading, guilt, and intimidation—to get Moreno to have sex with him.

Examples like this one indicate that the social science explanation inverts the relationship between sex and the hostility involved in acquaintance rape. It appears that the distal cause of rape is generally not the desire for power but the desire for sex. Aggression and hostility appear to be the tactics employed to achieve this end. The hostility, aggression, and violence that accompany rape seem to represent an attitude that short circuits the normal empathetic response, thus promoting coercive sexual behavior (Buss 1994).

A common trajectory for a rape scenario may go like this: A male is attracted to a female, but either his sexual advances are rejected or he expects that they would be. The male resents the strong sexual power that the female exerts over him and resents his inability to exert power reciprocally over her. Merely by virtue of her sexual attractiveness, the female appears to the male to be manipulating him—to be teasing him, tempting him. In reality, she may not even be aware he exists. The male consequently views the female as a *tease, bitch,* etc. He wants to regain control. The sexual intercourse he envisions becomes mixed with feelings of retribution. The male views himself as justified in sexually dominating the female because of what she has done to *him.* In his mind, she may even *want* him to overcome her sexual coyness because (again, in his mind) she has so clearly been sending sexual signals.

While these psychological factors culminate in a rape that is marked by aggression, violence, and overtones of power and domination, the entire causal cascade was set in motion by the rapist's initial sexual attraction to females who spurn (or are oblivious to) his advances. We can say, therefore, that in such cases rape is "an act of" aggression and dominance, and, contrary to the social science explanation, rape is simultaneously a sexually motivated act. Indeed, in the immediate chain of psychological motivations leading to such incidences of rape, the primary motivation appears to be sexual.

It is worth noting that rapists often report experiencing both a desire to dominate and a sexual desire for their victims (Thornhill and Palmer 2000). For instance, in one study, 84 percent of rapists reported sexual motivation as at least partly the cause of their actions (Smithyman 1978). But in fact, a feeling of sexual desire would not be necessary for sex to be considered the primary motive for rape. If rapists *only* felt the desire to dominate and humiliate their victims, we would still like to know why rapists preferentially desire to dominate and humiliate certain types of victims. The fact that sex acts are forced disproportionately on sexually desirable women suggests that the motives are sexual whether or not the perpetrators are conscious of these underlying motives.

Nor is it necessary that rapists entirely lack a sexual outlet for rape to be sexually motivated. Many rapists do have stable sexual partners. As discussed in Chapter 12, however, male sexual desire is not exhausted by a single sexual partner. As Symons (1979, p. 280) points out, "most patrons of prostitutes, adult bookstores, and adult movie theaters are married men."

Conflicts between Male and Female Reproductive Strategies

Despite its possible political benefits, the social science explanation for rape fails as a scientific hypothesis because it cannot explain why rape occurs. If rape is the result of culture-specific socialization patterns, why are males the rapists and females the victims across all human societies? Why don't we find any societies in which groups of women gang rape men more often than the reverse? Why does rape occur in other species, many of them without any socialization at all? If rape is not sexually motivated, why are women predominantly the targets of rape during their fertile years, rather than before puberty or after menopause? And why isn't this true of other forms of male aggression, such as aggravated assault? Perhaps most significantly, why would natural selection design males to learn a potentially costly act like rape merely because, as the social science explanation suggests, it furthers the sexual dominance of *other* males?

Let's begin again, this time equipped with the knowledge gained from Unit IV about the evolved reproductive strategies of men and women. Recall from Chapters 12 and 13 that men's and women's reproductive strategies often interfere with one another. When this happens—that is, when the playing out of a woman's reproductive strategy impedes the playing out of a man's reproductive strategy or vice versa—*sexual conflict* is said to occur. Rape and other forms of male aggression toward women can be understood as consequences of sexual conflict. From a man's perspective, women's reproductive strategies sometimes interfere with his reproductive strategies. There appear to be two major contexts in which this occurs: threats to a man's sexual access to females and threats to paternity certainty. We will take each of these threats in turn and examine how some men employ aggressive tactics to countervail them.

Harassment, Coercion, and Sexual Access

Harassment as a Probe for Sexual Interest

As you learned in Unit IV, men are generally more interested in engaging in uncommitted sex than women are. Women are generally more particular about their mates, especially for purely sexual relationships when men's standards are lowest. One outcome of these sex differences is that men often wish to have sex with women who are not interested. Many of the tactics men employ to overcome women's reticence about sex are bothersome at best. Men frequently make sexually suggestive comments,

gestures, and other overtures to women, presumably probing women's sexual interest. Often, these overtures are unwelcome and constitute sexual harassment. The victims of sexual harassment are disproportionately young, physically attractive, single women (Buss 1994).

Of course, women are not always closed to a man's sexual advances. When they are not, their receptiveness appears to reflect their own underlying reproductive strategies. In a sample of 109 college women, women reported that they would be significantly more upset by persistent requests for a date by men of lower socioeconomic status, such as garbage collectors, cleaning men, gas station attendants, and construction workers, than by men with greater investment potential, such as rock stars, premedical students, and graduate students (Buss 1994). In this study, women also reported that they would feel much less harassed by overtures, such as nonsexual touching, looks, or flirting, that signal more than purely sexual interests than they would by purely sexual gestures.

The Use of Violence When Costs Are Low or as a "Desperate Alternative"

Men occasionally go well beyond sexual harassment and resort to threats of violence or actual physical aggression to obtain sexual access. As discussed previously, the victims of male sexual aggression are typically objects of sexual desire—attractive, young women. Eighty-five percent of rape victims, for example, are below the age of thirty-six (Thornhill and Thornhill 1983). Thus, the age distribution of rape victims seems not simply to reflect men's propensity for violence against women—it appears to represent their sexual attraction to women, coupled with their propensity for using physical aggression to accomplish their aims. The idea that rape reflects men's evolved reproductive strategies is further supported by evidence that rapes of fertile-age women more often involve penile-vaginal intercourse, ejaculation in the female reproductive tract, and repeated intercourse than do rapes of non-fertile-age women (Thornhill and Thornhill 1991).

Some cases of rape, such as acquaintance rapes like the one experienced by Eva Moreno, also appear to be precipitated by a systematic misinterpretation of women's behavior by men. Men read flirtation and sexual interest in the behavior of women even when these women report no such interest and when other women perceive little flirtation (Abbey 1982; Abbey and Melby 1986; Saal, Johnson, and Weber 1989). This tendency to overestimate the sexual interest of females may have evolved because it caused males to miss fewer sexual opportunities over human evolutionary history. In much the same way, smoke detectors are designed to be oversensitive, triggering false alarms when we burn a dish in the oven so that we don't miss a truly dangerous fire. The costs to ancestral men of missed mating opportunities may have been large relative to the costs of misreading women's behavior, so selection favored a male mating psychology that errs on the side of seeing more sexual interest than truly exists.

Selection also appears to have shaped male psychology so that, compared to women, men experience greater interest in uncommitted sex and a desire for more mates. Added to men's capacity to use aggression to accomplish their goals, these facts help explain why rapists are men and not women. Selection also seems to have designed men to prefer the types of sex acts most likely to lead to fertilization with the women who are most likely to be fertile. This helps explain why young women are more likely to be raped than are females in other age groups and why specific sex acts (repeated penile-vaginal intercourse with ejaculation in the female reproductive tract) are more likely to be forced on fertile-age women.

But these facts go only part of the way to explaining the occurrence of rape. Most men will never rape. Yet, from a fitness-maximizing perspective, it seems that if rape sometimes resulted in conceptions over human evolution, then a tendency to rape fertile females would have conferred benefits to all males. So why are some men more likely than others to be rapists? Evolutionarily speaking, why don't more men commit rape? The answer, of course, is that there are enormous potential costs to rape. Rapists risk being punished or killed by the mates, friends, and family members of rape victims or by other members of the community. Like any facultative behavior, we expect the occurrence of rape to depend on the fitness costs relative to the benefits. Thus, we expect rape to depend heavily on the likelihood and severity of punishment.

When we look across cultures, the occurrence of rape appears to correspond to the likelihood of punishment. For example, rape is common during wartime among men who invade new territories and encounter unprotected women. And rape occurs in many small-scale societies in which men raid neighboring villages for wives (Sanday 1981, Smuts 1996). Women captured from another village lack nearby friends or family members to protect them from rape at the hands of their captors. Wartime rape and wife raiding may represent opportunities for sexual access in which the aggressors perceive few potential costs of their actions. The cases of "date rape" that occur in our own society also fit these conditions. Date rapes typically occur in cars, dormitory rooms, apartments, and other secluded locations where there are no witnesses and there is no protection for the victims.

In some cases of "stranger rape," the rapists are lower income, lower class men with little self-esteem (Buss 1994) who have had poor heterosexual interactions (Malamuth and Heilman 1998). For some of these men, rape may represent a "desperate alternative" to attracting a mate (Buss 1994). According to one serial rapist, "I felt that my social station would make her reject me . . . I didn't know how to go about meeting her . . . I took advantage of her fright and raped her" (quoted in Buss 1994). In such circumstances, punishment imposes relatively low fitness costs to rapists because winning mating opportunities by alternative methods such as mate attraction is unlikely to be successful. In other words, such men do not risk giving up much in the way of future mating opportunities if they are caught.

Is Rape an Adaptation?

Some cases of rape, such as preferential rape, appear to be caused by a mental disorder resulting from a disturbance in normal psychological development (Freund and Seto 1998). But in many contexts, rape seems to be an extreme manifestation of the coercive tactics employed by men pursuing a reproductive strategy of obtaining multiple sex partners with minimal investment. On the other hand, Randy and Nancy Thornhill (1983) have suggested that rape might represent a specialized male adaptation for obtaining sex when costs are low or when other tactics are unlikely to be successful. Thus, Thornhill and Palmer (2000, pp. 59–60) suggest two ultimate explanations for rape:

1. It may be an adaptation that was directly favored by selection because it increased male reproductive success by way of increasing mate number. That is, there may be psychological mechanisms designed specifically to influence males to rape in ways that would have produced a net reproductive benefit in the past.

2. It may be only a by-product of other psychological adaptations, especially those that function to produce the sexual desires of males for multiple partners without commitment. In this case, there would not be any psychological mechanism designed specifically to influence males to rape in ways that would have produced a net reproductive benefit in the past.

If rape were adaptive in the past—that is, if the fitness benefits from increased fertilizations outweighed the risks—then we would expect to see psychological adaptations in males that were designed specifically for this function. Thornhill and Palmer (2000, pp. 65–66) suggest several such adaptations, including:

1. psychological mechanisms that help males evaluate the vulnerability of potential rape victims

2. psychological mechanisms that motivate men who lack sexual access to females (or who lack sufficient resources) to rape

3. psychological mechanisms that cause males to evaluate sexual attractiveness (as indicated by age) differently for rape victims than for consensual partners

4. psychological and/or physiological mechanisms that result in differences between sperm counts of ejaculates produced during rape and those of ejaculates produced during consensual copulation

5. psychological mechanisms that produce differences between the sexual arousal of males caused by depictions of rape and that caused by depictions of consensual mating

6. psychological or other mechanisms that motivate males to engage in rape under conditions of sperm competition

There is some supporting evidence for these predictions of the rape-adaptation hypothesis (reviewed in Thornhill and Palmer 2000). But such evidence does not necessarily rule out the by-product hypothesis. The difficulty of disentangling the predictions of the rape-adaptation hypothesis from those of the by-product hypothesis is illustrated by predictions 3 and 4. While we might expect to find these psychological mechanisms if rape had been adaptive in the past, such mechanisms could also be by-products of male psychological adaptations for short-term sexual relationships in general. For example, the rape-adaptation hypothesis predicts that the age of rape victims should be near peak fertility (early to mid twenties) rather than near peak future reproductive potential (late teens). As noted previously, this prediction has been verified. But as Thornhill and Palmer (2000, p. 71) point out,

it is still possible that the mechanism involved has been designed for selecting consenting one-time sex partners or other short-term mates rather than rape victims, because a high-fertility choice would have increased male reproductive success in any short-term mating situation in human evolutionary history.

Thus, whether rape is now or was ever adaptive, or whether it merely represents a maladaptive extreme in the repertoire of evolved male sexual behaviors, remains controversial. It should be noted that what is at issue is *not* whether rape is the result of selection on male psychology. Rape *must* be either the result of psychological mechanisms designed, entirely or in part to function in rape *or* the maladaptive by-product of psychological mechanisms designed by selection for other functions. Nor, of course, is the morality of rape at issue in this debate. What is at issue is how the male mind is designed—an issue that will almost certainly have important consequences for understanding how to reduce the incidence of rape.

Whichever hypothesis turns out to receive the most empirical support, rape and male sexual coercion have probably been pervasive features of sexual relations throughout human evolutionary history. As Barbara Smuts (1996) notes, male sexual coercion is common among humans' closest living relatives, the apes, so it likely characterized our common ancestor with them as well. Moreover, sexual coercion appears to have been frequent enough in our evolutionary past for women to evolve counter-adaptations to it. Some apparent female counter-adaptations to rape will be discussed later in this chapter.

Abuse and Paternity Certainty

Male aggression against women, in addition to being caused by conflict over sexual access, may result from sexual conflict over paternity certainty. When men channel their resources into reproduction through bride-price, bride-service, or direct investment in their mates or offspring, they have an interest in protecting their investments. Remember, in the evolutionary past, investing males who were not vigilant against the mixed reproductive strategies of women and

the reproductive striving of other men risked being cuckolded and channeling their resources into other males' offspring (see Chapter 12). Consequently, selection favored counter-tactics in the behavioral repertoires of men.

Cooperative Anti-Cuckoldry Tactics

Sometimes these tactics may not be entirely objectionable to women. Gangestad, Thornhill, and Garver (2002) found that men increase attention to their mates when their mates are near the ovulatory phase of their menstrual cycles. As you may recall from Unit IV, this is the time when men would have been at the greatest risk of being cuckolded throughout human evolution because women are less faithful near ovulation when their fertility is highest (Baker and Bellis 1995). Gangestad and colleagues showed that men increase their vigilance when their mates are near ovulation by phoning their mates unexpectedly, spending more free time with them, and giving them unexpected gifts.

Selfish Anti-Cuckoldry Tactics

Often, however, the tactics that men use to protect against cuckoldry are far less chivalrous. Recall from Chapter 12 that men's jealousy about their mates' interactions with other men seems specifically designed to prevent cuckoldry. Men report greater feelings of jealousy over the prospect of their mates having sex with another man than over their mates developing emotional commitment to another man. And men's physiological responses corroborate their statements (Buss et al. 1997). Goetz and Shackelford (2006) found that men were more likely to use sexually coercive tactics (for example, threatening to have sex with another woman if their mate did not have sex with them) when they suspected their mates of sexual infidelity and when their mates reported greater infidelity. Furthermore, the use of these coercive tactics was related to mate retention behaviors, such as not letting their partner talk to other men and holding her hand when other men were around.

These observations suggest that male sexual coercion may sometimes function to prevent cuckoldry.

Physical Abuse

Men's sexual jealousy can also boil over into abuse. Abuse can take the form of psychological abuse, as when a man derogates his mate, apparently so that she will feel reliant on him and perceive her chances of obtaining a better mate to be unfavorable (Buss 1994). And of course, abuse can be physical. In the United States and Canada, physical battering of women by their mates is usually precipitated by the man's sexual jealousy (Cousins and Gangestad 2007) and is very often associated with accusations that the woman is having sex with other men (Buss 1994). This seems to be a widespread phenomenon across cultures (Daly and Wilson 1988, Smuts 1996).

Physical abuse as an anti-cuckoldry tactic reached extremes among some American Indian buffalo hunters, in which husbands are reported to have punished their adulterous wives by gang raping them with a group of unmarried men (reviewed in Sanday 1981). In several indigenous South American and New Guinea societies, men also use the threat of gang rape to control women's sexuality (Sanday 1981). These tend to be egalitarian societies characterized by strong male alliances. Because men rely on one another in warfare against other groups, it may be important for them to minimize potential sources of conflict among themselves, such as disputes over adultery (Smuts 1996). In many of these societies, men seem to accomplish this by propagating belief systems in which men's and women's lives are ideologically and physically segregated.[1] Men perpetuate the belief that women are dangerous and polluting and must be avoided whenever possible. Of course, individual men have an interest in reinforcing this belief to prevent other men from cuckolding them, while they themselves surreptitiously disregard it. Men also protect their paternity by enforcing the physical segregation of men from women. Men spend a great deal of time performing sacred rituals in men's houses, which are forbidden to women. Women are threatened with gang rape for violating men's space. And the threat itself generally seems sufficient for controlling women's behavior.

Female "Circumcision"

Men's sexual jealousy can also indirectly result in practices that many consider abusive to women. In Chapter 17, Rogaia Abusharaf describes female "circumcision" in the Sudan. Female circumcision is a form of genital surgery practiced in many African nations and several Asian cultures that involves one or a combination of the following: removal of the clitoris (clitoridectomy), amputation of the labia minora, and stitching together of the labia majora (infibulation) (Babatunde 1998). Female circumcision is painful, and it is also often unsanitary and can lead to infection and complications during childbirth.

As Abusharaf discusses in Chapter 17, men are usually not directly involved in the process of female circumcision; a girl's female relatives typically subject her to the ritual. But female circumcision is designed to protect the virginity of a girl by making sex unpleasant—if not impossible—for her before marriage. Because female circumcision supposedly protects virginity, it is intended to make women more attractive as wives to men who demand paternity certainty for their investment. In societies where females have little socioeconomic power and are dependent on men, it is important for women to secure this investment through marriage. Thus, Abusharaf suggests that attempts at the abolition of female circumcision may be unsuccessful until women are freed from economic dependence on men.

Mitigating Factors: Female Counter-adaptations and Social Constraints on Male Sexual Aggression

We have considered some of the ways in which men use aggression or threats of aggression against women to pursue their own reproductive strategies. We have also considered some of the motives behind male aggression against women, including the perception of limited alternatives or low costs to sexual coercion and the suspicion of a mate's infidelity. Given these possible causes, we might also ask what factors constrain a man's ability to coerce women sexually. There are at least two categories of mitigating influences on male sexual aggression: female counter-adaptations and social constraints.[2]

Female Adaptations against Rape

Although women may have evolved counter-adaptations to many different forms of male aggression, the best studied female counter-adaptations are those that reduce the risks or mitigate the costs of rape. Women suffer several potential fitness costs from rape. Most obviously, rape eliminates a woman's ability to choose her mates (or whether to mate at all). Rape resulting in pregnancy imposes the opportunity cost of not being fertilized by a more suitable mate or of not engaging in some other fitness pursuit such as investing in current offspring. Second, rape imposes the risks of injury and sexually transmitted diseases. Third, rape lowers the paternity certainty of a woman's mate, and this tends to decrease his investment

in her (see Chapters 12 and 13). Finally, given that men often invest in their short-term mates in exchange for sexual access, some cases of rape may be viewed as attempts to steal sex without paying for it. Thus, rape can limit a woman's ability to extract investment from short-term mates.

In response to these fitness costs, women appear to have evolved some counter-adaptations to rape and other forms of sexual coercion. Several female traits seem to represent counter-adaptations to the rape-imposed cost of not being able to choose when and with whom to mate.

Strength

For example, Sandra Petralia and Gordon Gallup, Jr. (2002) demonstrated that women's strength increases after exposure to a sexual assault scenario, but not after exposure to a similar scenario without sexual assault. The female participants in this study were first asked to squeeze a handheld device used to measure handgrip strength. Participants then read one of two passages—either a passage about a woman walking back to her car at night and being pursued by an unknown male or a passage about a woman walking back to her car in the daytime with plenty of people nearby. Next, the participants were asked for a second measure of their handgrip strength while they thought about the passage they had just read. Finally, participants were asked to take a self-administered urine-based ovulation test. Menstrual cycle phase was determined using this ovulation test and by counting forward from the onset of each participant's self-reported last menses. Participants who were between 13 and 17 days into their menstrual cycles and who tested positive for ovulation were considered in the ovulatory phase of their menstrual cycles.

Petralia and Gallup found that only women in the ovulatory phase of their cycles experienced a strength increase. And the strength

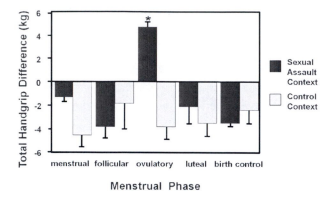

Figure 15.1 Women exhibit greater hand strength in response to reading a sexual assault scenario compared to a neutral scenario, but only during the fertile phase of their menstrual cycle.

(Redrawn from Petralia and Gallup 2002.)

increase occurred only in the group of ovulating participants who had read the sexual assault scenario. In other words, women appear to be most capable of physically resisting sexual assault when they are capable of becoming impregnated (Fig. 15.1).

Adjustment of Risk-taking Behavior

Another female trait that apparently lessens the chance of being impregnated by a rapist is the tendency of women to engage in less risk-taking behavior around the time of ovulation (Chavanne and Gallup 1997, Broder and Hohmann 2003). This tendency probably contributes to the fact that women have a reduced chance of being in the ovulatory phase of their menstrual cycles at the time of sexual assault (Rogel 1976, Morgan 1981).

Psychological Trauma

Rape-related psychological trauma may represent a third female adaptation against rape. Randy and Nancy Thornhill (1989) hypothesized that psychological distress is caused by threats to fitness and functions to direct attention toward these threats and produce behavior that minimizes them. According to Thornhill and Thornhill, the psychological trauma experi-

enced by rape victims functions to minimize fitness costs of rape. Several lines of evidence support this hypothesis.

Two facts suggest that the psychological trauma experienced by rape victims depends on the relative risk of losing male investment after being raped. First, married women are more traumatized by rape than are unmarried women (Thornhill and Thornhill 1990a). Second, married women who were violently raped experience *less* psychological trauma than do married women of similar age groups who were less violently raped (Thornhill and Thornhill 1990c). This startling finding makes sense when one considers that visible injuries give rape victims credibility with their current mates that the sex was forced on them and was not the result of infidelity. The increased psychological trauma experienced by married rape victims sustaining few visible bodily injuries may, as Thornhill and Thornhill suggest, serve to direct the victims' attention toward the potential loss of their husbands' investment. Moreover, outward expressions of psychological trauma may partly serve to establish the victims' credibility with their mates in the absence of other signs of rape.

The finding that women of reproductive age are more traumatized by rape than are prepubescent girls and older women (Thornhill and Thornhill 1990a, 1990b) also supports the hypothesis that psychological trauma functions to minimize the fitness costs of rape. For instance, rape victims of reproductive age report greater fear of unknown men and of being home alone. Loss of male investment is probably costlier to reproductive-age women than it is to non-reproductive-age women. But it is also likely that such age-related trauma is associated with the risk of becoming impregnated by the rapist. For example, reproductive-age victims are also more traumatized by penile-vaginal copulation than by anal intercourse, fellatio, or cunnilingus, whereas pre- and post-reproductive females are not differentially traumatized by these acts (Thornhill and Thornhill 1991).

Social Factors That Mitigate Male Aggression against Women

Barbara Smuts (1996) proposed several social factors that may affect the outcome of conflict between women's and men's sexual strategies. Smuts reviewed male sexual aggression against females in nonhuman primates and used this analysis as a source of hypotheses about cross-cultural variation in male violence against women.

For example, male aggression against females appears to be less pronounced in primate species in which females remain in their natal groups their whole lives and are thus able to receive aid from related females. Smuts hypothesized that male aggression against women will be reduced when women can obtain aid from close relatives, including male relatives such as brothers, sons, and fathers. As Smuts points out, female relatives can contribute to a man's fitness both directly through the reproductive benefits he receives from economic cooperation with them and indirectly through the inclusive fitness benefits he receives when he helps them to reproduce. Thus, men might be expected to aid their female relatives in disputes with other men. For example, among the Yanomamo Indians of Venezuela, women are regularly beaten by their husbands for suspected infidelity (Chagnon 1992). When a woman's husband is unusually cruel, however, her brothers often come to her defense. Consequently, women fear being promised to a man in another village where they will be cut off from this source of help.

Smuts (1996) also suggested that the importance of strong male alliances may contribute to incidences of male aggression against females. Males may be less willing to come to the aid of their female relatives if doing so will jeopardize valuable relationships with other men. According to Smuts, this may be especially true when men rely heavily on one another in intergroup

relations, including warfare. Such conditions may characterize some small-scale societies in which all men can effectively act as a unit against other groups of men in wife-raiding and the like.

Even within larger-scale societies with high levels of *within*-group competition among males, however, strong male coalitions may serve to curb male defense of female relatives against other males. In highly stratified societies in which some males are much more powerful than others, powerful males can gain access to multiple wives. Such males may ally with one another to enforce sanctions against adultery, both on the part of their wives and on the part of less powerful males. At the same time, economically and politically powerful males may be unwilling to jeopardize their alliances by protecting their sisters and other female relatives from spousal abuse (Smuts 1996).

This may be especially true if males invest heavily in reproduction through bride-price, bride-service, or direct investment in wives or offspring. Unlike nonhuman primate females, human females typically rely on males for at least some essential resources. Not only do heavily investing males have the greatest incentive to ensure their paternity by controlling their mates' sexuality (Dickemann 1981), but females who are highly dependent on male investment may also be faced with few viable alternatives to coercion by their mates (Irons 1983, Lateef 1990, Counts 1992). Thus, as Smuts concludes, "Cross-cultural analyses generally support the hypothesis that male control of resources makes women more vulnerable to male aggression" (1996, p. 250).

However, Smuts cautions, "This relationship between male control of resources and the frequency of wife beating does not necessarily hold . . . in industrial societies or societies undergoing modernization" (p. 250). According to Smuts, as female dependence on men decreases, men may use violence to suppress women's efforts to free themselves from male control. Thus, Smuts remarks,

> This . . . cautions us against the naïve hope that changes in a single variable will reduce women's vulnerability to male aggression. Rather, we must consider how numerous variables, including the ones suggested here, interact to increase or decrease the frequency of male aggression against women. (p. 251)

Summary

Approaching male violence against women from the perspective of evolved reproductive strategies promises to clarify both the circumstances that motivate some men to commit aggression against women and the social conditions that enable us to prevent it. For example, this perspective helps distinguish between acts of sexual aggression that have similar expressions but different motivations. The threatened gang rape of women trespassing into men's houses in the Highlands of New Guinea and the date rape of an undergraduate woman after a college fraternity party in the United States are both potential instances of rape. However, the former may be motivated by a male strategy to ensure certainty of paternity, whereas the latter may be motivated by a male strategy of obtaining multiple sexual partners.

Understanding the motives behind male sexual aggression against women is essential, but it is only the beginning. This knowledge must be combined with knowledge of the reproductive strategies and counter-strategies possessed by women and the social factors that influence the outcomes of sexual conflict. Looking at male aggression against women from the perspective of conflicts between evolved reproductive strategies promises to be a fertile ground for hypotheses about the relationships between these factors

and male sexual aggression. As Barbara Smuts (1996, p. 256) notes,

> To the extent that this evolutionary framework proves useful in helping to identify the conditions that favor male aggression toward women, it can also contribute to the formulation of strategies to alter those conditions.

Notes

1. This is not to say that women do not also benefit from perpetuating these belief systems. For example, the idea that women are dangerous and polluting may actually give women some power over men and protect women from male harassment. But such sexual segregation is almost certainly supported by men because it reduces the access of other males to fertile females. And the enforcement of sexual segregation represents yet another example of males protecting their paternity by controlling female sexuality through threats of violence.

2. The distinction between female counter-adaptations and social constraints on male sexual aggression is pedagogical; these categories are not mutually exclusive. For example, an evolved female tendency to form supportive alliances with other women could be construed as both a counter-adaptation and the basis of a mitigating social factor of male sexual aggression.

References

Abbey, A. 1982. Sex differences in attributions for friendly behavior: Do males misperceive females' friendliness? *Journal of Personality and Social Psychology* 32:830–38.

Abbey, A., and C. Melby. 1986. The effects of nonverbal cues on gender differences in perceptions of sexual intent. *Sex Roles* 15:283–98.

Babatunde, E. 1998. *Women's rites versus women's rights: A study of circumcision among the Ketu Yoruba of South Western Nigeria.* Trenton, NJ: Africa World Press.

Baker, R. R., and M. A. Bellis. 1995. *Human sperm competition: Copulation, masturbation and infidelity.* London: Chapman and Hall.

Broder, A., & N. Hohmann. 2003. Variations in risk-taking behavior over the menstrual cycle: An improved replication. *Evolution and Human Behavior* 24:391–98.

Brownmiller, S. 1976. *Against our will: Men, women and rape*. New York: Bantam.

Buss, D. 1994. *The evolution of desire*. New York: Basic Books.

Buss, D. M., R. J. Larsen, D. Westen, and J. Semelroth. 1997. Sex differences in jealousy: Evolution, physiology, and psychology. *Psychological Science* 3:251–55.

Chagnon, N. 1992. *Yanomamo*. Fort Worth, TX: Harcourt Brace Jovanovich.

Chavanne, T. J., and G. G. Gallup Jr. 1997. Variation in risk taking behavior among female college students as a function of the menstrual cycle. *Evolution and Human Behavior* 19:1–6.

Counts, D. A. 1992. Beaten wife, suicidal woman: Domestic violence in Kaliai, West New Britain. *Pacific Studies* 13:151–69.

Cousins, A. J., and S. W. Gangestad. 2007. Perceived threats of female infidelity, male proprietariness, and violence in college dating couples. *Violence and Victims* 22:651–68.

Daly, M., and M. Wilson. 1988. *Homicide*. Hawthorne, NY: Aldine de Gruyter.

Dickemann, M. 1981. Paternal confidence and dowry competition: A biocultural analysis of purdah. In *Natural selection and social behavior: Recent research and new theory*, ed. R. D. Alexander and D. W. Tinkle, 439–75. New York: Chiron Press.

Freund, K., and M. C. Seto. 1998. Preferential rape in the theory of courtship disorder. *Archives of Sexual Behavior* 27:433–43.

Gangestad, S. W., R. Thornhill, and C. E. Garver. 2002. Changes in women's sexual interests and their partners' mate retention tactics across the menstrual cycle: Evidence for shifting conflicts of interest. *Proceedings of the Royal Society: Biological Sciences* 269:975–82.

Goetz, A. T., and T. K. Shackelford. 2006. Sexual coercion and forced in-pair copulation as sperm competition tactics in humans. *Human Nature* 17:265–82.

Groth, N. 1979. *Men who rape*. New York: Plenum.

Irons, W. 1983. Human female reproductive strategies. In *Social behavior of female vertebrates*, ed. S. Wasser, 169–213. New York: Academic Press.

Lateef, S. 1990. Rule by the *Danda*: Domestic violence among Indo-Fijians. *Pacific Studies* 13:43–62.

Malamuth, N., and M. Heilmann. 1998. Evolutionary psychology and sexual aggression. In *Handbook of Evolutionary Psychology*, eds. C. Crawford and D. Krebs. Mahwah, NJ: Erlbaum.

Morgan, J. B. 1981. *Relationship between rape and physical damage during rape and phase of sexual cycle during which rape occurred*. Unpublished doctoral dissertation, University of Texas at Austin.

Palmer, C. 1989. Is rape a cultural universal? A re-examination of the ethnographic evidence. *Ethnology* 28:1–16.

Petralia, S. M., and G. G. Gallup, Jr. 2002. Effects of sexual assault scenario on handgrip strength across the menstrual cycle. *Evolution and Human Behavior* 23:3–10.

Rodabaugh, B. J., and M. Austin. 1981. *Sexual assault: A guide for community action*. New York: Garland STPM Press.

Rogel, M. J. 1976. *Biosocial aspects of rape*. Unpublished doctoral dissertation, University of Chicago.

Saal, F. E., C. B. Johnson, and N. Weber. 1989. Friendly or sexy? It may depend on whom you ask. *Psychology of Women Quarterly* 13:263–76.

Sanday, P. R. 1981. The socio-cultural context of rape: A cross-cultural study. *Journal of Social Issues* 37:5–27.

Smuts, Barbara. 1996. Male aggression against women: An evolutionary perspective. In *Sex, power, conflict. Evolutionary and feminist perspectives*, ed. David M. Buss and Neil M. Malamuth, 231–68. New York: Oxford University Press.

Smithyman, S. 1978. The undetected rapist. Doctoral dissertation, Claremont Graduate School. University Microfilms International.

Symons, D. 1979. *The evolution of human sexuality*. New York: Oxford University Press.

Thornhill, R., and C. T. Palmer. 2000. *A natural history of rape: Biological bases of sexual coercion*. Cambridge, MA: MIT Press.

Thornhill, R., and N. W. Thornhill. 1983. Human rape: An evolutionary analysis. *Ethology and Sociobiology* 4:137–73.

Thornhill, R., and N. W. Thornhill. 1989. The evolution of psychological pain. In *Sociobiology and the social sciences*, ed. R. Bell and N. Bell. Lubbock: Texas Tech University Press.

Thornhill, R., and N W. Thornhill. 1990a. An evolutionary analysis of psychological pain following rape I: The effects of victim's age and marital status. *Ethology and Sociobiology* 11:155–76.

Thornhill, R., and N. W. Thornhill. 1990b. An evolutionary analysis of psychological pain following rape II: The effects of stranger, friend, and family-member offenders. *Ethology and Sociobiology* 11:177–193.

Thornhill, R., and N. W. Thornhill. 1990c. An evolutionary analysis of psychological pain following rape III: The effects of force and violence. *Aggressive Behavior* 16:297–320.

Thornhill, R., and N. W. Thornhill. 1991. An evolutionary analysis of psychological pain following rape IV: The effect of the nature of the sexual act. *Journal of Comparative Psychology* 105:243–52.

16

Rape in the Field
Reflections from a Survivor

Eva Moreno*

Through field work at the pleasure of the host culture one learns one's place there and that it is one's only vantage point for penetrating the culture. Mistakes and mishaps in the field are great lamps of illumination if one survives; friendships there are the only greater source, besides being a divine comfort. (Landes 1986:139)

Aside from outright murder, rape is the ultimate sanction used by men to maintain the gender order.[1] Fear of rape forces women to abide by restrictions on physical movement and demeanor, and to conform to behavioral rules that govern most aspects of their entire lives.[2] That women are themselves to be blamed for rape is a prevalent notion in many societies, one that stems from the idea that it is the responsibility of women to make sure that they are not "in the wrong place at the wrong time." In other words, there are times, places, and situations out of bounds for women, which they traverse only at their own risk.

Rape and Female Anthropologists

Anthropologists who do fieldwork in foreign societies or among unfamiliar groups find themselves outside the bounds of their own gender order. They seldom conform completely to the gender conventions of the society in which they do fieldwork. An acute problem for female anthropologists, like myself, is that members of the host society may try to force us into a local gender order, in precisely the same way as local women, who wittingly or unwittingly provoke and challenge the existing order, are punished and brought into line. To some female anthropologists this can be a familiar situation, since we, in our home environment, may be perceived as recalcitrant rebels against a gendered order

*The author's name and all other names in this chapter are pseudonyms.

that does not easily allow independent, able women to rise above the prestige levels of our peers, and where sexual harassment is a standard measure taken by men to keep a male-dominated gender hierarchy intact. The potential for sexual violence against women, from harassment to rape-related murder, is present everywhere. In a field situation, the mere fact that one is a single female anthropologist doing her own thing may present an intolerable provocation to some individuals. Knowing that such risks face female fieldworkers, it is surprising that the anthropological literature is almost devoid of references to sexual violence to anthropologists.

There are many good reasons for this silence, some of them mentioned in other contributions to this volume. The element of blame that still attaches itself to the rape survivor means that women who have suffered sexual violence are afraid to damage their professional standing by talking about it. Among anthropologists, there is a tacit assumption often at work that a competent anthropologist would not place herself in a position where she could be raped in the first place (cf. Howell 1990:93). There is also a predominant masculine view that equates vulnerability with weakness, which makes many women afraid to confront vulnerability for fear of being considered lesser anthropologists than our male colleagues. In the "West," rape is still a stigmatized topic and victims often expect (and receive) little sympathy for their descriptions of assault. The recent reaction of some colleagues to reports of other kinds of personal violence against anthropologists in field situations, where the violence was seen as somehow the author's "fault," suggests that the silence of rape victims is based on fairly accurate assumptions (Kulick 1994). The two instances of rape and attempted rape mentioned in Howell's book both led to the death of the victims, which may, sadly enough, be the reason why they are reported, since no further damage can be done to the professional lives of the victims, and they cannot themselves control what is written about them.

Besides concern about one's professional reputation, a further, major reason for the silence on rape and sexual assault is that those who have experienced such assault are very likely suffering from rape trauma syndrome. In describing the rape inflicted on her and her subsequent attempts to cope with it, Cathy Winkler observes that,

> Rapists overrule not only the words and actions of their victims but also attack victims' definition of their body and their sexual self. Rapists' threats extend beyond superficial retorts and mentally and psychologically invade victims' beings and self-definition. (1991:12)

At the best of times, it takes a long time to overcome a rape trauma syndrome. Such an experience is devastating enough if it occurs in familiar surroundings. If it happens in a situation such as fieldwork, where one's sense of self is already under attack (Wengle 1988), many dimensions of the trauma, such as feelings of guilt, responsibility, and self-loathing, will be further aggravated. Unless the purpose of the writing is therapeutic or to provide legal testimony, it is almost impossible to write about the rape before the trauma is somehow brought under manageable control.

Then there is pure fear, a generalized fear by the survivor and an insidious relationship of fear between rapist and survivor that is likely to last until the death of either party. For the victim, this is fear of being raped again, or killed. Winkler writes that "rapists bury land-mines in the bodies of their victims," land mines that explode in confusion, nausea, nightmares, tremors, depression, and shakiness (Winkler 1991). If the victim reports the crime, she fears retribution from the rapist. If the rapist should be brought to trial, not only does the survivor have to relive the experience publicly and see the assailant once again, but he may be acquitted of the crime, perhaps with a mind to seek revenge on her for turning him in. And even if the rapist is convicted, the survivor knows he will soon be out, perhaps ready to take revenge on his accuser.

Twenty years have passed since the events I am about to describe took place. After all that time it has still been difficult to write this piece. It is impossible to be a participant observer and eventual reporter in a situation where your life and self are at stake. Your emotions and fundamentally disturbed equilibrium are too private to be traded in for anthropological credits.[3] Nevertheless, time does make a difference. I can look back on the young person who was me, with sadness and fear, but also tolerance and a profound gratitude to the people in the field who interfered and stood by me. I now feel that I owe it to that young woman who was me, and to many other fledgling anthropologists, to recount this story as I understand events after two decades of trying to come to grips with what happened and why.

A Fieldwork Experience

I first went to Ethiopia in 1964, on a five-week stay. I was 20 years old and propelled by an acute infatuation with an Ethiopian student in Sweden, my home country. A year later, I went back as a member of the Swedish Volunteer Service, to work for two years as a social scientist in a development-aid-funded technical organization. After those two years, I returned to Sweden to finish my undergraduate studies in sociology, but I was soon back in Ethiopia for several months in 1968 to do fieldwork for my final research paper.

When I returned to Ethiopia in February 1972 to do fieldwork for my doctoral dissertation, I had used the intervening years to delve into social anthropology for the Africanist knowledge I could not find in Swedish sociology. The goal of my research was to do an urban study, in the small southern town of Ketema, using both survey methods and life history interviews. To do this work, I needed an assistant to help me, preferably a person with a high level of education and a good command of English.

I would have preferred to work with a woman, and I spread that word through my contacts at the university and elsewhere. My networks came up with a couple of female candidates for the job; but in the end neither was interested in prolonged sojourns outside the capital. To most young, educated persons in Ethiopia, living outside the capital was extremely unappealing. If work "in the provinces" was unattractive to young men, it was nearly impossible for young women. Educated girls, like all girls belonging to the upper echelon, were kept, as far as was possible, within their families until they were married. The few who were not under the guardianship of their families had other concerns that made them unwilling to leave the urban scene.

In the end, I had two young men to choose between, both of whom had been suggested by my university contacts. One was several years younger than myself, a sociology major with a high Afro hair-style, flared trousers, nervous at the interview: the very picture of a dandy from the city. The other—whom I will call Yonas—was a man my own age, unobtrusively dressed and coiffed, with previous experience as a fieldworker for one of the national government agencies. Yonas professed to be politically interested (which at that time meant that he was leftist) and did not seem nervous when we spoke. Both Yonas and my other prospective assistant had recently been thrown out of the university, the younger man for the first time, Yonas for the third.

Being expelled from the university was common in those days of political tension, as university students in Ethiopia took the lead in protesting against autocratic political regimes. To be expelled three times, however, was odd. At the time, though, I interpreted this as a sign that Yonas was possessed by a commendable zeal in the pursuit of truth and justice—an interpretation no doubt encouraged by Yonas himself. After some consideration of which of the two men to choose, I finally decided on Yonas, on the basis of this zeal, his experience, his apparent calmness, and his professed interest in the study.

From the very beginning of my relationship with Yonas, I had problems with authority. In my mind, and consequently in my behavior and talk, several conflicting conceptions of authority were superimposed. In my own society, differences of social and economic class certainly existed but were only subtly marked. In the 1940s and 1950s, the existence of class differences in Sweden had been ignored in official political rhetoric. This had changed drastically in the 1960s. Heightened awareness of class differences propelled attempts to eliminate the class markers and undermine the social and economic dynamics that reproduced class inequalities. This effort took many different forms, both officially and informally, from far-reaching reforms of the educational system, to an abolition of the formal, polite *vous* pronoun of address in speech.

In workplaces, this meant doing away with the markers of rank. One newly built university campus, for instance, had no separate dining or meeting spaces reserved for faculty; the same conditions were meant to apply to everyone. Although we never quite reached the point of addressing one another as "comrade," titles were no longer used in face-to-face communication, and employees of all ranks within the same organization used first names to address one another.

But things were not really what they seemed to be. Beneath the professed equality we all knew perfectly well who the boss was and who the subordinate was; who decided and who was compelled to follow "suggestions." All we had done was set aside the more obvious markers of class and status. This worked, in an odd kind of way, because Swedes were a fairly homogeneous people with one religion, one language, and one race; descendants of the two-thirds that were left behind while the more daring lot disappeared to the United States at the turn of the century.

In addition to this confusing and contradictory stance toward authority that I brought with me from home, I also possessed a familiarity, mostly on a subconscious level, with the modern Ethiopian systems of stratification. Ethiopia was, and is, an extremely complex society where different kinds of hierarchies intersect, enforce, and contradict each other. In the 1960s, the most prominent of those hierarchies was the political ("feudal") hierarchy, with the Emperor at the apex. Relatives of the Emperor made up the upper segments of this hierarchy.[4] Other hierarchies were the ethnic ones, the religious ones, the one based on modern secular education, and the one based on wealth. Superimposed on all of these were the gender orders, which were distinct for each ethnic group, including a separate gender order for the urban, "modern" sector of society in which I had planted my roots.

This intricate webwork of hierarchy permeated every aspect of social life. It was everywhere, and was continually reinforced by practices of deference and domination that were inescapable if you were part of Ethiopian society. To be sure, my Ethiopian cronies abroad and in the capital were appalled at the open and ruthless exploitation built into and sustained by the manifold hierarchies; nevertheless, they—and I along with them—were part of the system and we all acted our part in dealing with ministers, beggars, officials, bosses, servants, prostitutes, brokers, thieves, husbands, and wives.

Without being aware of it, I had adopted the same attitudes and behavior towards people around me as my Ethiopian middle-class friends and companions. Unthinkingly, I expected the same kind of response from subordinates as they would have expected and received. I did not realize that the status I had held while living in Ethiopia before had been status by association, derived from the organization I worked for and from the status of the Ethiopians I associated with. Initially, my interaction with others as a solitary foreign researcher, equipped with a car and official permits and certificates, appeared to make most people accept the status I claimed.

After three months in Ethiopia, and one month working with Yonas in the capital on some archives, all preparations were over and I finally moved on to Ketema, with Yonas in tow.

Ketema twenty years ago was a busy town, expanding almost as one stood watching. It had about 12,000 inhabitants, from all of the major ethnic groups in the country. Its structure was typical of African roadside towns, a narrow belt of one-story adobe buildings with tin roofs that clung to a one-kilometer strip of all-weather highway. Nowhere did the town extend more than 500 meters from the highway.

The inhabitants of Ketema earned their living through trade, communication, services, and administration. The town was a town of newcomers, divided along class, ethnic, religious, and neighborhood lines. It catered to travelers and traders; it was full of eating places, dormitories, "nightclubs," and it hosted many one-room bars, run by single women who served local beer—and themselves—on demand. There were also a couple of banks, several gas pumps, two elementary schools and one junior high school, a police station, a sizeable daily market, and a very large weekly market. You could eat out in Ketema on anything from 5 US cents to 1.5 US dollars; you could spend the night in a dormitory for 10 cents or in a highly respectable hotel for 2 dollars.

When Yonas and I first arrived in Ketema, I decided to stay in the respectable hotel. I rented a room for Yonas in the same place, thus introducing a firm note of (assumed) equality into our relationship from the very start. Once we were established in the hotel, the first task that faced me was to find some place to live. I felt that as an anthropologist, I was expected either to live with a family or to have a household of my own. After all, who among us has not been appalled at backstage rumors of senior anthropologists working out of hotels? I realized later that in my situation in Ketema, the obvious thing would have been to set up permanent camp in one of the lesser hotels. But I had no eye for the obvious. I was set on doing things according to the book, and thus began house-hunting.

After having gone through the available dwellings in the town itself, I decided on a house a few hundred meters outside the town, even though it did not fit my idea of an ideal anthropological residence. The house was set apart from the town, and it was nice, spacious, and expensive. It was a stone construction, built by a minor official in a subdivision neighboring that of Ketema, for his eventual retirement. In the meantime, he wanted to rent out the house for a cost corresponding to that of his bank loan. With the house came the official's uncle and the uncle's wife, who lived in the servants' quarters in the back of the house and who looked after the house when it was empty. On one side of the building was an unfinished hotel, on the other a plot of land used for growing potatoes.

The house was big enough for both me and my assistant, so I invited Yonas to have a room in the building. My rationale was that I could not afford to find him a reasonable place in town. In addition, however, I also felt that I might become very lonely in the evenings, so I wanted him around to have someone to talk to. I discussed the advisability of this arrangement with Yonas because I feared that living together might signal to the townspeople that the relationship between Yonas and myself was more than one of employer-employee. Yonas told me that people in town would assume that we had sexual relations regardless of whether he shared the house with me or not, and that I therefore should choose the arrangement that was most practical. My apprehension was eased by the reactions of the old uncle, Benjamin, who was the caretaker of the house. Benjamin obviously did not imagine that Yonas and I were a couple; instead it was clear that he perceived Yonas as a kind of combination bodyguard/staff member.

Ketema, being the transient roadside town that it was, had nearly all essentials for hire. Before long, I had set up office, bedrooms, and kitchen with the aid of the local rental agency and some strong-armed daily laborers.

Early on, I developed serious doubts about Yonas' suitability as a field assistant. He was brooding, moody, excessively flattering, and habitually bragging—often of how he had got the better of someone who had insulted him. This was uncomfortable at the time. In hindsight, it was ominous. But time was short and I felt that I had no real alternative with whom I could replace him. I simply hoped for the best, calmed by my previous positive experience of working relations with young men who seemed superficially similar to Yonas.

One of the first nights in Ketema, while we were still in the hotel, Yonas appeared in my room one evening, dressed only in his underwear. This was my first indication that his interpretation of our relationship was very different from my own. In his view, he explained, the time had come for me to become his lover. I did not take his advance seriously, and I fended him off easily by reiterating my position: I had a permanent partner at home and I had no intention of having other relations while in Ethiopia. He went back to his room with no further protestations.

In retrospect, it seems incredible that this instance did not make me react more definitely. Thinking back, I realize that as a young woman I was so accustomed to men making unwelcome advances toward me that I considered Yonas' proposition quite "normal." It never occurred to me that, as his employer, I was actually in a position to demand that he stop bothering me with requests for sex. In addition, part of my own cultural baggage was an astonishing lack of fear. My generation of young women in Scandinavia felt safe, and was safe,[5] in our own countries. We carried our insouciance with us from the Arctic circle to the Sahara, fearing nothing, and usually getting away with it. Maybe our very innocence protected us. In addition, I had received no relevant field training, nor did I have any senior colleague at home or in the field to whom I could turn for advice. And furthermore, I was also reassured by the chivalrous courtship I had experienced during my earlier years in Ethiopia. What I did not realize was that during those earlier years, I had seemed very young to my Ethiopian friends. They often thought me no more than a teenager—that is to say, inexperienced and in need of protection. Now, four years later, I was clearly a mature woman with no husband or male guardian present. Therefore, I appeared available.

At any rate, as far as Yonas was concerned, this was clearly the case, and soon his campaign was launched. For several weeks it consisted mainly of nagging—interminable "why nots?"—and of not heeding my persistent refusals—refusals that became more determined, definite, and exasperated as time went on. I did not understand why he would not give up. He did not understand why I would not give in.

While all this was going on, data collection got under way. My aim in gathering data was to trace as many of the respondents as I could from a household survey that had been conducted several years previously by the national statistical agency. I wanted to check on the reliability of the survey technique in a setting such as Ketema, and to get an inkling of different kinds of change in the population.

To help with this work, I had employed a middle-aged messenger from the Community Development Center. He was the scout; he went around town with a list of the respondents, starting out by finding the ones he already knew, and then locating others in a snowball fashion. His work was absolutely crucial; not only did he find or get information on 80 percent of the original respondents, he explained the study to the respondents, persuaded them to agree to a second interview, and set the time for that interview. The messenger, Yonas, and I would then interview the respondent with a modified version of the original questionnaire.

As time went by, I felt that my presence was not required during the interviews and I increasingly left Yonas and the messenger to carry them out on their own, while I devoted myself to checking and organizing the compiled data. I was gradually recovering the language skills I had possessed when I left Ethiopia in 1968, but I had not mastered the art of conducting a formal interview with strangers. In the unnatural situation of a formal interview, I realized that I was using Amharic as if it had been Swedish, in a manner as alien to Ethiopians as if I had in fact been speaking a foreign language. Furthermore, hardly any of the respondents had spoken to a foreigner before and the experience affected them greatly. Some simply did not hear me and merely stared, or mumbled that they did not speak English. After proddings from the people listening in on the interview (there were always people listening in) they would listen and respond, but the situation clearly made them feel uncomfortable. I could not have carried out this work on my own. Not that Yonas was much of an interviewer himself, being much too direct and brusque. Without the preparations done by the messenger we would probably have ended up with a large number of refusals. As an interviewer, I think Yonas was conditioned by his previous role as an official in interview situations where the respondents had no choice about whether they wanted to partici-pate or not. At this point in the work, however, I was not yet aware of Yonas' faults as an inter-viewer. That insight came later, when I could compare his style with that of other persons working with me.

After weeks of daily nagging, Yonas quieted down, and for a while I thought he had given up the idea of sexual conquest. I later under-stood that he had merely changed his tactics. He now embarked on impressing on me how crucial his presence was to my work. In the picture he painted, the townspeople identified the study with him, not with me. He led me to believe that our industrious messenger would take orders only from him, and that I would have to start all over, from scratch, in another town, if he decided to quit and leave me.

What went on in the town I did not know. I was used to being stared at, to parents picking up their children to show them the ferenji, the foreigner. Ketema was not a friendly place. It was a town of strangers, with different languages and habits, full of prejudice and mutual suspi-cion. Although I was uneasy about the way the townspeople ignored me, I was not surprised. I blamed it on my own ineptness and inherent timidity. Increasingly I felt that I lived in a glass bowl, with people looking in on me and me looking out at them, but with no real contact, no genuine communication.

By the time we had been at work in Ketema for two months, I was beginning to feel quite shaken. My uneasiness about my isolation was compounded by Yonas' broodiness, which seemed to grow by the day. He had frightening, screaming nightmares, easily audible in my room, which was next to his. When he went out at night, he had taken to carrying a gun. The gun worried me, even though I knew that Ethiopian men prided themselves on being armed, and I had often seen other educated men from the capital bringing hand-guns along when they went out of town. My concern was over what Yonas, in his agitated and surly frame of mind, might do with his gun.

Lacking effective authority, I tried to handle the situation with quasi-psychological tech-niques that were meaningless, inefficient, and condescending under the circumstances. For instance, thinking/hoping that showing trust would generate trustworthiness, I did not lock my bedroom door. Sure enough, I woke up one night to find Yonas in the middle of the room, furiously accusing me of sleeping with every-body else except him.

I do not remember how I repelled this par-ticular advance, but Yonas left the room after a few minutes of loud complaining about my sex-ual discrimination against Ethiopian men. He believed me to be promiscuous: why, he demanded to know, would I not be promiscuous with him? Henceforth I locked my room care-fully, with a bitter feeling of failure and guilt.

Then, one day, Yonas suddenly announced that he quit. The next day he left.

At first, his decision to leave the job made me frantic. His continual insistence that I was dependent on him had influenced me pro-foundly: I had no doubt that my work in Ketema was linked to his person and that I would have to start all over again in another town if he left. Months into fieldwork, I still seemed to be com-pletely incapable of establishing rapport with anybody. The townspeople were distant; even though most respondents answered our ques-tions, they did so with little enthusiasm and the interviews led to no further contact. At this point I believed that this was because the townspeople wanted nothing to do with me.

Besides Yonas, the only people in Ketema with whom I had any kind of social relationship were Benjamin, the old guard who had come attached to my house, so to speak, and his wife. Benjamin was a retired soldier in his late seventies who used to be in the Emperor's service. Upon retiring, he had been promised a piece of land near Ketema where he would be able to support himself farming. Once actually there, however, the local officials would not honor his claim, and he was left without means of support. It was his firm opinion that "if the king only knew" things would be put right. But he had no ways of reaching the king, and while waiting for imperial intercession, he had accepted the position of guard for his nephew's house. Not that he held a very high opinion of his nephew, whose apparent wealth implied advanced levels of corruption, but . . .

His wife Sofia was many years his junior. They had been living together for a year when we met. She had only one eye, and was energetic, industrious, and realistic. She saw the old man as a gullible dreamer but a good man, to be respected for his bravery and his old age. She told Yonas that she had had offers from wealthier, and therefore more attractive, men, but that she felt it her duty to stay by the old soldier, who, in her opinion, could not possibly manage on his own.

The two of them had an easy-going, friendly relationship. Sofia supplemented their income by going around baking in wealthier households several times a week. She also distilled spirits in an ingenious still, composed mainly of bamboo sticks, calabashes, and cow dung. The couple consumed much of what they produced themselves; they often called me in for a snort on my route to and from the latrine ("Good for the heart!"). What they did not drink themselves went to supply some of the simple drinking places in town. The old man, in addition, furthered their economy by renting a piece of land where he grew cereals for their own use and for the market.

Sofia helped me out with washing, cleaning, and shopping. She was very interested in the doings of other people, and was lively and talkative, making her a wonderful source of information about everyday life in Ketema. Through her I learnt many things, including some of the strategies the townspeople used to manage economically.

Benjamin took his guarding seriously. When I told him that Yonas was no longer going to work for me and had left the house, he made no comments. Yet the same night when it was time to go to bed, he came into the house, bringing his big coat and blanket (and a kitten for company), and proceeded to bed down in front of my bedroom door. I was touched, of course, but also deeply embarrassed. The guard did not budge; there was no other way to keep me safe at night, he explained: he could not hear me from his home should anything happen, and it was his responsibility to see that nothing did. In the morning he wrapped up his bedding and went home.

After a couple of days on my own, I was beginning to collect my wits again and, to my surprise, I actually began to feel relieved at Yonas' departure. It looked as if I was finally getting out of what had become an insufferable situation. Changing towns might not be such a bad idea. I was beginning to think that I could start anew with an assistant from whatever town I might choose to work in. A real worry, however, was the short time at my disposal for my fieldwork. My whole project had already been delayed substantially because of the Ethiopian government's reaction to some critical articles that my anthropology supervisor had published in Swedish newspapers. Because of those articles, my research visa had been put on ice, and I spent nine months at home, waiting for the visa and consequently using up my research grant money. Moving to a new town and starting over would mean risking running out of money. However, my plan was simply to be less ambitious, and to try to make as much use as possible out of the material that had already been gathered in Ketema.

At that point, as I was actually beginning to feel happy at the prospect of starting over again,

Yonas came back. He returned nonchalantly, as if nothing had happened, to see if I had changed my mind. Of course, he told me, he never really intended to quit. He was just upset because I would not sleep with him. But now he was ready to get to work again.

In spite of my relief that Yonas had gone, I realized that to take him back would be the "easy" way out. I was going to be leaving Ethiopia soon for a month-long vacation. Yonas and the messenger could wrap up the re-study phase on their own, I reasoned. In a month or so, the first phase of the investigation would be over. Some sort of study seemed possible even if I had completely abandoned the notion of doing fieldwork with the depth I had intended, or the way I assumed all other anthropologists did it. I acquiesced to Yonas' return.

I returned to Ethiopia a month later and found the situation in Ketema as I had left it. Yonas was, if possible, more aggravated than before, and he resumed his campaign of sexual conquest immediately. He began taking out his gun at home. Glowering, he would put it on the table, together with his stock of bullets—five or six—and polish them, trying at the same time to impress me with the potential danger of gun use. I hysterically refused to admit even to myself that this little arms demonstration in any way concerned me. Gradually my sense of reality was giving way until I became just as preoccupied with Yonas, his moods, threats, resignations, and pleadings, as he had become obsessed with me and my resistance to his desires.

Our situation resembled that of a battered wife and her assailant. Seen from the outside, I could have stepped out of the situation at any time. But inside the circle cast by our grotesque relations, I had no ability to defend myself against his manipulations. I could not understand what was going on, except that Yonas seemed to be in the grip of a neurotic, fixed idea and could not be reached by reason or argument. All I could hope for was that the first phase of the study would soon be completed, so that I would have an excuse to put an end somehow to my association with Yonas.

In trying to cope with the extreme stress I felt, I found pretenses to visit the capital. I also fled regularly into writing and reading, and I could bring myself to make no decisions about the next step in the investigation. Gloom.

Finally, one of my oldest Ethiopian friends managed to break through my inertia. I had dropped in at his office in the capital for a cup of coffee and a chat. Casually I told him, as a joke, no doubt, about the bullet-polishing sessions. My situation in Ketema was assuming an eerie quality of normality as my vision of anthropological fieldwork receded. My friend Michael's reaction was unequivocal: "Get rid of the man at once! If you don't he is likely to kill you." Michael offered to lend me a gun. In his view, the situation was too serious for me to be unarmed. I declined, but I returned to Ketema finally realizing that I was in danger.

Even now, though, I was not up to firing Yonas. The many months in Ketema had locked us in a ghastly struggle of wills over which of us would be the one to define our relations. This ongoing battle had left me with a sense of Yonas' inevitability. During the previous several months, however, I had made the acquaintance of two expatriate ladies living in the neighboring town of Woha, 20 kilometers away. They were seasoned in the service of British Overseas Aid and the World Health Organization (WHO), and had worked for more than fifteen years in Asia and Africa. Seeking temporary escape from my glass bowl, I had taken to visiting them during weekends, in what provided a tremendous release from the pressures of "home." I had a car, and the younger of the two had a spare bedroom. Ketema was less than 20 minutes away by car. To break up our incongruous household, I decided to leave Ketema and accept the younger woman's standing offer of bed and breakfast, even if this act felt like the final betrayal of my own neurotic fixed idea—that of fieldwork "according to the book."

On the morning of 4 October, I told Yonas that I was dissolving the household. Furthermore, I would do it the next day. To my surprise, Yonas seemed to accept the new arrangement. But the same night I woke up. Someone was knocking at my door. I turned on the light and looked at my watch. It was one o'clock in the morning.

"What is it?"

"It is me, Yonas! I'm being eaten alive. Hand me the flea spray!"

The flea spray? Was it in my room? Why was it in my room?

I put on my dressing gown. Flea spray in hand, I unlocked and opened my door. Yonas pushed the door with all his strength and forced his entry into the room.

Time stopped. My room was fairly large and bare. My bed was in a corner. The window facing the front garden was shuttered from the inside. The guard Benjamin was sleeping in his own shuttered house, an unreachable 20 meters from where we were. My outer wall on the gable had no window. We were alone.

Yonas grabbed me, my gown, my hair. I was paralyzed. All I could bring myself to do was to retreat into the room, trying to loosen his hands from around my throat.

And then I screamed. Or rather, someone in me screamed. I heard myself screaming—an inarticulate scream, not calling for help, but shrill, loud, like a siren. My whole body seemed to have taken on a life of its own, refusing to move, to kick, to fight back—to do any of the things I knew that it could do. And that horrible scream. Even as I heard the screaming, though, I realized that there was nobody to hear me. There was a potato field just outside the house, but nobody was in that. Benjamin did not hear well, anyway there were three walls and many meters between us; his wife could not possibly hear me either. And what if someone did hear? Yonas had told me many times that people believed we were lovers anyway. Men regularly beat their wives; they would side with Yonas, thinking that I had earned whatever was coming to me.

Yonas made no headway with me. We were the same height, he was no heavier than me and no stronger. My body was stiff as a tree trunk. It kept up its shrill, piercing screaming.

Cold sweat poured down Yonas' face and made his hands slippery. His eyes were huge, bulging, mad. He was beside himself with rage and determination. Unreachable.

He was wearing striped pajamas with pockets. From one of those pockets, he now brought out his gun, almost reluctantly, making sure which way it pointed so as not to shoot himself accidentally. Backing up a few steps, he pointed the gun at me.

The screaming stopped; my mind and body reunited with the realization that my life was at stake, whether he shot me deliberately or not. If the gun went off accidentally, I might bleed to death.

As I looked at the mouth of the gun I had a vision of being directly beneath the black night and the cold, distant stars, cool, clear-headed, with death minutes, maybe seconds, away. And what for? A fixed idea, a manic determination not to give up, to uphold my definition of who I was at any cost?

Yonas began speaking. He told me that since I had decided to leave the house in Ketema he knew this was his last chance to have me. And he would have me now, whatever the cost to himself. He did not care anymore if he lived or died as long as he finally had me. I replied, coldly and perfectly numb, that he could have anything he wanted, anything at all.

At precisely that moment, there was a tremendous pounding on the shutters. Loud voices, many voices, pummeling, shouting. Yonas momentarily lost his step. We were both astounded. Who could it be? Who? To me it was as if the black, void sky had opened and angels had descended to interfere. A fraction of a second passed. Then Yonas recovered and began shouting commands to the people outside. He was absolutely certain they would obey.

"Go back to your beds!," he ordered them, "she only had a bad dream. She is alright. Go home!"

They did not oblige him at once. "We can't hear her!," they shouted back, "She is dead! You have killed her!"

Yonas grew more adamant, "Go back to your beds! I am telling you, she is alright!"

The noise subsided. My hopes died. It was as I feared; the angels were of lesser rank than Yonas; they would have to obey. They would believe what he told them.

But then the voices came back, shouting, "We can't hear her! We are going for the police!"

While this was going on, Yonas kept poking the gun at me, gesturing me toward the bed. His frenzy appeared to be fueled in part by the interference from outside. He let off a seemingly endless stream of words, accusations, explanations. Still beside himself, shaking, clammy, eyes popping, he told me his version of our fieldwork from the moment he had decided to apply for the job. He threw back at me words I had said to fend him off, and emphasize my determination not to have sex with him, but he twisted my words, interpreted them to mean the opposite of what I had intended. All I had said he understood against his image of me as an indiscriminate, promiscuous woman.

I moved toward the bed and sat down. He came toward me, holding me at gunpoint, and still talking, pausing in his tirade only long enough to fling occasional commands to the people outside, who had now gone back to pounding the shutters. He let his pajama bottoms drop. I pulled up my nightgown and dressing gown. At the sight of my genitals his movements were arrested for a moment.

He fell on top of me but had problems with the gun. He tried to push the gun between our bodies to be sure of control while raping me.

But he had stretched his capacity to the limit. Keeping me subdued, telling his story, calming the people outside, and penetrating an unwilling woman—all at the same time—could not be done. The moment our genitals touched he ejaculated. I think. Perhaps his erection collapsed and all that wetness was my body's reaction to rape. I don't know.

And then Yonas' frenzy was over. His features returned to normal. His eyes became comprehending again. He was afraid. He wanted to

be comforted, so he sat on my lap, with the gun still in his hand but no longer pointed at me. After a while he pulled up his pajama pants, went to the front door, and unlocked it to let the people see for themselves that I was alive and "alright."

Yonas must have been a frightening sight, disheveled and pouring with sweat, with a gun in his hand. The people outside drew back. For all they knew he had a corpse inside.

Then Benjamin stepped forward, with all the authority of a royal soldier, erect and tall. "Let me in to see her," he commanded.

And Yonas did. Then he turned on his heels and rushed away into his own room, locking the door behind him.

Benjamin entered my bedroom, and stretched out his arms towards me. "My dear child," he cried, "has he raped you?"

I fell into his arms, not weeping, but shaking uncontrollably. I wanted to get out of the house immediately. I dressed hurriedly, with difficulty.

Benjamin went past Yonas' room to get me a glass of water. As he returned from the kitchen, Yonas stormed out of his room, again frantic, prepared to shoot. The old man stepped between us, and told Yonas to return to his room. He did, and I went out to the car and drove the 20 minutes down to Woha where I found refuge with Sally, one of my two foreign friends.

I never saw Yonas again.

I later learnt that after I left, Yonas appeared from his room again and agreed to hand over his gun to the old man. Benjamin promptly carried the gun outside and buried it under the dirt floor of his own house. He then locked the doors to my room, the kitchen, and the office inside the house so that Yonas could not enter any room other than his own.

In the morning, Yonas asked to be let into the other rooms, claiming he had personal belongings in the office. The old man refused to let him in, saying that I had locked the doors and taken the keys with me when I left. He was afraid, as I was, that Yonas would destroy the material we had already collected. Yonas then took off for Woha himself, seeking shelter with some co-ethnic friends of his who were teachers and officials in that town.

Perspectives on the Rape

Rape in any form is about power and male domination. From the literature, it appears that the most common form of rape is for a man to violate a woman he already knows. One frequent scenario is that of a man who considers himself entitled to sex with a woman who does not accept what he perceives as sexual obligation. These men's demands to have their expectations fulfilled fuel their sense that they have the right to obliterate the will of women under their domination (Brownmiller 1975). Seen in this light, what happened to me in Ketema differs little from what happens to thousands of women annually in every country in the world.

Nevertheless, Ketema is in Ethiopia, and an interpretation of the outrage must be peculiar to that country and the circles to which I and Yonas belonged. Having different Ethiopian interpretations spelled out for me immediately after the events helped me survive, cope, and eventually return to a "normal"—but different—life as an anthropologist. The openness I encountered was triggered by the assault itself, then by my making the crisis public, by the genuine gratification people felt at pointing out what I ought to have done, and, I think, by the fact that Yonas had broken a series of taboos.

Yonas' Justification of the Rape

The following account of the way Yonas justified his act and intended to wreak revenge on me was given to me by Yonas himself during the rape, as described above. Although throughout the rape he appeared to be completely beside himself with fury and determination, he was absolutely

lucid, clear, and comprehensible in his speech. He wanted to make certain that I understood exactly what he was saying. What he told me was burnt into my memory, because of the extreme situation, and because of the shock I experienced as he made me understand how I had been manipulated and maneuvered by him from the very beginning of our relationship.

Long afterwards, I wondered about Yonas' need to tell why he must rape me. Maybe it was not so remarkable. When rape is punishment, then surely it must be imperative for the assailant to assure himself that the object knows why she is being punished.[6] What follows is the essence of what Yonas said during the rape situation; this is his view as he stated it.

Yonas had taken the job as my field assistant and accepted the prospect of months of work in the provinces because he wanted to have a foreign lover. This was the premise on which he went to work for me. He did not say why he was so keen on having a foreign woman. I can only assume that he had accepted the imagery which circulated among some Ethiopian groups that foreign, uncircumcised, independent women were sexually adventurous and promiscuous. He wanted me to understand that there was no other reason why he had applied for the job as my field assistant.

From the beginning of our association I had, in his view, implied that a sexual relation was a real possibility; we only had to wait for the right time and place. He quoted verbatim my turns of phrase or choice of words that on numerous occasions had confirmed his belief that I did eventually intend to gratify his desire. His memory was astounding. I felt intense shame when I heard my own words accurately repeated but distorted to imply meanings that were never intended. He started looking for significance and collecting signs that I would relent on my position when we met, and had continued until he began to suspect that he was going to be "cheated."

Yonas firmly believed that a woman will never reveal her true intentions to a man; therefore everything I said he understood in every way except the literal. All his friends, and his girlfriend in the capital, believed that we were living together as lovers. His girlfriend had therefore left him. The world pointed fingers at him. He had felt deep humiliation and failure when he was assumed to be my lover. In his view, no one would have believed him if he had said that it was not true. (I doubt that he had done much to inform his acquaintances about the true state of affairs. Not being able to seduce such a sexually voracious person as he had convinced himself that I was would not have improved his image as a man.)

He was positive that I had had sex with multitudes of other men. He had spied on me in the capital, and other persons had helped him follow me around. He knew exactly who I had seen. I met many white men unchaperoned; this meant that I had to be sleeping with them.

It was at this point I discovered the source of my isolation from the townspeople. Yonas explained to me that he wanted to keep me dependent on him. Therefore, he had actively worked to keep me isolated in Ketema. With great relish he told me how people had sought him out many times because they were keen to get to know me and to find out what my work in Ketema was all about. He had told them that I was not interested in the townspeople, that I did not want to talk to them or have anything to do with them. He was explicit on this point, wanting me to know how clever he had been in keeping me to himself. He probably also found satisfaction in making me understand how completely I had been in his power. *He* could make or break my work.

He was deeply disappointed and bewildered when I did not live up to my "promises" of sex. He had come to the conclusion that my people were prejudiced against men who were not white. Racial prejudice became the only possible explanation for why I consistently refused his sexual overtures. He concluded that Swedes were as prone to racial prejudice as Americans or Britons, from whom one could expect no better.[7]

Once he had understood that I was not going to fulfill what he saw as his legitimate demands, he had begun planning his revenge. He told me that he had been planning the assault for months. He actually explained his entire scheme before he had brought it to completion because he was so certain that I was in his power, that no one would believe me. I think he was afraid that I might not understand that these events had happened because he willed them and because he was in absolute control.

Yonas had not only manipulated the past, but intended to control the future as well. This is how he predicted the chain of events following the rape: I would fire him. Since we had an employment contract, he would then take me to court for breach of contract. He would dispute my right to fire him. I would then say that he had raped me. He would deny the accusation and no one would believe me. I would have to pay him heavy compensation for firing him unfairly and maybe be made to take him back. My humiliation at his hands would then be total.

About six weeks prior to the attack, he had asked me to make some changes in our contract. I did not understand the reason for this at the time, but saw later how those changes, which in effect made it more difficult for me to end his employment, had strengthened Yonas' plan. When I suddenly announced to him that I was dismantling the household, I had forced his hand. He would either have to carry out his plan that last night or lose the opportunity.

Yonas' story poured out of him as he was pacing the floor in front of the shuttered window, gesticulating with the pistol, and pausing every once in a while to order the people outside to go away. I was sitting on the edge of my bed, waiting for what was going to happen next. On some level, I do not think I really believed that Yonas would complete the rape within earshot of the people outside. At the same time, though, I was beyond caring. My entire concern was about getting out of the situation alive.

Once the fire had gone out of him and his senses returned to normal, Yonas stopped talking.

Benjamin's and Sofia's Reactions to the Rape

Benjamin and Sofia later told me that they had not heard my screams. But on the other side of the fence that separated my compound from the potato fields was a temporary camp of farm laborers, men who had been hired to pick potatoes. Benjamin had visited them when they first came, and had invited them into the compound.

It is very significant that neither Yonas nor myself "remembered" these farm laborers. In Ethiopia, not everybody is a person, a somebody. Servants, paupers, beggars, people from low-status ethnic groups, and "heathens" do not count. As I had understood it, persons below one in ethnic, economic, or occupational rank were not regarded as "people," whereas those equal and above always were. If you were a "nobody" you might as well be part of the furniture as far as your superiors were concerned. Yonas knew the potato pickers were there. Still, he clearly did not recognize them as people who might intervene, and therefore he went ahead with his plan as if the field had, in fact, been empty. He had simply forgotten all about them.

But the field was not empty, and the farm laborers had been aroused at once by my screams. From Benjamin, they knew very well who I was. They also knew that the old man considered himself my ultimate guardian. Therefore, they lost no time in forcing the fence and waking the old man from his sleep.

Benjamin was horrified at Yonas' assault. He had not for an instant believed that I had sexual relations with Yonas. After the rape, again and again, the old man complained bitterly of how Yonas had failed him. "I trusted him as I trusted myself," he said, "I was sure you were safe with Yonas in the house. How could I otherwise have allowed you two to be alone in there?"

Once the old guard was aroused, he lost no time in coming to my rescue. He said that he and the others were certain that I was dead, because of the way my screams rang out and then stopped completely. Still, they had all hesitated about bringing in the police until they knew for certain what had happened.

I was profoundly moved by Benjamin's reasoning and his unquestioning solidarity with me. I probably owed him my life,[8] and had myself seen him put his life at stake for me.

Men's Reactions to the Rape

As the rape became known in Ketema, I received a number of reactions from both men and women. How men reacted depended on how close they were to me and to the drama itself, and how they perceived Yonas.

Benjamin, as I have just noted, was shocked and prepared to act. He voiced no opinions about what I should do afterwards; as far as I understood him, he thought my own shock and near breakdown were correct and adequate reactions to what happened. He agreed that he had indeed saved my life and recognized the deep obligation I had incurred because of this.

The only person who insisted that I go to the police was a young man in town, a teenager whom I had supported since my volunteer days. This man became very upset when I chose not to report the rape to the police. There were several reasons behind my decision not to report to the police. At the time of the rape, in the middle of the night, the main reason was that the only other rape of a foreign woman that I had heard about until then had taken place in a police station, with the police as rapists. I was afraid that the local police would simply carry on where Yonas had left off. Later on, other reasons became more important, such as not wanting to be held up in Ethiopia for months, maybe years, waiting for an uncertain trial. My fear of what would happen if Yonas were acquitted was very strong. I felt that he would be quite likely to seek revenge if I tried to turn him in. Indeed, months later I received an anonymous note from Yonas, handed in at the post office in Ketema, containing the single line, "Stop your slander, or else."

Among other men in town, more distant, the consensus seemed to be that something like rape had been bound to happen. I remember one civil servant telling me that Yonas and myself were like a young bull and a heifer locked in a corral. When I asked why no one had warned me of what they saw as an inevitability, he replied, "You know us, you know our habits and our culture. We did not want to insult you by coming with advice."

Once the rape had occurred, I noticed no change in the behavior of people I regularly dealt with, such as the old messenger, officials at the local bank, post office, etc. It turned out that Yonas was not at all liked.

His hauteur and successful attempts at keeping me isolated had earned him no friends.

The day after the assault, after I definitely decided I did not want to involve the police, a bank official in the nearby town of Woha agreed to act as go-between, to help me terminate my employer-employee relationship with Yonas. The reason why I needed to contact Yonas again was because his story about how he would sue me for compensation haunted me. Until our contractual relations were dissolved, I lived in absolute panic about what he might do next. Maybe he would still find a way of hauling me into court to claim the official compensation he had been dreaming about. Or maybe the fact that he had not been able to penetrate me during the rape had left him in a worse position than when he was merely rejected. Would he try again, then? Or would he kill me to make me shut up?

The banker met Yonas two days after the events. Yonas denied that anything untoward had happened; he told the banker that he could not understand why I did not want to continue working with him. He very much wanted to continue assisting me. Yonas appeared completely calm and reasonable, there was no indication that things were not as he presented them. The banker believed him.

The banker then escorted me back up to Ketema, to pick up some necessities and to find out what had happened after I left. The house was exactly in the same state as it had been when I rushed off in the middle of the night. Benjamin had not opened the doors to my bedroom and the office since then. When the banker saw the confusion in my room, tufts of hair lying about,[9] and the remains of my torn dressing gown, he apologized. And if he had still had any doubts about the veracity of my tale he would have been convinced by Benjamin, who was bursting to tell all. This was the first time I found out how my rescue had been organized.

The banker's reflections were then typical of what I was told by several other men. "We Ethiopians only rape women we know," he explained. His advice was that I should not have remained in one place for as long as I had. I think the maximum "rape-safe" time he mentioned was three weeks. In order to escape molestation, I should have moved between towns, doing as much work as I could in that limited time. He failed to see that I had come to no harm at the hands of the local men from Ketema. The fact was that Yonas was much more like the banker than he was like the locals. Listening to other accounts of threats and assaults among women anthropologists and volunteers in Ethiopia, it later became clear to me that the most serious danger has always come from officials, assistants, and boyfriends—persons belonging to the section of educated, "modern" men whom foreign women are most likely to depend on and befriend.

When I protested at the banker's advice, saying that no serious fieldwork could be done hopping from one place to the other, he suggested that the only other alternative was to "do what our women do." To observe and adjust. To create a "family" and stay within its confines, protected by kinsmen and servants. This was in effect what Benjamin had tried to do for me, as he attempted to create a protective group that ensured that no ill-intended men could reach me. In Benjamin's eyes, I did not blunder when I allowed Yonas a room in the house. It was instead Yonas who was to be blamed and punished for not living up to the protective role that he had been expected to fulfill.

Another clue to the complex of sexual conquest and male domination was given to me by an old acquaintance, who, lamenting the fact that he had not propositioned me when we had

had official dealings with one another six years earlier, explained that he had not made clear his intentions then because he was not certain I would have accepted him. "You see," he told me, "we do not ask until we are certain of being accepted. It is difficult for an Ethiopian to face being turned down."

One dimension of the rape that prompted men to heap scorn on Yonas was the fact that he had used a gun. Rape is one thing, I came to learn, using a gun to subdue a woman is quite another. That, for many men, was what made this rape particularly inexcusable and shameful. Men should master women with words and the dula, a big stick that is a common means of defense and attack, one that looks more like a baseball bat than anything else. Many times I had heard Ethiopian men quote the saying, "With donkeys and women you talk with a dula."[10]

It seems as though, for some men who commented on the rape, the very masculinity that was to be proven by the rape was put in question by the use of the gun. What sort of man was this, who could not make it without threatening a woman with a gun? On this count I had men's unquestionable sympathy. Guns spelled death, which was something quite different from proving your point to a reluctant woman.

On a visit to Ethiopia many years after the rape, I discovered that Ethiopian legal praxis does not recognize "rape" as a crime against women unless the woman concerned is a proven virgin. This was true in the 1970s and it is still true today.

Women's Reactions to the Rape

The rape in Ketema altered my relations with women in Ethiopia completely. My introduction to Ethiopian society had been through men. During my early years in the country, working as a volunteer, all my workmates were men. When I gathered material for my final research paper, in 1968, all my contacts had been men. My original fascination with Ethiopia was powered by intense infatuation with an Ethiopian man. Men, men, men. Women in this world of men were secretaries, servants, relatives,—to me "non-persons," in effect.[11]

All of this now changed. If the women in my immediate surroundings, with the exception of Benjamin's wife Sofia, had until now demurred, served, kept quiet, looked down, and been "nice," they now stood erect, left the shadows, looked me straight in the eye, spoke up, and were furiously cynical.

What they said was simply that this is what we all suffer for being women. As long as we are women we are at the mercy of men. There was no need for me to feel ashamed or unhappy. What had happened to me was horrible and dreadful, but, unfortunately, normal. "As long as we are women . . ."

After the rape, women told me many tales of sexual violence at the hands of men. Their lack of trust in men was absolute. For many women, the prospect of a happy life was the possibility of a life without permanent bonds to men. Economic independence, surrounded by a family of your own, lovers if you wanted them, but no men with rights through marriage or the like—this was their utopian goal.

I felt guilty and ashamed of having been taken in by the male vision of the world, and the picture of sexual warfare painted by the women to whom I spoke was strangely comforting. In my conversations with women, the focus was frequently off me and on the iniquitous sexual organization of female dependency, where sex and domestic services are exchanged for economic security, and where the dependent woman loses her self-determination when she submits to a bond to an individual man. The man, in this contract, loses nothing except maybe his peace of mind, since he continually fears being "outbid" by wealthier, more powerful, and therefore more attractive men.

My Own Reactions to the Rape

After the rape, I was overwhelmed by a flood of information on gender relations and sexuality, but I was in no position to record, understand, or utilize the material. I felt naked, a simple civilian, a deserter from the anthropological field. Any idea that I should put my situation to anthropological use felt blasphemous, a continuation of the rape situation. There was nothing professional in what I was going through. I could barely hold myself together. I was dependent on my surroundings for security and my mental health. The rape had reversed a hierarchy where until then I had held the dominant position as researcher, professional, and foreigner. Now I was just a woman, looking to other women around me for guidance, safety, and advice.

Immediately after the assault, I had two strands of feelings. One was a tremendous fury. If I had had the gun my friend Michael had wanted to lend me, I felt capable of shooting Yonas on the spot. This rage remained with me for years.

The other was immense fear. Part of it was irrational. I felt I would die if I ever laid eyes on Yonas again. I know now that this is a standard reaction among rape survivors. Part of the fear was probably well founded. Yonas had set out to punish me and had constructed an elaborate plan of how this would be done. His plan had failed. If he started out by being humiliated by my refusal to accept him sexually, he left with a humiliation increased manifold. His social inferiors had intercepted him, disobeyed him, and refused to accept his definition of our relations. He had been disarmed by a servant. He had been tricked and fooled. He had failed sexually. And I knew all this and could easily reveal it.

Intuition told me that I was in much greater danger after the assault than before, and that I would continue to be in danger until I was out of the country, a continent away. Or until one of us was dead.

As mentioned above, I used the regional manager of one of the national banks as intermediary to establish contact first with Yonas' intermediaries and then with Yonas himself. Yonas finally agreed to sign a paper releasing me from all further obligations, but to do so, he demanded two months' pay and a letter of rec-ommendation. I paid and wrote the recommendation. He even had the audacity to amend the letter.[12]

The days until these matters were settled were days of panic. I recall crouching in the locked bathroom in the house of my hostess for hours, not daring to be alone in the rest of the house for a minute. "There are those who cope, and those who don't," she told me, recalling incidents from her fifteen years as headmistress in a school in Tanzania. I was not sure that I belonged among those who coped.

With the release paper signed, I felt free to leave. I returned the rented furniture and sold the remaining household utensils. The research material I stored with friends. I made an agreement with Benjamin to continue paying his salary, and turned over the house to his nephew. I then returned to my home country to recover.

I came back to Ethiopia two months later, my morale bolstered by the presence of my mother and my partner from home, who had long planned to visit me in the field anyway. For the duration of their month-long visit, I debated whether or not I could bear to pick up the threads and continue work in Ketema. In the end I decided to stay.

I finished a second survey phase in Ketema, which took another few months. Without Yonas to isolate me, I developed a great number of contacts in the town and could easily have gone on to more intensive work if my mental equilibrium had not been so precarious. It seemed that the rape drama had made me a real person in the eyes of the townspeople, who no doubt had debated events thoroughly in my absence. I sensed neither lack of respect nor moral judgment of me, which, of course, does not mean that negative opinions were absent. After four months my time was up and I left Ethiopia.

I managed quite well as long as I was in Ketema, which ironically became the only place in Ethiopia where I really felt safe, since I was convinced Yonas would not dare to appear in the town again. Once home in Sweden after fieldwork, however, I suffered a delayed reaction. In part, this was similar to what any rape survivor goes through. I had nightmares for years, and for many months I was unable to think about anything else. "Normal" guilt feelings were exacerbated by my thinking that I had created the situation myself, that I had in fact set up Yonas in the rapist role. Emotionally, I somehow felt that Yonas had the right to be seeking revenge. In fact, it was only in the course of writing this chapter that it has finally dawned on me that it was Yonas who maneuvered the whole relationship from the moment he first heard of a foreign woman wanting an assistant. I have known this ever since hearing Yonas' tale on that fateful night. Somehow, however, I have not understood what it meant until now.

Discussion

Despite the twenty-odd years since the start of the second wave of feminist anthropology, and despite the fact that "gender," as a consequence, has definitely been brought into much of anthropological understanding and analysis, anthropology has yet to come to terms with the fact that anthropologists are themselves gendered.[13] The demographic breakdown of social and cultural anthropology is similar to that of many other disciplines in the humanistics and social sciences: there is a majority of young women among students, but a gradually decreasing proportion of women as one approaches the apex of the academic hierarchy (Sanjek 1982). This kind of gendered pyramid structure ensures that female dominance in numbers does not translate into corresponding influence on the academic establishment.

Anthropologists "at home," in universities and departments, and in our lives outside academic institutions, are part of gender orders specific to the times and societies we live in. A central aspect of academic life, however, is the denial of gender at work. That is to say, we are expected to study, administer, write, and teach as if gender did not matter. This fiction is an integral part of academic life, and it can be upheld because we only spend part of our lives at the university. We leave the supposedly "gender-free" world of academia at the end of the day to go out and assume a multitude of gendered roles. Some go home to put their feet up, read the evening newspaper, and delve into the latest anthropological periodicals after dinner has been provided. Others go home to shop, cook, and do dishes, laundry, and whatever else is necessary for life to go on.[14]

For female anthropologists, one of the consequences of the fictitiously "gender-free" life we lead at university is that, if we bring up issues that are specific to us as women in the academic context, we run the risk of doing damage to our identities as anthropologists. This is, of course, because the archetypal anthropologist is a man. Part of the hidden agenda for female anthropologists is, therefore, to avoid drawing attention to ourselves as women when we establish our professional identities. After all, who wants to be a *female* anthropologist when it seems possible to be a "real" anthropologist?[15] As far as the danger of sexual violence is concerned, it may be part of a woman's daily life, but it is not seen to be relevant to the professional part of ourselves—the "anthropologist" part. "Anthropologists" don't get harassed or raped. Women do.

In the field, the false division of time and space between the "professional" and the "private" that underpins the supposedly gender-neutral identity of the anthropologist collapses completely. In the field, it is not possible to maintain a fiction of a genderless self. It is not possible to be an unmarked "anthropologist." In the field, one is marked. One is perceived to be, and one perceives oneself to be, a gendered anthropologist—a female anthropologist or a male anthropologist. And as gendered anthropologists, we cannot only be attractive to others and feel attraction ourselves—we can also be the target of sexual violence; violence that is directed, as it was in my case, as much at our "professional" selves as it is at our "private" selves (where, indeed, is the difference?).

The multidimensional meanings of sexual relations in the field can never be the same for female and male anthropologists. The thundering silence of heterosexual men on the subject is in itself ominously meaningful. Field accounts from women have frequently mentioned sexual aspects of the field situation, probably because in many fields the sexual problematic is forced on female anthropologists and shapes the kind of work we are able to do. The possibility of sexual violence, explicit or implied, is a means by which the movement and activities of women are restricted in many social contexts, and it is therefore an issue that most female anthropologists must deal with, where male anthropologists need not.[16] The question of whether to have sexual relations in the field is something that many female anthropologists have to deal with not occasionally, or once in a while, but more or less continuously, as males like Yonas ask, nag, and demand. All of this is different for men. Other sexual activities are different as well. Commercial sex, for example, might be available for men but never for women.

Rape is a vicious, murderous relation. Rape creates a chasm of mutual incomprehension between women and men. The will to rape is impossible to comprehend for women, and the consequences of rape for the victim-survivor may be equally difficult to understand and to empathize with for men. This being the case, maybe it is not strange that rape has remained a non-subject within our discipline, all other considerations apart. When I returned to my university department in Sweden after the assault in Ethiopia, I told my colleagues what had happened. My female colleagues all expressed shock, concern, and support. My two academic supervisors, on the other hand (both of whom were men), listened to me recount the tale of the attack, but offered little sympathy and never mentioned the topic of rape again. I later heard that one of them told a female graduate student that I must have acted like a fool in the field. Another senior male anthropologist, upon hearing about the rape, sighed that "Such things happen to women in the field."

When I set out to do fieldwork in the 1970s, I worked in Ethiopia with no understanding that my own gender might be an important factor in the fieldwork I did. All I had heard on the topic was my male supervisor telling me that female fieldworkers had advantages over male fieldworkers, because female anthropologists often had access to both female and male social circles. In actuality, the niches open to female fieldworkers vary from field to field, just as the backgrounds of anthropologists vary, and as the fit between the anthropologist and her or his field varies.

What does not vary is the fact that women must always, everywhere, deal with the spectre of sexual violence in a way that fundamentally differs from anything that our male colleagues have to contend with. This does not mean that sexual violence is, by definition, a "woman's problem." On the contrary, rape is most certainly part of a profoundly male problematic. And the point of this chapter is that, whatever else sexual violence against anthropologists may be, it is *by definition* an anthropological problem. It concerns all of us, women and men, and it warrants a strong place on the mainstream anthropological agenda.

Afterword

Well after this chapter was completed and sent into the publishers with the book manuscript, I was suddenly confronted with another, quite unanticipated reason why sexual violence in the field is so rarely discussed in the anthropological literature. Just before the proofs were about to be set, Routledge contacted me and suggested that my contribution be changed to make "Yonas" even more impossible to identify. Calling him by a pseudonym, as I had done (and continue to do), was not considered sufficient to ward off a possible slander suit against Routledge from "Yonas"—even though the events described in my contribution took place twenty years ago and in a country in which, as I have noted, legal praxis does not recognize rape as a crime against women who are not proven virgins. Instead of introducing fictional elements into the text that would have distorted the dynamics of the situation that ultimately led to the assault, I chose to publish the chapter using a pseudonym for myself. My use of a pseudonym is therefore not to protect my own identity but, rather (and I hope that the weighty irony here is not lost on anybody), to protect the identity of the rapist.

Acknowledgments

I would like to thank Margaret Willson and Don Kulick for the encouragement and collaboration they have offered in the writing of this chapter.

Notes

1. Rape always implies death. In this chapter I discuss rape as a means to punish, chastise, and reform individual women. Men and children are also raped, and rape is used on collectives of women in war, but these instances are beyond the reflections made here.

2. See, for instance, Gearing's contribution to this volume.

3. In her contribution to the groundbreaking anthology *Women in the Field,* Diane Freedman writes about how she returned to the field soon after the death of her husband, and how she was overwhelmed with information on death and mourning, as her informants tried to comfort her. She could take no notes and made no professional use of all this. It was real life, aimed at her, not coins for the anthropological market (Freedman 1986).

4. See, for instance, Markakis (1974) for an authoritative description of the Ethiopian polity prior to 1974, or Kapuscinski (1983) for a picture of the atmosphere surrounding the imperial palace.

5. I am not implying that there was no sexual violence against women in Scandinavia at this time, only that the incidence was low—very low compared to the United States, for instance.

6. The man who raped Winkler also spoke to her at length.

7. I have not encountered this kind of interpretation from other Ethiopian men. Ethiopians are very color conscious, but *white* is certainly not at the apex of the color hierarchy. When I worked as a volunteer for the Swedish volunteer service, a number of my Ethiopian workmates told me that their families were afraid they would marry a foreigner and thereby "ruin the blood" of the family. In a similar vein, Ethiopians are fond of telling foreigners of how God, when creating humankind, cast aside the black and the white man alike, preferring the brown Ethiopian, who was created with exactly the "right" color. Yonas' accusations of racism may have arisen from conversations with his friends who had experienced racial prejudice outside Africa.

8. No matter what Yonas' plans had been before the rape, I honestly believe that had we been alone he would not have been able to extricate himself from the situation without killing me.

9. I did not feel Yonas pulling my hair out while trying to subdue me with his hands.

10. This saying was part of the reason why I expected no help, even if someone heard my screaming.

11. To be truthful, this was no great change from how I saw the world of meaning and consequence at home.

12. It never occurred to me that there was actually an alternative to resolving the situation in the very Ethiopian way that I opted for. I could have gone all foreign—involving the embassy and the university that sponsored my stay, invoking all those

beautiful letters of permission and protection that had circulated in the bureaucratic structure prior to my arrival in Ketema. In fact, while I felt I was only floundering about in Ketema, miserably failing my anthropological mission, I had actually acquired a thorough knowledge of many salient aspects of Ethiopian urban life. Maybe participant observation is often like this. We have our minds set on the goals of research agendas, invested in long before we ever arrive in the field, and so we do not appreciate the knowledge and insights that are thrust upon us, since it is the "wrong" knowledge and insight, not primarily about the topics we had set our hearts on studying.

13. There are certainly many other important distinctions largely ignored or unrecognized.

14. Micaela di Leonardo writes in the acknowledgements of her 1991 anthology: "Most of the contributors (and I) are women in 'sandwich generation' positions: especially subject to medical and personal crises—and to those of kin and friends of both parents' and children's generations" (di Leonardo 1991:xi). It goes without saying that there is as yet no "sandwich generation" of men.

15. Dorothy Smith has coined the phrase "bifurcated consciousness" to describe how women in social science manage to take part in an academic enterprise that denies the validity of our life experience as women, and where we are brought to accept male definitions of academic standards in the theory and practice of our disciplines (Smith 1987:6).

16. Unless they are accompanied by wives or daughters. But again, that is "private," and they might not consider their safety to be part of the fieldwork.

References

Brownmiller, Susan (1975) *Against Our Will: Men, Women and Rape.* New York: Simon and Schuster.

di Leonardo, Micaela (1991) "Introduction," in *Gender at the Crossroads of Knowledge: Feminist Anthropology in the Postmodern Era.* Berkeley, Calif.: University of California Press.

Freedman, Diane (1986) "Wife, Widow, Woman: Roles of an Anthropologist in a Transylvanian Village," in Peggy Golde (ed.) *Women in the Field: Anthropological Experiences.* Berkeley, Calif.: University of California Press.

Howell, Nancy (1990) *Surviving Fieldwork: A Report of the Advisory Panel on Health and Safety in Fieldwork.* Special Publication of the American Anthropological Association No. 26. Washington, D.C.: American Anthropological Association.

Kapuscinski, Ryszard (1983) *The Emperor: The Downfall of an Autocrat.* New York: Harcourt Brace Jovanovich.

Kulick, Don (1994) "Response to David Lipset's letter to Anthropology Today, December 1993." *Anthropology Today* Vol. 10, No. 1, p. 13.

Landes, Ruth (1986) "A Woman Anthropologist in Brazil," in Peggy Golde (ed.) *Women in the Field: Anthropological Experiences.* Berkeley, Calif.: University of California Press.

Markakis, John (1974) *Ethiopia: The Anatomy of a Traditional Polity.* London: Oxford University Press.

Sanjek, Roger (1982) "The AAA Resolution on the Employment of Women: Genesis, Implementation, Disavowal and Resurrection." *Signs: Journal of Women in Culture and Society* Vol. 7, No. 4, pp. 845–68.

Smith, Dorothy E. (1987) *The Everyday World as Problematic: A Feminist Sociology.* Milton Keyes: Open University Press.

Wengle, John L. (1988) *Ethnographers in the Field: The Psychology of Research.* Tuscaloosa, Ala.: University of Alabama Press.

Winkler, Cathy (1991) "Rape as Social Murder." *Anthropology Today* Vol. 7, No. 3, pp. 12–14.

17

Unmasking Tradition

A Sudanese Anthropologist Confronts Female "Circumcision" and Its Terrible Tenacity

Rogaia Mustafa Abusharaf

In her essay on female circumcision, Rogaia Abusharaf brings to light an embedded cultural tradition meeting with conflict in today's world. Many African immigrants to the United States have made the general public aware of female circumcision and there is a growing movement to end the practice.

Is female circumcision mutilation or a rite of passage and/or purification? What action is being taken against female circumcision?

I will never forget the day of my circumcision, which took place forty years ago. I was six years old. One morning during my school summer vacation, my mother told me that I had to go with her to her sisters' house and then to visit a sick relative in Halfayat El Mulook [in the northern part of Khartoum, Sudan]. We did go to my aunts' house, and from there all of us went straight to [a] red brick house [I had never seen].

While my mother was knocking, I tried to pronounce the name on the door. Soon enough I realized that it was Hajja Alamin's house. She was the midwife who performed circumcisions on girls in my neighborhood. I was petrified and tried to break loose. But I was captured and sub-

dued by my mother and two aunts. They began to tell me that the midwife was going to purify me.

The midwife was the cruelest person I had seen. . . . [She] ordered her young maids to go buy razors from the Yemeni grocer next door. I still remember her when she came back with the razors, which were enveloped in purple wrapping with crocodile drawing on it.

The women ordered me to lie down on a bed [made of ropes] that had a hole in the middle. They held me tight while the midwife started to cut my flesh without anesthetics. I screamed till I lost my voice. The midwife was saying to me, "Do you want me to be taken into police custody?" After the job was done I could not eat, drink or even pass urine for three days. I remember one of my uncles who discovered what they did to me threatened to press charges against his sisters. They were afraid of him and they decided to bring me back to the midwife. In her sternest voice she ordered me to squat on the floor and urinate. It seemed like the most difficult thing to do at that point, but I did it. I urinated for a long time and was shivering with pain.

Reprinted with the permission of the New York Academy of Sciences. 7 World Trade Center. 250 Greenwich St., 40th Floor. New York, NY 10007. www.nyas.org

Rogaia Mustafa Abusharaf is a Sudanese-born anthropologist. She is a visiting scholar at the Pembroke Center for Teaching and Research on Women at Brown University in Providence, Rhode Island, and a lecturer at the University of Connecticut in Storrs.

It took a very long time [before] I was back to normal. I understand the motives of my mother, that she wanted me to be clean, but I suffered a lot.

—from a 1989 interview with Aisha Abdel Majid, a Sudanese woman working as a teacher in the Middle East

Aisha Abdel Majid's story echoes the experience of millions of African women who have undergone ritualized genital surgeries, often as young girls, without anesthesia, in unsanitary conditions, the surgical implement a knife, a razor, a blade or a broken bottle wielded by a person with no medical training. The pain and bleeding are intense; the girls sometimes die. Survivors are prone to a host of medical complications that can plague them throughout their lives, including recurrent infections, pain during intercourse, infertility and obstructed labor that can cause babies to be born dead or brain-damaged.

Female circumcision, also known as genital mutilation, is a common practice in at least twenty-eight African countries, cutting a brutal swath through the center of the continent—from Mauritania and the Ivory Coast in the west to Egypt, Somalia and Tanzania in the east. The ritual also takes place among a few ethnic groups in Asia. Where it is practiced, female circumcision is passionately perpetuated and closely safeguarded; it is regarded as an essential coming-of-age ritual that ensures chastity, promotes cleanliness and fertility, and enhances the beauty of a woman's body. In Arabic the colloquial word for circumcision, *tahara,* means "to purify." It is estimated that between 100 million and 130 million women living today have undergone genital surgeries, and each year two million more—mostly girls from four to twelve years old—will be cut.

Last December genital mutilation became illegal in Egypt, thanks to a closely watched court decision, and women's groups in Africa and abroad hope that the landmark ruling will bolster eradication efforts worldwide. But most people working for change recognize that government action, though an important and useful symbol, is ultimately not the answer. Barbaric though the ritual may seem to Westerners, female circumcision is deeply enmeshed in local traditions and beliefs. Treating it as a crime and punishing offenders with jail time would in many cases be unfair. Mothers who bring their daughters for the operation believe they are doing the right thing—and indeed, their children would likely become social outcasts if left uncut. You cannot arrest an entire village.

Make no mistake: I believe that genital mutilation must end if women are to enjoy the most basic human rights. But it does little good for a Westerner, or even an African-born woman such as myself, to condemn the practice unilaterally. We must learn from history: when colonial European powers tried to abolish the surgery in the first half of this century, local people rejected the interference and clung even more fiercely to their traditions. Without an understanding of indigenous cultures, and without a deep commitment from within those cultures to end the cutting, eradication efforts imposed from the outside are bound to fail. Nothing highlights the problem more clearly than the two terms used to describe the procedure: is it circumcision, an "act of love," as some women call it, or mutilation? Contradictory though the answer might seem, it is both.

Because genital cutting is considered an essential aspect of a woman's identity, abolishing it has profound social implications. Think of the politics and emotions in Western countries that have swirled around issues such as abortion, the right of homosexuals to be parents and the ethics of human cloning. Any change that requires a readjustment of long-established social mores makes people highly uncomfortable.

The justifications for female circumcision vary. Some ethnic groups in Nigeria believe that if a woman's clitoris is not removed, contact with it will kill a baby during childbirth. Other people believe that, unchecked, the female genitalia will continue to grow, becoming a grotesque penislike organ dangling between a woman's legs. Vaginal secretions, produced by glands that are often removed as part of the surgery, are thought to be unclean and lethal to sperm.

Circumcision is also intended to dull women's sexual enjoyment, and to that end it is chillingly effective. In a survey conducted in Sierra Leone, circumcised women reported feeling little or no sexual responsiveness. The clitoris is always at least partially removed during the operation, and without it orgasm becomes practically impossible. Killing women's desire is thought to keep them chaste; in fact, genital cutting is so closely associated with virginity that a girl who is spared the ordeal by enlightened parents is generally assumed to be promiscuous, a man-chaser.

Such beliefs may seem absurd to outsiders. But in the nineteenth century respected doctors in England and the United States performed clitoridectomies on women as a supposed "cure" for masturbation, nymphomania and psychological problems. Today some girls and women in the West starve themselves obsessively. Others undergo painful and potentially dangerous medical procedures—face lifts, liposuction, breast implants and the like—to conform to cultural standards of beauty and femininity. I am not trying to equate genital cutting with eating disorders or cosmetic surgery; nevertheless, people in the industrialized world must recognize that they too are influenced, often destructively, by traditional gender roles and demands.

Local custom determines which kind of genital surgery girls undergo. Part or all of the clitoris may be removed; that is called clitoridectomy. A second kind of operation is excision, in which the clitoris and part or all of the labia minora, the inner lips of the vagina, are cut away. Clitoridectomy and excision are practiced on the west coast of Africa, in Chad and the Central African Republic, and in Kenya and Tanzania.

The most drastic form of genital surgery is infibulation, in which the clitoris and labia minora are removed, and then the labia majora,

the outer lips of the vagina, are stitched together to cover the urethral and vaginal entrances. The goal is to make the genital area a blank patch of skin. A Sudanese woman in her sixties I interviewed told me that the midwife performing the surgery is often reminded by a girl's kinswomen to "make it smooth and beautiful like the back of a pigeon." A new opening is created for the passage of urine and menstrual blood and for sex—but the opening is made small, to increase the man's enjoyment. After the operation a girl's legs may be tied together for weeks so that skin grows over the wound. Women who have undergone infibulation must be cut open before childbirth and restitched afterward. Infibulation is practiced in Mali, Sudan, Somalia and parts of Ethiopia and northern Nigeria.

Genital surgery is usually performed by a midwife, either at her home, in the girl's home or in some cases in a special hut where a group of girls is sequestered during the initiation period. Midwives often have no medical training and little anatomical knowledge; if a girl struggles or flinches from the pain, the surgical instrument may slip, causing additional damage. There is also concern that unsterilized circumcision instruments may be spreading the AIDS virus. Among affluent Africans there is a growing trend to have the operations performed by physicians in private clinics—sometimes as far away as Europe—where general anesthesia is administered and conditions are hygienic.

The word circumcision (literally, "cutting around"), which was borrowed from the male operation, is a striking misnomer when applied to the procedures performed on women. Male circumcision, in which the foreskin of the penis is removed, is not associated with health problems, nor does it interfere with sexual functioning or enjoyment. By contrast, the immediate complications of female genital surgery include tetanus and other infections, severe pain, and hemorrhaging, which can in turn lead to shock and death. In July 1996 the Western press reported that an eleven-year-old Egyptian girl had died following a circumcision performed by a barber. The following month a fourteen-year-old girl died, also in Egypt. Countless other deaths go unreported.

Long-term complications of genital surgery are also common, particularly for women who have been infibulated. Scar tissue blocking the urethral or vaginal opening can lead to a buildup of urine and menstrual blood, which, in turn, can cause chronic pelvic and urinary-tract infections. The infections can lead to back pain, kidney damage, severe uterine cramping and infertility. If sebaceous glands in the skin become embedded in the stitched area during the surgery, cysts the size of grapefruits may form along the scar. Nerve endings can also become entrapped in the scar, causing extreme pain during sex.

Childbirth poses many special dangers for the infibulated woman. The baby's head may push through the perineum, the muscular area between the vagina and the anus. Sometimes a fistula, or abnormal passage, between the bladder and the vagina develops because of damage caused by obstructed labor. Women who develop fistulas may suffer frequent miscarriages because of urine seeping into the uterus. In addition, they smell of urine and often become outcasts.

Not surprisingly, depression and anxiety are also frequent consequences of genital surgery—whether spurred by health problems, fears of infertility, or the loss of a husband's attention because of penetration difficulties.

In spite of its grim nature, female circumcision is cloaked in festivity. Girls are feted and regaled with gifts after the operation. In some societies the experience includes secret ceremonies and instruction in cooking, crafts, child care and the use of herbs. After circumcision adolescent girls suddenly become marriageable, and they are allowed to wear jewelry and womanly garments that advertise their charms. Among the Masai of Kenya and Tanzania, girls undergo the operation publicly; then the cutting becomes a test of bravery and a proof that they will be able to endure the pain of childbirth. Cir-

cumcision gives girls status in their communities. By complying, they also please their parents, who can arrange a marriage and gain a high bridal price for a circumcised daughter.

The consequences of not undergoing the ritual are equally powerful: teasing, disrespect and ostracism. Among the Sabiny people of Uganda, an uncircumcised woman who marries into the community is always lowest in the pecking order of village women, and she is not allowed to perform the public duties of a wife, such as serving elders. Uncut women are called girls, whatever their age, and they are forbidden to speak at community gatherings. The social pressures are so intense that uncircumcised wives often opt for the operation as adults.

Girls, too, can be driven to desperation. A Somali woman identified as Anab was quoted in a report by a local women's group:

> When girls of my age were looking after the lambs, they would talk among themselves about their circumcision experiences and look at each other's genitals to see who had the smallest opening. Every time the other girls showed their infibulated genitals, I would feel ashamed I was not yet circumcised. Whenever I touched the hair of infibulated girls, they would tell me not to touch them since I was [still] "unclean." . . . One day I could not stand it anymore. I took a razor blade and went to an isolated place. I tied my clitoris with a thread, and while pulling at the thread with one hand I tried to cut part of my clitoris. When I felt the pain and saw the blood coming from the cut I stopped . . . I was seven years old.

Yet despite the peer pressure and the benefits to be gained from being circumcised, the prospect of the operation can loom threateningly over a girl's childhood, poisoning everyday activities and filling her with fear and suspicion. Memuna M. Sillah, a New York City college student who grew up in Sierra Leone, described in a recent story in *Natural History* how as a child, whenever her mother sent her on an unusual errand, she feared that it might be a trick, that this might be the moment when strange women would grab her and cut her flesh. And Taha

Baashar, a Sudanese psychologist, has reported the case of a seven-year-old girl who suffered from insomnia and hallucinations caused by fear of the operation. The problems reportedly improved when the girl was promised she would not be circumcised.

The origins of female circumcision are uncertain. Folk wisdom associates it with ancient Egypt, though the examination of mummies has so far provided no corroboration. Ancient Egyptian myths stressed the bisexuality of the gods, and so circumcision may have been introduced to clarify the femininity of girls. (In some African countries the clitoris is considered a masculine organ, and in the fetus, of course, both clitoris and penis develop from the same precursor tissue.) At any rate, the ritual certainly dates back more than 1,000 years: the eighth-century poet El Farazdaq denounced the tribe of Azd in the Arabian peninsula in one of his lampoons, writing that their women had never experienced the pain of circumcision and were therefore "of inferior stock."

Although female circumcision is practiced by Africans of all religions—Muslims, Christians and Ethiopian Jews, as well as followers of animist religions, such as the Maasai—it is particularly associated with Islam. Many Muslims believe the ritual is a religious obligation. In fact, however, female circumcision is not mentioned in the Koran, and it is unknown in predominantly Muslim countries outside of Africa, such as Saudi Arabia and Iraq. What seems likely is that when Islam came to Africa, its emphasis on purity became associated with the existing practice of genital cutting—much the way early Christianity assimilated existing pagan rituals such as decorating evergreen trees.

Female circumcision came to European attention long ago. An early historical record can be found in the writings of Pietro Bembo, the sixteenth-century Italian cardinal:

They now . . . sailed into the Red Sea and visited several areas inhabited by blacks, excellent men, brave in war. Among these people the private parts of the girls are sewn together immediately after birth, but in a way not to hinder the urinary ways. When the girls have become adults, they are given away in marriage in this condition and the husbands' first measure is to cut open with a knife the solidly consolidated private parts of the virgin. Among the barbarous people virginity is held in high esteem.

Other Europeans also wrote about genital cutting in accounts that were read by generations of foreign travelers to Africa. But despite some attempts by Christian missionaries and colonial powers to intervene, genital mutilation remained largely unknown abroad until the 1950s, when nationalist struggles gave rise to the women's movement in Africa. It was then that local activists and medical professionals began publicly condemning the practice.

After college I lived in Khartoum and worked for two years at a development corporation. A secretary I became friendly with there, whom I will call Shadia, confided in me that she found intercourse painful because of the effects of her circumcision. She and her husband had agreed, she told me, that any daughters of theirs would not be cut.

Two years ago I returned to Sudan to visit friends and I looked up Shadia. We had not seen each other for a decade. We embraced; I asked about her children and she pulled out a photograph. I gasped. The three girls, the youngest of whom was about six, were dressed in jewelry and fancy clothes, their hands and feet patterned with henna, and around their shoulders they wore traditional maroon-and-gold satin shawls called *firkas*. It was unmistakably a picture from a circumcision celebration. How could my friend have had such a change of heart? I was shocked.

Shadia explained. One day while she was at work, her mother-in-law, who lived with the family, had secretly taken the girls to be circumcised, in defiance of their parents' wishes. When Shadia's husband, a truck driver, returned home, he was so distraught that he left the house and did not return for a week. Shadia was also heartbroken but she consoled herself that the girls had "only" been given clitoridectomies; at least they had not been infibulated, as she had. "It could have been worse," she told me resignedly.

Entrenched customs die hard, and the task facing anticircumcisionists is daunting. They can take heart, however, from the precedents: foot binding and widow burning, once widespread in China and India, respectively, have been abolished.

International efforts to end genital mutilation began in 1979, when the World Health Organization published statements against it. Then, after a gathering of African women's organizations in Dakar, Senegal, in 1954, the Inter-African Committee Against Traditional Practices Affecting the Health of Women and Children was formed; since then, affiliates in twenty-three African countries have been working to end the practice. In 1994 the International Conference on Population and Development in Cairo adopted the first international document to specifically address female genital mutilation, calling it a "basic rights violation" that should be prohibited.

A variety of projects have aimed to end genital cutting:

- *Alternative initiation rituals:* In 1996 in the Meru district of Kenya, twenty-five mother-daughter pairs took part in a six-day training session, during which they were told about the health effects of circumcision and coached on how to defend the decision not to be cut. The session culminated in a celebration in which the girls received gifts and "books of wisdom" prepared by their parents.

- *Employment for midwives:* In several African countries, programs have aimed at finding other ways for midwives and traditional healers to make a living. A soap factory set up near Umbada, Sudan, with help from Oxfam and UNICEF is one example.

- *Health education:* Many African governments have launched public-information

campaigns. In Burkina Faso, for instance, a national committee has held awareness meetings and distributed teaching materials. A documentary film, *Ma fille ne sera pas excisée* ("My daughter will not be excised"), has been shown on national television. And in Sierra Leone, health workers found that when it was explained to women that genital surgery had caused their physical ailments, they were more willing to leave their daughters uncut.

So far the success of such pilot projects remains uncertain. The available statistics are disheartening: in Egypt, Eritrea and Mali the percentages of women circumcised remain the same among young and old. Attitudes, however, do seem to be shifting. In Eritrea, men and women under twenty-five are much more likely than people in their forties to think the tradition should be abandoned. And in recent years in Burkina Faso, parents who are opposed to circumcision but who fear the wrath of aunts or grandmothers have been known to stage fake operations.

Refugees and immigrants from Africa who arrive in Australia, Canada, Europe or the United States have brought genital mutilation more immediately to Western attention. On the basis of the 1990 U.S. Census, the Centers for Disease Control and Prevention in Atlanta, Georgia, has estimated that at least 168,000 girls and women in the United States have either been circumcised or are at risk. In the past four years the U.S. Congress and nine state governments have criminalized the practice, and similar laws have been passed in several European countries. So far in the United States, no one has been prosecuted under the new laws.

Meanwhile, Fauziya Kassindja, a twenty-year-old woman from Togo, spent more than a year behind bars, in detention centers and prisons in New Jersey and Pennsylvania, after fleeing to the United States in 1994 to avoid circumcision. Her mother, who remained in Togo, had sacrificed her inheritance and defied the family patriarch to help her escape. A U.S. immigration judge initially denied Kassindja's claim of persecution, saying her story lacked "rationality." Later, his ruling was overturned, and Kassindja was granted political asylum.

Western ignorance and incredulity regarding female circumcision have made life difficult and even dangerous for immigrant Africans. I recently met an infibulated Sudanese woman living in New England who was having trouble finding a gynecologist trained to treat her. "I am six months pregnant and I don't know what to expect," she told me fearfully. While pressing for an end to the practice, advocates must not ignore its victims. Perhaps exchange programs should be arranged for American gynecologists and obstetricians, to enable them to learn appropriate prenatal care from their African counterparts.

Every society has rules to which its members are expected to conform. But for African women, belonging exacts too high a price. Whereas African men often have more than one wife and freely engage in extramarital sex, "the acceptable image of a woman with a place in society [is] that of one who is circumcised, docile, fertile, marriageable, hardworking, asexual and obedient," writes Olayinka Koso-Thomas, a Nigerian physician.

The irony is that, in a society that forces women to reconstruct their bodies in order to be socially and sexually acceptable, most men prefer sex with uncircumcised women. In a study of 300 Sudanese men, each of whom had one wife who had been infibulated and one or more who had not, 266 expressed a strong sexual preference for the uninfibulated wife. A second irony is that circumcision does not guarantee a woman a secure marriage; in fact, the opposite may be true. Infibulated women are more prone to fertility problems, which in Africa is grounds for being cast off by a husband. One study has shown that infibulated women in Sudan are more than twice as likely as other women to be divorced.

It might seem odd that women, not men, are the custodians of the ritual—in fact, a Sudanese man recently made headlines by filing a criminal lawsuit against his wife for having their two daughters circumcised while he was out of the country. Why do women subject their daughters to what they know firsthand to be a wrenchingly painful ordeal? Many are simply being practical. "I think that it is very important for the virginity of women to be protected if they want to get husbands who respect them," a fifty-five-year-old Sudanese mother of five girls told me. To get married and have children is a survival strategy in a society plagued by poverty, disease and illiteracy. The socioeconomic dependence of women on men colors their attitude toward circumcision.

But male oppression is not the biggest problem women face in Africa. Africans—men and women alike—must still cope with the ugly remnants of colonialism, the fact that they and their land have been exploited by Western nations and then abandoned. They are struggling to build democratic systems and economic stability from scratch. For African feminists, Western outrage about genital mutilation often seems misplaced. On a continent where millions of women do not have access to the basics of life—clean water, food, sanitation, education and health care—genital mutilation is not necessarily the top priority.

Studies have shown that the more educated women are, the less willing they are to have their daughters circumcised. I have no doubt that when African women have taken their rightful places in the various spheres of life, when they have gained social equality, political power, economic opportunities, and access to education and health care, genital mutilation will end. Women will make sure of that.

Problem Set #9

Proximate Motivations for Reproductive Strategies and Sexual Conflict

To do this problem set, you will need to read the introduction to Unit V and Chapters 15 and 16.

1. Many behavioral traits of men and women (e.g., certain mating preferences) should be regarded as evolved adaptations.

   a. What does the idea that such traits are adaptations require?

   b. Does it require any conscious awareness of their evolutionary function?

   c. Why might male choice have shaped the evolution of female breasts and buttocks?

   d. Why might people adopt unrelated offspring?

2. The following questions concern the naturalistic fallacy (Chapter 1).

   a. What is the naturalistic fallacy?

   b. Why is it important to guard against it when exploring the adaptive basis of human behavior?

3. Rape is an extreme form of conflict between the sexes, but not all researchers want to view it as "sexual conflict."

   a. What is the conventional social science explanation of rape?

   b. Are there any problems with this model; that is, do its predictions match the occurrence of rape?

   c. Outline an adaptive explanation for rape and explore the degree to which it fits or does not fit the evidence.

   d. If rape were adaptive, would all men be expected to be rapists?

   e. If the adaptive explanation of rape were correct, what societal changes might it suggest for reducing the frequency of rape?

Unit VI
Sexual Orientation

The first reading of this unit considers the development and evolution of homosexuality. This reading begins by defining homosexuality and then discusses the genetic, hormonal, and neuroanatomical bases of homosexuality. Is sexual orientation heritable? If so, what are the mechanisms that mediate the relationship between genotype and sexual phenotype, leading to homosexuality or heterosexuality? Although this area is still not fully understood, current data bearing on these issues—the results of experiments using animal models and studies of natural human variation—are discussed. Human data on male and female homosexuality are both considered, although data on female homosexuality are relatively scarce. Finally, some hypotheses are discussed that attempt to explain the existence of "gay genes"—genes that are statistically associated with homosexuality. This is a question of considerable interest to human evolutionary biologists, given the apparent fitness costs of homosexuality.

In the next reading of this unit, Gilbert Herdt and Andrew Boxer delve into bisexuality, to them a "perpetual quagmire of sexual theory." Herdt and Boxer examine how the *sexual identities* of people classified as bisexual are related to the cultures in which they live. To Herdt and Boxer, sexual identity includes erotic desires, sexual orientation, sexual object choice, and sexual drive. Sexual identity also involves the transformation of these sexual desires into behavior or *sexual action,* a process that can be understood only within a particular cultural context.

Herdt and Boxer distinguish four "ideal types" of same-sex sexual action: age-structured, gender-structured, role- or class-structured, and gay or egalitarian-structured. Age-structured same-sex behaviors are represented by the Sambia of New Guinea, about 50 nearby Melanesian cultures, Ancient Greece and Tokugawa, Japan, in which men regularly practice or practiced same-sex behavior as part of male initiation rituals. Herdt and Boxer consider the Sambia culture, in which boys undergoing initiation are removed from their mothers and other women and brought into the men's house, which is forbidden to women. At several times during their initiation, boys are expected to perform fellatio on older boys and unmarried men.

Herdt and Boxer argue that to refer to this practice as "homosexuality" seems "inelegant and unreflective." Indeed, after marriage,

> . . . the vast majority of [Sambia] males do terminate their relations with boys. Perhaps 90% or better of men do so, in part because of exclusive sexual access to one or more wives, with genital pleasure being conceived of as more exciting than intercourse with boys.

In other words, even though they engage in same-sex *sexual action*, most of the participants (predominantly adolescent boys) are probably heterosexual in terms of their *sexual orientation*. This practice appears to represent a more general pattern among men (especially young men), whereby sexual gratification is obtained rather indiscriminately in relation to the object of gratification (e.g., through boys, animals, masturbation, inanimate objects, and in prison, other men).

But why, in cultures such as the Sambia, are same-sex practices so institutionalized? The motivation for these practices is clarified by asking whose reproductive strategies (see Chapter 12) they benefit. The answer seems clear; older, married, heterosexual men benefit. By maintaining these traditions, older men can minimize competition for women and threats to paternity by effectively removing young men from the mating pool. Indeed, the many unmarried young men are likely to be attracted to older men's wives, who are often much younger than their husbands. Among the Yanomami of Venezuela, for example, age differentials between men and their wives are also large, and unmarried boys "expend much effort attempting to seduce girls of their own age—who are generally married women, often with several children" (Peters-Golden 1997, p. 245). Sambia men appear to solve this problem by forbidding initiates from all heterosexual activity and by warning them of "the most fearful supernatural power" that brings death to adulterers (Herdt 1987, p. 156).

The ritualized homosexual behavior of the Sambia thus appears to be a tradition perpetuated largely by men with *heterosexual* orientations. This is not to say, however, that men with relatively exclusive homosexual preferences do not exist among the Sambia and similar cultures. The few men who continue having sexual relations with young men may constitute examples. "One such man, Kalutwo, has been studied in depth, and his sexual and social history reveals a pattern of broken, childless marriages, with an exclusive attraction to boys."

Next, Herdt and Boxer discuss the results of their interviews with 202 fourteen- to twenty-year-old gays and lesbians who attended a gay and lesbian community center in Chicago. Many gays and lesbians had engaged in opposite-sex sexual behavior in accord with societal norms, though heterosexual sex was "discrepant with their erotic desires and feelings." Thus, Herdt and Boxer find that sexual fantasy and preference are more temporally stable than behavior. They state that sexual orientation is "intrinsic," by which they seem to mean relatively predetermined from birth. Herdt and Boxer find that, among Chicago youths, sexual fantasy and preference are more bimodally distributed than is sexual behavior. To the gay and lesbian youths, bisexuality represents a transitional stage in the formation of a gay or lesbian identity. As Herdt and Boxer quote an informant, "Bisexuality is what you say until you are OUT." Thus, although the *sexual action* of American gays and lesbians and of the Sambia may be described as bisexual, the *sexual orientation* of very few seems to be reasonably described as bisexual.

In the final reading of this unit, Evelyn Blackwood considers how her homosexuality enabled her to close the social distance between herself as an anthropological researcher and the subjects of her ethnographic fieldwork. As you may recall from Chapter 1, cultural anthropologists employ participant observation as a method of gathering information about another culture. For Blackwood, learning about another culture requires finding similarities between oneself and the people being studied. Blackwood describes how she was able to do this through her romantic involvement with another lesbian in West Sumatra, Indonesia, where she carried out her fieldwork.

Despite their common homosexual orientation, however, Blackwood and her lover, "Dayan," have many different expectations about their identities as lesbians. For example, Dayan expects their relationship to take the masculine/feminine form characteristic of heterosexual relationships along with many of the associated gender-differentiated roles. Blackwood rejects the necessity of this masculine/feminine model. The differences between Blackwood's and her lover's beliefs and expectations surrounding lesbian relationships illustrate the distinction made by Herdt and Boxer between sexual orientation (which was shared) and sexual identities (which differed and had to be negotiated).

References

Herdt, G. 1987. *The Sambia: Ritual and gender in New Guinea.* Fort Worth, TX: Holt, Rinehart and Winston.
Peters-Golden, H. 1997. *Culture sketches: Case studies in anthropology,* 2nd ed. Boston: McGraw-Hill.

18

The Ontogeny and Evolution of Homosexuality

David A. Puts

In this chapter, we will consider the causes of homosexuality. What are the proximate causes? How are genetic, hormonal, neuroanatomical, and environmental factors related to sexual orientation? Is homosexuality heritable? If so, what are the ultimate causes of its persistence despite the apparent fitness costs? Before we explore answers to these questions, let's first be clear about what we mean by homosexuality.

Who's Gay?

What is homosexuality? Should people be considered homosexual simply because they identify themselves that way? Does it relate to whom they are attracted—or about whom they fantasize? Or is it because of their sexual behavior? Is sexual orientation a relatively stable trait, or does it fluctuate over a person's lifetime? For that matter, is homosexuality really a discrete phenomenon, or merely one end of a continuum?

Dimensions of Sexuality

Sexual Stability in Men

Four dimensions of sexuality are conventionally used to assess sexual orientation via the *Kinsey Scale* (Kinsey, Pomeroy, and Martin 1948). These dimensions include self-identification, attraction, fantasy, and behavior. According to the Kinsey Scale, a subject is assessed for each of the four dimensions, from 0 for exclusive heterosexuality to 6 for exclusive homosexuality. Dean Hamer and his colleagues (1993) used the Kinsey Scale to evaluate sexual orientation in a sample of 144 North American gay men and 22 of their heterosexual relatives. These researchers found a high degree of consistency between each individual's score on one dimension and his scores on the others. For example, men who self-identified as exclusively homosexual (a score of 6 for the self-identification dimension) were very likely to be attracted to and fantasize only about men and to have engaged in sex primarily with men (scores of 5 or 6 for the attraction, fantasy, and behavior dimensions).

Moreover, these scores appeared to remain stable over time; when men were asked questions designed to assess these four sexuality dimensions in the past, present, and ideal future, there was little change. Straight men were most stable over time for self-identification, sexual attraction, and fantasy. Some straight men had engaged in homosexual activities in the past, especially during puberty when boys tend to experiment sexually (Hamer and Copeland 1994). Gay men were most stable for sexual attraction and fantasy. This was probably due in part to the stigma attached to homosexuality. Many gay men did not at first acknowledge to themselves that they were homosexual, and most had tried sex with women in the past. For gay men, self-identification as "gay" or "homosexual" typically occurred well after their attraction to men began. The median age of self-acknowledgment was 16, but ranged from 4 to 30 years. The mean age of acknowledgement to others was 21 years (Hamer and Copeland 1994). For men attracted to women, self-identification as "straight" or "heterosexual" was generally taken for granted.

Sexual Stability in Women

When the four dimensions of sexuality measured by the Kinsey Scale are evaluated in women, they appear to be similar to men in that they exhibit the greatest temporal stability for the attraction/fantasy dimensions. Lisa Diamond (2000) performed a longitudinal study in which she interviewed 80 self-identified "nonheterosexual" women, ages 16–23, and then reinterviewed them two years later. Diamond found that one-third of the women had changed their sexual identities since the first interview, and one-half had changed their sexual identities more than once in their lives. Diamond also found that one-fourth of the women had sexual contact with men during the two-year interval, although the women's sexual behavior was generally consistent with their sexual attractions. In contrast with sexual identity and behavior, the sexual attractions of these women remained fairly stable over time, especially for those women who identified themselves as lesbian, rather than bisexual or unlabeled.

Defining Homosexuality

While early sex researchers (e.g., Kinsey, Pomeroy, and Martin 1948) emphasized a broader range of psychological and behavioral attributes in their consideration of sexual orientation, most now adopt a narrower definition in terms of sexual attraction (e.g., Hamer et al. 1993; Bailey, Dunner, and Martin. 2000; Herdt and Boxer, Chapter 19, this volume).

There are several advantages to defining sexual orientation in terms of attraction rather than other sexuality dimensions (or combinations of them). First, because sexual attraction and fantasy are more temporally stable for both sexes, they are more representative of, as Herdt and Boxer (Chapter 19) say, "intrinsic desires and feelings." Considering only attraction thus makes it easier to agree on what a person's sexual orientation is, because it is not liable to be different tomorrow or to have changed from yesterday. Focusing on attraction instead of behavior also has a practical value in that it does not require people to have had sex. Otherwise put, if sexual orientation were defined using behavioral criteria alone, virgins might be said not to *have* sexual orientations. Finally, definition in terms of attraction is useful in distinguishing sexual orientation from sexual behavior across cultures (see Chapter 19). The expression of same-sex sexual behavior varies considerably cross-culturally in relation to cultural expectations and gender roles. For example, in about fifty Melanesian cultures, all boys are expected to perform fellatio on men as part of the boys' initiation into manhood (see Unit VI introduction and Chapter 20). But a more-or-less exclusive preference for homosexual activity appears to characterize a relatively small proportion of the population in every human society (Whitam 1983).

Hamer and colleagues (1993) estimated the frequency of homosexuality (defined in terms of a Kinsey score of 5 or 6 for sexual attraction) to be approximately 2 percent in men and 1 percent in women. This is close to estimates by Bailey, Dunner, and Martin (2000) of 3.6 percent for men and 1 percent for women.

Sexual orientation differs between men and women in its relation to genital arousal. Chivers, Rieger, and Bailey (2004) measured genital arousal in response to male-male and female-female sex film clips. Women's sexual arousal was measured using a photoplethysmograph, a small device placed in the vagina that both emits light and measures the wavelengths reflected back. When the vagina becomes engorged with blood during sexual arousal, it becomes redder, and these pulsatile color changes can be detected with a photoplethysmograph. In men, sexual arousal was measured with a mercury-in-rubber strain gauge, a device composed of a ring placed over the penis that stretches as the penis becomes more erect.

Chivers, Rieger, and Bailey found that women became aroused to both male-male and female-female sexual stimuli. Men, on the other hand, showed far greater arousal to their preferred sex. That is, gay men became more aroused to the male-male films and straight men became more aroused to the female-female films. Interestingly, homosexual women showed an arousal pattern more like that of men; they tended to become more aroused to their preferred sex, women (see Fig.18.1).

Is Sexual Attraction Discrete or Continuous?

In short, sexual orientation shows little temporal fluctuation in individuals. Some people consistently prefer members of their own sex, while others always prefer members of the opposite sex.

But what about the variability of sexual orientation in the population? What does the frequency distribution look like? Are people either homosexual or heterosexual, attracted virtually exclusively to members of the same sex or the opposite sex? Or do a substantial number of people occupy the range in between complete homosexuality and complete heterosexuality? The answers to these questions depend on whether we are asking about males or females, as you will see.

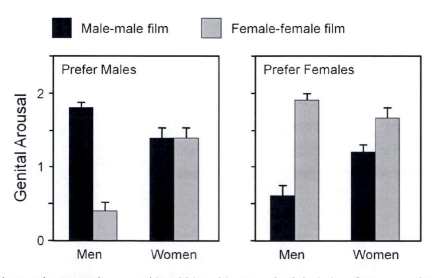

Figure 18.1 Genital arousal patterns (measured in within-subject standard deviations from arousal to neutral stimuli) in response to films of two men or two women performing various sexual acts. Arousal is less category-specific for women than it is for men. Men and homosexual women show greater genital arousal to their reported preferred sex. Heterosexual women are equally aroused by male and female sexual stimuli.

(Figure based on Chivers, Rieger, and Bailey, 2004.)

Sexual Attraction Is a Discrete Trait in Males

Hamer and his collaborators (1993) found male sexual orientation to be very *bimodal*—that is, having two modes. (You may remember the term *mode* from math courses; in mathematical terms, it refers to the most common value.) Most men fell either well toward the exclusively heterosexual or well toward the exclusively homosexual end of the continuum for all of the four sexuality dimensions measured by the Kinsey Scale. The least bimodal variable was sexual behavior, but even this measure was quite dichotomous. Hamer and his collaborators found the greatest bimodality for sexual fantasy. That is, when men think about having sex with someone else (for example, when masturbating), there is a strong tendency to think only about women or only about men (Hamer and Copeland 1994). These results corroborate previous studies by Pillard and Weinrich (1986) and Bailey and Pillard (1991). More recently, Bailey, Dunner, and Martin (2000) replicated the finding that male sexual attraction is bimodal in a large sample of 1,341 Australian men recruited without regard to sexual orientation (Fig. 18.2).

Of course, self-report is not perfectly reliable. Some people might report attraction toward both sexes, for example, when they actually experience sexual arousal only toward men. Rieger, Chivers, and Bailey (2005) examined men's genital arousal (measured by changes in penile girth during erection) in response to male or female sexual stimuli. As one would expect, self-reported heterosexual men tended to become sexually aroused to female but not male stimuli, and self-reported homosexual men tended to become aroused to male but not female stimuli. Interestingly, self-reported bisexual men also tended to become aroused *either* to male *or* to female stimuli, but not both. These results suggest that sexual orientation in men is an even more discrete trait than the self-report data indicate. As Rieger, Chivers, and Bailey state, "With respect to sexual arousal and attraction, it remains to be shown that male bisexuality exists (p. 582)."

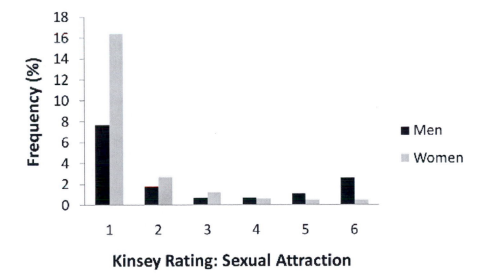

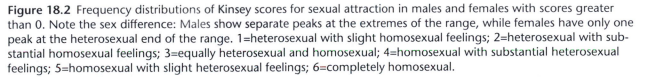

Figure 18.2 Frequency distributions of Kinsey scores for sexual attraction in males and females with scores greater than 0. Note the sex difference: Males show separate peaks at the extremes of the range, while females have only one peak at the heterosexual end of the range. 1=heterosexual with slight homosexual feelings; 2=heterosexual with substantial homosexual feelings; 3=equally heterosexual and homosexual; 4=homosexual with substantial heterosexual feelings; 5=homosexual with slight heterosexual feelings; 6=completely homosexual.

(Data from Gangestad, Bailey, and Martin, 2000.)

Sexual Attraction Is a Continuous Trait in Females

In contrast to sexual attraction in males, sexual attraction in females appears to be more a matter of degree. In the Australian study mentioned previously, Bailey and his collaborators (2000) obtained Kinsey scores for the attraction and fantasy sexuality dimensions for 2,441 women. These researchers found decreasing numbers of women at progressively higher (more homosexual) scores. Another study, by Gangestad, Bailey, and Martin (2000), published the numbers of men and women at each of the seven possible Kinsey scores for 1,759 men and 2,742 women recruited from the same source, the Australian Twin Registry, used by Bailey, Dunne, and Martin (see Fig. 18.1 and Table 18.1). This study showed that about 78 percent of women had exclusively heterosexual attractions (Kinsey score = 0), about 16 percent had scores of 1, about 3 percent had scores of 2, about 1 percent had scores of 3, and less than 1 percent of women had each of the remaining scores. Thus, for women, frequencies decreased as sexual orientation went from exclusive heterosexuality to exclusive homosexuality. This pattern differs markedly from men, who showed progressively *increasing* frequencies at scores higher than 4, from less than 1 percent at a score of 4, up to 2.6 percent at a score of 6. This sex difference in the frequency distributions of sexual attraction is significant because, as Bailey and his collaborators (2000) point out, it suggests that the devel-opmental causes of male and female homosexuality are different.

Ontogeny

How can the frequency distributions of traits help us understand their developmental causes? Recall our discussion of discrete and continuous traits from Chapter 3. Variation in discrete traits is often due largely to differences in a single gene—that is, discrete traits are often *monogenic.* For example, whether the flowers of one of Mendel's pea plants were white or purple depended on the plant's genotype at a single locus, the *P* locus. Because sexual orientation in males appears relatively discrete, we might similarly expect differences at a single genetic locus to explain a substantial portion of the phenotypic variation in male sexual orientation. In contrast, the variation in continuous traits more often results from variation among individuals at multiple genetic loci—in other words, continuous traits are often *polygenic.* Thus, we might expect female sexual orientation to be a polygenic trait, because it has a fairly continuous frequency distribution.

There are other possible explanations for the observed frequency distributions of male and female sexual orientation. For example, some discrete traits are nonetheless polygenic. How is this possible? Sometimes variation at multiple genetic loci, along with environmental differences, produces a single phenotype unless a sufficient number of these contributing factors exceed a particular threshold. Individuals whose combined genetic and environmental "predisposition" exceeds the threshold have a different phenotype. Thus, these traits are called *threshold traits.* Threshold traits are not uncommon. The tendency for cows to give birth to twins rather than single calves is a threshold trait, for example, as are adult onset diabetes, schizophrenia,

Table 18.1 Frequencies of Kinsey Scores for Attraction and Fantasy

Kinsey Score	Males		Females	
	N	%	N	%
0	1,502	85.4	2,142	78.1
1	136	7.7	451	16.4
2	31	1.8	75	2.7
3	12	0.7	33	1.2
4	12	0.7	16	0.6
5	20	1.1	15	0.5
6	46	2.6	15	0.5

Data from Gangestad, Bailey, and Martin (2000)

and spina bifida in humans (Hartl and Jones 1988). Bailey and Pillard (1991) proposed that male sexual orientation could be such a threshold trait.

Environmental differences could cause variation in sexual orientation, as well. There is evidence that a substantial proportion of the variation in sexual orientation is due to environmental differences; heritability estimates for sexual orientation are always significantly lower than 1 (see the following discussion). But because people with primarily homosexual preferences occur universally regardless of cultural expectations and gender roles, sexual preferences must be at least partially independent of these cultural factors. Moreover, no environmental variable, with the exception of birth order, has been identified that reliably explains why some individuals in a particular society become homosexual while others become heterosexual (Blanchard 2001).

Genes

On the other hand, there is accumulating evidence that sexual orientation varies among individuals because of genetic differences. Pillard and Weinrich (1986) found that the brothers of male homosexuals are about four times as likely to be homosexual themselves as are the brothers of heterosexual males. This evidence by itself does not rule out the possibility of shared environmental factors contributing to the similarity between homosexual brothers. After all, religious beliefs, political affiliation, and native language run in families, as well.

However, Heston and Shields (1968) and Bailey and Pillard (1991) found that *monozygotic* (identical) twin brothers of homosexuals are approximately twice as likely also to be homosexual as are *dizygotic* (fraternal) twin brothers. This finding indicates that differences in male sexual orientation are related to genetic differences, because monozygotic twins share twice as many genes as dizygotic twins (100 percent vs.

50 percent). In other words, male sexual orientation is heritable. Using various genetic models, Bailey and Pillard (1991) estimated the heritability of male sexual orientation be in the range of 31 to 74 percent. These estimates are comparable to those for female homosexuality, which range between 27 and 76 percent (Bailey and Benishay 1993, Bailey and Pillard 1991), and those for "nonheterosexuality" in both sexes combined, which range from 28 to 65 percent (Kendler et al. 2000).

Finally, Hamer and colleagues (1993) found that a gene on the X chromosome may influence male sexual orientation. These researchers recruited pairs of brothers and their mother, and used DNA analysis to determine which X chromosome alleles they shared. Where the mother was heterozygous, the researchers determined whether her sons inherited the same allele from her (were *concordant*) or inherited different alleles (were *discordant*). The prediction was simple: Randomly chosen pairs of brothers should be concordant about 50 percent of the time. But if there is an allele on the X chromosome that is associated with sexual orientation, then pairs of homosexual brothers should be concordant for the allele significantly more often than 50 percent of the time.

Hamer and his colleagues found that pairs of homosexual brothers were concordant for one genetic marker, "Xq28," about 83 percent of the time, and the probability of getting this apparent linkage by random chance was about 1 in 100,000—an "extremely significant" result, in the language of statistics (see Fig. 18.3). These results were replicated by members of Hamer's laboratory (Hu et al. 1995) and by another laboratory (Sanders et al. 1998), but Rice and colleagues (1999) failed to find a linkage between Xq28 and male homosexuality. With all of these results pooled, however, there appears to be an increased frequency of the Xq28 marker in gay men (Hamer 1999).

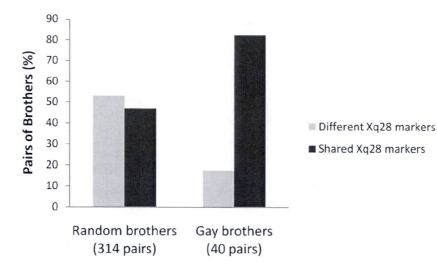

Figure 18.3 Brothers who are both homosexual are also more likely to have inherited the same Xq28 genetic markers from their mother. Random pairs of brothers inherit the same Xq28 markers about 50 percent of the time—no more than chance.

(Redrawn from Hamer and Copeland, 1994.)

Hormones

In general, the evidence strongly indicates that some men and women may be homosexual while others are heterosexual because of genetic differences. But how do these genetic differences lead to differences in sexual orientation? A good possibility is that genetic variation affects hormonal signaling during prenatal development. Several studies on nonhuman animals have demonstrated that prenatal hormones affect sexual orientation. For example, Elizabeth Adkins-Regan and Juli Wade (2001) caused same-sex partner preference in female zebra finches by manipulating sex hormone levels in eggs. And early manipulation of hormonal levels in both male and female rats affects adult sex partner preferences (Brand et al. 1991, Brand and Slob 1991). Recent research suggests that sex hormone signaling affects sexual orientation in humans, as well.

Hormones in Women

Some evidence comes from studies of women who were exposed to high levels of masculinizing hormones *in utero* because their mothers took drugs to prevent miscarriage. These girls show increased rates of homosexuality (Meyer-Bahlberg et al. 1995). Other evidence comes from studies of girls with congenital adrenal hyperplasia (CAH). CAH is a condition that causes abnormally high levels of androgens ("male hormones") beginning early in fetal development and continuing until treatment begins, usually soon after birth (Miller 1994, Pang 1997). Dittmann, Kappes, and Kappas (1992) found that girls with CAH are more likely to have homosexual fantasies and preferences than their unaffected sisters.

It is tempting to conclude that the high levels of prenatal androgens in girls with CAH, or in girls whose mothers took drugs to prevent miscarriage, were a direct cause of homosexual tendencies. If there were no other differences between "normal" girls and girls exposed to high prenatal levels of masculinizing hormones, this would be a fair assumption. However, girls with CAH and girls whose mothers took miscarriage medication are often born with *virilized* (somewhat masculine) genitalia. Thus, it is also possible that parents respond to this abnormality by treating virilized girls in a more masculine fashion and that this masculine treatment is the more immediate cause of the girls' homosexuality (Quadagno, Briscoe, and Quadagno 1977).

Several lines of evidence challenge this scenario. First, one animal study has specifically looked for effects of virilized genitalia and childhood treatment on behavior. Goy, Bercovitch, and McBrair (1988) found that female rhesus macaques treated prenatally with androgens exhibit masculinized behavior, but these behavioral effects are unrelated to genital masculinization or treatment by their mothers. Second, human parents do not report any difference between the treatment of daughters with CAH and the treatment of unaffected sisters (Ehrhardt and Baker 1974, Berenbaum and Hines 1992). Third, the degree of genital virilization in girls with CAH does not appear to be related to their behavior (Slijper 1984, Dittmann et al. 1990, Berenbaum and Hines 1992, Leveroni and Berenbaum 1998).

All of these lines of evidence are only indirect, and there are problems with each. Macaques are not humans, and parents' reports may be unreliable. However, Sheri Berenbaum (1999) tested the hypothesis that early hormone exposure in girls with CAH causes lifelong differences in preferences and behavior. Berenbaum hypothesized that if the sex-atypical behavior characteristic of girls with CAH is due to masculine treatment by their parents, then behavior should become less atypical as these girls age. This is because girls with CAH are reared and treated as females and have increasing interactions outside of the home with people who know nothing about their childhood genital abnormalities. Instead, Berenbaum found that large differences between girls with CAH and unaffected girls persist into adolescence. She concluded: "The results strengthen the argument that the behavioral changes seen in females with CAH reflect direct effects of androgens on the developing brain rather than social responses to the girls' physical condition or genital appearance" (p. 107).

More recently, Williams and colleagues (2000) showed that lesbians have a shorter index finger relative to the length of their ring finger (second-to-fourth digit length, or 2D:4D) than do heterosexual women. A variety of evidence indicates that a low 2D:4D reflects high prenatal androgen exposure. For example, 2D:4D is lower in males than in females by the end of the first trimester of gestation and is lower in females with CAH than in their unaffected female relatives (reviewed in Puts et al. 2008). Thus, lesbians seem to have been exposed to high androgen levels during prenatal development, but most lesbians presumably had normal-looking genitalia and were otherwise normal in appearance at birth. Brown and collaborators (2002) subsequently found that lesbians who identified themselves as "butch" (masculine) had significantly lower 2D:4D than did those who identified themselves as "femme" (feminine). These researchers concluded that early androgen exposure was likely to have played a role in the sexual orientation of butch lesbians but not femme lesbians.

Hormones in Men

Williams and colleagues (2000) also found that 2D:4D decreases with fraternal birth order. In other words, later-born brothers may have been exposed to higher prenatal androgen levels than have their older brothers. The likelihood of male homosexuality also increases with birth order (Blanchard and Bogaert 1996, Blanchard 1997), the only known reliable environmental correlate of male homosexuality (Blanchard 2001). Williams and colleagues therefore proposed that high prenatal androgen levels lead to homosexuality. This possibility was supported by Robinson and Manning (2000), who found a lower 2D:4D in homosexual than in heterosexual men.

However, Williams and colleagues (2000) did not obtain this result, nor did Robinson and Manning (2000) find the fraternal birth order effect on 2D:4D. Robinson and Manning suggested that they and Williams and colleagues may have failed to reproduce each others' findings because the relationships between 2D:4D and sexual orientation and between birth order and 2D:4D were weak. Robinson and Manning concluded that further work must be done to show whether these results are replicable. In general, relationships between 2D:4D and sexual orientation appear less replicable in men than they are in women (e.g., McFadden et al. 2005). Most researchers of sex differences and sexual orientation (e.g., Kimura, Chapter 8, this volume) agree, however, that differences in sexual orientation are probably associated with differences in prenatal hormonal signaling.

Fraternal Birth Order and the Maternal Immune Hypothesis

Recall that fraternal birth order is associated with male homosexuality; the more older brothers a man has, the likelier he is to be homosexual. Why do you think this peculiar phenomenon occurs? One possibility is that younger brothers are treated differently by their parents, siblings, or others. Perhaps younger brothers are "babied" by their mothers, and such treatment leads to homosexuality, for example. This is unlikely, however, as we will see.

Does Differential Upbringing Explain the Fraternal Birth Order Effect?

Ray Blanchard and Lee Ellis (2001) discovered an odd fact that bears on the proximate causes of the fraternal birth order effect: Homosexual men with older brothers are significantly smaller at birth than are heterosexual men with older brothers. Blanchard et al. (2002) subsequently corroborated this finding. This tells us there is a difference in fetal development between heterosexual men and homosexual men with older brothers. In turn, this suggests that the fraternal birth order effect is not due *only* to different upbringing of younger and older brothers. It seems too big of a coincidence for the prenatal developmental differences between homosexual and heterosexual men to have nothing to do with later differences in sexual orientation.

But these results do *not* rule out the effect of differential upbringing on sexual orientation. Consider an analogous situation: Recall from Chapters 7 and 8 that differences in fetal development lead to sex differences. Daly and Wilson

(Chapter 7) presented data indicating that some behavioral sex differences would persist even if women and men were treated the same. For example, there are some quite large sex differences in spatial thinking ability that persist even when the effects of differential experience are removed (Kimura 1999). Here's another sex difference: Women more often wear dresses than men. Do you think this sex difference would persist if males and females were treated the same? Of course not. But this sex difference *is* due to a difference in fetal development. Can you see why? Boys and girls can only be treated differently if they can be identified as boys and girls, and this is due to a difference in fetal development. In other words, some features of the phenotype can elicit certain kinds of treatment, and that treatment then constitutes a special environment, which can have further effects.

Now let's return to the fraternal birth order effect on male homosexuality. Male homosexuals with older brothers are born at lower weights than heterosexual males with older brothers. Most likely, this difference at birth, or some other consequence of differential fetal development, leads to homosexuality. But it may do so by causing parents, siblings, or others to *behave* differently toward these males. Perhaps small sons with older brothers are especially babied by their mothers.

As if things weren't strange enough already, there is another relevant peculiarity of the fraternal birth order effect. Daughters have absolutely nothing to do with the phenomenon. The number of older sisters a man has does not affect his probability of being homosexual. And the number of older brothers a woman has does not affect her probability of being homosexual. If different treatment associated with birth order leads to differences in sexual orientation, don't you think that females would factor in somehow?

A seemingly fatal blow to the differential upbringing hypothesis was dealt by Blanchard's collaborator, Anthony Bogaert (Bogaert 2006; Puts, Jordan, and Breedlove 2006). Bogaert examined sexual orientation in several samples totaling 944 men and found that sexual orientation was related to a man's number of biological older brothers through his mother, regardless of whether he was raised with these brothers. No other sibling variables, including number of nonbiological older brothers and the amount of time a man was raised with each type of sibling, were related.

Given that the social influence of older brothers is unlikely to explain the fraternal birth order effect, what is? Blanchard (2001) suggested an intriguing alternative hypothesis, the *maternal immune hypothesis*.

The Maternal Immune Hypothesis

Let's summarize what needs to be explained: First, why does the number of prior sons a woman has carried affect her present son's chance of being homosexual? And second, why don't daughters factor into the equation? Blanchard and Bogaert (1996) ruled out the possibility that maternal or paternal age causes the relationship between number of older brothers and male homosexuality. And Blanchard and Bogaert (1997) ruled out birth interval. According to Blanchard and Bogaert (1996), mothers may develop a progressive immune reaction to fetal sons, and this immune reaction may lead to smaller birth weights and homosexuality in sons.

To see how this could be, let's briefly review a typical immune response. Our immune systems recognize invaders through molecules called *antigens* on the surfaces of foreign cells. Our immune systems produce millions of different proteins called *antibodies*, each capable of binding to and recognizing a different antigen. When antibodies recognize their specific antigen, an immune reaction begins. The immune system produces more antibodies, a clone of infection-fighting effector cells, and a clone of long-lived *memory cells*, all specific to the antigen. Memory cells enable the immune system to respond more rapidly and forcefully to a subsequent infection by the same invader.

Blanchard and Bogaert (1996) proposed that some cells from a male fetus enter the mother's bloodstream, causing her immune system to react. Because the mother lacks a Y chromosome, her immune system recognizes any antigens encoded on the Y chromosome as foreign and produces antibodies to attack cells bearing them. Blanchard and Bogaert conjectured that maternal "antimale" antibodies subsequently enter the bloodstream of the fetus and affect its development (see Fig. 18.4). This idea is appealing because the mother's immune response would increase with repeated exposure to male fetal cells due to the buildup of memory cells specific to Y-linked antigens. In other words, the immune system provides a mother's body a way of "remembering" how many sons she had. And specific immune reaction to Y-linked antigens explains why daughters are irrelevant to the birth order effect.

How does the maternal immune response cause later-born brothers to become homosexual and to have lower birth weights? Blanchard and his colleagues (Blanchard and Bogaert 1996, Blanchard 2001, Blanchard et al. 2002) suggested two possibilities. First, maternal antibodies may interfere with Y-linked antigens that are directly involved in brain development in the fetus. For example, some male-specific cell surface proteins function in establishing connections between neurons. These researchers presented evidence that Y-linked antigens are involved in the sexual differentiation of the brain and also affect fetal birth weight. Alternatively, Blanchard and his colleagues suggested that maternal antibodies mimic the effects of androgens. Thus, homosexual males could appear to have been exposed to high prenatal levels of androgens without actually having been.

A third possibility is that maternal antibodies could attack and destroy tissue associated with testosterone production or reception. Thus, *low* prenatal androgen signaling might cause sexual attraction to males and low birth weight, as they do in females. After the body of the fetus has dealt with the maternal assault, it may attempt to compensate by increasing androgen levels—too late in some cases to reverse the effects on sexual orientation and birth weight,

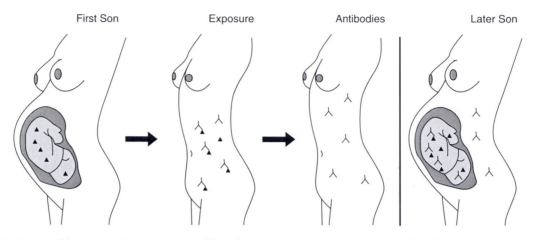

Figure 18.4 Maternal immunization hypothesis. The placenta protects the mother and her first son from exposure to each other's proteins. Mixing of blood upon delivery exposes the mother for the first time to male-specific proteins (triangles), including those encoded on the Y chromosome. If her immune system produces antibodies to these proteins (inverted "Y"s), then the placenta may transport those antibodies to subsequent offspring in utero, potentially affecting development of later-born sons, but not later-born daughters.

(From Puts, Jordan, and Breedlove, 2006.)

but early enough to lead to otherwise normal sexual development.

While some evidence supports all of these possibilities, it is still unclear whether any are correct. Certainly, a maternal immune response to fetal Y-linked antigens is a promising explanation for the fraternal birth order effect. But what mediates the connection between maternal immune response and male homosexuality? The most parsimonious explanation is that the maternal immune response affects sex hormone signaling in the fetus. This is consistent with evidence from experimental hormonal manipulation in nonhuman animals and with natural variation in hormonal levels in human females (e.g., girls with CAH). On the other hand, homosexuality could result from different developmental events in difference cases.

The Brain

Previously, we asked how genetic differences lead to differences in sexual orientation. We suggested that alternative genes have different effects on prenatal hormonal signaling, which can lead to variation among individuals in sexual orientation. But this story is incomplete. How do prenatal hormonal levels affect sexual orientation later in life? Recall from Chapter 8 that testosterone, an androgen, has important organizing effects on the brain. Divergent testosterone levels during fetal development, then, may contribute to differences in brain structure associated with sexual orientation. Indeed, several brain structures have been found to differ between heterosexual and homosexual men (Swaab and Hofman 1990, Allen and Gorski 1991, LeVay 1991, Zhou et al. 1995).

However, the relationships between these structural brain differences and sexual orientation remain unclear. While differential brain development may lead to variation in sexual orientation, sexual orientation may conversely influence the growth and structure of the brain. A third possibility is that brain structures that are known to differ with sexual orientation are not directly related to sexual orientation. In fact, many of these brain areas do not appear to be directly associated with sexual behavior at all (Hamer and Copeland 1994). Instead, variation in early hormonal regimes may lead to multiple brain differences between heterosexual and homosexual men, and only some of these differences may be directly associated with sexual orientation.

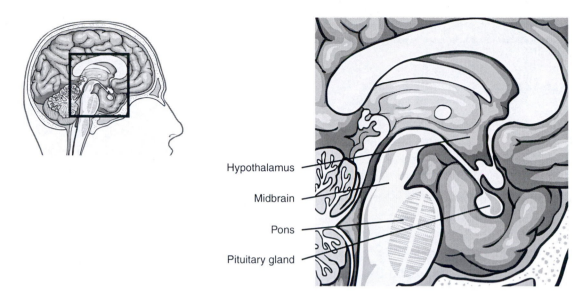

Figure 18.5 The hypothalamus is a brain region that has been found to differ between homosexual and heterosexual men.

(Image © Ogus Aral, 2008. Used under license from Shutterstock, Inc.)

Several lines of evidence implicate at least one brain structure, however—the third interstitial nucleus of the anterior hypothalamus, or INAH-3 (LeVay 1993). The *hypothalamus* (Fig. 18.5) is a small structure at the base of the brain associated with basic impulses such as hunger, thirst, and sex. LeVay (1991) found the INAH-3 to be approximately two to three times as large in heterosexual men as in women and homosexual men. More recently, Byne and colleagues (2001) replicated LeVay's findings of a sex difference in the size of the INAH-3, but found only a statistically nonsignificant "trend" toward smaller INAH-3 volume in homosexual men.

The INAH-3 is part of the hypothalamus located toward its front in a region called the *preoptic area.* When an experimenter electrically stimulates the preoptic area of a male monkey presented with a female in heat, the male mounts the female. Moreover, brain activity in this area increases when a male monkey presses a button to bring a female closer to him, but not when the male equally eagerly presses the button to bring a banana closer to him (reviewed in LeVay 1993). In rats, the size of this region of the brain increases in response to androgens, decreases in response to castration, and is associated with male sexual behavior (Jacobson et al.

1981). As in humans, this region is several times as large in male rats as in females (Gorski et al. 1980). Because the sexual differentiation of the preoptic area is accomplished in rats well before sexual maturity, it seems likely that the structural differences in the presumably analogous region in humans (INAH-3) develop before sexual orientation (LeVay 1993). Thus, INAH-3 appears to be related to sexual motivation, although it is far from clear whether differences in the size or structure of this region directly result in differences in sexual orientation.

We have the feelings, thoughts, and emotions we do because of the physiology of our brains, so differences in sexual feelings must come from differences in our brains. The locations of the relevant brain regions for sexual orientation are not known with certainty, but one such brain region may be the hypothalamus. Brain differences between homosexuals and heterosexuals seem to be at least partly due to differential prenatal exposure to sex hormones and are possibly caused directly by maternal antibodies. Genetic differences between homosexuals and heterosexuals, and perhaps nongenetic factors related to birth order and maternal condition, are likely causes of variation in sexual orientation.

Evolution

If sexual orientation is heritable, why is homosexuality still around? Bell and Weinberg (1978) found that male homosexuals reported approximately one-fifth as many children as male heterosexuals. If homosexuals have fewer children than heterosexuals do, natural selection should eventually remove genes associated with homosexuality from populations. Why hasn't it already? This question has intrigued many researchers, and several hypotheses have been suggested for the maintenance of "gay genes" by natural selection.

Heterozygous Advantage

Hutchinson (1959) proposed that gay genes persist due to *heterozygous advantage*. According to this hypothesis, individuals who are homozygous for a gay gene are homosexual and suffer a reduction in fitness. But individuals who have only one copy of the gay gene and one copy of its allele (heterozygotes) are heterosexual and average higher fitness than heterosexuals with no copies of the gay gene, thus maintaining the gay gene in the population. Although this hypothesis is plausible, it has received little support.

Kin Selection

Edward O. Wilson (1975) suggested another hypothesis. Wilson proposed that gay genes could be maintained by kin selection if homosexuals compensate for their lowered fitness by altruistically increasing the fitness of their close genetic relatives. If some of the recipients of this kin-directed altruism also possess the gay genes but are not homosexual themselves, then their increased reproduction could maintain the gay genes in the population.

This hypothesis is more appealing in light of the fraternal birth order effect (Blanchard and Bogaert 1996); genes that increase susceptibility to the fraternal birth order effect would elevate the odds of homosexuality in proportion to a man's number of older siblings in whose children he can invest. In other words, homosexuality should be most common in men who have many nieces and nephews, and thus where kin-directed altruism can most benefit their inclusive fitness.

Initially, the kin selection hypothesis failed to obtain empirical support in Western populations; homosexual men did not seem any more inclined to contribute to the reproduction of their relatives than did heterosexuals (Werner 1979, Bobrow and Bailey 2001, Rahman and Hull 2005). More recently, however, Vasey, Pocock, and VanderLaan (2007) found some support for this hypothesis on the small island nation of Independent Samoa. Here, the researchers found that homosexual men reported greater investment in their nephews and nieces than heterosexual men did.

The increased altruism found in homosexual Samoan men does not appear sufficient to outweigh the reproductive costs of homosexuality. However, it is possible that gay genes would have produced higher levels of kin altruism, or had some other adaptive consequence, in the small, hunter-gatherer groups in which humans spent the majority of their evolution. For example, the benefit of kin-directed altruism could be greater in societies where men's paternity certainty is low. If men were to mate heterosexually and invest in their mate's offspring, they might unwittingly be investing in the offspring of their competitors—that is, they might be cuckholded. When paternity confidence is low enough, the scales may tip so that investing in siblings, nieces, and nephews nets a better expected inclusive fitness payoff than investing in one's "own" putative offspring. Of course, this would be true only if men were to invest in siblings through their mothers or in nieces and nephews through their sisters. Otherwise, men would run the same risk of investing in genetically unrelated individuals, because their male relatives' paternity certainty should be as low on average as theirs would be. It remains to be seen whether Independent Samoan homosexual men invest more heavily in siblings through their mothers or in nieces and nephews through their sisters or whether paternity confidence is low enough to explain investment in kin rather men's own reproduction.

On the other hand, the kin selection hypothesis does not explain how gay genes are maintained in present large-scale societies in which paternity certainty is high. In addition, homosexuality seems an inefficient means of channeling reproductive effort into investment in kin. After all, homosexuals are likely to expend time, energy, and resources attracting and keeping same-sex partners. Wouldn't selection for such kin-directed altruism favor a lack of sexual interest rather than preferences for sexual behaviors that cannot increase inclusive fitness?

Maladaptive Extreme

Recall that Bailey and Pillard (1991) proposed that male sexual orientation may be a threshold trait. In other words, male sexual orientation may be polygenic despite having a bimodal frequency distribution. And because female sexual orientation is continuous, its variation is also likely to be polygenic. Also recall that sexual orientation—at least in women—seems to be affected by prenatal hormone signaling. Perhaps a person's number of alleles that affect prenatal testosterone production, for example, influences sexual orientation. In women, sexual orientation could vary more or less in direct proportion to the number of such alleles in their genotype. And in men, a sufficient number of such alleles could push the phenotype past a sexual orientation threshold from heterosexuality to homosexuality. How could continuous variation in a developmental factor like testosterone production lead to a discrete psychological trait in men? Bailey and Pillard (1993) suggested one possibility: A developmental process that causes attraction to females could simultaneously inhibit the development of an attraction to males (Fig. 18.6).

If sexual orientation is polygenic in women or men, then it is possible that natural selection has not favored homosexuality per se. Rather, selection may have favored genes for testosterone production or some other developmental process that underlies variation in sexual orientation and is, on average, adaptive. If an intermediate level of this developmental process is

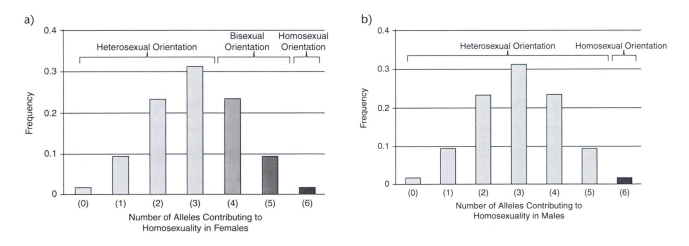

Figure 18.6 Homosexuality as a maladaptive extreme. Genes underlying variation in a trait are likely to affect other traits. If selection operates in opposing directions on these different aspects of the phenotype, it will favor an intermediate number of contributory alleles. Although the number of contributory alleles possessed by the average individual may be optimal under selection, the extremes will be less fit. High numbers of alleles contributing to homosexuality may cause females to be increasingly homosexual (a) or cause males to exceed a threshold (b).

favored by selection, both alleles that increase it and those that decrease it are maintained in the population. Through meiosis and recombination, sexual reproduction produces a variety of genotypes, with some individuals possessing few alleles that increase this process and some individuals possessing many such alleles. An extreme number of alleles contributing to such a developmental process could lead to a maladaptive phenotype. This hypothesis will be supported or rejected as more evidence about the genetics and development of sexual orientation accumulates.

Antagonistic Pleiotropy

On the other hand, perhaps gay genes are maintained because they have different effects in different bodies—a common phenomenon with an unusual name: *antagonistic pleiotropy*. For example, a gay gene that decreases the fitness of gay men could increase the fitness of their nongay brothers, fathers, uncles, and other relatives who also possess the gay gene. Alternatively, a gay gene could increase the fitness of the sisters and other female relatives of gay men. As Robert Trivers and William Rice have pointed out (in Hamer and Copeland 1994), this latter possibility is especially appealing if a gay gene resides on the X chromosome, as the research of Hamer and colleagues (1993) indicates. A gay gene on the X chromosome would have to increase the fitness of females by only half as much as it decreased the fitness of males in order for the gene to be maintained by selection. This is true because, whereas men possess only one X chromosome, females possess two copies and so would be twice as likely to possess the gay gene.

A study by Camperio-Ciani, Corna, and Capiluppi of the University of Padova, Italy, supports the antagonistic pleiotropy hypothesis. Camperio-Ciani and colleagues (2004) found elevated reproductive success in the maternal relatives of male homosexuals. Because variation in sexual orientation may result from genetic differences as well as from nongenetic differences associated with birth order, such as genomic imprinting or maternal hormonal constitution, the researchers considered only the families of homosexual men with no older brothers. They found significantly higher reproductive success in the mothers, maternal aunts, and nongay maternal uncles of homosexual men.

Summary

Homosexuality can be defined as exclusive or nearly exclusive sexual attraction to members of one's own sex. Homosexuality is a stable personality trait that is distributed differently in the sexes and is rarer in females. These sex differences hint at separate developmental causes. Homosexuality in both males and females appears to be partly heritable. Genes associated with homosexuality, along with the intra-uterine environment, seem to affect sexual orientation, perhaps by affecting the hormonal regimes impinging on the developing nervous system of the fetus. Although a great deal has been learned about the genetic, hormonal, and neuroanatomical bases of homosexuality, much has yet to be discovered, particularly regarding homosexuality in females. Even less is known about the evolution of homosexuality. But at least two evolutionary hypotheses for the maintenance of genes associated with male homosexuality have received some empirical support. These areas promise many fascinating future discoveries.

References

Adkins-Regan, E., and J. Wade. 2001. Masculinized sexual partner preference in female zebra finches with sex-reversed gonads. *Hormones and Behavior* 39:22–28.

Allen, L. S., and R. A. Gorski. 1991. Sexual dimorphism of the anterior commissure and massa intermedia of the human brain. *Journal of Comparative Neurology* 312:97–104.

Bailey, J. M., and D. S. Benishay. 1993. Familial aggregation of female sexual orientation. *American Journal of Psychiatry* 150:272.

Bailey, J. M., M. P. Dunner, and N. G. Martin. 2000. Genetic and environmental influences on sexual orientation and its correlates in an Australian twin sample. *Personality and Individual Differences* 78(3):524–536.

Bailey, J. M., and R. C. Pillard. 1991. A genetic study of male sexual orientation. *Archives of General Psychiatry* 48:1089–1096

Bailey, J. M., R. C. Pillard, M. C. Neale, and Y. Agyei. 1993. Heritable factors influence sexual orientation in women. *Archives of General Psychiatry* 50:217.

Bell, A. P., and M. S. Weinberg. 1978. *Homosexualities: A study of diversity among men and women.* New York: Simon and Schuster.

Berenbaum, S. A. 1999. Effects of early androgens on sex-typed activities and interests in adolescents with congenital adrenal hyperplasia. *Hormones and Behavior* 35:102–110.

Berenbaum, S. A., and M. Hines. 1992. Early androgens are related to childhood sex-typed toy preferences. *Psychological Science* 3:203–6.

Blanchard, R. 1997. Birth order and sibling sex ratio in homosexual and heterosexual males and females. *Annual Review of Sex Research* 8:27–67.

Blanchard, R. 2001. Fraternal birth order and the maternal immune hypothesis of male homosexuality. *Hormones and Behavior* 40:105–14.

Blanchard, R., and A. F. Bogaert. 1996. Homosexuality in men and number of older brothers. *American Journal of Psychiatry* 153:27–31.

Blanchard, R., and A. F. Bogaert. 1997. The relation of closed birth intervals to the sex of the preceding child and the sexual orientation of the succeeding child. *Journal of Biosocial Science* 29:111–18.

Blanchard, R., and L. Ellis. 2001. Birth weight, sexual orientation and the sex of preceding siblings. *Journal of Biosocial Science* 33:451–467.

Blanchard, R., K. J. Zucker, S. A. Cavacas, S. J. Bradley, and D. C. Schacter. 2002. Fraternal birth order and birth weight in probably prehomosexual boys. *Hormones and Behavior* 41:321–27.

Bobrow, D., and J. M. Bailey. 2001. Is male homosexuality maintained via kin selection? *Evolution and Human Behavior.* 22(5):361–68.

Bogaert, A. F. 2006. Biological versus nonbiological older brothers and men's sexual orientation. *Proceedings of the National Academy of Sciences of the USA,* 103(28):10771–74.

Brand, T., J. Kroonen, J. Mos, and A. K. Slob. 1991. Adult partner preference and sexual behavior of male rats affected by perinatal endocrine manipulations. *Hormones and Behavior* 25:323–41.

Brand, T., and A. K. Slob. 1991. On the organization of partner preference behavior in female Wistar rats. *Physiology and Behavior* 49:549–55.

Brown, W. M., C. J. Finn, B. M. Cooke, and S. M. Breedlove. 2002. Differences in finger length ratios between self-identified "butch" and "femme" lesbians. *Archives of Sexual Behavior.* 31(1):123–27.

Byne, W., S. Tobet, L. A. Mattiace, M. S. Lasco, E. Kemether, M. A. Edgar, S. Morgello, M. S. Buchsbaum, and L. B. Jones. 2001. The interstitial nuclei of the human anterior hypothalamus: An investigation of variation with sex, sexual orientation, and HIV status. *Hormones and Behavior.* 40:86–92.

Camperio-Ciani, A., F. Corna, and C. Capiluppi. 2004. Evidence for maternally inherited factors favouring male homosexuality and promoting female fecundity. *Proceedings of the Royal Society of London* B, 271:2217–21.

Chivers, M. L., G. Rieger, and J. M. Bailey. 2004. A sex difference in the specificity of sexual arousal. *Psychological Science,* 15(11):736–44.

Diamond, L. 2000. Sexual identity, attractions, and behavior among young sexual-minority women over a 2-year period. *Developmental Psychology* 36(2):241–50.

Dittmann, R. W., M. E. Kappes, and M. H. Kappes. 1992. Sexual behavior in adolescent and adult females with congenital adrenal hyperplasia. *Psychoneuroendrocrinology* 17:153–70.

Dittmann, R. W., M. H. Kappes, M. E. Kappes, D. Borger, H. Stegner, R. H. Willig, and H. Wallis. 1990. Congenital adrenal hyperplasia 1: Gender-related behaviors and attitudes in female patients and their sisters. *Psychoneuroendrocrinology* 15:401–20.

Ehrhardt, A. A., and S. W. Baker. 1974. Fetal androgens, human central nervous system differentiation, and behavior sex differences. In *Sex Differences in Behavior,* ed. R. C. Friedman, R. R. Richart, and R. L. Vande Wiele, 33–51. New York: Wiley.

Gangestad, S. W., J. M. Bailey, and N. G. Martin. 2000. Taxonometric analysis of sexual orientation and gender identity. *Journal of Personality and Social Psychology.* 78(6):1109–21.

Gorski, R. A., R. E. Harlan, C. D. Jacobsen, J. E. Shryne, and A. M. Southam. 1980. Evidence for a morphological sex difference within the medical preoptic area of the rat brain. *Journal of Comparative Neurology* 193:529–39.

Goy, R. W., F. B. Bercovitch, and M. C. McBrair. 1988. Behavioral masculinization is independent of genital masculinization in prenatally androgenized female rhesus macaques. *Hormones and Behavior* 22:552–71.

Hamer, D. H. 1999. Genetics and male sexual orientation. *Science* 5429(6):803.

Hamer, D., and P. Copeland. 1994. *The Science of desire: The search for the gay gene and the biology of behavior.* New York: Simon and Schuster.

Hamer, D. H., S. Hu, V. L. Magnuson, N. Hu, and A. M. L. Pattatucci. 1993. A linkage between DNA markers on the X chromosome and male sexual orientation. *Science* 261:321–27.

Hartl, D. L., and E. W. Jones. 1998. *Genetics: Principles and analysis.* Sudbury, MA: Jones and Bartlett.

Heston, L. L., and J. Shields, J. 1968. Homosexuality in twins: A family study and a registry study. *Archives of General Psychiatry* 18:149–60.

Hu, S., A. M. L. Pattatucci, C. Patterson, L. Li, D. W. Fulker, S. S. Cherney, L. Kruglyak, and D. H. Hamer. 1995. Linkage between sexual orientation and chromosome Xq28 in males but not in females. *Nature Genet.* 11:248–56.

Hutchinson, G. E. 1959. A speculative consideration of certain possible forms of sexual selection in man. *American Naturalist* 93:81–91.

Jacobson, C. D., V. J. Csernus, J. E. Shryne, and R. A. Gorski. 1981. The influence of gonadectomy, androgen exposure, or a gonadal graft in the neonatal rat on the volume of the sexually dimorphic nucleus of the preoptic area. *Journal of Neuroscience* 1:1142–47.

Kendler, K. S., L. M. Thornton, S. E. Gilman, and R. C. Kessler. 2000. Sexual orientation in a U.S. national sample of twin and nontwin sibling pairs. *American Journal of Psychiatry* 157:1843–46.

Kimura, D. 1999. *Sex and Cognition.* Cambridge, MA: MIT Press.

Kinsey, A. C., W. B. Pomeroy, and C. E. Martin. 1948. *Sexual behavior in the human male.* Philadelphia: W. B. Saunders.

LeVay, S. 1991. A difference in hypothalamic structure between heterosexual and homosexual men. *Science* 253:1034–37.

LeVay, S. 1993. *The sexual brain.* Cambridge, MA: MIT Press.

Leveroni, C., and S. A. Berenbaum. 1998. Early androgen effects on interest in infants: Evidence from children with congenital adrenal hyperplasia. *Developmental Neuropsychology* 14:321–40.

McFadden, D., J. C. Loehlin, S. M. Breedlove, R. A. Lippa, J. T. Manning, and Q. Rahman. 2005. A reanalysis of five studies on sexual orientation and the relative length of the 2nd and 4th fingers (the 2D:4D ratio). *Archives of Sexual Behavior* 34(3):341–56.

Meyer-Bahlberg, H. F. L., A. A. Ehrhardt, L. R. Rosen, R. S Gruen, N. P. Veridiano, F. H. Vann, and H. F. Neuwalder. 1995. Prenatal estrogens and the development of homosexual orientation. *Developmental Psychology* 31:12–21.

Miller, W. L. 1994. Genetics, diagnosis, and management of 21-hydroxylase deficiency. *Journal of Clinical Endocrinology and Metabolism* 78:241–46.

Pang, S. 1997. Congenital adrenal hyperplasia. *Endocrinol. Metab. Clin. North America* 26:853–891.

Pillard, R. C., and J. D. Weinrich. 1986. Evidence of the familial nature of male homosexuality. *Archives of General Psychiatry* 43:808–812.

Puts, D. A., C. L. Jordan, and S. M. Breedlove. 2006. O brother, where art thou? The fraternal birth-order effect on male sexual orientation. *Proceedings of the National Academy of Sciences of the USA,* 103(28): 10531–32.

Puts, D. A., M. A. McDaniel, C. L. Jordan, and S. M. Breedlove. 2008. Spatial ability and prenatal androgens: Meta-analyses of congenital adrenal hyperplasia and digit ratio (2D:4D) studies. *Archives of Sexual Behavior* 37(1):100–111.

Quadagno, D. M., R. Briscoe, and J. S. Quadagno. 1977. Effects of perinatal gonadal hormones on selected nonsexual behavior patterns: A critical assessment of the nonhuman and human literature. *Psychological Bulletin* 84:62–82.

Rahman, Q., and M. S. Hull. 2005. An empirical test of the kin selection hypothesis for male homosexuality. *Archives of Sexual Behavior* 34:461–67.

Rice, G., C. Anderson, N. Risch, and G. Ebers. 1999. Male homosexuality: Absence of linkage to microsatellite markers at Xq28. *Science* 5414(23):665–67.

Rieger, G., M. L. Chivers, and J. M. Bailey. 2005. Sexual arousal patterns of bisexual men. *Psychological Science,* 16(8):579–84.

Robinson, S. J., and Manning, J. T. 2000. The ratio of 2nd digit to 4th digit length and male homosexuality. *Evolution and Human Behavior* 21(5):333–45.

Sanders, A. R., et al. 1998. In Hamer, D. H. 1999. Genetics and male sexual orientation. *Science* 5429(6):803.

Slipjer, F. M. E. 1984. Androgens and gender role behavior in girls with congenital adrenal hyperplasia (CAH). In *Progress in Brain Research,* ed. G. J. DeVries, J. P. C. DeBruin, H. B. M. Uylings, and M. A. Corner, 61:417–22. Amsterdam: Elsevier.

Swaab, D. F., and M. A. Hofman. 1990. An enlarged suprachiasmatic nucleus in homosexual men. *Brain Research* 537:141–48.

Vasey, P., D. S. Pocock, and D. P. VanderLaan. 2007. Kin selection and male androphilia in Samoan fa'afafine. *Evolution and Human Behavior* 28:159–67.

Werner, D. 1979. A cross-cultural perspective on theory and research on male homosexuality. *Journal of Homosexuality* 1(4):345–62.

Whitam, F. L. 1983. Culturally invariable properties of male homosexuality: Tentative conclusions from cross-cultural research. *Archives of Sexual Behavior* 12(4):207–26.

Williams, T. J., M. E. Pepitone, S. E. Christensen, B. M. Cooke, A. D. Huberman, N. J. Breedlove, T. J. Breedlove, C. L. Jordan, and S. M. Breedlove. 2000. Finger length patterns indicate an influence of fetal androgens on human sexual orientation. *Nature* 404:455.

Wilson, E. O. 1975. *Sociobiology: The new synthesis.* Cambridge, MA: Harvard University Press.

Zhou, J. N., M. A. Hofman, L. J. G. Gooren, and D. F. Swaab. 1995. A sex difference in the human brain and its relation to transsexuality. *Nature* 378:69–70.

Bisexuality

Toward a Comparative Theory of Identities and Culture

Gilbert Herdt and Andrew Boxer

The understanding of human sexual behavior and identity has been troubled by the confound of some unusual problems in conceptualizing and representing the relationship between erotic potential and expression, on the one hand, versus developmental identity and social surrounding, on the other; and nowhere are these problems more confusing, condensed, and worth pondering than in that perpetual quagmire of sexual theory, "bisexuality."

From the mid-nineteenth century to the present, sexology, followed by psychoanalysis, and later survey sociology and international health epidemiology, have consistently endeavored (without great success) to map out and represent the relationship between the erotic identities, behaviors, and cultures that surround the "black box" of bisexuality (CDC 1989; Gagnon 1989; Herdt 1990; Klein and Wolf 1985; Parker, Herdt and Caballo 1991; Tielman *et al.* 1991). This chapter attempts a preliminary analysis of the interactive processes involved in one aspect of the problem: developmental relations between sexual/gendered identities and the cultures of persons either classified as bisexuals by investigators or self-identified as such.

Four Notions of Bisexuality

Bisexuality is uniquely suited to serve as a paradigm of both theorizing and empirical work because it represents the locus of several quite distinctive and divergent domains of study. Research scholars in the area of human sexuality have argued repeatedly, particularly with the onset of the AIDS epidemic, that bisexual behavior is a central element of the research, education and prevention effort needed to break the chain of HIV transmission across populations, and within subcultures or generations of the same population (see Gagnon 1989; Herdt and Lindenbaum 1992; Turner *et al.* 1989).

Anthropologists, historians, and symbolic sociologists have labored to deconstruct the category "bisexuality," seeing within it the particular formations of local cultures and historical periods (Weeks 1985; Herdt 1991a, 1991b). By contrast, sexologists and medically oriented gender theorists have tended to reproduce earlier cultural representations, most of which derive from the nineteenth century (reviewed in Weeks 1985).

We may speak of four dimensions of "bisexuality" in attempting to capture these conceptual valences and divergent perspectives. "Bisexuality" will now be placed in quotation marks to indicate the attempt to distinguish these levels and to untangle their meanings (and behavioral consequences) across the course of life in particular cultures. Thus, the following levels of analysis have been documented in the research literature as "core" areas of "bisexuality":

- Biological Bisexuality
  Sexual attraction to both sexes as innate drives.
- Psychological Bisexuality
  Relations with both sexes as self-function.
- Behavioral Bisexuality
  Relations with both sexes as interpersonal behavior.
- Cultural Bisexuality
  Relations with both sexes as cultural ideas.

Furthermore, there is a historical series or sequence in these levels: the biological level derives earliest, in the nineteenth century, followed by the other levels in historical time. The earliest literature of the last century, especially concerned with biological factors of bisexuality and inversion, is typical of the first level of study described above (reviewed in Stoller 1975; see also Freud 1905; Money 1987). By contrast, the research literature suggests that most contemporary investigations have been concerned with the second and third levels of bisexuality, as instanced in the significant volume edited by Klein and Wolf (1985). (Many publications in this area, however, often confuse or conflate the first two levels, sometimes lumping with them factors or variables deriving from the first and fourth levels.) Kinsey and his colleagues, for instance, were primarily interested in level three, though Kinsey's notion of "sex drive" obviously borrowed from Freudian and zoological principles to highlight an individual's typical threshold of sexual arousal and behavior potential (Kinsey *et al.* 1948; reviewed in Herdt 1990). The fourth level is newer and more difficult to map. The reasons for this have to do with the conceptualization of "identity" as a later twentieth century sociopolitical concept that articulated social diversity and sexual heterogeneity in complex societies, such as the United States, in a time when scholars such as Erikson (1963, 1982) were attempting to refine gender development in society during the intense social controls following the onset of the Cold War (D'Emilio and Freedman 1988; Herdt and Boxer 1993).

Now let us contrast these levels further. In the first level, the idea of biological bisexuality is strongly associated with medical sexology, with Lamarkian and Darwinian thought in the effort to describe natural selection in human phylogeny.

In the second level, psychological bisexuality has sometimes been conceptualized to mean areas of self-function and regulation, at any of several distinctive levels of biological and psychological development. Freud's (1905) "folk" notion of libidinal bisexuality is an effort to position sexual attraction potential for both sexes as part of a generalized "hard wired" image of human nature. Current work by John Money (1987) continues this line of thinking, with aspects of psychobiological development conceptualized as being part of the deep structure of human nature.

The emergence of the idea of psychological bisexuality is strongly associated with psychoanalytic and psychological discourse on sexuality, and this has tended to pathologize the relevant phenomena. In Freud's work, the emphasis was upon drives and their expressions, which sometimes meant (as it did in the writings upon homosexuality by psychoanalysts) the fixations of arrested development. Academic psychology largely avoided work in this area, though sexologists, most notably John Money (1987) and colleagues, studied the topic. In the work of the psychoanalyst Heinz Kohut (1971), by contrast, the emphasis shifted to the more positive study of self-psychology, so that one could speak of a different line of thinking about psychological bisexuality. Here, work would center on the regulation of self-esteem in the individual's effort to achieve satisfaction from having intimate relations with one or both sexes. The need to derive self-esteem from, sexual and intimate relations with both genders in this paradigm must be distinguished from the "pathological" forms of "bisexuality" commonly identified with the clinical experience of a few individual patients. Typically, in these latter cases individuals with diffuse and weak boundaries of self and fluid self-representations may wax and wane in their sexual desires according to tension states which are associated with sexual intimacy with both genders. (Frequently this is identified clinically with the so-called "borderline" personality, a form of psychopathology that should not be confused with other developmental expressions of sexual contact with both genders.)

In the third level, bisexuality has increasingly indicated interpersonal sexual relations with both sexes. This category is itself confounded by the problem that sexual intercourse typically does not occur with both sexes at the same moment in time. The same individual may, on occasion, be involved with only one sex, and not the other, which may perdure for a significant phase of the development life-course, only to be followed by a "crossing over" to erotic relations with the other sex again. This individual history of sexual interactions is often not aggregated within research for the same individual (as indeed Kinsey *et al.* 1948 did not do), with the effect that bisexuality emerges as a situational or functional outcome, rather than as a product of the life-history of the individual.

In the fourth and most recent level, bisexuality may refer to cultural ideas about sexual relations, or to ideals regarding what a proper, moral person should or should not do, with both sexes. This ideal type of "cultural bisexuality" obviously intersects with conscious desires

of the second level, and behavioral interactions of the third level. Yet the cultural level remains autonomous of these and distinct. Indeed, in the history of the study of bisexuality, study of cultural context and historical setting were typically omitted until the advent of "social constructionism" in the past several decades. In the accounts of social psychologists, for instance, they often strip away the meanings of the sociological and cultural "scripts" of the actors (Gagnon and Simon 1973). In short, what the newer fourth level has done is to problematize "bisexuality" as a matter of collective, rather than purely individual, meanings, agency, and conduct.

Sexual Identity and Bisexuality

In our multi-dimensional perspective on bisexuality we are positioning identity theoretically as a primary mediator of sexual development and cultural identity.[1] However, we are not claiming that this is the "core" or "determinant" of sexual interaction. Bisexual identity is here linked to a general model of sexual identity development and of the expression of desires. Sexual identity is represented as including modes of sexual being, which encompass such matters as erotic desire, sexual orientation, sexual object choice, and sexual drive; and sexual action, which includes such phenomena as erotic practices and tastes, sexual sequences of behavior, and sexual lifestyles. Where the former impinges upon the inner world of sexuality, the latter evokes much of what is important in the social construction of sexuality. Desires, according to recent work, are associated with three kinds of symbolic action in the person: at the level of fantasy, such as thinking about pleasures and "rehearsing" them in the person, in the manner of what John Gagnon and William Simon (1973, 1990) call "scripts"; at the level of the formation of object images and representations, such as the persons (real or fictitious) who the individual daydreams about; and at the level of participation in cultural activity, when individual desires are inserted into social relations.

Such a schema may be seen in historical perspective, for example, in generational age cohorts (Elder 1980) influenced by the changing meanings of sexuality, objects, and cultural practices in their real-life worlds. In Chicago, for instance, we have found that a major difference distinguishing older from younger persons who desire the same sex is that the older cohort consistently hides its desires from biological parents whereas the younger cohort typically reveals these desires to parents or expects to do so within the near future (Herdt and Boxer 1993).

Desires and identity are thus much more a part of the social production of life course development and its vicissitudes in culture, a view we have developed in our work (Herdt and Boxer 1993). Physical transformations of sexual being associated with the onset of puberty have long provided a paradigm for this area of modeling. Puberty involves a rather dramatic set of changes in which a child's body gradually comes to approximate that of an adult. Physical maturation presages other changes; for example, one of the outcomes of puberty is the attainment of mature reproductive potential. The adolescent's self-image is affected, as well as assumptions and expectations regarding sexual behavior and social interactions. The new physical status of the postpubertal adolescent (physical size, body shape, etc.) is accompanied by a variety of social and psychological expectations. Significant others, such as friends, teachers, and family members, may begin to react differently to a young adolescent, effecting a shift in the socially shared definitions of the self (reviewed in Boxer *et al.* 1993).

The concept of identity, as used by Freud and his daughter Anna Freud, Erikson, and later developmentalists such as Robert Stoller, is generally conceived of as an intrinsic process, necessary for full formation of the person. It is not seen as culturally constitutive. Our approach by contrast straddles halfway between ideas of culturally constructed identity and ideas of internal self. With regard to sexual identity, we are concerned with the significant process of transforming desires into sexual being and doing; but what we mean by sexual identity is not the same as gender-identity or sexual orientation, as used by many others (e.g., Kinsey, Stoller, Erikson). Sexual identity is thus more holistic than it was often characterized, at least until the onset of the AIDS epidemic led to significant new areas of research and education which have in turn opened up new questions about the conceptual position of the identity in context. In short, significant attention is needed to further clarify the cultural dimension of bisexuality in these studies.

Identity Systems in Culture

Let us continue the discussion of bisexual identity with the insight that virtually all studies of bisexual conduct or sexual interaction have neglected significant study of the cultural context in which this occurs. Bisexual identity has conventionally signified, that is, individual acts or individual meanings—the psychological level—rather than sexual acts in cultural context, which would include individual acts and meanings as two parts of a whole. Another way of arguing this view is to suggest that bisexuality is an identity system that must be described as including both historical-cultural context and individual actions (see Herdt 1984).

Thus, our problem is to conceptualize the actor or agent in cultural context as a total unit of analysis. For this purpose, we may rethink bisexuality not as a lone child in "nature," but rather as one of a series of categories of identity (heterosexual/homosexual; gay/straight, as argued by Herdt

1992), conceptualized as a cultural system. Such a system links features and components of individual persons' experiences with their conduct in social settings and networks.

Paradigm One: The Sambia of Papua New Guinea

Over a period of approximately fifteen years, one of us, Gilbert Herdt, has described aspects of the ritual traditions and sexual and gendered lives of the Sambia of Papua New Guinea, especially of male development.[2] The overall theme of this work has been to show the relation between cultural context and social practices, and the unfolding of sexual desire and behavior. Same sex relations in particular have been the subject of study because of the widespread practice, universal among Sambia males in earlier development, of relations between older and younger unmarried males (Herdt 1981). Originally, these practices were termed "ritualized homosexuality," and "ritual homosexual behavior" (Herdt 1984). It turns out that approximately fifty different cultures in the South Seas area of Melanesia practice a variant of this age-structured same-sex relation. Conceptual discussions of the phenomena have been provided by Barry Adam (1986) and David Greenberg (1988), among others (reviewed in Herdt 1993). Greenberg in particular has pointed out the failure of anthropologists to provide descriptions of the erotic component of theses activities, which Herdt and Stoller (1990) have also criticized. Greenberg has also rightly critiqued the tendency of anthropologists to abstract the practices and treat them as social matters, rather than as activities having to do with "sexual behavior."

These studies in Melanesia represent a watershed that broke through a critical impasse (Read 1980). The structural trend in Western epistemology has been to collate, consolidate, and wrest from a comparison of Western sexuality with these other sexualities the supposedly shared common denominators of human sexual nature, suggesting that, ultimately, a rose is a rose no matter what its color.[3] "Homosexuality" has been especially problematic for anthropologists because we have remained divided over whether this is a universal or local condition of culture and "human nature" (Herdt 1991a, 1991b). It remains as controversial today as it was a decade ago, in part because the AIDS epidemic has thrust itself into the cultural representation of same-sex relations.[4]

It is now clear from study of the Sambia and other cases that we must place the term "homosexuality" in quotation marks because its folk theory merges the distinction between kinds of cultural identity and types of sexual practice. What we once thought of as a unitary entity— homosexuality—is in fact not one but several "species" of same-sex relations. They differ not only in symbolic form, but also in their deeper nature. Thus, the received category "homosexuality" known in Western culture must now be represented as one of several different sociocultural types known around the world. It is now argued by many experts that such "traditional" forms of culturally conventionalized same-sex erotic practices as appear among the Sambia occur in clusters and culture areas of the world (Adam 1986; Greenberg 1988).

Indeed, four ideal types of same-sex practice can be contrasted: age-structured, gender-structured, role- or class-structured, and gay or egalitarian-structured homosexualities.[5] In the Austro-Melanesian area, "age" is the key to "cultural homosexuality," and is the defining factor in the same-sex relation between the boy and his sexual inseminator, just as in Ancient Greece and Tokugawa Japan (see Herdt 1984). To refer to this practice as "homosexuality" seems now inelegant and unreflective (see Herdt 1993); it is better to represent this symbolic type of same-sex practice as boy-inseminating rites (Herdt 1991b). Here is why.

The Sambia are a hunting and gathering tribe of the Papua new Guinea highlands, marked by an emphasis upon war and sexual antagonism. Their kinship system traces descent through the male line. All marriages are politically arranged with neighboring groups, who may be classified as hostile or even enemy villages. The division of labor is entirely gender coded, with men hunting and warring, and women gardening and tending children. The villages, often no larger than one hundred persons in number, are sex segregated, with men's clubhouses off-limits to women and children, and women's menstrual huts forbidden to men and older children. As in other New Guinea societies, this complex of warfare, marriage, and ritual practices creates an extraordinary context for individual development and social elaboration, which presents a curious mixture of ideas that emphasize both pleasure and reproduction, with the difference that "reproduction" is symbolically defined to include the insemination of boys.

Boy-inseminating rituals implemented in a series of initiations have made the Sambia notable for their acceptance of men's pleasures with both sexes. Like the Ancient Greeks, the Sambia recognize a range of sexual practices having different functions and eventual outcomes. The following ideas are reviewed extensively in Herdt (1981, 1984). On one level the practice of placing semen in the bodies of boys is a necessity due to the local belief system. Sambia believe that the male body is inherently incapable of the manufacture of semen. Since semen is not only the main stimulant to male growth and the masculinization of the body (including the attainment of puberty and the growth of secondary sex characteristics, such as facial hair and muscles) but also an elixir of life—the greatest power for human growth and vitality—the need to artificially introduce semen into boys is enormous. Beginning at ages seven or eight, and continuing until their mid-teens, boys are placed in the role of being orally inseminated by older bachelor males, in a sequence of secret initiations. During this time they com-

pletely avoid women and children, on pain of death. They experience six initiations in all, leading from childhood to manhood in their early twenties. During middle adolescence the boys undergo a third-stage initiation which results in their "switching" roles to become the active inseminators of a new crop of younger boys. They also learn ritual techniques, such as nose-bleeding rites, to rid themselves of the pollution of women's menstrual blood, as well as semen-replenishing techniques, such as the drinking of white tree sap milk (believed to be functionally like semen), in order to maintain their vitality.

Sexual intercourse has three functions for the Sambia. First is to reproduce, to create boys who will be heirs and warriors, and girls who will be traded in the marriage exchange system. Second is to grow masculine boys. And third is to have pleasure: first with boys (orally) and later with women (orally and genitally). In fact, a hierarchy of functions of semen transactions suggests that Sambia do not privilege sexual procreation any more than they do other sexual transactions. Why is this so? Primarily it is because the creation of a new cohort of young warriors to protect village and tribe is always pivotal in the minds of Sambia, men and women alike. They know that the village may be attacked at any time; and they believe that boys will not "naturally" achieve adult competence without the interventions of ritual. As Herdt and other ethnographers have demonstrated in describing these practices, the arousal of youth and men is strong and they experience the inseminating of boys as highly pleasurable. We must not think that their sexual practices are merely a product of sexual seclusion from women or sexual exploitation of boys and women by men. Rather, parallel lines of sexual pleasure develop in Sambia culture, supporting the idea that there are multiple functions of sexual practice, with sexual pleasure being a significant but not overriding function. Women and boys are sexual objects and in some ways are treated by men as a sexual commodity. Yet these women and boys also experience their own pleasures and necessities, including masculine growth (boys) and sexual pleasure and reproduction (women) (reviewed in Herdt and Stoller 1990).

The insemination of boys ideally ends when a man has married and fathered a child. In fact, the vast majority of males do terminate their relations with boys. Perhaps 90 percent or better of men do so, in, part because of taboos, and in part because they have "matured" to a new level of having exclusive sexual access to one or more wives, with genital sexual pleasure being conceived of as more exciting than intercourse with boys. Nonetheless, a small number of individual men continue inseminating boys, some of them boys exclusively, in defiance of custom. One such man, Kalutwo, has been studied in depth, and his sexual and social history reveals a pattern of broken, childless marriages, with an exclusive attraction to boys. Another, larger, category of men are best designated as "bisexual" after marriage in the sense that they enjoy pleasure and reproduction with their wives, but they continue to enjoy oral sex with boys on the sly. These men seem unable to give up the pleasures of intercourse with both sexes, and they do not appear to experience any loss of self-esteem or social approval as a result. They most nearly match the "polymorphous perverse" of having a multifaceted sexuality, though always in the dominant position of being the active inseminator (see Herdt 1981, 1993).

Paradigm Two: Urban Adolescents in Chicago, USA

Between 1987 and 1990, we conducted a cultural and developmental study of 202 gay and lesbian identified adolescents (aged 14–20) and their families in Chicago. We also conducted an historical and cultural study of the setting within which the project took place: Horizons Social Services, a large gay and lesbian community center. We used a modified "Kinsey" type identity scale. Our work in Chicago suggests the existence of three historically specific processes of culturally constituted sexual development in youth (Herdt and Boxer 1993). We follow the sexual identity model referred to above to denote three distinct levels. The first process is largely concerned with the emergence of aesthetic tastes, preferences and appetites from birth to puberty. The second process is focussed upon the experience of the erotic as this begins in childhood and continues through puberty. The third process focussed upon postpubertal experience and the social desires and adjustments which match social selves to real-life worlds. The first and second processes, we believe, are more strongly influenced by intrinsic desires and feelings, signified by the concept of "sexual orientation." However they are also heavily controlled by performative factors in culture. The third process is more sociocentric, but must still invoke the inner world of awareness and desire.

The Horizons Center was founded in the early 1970s by gay activists in Chicago who, in turn, created the first coming out support group for youth. Approximately 700 adolescents attended the informal drop-in meetings on Saturday afternoons which we observed. These are extremely diverse youth, most of whom live at home and attend school. We drew a sample of ethnically diverse youth from a variety of backgrounds, of both genders, to implement our interview study. Interviews with individuals were in-depth, narrative one-to-one and paper and pencil format. Most youth reported that this was a positive experience, the first time they had told their "whole story" of being gay, lesbian, or bisexual.

In the youth settings of Chicago, bisexuality has a specific meaning, which historical and ethnographic study has shown to be dramatically changing at the present time. In the Horizons youth group, as in American society in general, bisexuality is a contentious state of identity. The bisexual is "betwixt and between" sexualities; and at Horizons it follows that for many, though by no means all, youth, bisexuality is a social phase and certain developmental step into the formation of gay or lesbian identified social selves and relationships.

The meaning system of self-identifying as bisexual at Horizons depends upon the social surrounding and the particular individual. Before the existence of Queer Nation, this was "gay turf" to use Richard Herrell's (1992) term; youth found it perplexing to desire both sexes erotically. Hardly anyone desires the opposite sex as much as the same sex, at any rate (see Herdt and Boxer 1993). Rare is the youth who desires both sexes equally at the same point in development. No wonder many youth poke fun with a favorite saying—to quote one young informant on this point, "Bisexuality is what you say until you are OUT." Cultural factors that govern the general process of coming out play a part in the reliance upon bisexuality. Adolescents of color and the working class have a harder time emerging from secrecy, because of the traditional standards of their ethnic communities, with the effect that there is a somewhat greater tendency for younger Black men and women refer to themselves as "bisexual" (see also Peterson 1992). Young Anglo women experience difficulties because of the gender role pressures that make them conform to heterosexual standards enforced by boyfriends and families. Social oppression and internal repression thus combine, leading to an alienation from the desires of the self.

The puzzles of development and bisexuality are embodied in "Straight Sam," a member of the youth group. The group gave him this nickname in part to poke fun at him, and in part to mock his often repeated saying, "I'm straight." Sam was an intelligent but awkward nineteen-year-old white youth. He was the original "nerd" in the group—acne, rumpled clothes, horn-rimmed glasses, and a big mop of uncombed brown hair, a stark contrast to the other, usually carefully coiffured youths. In both his formal interview (done with the rest of the group) and

in two additional, informal interviews conducted alone with Herdt, Sam consistently maintained that he was heterosexual.[6] In his sexual identity scores, he rated a strong heterosexual interest in almost all domains, except in his social life, where he preferred to interact with gays. Sam had doubts about his sexuality; but upon questioning, he said that he had never been involved with the opposite or same sex intimately. He "had not had sex." He came to the group on Saturdays, he said, to "get rid" of his homophobia, which he "inherited" from his lower middle-class parents in the suburbs. In fact, Sam enjoyed being around gay and lesbian teens; that was clear. He suggested at one point that he liked his "gay friends better than his straight friends." We discovered that Sam was actually the target of harassment at high school—the "school fag," as it turns out. The youth at Horizons sometimes tried to discover his sexuality, as when one of the boys suggested that Sam might like to come to a party, insinuating something sexual. Sam turned him down. Sam's interest was not sexual, and he would not get closer to the other youth. Sam desired a gay symbolic space but had the cultural identity of being bisexual—a refugee from suburban life who was transforming along the way.

Same-sex contact between heterosexually active adolescent males is typically not defined as "homosexuality" and does not necessarily lead to the sexual identity "gay" or "homosexual" (Gagnon and Simon 1973). Conversely, at Horizons the youth's descriptions of their participation in opposite-sex activity revealed the normative socialization of the larger society toward participation in heterosexual activity. Many youth engage in such behavior, but only transiently, since it is discrepant with their erotic desires and feelings. The participation in heterosexual experience suggests that these youth were testing their own homoerotic desires, simultaneously engaging in expected behavioral outcomes of heterosexuality, and that these experiences served as a benchmark of comparison. As the cultural identity of "bisexuality" has emerged, this has afforded an alternative pathway of development.

From our quantitative analysis, we have begun to build a model of sexual and identity pathways that help us to understand bisexuality. The youths' accounts of their feelings about the same and opposite-sex experiences highlighted the comparisons that they made. Many youth who tried heterosexual intercourse commented on the lack of feeling and passion they encountered; often, this was magnified if it was preceded by a satisfying homosexual experience with which to compare it. We found that most youth in our sample of 202 teens reported a sequence that began with an awareness of their same-sex desires, proceeded to sexual fantasies, and progressed to some type of same-sex experience. On average, this began between the ages of nine and a half to ten years of age for both males and females. The one significant gender difference occurred with regard to age at first same-sex activity, with males reporting an average age (13.1) significantly younger than did females (15.2) ($t = 3.64$, $p < .001$).

Experiences with the opposite sex are illuminating. A significant number (fifty-five percent) of our gay and lesbian identified youth (thirty-seven females and seventy-four males) reported having had some type of opposite sex experience. Such heterosexual experimentation may be parallel to the same-sex encounters described by heterosexual youth (Kinsey *et al.* 1948). Sixty-seven percent of all females and fifty percent of all males reported these experiences. For males this occurred at 13.7 years on average, very close to the average age of 13.6 years for females. Both males and females reported mixed reactions to opposite-sex relationships. Kevin, a white (twenty-year-old) male described his first heterosexual experience at age thirteen this way:

> It was just kissing, she felt me out, I didn't put my hands in her pants or any of that. I was a little turned on by it, but it wasn't great for me really.

Gay and lesbian youth appear to diverge from psychological bisexuals in their cultural pathways to the sexual. The difference between boys and girls is one way of seeing this. The divergence of average ages for first same-sex but not first opposite-sex experiences indicates that, for males, first homoerotic sex typically preceded first heteroerotic sex. For girls, however, the average age of same-sex experience is later than the average age of first sex with a male, thus confirming the existence of divergent developmental pathways into sexual identity formation.

In classifying youth according to which of a series of three sequences occurred in their initial sexual encounters, we begin to perceive this. Thirty-five percent of the youth were categorized in the "first homo then hetero" sequence; twenty-eight percent were in the first "hetero then homoerotic" sequence; and thirty-seven percent in the "homoerotic" experience only sequence. Larger proportions of male teenagers were found in the homoerotic/heteroerotic, and homoerotic-only groups, while the percentage of females was higher in the first hetero-then/homoerotic group. Thus females were significantly more likely to have had a heterosexual experience before a homosexual one. Previous analyses of these data have confirmed that gender is significantly related to the youth's sequencing of first same-sex and opposite-sex experiences, regardless of the influence of other factors, such as the youths' minority status, employment status, or age at the time of the interview (Boxer 1990). Only twenty-seven (13%) of the teens did not fit into any of these sequences, for reasons such as having had no sexual experiences (neither heterosexual nor homosexual) at the time of the interview ($N=6$); having had heterosexual experiences exclusively ($N=11$); having had their first heteroerotic and homoerotic experiences at the same age ($N=9$), or because of missing information regarding sexual sequencing ($N=1$). The youths' descriptions of the feelings and experiences regarding same-sex and opposite-sex initiations suggest that their comparisons of these experiences were used to help clarify their feelings about their sexual identities.

For teenagers ambivalent or less positive about their first same-sex relationship, their comparing of this to opposite-sex experiences helped clarify feelings otherwise difficult to admit or accept. A boy in the "first homoerotic then/heteroerotic" category, for example, described his first same-sex experience as one in which "we enjoyed the act but didn't enjoy thinking about it." In these narratives, differing sexual identity pathways serve as developmental milestones through which the self compares erotic experiences. One's basis for comparison may affect how positively or negatively same-sex and bisexual relations, especially intimate ones, are experienced (Herdt 1984). How the youth regarded their first sexual experience may have thus been influenced by these comparisons. Likewise, these initial sexual encounters may also have been formative of how Horizons youth constructed their gay and lesbian identities in contrast to others who self-identify as bisexual.

These youth describe first heteroerotic experiences as "sex without feelings." Regardless of whether it was preceded by a same-sex experience or not, a feeling of "unnaturalness" and lack of affective intensity in their first heterosexual sex was mentioned repeatedly. This theme was present in the accounts of both males and females—although females tended to describe heterosexual experiences as something that they simply expected to happen, whereas males often sought out these experiences.

What if the teens' first homoerotic experience was initiated at a later age, but still prior to their opportunity to experience opposite-sex relations? To examine this possibility, we compared the mean ratings of feelings about first same-sex and opposite-sex activity for "ambivalent" youth in each of the three pathways. These self-ratings ranged from 1 through 5 (1 = very bad, 2 = bad, 3 = OK/mixed positive and negative, 4 = good, and 5 = very good). Respondents in all three groups rated their initial homosexual experiences fairly positively, in the 3.5 to 3.7 range (between okay and good). They are also similar in the uniformly lower ratings they give to their first heterosexual activity. There is nearly a one-point drop in the mean rating from homoerotic to heteroerotic activity for both the "homosexual/ heterosexual" and "heterosexual/ homosexual" groups (from 3.6 to 2.8 among the heterosexual/homosexual youth, and from 3.7 to 2.8 among the homosexual/ heterosexual youth.) The sequencing of the youths' first sexual experiences does not therefore appear related to the ages at which same and opposite-sex activity first occurred, nor to the youths' feelings regarding these first experiences. It is, rather, gender that plays the key role in the sequencing of first same-sex and opposite-sex relations, independent of other factors.

Boys revealed that they often sought heterosexual experiences, while girls often described heterosexual sex as something that had only happened to them at an earlier age. It is possible that the greater likelihood of sexual pressure and coercion experienced by females from heterosexual males predisposes them to the heterosexual/ homosexual sequence, as a consequence of growing up in a society where females encounter such experiences much more commonly than males. Sexual socialization of young females, in public schools for example, typically prepares them to experience their sexuality in passive, non-agentic ways (Fine 1988). Girl's initial (and relatively less pleasurable) heteroerotic activity may serve as a basis of comparison that facilitates the translation to lesbian identities. For the first time, they may express what they want to desire as agents of their own desires. While both males and females are the object of heterosexual assumptions from family, peers and significant others in their milieu, males may experience greater cultural and familial expectations for heterosexual behavior, impelling them to engage or experiment with it regardless of their desires. Similar to the subject of reports on gay and lesbian adults (Weinberg and Williams 1974; Bell, Weinberg and Hammersmith 1981), some teens have told us that their wish was that, by engaging in opposite-sex behaviors, they would make the same sex desires go away.

The youths struggle beyond the feeling of hiding and remorse, facing for the first time how to relate their experiences to existing practices and structures in the culture. The fear that they are "really bisexual" and not gay or lesbian is important for two fundamental reasons. Historically, as we have seen, bisexual represents the nineteenth century mediation between "homosexual" and "heterosexual" in the conventional American cultural system. But as a new twentieth-century species, the liberated hedonist, the "bisexual" mediates "gay" and "straight" in the emergent cultural system of sexuality in the United States. Here, the new emphasis is upon an ideology of hedonism. There is, however, another factor: the sense in which to "come out," youth must confront whether he or she is not bisexual, rather than gay or lesbian, in terms of cultural roles and desires. Here, it is in this sense that contemporary "bisexuality" represents states of becoming and being that are transitional: the essence of liminal passage both for individuals and for cultures.

Conclusion

This paper compares the assumptions about bisexuality present in the research literature, with the greatly differing cultural realities of New Guinea and gay and lesbian-identified youth in Chicago. We have suggested that four views of bisexuality can be contrasted. With the exception of the first biological level, the other three are critical in social and behavioral research on sexuality and recent study of health and sexually transmitted diseases. We have suggested that the concepts of desire and identity have been conflated in sexual theory until recently, and sexual identity has had a floating meaning that undermines the nature of empirical data related to observed development, at least in Western urban populations. Culture has often been left out of the description of these phenomena. This has caused the investigation of "bisexuality" to leave the study of cultural

action and historical context out of its total system of analysis. We claim that this was a critical error in the scientific modeling and research of past generations. New efforts should be devoted to investigating the cultural and historical contexts of bisexual identities, sexual interaction, and sexual cultures in Western and non-Western settings, in order to further understand the significance of bisexual conduct for the human species as a whole.

Notes

Acknowledgments: Some of the data presented in this paper were collected under the auspices of the project, "Sexual Orientation and Cultural Consequence: A Chicago Study," G. Herdt, principal investigator, and we should like to thank the Spencer Foundation for their support. The arguments and supporting material from the two case studies of this paper are drawn in modified form from material discussed in two sources: see G. Herdt, "Introduction to the Paperback: Ten years After *Ritualized Homosexuality in Melanesia*," in Herdt, *Ritualized Homosexuality in Melanesia,* 2nd ed. (Berkeley: University of California Press, 1993); and Gilbert Herdt and Andrew Boxer, *Children of Horizons* (Boston: Beacon Press, 1993). The writing of this chapter was made possible by Gilbert Herdt's sabbatical from the University of Chicago. Special thanks to Provost Edward O. Laumann for his support of this leave. For comments on the paper, we are especially indebted to Jeffrey Weiss and Richard Parker.

1. The material in this section is adopted in modified form from Herdt and Boxer 1993.

2. The material in this section is adopted in modified form from Herdt 1993.

3. Further, we may perhaps trace this desire for a common form (that is like the Western form) to our long-standing Western preoccupation with shared "psychic unity" and human nature (Herdt 1991a, 1991b; Spiro 1987).

4. See, especially, Herdt and Lindenbaum (1992) on AIDS and gays.

5. See, for a history of these typologies, the works of B. Adam, S. Murray, and more recently, D. Greenberg, reviewed in Herdt (1990, 1991a).

6. Herdt interviewed Sam in part because our graduate student interviewers were reluctant to take him on. They felt that he was a fake, and they could not understand his self-image; another manifestation of the issues related to transference and counter-transference in a project of this kind. In fact, Herdt found him tentative and confused, but interesting and benign.

References

Adam, B. 1986. Age, structure, and sexuality: Reflections on the anthropological evidence on homosexual relations. *Journal of Homosexuality* 11:19–33.

Bell, A. P., Weinberg, M. S., and Hammersmith, S. K. 1981. *Sexual Preference: Its Development in Men and Women.* Bloomington: Indiana University Press.

Boxer, A. M. 1990. *Life Course Transitions of Bay and Lesbian Youth: Sexual Identity Development and Parent-Child Relationships.* Ph.D. dissertation. University of Chicago.

Boxer, A. M. et al. 1993. Gay and lesbian youth. In *Research and Practice with Adolescents,* Tolan, P. H. and Cohler, B. J., eds., pp. 249–280. New York: John Wiley and Sons.

Centers for Disease Control (CDC) 1989. *Behaviorally Bisexual Men and AIDS.* Washington, D.C.: U.S. Department of Health and Human Services.

D'Emilio, J. and Freedman, E. 1988. *Intimate Matters: A History of Sexuality in America.* New York: Harper and Row.

Elder, G. H. 1980. Adolescence in historical perspective. In *Handbook of Adolescent Psychology,* Adelson, ed., pp. 3–46. New York: Wiley.

Erickson, E. 1963. *Childhood and Society.* New York: Norton.

Erickson, E. 1982. *The Lifecycle Completed: A Review.* New York: Norton.

Fine, M. 1988. Sexuality, schooling, and adolescent females: The missing discourse on desire. *Harvard Educational Review* 58:29–53.

Freud, S. 1905. *Three Essays on the Theory of Sexuality.* London: Hogarth Press.

Gagnon, J. H. 1989. Disease and desire. *Daedalus* 118:47–77.

Gagnon, J. H. 1990. The implicit and explicit use of the scripting perspective in sex research. *Annual Review of Sex Research* 1:1–43.

Gagnon, J. H. and Simon, W. 1973. *Sexual Conduct: The Social Sources of Human Sexuality.* Chicago: Aldine.

Greenberg, D. 1988. *The Construction of Homosexuality.* Chicago: The University of Chicago Press.

Herdt, G. H. 1981. *Guardians of the Flutes: Idioms of Masculinity.* New York: McGraw-Hill.

Herdt, G. H. 1984. A comment on cultural attributes and fluidity of bisexuality. *Journal of Homosexuality* 10:53–62.

Herdt, G. H. 1990. Developmental continuity as a dimension of sexual orientation across cultures. In *Homosexuality and Heterosexuality: The Kinsey Scale and Current Research,* McWhirter, D., Reinisch, J., and Sander, S., eds., pp. 208–238. New York: Oxford University Press.

Herdt, G. H. 1991a. Representations of homosexuality in traditional societies: An essay on cultural ontology and historical comparison. Part I. *Journal of the History of Sexuality* 2:603–632.

Herdt, G. H. 1991b. Representations of homosexuality in traditional societies: An essay on cultural ontology and historical comparison. Part II. *Journal of the History of Sexuality* 2:603–632.

Herdt, G. H. 1992. Introduction. In *Ritualized Homosexuality in Melanesia* (paperback edition), Herdt, G., ed., pp. vii–xiv. Berkley and Los Angeles: University of California Press.

Herdt, G. H. 1993. *Children of Horizons.* Boston: Beacon Press.

Herdt, G. and Linderbaum, S., eds. 1992. *The Time of AIDS.* Newbury Park, CA: Sage Publications.

Herdt, G. and Stoller, R. 1990. *Intimate Communications: Erotics and the Study of Culture.* New York: Columbia University Press.

Herrell, R. 1992. The symbolic strategies of Chicago's gay and lesbian pride day parade. In *Gay Culture in America,* Herdt, G., ed., pp. 225–252. Boston: Beacon Press.

Kinsey, A. C., Pomeroy, W. B., and Martin, C. E. 1948. *Sexual Behavior in the Human Male.* Philadelphia: W. B. Saunders.

Klein, F. and Wolf, T. J., eds. 1985. *Bisexualities: Theory and Method.* New York: Haworth Press.

Kohut, H. 1971. *The Analysis of the Self: A Systematic Approach to Psychoanalytic Treatment of Narcissistic Personality Disorders.* New York: International Universities Press.

Money, J. 1987. Sin, sickness, or society? *American Psychologist* 42:384–399.

Parker, R. G., Herdt, G. H., and Carballo, M. 1991. Sexual culture, HIV transmission, and AIDS research. *The Journal of Sex Research* 28(1):77–98.

Peterson, J. L. 1992. Black men and their same-sex desires and practices. In *Gay Culture in America,* Herdt, G., ed., pp. 147–164. Boston: Beacon Press.

Read, K. 1980. *Other Voices*. Novato: Chandler and Sharpe.

Spiro, M. 1987. *Culture and Human Nature: The Theoretical Papers of Melford Spiro*. Chicago: The University of Chicago Press.

Stoller, R. J. 1975. *The Transsexual Experiment, Vol. 2: Sex and Gender*. New York: Jason Aronson.

Tielman, R. A. P., Hendriks, A., and Carballo, M, eds. 1991. *Bisexuality and HIV/AIDS: A Global Perspective*. Buffalo: Prometheus Books.

Turner, C. F., Miller, H. G., and Moses, L. E., eds. 1989. *AIDS, Sexual Behavior, and Intravenous Drug Use*. Washington, D.C.: National Academy Press.

Weeks, J. 1985. *Sexuality and its Discontents: Meanings, Myths, and Modern Sexualities*. London: Routledge and Kegan Paul.

Weinberg, M. S. and Williams, C. J. 1974. *Male Homosexuals: Their Problems and Adaptation*. Oxford: Oxford University Press.

Falling in Love with an-Other Lesbian

Reflections on Identity in Fieldwork

Evelyn Blackwood

Being the supreme crossers of cultures, homosexuals have strong bonds with the queer white, Black, Asian, Native American, Latino . . . We are a blending that proves that all blood is intricately woven together, and that we are spawned out of similar souls. (Anzaldúa 1987: 84–5)

I conducted fieldwork in a rural Muslim Minangkabau village in West Sumatra, Indonesia.[1] I went there in 1989 to study social change, gender, and power, but I was also interested in exploring the gender identity of lesbians in West Sumatra.[2] I was fortunate to meet several lesbians, and in the process fall in love with one of them. An already challenging field experience then became more complicated as I shifted between the professional, straight identity I maintained in my research village, and the closeted, lesbian identity I possessed with my lover in her village. The instability of my identity and the necessity to reconstruct it in relation to the people with whom I interacted forced a recognition of the differences and similarities between us.

The question I want to explore here is how one's subjectivity in the field, in this case my own subjectivity as a lesbian and an anthropologist, exposes and challenges issues of exoticizing and identity in ethnographic fieldwork. I

attempt to understand the ways we reify distance between ourselves and our "subjects" to avoid asking uncomfortable questions about our presence in other cultures and the ways we exoticize Others. If the denial of our subjectivity enables exoticizing in anthropology, how does recognition of our subjectivity, our agency in relationships in the field, counter that practice? In particular, how does the subjective experience of sexuality in the field challenge the distance between "us" and "them"?

I will explore these issues through the disjunctures of the familiar and the alien that I encountered in my field experience. I was alternately a young, unmarried daughter who professed to be sexually naive and engaged to be married, and also a lover, who fell in love with an-Other lesbian. This essay is a reflection on life in the borders of gender and sexuality and how conflicts of identity lead to new meanings and deeper understandings of cultural differences and similarities.

In this essay I do not want to speak for my lover, although in my recounting of our relationship I ultimately represent her. These recollections, however, are my interpretation of our experience, not hers. Her experience of me differed from my experience of her; her conflicts and disjunctures may be other than the ones I highlight here. (It might have been troublesome to her that I was non-Muslim, but I do not raise that issue here.) Further, I do not pretend to understand precisely how she felt being with a lover whose affluence and power as a member of a First World country set the terms of the relationship. This essay, then, is an excursion into the subjectivity of the anthropologist. It is an attempt to recognize the multiplicity of genders, sexualities, and classes within which we operate as anthropologists and the ways in which we can use our subjective experience of these domains as a bridge to challenge the distance inscribed in ethnographic fieldwork.

Anthropological Privilege

Anthropology has long been accused of being a discourse in which the anthropologist holds a privileged position as bearer of the right to ask questions and make claims to knowledge about others. As Trinh so potently writes, anthropology is:

> a conversation of "us" with "us" about "them," of the white man with the white man about the primitive-native man . . . a conversation in which "them" is silenced. "Them" always stands on the other side of the hill, naked and speechless, barely present in its absence. (1989:65, 67)

This statement questions our right to speak for others and to assume in speaking that we convey some truth. As Trinh suggests, in the relation between anthropology and its subject there are two separate and distinct entities, a self and other, one unmarked, the other marked. This construction reinforces the distance between anthropologists and the people they "study." In his *Diary*, Malinowski (1989) expressed in contemptuous terms the gap he felt

between himself and the Trobrianders. Dubisch notes that, twenty years ago, she felt as if she occupied a different world from that of the people in Greece she went to study. As Kondo points out, "ethnographies commonly convey a subtle sense of superiority over the "people studied" . . . All too often, standards of scientific objectivity in ethnography have masked points of view that are merely distant and unsympathetic" (1986:84). Haraway eloquently defines this scientific objectivity as:

> the gaze from nowhere. This is the gaze that mythically inscribes all the marked bodies, that makes the unmarked category claim the power to see and not be seen, to represent while escaping representation. This gaze signifies the unmarked positions of Man and White. (1988:581)

As anthropologists, our presence in other cultures and our subjectivities as members of the First World elicit certain responses that are understandable only if we know how we are perceived. In reference to informants, the metaphor of "friend" appears frequently in writings about fieldwork by American anthropologists (see, for example, Geertz 1968). It is one way we define our relationship with the Other (and a way to find some solace for the loneliness we feel and replace relationships we had at "home"). We constitute ourselves as "friend," a neutral entity that embodies our belief that the relationship between ourselves and at least some of our informants is one of equality. But the category of "friend" that we so readily apply to cross-cultural situations actually masks a much greater complexity in our field relations.

The problems that arise from lack of recognition of one's position in fieldwork are apparent in Rabinow's *Reflections on Fieldwork in Morocco* (1977). In this book Rabinow uses his experience of fieldwork as a way to describe his initiation into, and growing understanding of, the ways of another people. Such confessional writing has become a standard genre for critical anthropologists; sometimes it provides other revelations than those intended. Rabinow argues that fieldwork is an experiential activity conducted by a culturally mediated and historically situated self (1977:5). So far, so good. But he fails to acknowledge the superior position from which he is operating. Further, he assumes that Moroccans are relatively unreflective about things that anthropologists want to know. Rabinow writes that the process of fieldwork requires a building up of common experiences in order for the informant to speak so that the anthropologist can understand (1977:152). In other words, the informant must come to see things in the way the anthropologist sees them to make their conversations intelligible. For Rabinow, it is his (male) informant who is required to bridge the gap, who should be brought to the (higher) level of understanding where the anthropologist dwells. Though Rabinow insists he only arrived at a partial understanding of his informants (1977:162), as with most ethnographies, it is nevertheless this partial understanding that is enshrined as true knowledge brought home from the field.

It is in part Rabinow's inability or refusal to position himself that creates the distance between himself and his subject. Rabinow established what he considered to be a friendship early on with the man who was his Arabic teacher. "Basically I had been conceiving of him as a friend because of the seeming personal relation we had," he stated (1977:29). His first disjuncture, which he identified as "one of my first direct experiences of Otherness" (1977:28), happened when his friend/teacher treated him as an exploitable source of income (someone who could provide a certain amount of status and financial reward), rather than the "friend" that Rabinow had convinced himself that he was. This disjuncture made him realize that they were operating under different assumptions, which he assumed meant something about his teacher's culture. On the contrary, Rabinow's disjuncture came from being reminded that he was not a neutral Self but a situated Other (the wealthy white man from America), something he attempted to downplay but which his informant understood quite well. Rabinow described this disjuncture as a meeting with

"culture," thus failing to recognize it as the result of his own positioning within another culture. By setting their interaction aside as distinctly belonging only to his informant's culture, he denies that they are both players at some level in the same world; his statement relegates his teacher to a cultural backwater that operates without connection to the larger world.

In contrast, Favret-Saada (1980) insists that there can be no ethnographic statement that is not upheld by its relation to the two (author and subject). Her work on witchcraft among French peasants caused her to rethink the relationship of the author and the subject. To understand, one has to "become one's own informant, to penetrate one's own amnesia, and to try to make explicit what one finds unstable in oneself" (1980:22). She was forced to understand her own motives, to question why she wanted to understand her subject; for her, simply seeking knowledge was not enough.

Reflexive anthropology, of which Favret-Saada's is one example, seeks to counter criticism "of the truth claims of Western representations of the 'other'" (Mascia-Lees *et al.* 1989:9) by bringing the anthropologist into the text and highlighting the interaction between anthropologist and subject. In another such attempt, Dwyer (1979) argues that understanding the dialectical relationship between Subject and Object provides an alternative to traditional anthropological practices. Dwyer implies a connectedness between Self and Other by suggesting that as ethnographers we are "at home" everywhere (1977:150). His vehicle for connection, a dialogic approach, goes a long way toward bridging difference. It is insufficient, however, because it only takes into account the will and subjectivity of the Other in the anthropological project, without fully accounting for the position of the anthropologist in this "confrontation with the Other" (1979:211).

It is not enough for the anthropologist to be visible asking the questions; we must acknowledge the position from which we ask our questions and make our interpretations. Our subjectivities form the core of anthropological theory and method. Haraway's challenge to feminists to search for situated knowledges is equally applicable to anthropological knowledge: "feminist objectivity is about limited location and situated knowledge, not about transcendence and splitting of subject and object" (1988:583). The position and identity of the ethnographer, as a member of a certain Western intellectual tradition and citizen of the "First World" (with all the implications of hierarchy that term carries), are critical to the shape of our work and the meaning it expresses. We have to locate ourselves because, as Kondo writes in her confessional on fieldwork, "knowledge is always knowledge from a particular perspective. Understandings are situated within culture, history, and biography" (1986:84). But the ethnographic experience is more than an identification of positionality or subjectivity; we occupy multiple positions and identities that transform over time, forcing us constantly to reconstruct who we are in relation to the people we study. Disjunctures, the moments at which we find ourselves uncomfortable, point the way to understanding these transformations and the differences between ourselves and others.

Marked Identities

My identity as a lesbian, feminist, and woman prevented me from assuming in the field situation that I was simply a neutral figure observing culture. As a lesbian, I am aware that I move in a world partially alien, one where the norms of heterosexuality and femininity are at odds with self-image. I have the sense that any role I take on is "drag," a costume one puts on to suit the occasion, not some inborn, natural part of me. As a lesbian and member of a marginalized community, I move within the dominant, straight (white) culture without comfortable inclusivity in it.

Consequently, I come to anthropology as an insider/outsider, an insider who was indoctrinated in American culture and its intellectual tradition, yet whose marginality as a lesbian makes me an outsider in many contexts. I am not allowed the luxury of perceiving myself as the center of the world, or as the "man" against which all others are measured, the person able to speak Truth (Trinh 1989). From a marginalized position on the borders of the dominant system, it is easier to recognize the categories that shape all of us and not just those categories that come under our scrutiny as anthropologists; it is harder to claim that one sees all, as Haraway's imagery of the Eye suggests (1988:581), and deny that one has any position relative to those being studied. Whitehead (1986), writing from a similarly marginalized position as a black American anthropologist, could not maintain the fiction that he occupied an unmarked, nonproblematic identity in his fieldwork. Instead, he used his identity and people's responses to him to gain a better understanding of Jamaican culture.

My lesbian identity was not openly part of my field identity, as Whitehead's identity as a black person was. I used it not as a personal criterion to judge other people's reactions but, rather, as an internal monitor that keyed me to the margins and disjunctures of culture. It made me extremely aware of the dominance of heterosexuality in Minangkabau culture and the careful gender distinctions that mark men and women as different. Later, when I met my lover, it also keyed me to the differences between her life and other women's lives and the forces that shaped her identity as a lesbian.

In preparing for fieldwork, I decided it would be better to hide my lesbian identity. I assumed Muslims would not accept an openly gay person and I did not want to hurt my chances of completing my research successfully. To those who asked, I identified myself as unmarried (I was, in fact, single at the time). I also allowed the cultural assumption of heterosexuality to slot me as heterosexual. Because my marriageability and high status as a foreigner made me a supposedly desirable target, it was suggested to me by other Indonesianists that I maintain a story about a fiancé whom I would marry as soon as I finished my dissertation. This story would hopefully discourage unwanted male advances and proposals of marriage. Since it is acceptable now in West Sumatra for women to finish their education before marriage, my excuse made sense to people in the village, although they still considered me to be rather old for an unmarried woman. I maintained this story throughout my fieldwork, although I was uncomfortable with it. It was a flimsy disguise at best (since I had no pictures of my fiancé and never received any letters from him) and at worst established my superiority over the people in the village because it implied they should not, or did not need to, know such things about "their" anthropologist. This notion that I was the knower and they the known reflects one of the ways we as anthropologists distance ourselves from those we study.[3]

As an unmarried, supposedly heterosexual woman living with an Indonesian family, I was expected to fulfill the ideals of the gender category to which I was ascribed. This situation is common for women anthropologists and always problematic. In many cases women anthropologists are forced to accept restrictions of movement as well as an inferior status vis-á-vis men that confronts a deeply held sense of self.[4] I tried to meet the expectations of people in the village concerning my gender because I wanted to maintain good relations, acquire access to any information I wanted, and, most of all, gain their love and acceptance. In a Minangkabau village, these expectations are not overly burdensome; within the rank hierarchy relations between women and men are egalitarian (see Blackwood 1993). As heads of lineages and controllers of ancestral houses and lands, women have power over the labor and activities of their kin; no decisions are made within the lineage without their consent. Consequently, women are prime movers in village social life, which is, however, sex-segregated in most social contexts.

Unmarried women in particular must protect their reputation and not associate freely with men, nor should they engage in activities typically identified with men, such as smoking, drinking, or gambling. I maintained these conventions quite easily in addition to my story that I had a "boyfriend" back home. At least my unavailability was amply supported by my lack of sexual interest in men in the village. I treated men my age as peers and older men as seniors and did not have to struggle with my sexual identity in relation to them.

At the same time I resisted constructing a field identity that conformed to their expectations for an unmarried woman. Although I cleaned my room and sometimes swept the floors in the house, I never cooked or did my own laundry; instead, I paid other women to take care of these domestic duties for me. This failing did not surprise my host, however, who assumed that "rich," privileged Americans would not be well trained in such matters. Where the gendered dress code was at odds with my lesbian self, however, I developed the most resistance to reconstructing my identity. I could not force myself to wear skirts, as any proper Indonesian woman does, except very occasionally. My host sometimes remarked on this lapse because it raised deeper questions for her about my womanhood. She expressed great satisfaction when I wore local dress on ritual occasions but eventually decided that my proclivity for pants was a harmless American custom. Her tolerance of my behavior showed a willingness to understand and overlook the differences between us that I had not expected.

My marginality in two cultures and my inability to conform to gender categories helped me to feel at ease moving between men's and women's spaces. At ceremonies I bridged the distance between men and women with equanimity. Women and men physically occupy different parts of a room during ceremonies. In some instances, I sat with the women and listened to their conversations, but when I had permission I would sit between the two groups. On one occasion I attended the male-only part of a ritual.

My presence with the men unnerved my Indonesian mother, who was helping with food preparations at the ceremony, yet she understood my need to collect data and sought to support me by crossing the boundary herself and sitting with me and the men.

While I recognized my own marginal gender identity, I resisted coming to terms with my privilege. Besides being a daughter to my Indonesian family, I was also the white American woman scholar, who, as a representative of the First World, had certain privileges and power over other people's lives. I was honored in a welcoming ceremony and sat in high-status positions at rituals. I was embarrassed by this treatment but took full advantage of it by boldly walking into anyone's house and asking them questions that were important only to me.

As have other women anthropologists during their fieldwork, I continually tacked back and forth between various assigned and constructed identities: researcher, friend, daughter, professional, American. I seemed to have no single identity but many, and none of them fit neatly into any of the ascribed categories for me. It was ultimately the instability of my identity that forced my awareness of the complexity of my position:

Sept. 7, 1989: I have to be here a year—make this my home and I'm such a stranger. Just dropped in on their world—I can share it but not really be a part of it. At another level I am just a researcher. I will go home again and leave all this behind—their worries, problems, needs. What an ambiguous role . . . I have to live with people who don't really understand who or what I am and have their own agendas in dealing with me. As I have mine. This is not my universe.[5]

In my journal I expressed the unease I felt in terms that emphasized the distance between myself and them: "their world," "not my universe." To me there was my home and this place that had no connection to it that occupied a different "universe." The problem of feeling alien was intensified, however, because I was a lesbian in a heterosexual world. I did not share a common sexual identity with the people in the village, which most ethnographers take for granted (although this assumed commonality has to be problematized, as other chapters in this volume point out). I felt as if I no longer recognized myself. My lesbian identity had totally disappeared:

Jan. 31, 1990: And who am I, this amorphous creature with few reality markers to cling to, yet somehow conspiring to present a self acceptable to people here. Much of who I am, or considered myself to be, goes unrecognized . . . . My gay identity is lost and crying out for recognition.

As Newton (1993) aptly points out in her discussion of the 'erotic equation in fieldwork,' there are few gay zones to retreat to in foreign field locales and thus no opportunity for lesbian or gay male anthropologists to relax in a safe and accepting environment. Every day I played the nice, polite, naive, heterosexual American woman and was thereby unable to share with anyone the part of my life that was about my lesbian identity and family. Indonesians always ask about family, parents, siblings, husband, and children; the silence I imposed on my own life story was a constant and painful reminder of my separateness; the denial of a significant part of my life was a tremendous blow to my self-esteem.

I lived with one family during my stay in Indonesia and the greater the emotional attachment between my Indonesian mother (whom I called Ibu, which means mother) and me, the more painful it was not to talk about my life. I cared deeply for Ibu; she was a guardian and good friend who willingly confided in me her hopes and fears, happinesses and sorrows. I tried to repay her for her kindness to me and did so through the best means available to me, by lending her money to keep her business solvent. Although this action played on the inherent inequality in our positions, it nevertheless seemed to restore some balance in my debt to her as my host and did not cause any rupture in our relationship, as it did with Rabinow.

Despite Ibu's friendship and the companionship of other women in the village, I felt cut off from myself and deeply lonely:

Nov. 2, 1989: Right now I want to go home. I want to be me again, with my friends, my house, my dyke world. I'm not tired of being here but I miss my life back home. I miss being in a familiar world where I know who I am . . . I can't talk about my lovers, about half my family experiences and that's what people relate to here. How can I share my life with Ibu who tells me all her life?

I missed everything that was part of the self I left behind. I was tired of being someone for somebody else, for professing to being sexually naive to suit Islamic notions of womanhood, for claiming to be engaged to avoid possible suitors, and for not being able to share who I was with people who shared so much of themselves.

In desperation one day, when Ibu and I were having a long conversation about American sexual practices, I told her I was a lesbian. I was tired of the deceit and the pretense of having a boyfriend. Instantly, I was afraid that I had lost the one person I could count on in the village. To my great relief, however, Ibu told me she was not upset. "That's what you do in America," she said, again refuting my understanding of the knower/known categories implicit in anthropology. She went on to warn me, however, that I should not engage in such practices here (meaning both her house and her country), effectively asserting the dominance of her cultural ideology and cutting off any further attempts to engage my vision of the world. Her response affirmed at once her own tolerance as well as the Islamic admonition to guide others in the right way, since according to Islam, homosexuality is a greater sin than adultery. She was also protecting herself and me, as a member of her household, from possible shameful repercussions. I adhered to her edict while I remained in her house, but her position on this issue later caused a strain in our relationship. Although I remained fearful for several days that the village head would come to my house and ask me to leave the village, nothing happened, and Ibu did not bring up the subject again.

The need to have my lesbian identity recognized, and the need for physical and emotional intimacy beyond the friendships I had, ultimately led me into a relationship with a Minangkabau woman in a village about an hour from my fieldsite. The significance of this relationship was far from clear to me during the nine months we were together. While I struggled to create a safe place and a new "home" where I felt sure of my identity, my relationship with an-Other lesbian decentered and displaced me, forcing me to recognize and resist the differences between us. At the same time, it helped me to regain my sense of self and establish a bond that bridged the distance between us.

Love in the Field

I had been in Indonesia for nine months before I was introduced to Dayan (a pseudonym). Early in my field stay I met several young gay men in town through a woman friend of mine. I asked this friend if she knew any lesbians, and when she said she did, I asked her to help me meet some of them. Months passed but nothing came of my request. Finally, I went into town one day and begged my friend to take me to see a friend of hers who she said was a lesbian. She collected another friend and after half an hour's bumpy ride on the local bus to a neighboring village, we got off the bus and walked a short distance down a dirt road to a dilapidated wood and cement house. We were greeted by a woman in her early thirties, Dayan's older married sister. Dayan was outside working on her chicken coop; she came in after a few minutes and shyly shook my hand. She had on shorts and a T-shirt, wore her black hair short; I thought she had a beautiful smile. We left her sister and several curious onlookers and children behind, and went up to her room.

Her room contained a small bed, a bureau, a chair, and a guitar (and, I later noticed, the largest spider I'd ever seen, hanging in its web about 12 feet above the bed in the rafters). Dayan's family owned some riceland but were not well off. She had posters of rock stars plastered on her walls: Billy Idol, Madonna, Sting. My friends went out for a short while to get cigarettes while we talked; Dayan asked me if I had some erotic photos of women that I could give her. She couldn't get any in Indonesia. Then my friends were back and it was time to leave—the buses don't run at night and they needed to get back to town. We said goodbye and I promised to come see her again.

My friends were pleased with their role in helping me meet Dayan. Young people in West Sumatra are generally more open about sexuality than the older generation, although most people in West Sumatra are aware that homosexuality exists. The words lesbi and gay have entered their lexicon through the national media, which frequently report on the lesbian and gay movement in Europe and America as well as provide portrayals of Indonesian lesbians. Lesbianism has been a topic in the media since the early 1980s. While some of the articles attempt to be sympathetic, most tend to criticize or condemn it as abnormal, deviant, or a reflection of Westernized lifestyles (Gayatri 1993). The Indonesian Criminal Penal Code does not forbid homosexual or same-sex relationships, however (Gayatri 1993). West Sumatran (and Indonesian) categories of gender and sexuality differ from the Western categories labeled "lesbian" and "gay," which refer to sexual identity. In West Sumatra, alternatively gendered males are called bujang-gadis (a term meaning boy-girl) or bencong. Both terms refer to a male transvestite or drag queen (in our terms), usually a male who dresses and acts like a woman; the term banci is also used, but more commonly in Java. Alternatively gendered females are called supik-jantan (a Minangkabau word meaning girl-boy) or tomboi (a more recent term from the English for a male-like woman). These terms are now used alternately with lesbi and gay, due to the close connection of alternative gender with homosexuality in West Sumatra and Indonesia (see also Gayatri

1993).[6] Alternatively gendered individuals find partners among same-sex individuals who appear straight-looking and are usually bisexual. The masculine (jantan or tomboi) partner in a lesbian couple is also called cowok, an Indonesian slang term for a young man meaning "guy," or laki-laki (man), while her feminine partner is called cowek, Indonesian slang for a young woman meaning "girl." This usage reflects the direct application of terms for man and woman to an alternatively gendered individual and her partner. Due to the tremendous pressure on children to marry, most bisexual individuals and some alternatively gendered individuals in Indonesia marry at some point in their lives and later may become involved with a lover of the same sex.

Homosexuality and alternative gender are more or less tolerated in rural West Sumatra as long as the person fulfills his or her duty to family by marrying and having children. Although Islamic law explicitly forbids homosexuality and Minangkabau are devoutly Muslim, Minangkabau tend to look the other way on this issue unless the individual strongly resists his or her marriage obligations. Pressure to marry and the strength of Islamic proscriptions, however, mean that most gay people conduct their relationships secretly to avoid shaming themselves and their families. According to Gayatri's study of lesbians in Java, whose lives have close parallels to those in West Sumatra,

the biggest risk is that they will be labeled as lesbian, scorned by friends and acquaintances, considered as sick, and thus become isolated within their own society. [They could also] lose their good name, especially if they happen to be public figures. The family name is also important, [as is] their respect for their parents. (1993:13)

Those who cannot conform to the heterosexual model move away from their families to urban areas to live with their lovers, if they can afford to. Others may be forced to marry and raise children, and only later be able to live with a lover, though they keep such a relationship hidden. Although gay people I met usually knew others in the area, there is no gay community as such, even in the large towns in West Sumatra. *Bencong* may have quite a following of bisexual men, and the parties they throw draw many other *bencong*, bisexual men, and some women. I met few lesbians in West Sumatra, a fact that probably attests to the greater pressure on women to marry and the fewer options for single women in rural communities.

Dayan, who grew up in a small rural town, was not open about her sexuality; in her village only her best friend knew she had women lovers, although several gays and bisexuals in the area knew she was a lesbian. All of Dayan's lovers were feminine. Dayan considered herself masculine. Some of her neighbors called her *cowok* ("guy") because of her masculine appearance. At 28, Dayan was well past marrying age and not living up to the model of womanhood expected of her as a Minangkabau woman. Because her family constantly pressured her to get married, she would leave home for months at a time in search of acceptance in urban areas. But she was never successful in finding decent employment, since she would not accept traditionally female jobs, and would be forced to return home.

When I met Dayan, she had recently returned from a several-month long stay in Jakarta, where she had been involved with a very feminine-looking woman (who, shortly after Dayan's departure, started seeing a man). She was in the middle of a new project to support herself: she was building a small chicken coop to house hens to collect their eggs for sale. Later I wrote in my journal about that meeting:

> *Jan. 29, 1990: I finally met my first gay woman— and I don't know how to write about it—because it was more personal than I expected. I don't want to make her a research object. I expected a mannish woman because [a friend] said they look like men, but [Dayan] wasn't at all . . . I didn't understand some of what she said—I don't know the language of emotions and lovers here. What would I do—I can easily imagine being lovers . . . I'm tired of only half of me being alive here.*

Our meeting made me anxious and happy at the same time. Here was someone I could share myself with, yet I wondered how to negotiate a cross-cultural relationship in which our common language was Indonesian, not English, and in which our ethnic and sexual identities were so different. I thought at first that it would be best to remain friends. I did not know whether I would have much time to spend with her, given the demands of my fieldwork and the necessity of maintaining secrecy. Further, I would be leaving in less than a year and was unsure what expectations might arise if we established a sexual relationship. But the bleakness of my daily life and my need and desire to be intimate overcame my caution and we became involved.

At first we saw each other infrequently, but as our relationship developed, I began to spend nearly every weekend at Dayan's house:

> *May 7, 1990: Sunday morning she asked when I was coming back and I said I didn't know. I felt torn by the expectations of people in [my fieldsite] and didn't think I should spend every weekend with Dayan. But the thought of not seeing her upset me so . . . that I decided[,] one week. I surprised myself at how achingly bad I wanted to be with her.*

I worked furiously all week so I could catch the bus on Saturday afternoons to go to her village. Monday mornings came too soon and I would reluctantly head back to pick up my research tasks again.

Dayan rarely visited me at my house. From the first time she met her, Ibu disliked Dayan. Feeling Ibu's antipathy, Dayan would only stay a short time and refused to eat with us, which Ibu took as a sign of disrespect. Ibu's rejection of Dayan highlighted for me how carefully distinctions are drawn between men and women. Ibu pointed out to me that Dayan never wore skirts, she drove a motorcycle, she smoked cigarettes and played cards, and she went out at night alone. All of these acts crossed the boundaries of gender and raised Ibu's suspicions that Dayan was not a proper woman. But her rejection of Dayan also came from a number of other sources. People tend to view outsiders, even other Minangkabau, with a certain level of mistrust; family ties, friends in common, or knowledge of a person's family background provide the foundation for acceptance, none of which Ibu had with Dayan. Further, Ibu's suspicions about Dayan were fueled by my own earlier confession and my frequent trips away from her home. Ibu asked me why I went to Dayan's village so often. Although I never talked to Ibu about my relationship with Dayan, in distancing Dayan from her house, Ibu indirectly communicated her discomfort with Dayan's presence in my life and her loss of my complete attention.

On our weekends together we stayed at her sister's, where Dayan had her own room slightly apart from the rest of the house. Her sister welcomed me but Dayan and I were very careful not to let her know that we were lovers. We maintained this secrecy because Dayan did not want her family to know she was a lesbian and was fearful of her family's reaction, particularly her brothers', if her identity became known. Dayan's male friends, who treated her as a cowok, visited her frequently to play cards or sing bluesy Minangkabau folk or pop songs. Sometimes we drank beer with her friends and listened to tapes of American rock music. Occasionally, she and I took off on he motorcycle, driving up into the nearby hills for a view of the checkerboard valley of rice fields and palm trees below.

When I met Dayan, I felt an instant bond with her. Here, I thought, was a woman who loves women: "January 29, 1990: Looking at her, I felt like I was with a sister, we both spoke the same language. Yes, she likes women." But beyond that simple identification lay a whole range of cultural differences and sexual expectations of which I knew little. From the start our relationship was not easy. When we talked, I struggled to understand her. The vocabulary of love and feelings was unfamiliar to me. Several times I had to wait until I returned home to my dictionary to find out what I had missed of her conversation. I did not know how to make small talk very well, much less express romantic feelings in Indonesian. The sense I had of not being

clearly understood nor of clearly understanding her created a distance between us that I found frustrating. But missing the nuances of language helped me initially to overlook the differences in our lesbian identities.

In addition to the constant vigilance to keep our relationship secret there were cultural practices that I found at times burdensome and other times useful. Women's practice of walking hand in hand was useful to me because it allowed us some freedom in public. On the other hand, cultural practices enjoining politeness and circumspection were burdensome when my actions or comments were misunderstood and I was accused of being rude. Our arguments sometimes left me bewildered and unable to bridge the gap in our differing expectations. When I once got tired of trying to resolve a misunderstanding, I made a show of leaving but then realized I did not want to return to my fieldsite, my only other option. Instead I walked in the woods near Dayan's house, to the dismay and embarrassment of her sister, who sent Dayan out to collect me on her motorcycle.

Little about our identities as "lesbians" coincided. I clung to a sense of our sameness, represented by our shared love of women, as the anchor to my lesbian identity and the means to assure me that I was operating in a familiar world. I resisted the knowledge of her difference and her attempts to make me fit her image of women lovers. But the differences in our lesbian identities continually decentered me even as I tried to construct our relationship to my own image. Dayan placed women into two categories, masculine and feminine, or cowok ("guy") and cowek ("girl"). We were forced to negotiate the differences between our lesbian identities because, although she was masculine, or "butch," as I persisted in calling her, I was not clearly "femme." I introduced the terms "butch" and "femme" to Dayan and used them partly to fit my own frame of reference and partly because she did not use any label for herself except cowok, which I resisted using. "Butch" and "femme" do not directly correspond with the cultural categories of *cowok* and *cowek* (or *tomboi* and woman).

On one occasion Dayan asked me if I was attracted to a rather pretty and feminine woman we both knew. I blithely said yes, not knowing I was slotting myself into a category. To Dayan, my response meant that I was *cowok,* since I clearly liked *cowek,* a perception that confused her because she was attracted to me. According to her understanding, *cowok* are not attracted to other *cowok.* When I later discovered my mistake, I told her I only meant that the woman was pretty, not that I was sexually attracted to her. I said I was attracted to Dayan, and that she was not so butch, using my categories, and I was not particularly femme. She politely ignored my slight to her identity and seemed to accept the notion that I might not be the model of womanhood she was used to.

Our differing gender and sexual identities turned out to be less easily managed than I imagined, however. We decided to have a party for Dayan's birthday. As the day approached, and her sister made the arrangements for the food, Dayan became increasingly offended that I was not taking charge of the preparations as a good wife should. I, however, was unaware of her expectations; once I began to understand, I tried to explain that I was abysmally ineffective in cooking or shopping, and preferred simply to pay for the food and drink. She interpreted my lack of participation as a lack of desire for her; her disappointment cast a pall over the entire day.

On another occasion we went to visit another lesbian and friend of Dayan's, a *cowok* who was living in a nearby town with a woman whose husband had died a few years earlier. Dayan had not wanted me to meet her friend because she was afraid I might find her more attractive. I remember feeling embarrassed and offended by the questions asked about me. Her friend asked if I was a good cook, if I was good in bed—questions that constructed me as *cowek* and reinforced their sense of being *cowok.* When I spoke to Dayan using her name, her friend raised her eyebrows and said, "She calls you Dayan?" Again I had stumbled on a practice of which I had no knowledge and embarrassed Dayan before her friend and rival by situating Dayan as a younger "friend" rather than an older male lover. Lovers call each other Ma and Pa (or other endearments), according to their gender identity in the relationship. When I later started to call Dayan Pa in an effort to please her and conform more to her expectations of me, she smiled with delight. The term, however, grated against my lesbian feminist sensibilities and my belief that we were both equal and both women.

Other disjunctures brought similar responses of disbelief and discomfort on my part. I was surprised on another occasion by Dayan's strong reaction to my presence in a male friend's hotel room. I had gone to the port town in West Sumatra on business and while there stopped to visit a friend of mine from the U.S., who was staying temporarily in town. Dayan was to meet me at my hotel room, but, arriving too late, she was given the message that I had gone to visit Bob. When she arrived at Bob's hotel room, she had little to say and I could sense that she was angry. We left shortly after and then she began to pester me with questions. Why hadn't I waited for her at my hotel? What had I been doing there in Bob's room? Were we lovers? Had we made love? I was shocked that she should even question that I might be attracted to Bob. I'm a lesbian, I said, as if that explained it all. But to her I was *cowok* and *cowok* all too often leave their female lovers for a man. She believed that I was bisexual and could not be convinced that I had no ulterior motive in visiting Bob.

It surprised me even more to find out that Dayan actually wanted to be a man. As a lesbian, I was repelled by her *cowok* identity and persisted in calling her butch to suit my own perceptions. The butches I knew back home did not really want to be men and I was not interested in a male lover. To me Dayan seemed soft and sweet, not at all like her *cowok* friend, whom I found too masculine. Dayan told me she had bound her breasts in high school so they would not get large. She wanted to be tough and enjoyed working with her hands and doing the things that men do. She regretted being female, she said, and wanted an operation to change her sex. I had to resist the temptation to talk her out of what I thought an odd desire.

Our sexual practices were informed by these differences in gender identity and gave me further insights into the gender distinctions that Dayan drew for herself. She preferred to take the "male" role in sex, as she understood it from men she had talked to, and was little interested in being touched. Acts that emphasized her female body made her uncomfortable; she perceived them as corporal negations of her maleness. My own practices reflected an American lesbian feminist's rejection of male-defined and hierarchical sexuality; however, my attempts to negotiate greater latitude in lovemaking, in effect, to insert "equality" into sex, were generally unsuccessful.

I tried to efface the differences between us even as I resisted her attempts to define me as *cowok*. Ultimately, it was the ethnic and class differences between us that defused her attempts to define our relationship as *cowok* and *cowek* and enabled me to set the boundaries of the relationship. The attractiveness and power of my status as a well-educated, middle-class, white American made me the dominant partner in our relationship. I had the money to pay for everything (I paid for her motorcycle and bought her cigarettes, among other things), the high-status job, and time constraints that could not be neglected. Consequently, I was able to call the shots about when we saw each other and what things we did that cost money.[7] She could refuse to meet my wishes, but she was invariably at home when I arrived on weekends. When we were together, Dayan had greater control of our movements and activities. She determined the pace of our days and where we went or whom we visited in her village. Though in some ways I reversed the *cowok*/*cowek* relationship, in other social and sexual contexts mentioned above her desires as *cowok* took precedence. Above all, I was dependent on her for creating the space for our relationship.

The struggle over our identities created a certain level of doubt about the meaning of our relationship. Was I exploiting her? Were we taking advantage of each other? When I told her I was doing research on lesbians in Indonesia, Dayan asked me if I was with her just so I could get data for my study. I told her no, that I did not have to be involved to get information, but I also gained much more information by being involved. Then I asked if she was with me because I was a "rich" American who could offer more than the limited opportunities she now had. She was offended by my asking and reminded me that I was leaving in a few months and she would be left alone.

Despite the differences in our identities and the struggles to understand each other, I felt closely bonded with Dayan at some basic level. With Dayan, I felt at ease in a way I never did with my Indonesian mother in her heterosexual world, even when I rubbed Ibu's arms and legs for her when she was ill, or plucked (timidly) at the grey hairs on her head that she insisted on having removed. For me Dayan represented a place to get away, to be lesbian, and to stop feeling so alien. I felt safe with her; when I buried myself in her arms, I could forget the loss of identity and loneliness I felt every day. We spent much of our time alone in her bedroom because it was only there that I truly felt at peace with myself and the knowledge of my lesbian identity. I resented the visits of her friends and the intrusions of her relatives, who came in even when the door was barricaded. I did not want to talk to anyone else, leave her house, or even go downstairs to eat with her family, because I felt exposed, vulnerable, and out of place. Any excursion threatened the fragile hold I had managed to gain on my lesbian identity. I needed to be with Dayan to remove the physical and emotional isolation I felt. She validated that part of me that went unrecognized everywhere else.

To me Dayan was a hero because she dared to believe in herself and maintain an identity for which there was no validation. I shared her pain when she talked about past lovers who had left her for boyfriends or marriage, or of the isolation that she increasingly faced in the village because she was not like other women, who at her age were all married and raising children. Yes, she was different from me and saw life as a lesbian differently from the way I did. But her love of women was unmistakable. Recognizing that similarity between us, I was able to move into a space that was at once familiar and alien, to find security and compassion in something that was and was not "lesbian."

By establishing a relationship with an-Other lesbian, I became both an insider and an outsider: an insider because I shared her marginalization as a lesbian and her love of women, and an outsider because of our different sexual identities and cultural frameworks. In a similar manner Rosaldo (1984) consciously uses his own experience of grief at his wife's untimely death to understand the Ilongot headhunter's rage and thus find a sense of shared humanness that recognizes the Other in ourselves. In a fascinating expose of her own field experience, Kondo argues that some elimination of difference, openness to Otherness, and a willingness to traverse the distance can be productive in fieldwork (1986:84). Her physical resemblance to the Japanese she studied and their assumption that she shared an identity with them helped her to bridge some of the differences between them. Yet she still carried with her her specifically American cultural framework. So I carried with me my Otherness to Dayan, my American tactlessness and refusal to be *cowek*, and she her Otherness to me, her desire to be a man and to make me her wife. But in our struggles together we found common ground and new meanings.

Conclusion

It has been five years since I returned to the U.S. alone, unable to bring my lover with me because she had no legally recognized relationship to me. Although some of my heterosexual colleagues have returned from the field with their partners, I was forced to leave Dayan behind, effectively severing our relationship, because the U.S. Embassy would not grant her a tourist visa. Since that time I have sought to understand the meaning of our relationship and the questions of identity and distance that it raised. I find it difficult to expose the wonderful and painful memories of our relationship, and yet am compelled to write about them to resolve my own confusion. My relationship with Dayan coalesced the identity conflicts that plagued me during my fieldwork. It helped to ease my sense of being ungrounded, restored to me my lost lesbian identity. I found a deeply rewarding and loving relationship that helped me survive the anomie and isolation of fieldwork, an isolation made more difficult by the need to keep my lesbian identity invisible.

My field experience revealed that identities are never stable, never simply undefined. Even the marked categories of gender, sex, race, and class are constantly shifting as our understanding of and distance from another culture shift. Manalansan's (1993) excellent piece on transmigration and the postcolonial bodies of Filipino gay immigrants shows that contact with another culture produces a new vision, a shift in perspective, and a need to make sense of one's place in the world that creates new distances and categories in the collision of race, class, ethnic, and gay identities. As anthropologists we may attempt to preserve unblemished our vision of culture from the top by remaining alien, but as with other travelers across cultural borders, we do not remain alien or undefined; we are forced constantly to reconstruct who we are in the field in relation to the people with whom we interact.

As an American in Indonesia, I felt strongly the loss of my lesbian identity. Thinking I had found it again with Dayan, I attempted to reconstruct that identity in a way that resonated with my own familiar categories. I wanted my relationship to be safe, to be home, and thus resisted many of Dayan's efforts to make me more familiar to her and construct me as her wife. By refusing the knowledge of her identity, and seeking, instead, comfortable familiarity, I reinscribed the distance and asymmetry between us. Because our negotiations were subtle, often subverbal, there was space for me to imagine a shared identity and overlook the differences between us. But while I persisted in defining our relationship and providing the categories, it refused to be simply "lesbian." Our relationship challenged my categories of experience as it continually decentered and repositioned me into new spaces. I was forced to examine our differences and recognize my privilege in relation to her. It was perhaps our sexual space that evoked the deepest expression of Dayan's identity and the clearest recognition of our different yet similar desires. Ultimately, in our mutual resistance we refashioned each other.

As members of a culture that downplays class differences, American anthropologists in particular tend to emphasize the egalitarian nature of relationships, assuming that in fieldwork most people will be friends or equals. Within the global context, however, anthropologists occupy a position of dominance that transcends attempts to be defined otherwise. If anthropologists are unable to erase differences of power, will recognition of these differences and positionalities bring greater understanding? I can use my position as an American woman and member of a minority in my own culture to sensitize me to the ways identities are shaped. I still speak for others, as ultimately I choose to do for Dayan, but in recognizing my position and the inequalities of power between us I can make choices about how I represent people and how I talk about their lives.

I have tried to situate myself in this encounter, to reflect on the power imbalances that existed within the relationship and what they meant for my relation to others in my fieldsite. My relationships with both Dayan and Ibu brought into view the boundaries of gender in West Sumatra, the assumption of heterosexuality, the dominance of marriage, and the masculine/feminine model of alternative gender relations. They also kept me from seeing the Minangkabau simply as Alien or Other. I could not and did

not want to remain alien or undefined. I was not just an observer; I constructed a family for myself, Dayan's family. Ultimately, it was this relationship that brought to the fore issues of identity and subjectivity that permanently altered my vision of myself in connection with an-Other lesbian.

I would suggest that many male anthropologists tend not to make the connection between their privilege and identity and the women with whom they have been sexually involved in the field. Rabinow (1977), who has been one of the few male heterosexual anthropologists willing to write about his sexual activities in the field, describes his sexual experience with a Moroccan woman as a one-night encounter noteworthy because it better secured his identity with other men. Whitehead (1986), who avoided involvements in the field, was surprised when he returned home to hear from a male colleague that "everybody gets laid in the field," a casual statement that carries all the overtones of the anthropological conquest of the Other, the Alien, Woman. Many male anthropologists, through their silence on the subject of sexuality in the field, have failed to make connections between their own privilege and power as situated (rather than unmarked) men and the very personal experience of sexual involvement. The paucity of articles by heterosexual men in this volume speaks to an unwillingness to acknowledge or question sexual and gender definitions. Having assumed the naturalness of gender categories, many heterosexual male anthropologists tend to be less able than those of us who are marked in our own culture to bridge the gap between Self and Other, particularly when Other is female. Reflexive anthropology is thus necessarily limited to the extent that its advocates are unwilling to situate themselves as gendered or ethnic beings (this criticism applies to, for example, Crapanzano 1977; Dwyer 1979; Clifford 1983).

Sexual connections do not always provide the insights I am suggesting, as any viewing of David Hwang's play *M. Butterfly* makes clear. In this play, a French diplomat falls madly in love with an image of exotic, submissive, oriental, feminine sexuality without ever piercing M. Butterfly's disguise until the truth of her gender is dramatically forced on him (Hwang 1986). (Did he ever understand "the Oriental"? See Kondo 1990 for further discussion of this point.) To find these insights, or at least make a beginning, we must be willing in our writing to expose our own privilege and power, and our own assumptions about the categories we occupy, whether they be categories of race, class, gender, or sexual orientation.

The ethnographic experience is about experiencing oneself with others, of knowing we are all different, yet recognizing the bonds among us rather than reifying the difference to make Others exotic or inferior. Finding the common ground through our subjective experience is the basis from which to build understanding and knowledge, as Haraway suggests (1988), and thus to avoid the stance that exoticizes other cultures. Anzaldúa (1987) argues that all people are border people, all sharing multiple selves, multiple identities. In recognizing our positions, our identities and shared humanness, we can displace the centrality of "the male, heterosexual cultural ego" of anthropology (Newton 1993) and replace it with many different marked perspectives.

Acknowledgements

I conducted fieldwork in West Sumatra for a year and a half during 1989 and 1990. I am extremely grateful to the people who gave comments on this chapter. They have pushed me (at times unwillingly) to explore and articulate more fully the meaning of my relationship with Dayan, a process that has been painful and rewarding. My heartfelt thanks go to Deborah Amory, Deborah Elliston, Patricia Horvatich, Joel Striecker, Mildred Dickemann, and Ellen Lewin. A special thanks to Don Kulick and Margaret Willson for excellent comments that carried this chapter to its final form.

Notes

1. The Minangkabau, comprising predominantly rural agriculturists, are one of the larger ethnic groups in Indonesia, numbering 3.8 million. They are also the largest matrilineal group in the world and devoutly Islamic. Descent and inheritance are reckoned from mother to daughter (see Blackwood 1993).

2. I use the term *lesbian* here with reservation because I do not wish to subsume other cultural categories under Western labels. The term *lesbian* does not adequately represent the women I met in West Sumatra, whose gender, and sexuality encompass a range of categories, including alternative gender, bisexuality, and homosexuality. Indonesians do use the term *lesbi* for female homosexuality, which is why I chose to use the term *lesbian* in addition to local terminology (cf. discussion on pp. 61–2). Some Indonesian women, however, are uncomfortable with the label because of its association in the Indonesian media with Western sexuality and promiscuity (Gayatri 1993).

3. It also reflects a reality of being lesbian or gay: it is sometimes safer to hide one's identity than to risk the rejection and even physical harm that could result if such were known. I could not say even now whether I would go to a fieldsite as an openly gay person.

4. See, for example, Abu-Lughod's (1987) experience conducting fieldwork in Bedouin culture and articles in Goldet (1986), Whitehead and Conaway (1986), and this volume.

5. All dated entries are from my field journal.

6. In addition to local terms, I also use the terms *lesbian* and *gay* in this chapter to refer to alternatively gendered individuals and their partners.

7. This situation is actually more complex. Although a Minangkabau husband is expected to provide money for his wife, most Minangkabau women make their own income as well. A wife may provide as much as or more than her husband to the household.

References

Abu-Lughod, Lila (1987) *Veiled Sentiments: Honor and Poetry in a Bedouin Society* Berkeley, Calif.: University of California Press.

Anzaldúa, Gloria (1987) *Borderlands/La Frontera: The New Mestiza*. San Francisco: Spinsters/Aunt Lute.

Blackwood, Evelyn (1993) *The Politics of Daily Life: Gender, Kinship and Identity in a Minangkabau Village, West Sumatra, Indonesia*. Ph.D. dissertation, Department of Anthropology, Stanford University.

Clifford, James (1983) On Ethnographic Authority. *Representations* Vol. 1, No. 2, pp. 118–46.

Crapanzano, Vincent (1977) On the Writing of Ethnography. *Dialectical Anthropology* Vol. 2, No. 1, pp. 9–73.

Dwyer, Kevin (1977) On the Dialogic of Fieldwork. *Dialectical Anthropology* Vol. 2, No. 2, pp. 143–51.

Dwyer, Kevin (1979) The Dialogic of Ethnology. *Dialectical Anthropology* Vol. 4, No. 3, pp. 205–24.

Favret-Saada, Jeanne (1980) *Deadly Words: Witchcraft in the Bocage*. Trans. Catherine Cullen. Cambridge: Cambridge University Press.

Gayatri, B. J. D. (1993) *Coming Out but Remaining Hidden: A Portrait of Lesbians in Java*. Paper presented at the International Congress of Anthropological and Ethnological Sciences, Mexico City, Mexico.

Geertz, Clifford (1968) Thinking as a Moral Act: Ethical Dimensions of Anthropological Fieldwork in the New States. *Antioch Review* Vol. 28, No. 2, pp. 139–58.

Golde, Peggy (ed.) (1986) *Women in the Field: Anthropological Experiences*, 2nd ed. Berkeley, Calif.: University of California Press.

Haraway, Donna (1988) Situated Knowledges: The Science Question in Feminism and the Privilege of Partial Perspective. *Feminist Studies* Vol. 14, No. 3, pp. 575–99.

Hwang, David (1986) *M. Butterfly*. New York: Plume.

Kondo, Dorinne K. (1986) Dissolution and Reconstitution of Self: Implications for Anthropological Epistemology. *Cultural Anthropology* Vol. 1, No. 1, pp. 74–88.

Kondo, Dorinne K. (1990) M. Butterfly: Orientalism, Gender, and a Critique of Essentialist Identity. *Cultural Critique* Vol. 16, pp. 5–29.

Malinowski, Bronislaw (1989) A Diary in the Strict Sense of the Term. *Trans. Norbert Guterman*. Reissue. Stanford: Stanford University Press.

Manalansan, Martin F., IV (1993) (Re)locating the Gay Filipino: Resistance, Post-colonialism, and Identity. *Journal of Homosexuality* Vol. 26, Nos. 2/3, pp. 53–72.

Mascia-Lees, Frances E., Patricia Sharpe, and Colleen B. Cohen (1989) The Postmodernist Turn in Anthropology: Cautions from a Feminist Perspective. *Signs Journal of Women in Culture and Society* Vol. 15, No. 1, pp. 7–33.

Newton, Esther (1993) My Best Informant's Dress: The Erotic Equation in Fieldwork. *Cultural Anthropology* Vol. 8, No. 1, pp. 3–23.

Rabinow, Paul (1977) *Reflections on Fieldwork in Morocco*. Berkeley, Calif.: University of California Press.

Rosaldo, Renato (1984) Grief and a Headhunter's Rage: On the Cultural Force of Emotions, in Edward M. Bruner (ed.) *Text, Play and Story: The Construction and Reconstruction of Self and Society*. Washington, D.C.: American Ethnological Society.

Trinh, T. Minh-ha (1989) *Woman, Native, Other: Writing Postcoloniality and Feminism*. Bloomington: Indiana University Press.

Whitehead, Tony Larry (1986) Breakdown, Resolution, and Coherence: The Fieldwork Experiences of a Big, Brown, Pretty-talking Man in a West Indian Community, in Tony Larry Whitehead and Mary Ellen Conaway (eds.) *Self, Sex and Gender in Cross-cultural Fieldwork*. Urbana and Chicago: University of Illinois Press.

Whitehead, Tony Larry and Mary Ellen Conaway (eds.) (1986) *Self, Sex and Gender in Crosscultural Fieldwork*. Urbana and Chicago: University of Illinois Press.

Problem Set #10

Sexual Orientation

To do this problem set, you will need to read Unit VI.

1. Let's begin by defining sexual orientation.

    a. What is the Kinsey Scale, and how can it be used to study sexual orientation?

    b. Based on Kinsey Scale data, do male and female sexual orientation look the same or different?

    c. Based on genital arousal, do male and female sexual orientation look the same or different?

    d. How temporally stable is sexual orientation in each sex?

2. Sexual orientation has a developmental course; individuals have their sexual orientations because of certain events or processes that happened to them.

    a. Outline some of the hypothesized developmental processes underlying variation in sexual orientation in each sex, separately.

    b. On the basis of what is known about these processes, can you venture an opinion about whether homosexuality is a facultative adaptation? Explain your logic.

3. Differences among men in sexual orientation seem to be partly due to genetic differences. There are three kinds of evidence that support this view. Detail evidence for each of the following:

    a. Pedigree evidence

    b. Heritability evidence

    c. Gene-sharing evidence

4. If there are genes for sexual orientation, and if gay men have lower fitness than straight men (as data indicate), why hasn't selection eliminated the "gay genes"?

5. Among the Sambia of Papua New Guinea, a homosexual phase is virtually universal for young men.

    a. Describe the situation.

    b. Does this practice affect men's sexual orientation?

    c. Does this practice have permanent effects on men's sexual behavior?

    d. Explain how this ritual affects the intensity of heterosexual mating competition.

    e. Given this, who would you expect to encourage this practice?

Unit VII

Marriage and Parenthood

This final unit begins with a reading (Chapter 21) that examines marriage and parenthood from an evolutionary perspective. The first major topic of Chapter 21 is a discussion of the ultimate causes of marriage across cultures. The potential reproductive benefits to husbands and wives, as well as the potential political, social, and economic benefits to their families, are considered. Because marriage often contributes to all of these ends, the relative importance of reproductive, economic, and social motives for marriage are evaluated and relevant evidence is discussed.

The second major topic of Chapter 21 is the use of evolutionary theory for understanding parental care and abuse. Evolutionary theory predicts that parental care will depend on the availability of other reproductive opportunities for parents, such as additional mating opportunities; the expected fitness benefits to children of parental investment; and the genetic relatedness of children to the caregiver. Each of these factors is discussed in detail, along with evidence for its influence on human parental investment.

Chapters 22, by Kathleen Gough, and 23, by Melvyn Goldstein, present two cultural oddities in the realm of marriage—"group marriage" among the Nayar of southwestern India and polyandrous marriage among Tibetans. Both the Nayar and the Tibetan examples serve to illustrate the social factors that influence marriage patterns. In Chapter 22, Gough describes Nayar marriage, which is unusual in many respects, including its absence of long-term wife-husband cohabitation, sexual exclusivity, and substantial paternal care. Nayar marriage illustrates that much of what we traditionally consider marriage rests on confidence in paternity. As you will see in Chapter 22 (and Chapter 21), the Nayar were a warrior caste, and the males were regularly absent from their villages for long periods. Such conditions would lower paternity certainty, which apparently had widespread consequences for sexual relations among the Nayar.

In Chapter 23, Goldstein discusses polyandry among Tibetans. Although polyandrous marriage is not limited to a single cultural group like the Nayar system, it is rare, occurring in less than 1 percent of human societies. Among Tibetans, several social, economic, and environmental constraints have traditionally made it easier for brothers who inherit land and other property to marry a woman jointly rather than take their shares of the inheritance and attempt to marry monogamously. Thus, polyandrous marriage has traditionally been much more common among landowning families than among the poor, who more often marry monogamously. Occasionally, jointly married brothers will later take on another wife, especially if the first turns out to be infertile. Like the Nayar case, Tibetan marriage illustrates the interaction of social and economic factors that determine marriage systems across cultures.

Finally, Lee Cronk considers the ultimate and proximate causes of parental favoritism toward daughters among the Mukogodo of Kenya. Cronk discusses the Trivers-Willard hypothesis, the idea that parents will produce more sons when reproductive conditions are favorable and more daughters when conditions are unfavorable (see also Chapter 21). Cronk illustrates how the Mukogodo case fits the predictions of the Trivers-Willard hypothesis. He examines the social conditions that lead to greater parental investment in daughters than in sons and discusses parental behaviors that may act as the proximate causes of female-biased sex ratios.

21

An Evolutionary Look at Marriage and Parenthood

David A. Puts

This chapter views the family through an evolutionary lens. We will begin by considering marriage, a human cultural universal. Why do people get married to one another? What do men get out of marriage, and what do women get out of it? Who else benefits from marriage? Why is importance so often placed on the social recognition of these relationships? How do marriage and marital transactions differ across cultures, and why?

Next, we will consider parenthood. What factors contribute to the variation within and across cultures in parental care? And, on the other side of the coin, why do parents sometimes commit child abuse?

Marriage

Social organization in humans is a bit odd. Long-term mating is rare among mammals. Yet, in almost every region of the world, men and women enter enduring relationships with members of the opposite sex that coexist relatively peacefully in a larger social group. When such relationships are formally recognized, we generally call them *marriage*. But there is substantial variability across cultures in the form that marriage takes. In most cultures (about 85 percent), a few men are able to acquire multiple wives *(polygyny)*. In a smaller number of cultures (around 15 percent), all marriages are monogamous. And in less than 1 percent of human societies, *polyandrous* marriages (two or more men married to the same woman) can be found (Murdock 1967) (see Fig. 21.1).

There is also a great deal of cross-cultural variability in other characteristics of marriage. According to Daly and Wilson (1983), marriages typically have the following features:

some degree of mutual obligation, some persistence in time, some formalized societal sanction, sexual access (usually, but by no means invariably, supposed to be exclusive), and some form of legitimization of the status of any offspring.

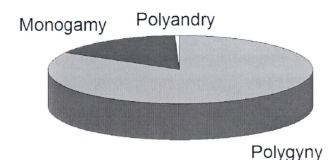

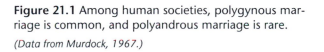

Figure 21.1 Among human societies, polygynous marriage is common, and polyandrous marriage is rare. *(Data from Murdock, 1967.)*

Kathleen Gough (Chapter 22) especially focuses on the social sanctioning of marriage and the role of marriage in legitimizing offspring. Gough attempts to define marriage in a way that is cross-culturally valid by considering an unusual case—the Nayar caste of southwestern India, during the period before the British took control of the region in 1792. Among the Nayar, girls at or near puberty were ritually married to a man from a lineage with social ties to their own. This marriage was mostly symbolic, and the man and woman had few obligations to one another. They did not live together and may never have had sex. Once a woman was ritually married, she became sexually available to men of the appropriate castes and may have had several sexual partners visiting her house at a given time. At the birth of a child, the woman and her family determined which man was most likely to be the father, and this man was expected to pay for the expenses of childbirth. By acknowledging paternity, the man—so long as he was of the proper caste—legitimized the child.

Marriage among the Nayar is certainly not typical of marriage cross-culturally. But such anomalous cases are often useful because they force us to look at practices as familiar as marriage as if we were seeing them for the first time. Previously, we may have been comfortable in saying, "I can't *define* marriage, but I know it when I see it." Now, we may want to ask, "Is Nayar marriage really *marriage*? For that matter, what is marriage? Why do people enter long-term relationships, and why are social rights and sanctions so often attached to these unions?"

As usual, evolutionary theory is a good place to begin looking for the reasons why any species, including humans, behaves as it does. In order to answer these questions, let's consider some potential inclusive fitness advantages of marriage and then examine cross-cultural evidence for their influence on marriage patterns.

Why Marry?

Why Do Men Marry?

David Buss (1994, 1999) gives five fitness benefits a man might obtain from marriage. First, because women are often interested in commitment from men, willingness to marry enhances a man's ability to attract a mate. Second, willingness to marry increases the number of potential mates a man can choose from, so he may be able to attract a higher quality mate. Third, marriage often affords a man more exclusive sexual access to a woman, thereby increasing his certainty of paternity. As you know, paternity certainty is a serious concern for investing males (see Unit IV introduction, Chapters 12 and 13). Fourth, human offspring are highly dependent on their parents and require a great deal of parental investment. Men who invest in their wives and children can thus increase offspring survival. Finally, through their investment, men can increase the mating success of their children by teaching them various skills, enhancing their social connections and status, and so on. To this list, we could also add that men often lower their costs of living (economically or in terms of time and energy) by living cooperatively with women and that marriage may help men build political alliances.

We can expect selection to have endowed men with psychological traits that track and maximize fitness-relevant variables such as attractiveness to the opposite sex, paternity certainty, and offspring fitness. But the relative importance of these variables is likely to differ across cultures. For example, attractiveness to women may be very important in a society like ours where women are free to choose their mates. However, in many societies women have less autonomy, and families may essentially sell their daughters to men (see the following discussion). In such societies, sexual access to women and paternity certainty are likely to be far more important benefits of marriage to men.

In many cases, men may actually think about such fitness benefits of marriage as attracting a better quality mate or increasing paternity certainty, but there is no need to assume that they would. Instead, natural selection has equipped humans, as it has other animals, with motivations to do what will win a mate, ensure our partner's fidelity, or increase the health of our children. In other words, natural selection has shaped our psychologies so we tend to *behave* as if we are concerned about our inclusive fitness, whether or not we actually have any such notions.

Why Do Women Marry?

Of course, women often stand to gain fitness benefits from marriage, so we also expect selection to have shaped women's psychology to extract these benefits. For example, men often support their wives economically. And as you may recall from Chapter 12, women consider economic potential an important criterion of mate choice across cultures. Another benefit that women can obtain from marriage is protection from other men against rape and against harm to their offspring (Smuts 1996). Male infanticide of unrelated offspring is prevalent among primates (Hrdy 1979), including humans (Smuts 1996), and the presence of the biological father provides protection for the offspring (Daly and Wilson 1988). It may very well be that widespread concern over the "legitimacy" of offspring has its evolutionary roots in the advantage gained by mothers of obtaining protection from male infanticide. This may also explain why there is such concern across societies about determining the biological father, even where men provide little or no resources to their children.

Arranged Marriage and Familial Influence

So far, marriage has been presented as if men and women simply decide whom they will marry, but this is frequently not the case. In most societies, parents or other family members play a major role in selecting a spouse for their unwed kin. Often, the criteria used by parents are quite close to those used by their sons and daughters. Parents want husbands who will be good providers for their daughters, and they want attractive, nurturing wives for their sons, for example. Among the !Kung San of Namibia and Botswana, parents carefully choose sons-in-law who are good hunters and who are not given to fighting (Lee 1984). This sort of selectivity is to be expected if humans, like the bee-eaters you encountered in Chapter 4, have evolved to be *nepotistic* strategists, acting in the interests of their close genetic relatives.

But marriages often present opportunities for parents to increase their inclusive fitness not only through their daughter or son to be married, but also through the formation of economic or political alliances that benefit the parents themselves or other family members. Among the Tiwi of Melville and Bathurst Islands off the northern coast of Australia, for example, fathers promise their infant girls in marriage to men with whom they wish to ally and who may have already promised a daughter of their own in exchange (Hart, Pilling, and Goodale 1988).

Evidence Regarding the Functions of Marriage

Using evolutionary theory, we can make sensible guesses about people's conscious or unconscious motivations for marriage. But what evidence do we have that these guesses are not far off the mark? Abstractly, we might imagine two potential sources of information: factors that initiate marriages and those that end them.

If you read Unit IV, you already know quite a bit about what men and women look for when they contemplate initiating long-term relationships such as marriage. Both tend to look for signs of good genes and investment capacity. But women emphasize a man's ability and willingness to invest economically, whereas men emphasize a woman's ability to invest physiologically in offspring. These mate choice criteria certainly suggest that marriage has much to do with people's evolved reproductive strategies. Indeed, the Betsileo of Madagascar often do not formally recognize marriages until after pregnancy occurs (Kottak 1980). But there are two additional sources of information about the conditions that initiate and terminate marriages that we have not yet considered: marital transactions and reasons for divorce. We will discuss each in turn.

Marital Transactions

Marital transactions provide evidence about the functions of marriage because the direction that goods or services flow at the time of marriage can tell what men, women, and their families hope to obtain from it. We can generally get a good idea of what people want by examining what they are willing to pay for. After all, knowing nothing about philately (stamp collecting), you could determine that philatelists want old stamps merely by noting that old stamps fetch the highest prices at auctions. Along the same lines, when people marry, who pays, and what are they paying for?

In most societies, men work for or purchase a wife from the wife's family through *bride-service* or *bride-price* (Murdock 1967, Daly and Wilson 1983) (see Fig. 21.2). In some societies, such as

the Tiv, a small bride-price is paid at marriage and additional installments are made with each subsequent childbirth (Daly and Wilson 1988). In other societies, such as the Kipsigis of Kenya, the amount of bride-price paid is related to the reproductive value of the bride (Borgerhoff Mulder 1988). Thus, the function of this male investment is clear: Males (or their families) are buying female reproductive potential.

In ranked or stratified societies in which some men are able to accumulate considerable wealth, a few men may be able to purchase multiple wives and achieve high levels of polygyny. You learned in Unit V that men probably evolved tendencies to control female sexuality because controlling women increased men's sexual access and certainty of paternity. The "ownership" of women through the purchase of wives from their families appears to be directly motivated by these goals.

Most of the remaining societies that do not practice bride-service or bride-price engage in either direct exchange of women or exchange of gifts, or no gifts are given at the time of marriage. These societies tend to be unstratified, relatively egalitarian societies in which few, if any, men are able to accumulate sufficient resources to achieve polygyny (Daly and Wilson 1983).

The small number of remaining societies practice *dowry*. Dowry is money or goods brought to the marriage by the wife or her fam-

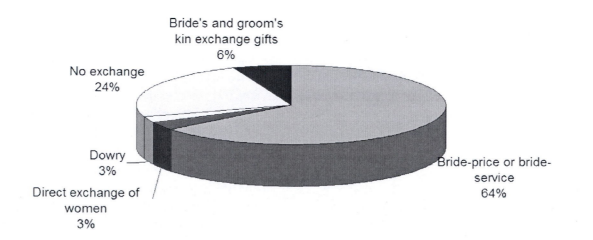

Figure 21.2 Men usually work for or purchase brides, although in many societies, families exchange gifts, exchange women directly, or no exchange takes place. Dowry is rare.

(Data from Murdock, 1967.)

ily. Thus, dowry is not quite the opposite of bride-price. Bride-price, remember, is paid to *the bride's family* by the groom or his family. Dowry, on the other hand, is paid to *the groom or the newlyweds* (but not to the groom's family) by the bride or her family. As you may recall from Chapter 13, Mildred Dickman (1981) hypothesized that dowry is a form of female-female competition for men. As Elizabeth Cashdan put it, dowry "sweetens the pot" for potential husbands. Gaulin and Boster (1990) tested this hypothesis by considering one of its predictions: Dowry should be most common in societies in which female competition for husbands is most intense. But which types of societies are these? Gaulin and Boster suggested two kinds of societies: those that regularly practice polyandry and those that exhibit "socially imposed" monogamy.

In polyandrous societies, some women are married to two or more brothers and so have multiple husbands. As you will learn in Chapter 23, polyandry generally occurs for economic reasons because single men lack the land and prosperity needed to comfortably support a wife of their own. Brothers will occasionally obtain additional wives later as they can afford them, especially if the first proves to be infertile. With multiple men married to a smaller number of women, there are many unmarried—though not necessarily childless—women in polyandrous societies. There is thus motivation on the part of women (or their families acting nepotistically on their behalves) to be one of the women married and supported by landed men.

Socially imposed monogamous societies are those that are highly stratified to the point that some men would be expected to have sufficient power or wealth to purchase, attract, or otherwise acquire multiple wives. Yet such men are unable to do so in these societies because of social restrictions on polygyny. Hence, monogamy is *socially,* as opposed to *ecologically,* imposed.

There is an important distinction here between the distribution of resources in polygynous and ecologically imposed monogamous societies and those with socially imposed monogamy. In societies with ecologically imposed monogamy, the ecological environment, subsistence technology, and the like limit men's abilities acquire wealth, and so there are not large wealth differences among men. Women can expect roughly equal access to resources no matter whom they marry. Surprisingly, the effect turns out to be much the same in polygynous societies. If men acquire wives in proportion to their wealth, then the resources of the wealthiest men are divided among many women, and the resources of less wealthy men are divided among fewer women. A woman who marries a wealthy man must share his great wealth with many women, whereas a woman marrying a poorer man shares with fewer women. As a result, all women have roughly equal access to resources, no matter to whom they are married.

The situation differs markedly for women in societies with socially imposed monogamy. Remember, in these societies, some men are fabulously wealthy. And because men are not allowed to take multiple wives, their resources will be available entirely undiluted for whomever they marry. In terms of resources, some women stand to win the marriage competition in a very big way, gaining access to tens, hundreds, or even thousands of times the resources available to women married to less wealthy men.

Therefore, Gaulin and Boster (1990) predicted that women or their families would tend to practice dowry as an *indirect mate competition tactic* (see Chapter 13) in societies with polyandrous or socially imposed monogamous marriage. They found precisely that. Dowry was much more common in polyandrous and in socially imposed monogamous societies than in any other type of society. In fact, the interaction of these two variables—marriage system and degree of socioeconomic stratification—are the best known predictors of the presence of dowry, with an accuracy rate of more than 95 percent (Fig. 21.3).

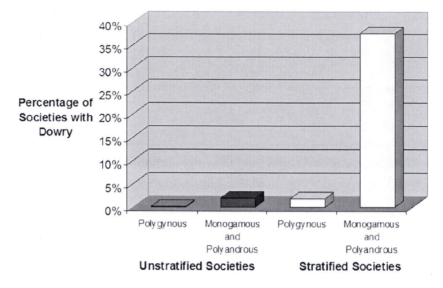

Figure 21.3 Dowry is most common in stratified monogamous and polyandrous societies. *(Data from Gaulin and Boster 1990.)*

Thus, while men often appear willing to exchange economic resources for a woman's reproductive investment, in societies where some women can gain much more male economic investment through marriage than others, they and their families tend to compete for the wealthiest men. In sum, when men pay, they pay for a woman's reproductive capacity, and when women pay, they pay for a man's investment capacity.

Grounds for Divorce

Motives for divorce provide an additional source of information about the functions of marriage. Laura Betzig (1989) performed a cross-cultural analysis of reasons for divorce using a sample of ethnographic data collected from 160 societies. Betzig found that a major reason for divorce across cultures is a failure on the part of men to provide their wives with economic support. This provides further evidence that women marry in part to secure a man's economic investment because they are willing to end the marriage when this benefit is not forthcoming.

Another leading cause of divorce is spousal infidelity (e.g., Betzig, 1989; Buckle, Gallup, and Rodd 1996). In fact, Betzig (1989) found infidelity to be the most frequently cited cause of divorce across cultures. Recall from Chapter 12 that for a woman, spousal infidelity can mean loss of male investment in her and her offspring. For a man, spousal infidelity means loss of paternity certainty. When a husband discovers that his wife has had sex with another man, the husband's estimation of his risk of cuckoldry shoots up dramatically. Suddenly, he concludes that his investment may be better spent elsewhere. Widespread divorce over spousal infidelity thus reinforces the notion that, for women, a function of marriage is the recruitment of male investment, and for men, marriage can function to increase paternity certainty.

Failure to produce offspring represents another common cause of marital dissolution across societies (Daly and Wilson 1983, Betzig 1989). In her cross-cultural analysis, Betzig (1989) found that infertility was the second largest cause of divorce. In some societies, a husband is within his rights to request a refund of any bride-price paid if his wife does not produce children, no matter whose fault it is. This expectation that marriage will result more or less directly in offspring highlights the fact that marriages are essentially, as Daly and Wilson (1983) say, "reproductive unions" in which men often literally purchase a woman's reproductive capacity from her family. The choice of young, healthy brides and wealthy, high-status grooms, concern for spousal fidelity, and so forth are all proximate goals to this ultimate reproductive objective. Thus, it should come as no surprise when men and women divorce after failing to produce children.

The Problem of the Nayars

Should the peri-pubescent betrothal practiced by the Nayars be considered marriage? Was a Nayar woman *married* to her visiting mates? Of course, the answers to these questions depend on how we define marriage. But marriage, however it is defined, is clearly the outcome of men, women, and their families, motivated by their evolved psychologies and acting within the constraints of their culture. Men strive to obtain fertile mates—sometimes more than one—and struggle to ensure their paternity. Women frequently wish to procure men of high status capable of affording them protection and investment. And parents tend to desire these things for their children but also promise their children in marriage to accomplish their own social and economic goals. In many ways, marriage is a contract—a set of reciprocal obligations. For this reason, the involved parties are typically interested in the marriage being socially sanctioned. The public recognition of marriage enforces obligations of investment and fidelity, for example, and solidifies family alliances.

Nayar marriage had many of these elements. As you will see in Chapter 22, men were obligated to invest monetarily in their "wives," for which they received sexual access. And because men dispensed a cash gift with each visit, they tended to invest in proportion to their probability of paternity. Moreover, men who were not merely passing through in the course of military operations, but who lived within the neighborhood, were expected to give additional gifts to maintain the relationship. Those men who were deemed most likely to be the father could, if they chose, acknowledge their paternity and

invest in the birth of their child and commit other gifts to their mate. While the marriage ritual itself apparently served to solidify alliances between families, the acknowledgment of paternity legitimized the child and thus may have served the underlying strategy of protecting the child from male infanticide.

But Nayar "marriage" was different in many ways from what we normally mean by marriage. There was no long-term husband-wife cohabitation, for example. Neither were there expectations about sexual exclusivity, nor substantial male investment. As Gough (Chapter 22) puts it, in these regards the Nayars were "highly unusual." Even within the region, these practices were confined to the central kingdom where they were apparently restricted to a single caste, the Nayars. Why did the Nayar caste have these unique marriage practices? Why were their traditions so different from what we normally expect?

Let's switch gears for a moment to refresh our memory about a relevant topic, and then we will return to these questions. Think back to the discussions of facultative reproductive strategies in Chapters 12 and 13. Do you remember what determines whether a woman is likely to commit to a single mate rather than pursuing multiple romantic relationships? One important variable is the probability that she will attract a faithful, investing male. If a woman's expectations about male investment are high, then she is likely to be sexually "restricted" and require emotional attachment before engaging in sex. On the other hand, if her expectations about male investment are low (for example because her father abandoned or divorced her mother), then she is likelier to have a more unrestricted reproductive strategy, forming short-term sexual relationships with multiple men, perhaps extracting a smaller amount of investment from each.

Now let's return to the Nayars. When we look at Nayar practices from the perspective of women's facultative reproductive strategies, the unrestricted sexual behavior of Nayar women makes perfect sense. Nayar women were merely playing out a feature of the evolved mating psychology of women everywhere. Substantial male investment was essentially nonexistent, so Nayar women formed less committed relationships with multiple men, obtaining some investment from each.

But this explanation begs the question: *Why was male investment among the Nayars so low?* One explanation immediately suggests itself: The Nayars were a warrior caste. The men were professional soldiers and spent part of the year away from their village. Because of their long absences, Nayar men would have had extremely low paternity certainty. And with low paternity certainty, men would not have been inclined to invest heavily in their mates.

In sum, rather than representing a puzzling anomaly, Nayar marriage provides an excellent illustration of the social variables that influence marriage patterns across cultures. Nayar marriage had many of the elements that characterize marriage in other societies, but it differed markedly in some important ways, including the absence of spousal cohabitation, sexual exclusivity, and substantial male investment. Yet these differences have sound explanations that follow from the logic of evolutionary theory—from the notion that females and males have evolved to be reproductive strategists.

Other Theories of Marriage

Alternative theories about the function of human marriage often stress the potential economic or political benefits that can be derived from it. For example, people may marry to raise children for the labor or economic support children can provide (e.g., Caldwell 1976, 1982). This, no doubt, is often a motive for marriage. However, people marry in *all* cultures, even in the many cultures (some with high fertility) in which children appear to cost more than they provide economically (Betzig 1989). Moreover, if the economic or social value of children were of primary importance in marriage, we might expect that

> *pregnant brides would be valued more than virgins and that wives who bore bastards would be rewarded rather than punished. Indeed, the collectors of exceptionally large harems . . . might be expected to reward men who donated semen to their hundreds and sometimes thousands of wives in order to help them make children. (Betzig 1989, pp. 661–662)*

As we have seen, quite the opposite is true with respect to each of these ideas.

Marriage may also serve social functions such as solidifying political alliances (Clignet 1970). As we have seen, this motive is often involved in marriage decisions, especially in arranged marriages. However, as Betzig (1989) points out, if the primary function of marriage were solidifying social alliances, both sexes would be hurt equally by their spouses jeopardizing the marriage through adultery. And men and women should be equally likely to divorce due to spousal infidelity. This is not the case. In fact, there is a very large sex bias in divorce due to infidelity; across cultures, males are far likelier than females to divorce when they suspect their spouses of adultery (Betzig 1989). Remember that infidelity costs males and females differently. If a man cheats but remains in the marriage, the wife stands to lose some (perhaps very little) of her husband's investment. Any investment that *she* makes will always be in her own children. On the other hand, when a woman cheats, the husband stands to lose not only *all of her investment* (gestation is not divisible) but *all of his investment* as well (he risks committing it to another man's offspring). The theory that marriages are fundamentally reproductive is the only theory that explains why men are so much more willing to terminate marriage when their mates have been unfaithful.

It seems clear that for married individuals the social, economic, and political functions of marriage are secondary, at least in evolutionary importance, to the immediate reproductive functions. In other words, selection has probably designed us to desire relationships like marriage mainly because these desires contributed to our fitness directly through the production of offspring rather than indirectly through social and economic status.

This is not to say these secondary social functions are not important. Indeed, they are often foremost in the minds of the families involved. For example, as you learned in Chapter 14, first marriages among the Taita of Kenya are frequently formed out of obligations to the family, although later marriages are more likely to "follow the heart." Because the interests of individual family members are seldom identical, marriages arranged by relatives can conflict with the desires of the betrothed. Thus, like the male bee-eaters in Chapter 4, humans are vulnerable to coercion by relatives. But there is often some recourse to extremely disappointed parties in arranged marriages. !Kung girls, for instance, occasionally run away at the conclusion of the marriage ceremony arranged by their parents, and this sometimes results in nullification of the marriage (Lee 1984). And divorce is cross-culturally a widespread phenomenon. Marriages are generally compromises between the fitness interests of brides, grooms, and their families.

Familial influence and the importance of social and economic alliances vary across cultures and therefore vary in their impact on marriage patterns. But the production of offspring seems to be the major adaptive function of marriage. This function has, over human evolution, shaped people's decisions about entering and remaining in marriages, whether or not they are aware of it. In fact, the idea that marriage ultimately functions in producing genetic progeny helps explain *why* marriages are so effective at cementing social bonds; they create offspring in which the father's and the mother's kin have a common inclusive fitness interest.

Parental Care and Abuse

We have seen that across cultures marriage is, in one way or another, about reproduction and that the marriage system can affect investment in offspring. In polyandrous and socially imposed monogamous societies, for example, parents are more likely to invest in their daughters though dowry. We have discussed in this book how humans are unusual in the amount of investment they provide to their offspring. But human parents, like investing parents across the animal kingdom, are not indiscriminate in their investment. As much as we may value the *ideal* of loving all children equally and caring for them impartially, the *reality* of parental care is frequently otherwise. Some children are abused in households in which other children are not. Some parents are loving caregivers, while others abandon their children or abuse them. Inheritance is passed on disproportionately to particular children, who in some cases are not even those of one's spouse. In Chapter 24, Lee Cronk discusses the Mukugodo of Kenya, who care for their daughters more than their sons, apparently leading to higher childhood mortality in boys than in girls.

Given that parental investment is discriminative, we should like to know what factors influence variation in parental investment. Again, the notion that people are nepotistic strategists can help. In general, we can expect parental investment to depend on (1) the availability of other reproductive opportunities, such as additional mating opportunities; (2) the expected fitness benefits to children of parental investment; and (3) the genetic relatedness of children to their caregiver (Alexander 1979). In a cross-culturally representative sample of 60 societies, Daly and

Wilson (1984) found that instances of infanticide by parents almost universally corresponded to one or more of these three categories or were coerced by a self-interested third party. We will discuss each of these categories in turn. Let's begin by considering the availability of other reproductive opportunities.

Investment Alternatives

Men's Alternatives

As you read in Chapter 6, organisms often face a choice between mating and parenting because effort expended in one pursuit usually cannot be used in the other. For men, the decision to invest in offspring is likely to depend partly on their chances of obtaining additional mating opportunities (see Unit IV). Because they have almost no obligatory biological investment in their offspring, men are capable of abandoning their mates and future children immediately after copulation (and thus even before conception). And because men do not create offspring through gestation and lactation as women do, men do not face having to commit this investment again if they choose to abandon a current child to begin a new reproductive venture.

You may recall from Unit IV that men who are most likely to be successful in obtaining extra-pair sex are least likely to invest in their mates (and thus, indirectly, in their offspring). This phenomenon was first discovered in non-human animals. For example, Nancy Burley (1986) found that male zebra finches whose attractiveness to females was experimentally enhanced subsequently decreased their parental investment and spent more time engaging in extra-pair sex. The same appears to be true of humans. Presumably because they are attractive to women, more symmetrical men have more extra-pair sex partners (Gangestad and Thornhill 1997, 1999) and invest less in their current mates (Gangestad 1993, Simpson et al. 1999).

Studies of circulating testosterone (T) levels in men provide further evidence that men's allocation of parental effort depends on the availability of mating opportunities. Recall from Chapter 8 that T is an important hormone for producing male bodies and behavioral patterns. Across a variety of species with male investment in offspring, high T levels are associated with mating competition behaviors, and low T levels are associated with paternal behaviors (reviewed in Gray et al. 2002). In humans, males with high T appear to have more mating opportunities, and this appears to result in lowered parental investment.

High T levels have been associated with greater *intrasexual* competitive ability in male primates generally (Ellis 1995) and in men particularly (Mazur, Susman, and Edelbrock 1997). That is, males with high T are more often victors in competitive interactions with other males for dominance and status, which as you know, tend to win mates. The relationship between intrasexual competitive ability and T levels is reciprocal; T increases a male's ability to win competitive interactions, and T levels are elevated as a result of victory (reviewed in Mazur, Susman, and Edelbrock 1997). Thus, we can expect men with high T to be successful intrasexual competitors not only because they are likelier to win future contests, but also because their present high T levels indicate that they may have won contests in the recent past. Some evidence suggests that males with high T have increased mating success beyond that which they would obtain through having more wives in polygynous societies. For example, high T men are more likely to obtain extramarital sex (Booth and Dabbs 1993).

High T males may have more mating opportunities, but they appear to invest less in their current mates. For example, men with high T levels are less likely ever to have been married (Booth and Dabbs 1993), and unmarried men have higher T levels than married men, with and without children (Gray et al. 2002). The latter fact raises an important question: In which direction does the causal arrow point? That is, are men with high T levels incorrigible philanderers who rarely settle down, get married, and have children? Or do marriage and childbirth lower a man's T levels, causing him to devote less effort toward mating and more effort toward investing in his long-term mate and offspring? Both may be correct. If T increases a man's tendency to compete for mates, then we can expect it to concomitantly decrease his tendency to invest in mates and offspring. (Remember, effort spent on mating is generally unavailable for parenting.) On the other hand, an interesting study suggests that the latter possibility is also correct—that opportunities for investment lower male T levels. Storey and colleagues (2000) found that men's T levels actually decline after new fathers have been exposed to their newborn infants. Thus, it seems that the relationship between T and parenting, as that between T and intrasexual competition, is reciprocal: T decreases parenting effort, and parenting decreases T.

To summarize, men with high T appear to have more sexual opportunities and invest less in parenting. But is a man's lowered investment in offspring really *caused* by an availability of sexual alternatives? Or are competitiveness and lowered investment both caused by high T levels? Both are likely, and both suggest that male parental investment is affected by available mating alternatives. T-related mating success may draw men's attention away from investment. And T levels may more directly cause men to invest less. But these *proximate* causes do not exclude mating opportunities as an *ultimate* cause of men's lowered investment. Consider this: Why would selection favor a male pattern of response to T in which competitive ability for mates was increased and paternal investment was simultaneously decreased? The answer is that mating and parenting are *alternatives*, and males who were likely to be successful in the mating realm left more progeny if they increased competitiveness and decreased parental investment.

Women's Alternatives

Women can also abandon a current reproductive venture, but they are much less likely than men to do so if they currently have an investing mate. In fact, the *absence* of an investing mate is one of the single best predictors of infanticide

by mothers across cultures (Daly and Wilson 1984). When women make decisions about investment in a child, they seem to weigh the current child-rearing conditions against future possibilities. Does the mother have the support of a mate? If not, it may be a better strategy to withhold investment in offspring until she does. Does she have too many children to care for already? Is she still nursing another child? A lack of support and too many mouths to feed are common causes of infanticide across cultures (Daly and Wilson 1984). Bereczkei (2000) showed in a sample of 590 Hungarian mothers that low current socioeconomic status also has a negative effect on maternal care, as measured by duration of breastfeeding and interbirth interval.

Women are also more likely to have abortions when they are young and unwed (Tullberg and Lummaa 2001). Tullberg and Lummaa found that, among Swedish women, young women were most likely to seek abortions. The researchers attributed this to the fact that young women were less likely to be married. It is worth noting that state assistance in Sweden is sufficient that women do not actually need male investment in their offspring (see Chapter 13). Thus, a desire for the support of a mate in child rearing appears to be a robust feature of women's evolved reproductive psychology.

Interestingly, women approaching menopause were also likelier to seek abortions than were women of intermediate ages. According to Tullberg and Lummaa, older women simply seemed less interested in having a child because they were "too old." Tullberg and Lummaa claim that older women's lack of interest in having children results from an overall decrease in women's desire to invest in new offspring over their lifetimes. This runs counter to the assumptions of others (e.g., Daly and Wilson 1988) that as women age they will place *greater* value on each new offspring because they have fewer reproductive opportunities ahead of them. But when the youngest (mostly unwed) women are removed from Tullberg's and Lummaa's analysis, it does indeed appear that the probability of seeking an abortion increases as women age.

According to Tullberg and Lummaa, this tendency may represent a shift in the focus of women's investment from producing new offspring to investing in their current children and grandchildren. This idea resonates with the so-called "grandmother hypothesis" for the evolution of menopause in women (see Hawkes et al. 1998). According to the grandmother hypothesis, menopause evolved in women because human infants need a great deal of parental care. If women continued to reproduce throughout their lives, when they died, they would often leave some dependent children unable to care for themselves. Reproductive effort might be better spent if instead women curtailed their own reproduction and diverted their energy into caring for their existing children and grandchildren.

So which hypothesis is correct? Do women generally want fewer new children as they age because selection has favored an increasing focus on grandmaternal activities? Or are older women more desperate for children as their reproductive clocks wind down? Certainly, the assistance of a mate, a woman's future reproductive opportunities, and the presence of existing children and grandchildren all affect the direction and intensity of a woman's parental investment. Work is still required to disentangle these factors, but it seems plausible that women's interest in children shows an initial upswing as they age, followed by a downward trend as they near menopause. Tullberg and Lummaa's (2001) data on abortion, the infanticide data of Bugos and McCarthy (1984) on the Aroyeo Indians of Bolivia and Paraguay, and the Canadian infanticide data of Daly and Wilson (1988) all show these trajectories (see Fig. 21.4).

Variation in Payoffs from Parental Investment

The same parental investment will not help all offspring equally. Consequently, parents are expected to be attuned to the probable payoffs from their investment and to direct their invest-

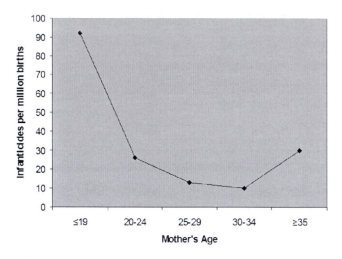

Figure 21.4 Risk of infanticide within the first year of life by natural mother as a function of mother's age. Canada, 1974–1983.
(Data from Daly and Wilson 1988.)

ment to children whose fitness will most increase as a result. The potential benefits of investment to the fitness of offspring depend largely on the condition, age, and sex of the child, as you will see.

Child's Condition

Children who are in poor condition, because they are sickly or born with a congenital handicap, for example, are less likely to be successful reproducers than are healthier children. Extensive investment in high-risk children over human evolutionary history would therefore have been less likely to augment a parent's inclusive fitness. As a result, we might expect parents to invest more heavily in healthy children, and we might expect unhealthy, high-risk children to more often be victims of parental neglect, abuse, and infanticide. Indeed, sickly or handicapped children are more likely to experience parental neglect and abuse across cultures (Daly and Wilson 1988). Bereczkei (2000) found that married, Hungarian mothers breastfeed children of low birth weight or with handicaps for a shorter duration than larger, unhandicapped children. Bereczkei also found that mothers waited longer to have another child if their previous child was healthy.

Child's Age

Younger children are also less likely to become successful reproducers than older children. This is because children sometimes die due to accidents or illness before they are able to reproduce. Let's say that people first reproduce on average when they are nineteen years old. Who is more likely to live long enough to reproduce, an eighteen-year-old or a two-year-old? The eighteen-year-old is, of course. She has only to live from her eighteenth year until her nineteenth year to expect to reproduce, whereas the two-year-old has a much longer road ahead of her. While childhood mortality is fairly low in modern industrial nations, it is much higher in nonindustrial nations and has undoubtedly been an important selective factor over human evolution. Thus, we can expect parents to invest in children who are most likely to live long enough to benefit from their investment, and these are disproportionately older children. Indeed, older children are much less likely to be the targets of their parents' deadly abuse, even when other factors such as the child's increasing ability to defend itself are considered. And mothers invariably choose to abandon newborns over older children across cultures (Daly and Wilson 1988).

The fact that parents often intervene on behalf of younger children in disputes between siblings may seem contradictory. But as Daly and Wilson (1988) point out, parents have interests in the well-being of all of their children. Parents are expected to distribute their investment on the basis of how much it will increase the fitness of their offspring, and the same investment is likely to help younger offspring more. But coming to the aid of a weaker child does not mean that the parent would choose similarly if the matter were life or death. Because older children have higher expected reproductive value, parents are predicted to favor them in such instances. The evidence on infanticide clearly indicates that they do.

Child's Sex

As you learned in our discussion of dowry, parents' investment in daughters depends on the expected fitness returns from their investment. Where daughters can gain a disproportionate share of men's resources though marriage, parents will often contribute to their daughters doing so. The same logic applies to parents' investment in sons. In highly polygynous societies, the men with the most wives have far higher reproductive success than any woman. In such societies, we might expect parents to invest preferentially in sons, so that their sons would be successful polygynous males rather than some of the many unmarried men. Hartung (1982) found that inheritance is indeed considerably more likely to be passed on to sons in highly polygynous societies than in either monogamous or polyandrous societies. More recently, Cowlishaw and Mace (1996) performed a similar study, this time controlling for the "nonindependence" of cultures. That is, the researchers controlled for the fact that cultures may resemble one another because they descended from the same culture (the way the United States, Canada, and New Zealand all have cultural roots in Great Britain), rather than because they developed similar cultural traits in response to similar conditions. When Cowlishaw and Mace controlled for nonindependence, they found an even greater cross-cultural relationship between marriage system and wealth inheritance pattern.

Robert Trivers and Dan Willard (1973) predicted that parents in good condition, capable of producing reproductively successful offspring, would invest more in sons. This is because male mammals typically have a higher variance in reproductive success than do females, so the most successful males almost always out-reproduce the most successful females. On the other hand, Trivers and Willard predicted that parents in poor condition would produce more daughters because, with a lower variance in reproductive success, daughters experience a smaller fitness loss due to low investment. This idea has become known as the Trivers-Willard Hypothesis (TWH). The TWH has been tested in nonhuman mammals and in people with generally positive results (reviewed in Keller, Nesse, and Hofferth 2001). In Chapter 24, Lee Cronk describes the female-biased sex ratios of the Mukugodo of Kenya, which fit the predictions of the TWH because the Mukugodo sit at the bottom of a regional economic hierarchy. Some support for this hypothesis has also been found in the Kipsigis of Kenya and in Hungarian gypsies (reviewed in Keller, Nesse, and Hofferth 2001).

However, higher investment in sons through inheritance has generally not been found among wealthy families in the United States and Canada (Keller, Nesse, and Hofferth 2001). Can you think of why this might be? As you know, in countries like the United States and Canada, monogamous marriage is socially imposed. Because some women can monopolize the resources of very wealthy men in these societies, we expect greater parental investment in daughters (for example, through dowry) than is found in polygynous or ecologically imposed monogamous societies. This effect of the marriage system may obscure an effect of parental investment capacity on which sex obtains more parental investment.

Genetic Relatedness and Parental Investment

The most obvious implication of kin selection theory is that parents will be predisposed to invest in their genetic offspring. Children, especially young ones, are extremely demanding of time and energy. But parental investment is a precious commodity, and parents are not expected to give it indiscriminately. Over human evolution—indeed over all of mammalian evolution—parents who withheld investment from genetically unrelated young and invested in their genetic offspring would have left more copies of their genes than parents who

did not. The tendency to care preferentially for one's genetic progeny characterizes mammals generally, and humans are no exception.

Abuse and Murder within Step-relationships

Kin-directed parental investment in humans is perhaps most clearly visible in rates of child abuse and murder. Kin selection theory predicts that parents will be less likely to abuse their natural children than they will be to abuse genetically unrelated children such as stepchildren. In families with stepchildren, conflicts between the needs of children and the reluctance of stepparents to invest are compounded. Not only are feelings of parental love for stepchildren often absent (Daly and Wilson 1988), but stepchildren represent a substantial drain on the resources, time, and energy of their natural parents, which conflicts with the interests of stepparents. In many species of birds and mammals, including many cat species and a variety of primates, a new mate simply destroys the eggs or kills the offspring left by a previous mate. In a few cultures, such as the Yanomamo of Venezuela, a new husband demands the death of his new wife's prior children (Daly and Wilson 1988).

A valuable source of information on the association between genetic relatedness and child abuse comes from comparisons of households with two biological parents to those with one biological and one stepparent. Instances of reported child abuse are rare regardless of the relationship between child and caretaker. But in Canada and the United States, a young child's risk of abuse is anywhere from seven to over forty times higher in a household with a step-parent and a biological parent than in a household with two biological parents (Daly and Wilson 1988) (see Fig. 21.5). The relative risk of fatal abuse to stepchildren is even greater. In Canada during the period from 1974 to 1983, a child's risk of being murdered by a stepparent was approximately one hundred times greater than his or her risk of being killed by a biological parent (Daly and Wilson 1988).

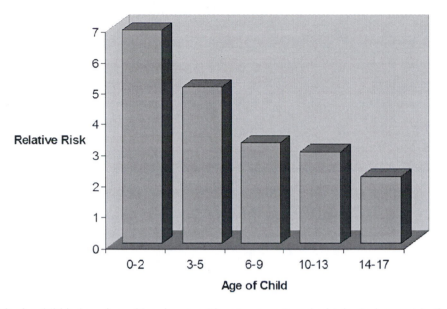

Figure 21.5 The risk of a child being abused in a home with a stepparent and a biological parent in the United States in 1976, relative to the risk of abuse in a home with both biological parents.

(Data from Daly and Wilson 1988.)

One sometimes hears that people who were abused as children grow up to be abusive parents. This may be true, but it does not explain the elevated rates of abuse by stepparents. A particularly informative study on this issue examined cases in which child abuse occurred in families containing two parents with at least one biological child and one stepchild in the household (Lightcap, Kurland, and Burgess 1982). Thus, each abusive parent was both a biological parent to at least one child and a stepparent to at least one child. The sample included 41 children—21 stepchildren and 20 biological children. In every one of the twelve reported cases of child abuse, the victim was the stepchild of the abuser.

The relative risk of abuse and murder incurred by stepchildren declines as children age (see Fig. 21.5). This probably has to do with the increasing ability of older children to defend themselves against abuse. It also probably results from the increasing value placed on older children by biological parents and their increasing willingness to defend their children. Finally, reduced risk of child abuse to older stepchildren almost certainly relates to the decreasing drain

(both present and future) on the investment of the biological parent, and therefore the reduced conflict between stepparent and stepchild.

Paternity Uncertainty and Paternal Investment

The fact that, before genetic testing, paternity was never certain is a recurrent theme in the evolutionary study of human behavior. While parents of both sexes are expected to invest preferentially in their genetic offspring, men are faced with the difficult task of determining just who their genetic offspring are (Fig. 21.6). Over the course of human evolution, men have had two primary "paternity tests" at their disposal: (1) information about the mother's sexual behavior around the time of conception and (2) phenotypic similarity between men and their putative offspring (Daly and Wilson 1998).

Although it is often difficult to recall the mother's behavior nine months before the birth of a child, men can certainly make judgments about the general promiscuity of their mates. Men who have perceived signs of infidelity are expected to be less willing to invest in their

Figure 21.6 Throughout most of human evolution, men could not be certain that they had fathered any particular child.

(Image © AGphotographer, 2008. Used under license from Shutterstock, Inc.)

mate's offspring. An interesting test of this hypothesis comes from ethnographic data on inheritance patterns across cultures. A particularly striking form of inheritance is *matrilineal* inheritance, in which men invest not in their wives' children but in their sisters' children. Matrilineal inheritance occurs in only about 10 percent of human societies. At first glance, this behavior seems to make little evolutionary sense.

Here's the logic: Under perfect monogamy, a man's child will share 50 percent of his genes. On the other hand, if his mate is unfaithful, a man may share none of his genes with his putative child. But a man always shares at least 25 percent of his genes with his sister (if they share one parent) and shares 50 percent of his genes with her if they share two parents. Because a man's sister always shares 50 percent of her genes with her children, a man will share between 12.5 percent (25 percent × 50 percent) and 25 percent (50 percent × 50 percent) of his genes with his sister's children. Thus, if a man's wife is unfaithful, he may be more closely related to his sister's children, who share at least 12.5 percent of his genes, than to his wife's children, who may share none of his genes. In societies in which female promiscuity is common, a man is also unlikely to share genes with his brother's children, because some of these chil-

dren are probably not his brother's genetic offspring.

The resulting prediction is that men acting in the interests of their inclusive fitness will be more likely to invest in their wife's children in highly monogamous societies and in their sister's children in societies in which women are highly promiscuous. John Hartung (1985) tested this hypothesis by looking at societies in which men pass on their property to their wives' children *(patrilineal inheritance)* and those in which men pass on their property to their sisters' children *(matrilineal inheritance)*. Hartung estimated men's probability of paternity in these societies by obtaining ethnographic data on the frequency and severity of punishment for extramarital sex. Hartung found that matrilineal inheritance was far more common in societies in which paternity certainty was low and that patrilineal inheritance was correspondingly high in societies in which paternity certainty was high (see Fig. 21.7).

As Gaulin and McBurney (2001) point out, cross-cultural variation in paternity certainty not only predicts where inheritance patterns will be found, it also explains why some inheritance patterns simply do not exist. For example, why don't women in some societies invest more in their sister's children than in their own children? Why are there no societies in which either men or women invest primarily in their brother's children? Because women are *always* more closely related to their children than anyone else's, we don't expect to find any societies in which women typically focus their investment on other people's children. And because, in promiscuous societies, a man's brother is as likely to be cuckolded as he is, men invest in their sisters' children rather than their brothers'. Thus, of all the inheritance patterns that could logically occur across cultures, inclusive fitness theory explains why we find only three (see Table 21.1).

In addition to keeping track of their mates' fidelity, men can make guesses about their relatedness to children by assessing phenotypic similarity. If a child has his or her "father's eyes," for

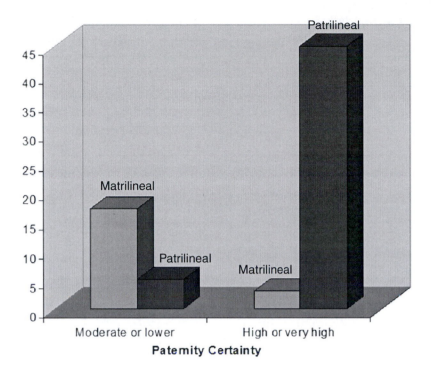

Figure 21.7 Number of societies with matrilineal or patrilineal inheritance as a function of paternity certainty. Matrilineal inheritance is most common in societies where paternity certainty is low, and patrilineal inheritance is most common where paternity certainty is high.

(Data from Hartung 1985.)

Table 21.1 Does a Particular Inheritance Pattern Exist in Some Societies?

	Give to "Own" Child	Give to Sister's Child	Give to Brother's Child
Women	+	−	−
Men	+	+	−

example, the father may be more likely to invest. Several studies have shown that men do appear more willing to invest in children who resemble them. Rebecca Burch and Gordon Gallup, Jr. (2000) found that men in a domestic violence treatment program were more likely to report positive relationships with children who they believed resembled them. Another study from this laboratory found that men were likelier to express willingness to invest in, and unwillingness to punish, children whose pictures resembled them (Platek et al. 2002). In this study, subjects were presented pictures of the faces of five "children," each of which had either been produced by a computer "morph-

ing" of the subject's face with the face of a child, or by morphing another adult's face with the face of a child. Male subjects showed a preference for investing in faces that resembled theirs, whereas female subjects showed no such preference. Interestingly, none of the twenty male and twenty female subjects had any idea that pictures of their faces had been used to produce some of the pictures of children's faces. And none of the males were aware that they had been selecting children for investment on the basis of similarity. However, although these authors were able to replicate their results (Platek et al. 2004), another laboratory (DeBruine 2004) found that facial resemblance increased willingness to invest for both men and women.

An intriguing question in this context is, What proximate mechanisms do men use to assess phenotypic similarity? In recent times, men have had access to mirrors (and in very recent times, photographs, video cameras, etc.). But throughout most of human evolution, as our psychologies were being shaped by selection, how did men know what they looked like? How could they tell whether a particular child resembled them or not? To what sorts of cues could men have attended? A good possibility is that men used natural reflecting surfaces, such as pools of water. Another possibility is that they used the phenotypes of other family members—fathers, mothers, brothers, sisters, uncles, and so forth—to form a mental image of what people with their genes looked like. If a man's putative child had features that ran in his family, the man could be more assured of his paternity.

Another mechanism by which men can assess phenotypic similarity is called the "social mirror" (Daly and Wilson 1982, Regalski and Gaulin 1993). Men can get information about the degree to which their putative child resembles them from comments from friends, family members, and other members of the community. Burch and Gallup (2000) found men's impressions of their children's resemblance to them to correlate strongly with their recollection of what others had said.

The problem with the social mirror as a reliable indicator of resemblance is that, in order to get a man's investment, the mother and her family should emphasize the similarities between the man and his putative children no matter what the actual resemblance is. Indeed, in maternity wards in the United States (Daly and Wilson 1982) and Mexico (Regalski and Gaulin 1993), the mother and her relatives and friends are more likely to comment on the child's resemblance to the putative father than to any other relative. The putative father's side of the family is less likely to make such comments, and fathers are more likely to express doubts about the resemblance.

Summary

In this chapter, we have explored the features of enduring relationships between men and women. Marriage is a reproductive alliance that can have different benefits for men and women and their families. Women can gain male investment and protection, and men can gain a female's reproductive capacity. Marital transactions and reasons for divorce provide evidence that men and women pursue and guard these potential benefits. Men and women invest differentially in mates and offspring depending on the availability of other opportunities, the expected benefits of investment to the child, and the relationship between the child and the caregiver. You have seen that social scientists are beginning to make sense of the tremendous cross-cultural diversity in the forms that marriage and parental investment can take. The evidence points to a common evolved human psychology.

References

Alexander, R. D. 1979. *Darwinism and human affairs.* Seattle: University of Washington Press.

Andersson, M. 1994. *Sexual selection.* Princeton, NJ: Princeton University Press.

Bereczkei, T. 2000. Maternal trade-off in treating high-risk children. *Evolution and Human Behavior* 22(3):197–212.

Betzig, L. 1989. Causes of conjugal dissolution: A cross-cultural study. *Current Anthropology* 30(5):654–76.

Booth, A., and J. M. Dabbs Jr. 1993. Testosterone and men's marriages. *Social Forces* 72:463–77.

Borgerhoff Mulder, M. 1988. Bridewealth variability among the Kipsigis. In *Human reproductive behaviour: A Darwinian perspective,* ed. L. Betzig, M. Bergohoff Mulder, and P. Turke. Cambridge, England: Cambridge University Press.

Buckle, L., G. G. Gallup, Jr., and Z. A. Rodd. 1996. Marriage as a reproductive contract: Patterns of marriage, divorce, and remarriage. *Ethology and Sociobiology.* 17(6):363–77.

Bugos, P. E., and L. M. McCarthy. 1984. Ayoreo infanticide: A case study. In *Infanticide: Comparative and evolutionary perspectives,* ed. G. Hausfater and S. B. Hrdy, 503–20. New York: Aldine de Gruyter.

Burch, R. L., and G. G. Gallup, Jr. 2000. Perceptions of paternal resemblance predict family violence. *Evolution and Human Behavior* 21(6):429–35.

Burley, N. 1986. Sexual selection for aesthetic traits in species with biparental care. *American Naturalist* 127:415–45.

Buss, D. 1994. *The evolution of desire.* New York: Basic Books.

Buss, D. 1999. *Evolutionary psychology.* Needham Heights, MA: Allyn and Bacon.

Caldwell, J. C. 1976. Toward a restatement of demographic transition theory. *Population and Development Review* 4:553–57.

Caldwell, J. C. 1982. *The theory of fertility decline.* New York: Academic Press.

Clignet, R. 1970. *Many wives, many powers.* Evanston: Northwestern University Press.

Cowlishaw, G., and R. Mace. 1996. Cross-cultural patterns of marriage and inheritance: A phylogenetic approach. *Ethology and Sociobiology* 17(2):87–97.

Dickemann, M. 1981. Paternal confidence and dowry competition: A biocultural analysis of purdah. In *Natural Selection and Social Behavior,* ed. R. D. Alexander and D. W. Tinkle, 417–38. New York: Chrion Press.

Daly, M., and M. Wilson. 1982. Whom are newborn babies said to resemble? *Ethology and Sociobiology* 3:77–81.

Daly, M., and M. Wilson. 1983. *Sex, eEvolution and behavior.* 2nd ed. Boston: Willard Grant.

Daly, M., and M. Wilson. 1984. A sociobiological analysis of human infanticide. In *Infanticide: Comparative and evolutionary perspectives,* ed. G. Haufater and S. B. Hrdy, 487–502. New York: Aldine de Gruyter.

Daly, M., and M. Wilson. 1988. *Homicide.* New York: Aldine de Gruyter.

Daly, M., and M. Wilson, M. 1998. *The truth about Cinderella: A Darwinian view of parental love.* New Haven, CT: Yale University Press.

DeBruine, L. 2004. Resemblance to self increases the appeal of child faces to both men and women. *Evolution and Human Behavior* 25: 142–54.

Ellis, L. 1995. Dominance and reproductive success among nonhuman animals. *Ethology and Sociobiology* 16:257–333.

Gangestad, S. W. 1993. Sexual selection and physical attractiveness: Implications for mating dynamics. *Human Nature* 4:205–35.

Gangestad, S. W., and R. Thornhill. 1997. The evolutionary psychology of extra-pair sex: The role of fluctuating asymmetry. *Evolution and Human Behavior* 18:69–88.

Gangestad, S. W., and R. Thornhill. 1999. Individual differences in developmental precision and fluctuating asymmetry: A model and its implications. *Journal of Evolutionary Biology* 12:402–16.

Gaulin, S. J. C., and J. S. Boster. 1990. Dowry as female competition. *American Anthropologist* 93:994–1003.

Gaulin, S. J. C., and D. H. McBurney. 2001. *Psychology: An evolutionary approach.* Upper Saddle River, NJ: Prentice Hall.

Gray, P. B., S. M. Kahlneberg, E. S. Barrett, S. F. Lipson, and P. T. Ellison. 2002. Marriage and fatherhood are associated with lower testosterone in males. *Evolution and Human Behavior* 23(3):193–201.

Hart, C. W. M., A. R. Pilling, and J. C. Goodale. 1988. *The Tiwi of North Australia.* New York: Holt, Rinehart & Winston.

Hartung, J. 1982. Polygyny and inheritance of wealth. *Current Anthropology* 23:1–12.

Hartung, J. 1985. Matrilineal inheritance: New theory and analysis. *Behavioral and Brain Sciences* 8:661–760.

Hawkes, K., J. F. O'Connell, N. G. Blurton Jones, H. Alvarez, and E. L. Charnov. 1998. Grandmothering, menopause, and the evolution of human life histories. *Proceedings of the National Academy of Sciences of the United States of America* 95:1336–39.

Hrdy, S. B. 1979. Infanticide among animals: A review, classification, and examination of the implications for the reproductive strategies of females. *Ethology and Sociobiology* 1:13–40.

Keller, M. C., R. M. Nesse, and S. Hofferth. 2001. The Trivers-Willard hypothesis of parental investment: No effect in the contemporary United States. *Evolution and Human Behavior* 22(5):343–60.

Kottak, C. 1980. *The past in the present.* Ann Arbor: University of Michigan Press.

Lee, R. B. 1984. *The Dobe !Kung.* New York: Holt, Rinehart and Winston.

Lightcap, J. L., J. A. Kurland, and R. L. Burgess. 1982. Child abuse: A test of some predictions from evolutionary theory. *Ethology and Sociobiology* 3: 61–67.

Mazur, A., E. J. Susman, and S. Edelbrock. 1997. Sex difference in testosterone response to a video game contest. *Evolution and Human Behavior* 18(5):317–26.

Murdock, G. P. 1967. *Ethnographic atlas.* Pittsburgh: University of Pittsburgh Press.

Platek, S. M., R. L. Burch, I. S. Panyavin, B. H. Wasserman, and G. G. Gallup, Jr. 2002. Reactions to children's faces: Resemblance affects males more than females. *Evolution and Human Behavior* 23(3):159–66.

Platek, S. M., D. M. Raines, D. M., G. G. Gallup, Jr., F. B. Mohamed, J. W. Thomson, T. E. Myers, et al. 2004. Reactions to children's faces: Males are more affected by resemblance than females are, and so are their brains. *Evolution and Human Behavior* 25:394–405.

Regalski, J., and Gaulin, S. 1993. Whom are Mexican infants said to resemble? Monitoring and fostering parental confidence in the Yucatan. *Ethology and Sociobiology* 14:97–113.

Simpson, J. A., S. W. Gangestad, P. N. Christensen, and K. Leck. 1999. Fluctuating asymmetry, sociosexuality, and intrasexual competitive tactics. *Journal of Personality and Social Psychology* 76(1):159–72.

Smuts, B. 1996. "Male aggression against women: An evolutionary perspective." In *Sex, power, conflict. Evolutionary and feminist perspectives,* ed. David M.

Buss and Neil M. Malamuth, 231–68. New York: Oxford University Press.

Storey, A. E., C. J. Walsh, R. L. Quinton, and K. E. Wynne-Edwards. 2000. Hormonal correlates of paternal responsiveness in new and expectant fathers. *Evolution and Human Behavior* 21(2):79–95.

Trivers, R., and D. Willard. 1973. Natural selection of parental ability to vary the sex ratio of offspring. *Science* 179:90–92.

Tullberg, B. S., and V. Lummaa. 2001. Induced abortion ratio in modern Sweden falls with age, but rises again before menopause. *Evolution and Human Behavior* 22(1):1–10.

22

The Nayars and the Definition of Marriage

E. Kathleen Gough

The problem of a satisfactory definition of marriage has vexed anthropologists for decades and has been raised, but not solved, several times in recent years.[1] Over time it became clear that cohabitation, ritual recognition, definition of sexual rights or stipulation of domestic services each had too limited a distribution to serve as a criterion for all the unions anthropologists intuitively felt compelled to call "marriage." For good reason therefore the *Notes and Queries* definition of 1951 makes no reference to any of these: "Marriage is a union between a man and a woman such that children born to the woman are recognized legitimate offspring of both parents."

Admirably concise though it is, this definition too raises problems in a number of societies. The Nuer institution of woman-marriage-to-a-woman would be a case in point. Here, both parties to the union are women yet, as Evans-Pritchard (1951, pp. 108–9) has shown, the legal provisions of the union are strictly comparable to those of simple legal marriage between a man and a woman. Few therefore would question Evans-Pritchard's logic in calling this union a marriage.

The *Notes and Queries* definition contains two criteria: that marriage is a union between one man and one woman, and that it establishes the legitimacy of children. Nuer woman-marriage does not conform to the first criterion but it does

to the second. At this point the problem therefore becomes: is a definition feasible which would insist only on the second criterion, that of legitimizing children?

In Europe,[2] Dr. Edmund Leach initiated the most recent chapter in this discussion (Leach 1955), and rather than review its whole history, it is pertinent for me to take up the argument where he and others have left it. In effect, Dr. Leach answered "no" to the question posed above. He argued not only against the vagueness of the phrase "legitimate offspring" but also against any use of potential legal paternity as universal criterion of marriage. He concluded in fact that no definition could be found which would apply to all the institutions which ethnographers commonly refer to as marriage. Instead, he named ten classes of rights[3] which frequently occur in connection with what we loosely term marriage, added that "one might perhaps considerably extend this list," and seemed to conclude that since no single one of these rights is invariably established by marriage in every known society, we ought to feel free to call "marriage" any institution which fulfills any one or more of the selected criteria.

There is, surely, a quite simple logical flaw in this argument. For it would mean in effect that every ethnographer might extend at will

Dr. Leach's list of marital rights, and in short define marriage in any way he pleased. This may be legitimate in describing a single society. But I would argue that for purposes of cross-cultural comparison, we do need a single, parsimonious definition, simply in order to isolate the phenomenon we wish to study.

In support of his argument against using the legitimizing of children as a universal criterion of marriage, Dr. Leach cited the Nayar case. On the basis of two of my papers on the Nayars (Gough 1952, 1955a), he stated that the Nayars traditionally had "no marriage in the strict (i.e., *Notes and Queries*) sense of the term but only a 'relationship of perpetual affinity' between linked lineages (Gough 1955a). The woman's children, however they might be begotten, were simply recruits to the woman's own matrilineage." He stated further, "The notion of fatherhood is lacking. The child uses a term of address meaning 'lord' or 'leader' towards *all* its mother's lovers, but the use of this term does not carry with it any connotation of paternity, either legal or biological. On the other hand the notion of affinity is present, as evidenced by the fact that a woman must observe pollution at her ritual husband's death (Gough 1955a)." Later Dr. Leach concludes that "among the matrilineal matrilocal Nayar, as we have seen, (to establish a socially significant 'relationship of affinity' between the husband and his wife's brothers) is the only marriage characteristic that is present at all" (Leach 1955, p. 183).

This paper has two objectives. It will begin by analyzing traditional Nayar marital institutions and thereby showing that in fact the notion of fatherhood is not lacking and that marriage does serve to establish the legitimacy of children. My analysis will, I hope, not only dispose of a misinterpretation on Dr. Leach's part, but will in general clarify what has always proved a crucial but difficult borderline case for theorists of kinship. The paper will conclude with a new definition of marriage which will again make the status of children born to various types of union critical for decisions as to which of these unions constitute marriage. The ultimate aim is not of course to re-define marriage in a dogmatic way to suit a particular case, for definitions are tools of classification and not aims of research. The aim is to show that there is a common element not only in the institutions anthropologists have confidently labelled "marriage" by the *Notes and Queries* definition, but also in some unusual cases to which that definition does not apply. Whether we call the element "marriage" does not much matter provided it is made explicit, but it would probably be convenient to do so.

Nayar Marriage in Central Kerala

This account will refer to Nayars in the former kingdoms of Calicut, Walluvanad, and Cochin in the centre of the Malabar Coast or Kerala. In the northernmost kingdoms (Kolattunad, Kottayam) and probably also in the southernmost kingdom of Travancore, Nayar residence appears to have been avunculocal even before the period of British rule, marriage was optionally polygynous but not polyandrous, and individual men appear to have had definite rights in and obligations to their children. Full information is not available for these northernmost and southernmost kingdoms in the pre-British period. But it seems probable that in the northern kingdoms at least, even the *Notes and Queries* definition of marriage was applicable to the Nayars. It was certainly applicable in the latter half of the nineteenth century for which I have accounts from informants.

My account of marriage in the central kingdoms is a reconstruction of a state of affairs which appears to have been general before 1792, when the British assumed government of the Coast. As I have shown elsewhere (Gough 1952), Nayar kinship was slowly modified in the nineteenth century and more rapidly in the twentieth. But in remote villages the traditional institutions persisted until towards the end of the nineteenth century and were remembered by a few of my older informants. Their reports are not contradicted and are substantially corroborated by writings of Arab and European travelers of the fifteenth to eighteenth centuries.

In this account I shall use the terms "marriage," "husband" and "wife" without definition. My reasons for doing so will appear later.

In each of the three central kingdoms the Nayar caste was divided into a number of ranked subdivisions characterized by different political functions. Chief of these were (a) the royal lineage, (b) the lineages of chiefs of districts, (c) the lineages of Nayar village headmen and (d) several sub-castes of commoner Nayars. Each of these last either served one of the categories (a) to (c) or else served patrilineal landlord families of Nambudiri Brahmans. I shall deal first with the commoner Nayars of category (d).

There were present in each village some four to seven exogamous matrilineages of a single sub-caste of commoner Nayars. These owed allegiance to the family of the head of the village which might be a patrilineal Nambudiri family a Nayar village headman's matrilineage, a branch of the lineage of the chief of the district or a branch of the royal lineage. The commoner held land on a hereditary feudal-type tenure from the headman's lineage and, in turn, had authority over the village's lower castes of cultivators, artisans, and agricultural serfs. Each retainer lineage tended to comprise some four to eight property-owning units which I call property-groups. The property-group formed a segment of the total lineage and was usually composed of a group of brothers and sisters together with the children and daughters' children of the sisters. The members owned or leased property, in common, lived in one house, and were under the legal guardianship of the oldest male (kāranavan) of the group. Both the property group and the lineage were called taravād.

Nayar men trained as professional soldiers in village gymnasia, and for part of each year they tended to be absent from the village in wars

against neighbouring kingdoms or for military exercises at the capitals. Only the kāranavan, the women and the children of the property-group remained permanently in their ancestral homes.

The Nayars of one village or of two adjacent villages formed a neighbourhood group (kara or tara) of some six to ten lineages. Each lineage was linked by hereditary ties of ceremonial co-operation with two or three other lineages of the neighbourhood. These linkages were reciprocal but not exclusive, so that a chain of relationship linked all the lineages of the neighbourhood. The lineages linked to one's own were called enangar, the total neighbourhood group, the enangu. At least one man and one woman of each linked lineage must be invited to the house of a property-group for the life-crisis rites of its members. Its linked lineages were also concerned if some member of a lineage committed a breach of the religious law of the caste. It was their duty at once to break off relations with the offending lineage and to call a neighbourhood assembly to judge and punish the offence. Its linked lineages thus represented the neighbourhood group as a whole to the offending lineage and were special guardians of its morality. Sometimes in small neighbourhoods the commoner Nayar lineages were all enangar to each other, but in larger neighbourhoods this was not feasible, for the heads of property-groups would have had too many ceremonial obligations to fulfil.

The linked lineages played their most important role at the pre-puberty marriage rite (tālikettakalyānam) of girls (Gough 1955b). At a convenient time every few years, a lineage held grand ceremony at which all its girls who had attained puberty, aged about seven to twelve, were on one day ritually married by men drawn from their linked lineages. The ritual bridegrooms were selected in advance on the advice of the village astrologer at a meeting of the neighbourhood assembly. On the day fixed they came in procession to the oldest ancestral house of the host lineage. There, after various ceremonies, each tied a gold ornament (tāli) round the neck of his ritual bride. The girls had for three days previously been secluded in an inner room of the house and caused to observe taboos as if they had menstruated. After the *tāli*-tying each couple was secluded in private for three days. I was told that traditionally, if the girl was nearing puberty, sexual relations might take place. This custom began to be omitted in the late nineteenth century, but from some of the literature it appears to have been essential in the sixteenth and seventeenth centuries. At the end of the period of seclusion each couple was purified from the pollution of cohabitation by a ritual bath. In Calicut and Walluvanad, each couple in public then tore in two the loin-cloth previously worn by the girl during the "cohabitation" period, as a token of separation. This rite appears to have been omitted in Cochin. In all three kingdoms however, the ritual husbands left the house after the four days of ceremonies and had no further obligations to their brides. A bride in turn had only one further obligation to her ritual husband: at his death, she and all her children, by whatever biological father, must observe death-pollution for him. Death-pollution was otherwise observed only for matrilineal kin. In Cochin, even if their mother's ritual husband never visited his wife again, her children must refer to him by the kinship term *appan*. Children in the lower, patrilineal castes of this area used this word to refer to the legal father, who was presumed also to be the biological father. In Walluvanad and Calicut I did not hear of this verbal usage and do not know by what term, if any, Nayar children referred to their mother's ritual husband.

The pre-puberty *tāli*-rite was essential for a girl. If she menstruated before it had been performed, she should in theory be expelled from her lineage and caste. In fact, however, my informants told me that in such a case the girl's family would conceal the fact of her maturity until after the rite had been performed. But it was a grave sin to do so and one which would never be publicly admitted.

The *tāli*-rite marked various changes in the social position of a girl. First, it brought her to social maturity. She was now thought to be at least ritually endowed with sexual and procre-ative functions and was thenceforward accorded the status of a woman. After the rite people addressed her in public by the respectful title *amma* meaning "mother," and she might take part in the rites of adult women. Second, after the *tāli*-rite a girl must observe all the rules of etiquette associated with incest prohibitions in relation to men of her lineage. She might not touch them, might not sit in their presence, might not speak first to them and might not be alone in a room with one of them. Third, after the *tāli*-rite and as soon as she became old enough (i.e., shortly before or after puberty), a girl received as visiting husbands a number of men in her sub-caste from outside her lineage, usually but not necessarily from her neighbour-hood. In addition she might be visited by any Nayar of the higher sub-castes of village head-men, chiefs or royalty, or by a Nambudiri Brahman. All of these relationships were called *sambandham*. Among commoner Nayar women, however, the great majority of unions were with men of commoner sub-caste.

Relations between any Nayar women and a man of lower Nayar sub-caste, or between any Nayar woman and a man of one of the lower, non-Nayar castes, were strictly prohibited. If a woman was found guilty of such a relationship her lineage's *enangar* carried the matter to the neighbourhood assembly. This temporarily excommunicated the woman's property-group until justice had been done. In the nineteenth century and early this century the property-group was re-accepted into caste only after its *kāranavan* had dismissed the woman from her household and caste, never to return. In pre-British times a woman so dismissed became the property of the king or chief and might be sold into slavery with foreign traders. Alternatively however, the men of her property-group had the right, sometimes exercised, to kill both the woman and her lover and thus preserve the good name of their lineage.

After the ritual marriage the bridegroom need have no further contact with his ritual wife. If both parties were willing, however, he might enter into a sexual relationship with his ritual bride about the time of her puberty. But he had no priority over other men of the neighbourhood group. There is some uncertainty as to the number of visiting husbands a woman might have at one time. Writers of the sixteenth and seventeenth centuries report that a woman usually had some three to eight regular husbands but might receive other men of her own or a higher caste at will. Hamilton in 1727 stated that a woman might have as husbands "twelve but no more at one time" (Hamilton 1727 I, p. 310). As late as 1807 Buchanan reported that Nayar women vied with each other as to the number of lovers they could obtain (Buchanan 1807 I, p. 411). A few of my older informants could remember women who had had three or four current husbands, although plural unions were being frowned upon and had almost died out by the end of the last century. There appears to have been no limit to the number of wives of appropriate sub-caste whom a Nayar might visit concurrently. It seems, therefore, that a woman customarily had a small but not a fixed number of husbands from within her neighbourhood, that relationships with these men might be of long standing, but that the woman was also free to receive casual visitors of appropriate sub-caste who passed through her neighbourhood in the course of military operations.

A husband visited his wife after supper at night and left before breakfast next morning. He placed his weapons at the door of his wife's room and if others came later they were free to sleep on the verandah of the woman's house. Either party to a union might terminate it at any time without formality. A passing guest recompensed a woman with a small cash gift at each visit. But a more regular husband from within the neighbourhood had certain customary obligations. At the start of the union it was common although not essential for him to present the woman with a cloth of the kind worn as a skirt. Later he was expected to make small personal gifts to her at the three main festivals of the year. These gifts included a loin-cloth, betel-leaves and areca-nuts for chewing, hair-oil and bathing-oil, and certain vegetables. Failure on

the part of a husband to make such a gift was a tacit sign that he had ended the relationship. Most important, however, when a woman became pregnant it was essential for one or more men of appropriate sub-caste to acknowledge probable paternity. This they did by providing a fee of a cloth and some vegetables to the low caste midwife who attended the woman in childbirth. If no man of suitable caste would consent to make this gift, it was assumed that the woman had had relations with a man of lower caste or with a Christian or a Muslim. She must then be either expelled from her lineage and caste or killed by her matrilineal kinsmen. I am uncertain of the precise fate of the child in such a case, but there is no doubt at all that he could not be accepted as a member of his lineage and caste. I do not know whether he was killed or became a slave; almost certainly, he must have shared the fate of his mother. Even as late as 1949, over a hundred and fifty years after the establishment of British rule, a Nayar girl who became pregnant before the modern marriage ceremony was regarded as acting within the canons of traditional religious law if she could simply find a Nayar of suitable sub-caste to pay her delivery expenses. But if no Nayar would consent to this she ran the danger of total ostracism, with her child, by the village community. I heard of several cases in which such a girl was driven from her home by her *kāranavan* at the command of the sub-caste assembly. Her natal kinsmen then performed funeral rites for her as if she had died. In each case the girl took refuge in a town before or shortly after her child was born.

Although he made regular gifts to her at festivals, in no sense of the term did a man maintain his wife. Her food and regular clothing she obtained from her matrilineal group. The gifts of a woman's husbands were personal luxuries that pertained to her role as a sexual partner—extra clothing, articles of toilet, betel, and areca—not the giving of which is associated with courtship, and the expenses of the actual delivery, not, be it noted, of the maintenance of either mother or child. The gifts continued to be made at festivals only while the relationship lasted. No man had obligations to a wife of the past.

In these circumstances the exact biological fatherhood of a child was often uncertain, although, of course, paternity was presumed to lie with the man or among the men who had paid the delivery expenses. But even when biological paternity was known with reasonable certainty, the genitor had no economic, social, legal, or ritual rights or obligations to his children after he had once paid the fees of their births. Their guardianship, care and discipline were entirely the concern of their matrilineal kinsfolk headed by their *kāranavan*. All the children of a woman called all her current husbands by the Sanskrit word *acchan* meaning "lord." They did not extend kinship terms at all to the matrilineal kin of these men. Neither the wife nor her children observed pollution at the death of a visiting husband who was not also the ritual husband of the wife.

In most matrilineal systems with settled agriculture and localized matrilineal groups, durable links are provided between these groups by the interpersonal relationships of marriage, affinity and fatherhood. The husbands, affines, fathers, and patrilateral kin of members of the matrilineal group have customary obligations to and rights in them which over time serve to mitigate conflicts between the separate matrilineal groups. The Nayars had no such durable institutionalized interpersonal links. This does not mean that men did not sometimes form strong emotional attachments to particular wives and their children. My information indicates that they did. I know, for example, that if a man showed particular fondness for a wife, his wife's matrilineal kin were likely to suspect the husband's matrilineal kin of hiring sorcerers against them. For the husband's matrilineal kin would be likely to fear that the husband might secretly convey to his wife gifts and cash which belonged rightfully to his matrilineal kin. This suspicion was especially rife if the husband was a *kāranavan* who controlled extensive property. Informal emotional attachments did therefore exist between individuals of different lineages.

But what I wish to indicate is that among the Nayars, these interpersonal affinal and patrilateral links were not invested with customary legal, economic, or ceremonial functions of a kind which would periodically bring members of different lineages together in mandatory forms of co-operation. Four special kinship terms did apparently exist for use in relation to affines acquired through the *sambandham* relationship, although, as I have said, there were no patrilateral terms for kin other than the mother's husbands. All men and women currently engaged in *sambandham* unions with members of ego's property group, and all members of the property-groups of these individuals, were collectively referred to as *bandhukkal* ("joined ones"). A current wife of ego's mother's brother was addressed and referred to as *ammāyi*, and a wife of the elder brother as *jyeshtati amma* (lit. "elder-sister-mother"). Finally, the own brother and the *sambandham* husband of a woman employed the reciprocal term *aliyan* to refer to each other but used no term of address. All the current *bandhukkal* of a property-group were invited to household feasts, but as individual affines they had no ceremonial or economic obligations and were not obliged to attend. As representatives of *enangar* lineages, however, some of these same individuals might be obliged to attend feasts and to fulfil ceremonial obligations as *enangar*. But as particular affines they had no obligations. In place, therefore, of institutionalized interpersonal patrilateral and affinal links, the Nayars had the hereditary institution of linked lineages. Whether or not, at a particular time, sexual relationships existed between individuals of linked lineages, the linked lineages must fulfil their obligations at household ceremonies and give neighbourly help in such emergencies as birth and death. In the patrilineal and double unilineal castes of Kerala, precisely the same obligations are fulfilled by the matrilateral kin and affines of individual members of the patrilineal group. The linked lineages of the Nayars must therefore, I think, be regarded as having a relationship of "perpetual affinity," which carried the more normal functions of affinity and persisted through the making and breaking of individual sexual ties.

In view of these facts, it is convenient to mention here that Dr. Leach's statement that Nayar marriage served "to establish a socially significant relationship between the husband and his wife's brothers" is not, strictly speaking, correct. The *sambandham* union did not establish "a socially significant relationship" between brothers-in-law, for in spite of the reciprocal kinship term, these persons had no institutionalized obligations to one another by virtue of the particular *sambandham* tie. Further, the *tāli*-rite did not establish a relationship between the ritual husband and the brothers of his ritual bride. The ceremony set up no special obligations between these persons; it was merely that their lineages were, hereditarily, *enangar,* both before and after any particular *tāli*-rite. What the rite did establish was a ritual relationship between the *tāli*-tier and his ritual bride, and, as I shall try to show later, a relationship of group-marriage between the bride and all men of her sub-caste outside her lineage. But a particular *tāli*-rite in no way modified the hereditary relationships between male *enangar*. It is for this reason that I call the *enangar* relationship one of "perpetual affinity" between lineages, which, though it carried the ceremonial functions of affinity, persisted irrespective of particular *sambandham*s and *tāli*-rites.

The Nayars of this area were thus highly unusual. For they had a kinship system in which the elementary family of father, mother and children was not institutionalized as a legal, productive, distributive, residential, socializing or consumption unit. Until recent years, some writers have thought that at least as a unit for some degree of co-operation in economic production and distribution, the elementary family was universal. This view has been put forward most forcibly by Murdock (Murdock 1949, chapter 1). Radcliffe-Brown, however, was one of the earliest anthropologists to observe that if the written accounts of the Nayars were accurate, the elementary family was not institutionalized among them.[4] My research corroborates his findings.

I turn briefly to marital institutions among the higher Nayar sub-castes of village headmen, district chiefs, and royalty. At various times during the pre-British period these lineages were accorded political office and set themselves up as of higher ritual rank than the commoner Nayars. The ritual ranking between these major aristocratic subdivisions was fairly stable, but the mutual ranking of lineages within each subdivision was in dispute. Most village headmen acknowledged the ritual superiority of district chiefs and most chiefs of the royal lineage. But some village headmen disputed among themselves for ritual precedence and so did many chiefs. As a result, each of these aristocratic lineages tended to set itself up as a separate subcaste, acknowledging ritual superiors and inferiors, but acknowledging no peers. In the course of time, moreover, following the vicissitudes of political fortune, such lineages could rise or fall in the ritual hierarchy. It was in these lineages therefore that hypergamous unions became most highly institutionalized, for most of these lineages refused to exchange spouses on equal terms. Instead, most of them married all their women upwards and all their men downwards. Women of a village headman's lineage entered *sambandham* unions with chiefly, royal, or Nambudiri Brahman men. Men of these lineages had unions with commoner Nayar women. Chiefly women had unions with royal "children." These fall into two categories: those of the *tāli*-rite and those of the *sambandham* union. In relations between spouses of the *tāli*-rite, the important rights are those of the woman. The ritual husband had, it is true, apparently at one time the right to deflower his bride. But the accounts of many writers indicate that this right was not eagerly sought, that in fact it was viewed with repugnance and performed with reluctance. The ritual husband also had the right that his ritual wife should mourn his death. But we may assume that this right had more significance for the wife than for the husband, for it was not attended by offerings to the departed spirit. These could be performed only by matrilineal kin. The ritual bride's rights were complementary to her husband's, but for her they were of supreme importance. She had, first, the right to have a ritual husband of her own or a superior sub-caste before she attained maturity. Her life depended on this, for if she was not ritually married before puberty she was liable to excommunication and might possibly be put to death. She held this claim against her sub-caste as a whole exclusive of her lineage, or (in the case of aristocratic lineages) against a higher sub-caste. This group must, through the institution of the linked lineages, provide her with a ritual husband of correct rank and thus bring her to maturity in honour instead of in shame. It was the duty of her lineage kinsmen to see to it that some representative from their linked lineages fulfilled this right. The ritual wife's second right was that of observing pollution at the death of her ritual husband. I interpret this as a mark of proof that she had once been married in the correct manner and that this ritual relationship had retained significance for her throughout her ritual husband's life.

The tāli-tier had no rights in his ritual wife's children except that they should observe pollution at his death. From the child's point of view however, his mother's ritual husband must have been a figure of great symbolic significance, because a child whose mother had no ritual husband could not acquire membership in his caste and lineage at all. The birth of a child before his mother's tāli-rite was absolutely forbidden and, in the nature of the case, can scarcely ever have happened. If it did occur, mother and child must certainly have been expelled and were most probably killed. The child's observance of pollution for his mother's ritual husband—like the use of the kinship term appan in Cochin—was a formal recognition that, for ritual purposes, he had been "fathered" by a man of appropriate caste.

Turning to the sambandham union, it seems clear that the husband had no exclusive rights in his wife. He had only, in common with other men, sexual privileges which the wife might withdraw at any time. Again it is the wife's rights which are important. The wife had the right to gifts from her husband at festivals, gifts of little economic value but of high prestige value, for they established her as a woman well-favoured by men. But most significant was the woman's right to have her delivery expenses paid by one or more husbands of appropriate caste, that is, to have it openly acknowledged that her child had as its biological father a man of required ritual rank. Her matrilineal kinsmen could if necessary press for the fulfillment of this right in a public assembly of the neighbourhood: in cases of doubtful paternity any man who had been currently visiting the woman could be forced by the assembly to pay her delivery expenses. But if no man of appropriate rank could be cited as potential father, woman and child were expelled from their lineage and caste.

The sambandham father had no rights in his wife's children. Here again, however, the child had one right in his possible biological fathers: that one or more of them should pay the expenses associated with his birth, and thus entitle him to enter the world as a member of his lineage and caste.

It is clear therefore that although the elementary family of one father, one mother and their children was not institutionalized as a legal, residential, or economic unit, and although individual men had no significant rights in their particular wives or children, the Nayars did institutionalize the concepts of marriage and of paternity, and gave ritual and legal recognition to both. It is here that I must contradict Dr. Leach's interpretation of the situation, for it is not true that "the notion of fatherhood is lacking" nor is it true that "a woman's children, however they might be begotten, were simply recruits to the woman's matrilineage" (Leach 1955, p. 183). For unless his mother was ritually married by a man of appropriate caste and, unless his biological paternity was vouched for by one or more men[5] of appropriate caste, a child could never enter his caste or lineage at all. As I pointed out in both the papers quoted by Dr. Leach, the Nayars were aware of the physiological function of the male in procreation and attached significance to it, for they expected a child to look like his genitor. Like all the higher Hindu castes of India, they based their belief in the moral rightness of the caste system in part upon a racist ideology which involved the inheritance of physical, intellectual, and moral qualities by a child from both of its natural parents, and which held that the higher castes were, by virtue of their heredity, superior to the lower castes. It was ostensibly for this reason that the Nayars forbade with horror sexual contacts between a Nayar woman and a man of lower caste, and that they expelled or put to death women guilty of such contacts. This racist ideology also provided a motive for hypergamous unions, for Nayars of aristocratic lineages boasted of the superior qualities they derived from royal and Brahmanical fatherhood.

Moreover, although individual men had no significant customary rights in their wives and children, marriage and paternity were probably significant factors in political integration, because hypergamous unions bound together the higher sub-castes of the political and religious hierarchies. Multiple sexual ties, as well as the *enangar* relationship, linked office-bearing lineages to each other and to their retainers in a complicated manner. And Nayar men phrased their loyalty to higher ranking military leaders, rulers, and Brahmans in terms of a debt owed to benevolent paternal figures whose forebears had collectively fathered them and whose blood they were proud to share. The generalized concept of fatherhood thus commanded the Nayar soldier's allegiance to his wider caste unit, to the rulers of his village, chiefdom and kingdom and to his religious authorities. It was associated with tender loyalty and with fortitude in war.

I cannot entirely blame Dr. Leach for underestimating the significance of Nayar paternity on the basis of his reading of my earlier papers. For in those papers I was concerned to emphasize the lack of rights of individual men in their spouses and children. It is true that in 1952 I wrote: "Marriage . . . was the slenderest of ties, while as a social concept fatherhood scarcely existed" (Gough 1952, p. 73). I had not then

realized the fundamental necessity to a Nayar of having both a ritual and a biological father of appropriate caste. Moreover, I myself confused the issue by referring to the *sambandham* partners as "husbands" and "wives" in my first paper (Gough 1952) and as "lovers" and "mistresses" in my second (Gough 1955a). For it was not until some time after I read Dr. Leach's paper that I decided to classify Nayar unions unequivocally as marriage and arrive at a definition of marriage which would include the Nayar case. In my own defense I must, however, note that in my paper of 1955 I mentioned that children must observe death pollution for their mother's ritual husband, and that in Cochin they used the kinship term *appan* for this ritual father. In both papers quoted by Dr. Leach, finally, I noted that sexual relations were forbidden between a Nayar woman and man of lower caste or sub-caste, and that the current *sambandham* husbands of a woman must pay her delivery expenses.

I regard Nayar unions as a form of marriage for two reasons. One is that although plural unions were customary, mating was not promiscuous. Sexual relations were forbidden between members of the same lineage on pain of death. It was also forbidden for two men of the same property-group wittingly to have relations with one woman, or for two women of the same property-group to have relations with one man. (This rule of course automatically excluded relations between a man and his biological daughter.) Further, relations were absolutely prohibited between a Nayar woman and a man of lower sub-caste or caste. These prohibitions are directly connected with my second and more important reason for regarding these unions as marriage, namely that the concept of legally established paternity was of fundamental significance in establishing a child as a member of his lineage and caste.

Granted that Nayar unions constituted a form of marriage, we must, I think, classify them as a clear case of group-marriage. This was the interpretation to which I inclined in 1952 (Gough 1952, p. 73) and it is, I now think, the only interpretation which makes sense of the descriptive material I have presented. The *tāli*-rite, as I see it, initiated for each individual Nayar girl a state of marriage to a collectivity of men of appropriate caste. First, the rite ceremonially endowed the girl with sexual and procreative functions. (The mock menstrual seclusion before the rite is relevant to this, as is the actual defloration.) Second, the woman's natal kinsmen surrendered the newly acquired rights in her sexuality, though not in her procreative functions, to a male representative from outside her lineage. This appears in that rules of etiquette associated with incest prohibitions came into force from this date. Third, rights in the woman's sexuality were received by her *enangan* as representative of the men of his sub-caste as a whole. This appears in that the individual *enangan*, as a special sexual partner, was dismissed at the end of the ceremonies and might approach the woman again only as one among a series of equal husbands. In the commoner sub-castes the *enangan* was of the same sub-caste as the woman, and through him, as representative, sexual rights in the woman were conferred on all men of her sub-caste as a collectivity. They were also in fact extended to any man of higher sub-caste who might favour her with his attentions. In aristocratic lineages the ritual husband was of a sub-caste higher than the woman's, and through him, as representative, sexual rights in the woman were conferred upon all men of higher sub-caste as a collectivity. Fourth, the *tāli*-rite, by providing the woman with a ritual husband who (in my view) symbolized all the men of his sub-caste with whom the woman might later have relationships, also provided her children with a ritual father who symbolized the correctness of their paternity. The children acknowledged their debt to him by mourning at his death.

The later *sambandham* unions, by this interpretation, involved the claiming of sexual privileges by men all of whom were potential husbands by virtue of their membership in a sub-caste. The husbands had, however, no individually exclusive rights and could be dismissed at the woman's wish. Their duties as members of their caste were to provide the woman and her lineage with children and to acknowledge their potential biological paternity through birth-payments which legitimized the woman's child.

The Definition of Marriage

I have called the Nayar unions marriage because they involved the concept of legal paternity. It is clear however that such a form of group marriage will not fit the *Notes and Queries* definition of "a union between a man and a woman such that children born to the woman are recognized legitimate offspring of both parents." For legitimacy in the case of the Nayar child required both a ritual father and a "legalized genitor" of appropriate rank, and indeed a child might have more than one "legal genitor" if two or more men had jointly paid the expenses of his birth.

As a tentative move toward a new definition which will have cross-cultural validity and will fit the Nayar and several other unusual cases, I suggest the following: "Marriage is a relationship established between a woman and one or more other persons, which provides that a child born to the woman under circumstances not prohibited by the rules of the relationship, is accorded full birth-status rights common to normal members of his society or social stratum."

A few footnotes to this definition may help to vindicate its inevitably clumsy phraseology "One or more persons" (in place of "a man") will bring into the definition both group-marriage of the Nayar type and also true fraternal polyandry.[6] It also brings within the definition such unusual types as woman-marriage-to-a-woman. "Under circumstances not prohibited by the rules of the relationship" would bring into the definition various problematic cases. It is possible for example that there are patrilineal societies in which a husband may legally repudiate a child illicitly begotten upon his wife by another man, without divorcing the wife herself. In this case the previous establishment of the marriage would not ensure full birth-status rights to the child, for the rules of the marriage relationship would have been broken through the circumstances which led to his birth. "Full birth-status rights common to all normal members . . ." is a compressed reference to all the social relationships, property-rights, etc., which a child acquires at birth by virtue of his legitimacy, whether through the father or through the mother. For patrilineal societies the phrase "full birth-status rights" will include the rights which a child acquires in his pater as a person and in his pater's group. It will include, that is to say, the legitimization of fatherhood, or more precisely, of "father-sonhood." The phrase is, however, broader than any concept of specific rights in a particular father. It will therefore take care of a case like the Nayar in which all rights are acquired through the mother but in which a relationship must be established between the mother and one or more other persons in order for these matrilineal rights to be ratified. Such a process may be called the legitimization of motherhood, or more precisely of "mother-sonhood." Moreover "full birth-status rights" is, I think, not only broader but more precise than "recognized legitimate offspring," to the vagueness of which Dr. Leach took exception. The inclusion of "society or social stratum" makes allowances for class or caste systems in which birth-status rights vary between strata. The case of the Nayars, who are a matrilineal caste in a predominantly patrilineal society, is an obvious example of this.

It should also perhaps be pointed out that this definition does not state that full birth-status rights cannot be acquired by a child except through the marriage of its mother but only that marriage provides for the acquisition of these rights. The definition does not therefore exclude societies like the Nuer in which a man may legitimize the child of an unmarried woman upon payment of a legitimization fee, without becoming married to the mother (Evans-Pritchard 1951, pp. 21, 26).

Prince Peter has objected to the *Notes and Queries* definition and, by implication, to any definition which would make the legitimization of children through the mother's relationship to another party the distinctive characteristic of marriage (1956, 46). His reason for objecting is that in some societies like the Toda, "marriage and legitimacy of the children can be looked upon as two different and separate concepts, and it may be necessary to go through a ceremony of legitimization of the offspring (the Toda *pursütpimi* ceremony) in order to establish who is the legal father, because marriage rites are insufficient in themselves to do this."

However, it seems from Rivers' account that precisely what distinguishes the Toda institution, which Prince Peter translates as "marriage" (*mokh-vatt*), from that which he translates as "concubinage" (*mokhthoditi*) (1957, 35), is that a "husband" holds the right to legitimize some or all of his "wife's" children by the *pursütpimi* ceremony, whereas a lover in the *mokhthoditi* union, being of a different endogamous group from the woman, does not hold this right (Rivers 1906, p. 526). A husband acquires the right to perform the *pursütpimi* ceremony, it seems, by virtue of arranged marriage to an infant or through payment of cattle to a former husband or to a group of former husbands of the wife. The Toda marriage union at its inception does therefore provide that a child born to the woman (under circumstances not prohibited by the rules of the relationship) must be legitimized before his birth; the *pursütpimi* ceremony confirms his legitimacy by attaching him to a particular father and giving him rights in the father's patrilineal group. In the Toda case, again therefore the concept of legal paternity is the distinguishing characteristic of marriage, even though the individual husband, because of polyandry, may be permitted to legitimize only some and not all of the children born to his wife. The Toda case therefore fits my definition,[7] whether we regard the *pursütpimi* ceremony as the final one of a sequence of marriage rites, or as a legitimizing act which, under circumstances not prohibited by the rules of the relationship, one or another of the woman's husbands is legally obliged to fulfil.

I do not argue that all societies must necessarily be found to have marriage by my definition. There may yet turn out to be whole societies—or more probably whole social strata—in which children acquire no birth-status rights except through their mother, by the simple fact of birth. It is possible for example that some slave populations do not have marriage in this sense of the term. What I do wish to suggest however is that for most if not all the societies for which we now have information, including the Nayar marriage as I have defined as a significant relationship, distinguished by the people themselves from all other kinds of relationships. My definition should therefore enable us to isolate marriage as a cross-cultural phenomenon, and from there to proceed to the more exciting task: that of investigating the differential circumstances under which marriage becomes invested with various other kinds of rights and obligations. Some of the most important of these Dr. Leach has already listed for us.

Notes

1. The fieldwork on which this paper is based was carried out in three villages of Kerala between September 1947 and July 1949 with the aid of a William Wyse Studentship from Trinity College, Cambridge. Writing it has formed part of a project financed by the American Social Science Research Council.

2. In America, Miss Alisa S. Lourié, Douglass College, Rutgers University, has recently worked on this problem, and I have been stimulated by correspondence with her and by reading an unpublished paper of hers, *Concepts in Family Sociology*. In this paper Miss Lourié formulates a definition of marriage which is narrower than mine, but when her work is published readers will see that I was helped toward my definition by her analysis. I have also profited much from discussion with my husband, David F. Aberle.

3. From *Journal of the Royal Anthropological Institute* V. 89, 1959, pp. 23–34. Reprinted by permission of Blackwell Publishing, UK.

    A. To establish the legal father of a woman's children.

    B. To establish the legal mother of a man's children.

    C. To give the husband a monopoly in the wife's sexuality.

    D. To give the wife a monopoly in the husband's sexuality.

    E. To give the husband partial or monopolistic rights to the wife's domestic and other labour services.

    F. To give the wife partial or monopolist rights to the husband's labour services.

    G. To give the husband partial or total rights over property belonging or potentially accruing to the wife.

    H. To give the wife partial or total rights over property belonging or potentially accruing to the husband.

    I. To establish a joint fund of property—a partnership—for benefit of the children of the marriage.

    J. To establish a socially significant "relationship of affinity" between the husband and his wife's brothers. (Leach 1955, p. 183).

4. Radcliffe-Brown expressed this view most recently and fully in his introduction to *African Systems of Kinship and Marriage* (1950 pp. 73 seq.)

5. I do not know whether the Nayars believed it possible for two or more men to contribute to the formation of one embryo. I think it possible that they did, for I found this belief among villagers of

the Tamil country. Among these castes it formed part of a belief that several acts of intercourse are necessary to "feed" the embryo and assist it to grow.

6. I agree with Dr. Leach that the Iravas of Central Kerala had true fraternal polyandry. My own enquiries produced evidence supporting Aiyappan's view that the brothers shared equally both sexual rights in the woman and also legal paternity of the children, in the same manner in which they were co-owners of the ancestral property. The eldest living brother at any given time was simply the legal representative of this corporation.

7. I agree with Dr. Fischer that Prince Peter's definition of marriage is a tautology and so of no assistance (1956, 92). All that Prince Peter's second note shows (1957, 35) is that several people of his acquaintance have different terms for different kinds of relationships between men and women. But unless we approach these with some guiding concepts of our own in mind, we cannot decide which of them to translate as "marriage" and which as "concubinage."

References

Buchanan, Francis (Hamilton) 1807. *A Journey from Madras through Mysore, Canara and Malabar.* 3 vols. London.

Evans-Pritchard, E. E. 1951. *Kinship and Marriage among the Nuer.* Oxford.

Fischer, H. Th. 1956. For a new definition of marriage. *Man* 1956, 92.

Gough, E. Kathleen 1952. Changing Kinship Usages in the Setting of Political and Economic Change among the Nayars of Malabar. *J. R. Anthrop. Inst* 82, pp. 71–87.

Gough, E. Kathleen 1955a. *The Traditional Lineage and Kinship System of the Nayars.* [Unpublished manuscript in the Haddon Library, Cambridge.]

Gough, E. Kathleen 1955b. Female Initiation Rites on the Malabar Coast, *J. R. Anthrop. Inst.* 85 pp. 45–80.

Hamilton, Alexander 1727. *A New Account of the East Indies,* 2 vols. Edinburgh.

Leach, E. R. 1955. Polyandry, Inheritance, and the Definition of Marriage. *Man,* 1955, 199.

Lourié, Alisa S. 1957. *Concepts in Family Sociology.* 1957. [Unpublished manuscript kindly made available to this author.]

Murdock, G. P. 1949. *Social Structure.* New York.

Notes and Queries in Anthropology 1951. 6th ed. London.

H. R. H. Prince Peter of Greece and Denmark for a New Definition of Marriage. *Man,* 1956, 46; 1957, 35.

Radcliffe-Brown, A. R. & Forde, D. (eds.) 1950. *African Systems of Kinship and Marriage.* Oxford.

Rivers, W. H. R. 1906. *The Todas.* London.

23

When Brothers Share a Wife

Among Tibetans, the Good Life Relegates Many Women to Spinsterhood

Melvyn C. Goldstein

Melvyn C. Goldstein, now a professor of anthropology at Case Western Reserve University in Cleveland, has been interested in the Tibetan practice of fraternal polyandry (several brothers marrying one wife) since he was a graduate student.

Eager to reach home, Dorje drives his yaks hard over the 17,000-foot mountain pass, stopping only once to rest. He and his two older brothers, Pema and Sonam, are jointly marrying a woman from the next village in a few weeks, and he has to help with the preparations.

Dorje, Pema, and Sonam are Tibetans living in Limi, a 200-square-mile area in the northwest corner of Nepal, across the border from Tibet. The form of marriage they are about to enter—fraternal polyandry in anthropological parlance—is one of the world's rarest forms of marriage but is not uncommon in Tibetan society, where it has been practiced from time immemorial. For many Tibetan social strata, it traditionally represented the ideal form of marriage and family.

The mechanics of fraternal polyandry are simple. Two, three, four, or more brothers jointly take a wife, who leaves her home to come and live with them. Traditionally, marriage was arranged by parents, with children, particularly females, having little or no say. This is changing somewhat nowadays, but it is still unusual for children to marry without their parents' consent. Marriage ceremonies vary by income and region and range from all the brothers sitting together as grooms to only the eldest one formally doing so. The age of the brothers plays an important role in determining this: very young brothers almost never participate in actual marriage ceremonies, although they typically join the marriage when they reach their mid teens.

The eldest brother is normally dominant in terms of authority, that is, in managing the household, but all the brothers share the work and participate as sexual partners. Tibetan males and females do not find the sexual aspect of sharing a spouse the least bit unusual, repulsive, or scandalous, and the norm is for the wife to treat all the brothers the same.

Offspring are treated similarly. There is no attempt to link children biologically to particular brothers, and a brother shows no favoritism toward his child even if he knows he is the real father because, for example, his other brothers

---

were away at the time the wife became pregnant. The children, in turn, consider all of the brothers as their fathers and treat them equally, even if they also know who is their real father. In some regions children use the term "father" for the eldest brother and "father's brother" for the others, while in other areas they call all the brothers by one term, modifying this by the use of "elder" and "younger."

Unlike our own society, where monogamy is the only form of marriage permitted, Tibetan society allows a variety of marriage types, including monogamy, fraternal polyandry, and polygyny. Fraternal polyandry and monogamy are the most common forms of marriage, while polygyny typically occurs in cases where the first wife is barren. The widespread practice of fraternal polyandry, therefore, is not the outcome of a law requiring brothers to marry jointly. There is choice, and in fact, divorce traditionally was relatively simple in Tibetan society. If a brother in a polyandrous marriage became dissatisfied and wanted to separate, he simply left the main house and set up his own household. In such cases all the children stayed in the main household with the remaining brother(s), even if the departing brother was known to be the real father of one or more of the children.

The Tibetans' own explanation for choosing fraternal polyandry is materialistic. For example, when I asked Dorje why he decided to marry with his two brothers rather than take his own wife, he thought for a moment, then said it prevented the division of his family's farm (and animals) and thus facilitated all of them achieving a higher standard of living. And when I later asked Dorje's bride whether it wasn't difficult for her to cope with three brothers as husbands, she laughed and echoed the rationale of avoiding fragmentation of the family and land, adding that she expected to be better off economically, since she would have three husbands working for her and her children.

Exotic as it may seem to Westerners, Tibetan fraternal polyandry is thus in many ways analogous to the way primogeniture functioned in nineteenth-century England. Primogeniture dic-

tated that the eldest son inherited the family estate, while younger sons had to leave home and seek their own employment—for example, in the military or the clergy. Primogeniture maintained family estates intact over generations by permitting only one heir per generation. Fraternal polyandry also accomplishes this but does so by keeping all the brothers together with just one wife so that there is only one set of heirs per generation.

While Tibetans believe that in this way fraternal polyandry reduces the risk of family fission, monogamous marriages among brothers need not necessarily precipitate the division of the family estate: brothers could continue to live together, and the family land could continue to be worked jointly. When I asked Tibetans about this, however, they invariably responded that such joint families are unstable because each wife is primarily oriented to her own children and interested in their success and well-being over that of the children of the other wives. For example, if the youngest brother's wife had three sons while the eldest brother's wife had only one daughter, the wife of the youngest brother might begin to demand more resources for her children since, as males, they represent the future of the family. Thus, the children from different wives in the same generation are competing sets of heirs, and this makes such families inherently unstable. Tibetans perceive that conflict will spread from the wives to their husbands and consider this likely to cause family fission. Consequently, it is almost never done.

Although Tibetans see an economic advantage to fraternal polyandry, they do not value the sharing of a wife as an end in itself. On the contrary, they articulate a number of problems inherent in the practice. For example, because authority is customarily exercised by the eldest brother, his younger male siblings have to subordinate themselves with little hope of changing their status within the family. When these younger brothers are aggressive and individualistic, tensions and difficulties often occur despite there being only one set of heirs.

In addition, tension and conflict may arise in polyandrous families because of sexual favoritism. The bride normally sleeps with the eldest brother, and the two have the responsibility to see to it that the other males have opportunities for sexual access. Since the Tibetan subsistence economy requires males to travel a lot, the temporary absence of one or more brothers facilitates this, but there are also other rotation practices. The cultural ideal unambiguously calls for the wife to show equal affection and sexuality to each of the brothers (and vice versa), but deviations from this ideal occur, especially when there is a sizable difference in age between the partners in the marriage.

Dorje's family represents just such a potential situation. He is fifteen years old and his two older brothers are twenty-five and twenty-two years old. The new bride is twenty-three years old, eight years Dorje's senior. Sometimes such a bride finds the youngest husband immature and adolescent and does not treat him with equal affection; alternatively, she may find his youth attractive and lavish special attention on him. Apart from that consideration, when a younger male like Dorje grows up, he may consider his wife "ancient" and prefer the company of a woman his own age or younger. Consequently, although men and women do not find the idea of sharing a bride or bridegroom repulsive, individual likes and dislikes can cause familial discord.

Two reasons have commonly been offered for the perpetuation of fraternal polyandry in Tibet: that Tibetans practice female infanticide and therefore have to marry polyandrously, owing to a shortage of females; and that Tibet, lying at extremely high altitudes, is so barren and bleak that Tibetans would starve without resort to this mechanism. A Jesuit who lived in Tibet during the eighteenth century articulated this second view: "One reason for this most odious custom is the sterility of the soil, and the small amount of land that can be cultivated owing to the lack of water. The crops may suffice if the brothers all live together, but if they form separate families they would be reduced to beggary."

Both explanations are wrong, however. Not only has there never been institutionalized female infanticide in Tibet, but Tibetan society gives females considerable rights, including inheriting the family estate in the absence of brothers. In such cases, the woman takes a bridegroom who comes to live in her family and adopts her family's name and identity. Moreover, there is no demographic evidence of a shortage of females. In Limi, for example, there were (in 1974) sixty females and fifty-three males in the fifteen- to thirty-five-year age category, and many adult females were unmarried.

The second reason is also incorrect. The climate in Tibet is extremely harsh, and ecological factors do play a major role perpetuating polyandry, but polyandry is not a means of preventing starvation. It is characteristic, not of the poorest segments of the society, but rather of the peasant landowning families.

In the old society, the landless poor could not realistically aspire to prosperity, but they did not fear starvation. There was a persistent labor shortage throughout Tibet, and very poor families with little or no land and few animals could subsist through agricultural labor, tenant farming, craft occupations such as carpentry, or by working as servants. Although the per person family income could increase somewhat if brothers married polyandrously and pooled their wages, in the absence of inheritable land, the advantage of fraternal polyandry was not generally sufficient to prevent them from setting up their own households. A more skilled or energetic younger brother could do as well or better alone, since he would completely control his income and would not have to share it with his siblings. Consequently, while there was and is some polyandry among the poor, it is much less frequent and more prone to result in divorce and family fission.

An alternative reason for the persistence of fraternal polyandry is that it reduces population growth (and thereby reduces the pressure on resources) by relegating some females to lifetime spinsterhood. Fraternal polyandrous marriages in Limi (in 1974) averaged 2.35 men per woman, and not surprisingly, 31 percent of the females of child-bearing age (twenty to forty-nine) were unmarried. These spinsters either continued to live at home, set up their own households, or worked as servants for other families. They could also become Buddhist nuns. Being unmarried is not synonymous with exclusion from the reproductive pool. Discreet extra-marital relationships are tolerated, and actually half of the adult unmarried women in Limi had one or more children. They raised these children as single mothers, working for wages or weaving cloth and blankets for sale. As a group, however, the unmarried woman had far fewer offspring than the married women, averaging only 0.7 children per woman, compared with 3.3 for married women, whether polyandrous, monogamous, or polygynous. While polyandry helps regulate population, this function of polyandry is not consciously perceived by Tibetans and is not the reason they consistently choose it.

If neither a shortage of females nor the fear of starvation perpetuates fraternal polyandry, what motivates brothers, particularly younger brothers, to opt for this system of marriage? From the perspective of the younger brother in a landholding family, the main incentive is the attainment or maintenance of the good life. With polyandry, he can expect a more secure and higher standard of living, with access not only to this family's land and animals but also to its inherited collection of clothes, jewelry, rugs, saddles, and horses. In addition, he will experience less work pressure and much greater security because all responsibility does not fall on one "father." For Tibetan brothers, the question is whether to trade off the greater personal freedom inherent in monogamy for the real or potential economic security, affluence, and social prestige associated with life in a larger, labor-rich polyandrous family.

A brother thinking of separating from his polyandrous marriage and taking his own wife would face various disadvantages. Although in the majority of Tibetan regions all brothers theoretically have rights to their family's estate, in reality Tibetans are reluctant to divide their land

into small fragments. Generally, a younger brother who insists on leaving the family will receive only a small plot of land, if that. Because of its power and wealth, the rest of the family usually can block any attempt of the younger brother to increase his share of land through litigation. Moreover, a younger brother may not even get a house and cannot expect to receive much above the minimum in terms of movable possessions, such as furniture, pots, and pans. Thus, a brother contemplating going it on his own must plan on achieving economic security and the good life not through inheritance but through his own work.

The obvious solution for a younger brother—creating new fields from virgin land—is generally not a feasible option. Most Tibetan populations live at high altitudes (above 12,000 feet), where arable land is extremely scarce. For example, in Dorje's village, agriculture ranges only from about 12,900 feet, the lowest point in the area, to 13,300 feet. Above that altitude, early frost and snow destroy the staple barley crop. Furthermore, because of the low rainfall caused by the Himalayan rain shadow, many areas in Tibet and northern Nepal that are within the appropriate altitude range for agriculture have no reliable sources of irrigation. In the end, although there is plenty of unused land in such areas, most of it is either too high or too arid.

Even where unused land capable of being farmed exists, clearing the land and building the substantial terraces necessary for irrigation constitute a great undertaking. Each plot has to be completely dug out to a depth of two to two-and-one-half feet so that the large rocks and boulders can be removed. At best, a man might be able to bring a few new fields under cultivation in the first years after separating from his brothers, but he could not expect to acquire substantial amounts of arable land this way.

In addition, because of the limited farmland, the Tibetan subsistence economy characteristically includes a strong emphasis on animal husbandry. Tibetan farmers regularly maintain cattle, yaks, goats, and sheep, grazing them in the areas too high for agriculture. These herds produce wool, milk, cheese, butter, meat, and skins. To obtain these resources, however, shepherds must accompany the animals on a daily basis. When first setting up a monogamous household, a younger brother like Dorje would find it difficult to both farm and manage animals.

In traditional Tibetan society, there was an even more critical factor that operated to perpetuate fraternal polyandry—a form of hereditary servitude somewhat analogous to serfdom in Europe. Peasants were tied to large estates held by aristocrats, monasteries, and the Lhasa government. They were allowed the use of some farmland to produce their own subsistence but were required to provide taxes in kind and corvée (free labor) to their lords. The corvée was a substantial hardship, since a peasant household was in many cases required to furnish the lord with one laborer daily for most of the year and more on specific occasions such as the harvest. This enforced labor, along with the lack of new land and ecological pressure to pursue both agriculture and animal husbandry, made

polyandrous families particularly beneficial. The polyandrous family allowed an internal division of adult labor, maximizing economic advantage. For example, while the wife worked the family fields, one brother could perform the lord's corvée, another could look after the animals, and a third could engage in trade.

Although social scientists often discount other people's explanations of why they do things, in the case of Tibetan fraternal polyandry, such explanations are very close to the truth. The custom, however, is very sensitive to changes in its political and economic milieu and, not surprisingly, is in decline in most Tibetan areas. Made less important by the elimination of the traditional serf-based economy, it is disparaged by the dominant non-Tibetan leaders of India, China, and Nepal. New opportunities for economic and social mobility in these countries, such as the tourist trade and government employment, are also eroding the rationale for polyandry, and so it may vanish within the next generation.

24

Parental Favoritism toward Daughters

Lee Cronk

Why do the parents of some cultures invest more in the offspring of one sex than the other? A case study of the Kenyan Mukogodo offers an evolutionary explanation

The birth of a healthy child is greeted with great fanfare in almost every part of the world. But not every birth inspires a celebration. In many cultures, the birth of a girl is merely shrugged off by a couple hoping to produce a son. In others, the favoritism toward boys is so strong that parents may resort to infanticide, refusing to invest energy and affection in a daughter. The question this behavior raises has always been an intriguing one for anthropologists. Why would parents show such strong bias toward children of one sex?

Although there have been many studies of cultures that favor boy children, the question of sex-biased parental favoritism arose in a different way, and unexpectedly, in my own research a few years ago. My wife and I had been studying cultural change among the Mukogodo people of central Kenya. Because the Mukogodo had recently shifted from hunting and gathering to sheep and goat herding, the people had experienced a drastic change in their lifestyle. It seemed to be a perfect opportunity to study the

Lee Cronk is a professor of anthropology at Rutgers University. He received his Ph.D. in anthropology in 1989 from Northwestern University. He received a Fulbright grant to continue his research among the Mukogodo, looking in detail at the effects of variations in parental behavior on children's health, nutritional status and development.
Address: Department of Anthropology, Rutgers University, 131 George Street, RAB 306, New Brunswick, NJ 08901-1414.

adaptive responses of a small society during a rapid economic transition.

While we were conducting a census of the population, however, we discovered a curious statistic: A survey of Mukogodo births in the previous year showed that 32 girls had been born, but only 13 boys! Intriguingly, the biased sex ratio persisted for children under four years of age. As of 1986 there were 98 girls and only 66 boys less than five years old. Whereas most cultures around the world have roughly equal or

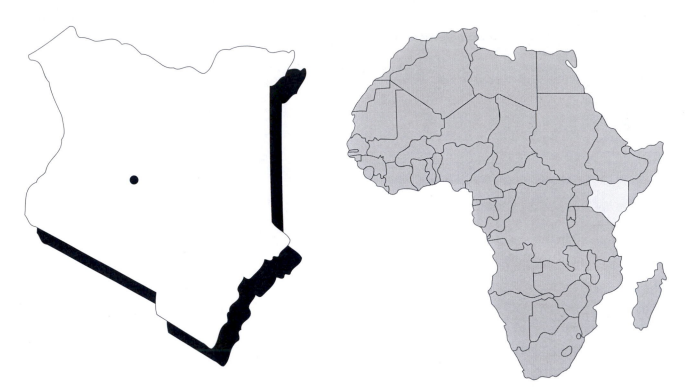

Figure 24.1 Mukogodo territory is located in a region of central Kenya that is inhabited by pastoralist Maasai-speaking peoples.

slightly male-biased childhood sex ratios, the Mukogodo had veered in the opposite direction in a very big way. Could parental favoritism account for the Mukogodo's lopsided sex ratios? If so, why did they favor girls?

The anomalous sex ratio of the Mukogodo instigated a course of research that I have pursued to the present day. In the course of my investigation, I discovered that female-biased parental favoritism is very rare. A few instances are known, however, in such disparate countries as Pakistan, New Guinea, and the United States. In recent years these and other cases of sex-biased parental investment have become the focus of a great deal of research, especially from an evolutionary point of view. There is in fact a body of evolutionary theory that offers a biological explanation for the lopsided sex ratio among the Mukogodo, even though the same explanation may not hold true for other examples of unequal treatment of daughters and sons in human society. The theory asks the question: Could the tendency to favor daughters or sons in particular circumstances be the product of our species' history of natural selection?

Parental Investment

The mix of males and females among newborns in a sexually reproducing population tends to be roughly 50-50. There are species, however, that exhibit different sex ratios, and evolutionary biologists have attempted to explain these differences. One way that parents might modify the sex ratios of their offspring is to invest different amounts of energy in activities that promote an offspring's survival.

At first glance, favoring or neglecting some offspring would seem to be a nonadaptive response. Shouldn't a parent want to produce as many offspring as possible, of either sex? As with so many important issues in evolution theory, Charles Darwin was the first to attempt an explanation of sex-biased parental investment and the closely related problem of offspring sex ratios. In this case, however, Darwin soon decided that "the whole problem is so intricate

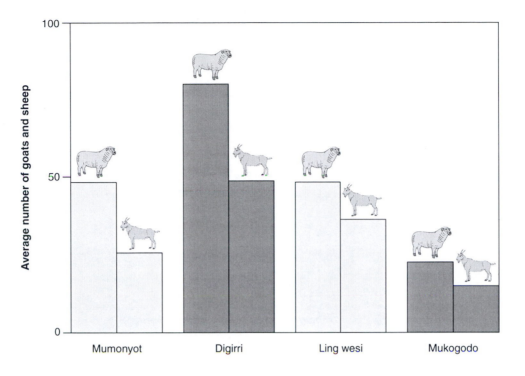

Figure 24.2 Relative wealth (measured in numbers of goats and sheep) of the Mukogodo and their neighbors finds the Mukogodo at the bottom of an economic hierarchy. Because of the economic status, Mukogodo men have difficulty accumulating the bridewealth necessary to arrange a marriage.

that it is safe to leave its solution for the future."

The British biostatistician Sir Ronald A. Fisher offered the first convincing explanation of sex-biased parental investment. Fisher began with the observation that because every individual in a sexually reproducing diploid (duplicate chromosome) species gets half of its genetic material from its father and half from its mother, selection should favor parents who invest equally in sons and daughters. In this view a single unit of investment in an individual of one sex will have the same effect on a parent's fitness (measured in terms of grandchildren) as a unit invested in the other sex. If daughters and sons cost the same to rear to adulthood (and provide an equal payoff in terms of grandchildren), then this would lead to equal numbers of sons and daughters.

On the other hand, if daughters and sons do not cost the same, selection should favor greater production of the cheaper sex so that the overall parental investment in the sexes is equal. For example, if sons cost half as much to rear as daughters, then the equilibrium sex ratio for the population would be two males for every female. Although an average male would leave only half as many offspring as an average female, males also cost only half as much to produce. So one unit of investment in a male yields the same number of grandchildren as one unit of investment in a female.

This idea, called "Fisher's principle of the sex ratio," assumes that all offspring of all parents have essentially the same reproductive prospects as other members of their sex. But what if the reproductive prospects vary among offspring of the same sex? This question was posed by evolutionary biologist Robert Trivers and mathematician Dan Willard in 1973. Trivers and Willard pointed out that in many species, male reproductive success is both more variable than that of females and more likely to be influenced by environmental conditions during the period of

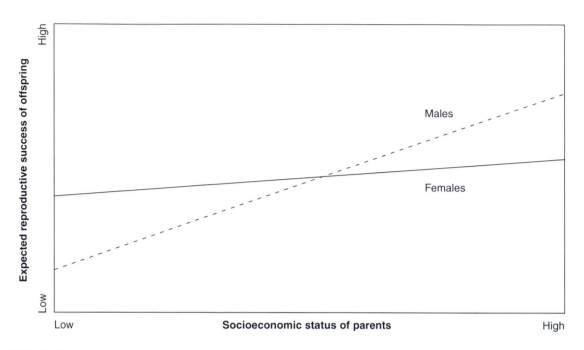

Figure 24.3 Socioeconomic status may predict sex biases in parental investment, according to a model first proposed by Robert Trivers and Dan Willard in the early 1970s. Male offspring typically have greater reproductive success than female offspring when their parents have high socioeconomic status. In contrast, female offspring are typically more reproductively successful than male offspring when their parents have low socioeconomic status. The Trivers-Willard model predicts that parents will favor the sex of offspring with the best reproductive prospects. The Mukogodo, who are at the bottom of a socioeconomic hierarchy, are predicted to favor daughters over sons.

parental investment. When conditions are good, both male and female offspring are likely to benefit reproductively, but males benefit more because of their greater reproductive potential. When conditions are bad, both male and female offspring are likely to suffer reproductively, but males usually suffer more. Given those conditions, parents who find themselves in good condition while raising their offspring would do best to favor their sons, whereas those who find themselves in poor condition should focus their energies on their daughters in order to have the most grandchildren.

Evidence for the Trivers-Willard hypothesis was thin and easily criticized until the 1980s, when a series of studies seemed to confirm the hypothesis among certain species. It was found that a large South American rodent, the coypu or nutria, adjusted its offspring sex ratio in a way that fit Trivers and Willard's predictions. In particular, when conditions are good, a fat, healthy female coypu selectively aborts small, mostly female litters but keeps small, mostly

male litters. Since small litters produce large offspring, and a large body size is probably more important for male reproductive success, it behooves the parents to invest more in male than in female offspring.

Steven Austad of Harvard University and Melvin Sunquist of the University of Florida observed a similar pattern when they experimented with the diets of female opossums. They found that female opossums receiving food supplements produced about 40 percent more male offspring than female offspring. In contrast, female opossums that were maintained on a normal diet produced equal numbers of male and female offspring.

Some of the best evidence for the Trivers-Willard effect among primates comes from studies of spider monkeys. Because male spider monkeys stay in the social group in which they are born, whereas female spider monkeys leave their natal troops, the reproductive success of a male is highly dependent on his mother's rank in the social hierarchy. Accordingly, low-ranking mothers produce all daughters, whereas high-ranking mothers have a balanced sex ratio. High-ranking spider monkey mothers also put more effort into raising their sons by carrying their sons for a longer period than their daughters and by waiting longer to get pregnant after the birth of a son than the birth of a daughter.

Trivers and Willard suggested that their model might also be fruitfully applied to the human species, with socioeconomic class replacing maternal conditions. In human beings, as in many other species, the variance in male reproductive success is typically greater than that of females. The reproductive success of a male is usually more affected by socioeconomic status than is the reproductive success of a female. This is especially true in societies where men are able to have more than one wife and where they must pay a bridewealth to the wife's family in order to marry. These conditions serve to enhance the advantages of being wealthy, powerful and prestigious.

The Mukogodo

The Mukogodo are neither wealthy, powerful nor prestigious. Until the early part of this century they were foragers and beekeepers, living in caves within the forest that bears their name. One British colonial settler described them as "a miserable tribe living in clefts in the rocks and subsisting on wild yams and honey and the chase."

Within a few years, however, the Mukogodo acquired cattle, sheep and goats—mostly as bridewealth when their daughters married men from neighboring herding groups. These groups—the Mumonyot, Ilng'wesi Digirri and Samburu—speak the same language and have a culture similar to the better-known Maasai of southern Kenya and northern Tanzania. The Mukogodo moved out of their caves which were inconvenient for maintaining livestock, and adopted the language and most of the other customs of their neighbors.

One result of the change was to put the Mukogodo firmly at the bottom of regional hierarchy of wealth, prestige, and, ultimately, marital and reproductive opportunities. A livestock census conducted by the British in the early 1930s clearly shows that the Mukogodo were the poorest people in the area at that time. A recent survey in the 1980s of the most economically important stock (goats and sheep) shows that the Mukogodo are still on the bottom rung of the socioeconomic ladder.

The Mukogodo also carry a stigma due to their history of hunting and gathering, an activity that the Maasai and other local groups consider appropriate for wild animals, not civilized people. Maasai-speakers refer to the Mukogodo as *il-torrobo* (anglicized as Dorobo), which translates roughly as "poor scum." Maasai-speakers associate Dorobo with all manner of negative characteristics—cowardice, envy, selfishness—and even with their version of the original fall from grace. In their mythology, a Dorobo is said to have shot an arrow that severed a cord by which God had been sending cattle from heaven to earth. The fact that the Mukogodo once spoke a different, now nearly extinct language makes them even more alien and suspect to their neighbors. Many of the Maasai-speakers falsely believe that the Mukogodo secretly speak their old language in private, mysterious ceremonies.

For Mukogodo men the consequence of their socioeconomic status is simple: It is harder for them to find wives than it is for other men in the area. Their lack of livestock means they do not have the bridewealth needed to pay for a wife, and the stigma attached to their Dorobo status means that the women of the other ethnic groups do not find them desirable. The situation is exacerbated because Mukogodo men must pay a higher bridewealth when they marry women from other groups in comparison to men from other groups who marry Mukogodo women. This may be due to the difficult bargaining position of the Mukogodo and the taint of their Dorobo label.

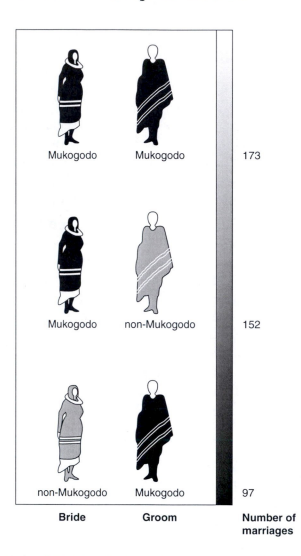

Figure 24.4 Inter-ethnic marriages occur most often between a Mukogodo bride and a non-Mukogodo groom. In contrast, Mukogodo men marry non-Mukogodo women much less frequently. The highest proportion of marriages consists of a Mukogodo bride and groom. Ultimately, it is easier for a Mukogodo woman to marry than it is for a Mukogodo man because the bridewealth for a Mukogodo woman is relatively low, and Mukogodo men have difficulty acquiring the livestock required to marry a woman of higher status.

Women in the Mukogodo area, in contrast, are always in short supply since men can have as many wives as they can afford. As a result, Mukogodo women all find husbands—often among their wealthier, higher-status neighbors—despite their Dorobo origins. In the end, the average Mukogodo woman has more children than the average Mukogodo man.

Favored Daughter

The Mukogodo situation clearly fits the preconditions set by Trivers and Willard for sex-biased parental investment. But what is it that the Mukogodo do, if anything, to produce such a female-biased sex ratio among their children?

Given the imbalance in births during the year of our fieldwork, it would be tempting to say that something physiological is taking place. Perhaps there are more female conceptions or more male miscarriages than normal. Unfortunately, the data to test this idea are simply not available (partly because the Mukogodo women are reluctant to talk about the details of reproduction). The data we do have suggests that the sex ratio at birth is just about normal, with slightly more males than females at birth. (The sex ratio of births during 1986 may be a statistical anomaly.)

That leaves the time after the babies are born. One possibility, seen in many other parts of the world, is infanticide: Mukogodo mothers could be killing their sons. But there is no evidence of this. The Mukogodo have no tradition of infanticide, they do not admit having practiced it, and there is no physical evidence of it. Mukogodo parents are also not overtly abusive of their children and corporal punishment is rare.

It is more likely that their sons are dying at a higher rate than normal because of a broad tendency to favor daughters over sons. The best evidence for this comes from the records of health facilities run by a local Roman Catholic mission. Mukogodo parents show a clear and statistically significant tendency to take their daughters more often than their sons for treatment at a dispensary. Mukogodo parents also enroll their daughters more frequently in the mission's monthly traveling baby clinic, which provides mothers with some food and child-care lessons.

In contrast, the non-Mukogodo people in the region show no bias toward sons or daughters when they take them to the dispensary or clinic. Since the Mukogodo and their neighbors share the same views about children and child-rearing, it seems unlikely that the Mukogodo's female bias could be due to a belief that girls are more sickly than boys.

For the Mukogodo, taking a child to the dispensary or the clinic is a major investment. The dispensary charges a fee of five Kenyan shillings (equivalent to 30 U.S. cents in 1986) for every visit. The fee is intended to discourage frivolous visits, but in combination with the time it takes to travel to the dispensary (from half a day to three days) it amounts to a substantial bother and expense to take a child to see the doctor. The clinic is also relatively expensive, charging a monthly fee of 22 Kenyan shillings (about $1.38), and requires nearly a full day of travel.

Mukogodo mothers also tend to breastfeed their daughters longer than their sons. In one instance a two-and-one-half-year-old girl was still being nursed. Nearly 84 percent of all girls, but only 70 percent of all boys less than two-and-one-half years old were being nursed.

Although Mukogodo standards of child-care are different from our own, there were three clear cases of child neglect, all of which involved boys. One little boy was made miserable for months by a chronic eye infection because his mother refused to take him to the dispensary. Another infant boy was visibly underdeveloped, listless and easily frightened, whereas his older sister was bright, healthy and well fed. A physician had diagnosed the boy's problem as malnutrition. In the third instance, a five-year-old boy had a large festering wound behind one ear for the entire year we were among the Mukogodo because his parents refused to take him for medical treatment. (Although we tried to bandage the wound several times, it did not heal until it was treated by a health worker from the Catholic mission who was passing through the village.)

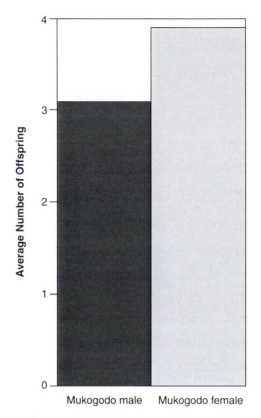

Figure 24.5 Fertility of the average Mukogodo woman is greater than that of the average Mukogodo man. The greater reproductive success of Mukogodo women means that Mukogodo parents can produce a greater number of grandchildren by having more daughters than sons.

Other Societies

In my perusal of the literature, I have discovered the existence of other societies in which the sex ratios of the population did not follow the standard bias in favor of boys. In an attempt to understand these aberrant societies, I have tried to interpret their circumstances in the light of the Trivers-Willard model.

The Cheyenne Indians of the nineteenth century offer a striking example. These people were divided into two groups, lower-status "war bands," led by "war chiefs," and upper-status "peace bands," led by "peace chiefs." Peace chiefs naturally tended to survive longer than war chiefs, they tended to have more wives, and their bands were generally wealthier than those of the war chiefs. Interestingly, a census from 1892 shows that the childhood sex ratios in the peace bands were about even, with 97 boys for every 100 girls, whereas the ratio in the war bands was about 69 boys for every 100 girls.

In other instances where parents favor their daughters over their sons, the Trivers-Willard model does not apply since girls do not have better reproductive prospects than their brothers. In such cases, it appears that in one way or another girls are either cheaper to raise than boys or provide more benefits to their families than boys do. In rural areas of nineteenth-century America, sons were more valuable to their families than daughters because of the important farm work they were called upon to do. In more urban areas, in contrast, the economic value of girls was higher since they could get jobs in the many new industries that were arising. Demographic data suggest that parents directed more investment toward the economically more productive sex. In non-urbanized regions, there were more boys than girls in the United States between 1800 and 1860, whereas in urbanized regions such as New England there were more girls than boys. The life expectancy was higher for girls in towns of 10,000 people or more, but higher for boys in towns with fewer than 10,000 people.

A more colorful example is provided by the Kanjar of Pakistan and northern India who travel from town to town selling ceramic and papier-mâché toys, dancing, begging and occasionally offering carnival rides and engaging in prostitution. Almost all of these activities are the realm of girls and women, who provide more than half of the income of most Kanjar families. As a result, Kanjar society presents one of the clearest recorded examples of a reversal of the usual sex roles in human societies. Kanjar men are passive, cooperative and subordinate to females, whereas Kanjar women dominate public and private affairs and are socialized to be aggressive and independent.

Kanjar girls also help their brothers get married. Bridewealth payments are very high for the Kanjar, sometimes amounting to ten times a family's annual income. To reduce their costs, two families will often exchange daughters. As one Kanjar woman explained, "The only way I can avoid paying a fortune for my son's bride is to arrange his marriage with my brother's daughter and to give my daughter to my brother's son. We call this *wady de shadi,* or exchange marriage."

When Kanjar girls do marry for bridewealth, they bring a great deal of wealth to their parents. It is not surprising, then, that the Kanjar buck the general trend in South Asia of favoritism toward sons. This is best seen in their response to the birth of a child. A newborn girl is greeted with celebrations, but the birth of a boy is received with no fanfare.

One of the strangest examples of female-biased parental investment was provided by Margaret Mead and Reo Fortune in their study of the Mundugumor of New Guinea in the 1930s. According to Mead and Fortune, Mundugumor mothers and fathers had different opinions about the value of sons and daughters, with fathers tending to favor daughters and mothers favoring sons. Father-daughter relationships were reportedly very close; fathers tried to favor their daughters in inheritance and tried to allocate more property to them. Mundugumor mothers, in contrast, were closer to their sons and tried to give them more of the family's property.

The explanation for this may lie in the Mundugumor marriage system, which involved the exchange of women between families and pitted fathers against sons for access to brides. Traditionally, daughters were to be used as currency to obtain wives for their brothers. However, since men were allowed to have multiple wives, they could also use their daughters to obtain more wives. Sons had to be vigilant to ensure that their fathers did not cheat them. As a consequence, father-son relationships were stiff and formal.

Conclusion

Although many human societies show a disturbing amount of favoritism toward their sons, this is by no means a universal human pattern. Societies in which daughters are favored clearly exist. Moreover, it is also possible to identify some of the reasons for the parents' bias.

In all of these examples, I have focused on the *behavior* of the parents when they favor their daughters or sons. Another approach to studying biases in parental investment is to note the parents' *opinions* in response to questions about the number of sons and daughters they would like to have. Although the survey approach is commonly used by demographers, the statements of the Mukogodo parents suggest that there is a problem with it. Despite their behavior, most Mukogodo mothers claim to prefer sons rather than daughters. The discrepancy makes sense only in the light of the pervasiveness of the Maasai-speaking culture, which is extremely male-biased.

Since the Mukogodos' statements clearly do not reflect their behavior, it may be that the Mukogodo parents are not aware of their favoritism toward daughters. Whether or not the Mukogodo are aware of the contrast between their statements and their actions, research on the psychology of sex-biased parental investment could provide some fascinating insights into the phenomenon. It also stands as a caveat to the demographer's practice of using a parent's statements as a substitute for observations of the parent's behavior.

In the future I intend to return to the Mukogodo to understand whether subtle variations in parental behavior can affect a child's health. For example, is there any measurable relationship between the amount of time spent holding and nursing a child and the child's health, nutritional status or cognitive development? Through continued research on the causes and consequences of sex biases in parental behavior, we should be able to determine which children are likely to be at risk and how we might be able to help them and their parents cope with their situation.

Bibliography

Austad, S., and M. E. Sunquist. 1986. Sex-ratio manipulation in the common opossum. *Nature* 324:58–60.

Austad, S., and M. E. Sunquist. 1988. More sons for plump possums. *Natural History* 97(4):74–75.

Berland, J. C. 1982. *No Five Fingers Are Alike: Cognitive Amplifiers in Social Context.* Cambridge: Harvard University Press.

Berland, J. C. 1987. Kanjar Social Organization. *In The Other Nomads: Peripatetic Minorities in Cross-Cultural Perspective*, ed. A. Rao, pp. 247–265. Köln: Böhlau Verlag.

Cronk, L. 1989. Low socioeconomic status and female-biased parental investment: The Mukogodo example. *American Anthropologist* 91:414–429.

Cronk, L. 1991a. Intention vs. behaviour in parental sex preferences among the Mukogodo of Kenya. *Journal of Biosocial Science* 23:229–240.

Cronk, L. 1991b. Preferential parental investment in daughters over sons. *Human Nature* 2(4):387–417.

Fisher, R. A. 1958. *The Genetical Theory of Natural Selection.* 2nd ed. Oxford: Clarendon.

Gosling, L. M. 1986. Selective abortion of entire litters in the coypu: Adaptive control of offspring production in relation to quality and sex. *American Naturalist* 127:772–795.

Hammel, E. A., S. R. Johansson and C. A. Ginsberg. 1983. The value of children during industrialization: Sex ratios in childhood in nineteenth-century America. *Journal of Family History* 8:346–366.

Hrdy, S. B. 1987. Sex-biased parental investment among primates and other mammals: A critical evaluation of the Trivers-Willard hypothesis. In *Child Abuse and Neglect: Biosocial Dimensions*, ed. R. J. Gelles and J. B. Lancaster, pp. 97–147. New York: Aldine De Gruyter.

Hrdy, S. B. 1988. Daughters or sons. *Natural History* 97(4):63–83.

McDowell, N. 1991. *The Mundugumor: From the Field Notes of Margaret Mead and Reo Fortune.* Washington, DC: Smithsonian Institution Press.

McFarland Symington, M. 1987. Sex ratio and maternal rank in wild spider monkeys: When daughters disperse. *Behavioral Ecology and Sociobiology* 20:421–425.

Mead, M. 1935. *Sex and Temperament in Three Primitive Societies.* New York: Morrow.

Trivers, R. L., and D. E. Willard. 1973. Natural selection of parental ability to vary the sex ratio of offspring. *Science* 179:90–92.

Vinovskis, M. A. 1972. Mortality rates and trends in Massachusetts before 1860. *Journal of Economic History* 32:184–218.

Problem Set #11

Marriage and Parenting

To do this problem set, you will need to read Unit VII.

1. Marriage is a human universal, presumably because it serves certain fitness-related functions.

   a. What are the possible benefits of marriage?

   b. Do these fitness benefits accrue equally to both sexes? Explain.

   c. How do patterns of divorce illuminate the functions of marriage?

2. Generally, humans provide lots of parental investment, but there are some exceptions.

   a. How might patterns of child abuse illuminate evolved parental motivations?

   b. What are the observed patterns?

   c. To what extent do they conform to evolutionary expectations?

3. Matrilineal inheritance is rare in human societies.

   a. What is it?

   b. Under what conditions is it most likely to be adaptive?

   c. Under what conditions does it actually occur?

4. Parents don't always invest equally in sons and daughters.

   a. Under what conditions might parents benefit by investing preferentially in one sex or the other?

   b. Discuss the extent to which the Mukugodo discussed by Lee Cronk conform to these expectations.